Praise for
Directorate S

Longlisted for the National Book Award for Nonfiction
A *Washington Post* Notable Book of the Year

"A spectacular account of fifteen years of secret CIA and U.S. military operations in Afghanistan and Pakistan by the investigative journalist and academic Steve Coll. . . . With impressive access to American, Afghan, and Pakistani intelligence, Coll reveals the extent of the surveillance undertaken by all sides. . . . *Directorate S* has a cast of characters that make the Bourne movies pale in comparison—from type-A CIA officers and paramilitaries to cigar-smoking and whiskey-drinking Pakistani generals to a dog nicknamed 'Lucky' because he was able to detect incoming missile strikes from drones before they hit." —*The Financial Times*

"Steve Coll has written a book of surpassing excellence . . . Drawing on some 550 interviews, Coll describes in granular detail how senior officials, intelligence operatives, diplomats, and military officers struggled to comprehend the problem at hand and to devise a solution." —*The New York Times Book Review*

"Definitive." —*The Washington Post*

"Coll's book is riveting." —Richard Cohen, *New York Daily News*

"This sequel to *Ghost Wars* might well become the definitive account of the CIA and America's secret wars in Afghanistan and Pakistan. . . . In the pages of *Directorate S*, the sequel to Coll's Pulitzer Prize–winning *Ghost Wars*, the story is delivered with a literary prowess that has been absent in previous western accounts of America's longest running war. The dance of blame, with the U.S. swaying at one moment towards Pakistan and the next towards Afghanistan, is a choreography familiar to CIA chiefs, U.S. presidents, and writers who have tackled the subject. Coll refuses to follow this tired tune, and the result is masterful." —*The Guardian* (UK)

"Spellbinding . . . It does for America in Afghanistan what Michael Gordon and Tom Ricks did for the Iraq misadventure in *Cobra II* and *Fiasco*." —*Evening Standard*

PENGUIN BOOKS

DIRECTORATE S

Steve Coll is the author of the Pulitzer Prize–winning *Ghost Wars* and a professor and dean emeritus of the Graduate School of Journalism at Columbia University, and from 2007 to 2013 was the president of the New America Foundation, a public policy institute in Washington, D.C. He is a staff writer for *The New Yorker* and previously worked for twenty years at *The Washington Post*, where he received a Pulitzer Prize for explanatory journalism in 1990. He is the author of seven other books, including *On the Grand Trunk Road*, *The Bin Ladens*, and *Private Empire*.

DIRECTORATE S

THE C.I.A. AND AMERICA'S
SECRET WARS IN AFGHANISTAN
AND PAKISTAN

STEVE COLL

PENGUIN BOOKS

PENGUIN BOOKS

An imprint of Penguin Random House LLC

penguinrandomhouse.com

First published in the United States of America by Penguin Press,
an imprint of Penguin Random House LLC, 2018
Published in Penguin Books 2019

Photograph credits:
Insert page 1 (bottom): Courtesy of David O. Smith; 2 (top): U.S. Department
of State; 2 (middle): Mian Kursheed/Reuters Pictures; 2 (bottom): Reuters
Photographer/Reuters Pictures; 3 (top): White House photo by Tina Hager;
3 (bottom left): By Heinrich-Böll-Stiftung via Wikimedia Commons; 3 (bottom
right): By U.S. Embassy, Kabul, Afghanistan (U.S. Department of State), via
Wikimedia Commons; 4 (top): AP Photo/J. Scott Applewhite; 4 (middle): AP
Photo/Anjum Naveed; 4 (bottom): U.S. Department of State; 5 (top):
Department of Defense photo by Tech. Sgt. Jacob N. Bailey, U.S. Air Force
(Released); 5 (middle): Baz Ratner/Reuters Pictures; 5 (bottom): Courtesy
of Cpt. Timothy Hopper; 6 (top): Pool New/Reuters Pictures; 6 (bottom):
White House Photo/Alamy Stock Photo; 7 (top): Courtesy of
Barnett Rubin; 7 (bottom): Courtesy of the Loftis family;
8 (top right): From personal collection of Marc Sageman;
8 (middle left and bottom right): Photos by Robert Nickelsberg

ISBN 9781594204586 (hardcover)
ISBN 9780143132509 (paperback)
ISBN 9780525557302 (ebook)

Printed in the United States of America

Designed by Amanda Dewey
Maps by Charles Preppernau

In Memory of Robert and Shirley

Everybody knows that the dice are loaded
Everybody rolls with their fingers crossed
Everybody knows that the war is over
Everybody knows that the good guys lost

—LEONARD COHEN, "Everybody Knows," 1988

AUTHOR'S NOTE

Two extraordinary colleagues contributed deeply to this book. Christina Satkowski, who earned an undergraduate degree at Wellesley College and a master's degree at Georgetown University, carried out important interviews and document analysis for more than two years. She was singularly responsible for the rich interviews that inform chapter 26, among many contributions. I could not have finished the book without her. The same is true of Elizabeth Barber, a graduate of the honors college at the State University of New York who also earned a master's degree from Columbia University's Graduate School of Journalism. Among other things, Elizabeth carried out a nine-month fact-check of the manuscript, recontacting sources and reaching out to new ones. She used this reporting to improve the manuscript from start to end, adding new scenes and revelations, and pushing tirelessly for accuracy, nuance, and completeness. Although I am solely responsible for what appears in these pages, *Directorate S* belongs to Christina and Elizabeth as much as it does to me. There are other colleagues from Columbia and elsewhere who made important contributions; I have tried to thank them all in the acknowledgments.

Contents

PART THREE

THE BEST INTENTIONS,
2006–2009

PART FOUR

THE END OF ILLUSION,
2010–2014

LIST OF MAPS

CAST OF CHARACTERS

AT THE C.I.A.

Frank Archibald, case officer, Kandahar, circa 2002; later Chief of Islamabad Station; C.I.A. liaison to Richard Holbrooke's office at the Department of State, 2009–2010

Jonathan Bank, Chief of Islamabad Station, 2010

John Bennett, Chief of Islamabad Station, 2009; later Deputy Director of Operations

Cofer Black, Director of D.C.I.'s Counterterrorist Center, 1999–2002

Rich Blee, Chief of ALEC Station, 1999–2001; Chief of Kabul Station, 2002; Chief of Islamabad Station, 2004–2005

John Brennan, Director of Central Intelligence, 2013–2017

Michael D'Andrea, Director of the C.I.A.'s Counterterrorism Center, 2006–2015

Porter Goss, Director of Central Intelligence, 2004–2006

Robert Grenier, Islamabad Station Chief, 2001; Director of C.I.A. Counterterrorism Center, 2004–2006

Michael Hayden, Director of Central Intelligence, 2006–2009

Michael Hurley, senior case officer, Kabul Station, 2002–2004

Stephen Kappes, case officer, Pakistan, 1980s; Deputy Director for Operations, 2004; Deputy Director of Central Intelligence, 2006–2010

Mark Kelton, Chief of Islamabad Station, 2011

Leon Panetta, Director of Central Intelligence, 2009–2011

David Petraeus, Director of Central Intelligence, 2011–2012

Jose Rodriguez, Director of C.I.A. Counterterrorism Center, 2002–2004; Deputy Director of Operations, 2004; Director of National Clandestine Service, 2004–2008

Tony Schinella, senior military analyst; director of District Assessments project mapping the Afghan war, 2009–2016

George Tenet, Director of Central Intelligence, 1997–2004

Greg Vogle, Chief of Base, Peshawar, Pakistan, 2001; C.I.A. liaison to Hamid Karzai, November–December 2001; paramilitary officer, Kabul Station, 2002; Chief of Kabul Station, 2004–2006 and 2009–2010; Director of C.I.A. paramilitary operations, 2014–

Brian Glyn Williams, consultant on suicide bombings in Afghanistan, 2006–2007

Chris Wood, case officer, Pakistan, 1997–2001; case officer, Northern Alliance Liaison Team, autumn 2001; head of operations, Kabul Station, 2002; Chief of ALEC Station, circa 2003–2004; Afghan specialist at the Office of the Director of National Intelligence, 2010; Chief of Kabul Station, 2011; Director of C.I.A.'s Counterterrorism Center, 2015–2017

AT OTHER U.S. INTELLIGENCE AGENCIES

Jeff Hayes, D.I.A. analyst on South Asia, assigned to National Security Council, 2009–2014

Peter Lavoy, National Intelligence Officer for South Asia, 2007–2008; Deputy Director of National Intelligence for Analysis, 2008–2011; Principal Deputy Assistant Secretary of Defense, 2011–2014; Senior Director for South Asia, National Security Council, 2015–2016

Marc Sageman, former C.I.A. case officer, consultant to U.S. Army intelligence, 2010–2012; consultant to International Security Assistance Force in Afghanistan, 2012–2013

David Smith, Defense Intelligence Agency representative in Islamabad, 2001; senior Pakistan analyst at D.I.A. and the Pentagon until 2012

AT THE PENTAGON AND THE ARMED SERVICES

David Barno, U.S. and coalition commander in Afghanistan, 2003–2005

Karl Eikenberry, U.S. and coalition commander in Afghanistan, 2005–2007; U.S. Ambassador to Afghanistan, 2009–2011

Michael Flynn, International Security Assistance Force intelligence chief, 2009–2010

Timothy J. Hopper, platoon leader, 320th Field Artillery Regiment, Combined Task Force "Strike"

Darin Loftis, chief plans adviser for the International Security Assistance Force, in the AFPAK Hands program, 2011–2012

Stanley McChrystal, Commander of Joint Special Operations Command, 2003–2008; Director of the Joint Staff, 2008–2009; Commander of I.S.A.F. and U.S. Forces Afghanistan, 2009–2010

Mike Mullen, Chairman of the Joint Chiefs of Staff, 2007–2011

Barry Shapiro, deputy for the Office of the Defense Representative–Pakistan, 2002–2003 and 2005–2008

AT THE WHITE HOUSE

Tony Harriman, senior director for Afghanistan at the National Security Council, 2005–2007

Jim Jones, National Security Adviser, 2009–2010

Doug Lute, Assistant to the President and Deputy National Security Adviser for Iraq and Afghanistan ("War Czar"), 2007–2009; Special Assistant to the President and Senior Coordinator for Afghanistan and Pakistan, 2009–2013; U.S. Ambassador to N.A.T.O., 2013–2017

Paul Miller, Director for Afghanistan and Pakistan on the National Security Council, 2007–2009

AT THE STATE DEPARTMENT

Wendy Chamberlin, Ambassador to Pakistan, 2001–2002

Hillary Clinton, Secretary of State, 2009–2013

Ryan Crocker, Ambassador to Pakistan, 2004–2007; Ambassador to Afghanistan, 2011–2012

James Dobbins, Special Representative for Afghanistan and Pakistan, 2013–2014

Robert Finn, Ambassador to Afghanistan, 2002–2003

Marc Grossman, U.S. Special Representative for Afghanistan and Pakistan, 2011–2012

Richard Holbrooke, U.S. Special Representative for Afghanistan and Pakistan, 2009–2011

Zalmay Khalilzad, Ambassador to Afghanistan, 2003–2005

David Kilcullen, Special Adviser to the Secretary of State, 2005–2009

Cameron Munter, Ambassador to Pakistan, 2010–2012

Ronald Neumann, Ambassador to Afghanistan, 2005–2007

Anne Patterson, Ambassador to Pakistan, 2007–2010

Condoleezza Rice, Secretary of State, 2005–2009

Barnett Rubin, Senior Adviser to the Special Representative for Afghanistan and Pakistan, 2009–2013

Frank Ruggiero, senior deputy special representative and deputy assistant secretary of state for Afghanistan and Pakistan, 2010–2012

IN PAKISTAN

Mahmud Ahmed, Director-General of Inter-Services Intelligence, 1999–2001

Benazir Bhutto, Leader of the Pakistan People's Party, 1988–2007

Ehsan ul-Haq, Director-General of Inter-Services Intelligence, 2001–2004

Ashfaq Kayani, Director-General of Inter-Services Intelligence, 2004–2007; Chief of Army Staff, 2007–2013

Pervez Musharraf, President of Pakistan, 2001–2008

Ahmed Shuja Pasha, Director-General of Inter-Services Intelligence, 2008–2012

Nadeem Taj, Director-General of Inter-Services Intelligence, 2007–2008

Asif Zardari, President of Pakistan, 2008–2013

IN AFGHANISTAN

Abdullah Abdullah, Minister of Foreign Affairs, 2001–2005; Chief Executive of Afghanistan, 2014–

Tayeb Agha, head of the Taliban political commission, 2009–2015

Engineer Arif, head of intelligence for the Northern Alliance, 1994–2001; head of the National Directorate of Security, 2001–2004

Abdul Rashid Dostum, Deputy Defense Minister, 2003; Vice President of Afghanistan, 2014–

Marshal Mohammed Fahim, Vice Chairman of the Interim Government, 2001–2002; Interim Vice President of Afghanistan, 2002–2004; Vice President of Afghanistan, 2009–2014

Ashraf Ghani, Minister of Finance, 2002–2004; President of Afghanistan, 2014–

Ibrahim Haqqani, representative for the Haqqani network, 2002–

Hamid Karzai, Chairman of the Interim Government, 2001–2002; Interim President of Afghanistan, 2002–2004; President of Afghanistan, 2004–2014

Ahmad Shah Massoud, Commander of the Northern Alliance, 1996–2001

Rahmatullah Nabil, head of the National Directorate of Security, 2010–2012 and 2013–2015

Amrullah Saleh, Intelligence Adviser for Ahmad Shah Massoud, 1997–2001; head of the National Directorate of Security, 2004–2007

Gul Agha Sherzai, Governor of Kandahar, 1992–1994 and 2001–2003; Governor of Nangarhar, 2005–2013

Introduction

I n 1989, I moved to New Delhi for *The Washington Post* to become the newspaper's South Asia correspondent. I was thirty years old and responsible for a phantasmagoria of news from India, Pakistan, Afghanistan, Bangladesh, Sri Lanka, and Nepal. For three years I hopped from capital to capital, and from one guerrilla war, coup d'état, and popular revolution to another. It was thrilling and affecting work.

In Afghanistan, the last units of the Soviet occupation forces had recently pulled out of the country. The war caused by the Soviet invasion had claimed an estimated one to two million Afghan lives, or up to 10 percent of the prewar population. Land mines and indiscriminate bombings maimed hundreds of thousands more. About five million Afghans became refugees. Soviet and Afghan Communists purposefully decimated the country's educated elites, executing or exiling traditional leaders. By the time I turned up, this culling had left much of the field to radical preachers and armed opportunists.

In Kabul, the Soviets had left behind a few thousand K.G.B. officers and military advisers to prop up a regime led by Mohammad Najibullah, a physician turned secret police chief. Najibullah's forces controlled the Afghan capital and an archipelago of cities. The countryside belonged to the mujaheddin, the anti-Communist rebels funded and armed by the C.I.A., as well as by Pakistani and Saudi intelligence. The war had settled into a grinding stalemate.

The Soviet troop withdrawal knocked the Afghan story off front pages and network broadcasts in the United States, but for the *Post* it remained a matter of running interest, not least because the C.I.A. was still smuggling guns and money to the rebels; the agency's career officers and analysts were among our subscriber base in Washington. Like other correspondents in those years, I covered the Afghan war from both sides. I flew periodically to Kabul, to interview Najibullah and his aides, or to travel around the country with Afghan Communist generals. From Pakistan, I went over the border to see the Islamist rebels' hold on the countryside. The work was generally safe, as correspondence from a medium-grade civil war goes. Yet during this period, Western reporters and humanitarian workers learned to be wary of the loose bands of Arab Islamist volunteers circulating among the Afghan mujaheddin. These international radicals sometimes staged roadside executions of nonbelievers they came across. We did not yet know them as Al Qaeda.

The C.I.A. subcontracted its aid to the Afghan rebels through Pakistan's main spy agency, Inter-Services Intelligence, or I.S.I. By 1989, the service had grown into a powerful, corrosive force within Pakistan, a shadowy deep state that manipulated politics on behalf of the army and increasingly promoted armed groups of Islamists, including the Arab volunteers we had learned to approach cautiously. I.S.I. officers were not easy to meet, but not impossible to track down, either. I became somewhat obsessed with reporting on the underbelly of the Afghan conflict. I wrote for the *Post* about how the C.I.A. program to arm the rebels functioned, why its escalation had helped to defeat the Soviet occupation, and how, simultaneously, the C.I.A.'s covert action had empowered the more radical factions in the rebellion, largely at I.S.I.'s direction.

In December 1991, the Soviet Union collapsed. The political upheavals in Moscow and Central Asia rippled into Afghanistan. Soviet cash, food, and arms supplies to Najibullah's government looked to be finished. This altered the civil war's balance. By late April 1992, the fall of Kabul to the I.S.I.-backed Islamist rebels seemed imminent. I flew in. The mujaheddin flowed into the capital unopposed on a Saturday. Kabul's wary residents had been governed for a decade by an officially secular regime. Hoping to avoid a bloodbath, they greeted the entering long-bearded rebels with flowers. Najibullah tried to flee but was arrested at the airport. His security forces took off their uniforms, abandoned their posts, and went home, trying to blend into the new order. The mujaheddin seemed uncertain initially about whether to trust their acceptance into Kabul. That first day of the takeover, I met a rebel straggler near the zoo. He said his name was Syed Munir. He was carrying an assault rifle. He turned in circles and insisted that anyone who wished to talk to him do so from a distance of ten feet. "Everyone is friendly," he admitted. "But maybe some people want to take my gun."

He was right to be wary. That night, a new round of war erupted among factions of the Afghan rebels. The fighting soon shredded Kabul, claimed thousands more innocent lives, and consigned Afghanistan to yet deeper poverty and international isolation. America, by now absorbed by victory in the Cold War and startling geopolitical changes such as the reunification of Germany, looked away.

I moved on as well, to London, to take up a position as an international investigative correspondent for the *Post*. I was stationed there on February 26, 1993, when a cabal of jihadists, some with ties to the Afghan war, detonated a truck bomb beneath the World Trade Center, killing six people and wounding many others. My editors asked for an investigation into the networks of Islamist radicals and financiers that seemed to lie behind the World Trade Center attack. I worked on some of that project with another reporter, Steve LeVine. We heard about a wealthy Saudi exile in Sudan, Osama Bin Laden, who was reported to be funding some of the groups we were looking into. Steve flew to Khartoum to ask for an interview. Bin Laden's bodyguards said he would not be available. After speaking with some of Bin Laden's aides and many other supporters and members of the jihadi movement from London to the Balkans to the Middle East, we wrote, "Arguably, the best way to think about Bin Laden's multistory Khartoum guest house is not as a centralized, string-pulling headquarters," but as "one among many scattered centers of gravity where militant Islamic radicals may find haven, succor or support." We still had not heard of Al Qaeda. Because of Bin Laden's rising notoriety, the United States soon pressured Sudan to kick him out of Khartoum. He went to Afghanistan in the summer of 1996, declared war on the United States, and soon found shelter with the Taliban.

By 2001, I had become the *Post*'s managing editor in Washington. That spring, the paper carried coverage of the New York trial of jihadi conspirators who had participated in the terrorist attacks on two U.S. embassies in Africa in August 1998. The prosecutors introduced evidence of Bin Laden's involvement in the terrorist plot, as well as his leadership of Al Qaeda, which was at last identified publicly. A defector testified in detail about how Al Qaeda worked and how Bin Laden and his aides doled out support to followers and allies. Yet the conventional wisdom in Washington held that the group was isolated in distant Afghanistan, and that it was most likely to continue to carry out attacks overseas—Al Qaeda was a serious nuisance, in other words, but not a major threat to American territory or security.

On the morning of September 11, I was at a desk in my home office in Maryland, typing notes for a book I was considering about genocide in Africa. I had CNN on mute on a small television to one side. When I saw the first reports about a plane that had smashed into the North Tower of the World Trade Center in clear weather, I assumed it was a freak accident. I scrambled to collect my keys and work materials, to rush to the newsroom. I was just about out the door when my wife called out as she watched United Airlines Flight 175 hit the South Tower. We stared at the terrible scenes for some minutes. "Oh, this is Bin Laden," it finally occurred to me to say. I drove downtown. Smoke rose from across the Potomac River, where American Airlines Flight 77 had struck the Pentagon.

Six weeks later, I went digging around in my garage, looking for old tape recordings of interviews with I.S.I. officers from the early 1990s. I found them. That discovery inaugurated research for the book that became *Ghost Wars: The Secret History of the CIA, Afghanistan, and bin Laden, from the Soviet Invasion to September 10, 2001.* My intention was to provide Americans, Afghans, and Pakistanis with a thorough, reliable history of the often-secret actions, debates, and policies that had led to Al Qaeda's rise amid Afghanistan's civil wars and finally to the September 11 attacks. I traveled back to Afghanistan and Pakistan to conduct some of the research. *Ghost Wars* came out in 2004.

At the time, Afghanistan and Pakistan appeared to be stable and relatively peaceful. During the next several years, the Taliban and Al Qaeda revived, plunging Afghan and Pakistani civilians into further violent misery and insecurity. It seemed evident that I.S.I. was, once again, interfering secretly in Afghanistan, exploiting the country's fault lines, and that the U.S. government, including the C.I.A., was again unable to forestall an incubating disaster. The Bush administration and then the Obama administration gradually escalated America's commitment to suppressing the Taliban and defeating Al Qaeda. Ultimately, hundreds of thousands of Americans volunteered to serve in Afghanistan after 2001 as soldiers, diplomats, or aid workers. More than two thousand American soldiers died alongside hundreds of contractors. More than twenty thousand soldiers suffered injuries. Of the much greater number who returned safely, many carried questions about whether or why their service had been worthwhile and why the seemingly successful lightning-strike American-led war of late 2001 had failed to vanquish the Taliban and Al Qaeda for good.

Directorate S: The C.I.A. and America's Secret Wars in Afghanistan and Pakistan, 2001–2016 is intended to address those questions, as best as the evidence allows. It is a second volume of the journalistic history recounted in *Ghost Wars*, starting from where that volume ended, on September 10, 2001. The new book can easily be read independently, but it also seeks to deliver to readers of the first volume a recognizable extension of the subjects, narrative approaches, and investigations they encountered there.

Directorate S seeks to provide a thorough, reliable history of how the C.I.A., I.S.I., and Afghan intelligence agencies influenced the rise of a new war in Afghanistan after the fall of the Taliban, and how that war fostered a revival of Al Qaeda, allied terrorist networks, and, eventually, branches of the Islamic State. The book also seeks to connect American, Afghan, Pakistani, and international policy failures to the worldwide persistence of jihadi terrorism. It tries to provide a balanced, complete account of the most important secret operations, assumptions, debates, decisions, and diplomacy in Washington, Islamabad, and Kabul. Like *Ghost Wars*, this volume asks the reader to traverse much territory. To keep things moving, I have again tried to prioritize action, vivid characters, and original reporting, without sacrificing depth and context.

After 2008, the United States and N.A.T.O. allies fought a large-scale overt conventional war against the Taliban, and, in a secret annex campaign waged mostly by armed drones, against Al Qaeda and its allies in Pakistan. This campaign could be the subject of a book in and of itself (and has been the subject of a number of excellent ones, including *Little America*, by Rajiv Chandrasekaran; *Obama's Wars*, by Bob Woodward; and *The Way of the Knife*, by Mark Mazzetti, which also provides a penetrating account of the C.I.A. during these years). In *Directorate S*, I have tried to offer new insights into that war, but not to recount it fully, concentrating instead on the less thoroughly treated trajectory of decision making at the C.I.A., the I.S.I., and the principal Afghan intelligence service, the National Directorate of Security. I have also had to consider how to absorb, but not regurgitate, the vast body of excellent journalism already produced by other reporters about Afghanistan and Pakistan since 2001. I traveled repeatedly to both countries after 2005 while carrying out the research for what became *Directorate S*, but I cannot possibly match here the granular, on-the-ground correspondence and books by the many intrepid field reporters and resident researchers who have done so much to deepen public understanding of South Asia's instability and political violence. I could not have written this volume without incorporating the insights and research of scores of other journalists and scholars, some of them colleagues and friends, including Ahmed Rashid, Peter Bergen, Dexter Filkins, Carlotta Gall, Anand Gopal, Felix Kuehn, Anatol Lieven, David Rohde, Owen Bennett-Jones, Sarah Chayes, Graeme Smith, Alex Strick van Linschoten, and Martine van Bijlert, as well as many others cited in the source notes. However, I have concentrated the narrative in *Directorate S* on my own reporting, and principally on the hundreds of interviews conducted for the book during the last decade, as well as new documentary evidence obtained from those sources. I have sought to ground my reliance on interviews and contemporaneous notes with secondary sources such as documents obtained from F.O.I.A. requests and the State Department cables released by WikiLeaks.

For many Americans and Europeans who have lived and worked in

Afghanistan and Pakistan before and after 2001, it is frustrating to hear discourse back home holding that Afghanistan and Pakistan are lands of "warring tribes" or "endless conflicts." The historical record belies such clichés. Independent Afghanistan was impoverished but peaceful and stable, untroubled by radical international violence, for many decades of the twentieth century, prior to the Soviet invasion of 1979. Its several decades of civil war since that invasion have been fueled again and again by outside interference, primarily by Pakistan, but certainly including the United States and Europe, which have remade Afghanistan with billions of dollars in humanitarian and reconstruction aid while simultaneously contributing to its violence, corruption, and instability. And for all of Pakistan's dysfunction, state-sponsored radicalism, and glaring economic inequality, it remains a modernizing nation with a vast, breathtakingly talented middle class and diaspora. If the army and I.S.I. did not misrule Pakistan, in alliance with corrupt political cronies, the country's potential to lift up its own population and contribute positively to the international system might today rival India's. The region's "endless conflicts" are not innate to its history, forms of social organization, or cultures. They are the outgrowth of specific misrule and violent interventions. They reflect political maneuvering, hubristic assumptions, intelligence operations, secret diplomacy, and decision making at the highest levels in Kabul, Islamabad, and Washington that have often been unavailable to the Afghan, Pakistani, American, and international publics. This is the story of Directorate S.

PART ONE

BLIND INTO BATTLE,

September 2001–December 2001

ONE

"Something Has Happened to Khalid"

I n the late summer of 2001, Amrullah Saleh flew to Frankfurt, Germany, to meet a man he knew as Phil, a C.I.A. officer. Saleh handled intelligence liaisons, among other tasks, for Ahmad Shah Massoud, the legendary Afghan guerrilla commander, who was then holding out against the Taliban and Al Qaeda from a shrinking haven in the northeast of his country. At twenty-eight, Saleh had a stern, serious demeanor; he was clean-shaven and kept his dark hair cropped short. He spoke English well, but deliberately, in a sonorous accent.

Saleh typically met his C.I.A. handlers at a hotel. He and Phil discussed a cache of spy gear the C.I.A. had organized for Massoud. The delivery included communications equipment and night-vision goggles that would allow Massoud's intelligence collectors on the front lines to better watch and eavesdrop on Taliban and Al Qaeda fighters. The C.I.A. had been training and equipping Massoud's intelligence directorate for several years, but the program was limited in scope. Under the policies of the Clinton administration and more recently the George W. Bush administration, the C.I.A. could not provide weapons to support Massoud's war of resistance against the Taliban. The agency could only provide nonlethal equipment that might aid the agency's hunt for Osama Bin Laden, the fugitive emir of Al Qaeda, who moved elusively around

Taliban-ruled areas of Afghanistan. One shipment had included a giant, remote-controlled telescope. At another point the C.I.A. considered supplying Massoud with a balloon fixed with cameras to spy on Al Qaeda camps, but between Afghanistan's heavy winds and the possibility that neighboring China might misinterpret the dirigible, they decided against it.

Frankfurt was a logistics hub. The C.I.A.'s supply lines for Massoud were jerry-rigged and constrained by caution at headquarters. By early 2001, Langley had ordered C.I.A. officers to stop flying in Massoud's helicopters because they weren't judged to be safe enough. Phil and his colleagues usually delivered equipment directly to Dushanbe, where Saleh ran an office for Massoud. Tajikistan was recovering from a bloody civil war and there was occasional political unrest in the capital. That could make it difficult for C.I.A. officers to travel there but for the most part they found a way. Once in a while, however, they had to ask Saleh to pick up equipment in Germany and carry it the rest of the way himself. The C.I.A. officers involved knew the German government was highly sensitive about anything the agency did on German territory without informing the B.N.D., the principal German intelligence agency. But the supplies to Massoud were uniformly nonlethal; some of the equipment might skirt the borders of export licensing rules, but it was not obviously illegal, as arms and ammunition would be. Massoud's lieutenants were experienced smugglers. Sometimes Saleh would have to figure out how to transport C.I.A. equipment on his own.

This made Saleh nervous. He did not relish answering the questions of German police or customs officers at Frankfurt Airport. *Where did you buy this?* He would have no answer. *Do you have any receipts?* No. *What will you use these night-vision goggles for?* It would be unwise to mention the Afghan war. *How did you obtain the funds to buy a $5,000 satellite phone and subscription?*[1]

Saleh had become an intelligence specialist only recently, but he was an avid student of the profession. In 1999, Massoud had selected him and eight other senior aides and commanders to travel to the United States to attend a C.I.A. training course put on by the Counterterrorist Center under strict secrecy rules; few people outside the center knew about it. The curriculum partly covered the arts of intelligence—identifying and assessing sources, recruitment, technical collection, analysis, and report writing. The paramilitary courses covered assessing targets, maneuvering and communicating in the field, and so on. In Nevada, the trainees climbed a mountain with a telescope to practice reconnaissance operations in conditions that replicated those in Afghanistan. The training reflected the C.I.A. Counterterrorist Center's hope—a quixotic one, in the view of many agency analysts familiar with Afghanistan—that Massoud's guerrillas might someday locate and trap Bin Laden, even though the Al Qaeda leader rarely traveled to the north of the country, where Massoud's guerrillas were.

At the C.I.A.'s school, Saleh was a bit bored by the paramilitary instruction. He was more drawn to the craft of intelligence collection. He wanted a fuller understanding about intelligence systems and methods. He peppered the C.I.A. officers on the faculty with questions. He found a few who were willing to give him extra time and he tried to understand how the C.I.A. worked. When the course was over, Saleh went to Borders to buy a stack of books about spy services and intelligence history. Since then, he had earned respect at the C.I.A. The officers with whom he worked assessed Saleh as tough, disciplined, honest, and professional, if also a bit young to command authority in Afghan society, which venerated age and experience.[2]

To solve his shipping problems in Germany, Saleh tried to draw on his self-education, particularly concerning the methods of Israeli intelligence. Mossad had networks of helpers around the world—not just employees and paid agents or informers, but friends of the service who could be called upon for ad hoc favors. Saleh telephoned an Afghan-German businessman in Frankfurt whom he had cultivated for such assistance.

"I have something I need you to do—I need your help," Saleh said. The man suggested they meet at a hotel.

"I won't lie," Saleh said when they were settled. "It's equipment. If I'm lucky, I can take it out of Frankfurt Airport. If I'm unlucky, they will confiscate it." The gear was not lethal, Saleh added, but it did constitute "war equipment."

"Brother, I had offered to help you—but not in smuggling," the businessman said.

"This is not smuggling," Saleh pleaded. "It's all plastic, there's no explosives, nothing. There are some goggles."

Still, the man declined. He wished Saleh luck.

Saleh transported the gear, which was about the size of a half sofa, to Frankfurt Airport. He booked himself on a flight to Tashkent, Uzbekistan, from where he would transfer to Dushanbe. This was typical of the struggle against the Taliban in which he and Massoud were engaged: They were fighting a D.I.Y. guerrilla war. Massoud and his men had resources; the commander and many of his top lieutenants kept bank accounts in London and elsewhere abroad, according to C.I.A. reporting, and Massoud was reported to control just over $60 million in London accounts. Yet they were effectively at war with the Taliban and Pakistan, a nuclear-armed state with a gross domestic product in 2001 of more than $70 billion.[3]

At the Lufthansa counter Saleh filled out forms. Then he answered many questions about his equipment. Had the C.I.A. tipped off the Germans and had the Germans agreed to go easy? He never knew. After a long colloquy, Lufthansa demanded only a considerable sum of money, which it calculated based on the weight of Saleh's cargo.

Amrullah Saleh had grown up in Kabul in a poor family from the Panjshir Valley. He was the youngest of five brothers. At seven, he was orphaned. Like many Afghans who came of age during the Soviet occupation of the country during the 1980s, he knew political violence intimately. One of his brothers disappeared, executed by unknown parties. Another of his brothers, who was an air force officer, fell to an assassin in Kandahar. At twenty-two, Saleh joined Massoud's guerrillas in the Panjshir Valley. The Panjshir is a gorge that occasionally widens into a valley. It slices from the north of Kabul toward Tajikistan. A tight kin network of ethnic Tajiks inhabited the valley and scratched out livings as farmers, emerald miners, smugglers, and traders. By the time Saleh arrived the Soviets had withdrawn their combat forces from Afghanistan, leaving behind advisers to shore up an Afghan Communist regime headed by President Najibullah, a former secret police chief. The war between mujaheddin guerrillas and the Communist government in Kabul continued but, increasingly, the guerrillas fought among themselves. They anticipated victory and competed for its prospective spoils. Massoud was perhaps the most politically savvy faction leader, the one who followed precepts of successful guerrilla leaders throughout history. He was a brilliant battlefield tactician, but he was equally concerned with food supplies and security for his civilian followers and with his popular credibility.

Because Saleh was bright and had already taught himself English, Massoud's lieutenants sent him to Pakistan in 1992, on a course provided by the United Nations titled "Post-Conflict Reconstruction and Management." Saleh studied how to run humanitarian operations, in the eventual service of northern Afghanistan. Gradually, Saleh became the youngest man in Massoud's circle of advisers.[4]

In the mid-1990s he moved to Russia. He learned Russian and tried to evaluate the potential for a new partnership with Afghanistan's former tormentor. (Russia had fallen into political and economic chaos under President Boris Yeltsin and Saleh returned to the Panjshir unconvinced that the Russian government could provide much help.) Later, Massoud dispatched Saleh to attend peace negotiations with the Taliban, sponsored by the United Nations. And Saleh began to work with the C.I.A.

The main C.I.A. unit tasked to interact with Massoud's guerrillas was called ALEC Station. Its mission was to capture or disrupt Osama Bin Laden and other Al Qaeda leaders. The station comprised about twenty-five operations officers and analysts, and it was based at C.I.A. headquarters in Langley, Virginia. Richard Blee, an experienced operations officer from the Africa Division of the clandestine service, took charge of ALEC in 1999. He inherited a group under rising pressure. After Al Qaeda bombed American embassies in Africa in 1998, C.I.A. officers working with foreign intelligence services from Egypt to Jordan to Kenya to Pakistan conducted raids on the homes of suspected Al Qaeda members and associates around the world. They seized computer drives and documents in Arabic, Urdu, English, and other languages and then dumped the materials on ALEC Station, to be sifted line by line for clues and names that might help to thwart upcoming terrorist attacks. By 2001, the station's analysts transmitted an average of twenty-three formal reports per month to the F.B.I. about Al Qaeda. The work combined high stakes with numbing detail. Senior officers found that if they did not work from 7:00 a.m. until 6:00 p.m. or later Monday through Friday, plus a few hours on Saturday and Sunday, they could not keep up with the traffic.

Blee had served multiple tours working the streets in unstable capitals. His C.I.A. tours had included postings to Bangui, the capital of Central African Republic; Niamey, the capital of Niger; Lagos, Nigeria; and Algiers. Blee was tall, with sandy hair. Some of his colleagues found him aloof and entitled. He was a second-generation C.I.A. officer, pegged by some to rise high in the agency, eventually. He was cerebral and well informed about international affairs, comfortable working in ambiguous conflict zones. Considering the problem of Al Qaeda's sanctuary in Afghanistan, a landlocked nation where the United States had no active embassy, Blee strongly favored working through Ahmad Shah Massoud, the most effective Afghan commander on the ground, who shared the C.I.A.'s antipathy toward Bin Laden.

Blee had led a covert team of C.I.A. counterterrorism officers who flew into the Panjshir to meet Massoud in October 1999. "We have a common enemy," Blee had told the commander. "Let's work together." He and C.I.A. officers who followed provided power supplies for Massoud's intelligence equipment, better intercept gear, and an encrypted communications link that connected Massoud's intelligence aides to ALEC Station, to send and receive secure typed messages. There was one encrypted terminal in Dushanbe and a second in the Panjshir. Massoud assigned Amrullah Saleh to be Blee's main contact.[5]

The following year, Al Qaeda suicide bombers supported from Afghanistan struck an American warship, the USS *Cole*, in the Yemeni port of Aden, killing seventeen American sailors. After that, in December 2000, Blee had drafted plans at the request of the expiring Clinton White House for a $150 million covert action program to arm, equip, and train Massoud for missions beyond the Bin Laden hunt, to help him fight the Taliban more effectively. Yet many American and European intelligence officers, generals, and diplomats did not see Massoud as a viable partner against Al Qaeda. Recalling the miserable fates of imperial Britain and the Soviet Union, they did not want to entangle the United States in Afghanistan's civil war. The Panjshiris had committed mass killings during a period when they shared power in Kabul during the mid-1990s. They continued to smuggle gems and heroin, to fund their war. Massoud's warnings about Al Qaeda could be dismissed as an element of a self-interested diplomatic campaign to win international aid for his losing factional struggle.

Blee became one of Massoud's most ardent defenders in Washington, regarding the commander as a great historical figure, comparable to Che Guevara. Massoud's wispy beard had grown gray and dark bags hung beneath his eyes, but he remained highly energetic on the battlefield. Massoud's argument was that the United States had a "huge problem" in Afghanistan, much bigger than Bin Laden. The essence of Massoud's message was: "You've got all of these extremists. You've got the Taliban. And I'm the only friend you've got in this neighborhood."

Blee agreed with Massoud entirely but he could not win the foreign policy argument in Washington. He told Massoud, "Look, nobody gives a damn about Afghanistan. They care about Bin Laden. I can't talk to you about taking over the government of Afghanistan. I'm only empowered to talk to you about getting Bin Laden. But we can build on that. Who knows where that goes?" Massoud understood. All of his allies and foreign suppliers were constrained in one way or another.[6]

ALEC Station ran some of its covert operations against Al Qaeda, including Predator drone surveillance flights, from the C.I.A. station in Tashkent, Uzbekistan. Amrullah Saleh worked with officers there as well as those in Virginia. That summer of 2001, amid the frustration over America's hesitancy to back Massoud fully, Saleh fell into conversation with one of Rich Blee's colleagues, Jim Lewis, a Counterterrorist Center case officer posted to Tashkent. Lewis urged Saleh to watch *The Siege*, a 1998 movie about terrorism written by the journalist and author Lawrence Wright and starring Denzel Washington and Bruce Willis. In the film, a terrorist group carries out bombings inside the United States and the government imposes martial law. Lewis predicted, "Something similar to that will happen to my country. But nobody is listening to us."[7]

From Frankfurt, Saleh returned to Dushanbe. He met Massoud there on Friday, September 7. Massoud had arrived to speak with a visiting Iranian delegation. In the absence of more robust American support, Massoud depended on Iran, India, and Russia for weapons, money, and medical aid. Iran was perhaps his most reliable ally. Iranian Revolutionary Guards and intelligence operatives worked in northern Afghanistan alongside Massoud's guerrillas.

While they were together in Dushanbe, Saleh asked Massoud, "Where shall I send the equipment?" He was referring to the C.I.A.'s latest gear. Massoud told him to keep it in Tajikistan for the time being and to invite some Panjshiri colleagues up to Dushanbe. "You can train them," Massoud instructed.[8]

That weekend Massoud returned to Afghanistan, to his compounds near the Tajikistan border in Khoja Bahauddin. Two Arab television journalists carrying Belgian passports had been waiting there for days to interview the commander.

On the morning of September 9, 2001, Muhammad Arif Sarwari, who was commonly referred to as Engineer Arif, because he had studied electronics at a technical university in Kabul before dropping out to join Massoud at war, was at work in his basement office, where he oversaw a wire-strewn rat's nest of ultra-high-frequency radios, intercept boxes, and satellite telephones. Arif was Massoud's senior intelligence operations leader, in charge of all reporting agents and intercept collection in the day-to-day war effort.

Arif was a gregarious, energetic man with thinning hair. A C.I.A. officer who worked with him called Arif "scruffy, verbose, crafty, corrupt, and a good, reliable partner." He was born to a Panjshiri family in Kabul in 1961 and grew up in Karte Parwan, the neighborhood where Ahmad

Shah Massoud had also lived as a boy. When the Soviet Union invaded Afghanistan in 1979, Arif was still in school, but in 1982 he left for the Panjshir to join the rebellion. Initially he worked as a guard and a clerk, but after a year, when Massoud learned that he was from a trusted Panjshiri family, spoke Russian, and knew electronics, the commander asked him to set up a listening post in the Panjshir, to monitor Russian military communications.[9]

The British foreign intelligence service, MI6, had recently provided Massoud with a Jaguar high-frequency radio network and computers. Someone needed to organize all this equipment and make tactical use of the intercepted messages. Arif became the Panjshir Valley's de facto intelligence chief, often at Massoud's side. Besides managing radio intercepts, he developed human sources. During the war's late stages, Massoud built secret ties to an Afghan Communist faction in Kabul known as the Karmalites. When the Communist regime collapsed in the spring of 1992, Massoud seized Kabul. For the next four years, Massoud served as Afghanistan's minister of defense while Engineer Arif worked as the number two at the Afghan intelligence and security service, formally known as Khadamat-i-Atala'at-I Dawlati, or Government Information Service, but notorious across the country by its acronym, K.H.A.D. Its officers had carried out brutal interrogations and thousands of extrajudicial executions during the Communist era. Arif kept some Soviet-trained Communist veterans in place. After the Taliban took Kabul in 1996 and Massoud retreated back to the Panjshir, Arif maintained contact with some of the former K.H.A.D. officers he had worked with; some of them now served as agents behind Taliban lines. Arif sent small satellite phones to agents in Kabul and Kandahar and arranged for them to cross into Panjshir to meet Massoud personally. "Are there Pakistani troops?" Massoud would ask. "What about Al Qaeda? What are their ammunition supplies?" Kabul was particularly easy to penetrate because of its mixed ethnic makeup and its proximity to the Panjshir. One of Massoud's reporting agents was the head of all intelligence for the Taliban in Kabul.[10]

Massoud owned thousands of books and was devoted to Persian poetry. In the early hours of Sunday, September 9, he stayed up with an old

friend—a longtime political aide named Massoud Khalili—and read poetry aloud in a bungalow, as the two of them did regularly. The next
morning, the commander summoned Engineer Arif to ask what should
be done about the United States, "how to advance that relationship, what
the issues were, what strategy to pursue."

The communications and radio intercept center Arif ran was located
on the ground floor of a concrete house he used as an office when he
stayed in Khoja Bahauddin. There was a reception room upstairs. Massoud said he was finally ready to grant the visiting Arab journalists an
interview. The journalists set up their tripods and cameras in the room
just above Arif's intelligence center. It was by now almost noon. Arif was
in and out. At one point, the commander took a call on his satellite
phone. He learned that a Taliban and Al Qaeda force had attacked their
front lines near Bagram Airfield and that eight Arabs had been seized.
He asked Arif, "See what you can learn about the fighting."

Arif went downstairs. He was on the satellite phone when suddenly
an explosion knocked the phone out of his hand. At first he thought it
was a bomb dropped by one of the Taliban's handful of fighter planes or
an enemy rocket launched from long distance; such attacks were commonplace in Khoja Bahauddin. Then Arif smelled smoke and heard
guards shouting. He ran upstairs to the reception room and saw Massoud's body lying inert, blood everywhere. His friend Khalili, who had
been translating for the commander during the "interview," also lay un-
conscious. Arif called out for the commander's Toyota Land Cruiser. He
and other men carried the victims outside. They laid Massoud on the
backseat of the Land Cruiser and put Khalili in the third-row seat. As
they drove off, Arif called for a helicopter. He ordered the driver to head
for a landing area five or six minutes away. By coincidence, there was a
helicopter in the air nearby.

"It's an emergency," Arif said. "We're going to need that helicopter—
but tell them not to shut down the engines. We're coming."

They loaded the wounded men aboard. Arif tried to prevent the helicopter pilots from learning what had taken place. He told them to fly
straight to a hospital not far from Khoja Bahauddin that had been built
by the government of India and to land in the garden. Then he returned

to his office and raised General Fahim Khan, Massoud's most important military commander, on a satellite phone. Arif used the code word they employed for Massoud. "Something has happened to Khalid," he said.[11]

September 9 is Independence Day in Tajikistan, a government and business holiday, so Amrullah Saleh was at home when his phone rang. It was a nephew of Massoud's. "Don't waste time packing—you are ordered to rush to the airport and fly to Kulyab," a city in Tajikistan about 120 miles southeast of Dushanbe. Saleh left immediately.[12]

In Kulyab, still following cryptic instructions, he made his way to a hospital. He found four or five of Massoud's commanders and aides there. A little later General Fahim Khan arrived. Engineer Arif turned up near sunset, his clothes still covered in blood. A liaison officer from Tajikistan's intelligence service joined the group, as did an officer of Iran's Revolutionary Guards. Abdullah Abdullah, a medical doctor and the longtime foreign policy adviser to Massoud who ran many of his overseas liaisons, had been summoned from a diplomatic trip to New Delhi. For the first time, the commanders told Amrullah Saleh the truth: Massoud was dead.

His corpse was inside the hospital. They had flown the body up from the Indian hospital on the Afghan border.

In the garden, they talked about what to do. There were now about a dozen of them gathered. They were in shock; some of the men wept. Al Qaeda and the Taliban had tried to kill Massoud many times before, but he had seemed invincible. (The two Arab suicide bombers, who had been prepped for their martyrdom by Al Qaeda, had hidden their explosives in their camera equipment.) As they talked, the Panjshiri leaders concluded quickly that they would have to lie publicly about Massoud's death. They would have to put out word that he had only been lightly injured and would survive. Otherwise they feared that their fighters on the front lines at the mouth of the Panjshir Valley, facing a mass of Taliban and vicious, death-seeking Al Qaeda volunteers, would panic and retreat, allowing the Taliban to swarm into the valley and carry out a slaughter. The Iranian Revolutionary Guards adviser with them volunteered that if it seemed too difficult to keep the secret of Massoud's killing while his corpse was lying in Kulyab, the guards and Tajikistan's intelligence service could transfer the body to Mashhad, in Iran, and "keep his death secret for one month, six months, whatever you need."

Others in the group suggested that they move the corpse back to the Panjshir Valley. Yet this carried the danger that the truth would leak out prematurely, before they had prepared commanders on the front lines. Abdullah had no doubt that the resistance would collapse if news spread that Massoud was gone. The officer from Tajikistan intelligence said there was a morgue nearby the hospital. They could secretly keep the body there for at least a few days while Fahim consulted with commanders. They all decided that was the best plan.[13]

They also agreed to inform the six countries that were most important to their cause about what had really happened: the United States, Russia, Iran, India, Tajikistan, and Uzbekistan. They gave instructions to Amrullah Saleh: Call the C.I.A. Tell them the truth about Massoud's assassination and ask for weapons. The argument Saleh was to deliver to ALEC Station was, in essence, "If resistance to the Taliban and Al Qaeda means something to you, we can hold. We can fight. We *will* fight. But if you wanted to help Commander Massoud only—he is not with us anymore. To compensate for his loss, we need *more* help than in the time when he was alive."

Saleh flew back to Dushanbe and put a message in for Richard Blee at the C.I.A.'s Counterterrorist Center. He said he needed to speak urgently. When Blee called on an encrypted line, Saleh followed the script given to him at Kulyab. He confirmed to Blee that Massoud was dead but emphasized that Panjshir's leaders wanted to keep the news secret as they tried to forestall a collapse of their lines.

After they hung up, Blee notified the White House. Within hours, news services quoted anonymous Bush administration officials saying that Massoud had probably been assassinated.

Saleh called back. You are causing me great difficulty with my comrades, he said evenly. My instructions were to keep this secret.

Blee agreed that it was unfortunate. The C.I.A. was obligated to inform policy makers of such important information as soon as it arrived but the agency had no control over how the White House or State Department handled reporters' questions.

Saleh pressed. He knew that Blee and ALEC Station had advocated for arms supplies to Massoud and had earlier taken their arguments to the White House and lost. But the Bush administration had now settled in and here was a new threat to American intelligence collection on Bin Laden—if the Panjshir fell, the C.I.A. would lose a vital listening station. Would America try to save the Council of the North, or would it leave the Panjshiris to their fate?

"The decision is that we will fight," Saleh said. "We will not surrender. We will fight to our last man on the ground. This resistance was not about Massoud. It was about something much, much bigger. We will hold."

Saleh was putting together a list of the weapons and logistical supplies they needed most urgently. "What can you do for us?"

Blee said he understood the question. It was Monday, September 10, the beginning of a new working week in Washington. He would need a day or two. "Let me come back to you on this," he said.[14]

TWO

Judgment Day

On September 11, ALEC Station held down a small area of the D.C.I. Counterterrorist Center, a windowless expanse of cubicles and computers on the ground floor of the New Headquarters Building. It was the worst office space at the C.I.A., in the opinion of some who worked there. It felt like a bunker. During the last days of the Cold War, the Soviet–East Europe Division had occupied the floor; its impermeability would thwart the K.G.B.'s eavesdroppers, the thinking went. The C.I.A.'s Russia hands eventually found better quarters and C.T.C. moved in. The center was a bureaucratic stepchild. It had been founded in 1986 as an experiment, a place where analysts—typically, writers and researchers with graduate degrees but no operating experience on the street—might work alongside or even supervise case officers, also known as operations officers, the career spies who recruited agents and stole secrets. The C.I.A.'s case officer cadre enjoyed the greatest prestige and power at the agency. It was not natural for them to collaborate with analysts. It was akin to creating teams of detectives and college professors to solve crimes. Senior C.I.A. leaders advised newly minted case officers to avoid C.T.C. because being assigned there might inhibit promotions and overseas assignments. Yet during the late 1990s, as terrorism evolved amid post–Cold War disorder, the Counterterrorist Center's budget more than doubled, including one-time supplemental appropriations, while the rest of the C.I.A. dealt with flat or declining budgets.

By September 2001 there were about 350 people working at C.T.C. About three or four dozen worked in overseas stations, but most of the rest were jammed into the New Headquarters bunker. Besides ALEC Station, the center housed branches and sections assigned to Sunni extremist groups other than Al Qaeda, such as Hamas, as well as ideologically diverse groups such as Hezbollah (a Shiite Islamic faction based in Lebanon), Colombian guerrillas (mainly Marxist and secular, yet operating within a Catholic country), the Tamil Tigers in Sri Lanka (Hindu and ethnically nationalist, yet fighting for autonomy in a Buddhist-majority country), the Japanese Red Army (a fragment of the Cold War), and more than six dozen other targets. The office featured low-grade industrial carpeting and cookie-cutter government cubicles. It was poorly lit and smelled vaguely sour. Wanted posters of grim-looking terrorist fugitives, including Osama Bin Laden, decorated the walls. In an attempt at relief, someone had mounted fake windows looking out on beaches and palm trees.[1]

A job at C.T.C. came with a certain dark glamour and a lifesaving mission, but the federal government's general schedule salaries were no better than those at the Department of Agriculture. The C.I.A.'s bureaucracy was thick and intrusive. The agency's counterintelligence division, charged with detecting traitors and other abusers of security clearances, surveyed the workforce and administered polygraphs that could be highly unpleasant, no matter how diligent and loyal the person examined might be. Mid-level C.I.A. managers could be lazy or cantankerous or stupid or all three. Federal employment rules made it difficult to do anything about poor performers, short of proof of theft or felony violence. Overall, C.T.C.'s employees liked their jobs better than typical C.I.A. employees did in the summer of 2001, according to an internal survey. They knew their mission mattered. Yet ALEC Station's analysts suffered from information overload. They handled more than two hundred incoming cables a day from other parts of C.I.A., plus another two hundred or more from the Pentagon, the State Department, the National Security Agency, and elsewhere. Dozens of these were "action cables" requiring a prompt reply or follow-up. The analysts often felt stressed. About a third of C.I.A. employees overall felt they handled too much work, but at ALEC Station, almost six in ten felt that way.[2]

The pressure and the sense of foreboding that informed office life at ALEC was not felt widely across the government or in Congress. The analysts and operators were strikingly small in number, considering that Al Qaeda had carried out several successful attacks against the United States claiming hundreds of lives. ALEC and its counterparts, equally modest in number, at the National Security Council, the F.B.I., and the National Security Agency were largely on their own, to grind out whatever detection, arrests, and disruptions they could deliver. The C.I.A.'s counterterrorism operations in the summer of 2001 often resembled the surveillance operations and criminal investigations carried out domestically by the F.B.I., with the difference that C.T.C. typically worked overseas, clandestinely, often without regard to the laws of other countries. A common C.T.C. operation involved intensified intelligence collection on a terrorist suspect in an impoverished, unfriendly city like Khartoum or Karachi. That meant operators built a file on a suspect by observing his movements and taking clandestine photographs of his visitors. They might also work with the National Security Agency to tap his phones or hack into his bank accounts or bribe a clerk for the records. A special roster of C.I.A. independent contractors—ex-soldiers, ex-cops, and assorted other adrenaline junkies—carried out the riskiest surveillance and break-in work overseas because full-time case officers, if caught in the act, likely would have their mug shots publicized by the host government, rendering their expensive training and years-in-the-making cover stories useless. In comparison to career case officers, the contractors were "sort of cannon fodder," as one of them put it.

Some of them specialized in "area familiarization," as it was called, meaning long stakeouts and detailed mapping of a suspect's neighborhood, routes, and routines. These C.I.A. operatives also observed local police and intelligence services so as to plan how to get away if caught. If burglary or planting a listening device was called for, that required a specialized C.I.A. team that resided offshore. These contractors were trained to break into a home or office or embassy, plant a device or steal documents, and get out of the country as fast as possible.

The C.T.C. analysts in the basement of New Headquarters supported these surveillance and profile-building operations by assessing and logging the photos, wiretaps, and reporting cables that poured in. If C.T.C. wanted to take a suspect off the streets, it typically relied on friendly governments to make arrests, but the center also had some capacity to detain and transport individuals on its own in a procedure called "rendition." The C.T.C.'s Renditions Branch would sometimes transfer a terrorism suspect from one country to another for interrogation, including to countries like Egypt, whose military dictatorship had a stark record of torturing detainees.[3]

The director of C.T.C. that summer was Cofer Black, a former Khartoum station chief who had worked the Al Qaeda account on and off since the mid-1990s. He was six foot three, perhaps twenty pounds overweight, with thinning hair and a pasty skin tone befitting a man whose office along one of the basement's walls now ensured that he rarely saw the light of day.

His father had been an international airline pilot. Black had spent his childhood in Germany and England, before attending boarding school. He had joined the C.I.A. after studying international relations at the University of Southern California. He had spent much of his career as an operations officer in the Africa Division, managing American allies, supplying arms, and working on Somalia's conflicts. The C.I.A.'s Africa Division also recruited Soviet, Chinese, Cuban, North Korean, and Iranian diplomats, spies, or defense attachés who were posted to African embassies, where the targeted individuals were far from headquarters and susceptible to compromise. During the Cold War, the division had a reputation among young operations officers as an exciting, unrestrained place of action, adventure, and professional opportunity, but also as a place untethered from headquarters and lacking the prestige and centrality of Moscow, Berlin, or Beijing.

After many years in Africa, Black's manner had become theatrical and self-dramatizing. He was the sort of C.I.A. officer one would expect to encounter in an Oliver Stone film. His years abroad had left him with a hard-to-place accent—a touch of South Africa seemed evident. He had proven to be an effective office politician as he rose within C.I.A. He had a subtler intelligence than his melodramatic speech might suggest, and because he could be funny and generous, he had won the loyalty of senior colleagues. George Tenet had sent him to run C.T.C. in 1999, at a time when the Seventh Floor, as the C.I.A.'s leadership was known, was becoming highly alarmed about Al Qaeda.

Black was not a Harvard Business School–inspired manager. Even more than most operations officers, who as a class prided themselves on their ability to freelance and improvise, Black considered it his mission to bend or ignore the C.I.A.'s bureaucracy, to concentrate on action and operations. Yet he also managed to keep many of his superiors on his side.

As Khartoum station chief, Black had overseen intelligence collection operations against Osama Bin Laden. He tried to infuse C.T.C. with the spirit of streetwise operational gusto that Africa Division considered its trademark. He brought in Hank Crumpton, who had spent more than a decade as an operations officer in Africa, as his principal deputy. At ALEC Station, he inherited Rich Blee, another familiar Africa hand. They recruited others from their old division as well.[4]

At 8:00 a.m. on September 11, 2001, Cofer Black convened a regular briefing meeting in his office. Each week, C.T.C. presented three separate update briefings on Al Qaeda to C.I.A. director George Tenet; James Pavitt, the head of the clandestine service; and A. B. "Buzzy" Krongard, the agency's executive director. Black asked for a read-in on each briefing before it was delivered. That morning they were scheduled to provide their weekly update to Krongard.

Rich Blee walked into Black's office. He was preoccupied by the aftermath of Ahmad Shah Massoud's assassination. Despite Amrullah Saleh's brave talk, Blee figured that without Massoud's leadership, the Panjshiri resistance to the Taliban would soon collapse. It seemed doubtful that the Bush administration would do anything to prevent that. Yet Blee owed Saleh an answer.

Also at the meeting was the head of analysis at C.T.C., Ben Bonk. He was a Detroit native who evangelized about its Corvettes and sports teams, and who had become a specialist in South Asia and Central Asia, at one point serving as national intelligence officer for the region.

Just after 8:46 a.m., Black's secretary came in to say that a private plane had crashed into the World Trade Center.

Black was a licensed pilot like his father. Glancing at the news coverage on a television mounted in the corner of his office, he could see a hole in the World Trade Center's North Tower. The weather looked clear. He figured the accident involved a light aircraft and that the pilot might have committed suicide. It was an oddity, not necessarily an act of terrorism.

A little before 9:00 a.m., several visitors arrived outside Black's office. They had no appointment but they wanted to make a short courtesy call. The group included U.S. Navy commander Kirk Lippold, who had been at the helm of the USS *Cole* the previous October when Al Qaeda suicide bombers attacked the ship. He had driven over to the C.I.A. that morning to receive an update from agency analysts about Al Qaeda.

Just as he prepared to greet Lippold, a phone on Black's desk rang. His desk had several secure telephone lines and he wasn't sure how all of them worked. Yet he knew that the one ringing was a nonsecure phone for sources or contacts that he didn't want to route through the C.I.A. switchboard. Most of the time when that line rang, the callers were selling credit cards or oil changes.

He picked it up. It was an old friend, an officer from the C.I.A.'s paramilitary division. They had worked together during the Angolan war. His friend had since risen to a senior position at the agency. He happened that morning to be visiting the C.I.A.'s station in New York, which was located in an office building next to the World Trade Center.

"Hey chief, we've got a problem," the officer said. "I watched this 737-like civilian airliner. I was watching the control surfaces of the aircraft. The pilot flew it into the World Trade Center."

He spoke in the clipped vernacular of battlefield operations. "We've been struck. I'm evacuating my position."[5]

———

Rich Blee walked across the hall to ALEC Station's cluster of cubicles. "That's Bin Laden or Al Qaeda," he said, pointing to a nearby television hanging from the ceiling.

"You can't say that," one of his colleagues objected. "It could be an accident. Every time something happens, you can't say that it's Al Qaeda."

They stood around arguing. There was a split verdict within ALEC Station, but most of the analysts credited the possibility of an accident. ALEC analysts had written warning report after warning report, briefing slide after briefing slide, for the White House and the Bush cabinet. They had provided insights for the article in the President's Daily Brief received by George W. Bush on August 6, 2001, headlined BIN LADIN DETERMINED TO STRIKE IN US.

"It's Bin Laden," Blee insisted to his colleagues.

They were still arguing among themselves at 9:03 a.m. when United Airlines Flight 175 struck the World Trade Center's South Tower.[6]

George Tenet raced up the George Washington Parkway to C.I.A. headquarters at about eighty miles an hour. His security detail had pulled him out of a breakfast at a downtown hotel after the first plane hit. Tenet called ahead and asked for the agency's senior leaders to assemble in 7D64, the director's conference room at Old Headquarters.

Cofer Black grabbed an experienced administrative colleague on the C.T.C. staff as he prepared to head upstairs. "Wherever I go today, you come right with me," he told her. "No matter who's there, you come in. I want you to write down every order people give me because I'm not going to remember them all."

At 9:37 a.m., American Airlines Flight 77 struck the Pentagon while flying about 530 miles per hour.

In Tenet's conference room, there was "a lot of yelling and screaming," as Charles Allen, a sixty-five-year-old agency veteran in charge of intelligence collection, put it.

"We have to get out of here!" one senior officer exclaimed. "They're heading for us!"[7]

At 9:40 a.m., Black and deputy C.I.A. director John McLaughlin spoke by secure video link with Richard Clarke, the lead counterterrorism expert at the White House. Clarke said the Federal Aviation Administration was uncertain how many other planes might have been hijacked and still in the air. Several planes were not responding to air controllers or were squawking signals that might indicate a hijack. There were rumors of a car bombing at the State Department.[8]

C.T.C. officers who accompanied Black upstairs mentioned to the group in 7D64 that Ramzi Yousef, the ringleader of the bombing of the World Trade Center in 1993, had once discussed flying a Cessna packed with explosives into C.I.A. headquarters. And here they all were packed in together on the building's highest floor.

"Let's get out of here," the head of Tenet's personal security detail recommended. "Let's evacuate."

Should we leave? Tenet asked his senior team.

"We should stay here and work on," Charles Allen argued. "Where are we going to go?"[9]

Tenet had risen in Washington as a staff member on Capitol Hill known for his charisma and his succinct, colorful briefings. He explained later that he "didn't want the world to think we were abandoning ship," yet he "didn't want to risk the lives of our own people unnecessarily," and "we needed to have our leadership intact and able to make decisions."[10]

He ordered the senior team downstairs. Around 10:00 a.m., he directed C.I.A. personnel to evacuate the grounds. Within minutes every computer at the agency flashed EVACUATE in red. Intelligence officers trudged down the stairwells. The evacuation did not sit well with all of them; it felt like running away. When they got outside, they saw a huge traffic jam as several thousand employees tried to drive out of the campus simultaneously.[11]

During the Cold War, the C.I.A. had maintained a secret, bunkered alternate campus to which its leaders could retreat in the event of nuclear war. The alternate campus had been eliminated from the federal budget after the fall of the Berlin Wall. The C.I.A. and its budgeters in Congress had failed to prepare for an emergency on this scale. Tenet's office had the agency's printing plant on the Langley campus as a nearby emergency site, if needed. Charles Allen's office had been working to build a new, survivable emergency site, away from the campus, for the C.I.A. and other critical agencies of government, but this was still a work in progress.[12]

Tenet now led a march of senior officers toward the C.I.A. printing plant, an outbuilding across the campus. When they reached there, a technician set up a secure terminal equipment, or S.T.E., line to the White House. Tenet raised Stephen Hadley, the deputy national security adviser.

President Bush was by now in the air aboard Air Force One, en route to a Louisiana air base. Vice President Dick Cheney had been hustled into a White House bunker. Secretary of Defense Donald Rumsfeld was inside the smoldering Pentagon. Secretary of State Colin Powell was traveling in Latin America. The country's leaders communicated only sporadically, and the attack still seemed to be in progress.

Hadley insisted that Tenet keep the S.T.E. line open to the White House continuously. Because that channel was occupied, Charles Allen had no way to collect securely the latest intercept reports from the National Security Agency about who might be responsible for the airplane hijackings. Michael Hayden, the N.S.A. director, wanted to send over reports providing preliminary evidence that Al Qaeda was responsible. Allen sent an N.S.A. liaison officer back into C.I.A. headquarters to pull these reports off a secure fax machine and bring them to the printing plant.

Tenet talked to leaders at the F.B.I., the Federal Aviation Administration, State, the National Security Agency, and other counterparts. He also tried to determine whether any C.I.A. officers in the New York station had been killed. (None had, it turned out.)

Cofer Black finally cornered him.

All summer, it had been obvious from intelligence reporting that something big and bad was coming. For weeks, Black had been thinking about how he would handle this day. He had tried to imagine in advance a moment of great pressure when a lot of people would be dead and he would have to speak forcefully to C.T.C.'s workforce and to his superiors on the Seventh Floor.

"Sir, we're going to have to exempt C.T.C." from the C.I.A.-wide evacuation, Black told Tenet. They would also need to exempt personnel from the Office of Technical Services, which supported C.T.C. "We need to have our people working the computers."

"They're going to be at risk," Tenet answered.

"We're going to have to keep them in place. They have the key function to play in a crisis like this."

"Well, they could die."

"Well, sir, then they're just going to have to die."

Tenet thought it over and replied, "You're absolutely right."[13]

Black walked back toward New Headquarters, into the swarm of evacuating C.I.A. employees.

Inside C.T.C., Black said that their job now was to explain to the president and his cabinet what had just happened to the United States, who did it, and what might be coming next.[14]

The Federal Aviation Administration had a liaison officer at C.T.C. He could access airline passenger manifests. Rich Blee and his ALEC Station analysts were by now certain that Al Qaeda had carried out the hijackings but to make that call firmly for the White House they needed proof.

Blee asked the liaison officer to access the F.A.A.'s computers and obtain passenger lists for the four known aircraft seized by hijackers. The officer said he could not do that. These were American airliners filled with American citizens and under the law the C.I.A. could not access private information about U.S. persons, he maintained. Blee was beside himself. He asked F.B.I. agents deployed to ALEC Station to see what they could obtain through the bureau's channels.[15]

The Hezbollah Branch's analysts at C.T.C. were as certain as the ALEC team that the hijackings had been carried out by *their* terrorists. The attack was a sophisticated, complex operation that required planning and resources. Hezbollah had thousands of fighters in southern Lebanon and a worldwide network strong enough to pull off such a feat. Just a week or two earlier, the branch's analysts had placed a provocative article in the classified *National Intelligence Digest* arguing that Hezbollah was a more serious threat to the United States than Al Qaeda. During the past two decades, Hezbollah units had bombed American facilities in Saudi Arabia, Kuwait, and Lebanon. The death toll from Hezbollah attacks since the 1980s was higher than the death toll from Al Qaeda strikes, the article had pointed out.

"This is Mughniyeh," one of the Hezbollah analysts assured Blee, referring to Imad Mughniyeh, then the notorious fugitive leader of Hezbollah's Islamic Jihad Organization.

"It's not Mughniyeh," Blee said. Intelligence about a spectacular Al Qaeda attack had been piling up all summer from multiple sources. There was no comparable threat stream about Hezbollah. Yet the Hezbollah analysts were adamant. "Go for it," Blee finally said. Prove your case.[16]

The analysts in ALEC Station's cubicles all knew the history of Ramzi Yousef, the architect of the first World Trade Center bombing in 1993. It was two years after that when Yousef had also discussed flying a plane into C.I.A. headquarters. The husband of one analyst worked at the Pentagon, which was now in flames. Other analysts had children at home or school.

Blee decided to speak to the group.

He was not an easy man to read. He could be blunt. This morning, he tried to be calm. The sensation of being under fire was not new to him. But for many Washington-bound analysts at ALEC, this was a first.

Blee told them he understood that not everyone would feel that they could stay at work, that some had families they would feel they needed to serve first. It was okay to leave, he said. Still, he continued, "The country needs you. We need you. It's hard, but try to stay here."

Blee had been reflecting on the fact that a hijacked plane might strike C.I.A. headquarters at any minute. Yet he felt they would survive. A plane would have to fly above the treetops around the C.I.A. campus and so it would almost inevitably strike the New Headquarters' upper floors. Even if the building pancaked, Blee figured, C.T.C.'s bunker-like ground floor would survive intact for a while and there would be time to get outside. Here at last was a reason to be grateful for this miserable office space: Five planes could land on C.I.A., Blee thought, and his workforce would probably crawl out unharmed, like cockroaches.

One of the analysts on the team asked him about the C.I.A.'s defenses. "One of those planes is probably headed our way. Are there surface-to-air missiles on the roof?"

"Sure, there are surface-to-air missiles," Blee lied. "They've got them at the White House. They've got them here, too." His response was spontaneous. He was trying to keep ALEC together. Also, lying was part of a case officer's profession.

"We're going to war," Blee said. ALEC's days of isolation were over. They would soon be catapulted to the center of national decision making. Any proposals for attacking Al Qaeda that had earlier been turned down by the Seventh Floor or the White House should be revived and reconsidered. "Use your imagination," Blee said.

All but two of the ALEC Station employees stayed at their desks, according to the recollections of Blee's colleagues.[17]

By noon it was clear that the threat of additional kamikaze attacks on Washington had passed. The F.B.I. sent over the passenger manifests for the four hijacked airliners by about 1:00 p.m. ALEC Station's analysts typically divided their work by geographical region. Some covered Asia, others the Middle East or Africa. An F.B.I. analyst on assignment to C.I.A. kept track of Al Qaeda's domestic ties. Just a few weeks earlier, while reviewing old cable traffic, she had recognized that a known Al Qaeda associate, Khalid al Mihdhar, had obtained an American visa and flown to the United States in early 2000. She had asked the F.B.I. to look for Mihdhar and a colleague, Nawaf al Hazmi, but the search had barely started. Now the analyst saw their names on the American 77 passenger list.

She approached Blee. "Here's the smoking gun," she said.[18]

D id September 11 vindicate the C.I.A.'s warnings about Al Qaeda or expose its failure to prevent a disaster the agency might have stopped?

Tenet, Black, and Blee warned the Bush administration about Al Qaeda clearly and repeatedly during 2001. They were not the only people in the government to issue such warnings. Richard Clarke at the National Security Council repeatedly urged Condoleezza Rice and other Bush administration leaders to focus on Bin Laden and take more aggressive action. Al Qaeda specialists at the F.B.I. and the Justice Department also understood well the threat Bin Laden posed.

In the two decades before 2001, the C.I.A. had sometimes failed in its mission to alert presidents in advance to strategic risks and threats abroad. The agency's analysts were late to recognize the forces that swept the Soviet Union away. They were timid about Soviet premier Mikhail Gorbachev's potential as a reformer. The agency failed to detect or predict India's decision to test a nuclear bomb in 1998. On Al Qaeda, however, in 2001, the C.I.A. had the big picture right and communicated warnings forcefully. In late June, C.T.C. had alerted all station chiefs worldwide about the possibility of an imminent suicide attack, and Tenet asked the chiefs to brief every ambassador. "Over the last several months, we have seen unprecedented indications that Bin Ladin and his supporters have been preparing for a terrorist operation," that C.T.C. bulletin reported. Other C.I.A. warning reports that month carried the headlines BIN LADIN ATTACKS MAY BE IMMINENT and BIN LADIN AND ASSOCIATES MAKING NEAR-TERM THREATS. A daily C.I.A. analytical product, the Senior Executive Intelligence Brief, carried an article on June 30 entitled BIN LADIN PLANNING HIGH-PROFILE ATTACKS.[19]

The C.I.A. did not know when or where the attack would occur, however. Blee said that Bin Laden's pattern in the past had been to have his suicide cells attack only when they were ready, not according to any hard schedule. Based on the totality of the intelligence available, Blee said, "Attack preparations have been made. . . . Multiple and simultaneous attacks are possible, and they will occur with little or no warning." Yet they had no concrete evidence of any plan to strike inside the United States; their best guess was that Al Qaeda would continue with its established pattern of striking American embassies or defense facilities abroad.[20]

Why did the C.I.A. have so little insight into the U.S. plot? Despite several years of field operations and the recruitment of more than one hundred reporting agents inside Afghanistan, ALEC Station had not penetrated Bin Laden's planning. Al Qaeda's counterintelligence against potential moles was formidable. In counterterrorism, strategic warning is vital, but tactical warning about dates and places saves lives. The C.I.A. had not attained that fidelity about Al Qaeda.

Worse, as the F.B.I. analyst's instant recognition of the "smoking gun" names on the Flight 77 passenger manifest indicated, agency analysts had possessed for twenty-one months intelligence that might have led to the disruption of the September 11 conspiracy. Yet C.I.A. analysts in multiple stations and branches had failed to act adequately on its importance.

In late 1999, operatives working with Malaysia's Special Branch police had photographed clandestinely a meeting of suspected Al Qaeda associates in Kuala Lumpur. In January, they discovered Mihdhar's name and the fact that he had a visa to travel to the United States. In March, they learned his colleague Hazmi's name as well and the fact that both men had already flown to Los Angeles. Yet they took no action until August 2001. Soon after the information about Mihdhar and Hazmi was discovered, Doug Miller and Mark Rossini, F.B.I. agents assigned to ALEC, drafted a cable reporting the facts to the F.B.I. But a C.I.A. officer blocked them from releasing the cable. It is unclear why. The failure to detect and locate Mihdhar and Hazmi would catalyze blame shifting between the C.I.A. and the F.B.I. for years to come.

According to an investigation by the C.I.A.'s Office of Inspector General completed in 2005 but not declassified for another ten years, fifty to sixty individuals "read one or more of six different C.I.A. cables containing travel information related to these terrorists," meaning Mihdhar and Hazmi. A majority of those who read the cables worked at C.T.C. They were mainly C.I.A. analysts but also included four F.B.I. agents on assignment to the agency.[21]

The C.I.A. failed to place either Mihdhar or Hazmi on a State

Department–managed terrorist watch list that might have caused the men to be denied entry to the United States or refused visas. (The list was not as significant as watch lists would become after September 11— it did not have a "no fly" provision that airlines could automatically access as passengers checked in, for example.) Mihdhar left the United States once after his initial arrival and then returned, so if he had been on the State Department list, he might have been refused entry the second time. "That so many individuals failed to act in this case reflects a systemic breakdown—a breakdown caused by excessive workload, ambiguities about responsibilities, and mismanagement of the program," the C.I.A. inspector general's investigators later concluded. "Basically, there was no coherent, functioning watchlisting program."[22] The investigators recommended that a C.I.A. Accountability Board review Cofer Black, among others, for failing to perform to professional standards, but Porter Goss, the C.I.A.'s director when the recommendation was made, chose not to do so. Goss's view was, first, that he was not interested in reprimanding anyone who was no longer at C.I.A. (Black had left government by then.) Second, Goss noted that no other agency involved in homeland security before September 11—not the F.B.I., not the Pentagon, not the Federal Aviation Administration—had felt it necessary to single out any individual for responsibility.[23]

Later e-mail records suggest C.I.A. officers believed the information about Mihdhar and Hazmi had been conveyed to the F.B.I. C.I.A. analysts told the inspector general that they had communicated the details informally, over the telephone. Yet there is no documentary evidence to support these recollections, according to the inspector general. His investigators "found no evidence, and heard no claim from any party, that this information was shared in any manner with the F.B.I. or that anyone in ALEC Station took other appropriate operational action at that time."[24] Well into 2001, various analysts reviewed the files but failed to recognize the significance of their information until it was too late.

These failures are an indelible part of the "what if" history of September 11, the possibility that the attacks might have been stopped, that thousands of lives might have been spared, and that America's foreign policy might not have pivoted in costly directions. Yet that counterfactual requires a context. The gross domestic product of the United States in 2001 was about $10.6 trillion. The budget of the federal government was about $1.8 trillion. In fiscal 2001, the government enjoyed a $128 billion operating surplus. Yet counterterrorism teams at the C.I.A. and the F.B.I. working on Al Qaeda and allied groups received an infinitesimal fraction of the country's defense and intelligence budget of roughly $300 billion, the great majority of which went to the Pentagon, to support conventional and missile forces. Bush's national security deputies did not hold a meeting dedicated to plans to thwart Al Qaeda until September 4, 2001, almost nine months after President Bush took the oath of office. The September 11 conspiracy succeeded in part because the democratically elected government of the United States, including the Congress, did not regard Al Qaeda as a priority.

In the first days and months after the attack, in any event, the country had scant appetite for reflection or accountability. President Bush needed answers and plans for retaliation and the C.I.A. had them. September 11 empowered the Counterterrorist Center and its leaders. It put the C.I.A. in a commanding position within the Bush national security cabinet, with a degree of influence over national policy the agency had not enjoyed at the White House since the days of anti-Communist proxy guerrilla war during the 1980s. Overnight, Cofer Black and Rich Blee and their colleagues, promoted by their persuasive boss, George Tenet, became vital authors of American military and foreign policy.

They proceeded under certain assumptions. They believed that C.T.C.'s covert action against Bin Laden after 1998 had been hamstrung by caution and fecklessness at the White House and among the C.I.A.'s leaders. They feared what might be coming next and believed they had to act quickly. Their aggression in the coming weeks "was not about violence," Black insisted later, "although we used the vocabulary of violence to shock and impress and inspire various constituencies." They needed to move fast in order to cause Al Qaeda's leaders to turn their attention away from planning or executing follow-on attacks, to concentrate instead on self-preservation. *The gloves are off*, they told colleagues, a phrase that rapidly spread around the agency and the capital as a dangerous, facile cliché.

The professional histories of Black, Blee, and others in leadership at the Counterterrorist Center that September included long exposure to unconventional war in Africa—arming and training proxy armies, working behind the scenes with small teams of paramilitaries, empowering strongmen while accepting that few guerrilla leaders were morally admirable. They preferred to let the locals carry the fight, enabled by the C.I.A.'s money and technology, following a script that traced back to the secret operations of the Office of Strategic Services during the Second World War, which laid the C.I.A.'s foundations. The Defense Department typically required weeks or months to build the logistics tail to support overseas ground operations. The C.I.A.'s value to the White House over decades—part myth, part valid history—had always been that a hundred operations officers with M4 rifles could go anywhere in a week and create mayhem without a lot of care and feeding. Black's conception of the C.I.A. as the "anti-military," as he put it, required improvising fast.[25]

The American public, shocked and angry on September 11, ready to support retaliation, had no acquaintance with the men in the C.T.C. bunker. Yet the center's leaders would define the country's initial reply to Bin Laden—a paramilitary war in Afghanistan, a counterterrorist campaign against Al Qaeda worldwide. And they would influence many of the legal, political, and diplomatic strategies that would shape those campaigns. The coming war in Afghanistan would follow Africa Division rules.

Shortly after 3:00 p.m. on September 11, Tenet told President Bush during a secure videoconference that the C.I.A. was certain Al Qaeda had carried out the hijackings. He went through the names and case histories of Mihdhar and Hazmi, and the fact that they had been passengers on Flight 77. This was an Al Qaeda operation, the C.I.A. director reported.

Rich Blee called Amrullah Saleh in Dushanbe on their secure line. Saleh had been watching the news coverage but he wasn't sure what the attacks would mean for America's willingness to arm the Council of the North. Saleh certainly did not expect the United States to invade

Afghanistan. At most, if Massoud's men were lucky, the C.I.A. might open its checkbook a little more generously, he thought. Saleh had made more lists since his last call with Blee. He had written up an inventory of weapons and military gear the Panjshiri guerrillas would need to hold the valley against the Taliban and Al Qaeda.

Saleh started to read off his list. Blee interrupted him. "This is a tragedy for my country but it is going to change your country forever," Blee said. The American response to the hijackings was going to involve much more than an increased supply of grenades and helicopters.

"This is now much beyond you," Blee continued. "Consult your leaders because this is going to come in ways—in scope and in scale—that you cannot imagine."[26]

There was a psychologist working at C.T.C., an expert on terrorism. She mentioned to Cofer Black that he should probably talk to the center's workforce to address their emotions.

Black asked her to walk around a little and take in the mood.

"Should I give one of my motivational speeches?" he asked after she had done so.

"These aren't operators," she advised him. They need reassurance. "You're their father. Speak to them like that."

Black was accustomed to supervising case officers doing risky work. The style of speech these officers appreciated was derived from fired-up football coaches exhorting young men in locker rooms. Yet the C.T.C. analysts at New Headquarters in Virginia had graduate degrees. They did not respond especially well to entering-the-jaws-of-hell talk. Black made some notes. He called the workforce together on September 13.

"It really pains me to tell you this, but by the time this is all over, at the victory parade, we will not all be there," Black said. He guessed privately that around four or five dozen C.I.A. personnel would perish or be captured in the coming fight in Afghanistan and elsewhere. He was trying to sensitize the group to the losses he foresaw and to encourage them to appreciate the friends and colleagues they saw in the hallway. There was silence. A few wept.

He tried to lighten the mood. He told them what he had been doing over the last forty-eight hours. He had met with President Bush. The president had already given him a nickname, "Heffer," because apparently Bush couldn't remember "Cofer" and "I am sort of a hefty guy."

Black also told them that his favorite movie was *Bill & Ted's Excellent Adventure*, a 1989 science fiction comedy about two teenage slackers who use a time machine to travel through history. Even those around him who were crying laughed.

"Be excellent to each other," Black went on. "Give everyone a break. We're all doing the best we can." He was thinking about a colleague on the analytical side of C.T.C. who had reported that a neighbor had confronted her and told her that she was partly responsible for September 11, sending her into tears. These were dark days, Black felt, many in C.T.C. were racked by guilt, the emotions were raw, and he struggled, too, to hold a measured tone.

He added, "If you remember one thing from this, I'd like it to be that we're the good guys, and we're going to win."[27]

THREE

Friends Like These

D ave Smith had an office on the third floor of the U.S. embassy in Islamabad, Pakistan, near the C.I.A. station, in the chancery's secure area. In September 2001, he was ten months into his fourth deployment to Pakistan. His business card read "Colonel David O. Smith, United States Army Attaché." This was slightly fictitious. He had served in the Army for thirty years and had risen to the rank of colonel but had recently retired. The Defense Intelligence Agency had recruited him as a civilian under a program designed to improve Pentagon reporting from hard countries, including Pakistan. After some rumination, the Pentagon's lawyers had signed off on a plan to allow Smith to call himself an active United States Army officer and even to wear his uniform in Pakistan when the occasion required.[1]

The D.I.A. was the Pentagon's intelligence arm, headquartered at Bolling Air Force Base, adjacent to Washington's low-income Anacostia neighborhoods. Its collectors and analysts provided intelligence to the secretary of defense and uniformed commanders, as well as to the White House and other government customers. The D.I.A.'s budget dwarfed the C.I.A.'s but it had none of Langley's fame and little of its influence. Its leaders struggled to reconcile the requirements of military discipline with the law-skirting tradecraft of human intelligence collection, or "humint." Yet the D.I.A. housed some of America's most experienced, best-sourced experts on foreign armies, among other subjects.

Dave Smith was one. He was a meticulous, balding man then in his midfifties. He was easily overlooked, useful for an intelligence officer. He had grown up in Missouri, where his father worked at an oil refinery. His ancestors had fought in many American wars, but Smith was the first in his family to graduate from college and the first to be commissioned as an officer. He served initially in the artillery but later joined the Army's Foreign Area Officer Program. It deployed mid-ranking officers to embassies worldwide, where they collected information on host country militaries and their intelligence wings.

In 1982, Smith enrolled at the Pakistan Army's prestigious Command and Staff College in Quetta, where he befriended Pakistani officers on track for promotion. He kept up those relationships when he deployed to the U.S. embassy in Islamabad as an attaché in the late 1980s, just as the C.I.A.'s covert action program to thwart the Soviet Union in Afghanistan was winding down, and then again in the mid-1990s, as the Taliban rose to power. By the time the D.I.A. recruited Smith in late 2000 to return to Islamabad under light cover, the Pakistan Army officers he had first met almost two decades earlier had risen to become commanding generals. One of them was Mahmud Ahmed, the director-general of the Inter-Services Intelligence Directorate, or I.S.I., Pakistan's most powerful intelligence agency, the locus of the country's covert operations to aid Taliban rule in Afghanistan.

Smith and Mahmud shared an interest in military history. Over the years, they had enjoyed dinner at each other's houses. During his tour in the mid-1990s, Smith had run a military history club for Islamabad expatriates. Mahmud was then director-general of military intelligence, a separate organization from I.S.I. that concentrated on battlefield information and India's military deployments. At that time, the United States had imposed economic sanctions on Pakistan because of its nuclear program; relations between the two countries were badly strained. Still, Mahmud visited Smith's house to talk to his history club about Pakistan's 1965 war with India, a subject the Pakistani general had studied closely. Mahmud also had an abiding interest in the American Civil War. He could talk for hours about the tactical decisions of Robert E. Lee and George Meade.[2]

Mahmud embodied all the contradictions and mysteries that Pakistan's top generals presented to their American counterparts. He wore a bushy gray mustache and aviator sunglasses, carried a swagger stick as part of his uniform, and salted his monologues about history and war with references to Western literature. He played tennis. His wife was well educated, as was his daughter. The general once told a C.I.A. officer in Pakistan that he and his daughter were reading Stephen Hawking's *A Brief History of Time* together so they could discuss its theories of the universe. At the same time, Mahmud served as the paymaster of the obscurantist Taliban and, through them, as Al Qaeda's enabler in Afghanistan.[3]

In this he carried out Pakistan's national policy. The country had lost three wars with India since its establishment as an independent Muslim homeland in 1947, birthed from the ashes of the British empire. Despite repeated battlefield failures, Pakistan's generals had enriched and empowered themselves over decades by cultivating a nationalism that stoked the fear that India sought to weaken and dismember their country. (After winning the 1971 Indo-Pakistani War, India had severely damaged Pakistan by fostering the establishment of independent Bangladesh, formerly East Pakistan.) By 2001, however, India was decoupling from its long rivalry with Pakistan. India's economy was booming. Its generals and foreign policy strategists professed to be more concerned about China than about their dysfunctional sibling neighbor to the west. Yet the Pakistan Army used fear of India as a justification for dominating Pakistan's politics.

Pakistan had a smaller population and a weaker industrial base than India. To compensate, the army had built nuclear bombs to deter an Indian military invasion. To destabilize its enemy, and to pursue Pakistan's decades-old goal of acquiring all of disputed Kashmir's territory, I.S.I. covertly armed, trained, and infiltrated Islamist rebels into Indian-held Kashmir, where the guerrillas blew up police stations, carried out kidnappings, and assaulted Indian Army posts.

Pakistan's top military leaders directed the I.S.I., an institution of about twenty-five thousand people. The spy service had three distinct categories of employees. There were senior leaders like General Mahmud who spent the bulk of their careers in the army, navy, or air force and then rotated through the intelligence service in supervisory roles, on tours of two to four years. The second group consisted of active military officers of the rank of colonel or below who had been directed into I.S.I. after failing to make the cut for promotion to generalship. Two thirds or more of Pakistan Army officers rising through the ranks were not destined to become generals, so at a certain point they were assigned to branches of service where they could rise as high as colonel. Some went into logistics, others into administration, and some entered into careers in intelligence, which allowed some of them to serve in uniform at I.S.I. for many years. The presence of these officers in the middle-upper ranks of I.S.I. further connected the institution to the Pakistan military's leadership. Still, the day-to-day work even within I.S.I.'s less secretive directorates could be very different from that of the military, because of the strict compartmentalization of information. An officer would not have any idea what the man in the next office was doing. Information was telescoped to the top, where only the most senior generals had complete visibility.

There was also a large civilian component of I.S.I., working under contract. These ranks included watchers and thugs who kept track of foreign diplomats and other surveillance targets in Islamabad, Lahore, Karachi, and elsewhere. They also included specialists who manipulated and intimidated politicians and journalists. The civilians cultivated an aura of menace and self-importance. They allowed military officers to keep their distance from the roughest business, including murder, if they chose.

The range of I.S.I.'s activity within Pakistan and outside the country was vast. The service was organized into a series of directorates underneath the director-general, who was always a serving three-star general, as Mahmud was. Two-star generals led the major directorates. There were full directorates or subsidiary wings dedicated to counterterrorism, counterintelligence, and Pakistani domestic politics, for example. The analysis directorate was a prestigious post that produced white papers and memos and managed international liaison. I.S.I. ran stations in Pakistani embassies devoted to spying abroad. A technical directorate managed eavesdropping in concert with the army's Signal Corps.[4]

Buried in this bureaucracy lay the units devoted to secret operations in support of the Taliban, Kashmiri guerrillas, and other violent Islamic radicals—Directorate S, as it was referred to by American intelligence officers and diplomats. It was also known as "S Wing" or just "S." (During the Cold War, the K.G.B. also had a "Directorate S" that ran the spy service's "illegals" operations, meaning espionage carried out by trained officers and agents who operated abroad under deep cover. The I.S.I. version had similar aspects, if an entirely different ideological basis.) Directorate S partially resembled the C.I.A.'s Special Activities Division, in charge of covert paramilitary operations. Officers inside I.S.I. sometimes used other names for the external operations units—the Afghan Cell, the Kashmir Cell, Section 21, or Section 24. Veterans of Pakistan's Special Services Group, a commando organization, primarily staffed the I.S.I.'s covert war cells, just as the C.I.A. drew its paramilitary specialists from the ranks of U.S. Special Forces.

To enlarge Pakistan's sphere of influence in Afghanistan during the 1990s, Directorate S covertly supplied, armed, trained, and sought to legitimize the Taliban. That a tennis-playing Gettysburg aficionado oversaw these operations was not remarkable. Black Label–sipping Pakistani generals with London flats and daughters on Ivy League campuses had been managing jihadi guerrilla campaigns against India and in Afghanistan for two decades. By 2001, however, C.I.A. and D.I.A. analysts were circulating reports that some I.S.I. and army officers had become increasingly influenced by the radical ideologies of their clients. This raised the possibility that generals with a millenarian or revolutionary outlook might capture the Pakistani state and its nuclear bombs. The classified reports singled out Mahmud Ahmed as one Pakistani general who had undergone a religious conversion, to the point where, in Mahmud's case, his "evident personal enthusiasm for the Taliban . . . appeared to go well beyond considerations of Pakistani national interest," as a C.I.A. officer who worked with the general later put it. Mahmud considered this a misunderstanding. He had not suddenly "become" religious. He had been conservatively faithful since school days. The issue arose, he felt, only because he had risen to command of I.S.I. and had therefore come under intense scrutiny.[5]

Dave Smith's superiors at D.I.A. had hoped that his long friendship with Mahmud might allow for deeper engagement with him. But after Smith arrived in Islamabad, Mahmud snubbed him. Smith thought he understood why: Mahmud had taken a lot of heat on visits to Washington over Pakistan's support for the Taliban, and he wanted to signal that he did not have much use for Americans anymore. The general's assistants told Smith he was too busy to meet and they pushed him off on I.S.I.'s director-general of analysis. Smith persisted. Finally, in May 2001, Mahmud had invited his old friend to his office at I.S.I. headquarters for tea and a chat.

slamabad is a planned capital dating to the 1960s, tucked into the Margalla Hills. It lacks the grandeur and beauty of Lahore, the Punjabi seat of Mughal tombs and gardens, and it evinces little of the ungoverned chaos of Karachi. It was designed as an international enclave, a kind of fantasy theme park of what a modernizing, prosperous Pakistan might eventually become. The city is laid out on a grid system. I.S.I.'s headquarters occupied an unmarked compound in the G/6 section, nestled behind a ten-foot wall. The main I.S.I. building was old and in need of renovation. It was so close to the main road, Khayaban-e-Shurawardy, that a well-placed truck bomb might damage it badly. The security measures at the I.S.I. entrance in mid-2001 were not rigid, especially if Smith called ahead and provided his diplomatic car's license plate number. The I.S.I. guards popped his trunk, used mirrors to check the chassis for any sign of explosives, made sure there were no unauthorized passengers in the vehicle, and waved him through. Smith's driver pulled inside and deposited the "colonel" at the front door. The I.S.I.'s chief of protocol escorted the American to the second floor.

Mahmud's modest-size office lay away from the street. A portrait of Mohammed Ali Jinnah, the founder of Pakistan, hung on the wall behind the desk, a standard decoration in government offices. There was a large wooden plaque carved with the names and service dates of previous spy chiefs. Mahmud directed Smith to a sofa. An aide joined them to take notes. Smith pulled out his own pad and pen. A *chaprassi* served tea, cakes, and sandwiches and then withdrew.

Smith said he hoped to hear Mahmud's views about the role of Islam in the Pakistan Army. Mahmud said he would be happy to discuss it, but first he had to provide some "context." Mahmud was notorious for long monologues; here came another.

"This part of the world is still going through a demographic metamorphosis. It is still recovering from colonialism," the I.S.I. director said. "There's a lot of resentment toward the West." Moreover, he continued, "Islam is misunderstood in the West. Islam sees no distinction between religion and the state." This had been true of Christianity in Europe for many centuries, until the Enlightenment, Mahmud added. "The Pakistan Army is not completely insulated from this thinking," he went on, meaning that the army enlists soldiers who have been raised in village settings where there is no separation of church and state. Enlisted men learn "all kinds of prejudices" from village mullahs before they even enter the army. In recent years, the army had tried to teach them a "moderate" faith, he said, and had placed a great deal of emphasis on reeducation. The great majority of Pakistanis and especially the rank and file of the army were motivated, conservative, and stable Muslims.

In the mid-1990s, he had been assigned command of Pakistan's Twenty-third Division, headquartered at Jhelum, near the heavily militarized Line of Control that divided Kashmir between de facto Indian and Pakistani sovereignty. There, on the front lines, Mahmud said, brother Pakistan Army officers had urged him to reexamine his faith. "I knew my military topics but was ignorant about religion. The men would come to me for military advice but go to the *maulvi* for moral guidance. In my pursuit of unity of command it was necessary for me to educate myself about religion. I took it upon myself to study Islam," he said. "I wanted unity of command—both tactical and moral." This was not an outlook that should alarm the United States, Mahmud continued. Islam in Pakistan was becoming "conservative and orthodox," not revolutionary. That is, it might be considered fundamentalist, but it did not seek political upheaval. The Taliban, Mahmud believed, represented a similar strain of faith—from the American perspective, an essentially harmless, inward-facing orthodoxy.[6]

Smith wrote up the conversation in reporting cables. His account did little to calm those at C.I.A. and the Pentagon who feared that I.S.I. was commanded by a politically restless, religiously recommitted general who oversaw what amounted to an alliance between a nuclear state and Al Qaeda.

That summer, following Smith's encounter amid the surge of alarming reports about Al Qaeda's plans for a big attack, the United States redoubled its efforts to cultivate Mahmud, in the hope that the I.S.I. chief might use his influence with the Taliban's leadership to persuade them to either expel or betray Osama Bin Laden. George Tenet flew secretly to Pakistan to meet with Mahmud. To reciprocate for his hospitality to Tenet, the C.I.A. invited Mahmud to Washington and promised to arrange high-level meetings across the new Bush administration and in Congress. The I.S.I. director's visit was to end on September 9 and Mahmud and his wife were booked on the Pakistan International Airlines flight out of New York on the evening of September 10. However, he stayed to accept a late invitation to have breakfast at the Capitol on the morning of September 11, with Porter Goss and Bob Graham, the chairs of the House and Senate Intelligence Committees, respectively. They were mid-meal when aides rushed in shouting that they had to evacuate immediately.[7]

Wendy Chamberlin, the newly arrived U.S. ambassador to Pakistan in 2001, was a career foreign service officer who had been posted previously to Laos, Malaysia, and Zaire. It was about 6:30 p.m. in Pakistan when United Airlines Flight 175 struck the South Tower. She called Dave Smith and half a dozen other senior aides to her upstairs living quarters within the embassy compound, where she had CNN on the television. As they watched in shock and discussed security measures, the ambassador's young daughters sat at a desk to one side, doing their homework.

General Tommy Franks, in charge of Central Command, the military headquarters that had responsibility for the Middle East, Afghanistan, and Pakistan, called her the next morning. "You need to tell Musharraf they're either with us or against us," Franks told Chamberlin, referring to General Pervez Musharraf, Pakistan's president and chief of army staff. "They need to get a very strong statement out as soon as possible." But Chamberlin did not report to the Pentagon. She waited for instructions from Colin Powell at the State Department before she telephoned Musharraf.

Musharraf was on a ship in the Arabian Sea, observing naval exercises. "You should be very clear that you support the United States at this time," Chamberlin said when she reached him by satellite phone.

"Come on, Wendy, Al Qaeda could not have done this," Musharraf said. "They're in caves. They don't have the technology to do something like this."

"General, frankly, I disagree. They did this with box cutters."[8]

The next afternoon, September 12, Dave Smith drove to the Pakistan Army's General Headquarters in Rawalpindi, near Islamabad, to meet Tariq Majid, the two-star general who ran military intelligence. He worked in an L-shaped building that also housed Musharraf's official army office. (As commander of the military and president, Musharraf had offices in both Rawalpindi and Islamabad.) The inevitable portrait of Jinnah hung on one wall. A small door led off the main office to a map room filled with current intelligence charts depicting Indian military deployments. Smith was the rare outsider who got a glimpse of the uncovered estimates. Majid was another of the Pakistani officers he had befriended two decades earlier.

Smith asked how the Pakistan Army's commanders were reacting to the attacks on New York and Washington. Majid said that India's external intelligence service, the Research and Analysis Wing, or R.A.W., was planting "false rumors" to implicate Pakistan in terrorism and the attacks. "There is concern that hostile states like India will use the attacks to gain an advantage over Pakistan," he said. He added that he was not convinced that Al Qaeda was responsible for the hijackings.

"It's one possibility, but there are others—the Red Army Faction or some similar European group," he said, referring to Marxist radicals of the Cold War era, now mostly defunct. He also mentioned Pakistanis who were living in Bolivia as possible suspects—a theory so far-fetched that Smith wasn't sure what to say.[9]

I n Washington, Powell and Deputy Secretary of State Richard Armitage drafted seven requirements to be presented to Pakistan as a "with us or against us" ultimatum. Armitage delivered the list to Mahmud in the form of a "nonpaper," or unofficial memo, at a "businesslike" State Department meeting on September 13. Mahmud pointed out "the inconsistency of U.S. attitudes toward Pakistan since our creation and the hostile feelings it has engendered among our people against the U.S." The same demands came to Wendy Chamberlin as written instructions. She had a previously scheduled meeting with Musharraf on September 13, Pakistan time, nine hours ahead of Washington. The meeting was a formal ritual of protocol where Chamberlin would present her credentials as the American ambassador.

First on the list of demands was "Stop Al Qaeda operatives at your border, intercept arms shipments through Pakistan and end all logistical support for Bin Laden." In addition, American warplanes should enjoy "blanket overflight and landing rights." The United States should have access to Pakistani naval and air bases "as needed." Also, Pakistan should "immediately" provide intelligence and immigration information about terrorist suspects. Pakistan should publicly denounce the September 11 attacks and "continue to publicly condemn terrorism against the U.S. and its friends or allies." I.S.I. should cut off all fuel shipments to the Taliban and block all Pakistani volunteers from fighting in Afghanistan. Finally, should the evidence "strongly implicate" Al Qaeda and should the Taliban continue to harbor Bin Laden, Pakistan should break diplomatic relations with the Taliban and help the United States "destroy Osama Bin Laden and his Al Qaeda network."[10]

Chamberlin departed the American embassy in a horse-drawn carriage; the pomp was part of the ceremony of presenting an ambassador's credentials. She clopped up to Musharraf's grand office at the Aiwane-Sadr, the recently built presidential palace on Constitution Avenue. In Musharraf's reception room, Chamberlin read out the demands, and asked, as she had been instructed to do, "Are you with us or against us?" She added, "Come on, General Musharraf, I know you are with us because we have talked."

"I am with you and not against you," Musharraf said immediately, but rather than address Chamberlin's specific requests, he filibustered. He launched into complaints about American "betrayals" of Pakistan in the past. The United States had used Pakistan as a frontline ally against the Soviet Union in Afghanistan, then abandoned the region when the war was won, leaving Pakistan with a massive burden of refugees, gun violence, and heroin addiction.

"That's in the past," Chamberlin said. Pakistan could now be either a "clear enemy" of the United States or a "clear friend." If it became a friend, many good things could result, she said.

Musharraf returned to his litany of complaints about America's unreliability.

"I'm not hearing anything different from what you said before these attacks," Chamberlin said. "What do we need to do? We can help you get what you want. We need *your* help to get what we want."

"It's hard for me to sign up to support a military operation that lacks any details," Musharraf argued. "I can't just send two brigades onto Afghan soil."

He said he was willing to cooperate with the United States, but he would require help to explain his betrayal of the Taliban to the Pakistani people. Washington had misunderstood his position on the Taliban, he said. India was mounting a strong propaganda effort to portray Pakistan as synonymous with extremism.

"Frankly, General Musharraf, I have not heard what I need to tell my president," Chamberlin finally said.

"Well, we will support you unstintingly," Musharraf answered. Yet he needed to consult with his generals and cabinet before he could formally answer the seven American demands.[11]

Pervez Musharraf had a formidable ego. He was a Pakistani nationalist but not especially pious. There was no suggestion that he had undergone a religious recommitment like General Mahmud's. Indeed, there was little evidence that Musharraf sought a unity of the "tactical and moral" in his life; he seemed above all to be a tactician. He had been educated in Catholic schools in Karachi and spent much of his boyhood in secular Turkey. Musharraf had faced expulsion from the army as a young officer because of discipline infractions. He salvaged his career in the Special Services Group, or S.S.G., as a commando. He won a gallantry award during the 1971 war for operating behind Indian lines. As he rose to become a four-star general and lead the army as chief of staff, he did not take advice easily. He remained a risk taker but did not always win. In 1999, he had authorized a reckless covert invasion of Indian-held Kashmir by Pakistani soldiers disguised as guerrillas; the operation touched off a small war with India and failed utterly. That same year, Musharraf had seized power from Prime Minister Nawaz Sharif in a coup d'état. General Mahmud had secured Musharraf's coup by leading forces into the streets of Islamabad. Musharraf then appointed him to I.S.I.

Musharraf presided over Pakistan as a military dictator that September but he still required support from his fellow generals, particularly the nine three-stars who constituted the corps commanders. They held direct control of the Pakistan Army's men and weapons.

After putting off Wendy Chamberlin on the 13th, Musharraf jawboned his generals and admirals, as well as his civilian cabinet, newspaper editors, and politicians, to prepare them for what he regarded as a necessary swerve in Pakistan's foreign and security policy. The essence of Musharraf's argument during these critical days was: If Pakistan did not manage this moment of crisis to its advantage, India would.

Musharraf faced resistance from several corps commanders, however, and from Mahmud at I.S.I. The dissenters believed it was unconscionable and dangerous for Pakistan to abandon the Taliban and align with the United States as it prepared to attack a Muslim country, an attack that would no doubt kill and maim many civilians. Musharraf tried to assure these doubters that he would preserve Pakistan's national interests, that he was only doing what was necessary. As he put it later, "We were on the borderline of being . . . declared a terrorist state—in that situation, what would happen to the Kashmir cause?"

The approach Musharraf sold in private was that he would tell the Americans, "Yes, but . . ." as the Pakistani journalist Ahmed Rashid characterized it. Recalled Abdul Sattar, then Pakistan's foreign minister, who heard Musharraf's sales pitch: "We agreed that we would unequivocally accept all U.S. demands, but then later we would express our private reservations to the U.S., and we would not necessarily agree with all the details."

"The stakes are high," Musharraf told Bush over a secure telephone. "We are with you." Yet it was obvious from the start that Musharraf saw Afghanistan and Al Qaeda through his own prism. "In almost every conversation we had," Bush recalled, "Musharraf accused India of wrongdoing."[12]

Wendy Chamberlin met Musharraf a second time on September 15, this time at his home, Army House, the whitewashed, colonial-era residence of Pakistan's top military officer, in Rawalpindi. "Yes, but" was already in full swing. Musharraf's posture was "I'm going to share with you my concerns, but these are not conditions." Chamberlin felt his caveats were not expressions of resistance but "gentle" reminders of Pakistan's interests as it turned from ally of the Taliban to collaborator with America.

On the Bush administration's demand to seal the Afghan-Pakistan border, Musharraf said, frankly, that was impossible. "The entire Frontier Corps is insufficient for such an operation," he said, referring to the tens of thousands of locally raised paramilitary troops that Pakistan maintained in forts and posts along the long mountainous border. "But we will try."

Allowing American planes to overfly Pakistani territory would be "no problem," Musharraf said, but he asked for the U.S. and Pakistani militaries to map out specific air corridors. "We are concerned that India might try to intrude into airspace the U.S. wants to use—we are sensitive about our nuclear installations." Musharraf said the United States should tell India to "lay off and stay off."

Musharraf had questions about what sort of war the United States intended to wage in Afghanistan. "Short and swift operations will be better than massive ones," he said. Would the United States go "after all the Taliban or just their leaders? It would be best to focus on just taking out terrorists like Al Qaeda." That, of course, would leave the Taliban, Pakistan's ally, largely intact.

He suggested inviting Saudi Arabia, Turkey, and the smaller Gulf States into the American-led coalition to fight the coming Afghan war. That would add other Muslim nations to the cause. "Neither India nor Israel should be part of any U.S. coalition," Musharraf insisted. "They are not friends of Pakistan."

India, he said at one point, is "not trying to help you so much as they are trying to fix us as terrorists."

Also, Musharraf urged, "Kashmir should be kept out of this." He urged the United States not to "equate terrorism in Afghanistan with terrorism in Kashmir." Finally, Musharraf wondered what Afghanistan was going to look like "when the operations are over." The postwar regime in Kabul "must be a pro-Pakistan . . . government that is inclusive of all Afghans."[13]

In the days ahead, Musharraf and Mahmud advanced these talking points relentlessly in meeting after meeting with American officials. One theme was: *The Taliban are not the same as Al Qaeda and can be engaged or at least divided in service of American goals in Afghanistan.* Another was: *India is spreading lies about Pakistan, seeking to exploit your tragedy.* A third went: *The Northern Alliance created and led by Ahmad Shah Massoud, the C.I.A. favorite, is made up of murderous thugs from the country's ethnic minorities and cannot govern Afghanistan.*

Musharraf considered the Taliban's emir, Mullah Mohammad Omar, to be a stubborn man with a tenuous grasp of international politics. Negotiating with him, Musharraf had found, was like "banging one's head against the wall."[14] Yet the broader Taliban movement was important to Pakistan, as the country's generals conceived of Pakistan's interests. Partly this was because the Taliban could be understood as an expression of ethnic Pashtun nationalism as well as of religious ideology. The Pashtuns were a tribally organized community bound by centuries of history along the Afghan-Pakistan border as well as by a distinct language.

Throughout British imperial rule in South Asia, they had managed to preserve a sense of independence and autonomy, including the right to mete out their own tribal justice under arms, and the right to enforce their own socially conservative mores. Almost all Taliban were ethnic Pashtuns. The Taliban had captured and exploited the grievances and anxieties of Pashtuns during the brutal Afghan civil war of the 1990s. Pashtuns lived on both sides of the Pakistan-Afghan border. In Afghanistan, they made up about half of the population, concentrated in the south and east. In Pakistan, they constituted a minority of about 15 percent, but an influential and restive one. The future of Pashtun politics would affect Pakistan's internal stability, and the Taliban's outlook had become a part of Pashtun politics. At the same time, while the Taliban's Islamic radicalism might pose a revolutionary danger to Pakistan, it also intimidated India—that was another reason for Pakistan's India-obsessed generals to support the movement.

The task facing Musharraf at that moment of crisis in September 2001 was not necessarily to preserve the life of Mullah Mohammad Omar, but to legitimize at least some Taliban elements in the eyes of the United States and the international community. Musharraf told Wendy Chamberlin at Army House that a postwar government in Afghanistan, in addition to being "pro-Pakistan," should also be "Pashtun dominated."[15] For two decades, I.S.I. had tried to control Islamist Pashtun parties to influence Afghan politics; it was not about to stop now.

"Extremism is not in every Taliban," Musharraf told Colin Powell as the American-led Afghan war neared. "One knows for sure that there are many moderate elements."[16]

Case officers in the C.I.A.'s Islamabad Station had been recruiting Taliban agents and contacts for several years, primarily to collect intelligence about Bin Laden and Al Qaeda in Afghanistan. The agency's most active recruiter until the summer of 2001 was Chris Wood, a second-generation C.I.A. officer. His father had risen into the Senior Intelligence Service before retiring. Wood had started out as a teenager working at headquarters in the security section, watching janitors and maintenance men in the hallways to make sure they didn't try to steal any classified materials. He moved over to the agency mail room while attending George Mason University in northern Virginia. As a young officer he learned Farsi, Iran's dominant language, a close cousin of the Dari spoken in Afghanistan. Wood worked Iranian operations for a number of years, but as penetrating the Taliban became a C.I.A. priority in the late 1990s he rotated to Islamabad, where he could use his Dari to recruit Afghan agents. He became renowned within the Near East/ South Asia division of the Directorate of Operations for taking a large number of "hostile meetings," as they were called in C.I.A. vernacular. These were meetings taken by career C.I.A. officers with paid reporting agents or informal contacts where it seemed possible that the individual might be armed and dangerous. Wood would drive a sport utility vehicle with the passenger seat unoccupied and an armed colleague—a contractor or a fellow case officer—would sit in the backseat, ready to shoot. They would wind through Islamabad, Rawalpindi, or Peshawar to an agreed-upon intersection, roll up to where the Taliban agent was waiting, invite him into the car, and drive away. From these tense, fractured conversations with informers, as well as less fraught meetings with anti-Taliban Pashtun activists and other local sources, the C.I.A. had developed insights about the Taliban's leadership and its attitudes toward Al Qaeda.[17]

In 2001, C.I.A. analysts reported to the Bush cabinet that "the Taliban is not a monolithic organization," as then–deputy C.I.A. director John McLaughlin recalled. Their analysis was "There are ideological adherents but many others are with them because it is how you get money and guns." The logic implied by this conclusion was "There has to be a way to drive wedges in the organization."[18]

The C.I.A. had identified individuals in the Taliban leadership who claimed to disagree with Mullah Mohammad Omar's policy of providing sanctuary to Bin Laden and Al Qaeda because harboring terrorists deprived the Taliban government—formally known as the Islamic Emirate of Afghanistan—of international recognition and aid.

Bob Grenier was the Islamabad station chief, in charge of the C.I.A.'s efforts from Pakistan to split the Taliban and somehow capture or kill Bin Laden. Grenier was a wiry, fit Dartmouth alumnus then in his late forties.

He was a forceful, clear writer who had studied professional management philosophies as he rose as a case officer into the Senior Intelligence Service. After a long career, Grenier found the C.I.A. could be "arrogant, insular and parochial," and while he "enthusiastically shared that culture," he was also "wary of it." He assessed himself as a "contrarian."[19] Grenier had wide field experience but he had arrived in Islamabad in 1999 after holding supervisory office roles in Virginia for the previous five years. The September 11 attacks thrust Grenier into sudden prominence on the Seventh Floor as an adviser to Tenet and the White House on critical questions about which the Bush administration had scant expertise.

For example: Could the I.S.I. be trusted for anything, and if so, what? To what extent should the United States accommodate Pakistan's demands as the war in Afghanistan unfolded? Could the Taliban be split or otherwise persuaded to betray Bin Laden and Al Qaeda, or should they be regarded as a unified enemy to be attacked without mercy or compromise?

Grenier maintained channels to Taliban leaders. In January 2001, at a U.S. embassy reception, he had met Mullah Abdul Jalil Akhund, the Taliban's deputy foreign minister. Grenier had suggested they stay in touch and had provided Jalil with an Immarsat satellite telephone. They spoke regularly.[20]

After the attacks on New York and Washington, Grenier called Jalil and suggested they meet in Quetta. Mullah Akhtar Mohammad Osmani, commander of the Taliban's Southern Zone, accompanied Jalil. Osmani said he had Mullah Mohammad Omar's permission to parley with the C.I.A., to develop proposals that might break the impasse over Al Qaeda. They talked for hours, exchanging threats and proposals. Grenier suggested the Taliban could stand aside while U.S. forces snatched Bin Laden. Grenier had no authority to make such a deal, but he was trying to develop a plan that could be presented to the White House as an option. The United States needed some kind of Pashtun strategy—an uprising, a deal with Mullah Mohammad Omar, some intervention closer to the heart of the Taliban–Al Qaeda nexus than working with Ahmad Shah Massoud's surviving commanders in the Northern Alliance was ever going to provide. The most Grenier could extract, however, was an assertion that the Taliban "would not risk the destruction of their nation for the sake of one man."

Mahmud Ahmed returned from Washington on September 15. He had used his time to lobby the C.I.A.'s leadership for one last chance to persuade Mullah Mohammad Omar to betray Al Qaeda. In Bob Grenier the I.S.I. chief now had an ally. They met as soon as Mahmud landed in Islamabad.

Grenier provided "a lengthy, arm-waving, account" of his discussions with the Taliban in Quetta. Here was the sort of opening I.S.I. had been hoping for, to preserve the Taliban without alienating the United States. Mahmud said he would fly to Kandahar on the 17th to negotiate directly with Mullah Omar.[21]

No American accompanied Mahmud, who provided nearly identical debriefings separately to Grenier and Dave Smith during the days after he returned to Islamabad on the night of the 17th.

He said his talks with Mullah Omar lasted four hours. They were well acquainted with each other. To Mahmud, Pakistan's core interests, managed through I.S.I., included the promotion of a peaceful Afghanistan and the reduction of poppy cultivation and heroin trafficking, which Omar had delivered. The Taliban controlled all of the country except a few pockets in the north, and drug production had been reduced. They had a basis for mutual confidence, in Mahmud's view.

Omar had sat on a large rectangular sofa at his pine-shrouded home on Kandahar's outskirts, with his legs pulled up and crossed beneath him. As they spoke, Omar picked at his toes. Mahmud relayed the main elements of America's position: Bin Laden had to be brought to justice or expelled. The same was true of fifteen to twenty other Al Qaeda leaders in Afghanistan. The Taliban had to close all Al Qaeda camps. Mullah Mohammad Omar "might have two to three days" to consider surrendering Bin Laden.

They had a detailed discussion about the possibility of Bin Laden's expulsion. Omar said he could not hand over Bin Laden to any non-Muslim authority, as Mahmud, as a Muslim, well knew.

The I.S.I. chief tried a lawyerly argument. Prayer is an absolute obligation on Muslims, he pointed out, which cannot be avoided even on one's deathbed. Mullah Omar agreed.

"But what if a snake approaches while you are in the midst of prayers?" the I.S.I. chief asked.

"You abandon your prayers and deal with the danger first and then resume your prayers," Mullah Omar answered.

"Don't you see this giant anaconda approaching Afghanistan?" Mahmud asked. He meant the United States. "As emir of 25 million Afghans, is your oath of hospitality to Osama more sacrosanct than protection of your people?"[22]

Mullah Mohammad Omar thought for a while and then remarked that an assembly of religious scholars was to gather in Kabul the next day, and that the I.S.I. chief should discuss the question with them. Mahmud did go to Kabul. The assembly issued a statement to the effect that Bin Laden was free to leave Afghanistan of his own free will. Mahmud considered it a momentous concession, but it barely registered in Washington.

To Smith and Grenier, Mahmud reported that Omar had said the current crisis represented "the will of God," and as for Bin Laden, "only his death or mine" relieved Mullah Omar of the obligation to protect a Muslim guest. That sounded like the end of negotiation, but Mahmud insisted that there was still reason to be optimistic:

"The United States has to give engagement with the Taliban a chance," Mahmud pleaded to Dave Smith. "The use of force should be an absolute last result. . . . Maybe he has used me, but I'm happy to be used if it will avert a greater tragedy."

The I.S.I. chief added, "I'm not a sleuth or a super spy. I'm a soldier and I will fulfill the commitment made by the president," meaning Musharraf's promise to side ultimately with the United States, if it came to that.[23]

On September 20, President Bush addressed a joint session of Congress, before a television audience estimated at eighty million. His national security cabinet and speechwriters had deliberated for nine days about how to frame the coming war. Bush named Al Qaeda and Osama

Bin Laden as responsible for the attacks on New York and Washington. The president explained that Al Qaeda enjoyed sanctuary in Afghanistan through its alliance with the Taliban.

"We condemn the Taliban regime," Bush said. "It is not only repressing its own people, it is threatening people everywhere by sponsoring and sheltering and supplying terrorists. By aiding and abetting murder, the Taliban regime is committing murder."

He continued, "Tonight, the United States of America makes the following demands on the Taliban: Deliver to the United States authorities all the leaders of Al Qaeda who hide in your land. . . . Close immediately and permanently every terrorist training camp in Afghanistan and hand over every terrorist and every person in their support structure to appropriate authorities. Give the United States full access to terrorist training camps, so we can make sure they are no longer operating. These demands are not open to negotiations or discussion. The Taliban must act, and act immediately. They must hand over the terrorists, or they will share in their fate."

It was highly unlikely that Mullah Mohammad Omar could meet these conditions in a matter of days, even if he wished to do so. Al Qaeda's brigades in Afghanistan were made up of determined fighters who would be no easy match for Taliban forces.

On September 24, Mahmud rode to the American embassy to meet with Chamberlin, Smith, and a visiting Pentagon team that had come to plan for the war. They gathered in a conference room in the chancery basement that had shelves of books about Pakistan. Mahmud spoke forcefully and emotionally.

"The Taliban are on the side of good and against terrorism," he declared. "You need the help of the Afghan people while U.S. forces are assembling. I beg you—I implore you—not to fire a shot in anger. It will set us all back many years. Don't let the blood rush to your head."

Mullah Mohammad Omar is frightened, Mahmud continued. "Reasoning with them to get rid of terrorism will be better than the use of brute force," he said. If the Taliban were destroyed, Afghanistan would revert to rule by warlords, he predicted. "We will not flinch from a military effort," Mahmud promised. "But a strike will produce thousands of frustrated young Muslim men. It will be an incubator of anger that will explode two or three years from now."

He mentioned Sun Tzu's aphorism about how the supreme art of war involved learning to win without firing a shot. Mahmud added, "Whatever decision you take, Pakistan will stand behind you."

"The most important sentence you spoke was the last one," Chamberlin answered. "The time for negotiating is over."[24]

The best-known I.S.I. operator in the Afghan units of Directorate S was a Special Services Group career officer named Colonel Sultan Amir Tarar, whose nom de guerre was Colonel Imam. He had collaborated closely with C.I.A. officers during the anti-Soviet war. He redirected his services to the Taliban after the Americans quit Afghanistan. Tarar was a tall man who kept a long graying beard and professed a deep religious faith. He was also a raconteur who enjoyed talking about the glory days of killing Soviet forces. He openly admitted that he had worked with Bin Laden during the 1980s. He found the Al Qaeda founder "rather like a prince, very humble."[25]

By 2001, Tarar served as Pakistan's consul general in Herat, Afghanistan, supporting the Taliban. He left Afghanistan early in October as the American bombing campaign neared. On his way home, Tarar ran into Grenier, the Islamabad station chief. They shared a flight to Islamabad on an I.S.I. plane. Tarar wore a Taliban-style turban of the sort Bin Laden often wore and spoke "excellent and colorful English." Tarar presented Grenier with a Special Services Group pin as a memento. The C.I.A. station chief found Tarar to be "marvelous company." He did not hold out any hope that they could work together on Bin Laden, but he was familiar with I.S.I. officers who hated American policy but got on well with American counterparts.[26]

Once back in Islamabad, Colonel Imam sought an appointment with the Taliban's ambassador to Pakistan, Mullah Abdul Salam Zaeef, an old friend and war comrade of Mullah Mohammad Omar's. Zaeef received the I.S.I. veteran at the Taliban's embassy.

After they exchanged greetings, Imam started to cry. Tears ran down his face and his white beard and he could not speak. When he finally composed himself, he said, "Almighty Allah might have decided what is to take place in Afghanistan, but Pakistan is to blame. How much cruelty it has done to its neighbor! And how much more will come!" The colonel laid the blame on Musharraf. He started to cry again. He said he would never be able to repent for what Musharraf had done by aligning himself with the Americans. He would suffer not only in this world but in the next.[27]

This was I.S.I. in microcosm: an institution well practiced at manipulating the C.I.A. and the Taliban simultaneously.

From the very first days after September 11, the United States adopted an ambiguous policy toward I.S.I. that would haunt its ambitions in South Asia for years to come. "We will make no distinction between the terrorists who committed these acts and those who harbor them," George W. Bush had declared. It was an emotionally satisfying position, but was it realistic? Bush's doctrine might be applied easily enough to the Taliban, a ragtag force that eschewed modern technology and had no air defenses or air force of significance. But how should it be applied to Pakistan, a nuclear-armed, highly nationalistic country of 150 million? Hadn't Pakistan "harbored" the Taliban, and didn't its desperate effort to prevent the movement's destruction signal that Pakistan's interests might not be aligned with those of the United States as war in Afghanistan unfolded? Bush's national security cabinet included experts on Russia, missile defense, military modernization, and the Middle East. It included nobody who knew Afghanistan well, however. Powell and Armitage had worked closely with Pakistan's military during the 1990–1991 Gulf War to expel Iraqi forces from Kuwait, a war in which Pakistan had participated as an American ally. Powell respected Pakistan's army and was sympathetic to Musharraf's pleadings. President Bush, for his part, concluded that by turning on the Taliban, however ambivalently, Musharraf was taking large domestic and political risks on behalf of the United States. He therefore deserved support and understanding.

There were pragmatic reasons for the Bush administration's restraint that September and October. The most important purpose of American military action in Afghanistan would be to assault Al Qaeda's leaders and guerrillas, to disrupt any additional terrorist plots against the United States that the group might have under way. Bin Laden's strongholds lay mainly in Afghanistan's south and in its eastern mountains. The seaports and air bases Musharraf offered the United States would make a war in Afghanistan much easier to fight than if the United States relied on more distant India (which had also offered basing support). Al Qaeda was the main enemy, and there would be time later to reconsider I.S.I.'s role in destabilizing the region. A shocked world had rallied to America's cause against Bin Laden. The war was coming. Don't let the blood rush to your head, Mahmud Ahmed had advised, self-interestedly. It was too late.

FOUR

Risk Management

Mullah Mohammad Omar spent his boyhood in Afghanistan's destitute Uruzgan Province, raised by an uncle who was an itinerant religious teacher. (His father died when he was very young and his mother married the father's brother.) He belonged to the Hotak tribe, a marginalized clan with little purchase on southern Afghanistan's power or resources. The farthest Omar ever traveled was Pakistan. Apart from Koranic studies, he had no formal education. He possessed a "rural mind," as one of his more widely traveled Taliban colleagues put it, "cut off, religiously and politically." After the Soviet invasion, as a teenager, he joined a group of insurgents he knew from Kandahar's madrassas and preaching networks. They fought in the irrigated desert west of Kandahar city, around Maiwand District. One day on the battlefield, the Russians pushed forward and Omar and his comrade Mullah Abdul Salam Zaeef could see them from their trenches. The area was covered with corpses. The Russians lobbed in shells. Shrapnel struck Omar in the face and wounded his right eye.

That night, the Afghan comrades held "a marvelous party," in Zaeef's description, and Omar, his face bandaged, sang a ghazal, or traditional poem:

> *My illness is untreatable, oh, my flower-like friend*
> *My life is difficult without you, my flower-like friend*[1]

Omar never regained the use of his eye. After the war he retired to a home without electricity near a mud-walled mosque in Sangesar, close to the battlefield where he had been wounded. He took four wives, raised many children, preached, and studied Islam. As Afghanistan collapsed into civil war after the Soviet withdrawal, criminals, predators, and warlords ruled Kandahar, extorting citizens and truckers at a maze of checkpoints, or kidnapping boys into sexual slavery. Omar's wartime comrades decided to challenge the abusers. They required a leader; a committee arrived one evening at his home. The members explained to him they had picked him. Zaeef watched as Omar hesitated, seeming to think before saying anything. It was one of his habits. Finally, Omar said that he agreed with what the committee proposed. Something needed to be done.[2]

As he created the Islamic Emirate of Afghanistan with support from the I.S.I. and Saudi Arabia, Omar surrounded himself with religious advisers and military commanders almost uniformly educated in rural Pashtun villages and madrassas. Searching for a purity of life partly drawn from village norms, and following religious instruction to imagine life as it prevailed in the seventh century, during the Prophet's lifetime, they evolved or invented a public Islam whose specific rules had an otherworldly character. An official Taliban gazette published a week before the September 11 attacks clarified the following list of items formally banned in the Islamic Emirate: "The pig itself; pork; pig fat; objects made of human hair; natural human hair; dish antennas; sets for cinematography and sound recording projectors; sets for microphotography, in case it is used in the cinema; all instruments which themselves produce music, such as the piano, the harmonium, the flute, the tabla, the tanbour, the sarangi; billiard tables and their accessories; chess boards; carom boards; playing cards; masks; any alcoholic beverage; all audio cassettes, video cassettes, computers and television which include sex and music; centipedes; lobsters (a kind of sea animal); nail polish; firecrackers; fireworks (for children); all kinds of cinematographic films, even though they may be sent abroad; all statues of animate beings in general; all sewing catalogues which have photos of animate beings; published tableaus (photos); Christmas cards; greeting cards bearing images of living things; neckties; bows (the thing which strengthens the necktie); necktie pins."[3]

Omar was an unusually tall man. He could be reticent and refused to meet most non-Muslim visitors. He sometimes cited his dreams in explaining his decisions. He saw his earthly life as a fate he did not control fully and he referred continually to God's will. Bashir Noorzai, an opium smuggler from Mullah Mohammad Omar's home district who supplied money and arms to the Taliban during the Islamic Emirate, believed that his leader "had one characteristic: He was very stubborn. . . . His attitude was that he knew better than anyone else. Now, power also makes one 'knowledgeable.'" He was an ardent Islamic rule enforcer yet he was not an ascetic zealot. He listened to Pashto folk songs on cassette tape. Apart from his exceptional height and his commitment to wars of resistance against non-Muslim invaders, Omar had little in common with Osama Bin Laden, who had grown up privileged and exposed to cosmopolitanism in booming Jeddah, Saudi Arabia. Omar was a few years younger than Bin Laden. He had not invited the Saudi to Afghanistan. Bin Laden initially entered Afghan territory not controlled by the Taliban in a chartered jet, carrying cash and a following of fighters. Mullah Mohammad Omar received him in Kandahar and gradually forged an alliance. The Taliban needed Al Qaeda's shock troops against the Northern Alliance. Omar also accepted Bin Laden's financial largesse to improve Kandahar. Yet there were tensions between them, over Bin Laden's provocative media interviews and the terrorist attacks Al Qaeda carried out abroad, which brought the Taliban under tightening diplomatic, economic, and travel sanctions.[4]

No Taliban or other Afghans participated in the September 11 attacks. The hijackers were Saudis and other Arabs. Khalid Sheikh Mohammed, the plot's mastermind, was a Pakistani who had lived for many years in Kuwait and attended college in North Carolina. It is not clear whether Mullah Mohammad Omar knew of the conspiracy in advance. Two European scholars who interviewed Taliban leaders extensively judged it "doubtful" that he did, but could not reach a firm conclusion. Hank Crumpton at the C.I.A.'s Counterterrorist Center had come to believe that "Al Qaeda, if anything, had co-opted the Taliban leadership and had taken advantage of their stunning ignorance of world affairs." Still, under the emerging Bush Doctrine, Omar's refusal to cooperate in Bin Laden's arrest condemned the Taliban to mass slaughter and indefinite imprisonment as enemy combatants. And the Taliban leader declined to yield. An edict issued in Mullah Mohammad Omar's name eight days after the attacks on Washington and New York required all offices of the Islamic Emirate, "in addition to being ready for sacrifices," to begin holding "Koran reading sessions in their mosques and ask great God for humiliation, embarrassment and defeat of the infidel powers."[5]

Mullah Zaeef had served Mullah Omar loyally as a minister and then as ambassador to Pakistan, the Taliban's most important diplomatic post. After the September 11 attacks, he traveled to Kandahar. Omar told him that he had summoned Bin Laden and asked him about the attacks on New York and Washington.

"He swore that he didn't do it," Omar explained. "I couldn't pressure him beyond that. If you have proof of his involvement, then show it to me. But I haven't seen any proof. . . ." In Omar's mind, "There was less than a 10 percent chance that America would resort to anything beyond threats," Zaeef concluded.

The Taliban leader clung to his position that Bin Laden had not been proven guilty: "Where is the evidence?" And, "If there was a crime, we are not supporting the criminal," so there was no reason for the United States to target the Taliban.

Zaeef predicted, "America would definitely attack."

Other Taliban leaders advised that even if Mullah Mohammad Omar produced Bin Laden, the Americans would still strike. The demand for Bin Laden, they argued, was "just an excuse" to overthrow the Taliban's Islamic State. A Taliban editorial published on September 23 posited that "Osama is a good pretext" for the United States, which had "colonizing objectives" and was "interested in establishing a military base in Pakistan at any cost in order to control this region."

In Mullah Mohammad Omar's advisory circle, "They believed that power had been given to them by Allah and that at any time Allah could take it away," said a former Taliban Foreign Ministry official then in

Kabul. "They were thinking, 'If Allah is not with us, then we will lose power.' Conversely, 'If He is with us, we can defy the world.'"⁶

The air war opened on the night of October 7 in Afghanistan, the afternoon in Washington. At the C.I.A., the center of action was the Global Response Center, the Counterterrorist Center's twenty-four-hour operations room on the sixth floor of Old Headquarters. Video screens hung on the center's walls. Officers and analysts—many from the agency, but some on assignment from the military—sat before classified computers and secure telephones. The atmosphere was alert but quiet; the operators mainly communicated by typing messages in a secure chat system.

George Tenet arrived at the center for the war's opening. Charles Allen, the C.I.A.'s assistant director for collection, who had helped develop the Predator drone program, turned up as well. As C.T.C. director, Cofer Black was the commanding officer in charge of the C.I.A.'s drone operations, which had recently acquired lethal capability. Predators and similar drones had been providing low-altitude aerial surveillance for the C.I.A. and the military for a number of years. The C.I.A. had been operating Predators on surveillance missions over Afghanistan out of an air base in Uzbekistan since the summer of 2000. The classified program was experimental. The ability of drones to hover over terrorist camps in otherwise remote and inaccessible territory gave rise to the idea that they might be equipped with weapons. A C.I.A.–Air Force team known most recently as the Summer Project had modified the drone's capabilities rapidly. The latest innovation, perfected over the summer, had been to equip Predators with Hellfire air-to-ground missiles that could strike buildings or vehicles. On September 17, President Bush had signed a Memorandum of Notification authorizing C.I.A. covert action against Al Qaeda and its allies, including targeted killing. Bush delegated the trigger-pulling decision to Tenet, who delegated it to the C.I.A. directorate of operations, which delegated it to Black. Under the Counterterrorist Center's command, pilots had been flying Predators armed with Hellfires over Afghanistan for several weeks, but the C.I.A. had refrained from shooting at any targets because doing so might risk exposing Uzbekistan's secret cooperation. Now, under the cover of a wider air war carried out by conventional American bombers, starting this night, the agency could fire when ready. Yet Black did not have authority to order Air Force or Navy bombers into action. That decision belonged ultimately to General Tommy Franks, the four-star general and career artillery officer who ran Central Command.

That afternoon in Langley, the Global Response Center screens showed infrared imagery of Mullah Mohammad Omar's home on Kandahar's outskirts. A C.I.A.-controlled drone transmitted the live video feed. It was a dark night in Kandahar. The drone sending the pictures was one of a small number the C.I.A. had put in the air over Afghanistan after September 11. The pilot and sensor operator controlling the flight sat in a metal container elsewhere on the C.I.A. campus, near a parking lot. Scott Swanson, a former Special Operations helicopter pilot, had the stick. The sensor operator was Jeff A. "Gunny" Guay, an Air Force imagery analyst.[7]

Omar's Kandahar compound was a well-known surveillance target. C.I.A.-directed pilots had been flying over the home regularly since 2000. The house was one of the few "obvious targets" known in Afghanistan, as a senior officer involved put it. The C.I.A. had placed the emir's compound on a list of targets for Central Command to bomb after September 11, but it was up to Tommy Franks to decide what to strike first this night. Osama Bin Laden and many of his Al Qaeda lieutenants had already fled to the White Mountains, along the border with Pakistan, according to the C.I.A.'s reporting. Yet Mullah Mohammad Omar had stayed put at his comfortable home in Kandahar, which had been built and decorated by Bin Laden, as a gift.

Some officers in the C.I.A.'s leadership hoped Central Command would bomb the compound in the very first strikes of the war, to eliminate Omar and his lieutenants. Instead, following more conventional doctrine, Franks approved initial bombing on October 7 of an airfield in Kandahar. Air Force doctrine typically sought to eliminate the enemy's air defenses in the initial strikes so that U.S. and allied planes could fly and bomb at will after that. The Taliban's air defenses were rudimentary, but Franks took the standard approach.[8]

The problem was, the initial bombing of the Kandahar Airfield effectively announced that the American air war had begun. As the C.I.A. Predator watched overhead, several turbaned men soon emerged from Mullah Mohammad Omar's house. The Taliban climbed into a pair of vehicles and drove away. The C.I.A. Counterterrorist Center's analysts judged that Mullah Omar was in the group. The intelligence case was "multiple stream, authoritative, comprehensive," in the assessment of a senior officer involved. The C.I.A.-directed Predator followed the small convoy. The vehicles drove initially to a home in downtown Kandahar that the C.I.A. had previously identified as the residence of Omar's mother. The men entered, stayed a brief time, and then left. This time, they departed Kandahar and drove about forty kilometers to the west of the city. They arrived at a compound that contained two one-story flat-roofed buildings separated by a rectangular open area about one hundred yards long and fifty yards across. One building appeared to be a madrassa, or Islamic school. The smaller building across the yard appeared to be a mosque.[9]

The presumed Taliban, possibly including Mullah Omar, went inside the school. There were other armed men and vehicles present. Later, participants would retain diverse memories of the number of presumed Taliban gathered, from a relatively small number to several hundred.

During the next several hours, the decision making about whether to attempt to kill Mullah Omar or, more precisely, the group of men that had emerged from his house and was judged to include him, became badly confused. The Predator's infrared cameras showed glowing images of distinct individuals but could not provide photographic clarity. This was a novel interagency operation in which a top secret C.I.A. drone program was attempting to coordinate its action with Air Force decision makers who sometimes didn't even know that the C.I.A. had a live camera on the target. Air Force imagery analysis was at its best when tasked with identifying enemy tanks in open areas on a conventional battlefield. Collaborative analysis with the C.I.A. about men out of uniform hanging around on the outskirts of Kandahar challenged the Air Force's standards of risk management.

The twenty-pound Hellfire missile the C.I.A. Predator carried had been developed for Apache attack helicopters, to penetrate tanks and kill their occupants. Its relatively light explosive payload would be ineffective against a large roofed building like the school the presumed Taliban had just entered. The alternative was to drop conventional bombs—each with massive, destructive explosive force, compared with a Hellfire missile. Air Force and Navy fighter-bombers were now circling outside Kandahar on standby. They carried such ordnance.

The C.I.A.'s Global Response Center had an open line to Central Command's joint intelligence operations center in Florida. C.I.A. officers talked with Brigadier General Jeff Kimmons, the director of intelligence or J-2 at Central Command. Kimmons was sitting inches from General Franks in a small secure room on the second floor, watching the same infrared Predator footage as the C.I.A.'s leaders. There were eight to ten intelligence officers, operations officers, and analysts in the Central Command operations room, as well as a Navy captain who was a military lawyer or judge advocate general. She was there to advise Franks about targeting rules. In larger adjoining rooms sat dozens of other Central Command officers and targeting analysts.

The C.I.A. requested a conventional bombing of the madrassa where it appeared Mullah Mohammad Omar had entered. A Central Command intelligence officer present said years later that he did not recall that request, but even if the C.I.A. had asked for such a strike, he would have advised Franks against dropping bombs on the target. The reason: "When someone enters a building you don't just strike and kill everybody under the assumption that they're all Taliban." Bombing the presumed school with so many unidentified people inside would have been irresponsible. Also, Central Command's on-site lawyer, the J.A.G., concluded that the nearby mosque would be damaged unacceptably. The scene required "tactical patience," as the military intelligence officer put it. "We were not eager to do something foolish and kill lots of innocent people. That mattered a lot to Franks. . . . The military was not out to kill [Mullah Mohammad Omar] at all costs. We were intent on killing him at a time and place where we could do so surgically."[10]

Moreover, Secretary of Defense Donald Rumsfeld and Tommy Franks had orders from President Bush to minimize collateral damage and

civilian deaths during the air war, to avoid inflaming Afghan and international opinion. In his final conversation with President Bush, Bush had
told Franks that the war was "not about religion. If you see Bin Laden go
into a mosque, wait until he comes out to kill him."

Now, as he watched the compound, Franks thought, "Wait till they
come out."[11]

Franks relayed to the C.I.A. that he had decided not to bomb the
school. An Air Force officer monitoring the events made notes of his
reaction to this decision: "CINC [commander in chief of CENTCOM,
i.e., Franks] not hitting building because of collateral damage. Amazing.
We could get Omar but the CINC's worried about collateral damage."[12]
The C.I.A. initiated an appeal, according to several officers involved, to
ask Rumsfeld and ultimately President Bush to overrule Franks. But it
would take an hour or so for that request to play out.

Black and the C.I.A. team running the Predator operation inside the
Global Response Center still had an opportunity to fire a Hellfire missile, even if the missile was not potent enough to take out the school
and kill all the men inside. Nobody had ever fired a missile from a remotely operated drone on a battlefield. They would make military and
intelligence history if they did. An officer watching the Predator feed at
Langley figured there "would be a lot of Monday morning quarterback-
ing" about whatever the C.I.A. did now. The feeling in the Global Response Center was "Have to be correct. . . . Don't mess it up."[13]

Cofer Black could have fired legally on his own authority. Yet Central
Command's senior intelligence officer had just announced that there
was an unacceptable risk of collateral damage. Officers watching the
C.I.A. feed recalled that the Global Response Center asked for permission to shoot at a pickup truck parked outside the assembly building.
"The purpose was psychological," according to an officer involved. They
would stun the Taliban.[14]

In Florida, Franks thought that maybe a Hellfire shot "will persuade
the people to leave the mosque and give us a shot at the principals." The
Air Force officer keeping notes recorded Franks's logic: "Perhaps use
Hellfires to scare them out to go to another hold site and then hit them."

Black gave the order. In the container on the C.I.A. campus, Swanson now counted down. "Weapon away," he said. The Hellfire missile fired off its rail. A truck exploded in a flash of light.

The Taliban in the flat-roofed building did indeed rush out. They took up positions in a standard 360-degree infantry defense. The glowing infrared figures "were all adult males, some carrying weapons. There wasn't another target like that for the rest of the war," in the judgment of an officer watching.[15]

The men drove off. They did not all go in the same direction, however. Swanson and Guay directed their Predator above one vehicle that they believed held Omar. There are two credible accounts of what happened next, drawn from the memories of participants. In one account, Central Command ordered the C.I.A. to return to watching the original school compound. In the other, the Predator followed the vehicles to a new compound with a mosque.

It is clear that at some point Franks spoke with Rumsfeld about whether to risk collateral damage by striking a mosque, given the possibility that they would kill Omar. According to a memo Rumsfeld composed two weeks later, the secretary of defense instructed Franks to wait a few minutes. Then Rumsfeld called President Bush to inform him. Bush concurred that the risk of innocent deaths or destroyed mosques was worth bearing if Mullah Mohammad Omar was in their sights. Rumsfeld relayed his own approval to Franks, without telling him that he had spoken to the president.[16]

Finally, on Franks's order, American fighter-bombers deposited two bombs on the mosque under C.I.A. surveillance. In any event, Mullah Omar was not there. The C.I.A. later assessed that after he departed the school west of Kandahar, he made his way to Gardez, in eastern Afghanistan. So far as is known, no other significant Taliban leaders died in the bombing on the first night of the war, either.[17]

Mullah Mohammad Omar's death on October 7 might have influenced the Taliban's evolution, given the divided opinions within the movement's leadership about how to manage their relationship with Al Qaeda after the shock of September 11. That alternative history might have turned out no better than what actually unfolded, but as the coming decade's failures and suffering unfolded, the lost opportunity of

October 7 gnawed at several of the military and intelligence officers involved that night. They wondered from time to time what might have been.

The hunt for Mullah Omar went on, but it seemed to be cursed. In
one instance, recalled Robert Grenier, then the C.I.A. station chief
in Islamabad, "our best human source in Kandahar" provided a precise
account of Omar's movement in a small convoy, but when Islamabad Station "put the target information out within minutes of our receiving it,"
the station "got no response" from headquarters.

The C.I.A. and I.S.I. also apparently tried to track Mullah Zaeef in
the hope the Taliban ambassador would lead them to Omar. As the air
war intensified, Zaeef traveled to Kandahar in a Land Cruiser to discuss
with Omar an offer Qatar had made to mediate an end of the fighting.
He was "followed all the way by Pakistani intelligence." He made his way
to a makeshift Taliban headquarters in Kandahar and asked for Mullah
Omar, but he was not there. Zaeef left. One hour later, a U.S. Air Force
strike destroyed the building.[18]

The Taliban emir had trusted his fate to Allah. It would be obvious to
him how to interpret the outcome: His role on this Earth was incomplete.
He told Taliban colleagues, according to one of them, "It is very strange
that I am not greedy, for I know my power; my position; my wealth; and
my family are in danger. . . . However I am ready to sacrifice myself and I
do not want to become a friend of non-Muslims, for non-Muslims are
against all my beliefs and my religion." He said he was "ready to leave
everything and believe only in Islam and in my Afghan bravery."[19]

"We are living in decisive days that will give rise to a manifest victory
for Islam and its people, if Allah wills," he prophesied in a letter he wrote
that autumn. "We will not submit nor become lenient. . . . The full moon
of victory has appeared on the horizon."[20]

That fall, the C.I.A.'s Counterterrorist Center grew chaotically, to
about 2,000 full-time personnel. Its Office of Terrorism Analysis
alone ballooned from 25 to 300. The office annexed entire groups of

regional and subject matter experts from the mainstream Directorate of Intelligence. *You were following Polish politics yesterday? Today you are analyzing terrorism issues in Central Asia.* For a few weeks, Cofer Black slept on a blow-up mattress in his office and some of his deputies slept on cots. Conference rooms became group offices with analysts and reports officers shoulder to shoulder. Computer wires spread like kudzu. Tenet ordered any Directorate of Operations personnel whose skills were tangentially related to terrorism—narcotics teams, illicit finance units—to be folded under Cofer Black's authority. Tenet thought Black was an enormously talented leader and trusted him. In some sections of the agency, Black's language and manner rubbed people the wrong way. The Directorate of Operations was a professional shark tank. "You have big personalities and everybody wants to drive the car," as one senior official put it.[21]

Black was trampling all over the C.I.A.'s organization chart that autumn, grabbing and dispatching talent, upending careers and prerogatives, not asking permission to have his officers travel across other divisions' turf. The traditional area chiefs—Senior Intelligence Service officers in charge of Latin America, Europe, or Asia—resisted surrendering their personnel to C.T.C., at least not without some kind of bureaucratic due process. The feeling among Black and his colleagues down at C.T.C. was, essentially: *Is it not obvious that we should put all hands on deck to prevent a second-wave Al Qaeda attack on American soil? Are you really going to waste our time on these personnel issues?* Black worked to control himself and not fight, "only because fighting was unproductive." Yet fights went on just about every day. At one meeting that became legendary at C.T.C., an area division manager asked whether the new terrorism-centric order at C.I.A. would affect flextime, a program that allowed employees to work at home some days.[22]

The prevailing assumption inside the Counterterrorist Center was that Bin Laden probably had additional attackers already in place. Threat reporting about possible follow-on Al Qaeda operations was off the charts. Partly this was a distortion caused by the C.I.A. and the National Security Agency increasing the fidelity on their collection. Both agencies suddenly solicited and listened for every scrap of information about Al

Qaeda that might be obtained worldwide. At C.T.C.'s urging, allied intelligence services from Jordan to Egypt to France to Malaysia detained Islamist suspects on whatever pretense was available and interrogated them for clues about Al Qaeda's next plot. Black, Ben Bonk, and other C.T.C. leaders flew to Libya, Pakistan, Jordan, Russia, Britain, and elsewhere to ask counterparts for every scrap of relevant information they might possess. They heard scary reports—some vetted, some not. But nobody wanted to be blindsided again, and the C.I.A.'s leadership feared that the agency's very existence would be at stake if they missed a big attack a second time. They were thoroughly convinced that there would be another attack inside the United States soon and that it would be even more spectacular than September 11.[23]

The panic gripping Washington that autumn had some basis in hard evidence. On September 18, the first of a series of mysterious envelopes containing lethal anthrax spores were mailed to two Democratic senators on Capitol Hill and to the *National Enquirer* in Florida. The anthrax attack spread to the three major broadcasting networks, ultimately killing five people who inhaled the spores. Nobody knew where the envelopes had originated. The C.I.A. had also learned within weeks after the attacks on New York and Washington that a retired Pakistani nuclear scientist, Sultan Bashirrudin Mahmood, and a retired nuclear engineer, Chaudiri Majeed, had met with Bin Laden in Afghanistan. They had discussed sharing materials for weapons of mass destruction. It appeared that these contacts "with the Taliban and Al Qaeda may have been supported, if not facilitated, by elements within the Pakistani military and intelligence establishment," as Tenet put it. The C.I.A.'s analysts judged that Al Qaeda wanted chemical, biological, and nuclear weapons "not as a deterrent but to cause mass casualties in the United States." I.S.I. detained Mahmood and allowed the C.I.A. to interrogate and polygraph him. When the scientist discussed his time in Afghanistan, the polygraph operator reported that Mahmood's answers showed "deception indicated."[24]

The Counterterrorist Center was thrust into an unusual position within the American national security state. It was a locus of government expertise about a poorly understood enemy. It was also the only institution in town that possessed the outline of a war plan to enter into Afghanistan quickly. At the Pentagon, there were no plans on the shelf that had been previously vetted by the chairman of the Joint Chiefs. Afghanistan was not well understood by the Pentagon's high command. The relationship between Al Qaeda and the Taliban was a mystery. The feeling among the chiefs of the Army, Air Force, Navy, and Marines, as a general involved put it, was "Where is Afghanistan? Where are the maps?" "The fact was that there was no existing war plan for Afghanistan," Rumsfeld admitted. "In some cases our analysts were working with decades-old British maps."[25]

The C.I.A. was in a better position to influence the White House. Four days after the Al Qaeda attacks, Tenet presented a slide deck entitled "Going to War" to President Bush and his national security cabinet. Rich Blee and Ben Bonk at C.T.C. had prepared the slides. They were adapted from memos composed months earlier in response to periodic requests from Richard Clarke at the White House for "Blue Sky" thinking about what C.I.A. would do to attack Al Qaeda if the agency could spend more money and felt no political constraints. The earlier memos had not been acted upon but they covered substantial ground, such as how to arm and support Massoud's guerrilla forces and how to identify more aggressive anti-Taliban allies in southern Afghanistan. The slide deck contemplated a light-footprint campaign in Afghanistan that would start quickly with Massoud's forces in the Panjshir and spread to include other anti-Taliban groups led by Afghan mujaheddin known to the C.I.A. from the 1980s. These warlords included the ethnic Uzbek commander Abdul Rashid Dostum, a former Communist general who had spent years in exile in Turkey; Atta Mohammad Noor, an ethnic Tajik commander allied with Ahmad Shah Massoud; and Ismail Khan, a former C.I.A. client who had been expelled by the Taliban from his stronghold in the western city of Herat. These were the most powerful men under arms who were implacably opposed to the Taliban. They had regional followings and could be used to stabilize and even rule Afghanistan after the Taliban were expelled from office.[26]

The plan embedded in the "Going to War" slides offered speed to Bush and his cabinet. A second attraction was that a light mobile force of guerrilla advisers with laser targeting equipment could bring to bear America's precision airpower while minimizing U.S. casualties. Operation Enduring Freedom, the ensuing Afghan campaign by small Special Forces teams, aided by C.I.A. paramilitaries and case officers, some riding on horseback, would later be well chronicled in books, memoirs, and military "lessons learned" reports. The C.I.A. started out in the leading role and transitioned slowly to a more familiar mission of collecting target intelligence, chasing Al Qaeda fugitives, and running off-the-books militia operations.

The C.I.A.'s first Northern Afghanistan Liaison Team, led by Gary Schroen, landed by helicopter in the Panjshir Valley on September 26. Schroen was a Dari speaker in his early sixties, the equivalent within the C.I.A.'s ranks of a three-star general. He had served several tours in Pakistan and had worked with Ahmad Shah Massoud and his aides for more than a decade. It would take weeks for Pentagon Special Forces units to join the fight. On October 17, Rumsfeld wrote a biting memo to the chairman of the Joint Chiefs, Air Force General Richard Myers. (General Hugh Shelton had already been scheduled to retire when September 11 took place.) "Given the nature of our world, isn't it conceivable that the Department ought not to be in a position of near total dependence on C.I.A. in situations such as this?" Rumsfeld asked. Black put Hank Crumpton in charge of the Counterterrorist Center's part of the war. Crumpton had been C.T.C. operations chief until the summer of 2001, when he rotated to become chief of station in Canberra, Australia. He returned to New Headquarters to work out of a "windowless room filled with maps, photos, books and stacks of paper. It looked like the office of an associate professor at a small, poorly funded liberal arts school." Once Crumpton arrived, Blee and his operations officer took charge of Al Qaeda missions outside Afghanistan. Their work was folded under a massive covert action program, perhaps the largest in C.I.A. history, under the code name of Greystone. As new officers poured into C.T.C., they organized two new units to track Al Qaeda's finances and experiments with chemical, biological, and nuclear materials.[27]

Cofer Black traveled abroad frequently, but when he was at Langley, he tried to buck up his workforce. Many case officers and retirees felt fired by an attitude of war-fighting volunteerism. (Black sent Billy Waugh, a legendary street operative he had worked with in Sudan, forward to Afghanistan, where Waugh celebrated his seventy-third birthday.) Yet some of the Counterterrorist Center's analysts—desk bound and responsible for finding terrorist needles in overnight cable haystacks—also felt pressured. Some felt guilt and embarrassment and heard even agency colleagues say that September 11 was their fault. "We were all angry, of course," as an officer then at C.T.C. put it. At the same time, "a kind of guilt feeling comes across. You feel like maybe you let people down, maybe you let the country down because you couldn't prevent it from happening. You're at the pointy end of the spear in the Counterterrorist Center. You would like to have thought you could prevent something like this from happening."

It was inevitable that C.T.C. would take arrows, Black told colleagues: "When the hearings and the retribution and the finger-pointing comes, we are going to get hammered." They should do what they could, without self-pity, in the time available, before their careers ended, his most ingloriously of all, he said.[28]

I n the Panjshir Valley, to support the Northern Alliance's drive on Kabul and the search for Al Qaeda leaders, Gary Schroen's team set up a joint intelligence cell with Amrullah Saleh and Engineer Arif. With Massoud dead and the C.I.A. on the scene, the two Northern Alliance intelligence leaders moved into critical positions, supporting the C.I.A. officers but also trying to keep track of what they were doing. Schroen's men had carried in $10 million in boxed cash. They handed out bundles like candy on Halloween. Schroen had recruited onto his team Chris Wood, the Dari-speaking case officer who had worked the Taliban account out of Islamabad. Wood ran the day-to-day intelligence reporting at the joint cell, collecting and synthesizing field radio reports about Taliban and Al Qaeda positions and movements.

Fahim Khan, Massoud's military chief, commanded the Panjshiris' war. His deputy on the front line was Bismillah Khan, whose men controlled the mouth of the Panjshir, facing the Shomali Plains. Beyond those plains lay Kabul. To the east, the Northern Alliance line was manned by about two thousand fighters loyal to Abdul Rasoul Sayyaf, a conservative mujaheddin leader from the anti-Soviet war who had once been close to Bin Laden. Schroen visited Sayyaf early on and gave him $100,000 in cash.

Sayyaf's men showed the C.I.A. team the shadow of an old airstrip near their section of the front line. Vacationing German trout fishermen had used the strip before the Second World War, some locals explained. Others said the owners of a German brewery had used it. Reading a history of Britain's wars in Afghanistan, one of Schroen's team eventually discovered that the German military had constructed the field around the time of the First World War. Now it consisted of barely visible ruts.

Schroen suggested to Chris Wood that they hire local men to dig out the field and make it operational. Wood became foreman. Every few days he rolled over to the construction site to check on progress and distribute a cash payroll. He by now sported a full blond beard. Whenever he got out of his S.U.V., his Panjshiri security detail followed him, toting assault rifles.

One mid-October afternoon, a C.I.A. colleague at their main Panjshir base interrupted Schroen. The colleague was on the secure phone to Langley. "This is the mission manager for Predator flights," the officer explained. "He wants to know if we have any information about a newly constructed airfield on the Shomali Plains near a village named Gul Bahar."

Schroen took the phone. "Sir, we have a Predator loitering above what appears to be a newly constructed Taliban airfield," the voice on the other end reported. "C.I.A. confirms this is a new Taliban facility, under construction for the past ten days or so. The Predator is looking at an S.U.V. parked on the dirt landing strip, and there are two men, dressed in Western-style clothing. . . . We think they may be Al Qaeda."

Schroen assured the caller he was wrong—they were tilting their Hellfire at two C.I.A. officers, including Chris Wood.

The caller asked if he was "sure" and Schroen assured him that he was "positive." He had forwarded reports on the airstrip's construction to C.I.A. headquarters, including geocoordinates, several times. Schroen was incredulous. He could understand how the U.S. military might not know about his clandestine airstrip project, but how could the C.I.A. not know about it? Had the officer on duty not thought to call the Panjshir base to check, the Predator might have killed his colleagues. In years to come, Wood would rise in the Senior Intelligence Service to become one of the C.I.A.'s most influential officers in the long Afghan war, serving multiple tours as station chief in Kabul and as an intelligence liaison to the Obama administration's National Security Council during a critical period of war planning. Wood later led the C.I.A.'s Counterterrorism Center, as it would be renamed in 2004, where he commanded the agency's worldwide drone operations. (The C.I.A.'s center was an internal unit, distinct from the interagency National Counterterrorism Center, which was created as part of a 2004 intelligence reorganization.) Wood had more reason than most to understand that not every tall bearded man surrounded by bodyguards was what he seemed to be.[29]

Back at Langley, operations that would come to change the character of global air war—lethal drone flights conducted by remote control from far away—evolved from the confusion of October 7 toward a steady tempo. In the Global Response Center, civilian intelligence officers who lived in tract homes and town houses and had never killed anyone followed and watched presumed militants on their screens. They heard the targets' deaths ordered by a colleague in a suit and tie. They watched the victims be consumed in balls of fire. It was hard to ignore the strangeness of this kind of warfare, the way it severed death and experience.

One day, an armed Predator tracked three Hilux trucks carrying fighters as they moved through Jalalabad. The C.I.A. officers on duty noted that, to avoid civilian deaths, they would have to wait for the trucks to clear out of the city and move into open territory before they took a Hellfire shot. As the officers watched the trucks, they spotted a large dog in the back of one of them. They talked disconcertedly about

the possibility that they might have to kill the dog while attacking the
guerrillas. Then the trucks stopped briefly and the dog decided he had
better things to do and jumped out. Cheers erupted in the C.I.A.'s
Global Response Center. After the wave of emotion subsided, at least
one officer in the room thought to himself: *That was weird.* The C.I.A.
officers named the dog "Lucky." It turned out to be not an unusual nickname for other Afghan and Pakistani dogs at the sites of drone-launched
Hellfire strikes. The animals' hearing was so acute that they sometimes
seemed to detect Predators overhead or picked up the whine of missile
launches when humans could not, and then got out of the way.[30]

In Virginia, one weekend afternoon, while watching one of his kids'
football games, Ric Prado took out a yellow legal pad and sketched out
a plan for a roving clandestine team that would hop around the world
and photograph and document Al Qaeda network members, much as
Counterterrorist Center contractors already did. Prado was the most
dangerous-looking senior officer working in the C.T.C. that fall. He
served as one of Black's key deputies. He was a Cuban-born fourth-
degree black belt in martial arts who had run paramilitary operations
with the Contras in Honduras during the 1980s. He was a trained expert
in parachuting, knife fighting, evasive driving, and extreme motorcycle
tactics. He was about five feet seven inches tall, then in his early fifties,
with a tattoo on one of his biceps. Prado's field experience in Honduras,
Costa Rica, Peru, ALEC Station, and Sudan had included close photographic surveillance operations against diverse targets. (In Sudan, Prado
wore elaborate masks that made him look like a black African and drove
around Khartoum in a battered car, watching Al Qaeda and other targets.) Prado had come to believe, he told Black, that there was little point
in concentrating counterterrorism operations on low-level Al Qaeda
shooters and street operatives. Those foot soldiers would always be replaced. Targeting Al Qaeda leaders was obviously the highest priority,
but the leaders would always be hard to locate. The plan Prado now
proposed would aim at upper-middle "facilitators," as they were called in

government jargon, meaning money traders, weapons suppliers, imams offering safe transit, forgers, bomb makers, counterfeiters, and the like.

After conducting close surveillance and building a case file, Prado's team would develop options for taking the targeted individuals off the street. One option would be to turn the file over to local police, if it seemed likely they would make an arrest. Another option might be non-lethal C.I.A. dirty tricks, such as planting bomb-making material in a target's trunk and then tipping off the local police anonymously. Prado also recommended that they develop the capacity to assassinate the target. Black approved Prado's plan, withholding final judgment about what to do if a target was fully documented and involved in violence. That fall, Prado and Jose Rodriguez, an old colleague from the Latin America division, who had recently joined C.T.C. as "chief operating officer," briefed the concept in the White House Situation Room. Rodriguez had no prior experience with Al Qaeda but he was a well-known figure in the Senior Intelligence Service, a hard-liner willing to back risky operations. The C.I.A. officers flashed photos of two potential targets, Mamoun Darkazanli, a Syrian in Germany who the C.I.A. believed was culpable for planning September 11, and Abdul Qadeer Khan, the father of Pakistan's nuclear program. Vice President Cheney approved the program, which Prado would lead until 2004. (It took some effort for Prado to persuade Black to let him back on the streets; he was now in the Senior Intelligence Service, the equivalent of ambassador or general. He had started as a GS-7, at a pay scale comparable to a truck driver's.) Most of the targets Prado's unit watched and documented were suspected Al Qaeda types, but C.T.C.'s Hezbollah unit also nominated a few candidates for investigation. In the end, the C.I.A.'s leadership declined to order any targets killed, but what other actions might have been taken remains unclear. This was a need-to-know campaign. Only the more seasoned among them reflected at the time that immunity from public scrutiny would not last long.[31]

George W. Bush "knew the war would bring death and sorrow," but he took comfort from his conviction that "we were acting out of necessity and self-defense, not revenge." On the front lines, inevitably, there was blood in the mouth. C.I.A. officers had not fought on such a violent battlefield as Afghanistan's since the 1980s. The agency had not planned assassinations since the early 1970s. Hank Crumpton, the agency's war commander, worked from day to day that fall "in a barely bounded rage." He felt "a burning need for retribution rooted in a sense of shameful violation."[32]

FIVE

Catastrophic Success

Pervez Musharraf forced I.S.I. director-general Mahmud Ahmed to retire about two hours before the American war began. He did not explain his decision. As to the way ahead, Musharraf told the Americans what they wanted to hear: He was going to "clean up" I.S.I. He appointed Lieutenant General Ehsan ul-Haq as his new spy chief. Haq was a clean-shaven Pashtun air defense officer in the Musharraf mold—a professional soldier and nationalist who gave off a rogue's air. He stood about five feet eight inches tall and wore dapper Western suits. His baritone voice carried British inflections. He had previously served as director-general of military intelligence and most recently as commander of the XI Corps, headquartered in Peshawar. In meetings with American counterparts that autumn, Haq denounced India and pleaded that Pakistan had little influence over the Taliban. As to Operation Enduring Freedom in Afghanistan, he emphasized, "It's in Pakistan's interest to resolve the present situation quickly."[1]

The Bush administration had demanded that Pakistan prevent its citizens from traveling to Afghanistan to fight against the United States, but it was clear by mid-October that more than ten thousand Pakistanis had gone across anyway. Ehsan ul-Haq denied in meetings with Dave Smith that anything like "thousands" of Pakistanis had joined the war. He made it clear that Pakistan would turn over all Arabs and other foreign radicals to the United States, but that it would absolutely not cooperate in the capture of Pakistani citizens. There were "maybe hundreds" of Pakistani volunteers fighting with the Taliban in any event, Haq estimated. Smith noted in silence that the I.S.I. chief was off by a few decimal points.[2]

Dave Smith continued to ride to I.S.I. headquarters as often as the service would have him. One of his objectives was to probe what Musharraf meant about his supposed reform campaign inside I.S.I. The Americans wanted Haq and Musharraf to come clean about the presence of its officers and agents on the battlefield in Afghanistan, so the Pentagon could understand more precisely what it was up against. How many Pakistani officers were there embedded with the Taliban? What was the Taliban order of battle?

Engineer Arif and Amrullah Saleh of the Northern Alliance's intelligence wing reported that hundreds of disguised Pakistani military officers had maneuvered and fought with Taliban and Al Qaeda units before September 11. European and United Nations intelligence officers working out of Kabul never found evidence of that scale of direct Pakistani participation. They typically encountered two to four I.S.I. advisers in plain dress when they met Taliban units. The Europeans estimated that I.S.I. advisers inside Afghanistan numbered about one hundred. Mahmud Ahmed insisted that I.S.I. never had so many officers inside Afghanistan.[3]

That autumn, Javed Alam, the two-star general in charge of I.S.I.'s Directorate of Analysis, told Smith that there had only ever been nine I.S.I. officers working inside Afghanistan. These officers had withdrawn, he added. Smith did not believe the number had been so low, but there was no way to document a precise figure. Neither American nor Afghan forces captured Pakistan Army officers on the battlefield that fall, at least none they could identify as such.

To avoid additional scrutiny, Smith later learned, I.S.I. moved its covert action cell supporting the Taliban out of the service's Islamabad headquarters to an army camp at Ojhri, near Rawalpindi. From the evidence available it seems most likely that I.S.I. did pull back many of its officers from Afghanistan during the American bombardment but kept its support for the Taliban viable. There were ample munitions depots inside Afghanistan for all combatants, the legacy of more than two decades of covert and overt war.

Javed Alam told Smith that most of the Pakistani volunteers who had swarmed into Afghanistan to fight against America had traveled from Southern Punjab, an area of the Pakistani heartland that was home to growing numbers of radical Islamists. "Most of them died," he said, without evident remorse. "They got their just deserts."

Alam and his analysts presented scenario forecasts of where the American invasion might leave Afghanistan. If the United States toppled the Taliban and departed quickly, it would leave chaos, as during the early 1990s, Alam predicted. Alternatively, the Bush administration could enable "de facto partition" of Afghanistan between north and south. In that case, a follow-on American military presence "would have to be sizeable, two hundred and fifty thousand soldiers," and would need to transition "from peacekeeping to peace enforcement." As it turned out, in the longer run, the general was not far off, not least because of I.S.I.'s continuing support for the Taliban.[4]

In early November, Pakistan mounted one last diplomatic effort to rescue the Taliban from destruction, this time with assistance from Saudi Arabia. Ehsan ul-Haq flew secretly to Washington with Prince Saud al Faisal, Saudi Arabia's foreign minister. They carried a four-page letter from Musharraf to President Bush that proposed another effort to resolve the Afghan conflict through negotiations with Taliban leaders willing to cooperate against Al Qaeda.

British prime minister Tony Blair encouraged their initiative, according to Pakistani officials involved, and volunteered to raise Musharraf's concerns privately with Bush. Blair arrived in Washington on November 7. But when Haq and his Saudi escorts landed soon after, Blair relayed bad news: There was no hope for negotiation, so far as the Bush administration was concerned. The war would go on until the Taliban surrendered unconditionally or were annihilated.[5]

C.I.A. frontline officers divided into factions on the I.S.I. question that fall. Some sympathized with Pakistan's position, recognizing that the country had legitimate interests in Afghanistan's future. Others regarded I.S.I.'s maneuvering as unacceptable. This played out primarily as a fierce conflict between senior officers at the Counterterrorist Center working with the Northern Alliance and Bob Grenier, station chief in Pakistan. Grenier lamented "the aggressive philistinism of C.T.C." The conflict had a personal edge—the men involved were Senior Intelligence Service peers, and they felt free to write and speak sharply to and about one another. They belonged to a generation of clandestine service officers who had grown up in a C.I.A. little constrained by human resources department norms about collegiality or inclusivity. Yet at the heart of their conflict was a genuine dilemma of war strategy. Should the Bush administration encourage the Panjshiri vanguard of the Northern Alliance to seize Kabul, or should it defer to Pakistan's position that it was necessary to delay Kabul's fall so that a more Pashtun-influenced post-Taliban political settlement in Afghanistan could be fashioned, one more aligned with Pakistan's goals?[6]

Grenier "felt strongly that a seizure of Kabul by the Tajiks and Uzbeks would make an eventual political settlement with the Pashtuns far more difficult." This was Musharraf's position and that of I.S.I. Colin Powell held the same outlook. Richard Armitage and George Tenet were also sympathetic to Grenier's analysis. Tenet thought it was not an either-or question: Let all the options play out. His logic was: The enemy is Al Qaeda; we need Pakistan's army and I.S.I. to dismantle Al Qaeda; and Pakistan's stability and interests are at least as important to the United States as Afghanistan's recovery from Taliban rule. Tenet had met regularly with I.S.I. before September 11 and seemed never to have encountered an intelligence liaison relationship he didn't value. For the C.I.A., keeping I.S.I. on side offered the opportunity to recruit agents from the service's ranks who might be well informed about Al Qaeda and allied militants. The Counterterrorist Center assumed that if anyone was likely to have a line on the whereabouts of Bin Laden, his deputy Ayman Al Zawahiri, Mullah Omar, and other targeted leaders, it would be officers inside I.S.I.'s Directorate S. They had to stay close to the service in order to identify, assess, and recruit I.S.I. informers.[7]

More broadly, this line of thinking went, Pakistan might be an imperfect ally, but it had more than five times Afghanistan's population, nuclear weapons, Middle Eastern networks, and a history of alliance with the United States. Because the objective of the war was to destroy Al Qaeda, not to manage post-Taliban Afghan politics as a neo-imperial power, surely the United States could afford to take account of Pakistan's interests.

This outlook did require credulity about I.S.I.'s potential as a good-enough partner in postwar Afghanistan, notwithstanding the service's long record as an incubator and enabler of extremism. In one top secret cable, Grenier wrote, as a C.I.A. colleague later summarized his argument, the "new, more moderate leadership" at I.S.I. under Ehsan ul-Haq was now motivated to "cooperate fully with the C.I.A. in the war on terrorism." Moreover, I.S.I. had "years of experience in dealing with the Afghan situation and were already working hard to build a broad ethnic 'Afghan Government in Exile' in Peshawar." The Bush administration "should work closely with the Pakistanis on that effort, concentrate on the south, and go slowly with our bombing." Grenier recommended: "This should be primarily a political struggle rather than a military one." Grenier was worried that if the United States came in wholeheartedly on the side of the Northern Alliance that that would only cause Pashtuns to coalesce around the Taliban. He also feared the Northern Alliance militias would carry out a bloodbath in Kabul, which would have the same effect. They were having enough trouble generating a Pashtun up-rising against the Taliban and Al Qaeda as it was.[8]

Grenier knew he had crawled out on a limb by making these arguments—his views put him firmly at odds with the newly powerful Counterterrorist Center. Hank Crumpton and other C.T.C. officers dismissed him as "Taliban Bob." Grenier had "taken the side of" I.S.I., but Crumpton and his colleagues "knew that I.S.I. was not the answer." Grenier was "suffering from a case of clientitis," meaning that he had lost his ability to separate his own thinking from that of his partners in the Pakistan Army. Yet Grenier's position remained influential throughout October. Tenet initially overruled C.T.C.'s objections in order "to give the Pakistanis some time to address the southern question," meaning the establishment of a Pashtun-influenced force that could emerge as an alternative to the Taliban. Tenet and his chief of staff, John Brennan, were impressed by the sophistication of Grenier's arguments; while pursuing a policy of "all options" they thought his case deserved some time.[9]

Forward in the Panjshir Valley, Gary Schroen, who had served three tours in Islamabad since the late 1970s, argued the Northern Alliance cause. The key to victory was in the north, he believed, yet Grenier "was loudly beating what I thought of as the Pakistani drum song." Grenier was sitting in a comfortable office in Islamabad (which Schroen had previously occupied), with all the technology needed to send in articulate cables to the Bush cabinet, while Schroen was working in primitive conditions with an old computer that took floppy disks; he was struggling to get his points across. Grenier's position was "a blueprint for failure and political confusion," Schroen concluded. "This push to allow the Pakistanis back into the Afghan game was disturbing and a real mistake. They had their own specific agenda for the country and it did not track with anything the U.S. government would want to see emerge there in the post-Taliban period."

Massoud's intelligence aides and generals knew about the debate within the C.I.A. and the Bush cabinet and pushed Schroen to resolve it in their favor. They would pursue their own war aims, regardless of where the Americans came down. Schroen and Chris Wood fumed as the weeks passed and Grenier's arguments seemed to influence Central Command's targeting decisions. The U.S. Air Force bombed and provided close air support for Northern Alliance commanders who sought to seize the northern cities Mazar-i-Sharif and Kunduz. The fall of those cities to the Northern Alliance presented no political complications, as the majority of the local population was non-Pashtun. Yet the bombing of Taliban positions defending Kabul seemed tepid by comparison. The first night of the air war, it was raining around Kabul. In the Panjshir, Schroen and his colleagues sat on a balcony and watched lights flash in the distance. There were only a few. They blamed the weather, but soon discovered that in fact it was a policy edict from Washington. The Bush administration did not actually wish to break the Taliban and Al Qaeda lines blocking the Northern Alliance from taking Kabul. "This is all the U.S. Air Force can do?" Massoud's lieutenants asked their C.I.A. liaisons. "We'll have to be here forever."[10]

T he Taliban imposed a night curfew inside Kabul but otherwise tried to keep up appearances. Taliban bureaucrats went to work at their ministries as usual. Kathy Gannon of the Associated Press, who had been traveling in and out of Afghanistan for almost two decades, arrived in the capital late in October and found residents paying their electricity bills at the telecommunications ministry even though the ministry itself had no power. Food supplies dwindled. Mullah Mohammad Omar remained in hiding around Kandahar, but his lieutenants to the north, inside Kabul, could see by the second week of November that if they held out too long they might become trapped. If that happened, they could be slaughtered and imprisoned in large numbers.

Just after nightfall on November 12, in Wazir Akbar Khan, a dozen or so Taliban leaders gathered to discuss a strategic retreat. They decided by consensus to withdraw right away to Wardak Province and to move from there toward Kandahar. Convoys of vehicles roared through the night, evacuating to the south and east, into the Pashtun heartland. Amrullah Saleh and Engineer Arif picked up the Taliban's radio traffic. They knew that a withdrawal had started. Yet the Panjshiris remained under pressure from the United States to hold back.

On November 13, when the Taliban appeared to have evacuated almost completely from Kabul, C.I.A. headquarters instructed an officer in Panjshir to meet with the Northern Alliance. The officer announced, "There is still concern back in Washington that there will be a wave of revenge killings by your forces if they move into Kabul." He cautioned, "The Pakistanis continue to complain to Washington about what will happen if the Northern Alliance takes Kabul."

The alliance's commanders assured the C.I.A. that there would be no brutality. They added that they were "going to Kabul no matter what your N.S.C. decides."[11]

The C.I.A. went with them—three officers packed into a sport utility vehicle carrying satellite phones and semiautomatic rifles. On November 14, around 6:00 p.m., they rolled past the shuttered American embassy building, abandoned since early 1989. They soon reached the

Ariana Hotel, in the heart of downtown, which Engineer Arif had agreed the C.I.A. could rent as a base of operations. That night, Kabul Station informally reopened after a hiatus of just under thirteen years. The Panjshiris controlled Afghanistan's capital. Musharraf and I.S.I. had failed to stop them.

Back in the 1980s, during the anti-Soviet war, Hamid Karzai was a university student and organizer, the privileged scion of an influential family in Kandahar of the Popalzai tribe. His father, Abdul Ahad Karzai, had sat in the Afghan parliament before the Communist takeover. Hamid studied politics at Himachal Pradesh University in India before moving to Peshawar, in 1983, to work as an aide to Sibghatullah Mojaddedi, one of the Afghan resistance's more moderate but less influential leaders. Karzai served as a foreign policy adviser, humanitarian aid organizer, and press contact. He was known as a snappy dresser and a well-liked participant in Peshawar's expatriate social scene, which was enlivened by Australian aid workers, Scandinavian nurses, British spies, I.S.I. watchers, unreliable journalists, and mysterious drifters, all of them energized by a liberation war and the smoky atmospherics of a Cold War *Casablanca*.

As the war raged Karzai saw the front lines but he thought of himself as a political and social analyst. His sense of politics was informed by the example of his father, who promoted the traditional power of Afghanistan's tribes and the country's royal family, while also supporting modernization. The Soviet war shattered and scattered the Karzais as it did so many other Afghan families. In a country as poor as Afghanistan, privilege and a touch of rank such as the Karzais enjoyed did not translate into seven-figure Swiss bank accounts. They were better off than many countrymen and yet financially insecure. Some of Hamid's brothers went abroad. One of them, Qayum, opened an Afghan restaurant in Baltimore. Another, Mahmud, opened fast-food outlets in San Francisco and Boston. Only Hamid and his younger brother, Ahmed Wali, settled in South Asia.

Hamid Karzai argued that Afghanistan should seek to recover from the

Soviet war by restoring tribes and the royal family as symbols of national unity—a strategy that would benefit previously elite Durrani Pashtun families such as his own. In 1988, he published an essay in the *Central Asian Survey*, an academic journal. His modest thesis concerned "the extraordinary resilience and persistence" of "the very deep-rooted traditional beliefs and religious values of the tribes, and indeed of the whole nation."[12]

In 1992, when Kabul fell to the C.I.A.-backed mujaheddin, Mojaddedi became president briefly. Karzai became a deputy foreign minister. I.S.I.'s favored Islamist guerrilla leader, Gulbuddin Hekmatyar, had been named prime minister but refused to join the new government. Hekmatyar's forces shelled Kabul mercilessly from a base to the south of the capital. The I.S.I. would eventually abandon Hekmatyar in favor of the Taliban, but at the time he was the most important client of Directorate S.

Ahmad Shah Massoud was then minister of defense. Fahim Khan and Engineer Arif, his intelligence aides, suspected that Hekmatyar had a secret network of supporters inside Kabul. One day, Arif summoned Karzai for "advice" about individuals who might be working for Hekmatyar, a senior Afghan official involved recalled. The idea was "to share intelligence" with Karzai "and ask him to do something about it" at the foreign ministry, meaning identify and help round up Hekmatyar sympathizers. But Karzai "was nervous," understandably enough, about being interrogated by Panjshiri musclemen.[13]

Afterward, Karzai took it upon himself to visit Hekmatyar to try to find a diplomatic solution. When he returned to Kabul, however, Fahim Khan arrested Karzai on suspicion of collaboration with the enemy. The intelligence service abused Karzai in a Kabul cell. Fahim regarded Karzai as a "weak figure" who could be intimidated, as a Western diplomat who worked closely with both men put it.[14]

After a short period of imprisonment, one of Hekmatyar's randomly aimed rockets hit the jail and knocked a hole in the wall, allowing Karzai to escape. He fled to Pakistan. There he expressed support for the Taliban. "I believed in the Taliban when they first appeared," Karzai later conceded. "I gave them fifty thousand dollars to help them out, and then handed them a cache of weapons I had hidden near Kandahar. . . .

They were good people initially, but the tragedy was that very soon after they were taken over by the I.S.I."[15]

As the years passed, the Taliban's hostility toward the Karzai family changed his thinking again. Hamid Karzai's aging father spoke out against the Taliban. One morning in 1999, assassins on motorbikes gunned him down. After that, Hamid opened contacts with Ahmad Shah Massoud, Fahim's commander. They discussed the possibility of Hamid Karzai's entering Afghanistan to build up a Pashtun-led resistance to the Taliban.

At the time of the September 11 attacks, Greg Vogle served as the C.I.A.'s chief of base in Peshawar. He worked from the U.S. consulate there. He was a man of medium height who had become well known in the Directorate of Operations for his spartan workouts and his bushy, Fu Manchu mustache. He looked like he might be a guitarist in a Lynyrd Skynyrd or Allman Brothers revival band. He had grown up in the Deep South and joined the Marine Corps reconnaissance force, a branch of the Special Forces. On one early assignment, in 1983, he flew into Beirut after Islamic Jihad bombed a Marine barracks there, killing almost three hundred. Vogle left the Marines after five years to become a C.I.A. officer. For the next twenty years he served mainly in the Special Activities Division, the agency's paramilitary wing. During a tour in Riyadh, Saudi Arabia, Vogle would ride for an hour on a stationary bike in the morning. At midday he would move the bike into the peak desert sun and ride for another hour. In the evening he would swim for a third hour using a device that rendered his legs inert so that he pulled through the water with his arms. Later, Vogle deployed to Africa and the Balkans. As he aged his hair grayed and his face sank, adding to his battered biker-rocker mien. "Easy day," he liked to say in parting.[16]

Paramilitary specialists in the C.I.A. were "a wary and misunderstood breed," who often struggled to be fully accepted by their liberal arts–educated colleagues, as Robert Grenier put it. Vogle "was among the few in his tribe who excelled in both intelligence and paramilitary operations." He was profane and had an imaginative sense of humor. Yet he also had "a rather thin skin, and a sensitive soul." According to Crumpton, Vogle could hold a blood grudge.[17]

Grenier made the "arbitrary" decision to assign Vogle to Hamid Karzai. They were not the most likely pair, except that Karzai, too, was a sensitive soul. Grenier insisted that Karzai was in no way a controlled C.I.A. agent, but rather a potential resistance leader in a common cause. After the assassination of his father, Karzai met with diplomats regularly and talked, not very convincingly, about plans to enter Afghanistan and link up with the Northern Alliance. I.S.I. caught wind of the planning and served Karzai with an eviction notice late in the summer of 2001. Then came September 11, which galvanized Karzai. He and Vogle discussed a new possibility: Karzai would move into Afghanistan to stir up a rebellion among tribesmen and allies in the Taliban's heartland—a more direct and risky version of the guerrilla strategy the pair had outlined earlier.

A few days before the air war started on October 7, Vogle called Karzai.

"I can't tell you why, but you've got to get inside now," Vogle said. The implication was obvious: The American bombing would start soon. Karzai had to be in position to take territory and rally followers as the Taliban reeled under the coming air assault.

Karzai said he had to check with contacts in Kandahar. The next day, he called Vogle back. "I'm going this afternoon," he reported.[18]

Unarmed, in the darkness, joined only by three friends, Karzai crossed by motorcycle into Afghanistan.

His courage made an impression on Vogle. It was one thing for a trained reconnaissance soldier to ride into the dark; it was another for a political science student with no military experience. Vogle and Grenier pressed to create a joint C.I.A.–Special Forces team of the sort that had earlier been inserted into the north, to aid the more experienced Panjshiris and their Uzbek and Hazara allies. Those helicopter-borne teams had landed in areas firmly controlled by the indigenous forces they would assist, however. Karzai had melted into vast Taliban country—he had no base of operations, no bodyguard, and no confirmed military allies inside Afghanistan. The idea was that as soon as Karzai had "rallied a sufficient number of fighters to hold territory and defend a landing zone," as Grenier described it, Greg Vogle and Pentagon special operators would follow by helicopter. "The truth was we were all making it up as we went along."[19]

Karzai initially toured rural Kandahar, hosting delegations and giving speeches, then moved toward Uruzgan's provincial capital of Tarinkot. He found modest support—perhaps a few dozen armed fighters traveled with him—but also ambivalence. Switching sides was an Afghan way of war, but the Taliban had showed no mercy to those who defected, and it wasn't yet clear to locals how this war would turn out. Where were the Americans?

Karzai and Vogle stayed in touch by satellite phone and text. Grenier believed that Cofer Black and Hank Crumpton were too slow to support Karzai, and that C.T.C.'s failure to supply him as he traveled was "beyond scandal." Crumpton was at odds with Grenier over the latter's caution about working with the Northern Alliance, but felt that he ordered "a lot of reconnaissance" to support Karzai. Between October 30 and November 2, Karzai's small band fought off a Taliban force sent to kill him. They barely escaped. "Everyone in the U.S. government supports you," Vogle texted him. "All we ask is that you maintain a continuous heartbeat."[20]

The next day, Karzai asked to be rescued—his phone was running out of batteries. Vogle flew on the Special Operations helicopter that extracted him and some followers. Back in Pakistan, they moved Karzai into an old schoolhouse at a Pakistani air base in Jacobabad, in southern Sindh Province. Karzai gave phone interviews to the BBC and other journalists, pretending to be still inside Afghanistan, until Secretary of Defense Donald Rumsfeld inadvertently blurted out that Karzai was actually in Pakistan.

By mid-November the Pentagon and C.I.A. had organized Team Echo, a paramilitary force drawn from the Army's Fifth Special Forces Group, Delta Force, and the C.I.A. Army captain Jason Amerine, a West Point graduate, would command the team. Greg Vogle would lead its small C.I.A. contingent. Team Echo flew into Uruzgan on the night of November 14.

At that point, besides Karzai, the only other Pashtun resistance leader the C.I.A. was prepared to back with an embedded military team was Gul Agha Sherzai, a strongman from southern Afghanistan's Barakzai tribe. Karzai and Sherzai were destined to become political rivals whose struggles would shape Afghanistan; it was the C.I.A.'s support that gave birth to this competition. Like Karzai's Popalzai tribe, the Barakzai had produced generations of Pashtun elites, particularly through the Mohammadzai subtribe. Gul Agha Sherzai was not of the elite, however. His father, Abdul Latif, was a small businessman who had risen during the anti-Soviet war as a commander, "exploiting the absenteeism of the Barakzai aristocracy," as two scholars of the family's history put it. In 1989, Abdul Latif's cook murdered him by poison. His son Gul Agha ("Flower" in Pashto, a name he adopted as a boy) inherited his networks of influence and added Sherzai ("The Lion's Son") to his name. He became governor of Kandahar after the Soviet withdrawal, a powerful figure in the coalition of checkpoint-extorting, neighborhood-menacing commanders the Taliban expelled from power. He went into exile. Sherzai relied on political influence and a "ragtag band of tribal militiamen with no organization and few heavy weapons." Through his networks, Sherzai had been gathering intelligence on the Taliban and Al Qaeda for the C.I.A. for more than a year before September 11. He lived in Quetta, enriched himself through business and espionage, and bided his time. The significance of his position that autumn was that, like the Panjshiris, Gul Agha Sherzai was already a vetted Counterterrorist Center partner with a track record of cooperation with the C.I.A. against the Taliban.[21]

Sherzai entered Afghanistan from Quetta, to Kandahar's south, a few days after Karzai landed by helicopter. Team Foxtrot, another Pentagon-commanded Special Forces–C.I.A. collaboration, joined Sherzai. To prepare, Sherzai's lieutenants met I.S.I. officers in Quetta to receive Pakistani weapons. The service had reluctantly come to play both sides in the American war against the Taliban, but few officers had changed their convictions. The I.S.I. officer handing over the guns told Sherzai's men "that they were making a serious mistake in trying to overthrow the Taliban, one which they should regret, and one which they should seriously reconsider."

In Grenier's judgment, the threat Karzai and Sherzai "posed to the Taliban was primarily political, not military." The Taliban had taken power five years earlier by persuading entire sections of the Pashtun population to join them, without firing a shot. Now the process might work in reverse. The problem was, as Grenier put it, "Our own understanding of this broad sociopolitical shift was hazy at best."[22]

The decisive battle of Hamid Karzai's improbable campaign took place less than two weeks after he returned to Afghanistan in the company of Vogle. A convoy of about fifty armed and highly irregular Taliban vehicles rolled up a highway from Kandahar to attack Karzai outside Tarinkot. It "looked like a snake slithering out of the pass," in the journalist Eric Blehm's description. "There seemed to be no end; it just kept coming, its numbers obscured by the dust storm it created as it advanced across the flat desert floor." Karzai's smaller militia carried "everything from AK-47s to bolt-action rifles that likely predated World War II." But F-18 fighter-bombers obliterated the Taliban trucks before their occupants could dismount, scattering dozens of charred bodies on the plain. The remaining trucks turned and fled.[23]

The victory brought yet more local leaders to Karzai's makeshift quarters, where Greg Vogle, who had taught himself some Pashto, was a constant presence—part bodyguard, part political adviser, and part reporting officer into C.I.A. channels. The political stakes he managed rose by the day. The Northern Alliance held Kabul. Kandahar lay open to Karzai and Sherzai. An interim post-Taliban government was now an urgent requirement, and the Bush administration appointed the diplomat James Dobbins to negotiate one, in partnership with the Algerian-born diplomat Lakhdar Brahimi. The United Nations scheduled a formal conference in Bonn, Germany. En route, Ehsan ul-Haq, the I.S.I. chief, and Abdullah Abdullah, the longtime political adviser to Massoud, each volunteered to Dobbins the name of Hamid Karzai as someone who might be an acceptable interim leader of Afghanistan. "We thought, 'If he's a Pashtun from Kandahar, and he's a C.I.A. guy, okay,'" explained one senior Northern Alliance leader. It was unlikely that there would be many other aspects of Afghan politics on which the I.S.I., the C.I.A., and the Northern Alliance would agree. Hamid Karzai's destiny was sealed.[24]

As he moved toward Kandahar, Karzai met tribal leaders hoping to pledge themselves to him early. On December 5, he had just sat down for another parley when an explosion shook the room, throwing him to the floor. Vogle leaped on top of Karzai's body to protect him, followed by a scrum of Afghan guards.[25] They feared a Taliban attack was under way.

It was friendly fire. An Air Force controller had inadvertently directed a two-thousand-pound bomb near Karzai's position. Three Americans and fifty Afghans died.

Karzai was shaken but not seriously hurt. During the next hour, a BBC reporter called his satellite phone from Kabul to inform him that he had been named chairman of the new Afghan interim government. That same day, a Taliban delegation arrived with a letter of surrender, as Karzai later characterized the document.

Karzai asked Mullah Naqibullah, the militarily powerful commander of an armed force in Kandahar, to speak with surviving Taliban leaders who had gathered in Shah Wali Kot, a redoubt of canyons and ridges to Kandahar's northeast. Mullah Mohammad Omar received him. Other senior Taliban leaders and advisers were also present. Karzai was inclined to accept Omar's terms of surrender.

The next day, at a Pentagon press conference, however, Donald Rumsfeld announced that any negotiated end to the war against the Taliban was "unacceptable to the United States." It remained American policy toward the Taliban "to bring justice to them or them to justice." This policy was soon felt in Kandahar. Some of the senior Taliban who offered to back Karzai's new regime were arrested and later sent to Guantánamo.

After tense negotiations, the C.I.A. helped to broker a deal in which Gul Agha Sherzai was restored as governor of Kandahar, Naqibullah yielded political power but maintained his armed force, and Hamid Karzai took over national leadership from Kabul. Mullah Mohammad Omar hid out for a few days, wrapped in a shawl, then climbed on a motorcycle and escaped into Pakistan.[26]

Hardly anyone in Washington or at the C.I.A.'s Counterterrorist

Center reflected on the Taliban's political fate or how the movement's exclusion from the country's new politics might later create a backlash. "Sadly, in terms of our policy, I don't think we thought much about them at all," Crumpton recalled, referring to the Taliban's surviving leadership. "We killed a lot of them, many thousands of them, including some of the key leaders. They were whipped." Unfortunately, "what we failed to do is to understand that we had to replace the Taliban with something better." As he worked with Karzai and the Northern Alliance to allocate cabinet seats in the new Afghan regime, James Dobbins believed the Taliban "had been so discredited by their performance in government and by the speed at which they had been displaced that they were not going to be a significant factor in Afghan politics. That turned out to be completely wrong."[27]

I n early October, Osama Bin Laden issued his first statement since September 11. "There is America, hit by God in one of its softest spots," he said. "Its greatest buildings were destroyed, thank God for that. There is America, full of fear from its north to its south."[28] He kept a low profile in the weeks that followed, receiving a few visitors but moving frequently. When Kabul fell, Al Qaeda's remnant army of Arabs, Uzbeks, Chechens, Africans, and other volunteers evacuated to the east, toward Jalalabad and then southeast into the White Mountains near the Pakistan border. Bin Laden had constructed underground bunkers there during the anti-Soviet war, at the complex known as Tora Bora.

On November 21, Central Command's Tommy Franks, who was planning air operations against Tora Bora, took a call from Donald Rumsfeld, who ordered him to start working on plans for an invasion of Iraq. Rumsfeld told him to have something ready within a week.[29] That dissonance set the tone for the following three weeks. The objective of Operation Enduring Freedom was not to seize Kabul; it was to destroy Al Qaeda. Yet Rumsfeld was ordering the campaign's commander to plan for a different war before he had completed the one at hand. Military history is rife with examples of generals and presidents who squander strategic advantage by failing to press a battlefield triumph to its

conclusion. Here was the same story again, involving not only complacency but also inexplicable strategic judgment, fractured decision making, and confusion.

The C.I.A.'s days-old Kabul Station attempted to track Al Qaeda as
its units fled the capital, but the atmosphere was highly improvised and
the station had new leadership. Schroen had pulled out after about six
weeks in the field, replaced by Gary Berntsen. The new chief had grown
up on Long Island, where he "drank, got into fights, and caused all sorts
of trouble, graduating next to last in a high school class of about
300, a functional illiterate." He did not know Afghanistan, but he
spoke Farsi and had worked on terrorism operations, where he "took a
grab-them-by-the-neck approach." Sending him to run C.I.A. operations at the end of October was Hank Crumpton's call. Crumpton
wanted aggression on the front line, and he got that. During his short
tour in Kabul, Berntsen may have advocated more forcefully than anyone in the U.S. government to put American boots on the ground at Tora
Bora to try to prevent Bin Laden's escape. Yet he also fought so bitterly
with colleagues and U.S. military commanders that he undermined his
own message.

On November 26 or 27, a C.I.A. officer who was a former Delta operator told Berntsen that the small American presence coordinating with
Afghan militias was not working. Berntsen sent in a "careful" cable asking for U.S. Rangers. "Let's kill this baby in the crib," he concluded.[30]

On November 29, Vice President Dick Cheney told ABC News that
Bin Laden "was equipped to go to ground" at Tora Bora. "He's got what
he believes to be secure facilities, caves underground. It's an area he's
familiar with." Around December 1, Crumpton took maps of Tora Bora
to the Oval Office and squatted on the floor before President Bush and
Cheney to review the terrain.

"Is there any way we can seal this border?" Bush asked.

"No army on Earth can seal this," Crumpton answered.

Delta Force, C.I.A., and other paramilitary and Special Forces units
were following the method that had already conquered Afghanistan's
northern cities: They embedded with Afghan militias. Hazarat Ali, a
commander in Jalalabad allied with the Northern Alliance, oversaw one

force; Haji Zahir, the son of a prominent commander who had initially welcomed Bin Laden to Afghanistan, oversaw a smaller one. Neither of them had the motivation or history of collaboration with the C.I.A. that the Panjshiris or Gul Agha Sherzai had.

The United States could deploy small reconnaissance units behind the caves and watch for Bin Laden and his followers with satellites and the C.I.A.'s two Predators, Crumpton told Bush, "but with such a vast territory and uncertain weather, we could miss their escape." Crumpton felt that he had made an intelligence case emphasizing the Pakistani border was porous and that he had doubts that Pakistani forces could seal it. He did not think it was his position to recommend directly that Bush deploy hundreds of U.S. troops in a blocking position; as an intelligence officer, he had laid out his analysis, but the decision about how to fight the war was up to the president and Franks. The alternative to an American ground assault force was airpower. But Tora Bora had been constructed fifteen years before to withstand heavy Soviet aerial bombardment.[31]

Franks ordered heavy bombers into action on December 3. Over the next four days B-52s and other high-altitude aircraft dropped about seven hundred thousand pounds of explosives on Al Qaeda's suspected positions. Small teams of Delta Force and C.I.A. officers working with reluctant Afghan militias pushed up the mountainside to observe what they could. The teams intercepted radio transmissions that included Bin Laden speaking to his followers, in the judgment of C.I.A. analysts. But Al Qaeda vastly outnumbered the small American spotting force on the mountain. So did the legions of foreign journalists covering the fight from around Jalalabad.

Several days after Crumpton's Oval Office meeting, around December 4, Berntsen demanded that the United States put more of its own soldiers on the ground. He "almost screamed" over the phone to Crumpton that U.S. Army Rangers or Marines were needed in the mountains. Crumpton briefed Cofer Black and then called Tommy Franks the next morning in Tampa. They had a long conversation; Crumpton urged the general to deploy American troops onto the mountainsides. Franks "expressed concern about the lack of planning and the time required to deploy substantial reinforcements," as Crumpton put it later.

When Crumpton described Central Command's reluctance to Berntsen, the Kabul station chief only cursed. Crumpton answered that Berntsen had to accept Franks's decision and "go with what we have."[32]

Bush later defended his own decision making on the grounds that he "asked our commanders and C.I.A. officials about bin Laden frequently" and "they assured me they had the troop levels and resources they needed." But Crumpton's view was that Central Command had to provide the critical blocking forces on the ground; that was well beyond the C.I.A.'s capacity.[33]

In Kabul, Berntsen met Major General Dell Dailey, who commanded Joint Special Operations Command, the subunit of Special Forces housing elite counterterrorism units such as Delta Force and the Navy SEALs. Dailey told Berntsen that he would not deploy more American troops to Tora Bora because it might arouse resentment from Afghan allies. "I don't give a damn about offending our allies!" Berntsen shouted. Dailey refused to change his mind; in fact, the decisions were being made at higher levels. "Screw that!" Berntsen answered.[34]

United States Senate investigators later concluded that about two thousand to three thousand American troops would have been required to make an effective attempt to block Al Qaeda's escape from Tora Bora. About a thousand soldiers from the Tenth Mountain Division had deployed nearby to Uzbekistan, where they had no significant mission. A thousand Marines sat at Camp Rhino, southeast of Kandahar, with no significant mission. With reinforcements from the U.S. Army Rangers and the 82nd Airborne flying out of the United States, a substantial blocking force was available. Organizing enough high-altitude helicopter lift, supplies, and medical support would have been challenging and risky under such time pressure. The peaks at Tora Bora rose as high as fourteen thousand feet, meaning that American soldiers training at lower altitude and dropped there suddenly might suffer from altitude sickness. Because of the harsh weather and rough terrain, close air support would have been difficult to deliver, leaving ground troops vulnerable to ambush or capture.[35]

Yet various accounts given by Franks and his lieutenants indicate that Central Command's reluctance to bear risk was as much the product of a political judgment as it was about logistics. The generals feared the deployment behind Tora Bora might provoke a tribal revolt in the mountains or otherwise destabilize Afghan politics. History misguided them: The cataclysms and mass slaughters suffered by Soviet and British invaders of Afghanistan led Franks and Lieutenant General Michael DeLong, his deputy, to believe that the sudden arrival of hundreds of American soldiers among armed Pashtun tribesmen might stir a spontaneous uprising, they said later. As DeLong put it: "We wanted to create a stable country and that was more important than going after Bin Laden at the time." He feared that "this tribal area was sympathetic to Bin Laden."

The reluctance to go in heavy with American forces began at the top, with Rumsfeld and Franks. According to Major General Warren Edwards, who was involved in the operation, "The message was strong from the national level down: 'We are not going to repeat the mistakes of the Soviets. We are not going to go in with large conventional forces.'" This precept was "embedded in our decision-making process, in our psyche." In fact, the pattern of local responses to heavily armed N.A.T.O. troops deploying for short periods in Pashtun regions would later make clear that even where locals were sullen or hostile, they did not typically have the means or will to mount a spontaneous armed uprising. That would only invite bombing and other deadly retaliation from a vastly superior American force. In the longer run, alienated Pashtuns across the south and east would join or aid the Taliban against the United States, but those populations almost certainly did not pose the threat to a short-term deployment at Tora Bora in December that DeLong and others feared.[36]

On December 9, Crumpton informed Berntsen that he was being replaced after only a few weeks in country. Berntsen had alienated analysts and operators at the Counterterrorist Center and ALEC Station. When he learned of his removal, he felt "as though someone had just thrown a bucket of cold water in my face." He could not understand the decision. "Why was headquarters pulling us out? And why was Washington hesitant about committing troops to get Bin Laden?"

Crumpton felt Berntsen had "done a magnificent, heroic job," but Afghanistan was about to form a post-Taliban government, and there would be a "new mission" for the C.I.A. in Kabul that required "a strong station chief." Crumpton believed he had to manage "sudden success" and the "impending political transformation from a Taliban-occupied country to a liberated proto-state in need of a central authority." This required a chief of station who "could engage across the entire U.S. national security spectrum and forge a close working relationship with the emerging Afghan national government." That might be so, but it did not explain why it was necessary to deliver this news to Berntsen and his frontline team before the Tora Bora battle was resolved. Berntsen was furious, and punched a hole in a door at the Ariana Hotel. He had to sheepishly watch Afghan workmen repair it the next day while he ran a meeting. But he turned back to the fight. He was "pretty angry" about being ordered back, but "3,000 people had been killed" on September 11, so the decision "had no negative effect on my performance." He had a sore fist, however.[37]

Tommy Franks said later that, in addition to heavy bombing, his plan was to help Pakistan's army block Al Qaeda's exit. He thought it was "a pretty good determination" to work with the Pakistanis. But the C.I.A. reported immediately that the plan would fail, according to Charles Allen, who was in charge of agency intelligence collection at the time. On December 11, at C.I.A. headquarters, Allen's directorate composed the first edition of what would become a daily "Hunt for Bin Laden" classified memo, intended for Tenet, Bush, and key members of the national security cabinet. The early editions concentrated on Tora Bora and emphasized that "the back door was open," by Allen's account.

The Pakistani generals in charge of closing the back door had no means to airlift troops high into the Hindu Kush Mountains in the time available. When they asked the United States for help, they were turned down. Pakistan's then director-general of military operations, in charge of all day-to-day military movements, later said that he "first learnt about Tora Bora from the television," and that the Pakistan Army command's reaction to the battle was one of alarm. This account is supported by other Pakistani generals then stationed along the border. Only by December 8 or 9, after days of heavy bombing had taken place, did Franks ask the Pakistan Army's XI Corps to seal the border. Pakistan had few troop-carrying helicopters. The army did move ground forces into the region by truck, but this only blocked a few routes of escape from Afghanistan.[38]

Was Bin Laden really there? Charles Allen and a Delta Force major who at the time scrutinized intercepts of a radio speech Bin Laden apparently delivered on December 10 concluded that he was, as did the operations officers and analysts back at ALEC Station. It later materialized that Bin Laden wrote his last will and testament on December 14. The document's tone and content suggest he thought he would die soon. "Allah bears witness that the love of jihad and death in the cause of Allah has dominated my life and the verses of the sword permeated every cell in my heart, 'and fight the pagans all together as they fight you all together,'" he wrote. He apologized to his children for the hardship he had created in their lives and asked his wives never to remarry. It was probably the next day that he left for Pakistan. The C.I.A.'s Allen hypothe-

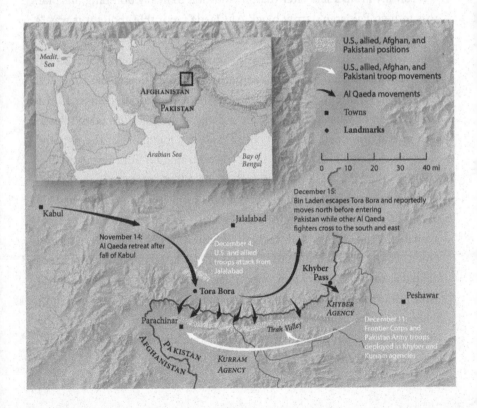

sized that Bin Laden moved north, inside Afghanistan, into Kunar and Nuristan provinces before crossing over to Pakistan. Scores of Bin Laden's Al Qaeda followers who survived the bombing walked or rode into Pakistan—Arabs, Chechens, Uzbeks, some wounded and ill, all seeking shelter.[39]

Tommy Franks flew into Islamabad to meet Musharraf over lunch in the midst of this migration. Chamberlin attended. Musharraf asked, "General Franks, what are you doing? You are flushing these guys out and there are one hundred and fifty valleys for them to move through. They are pouring in to my country." Franks did not have an answer. Musharraf asked Franks if Central Command could hurriedly provide helicopters to lift sixty thousand Pakistani troops to the Afghan border. Trapping Al Qaeda's thousand-odd hard-core survivors inside Afghanistan was as much in Pakistan's interest as it was in America's, since Al Qaeda's migration into Pakistan could wreak havoc. Franks did not answer at the time but later communicated to Musharraf that it could not be done. Helicopters were in short supply.[40]

President Bush heard conflicting advice throughout the fall of 2001 about how much Osama Bin Laden mattered as an individual target. Some of his advisers argued that Bush should avoid equating Al Qaeda with the United States by singling Bin Laden out. It is true that Bin Laden's position was not that of a commanding general or even a guerrilla leader comparable to Mao Zedong or Fidel Castro. He was the chairman of a force of multinational volunteers who sometimes worked autonomously and had no political territory of their own. After Bin Laden disappeared, it was tempting for Bush and his advisers to believe that his survival didn't matter much, apart from the need to deliver justice on behalf of Al Qaeda's victims in New York, Washington, Nairobi, Dar es Salaam, and elsewhere. But the failure at Tora Bora ran deeper than justice delayed. As Senate investigators later concluded, the events at Tora Bora "forever altered the course of the conflict in Afghanistan and the future of international terrorism."[41]

It also altered the future of Pakistan. On the eve of the American attack on Afghanistan, Dick Cheney had warned Bush's war cabinet that the war could spill over into Pakistan, "causing the government to lose control of the country and potentially its nuclear arsenal." Stephen Hadley, Bush's then–deputy national security adviser, called this "the nightmare scenario." Pentagon planners had listed "the collapse of the Pakistani government" as one of the risks of the campaign. Now the migration of hundreds of Uzbeks, Chechens, Arabs, and other foreign fighters from the eastern mountains of Afghanistan into Pakistan's tribal areas and cities brought that "nightmare scenario" into being. Al Qaeda's arrival created conditions that would further destabilize Pakistan. It connected the country's indigenous radical networks with Al Qaeda's international ideologists. It deepened resentment among Pakistan's generals, who would come to see their country's rising violence as a price of American folly in the fall of 2001. The potency of Al Qaeda's ideas and tactics further challenged a Pakistani state that was weak, divided, complacent, and complicit about Islamist ideology and violence. These consequences were not fully apparent that December, but they would rapidly metastasize.[42]

American politicians and media celebrated Operation Enduring Freedom as a great and stunning campaign, a harbinger of a new kind of war. The operation did succeed faster and at a lower cost in American lives than any comparable war in the country's history. The C.I.A., Navy, and Air Force planners and Special Operations Command developed and executed in less than four weeks an improvised, successful attack in a large, distant, landlocked country. Special Forces teams fought remarkably alongside Afghan forces that were themselves courageous and daring. Of course, the Taliban had no modern air defenses, no significant air force, no economy, and no powerful allies. Even so, few would have ventured to predict on the night of October 7 that by mid-December the Taliban would be out of power entirely, or that an opposition government led by Hamid Karzai and recognized by the United Nations would be installed, or that the U.S.-led coalition would have suffered only twelve military deaths, as well as the death of one C.I.A. officer, Johnny Micheal Spann. Operation Enduring Freedom was a military-political-intelligence endeavor of great ingenuity, luck, and tactical skill.

Its success blinded many American politicians, commanders, and C.I.A. leaders to the losses inflicted on Afghans and the political risks of their strategy. The U.S.-led coalition dropped about twelve thousand bombs on Afghanistan that autumn, about 40 percent of them "dumb," or unguided, according to an analysis by Carl Conetta of the Center for International Policy. Hank Crumpton at the Counterterrorist Center estimated that the campaign killed "at least ten thousand" foreign and Taliban fighters, "perhaps double or triple that number." By the conservative estimate of Boston University political scientist Neta Crawford, between 1,500 and 2,375 Afghan civilians also died. Some perished in plainly avoidable mistakes when American bombers destroyed civilian villages and extended families. The arbitrariness of these civilian deaths planted seeds of bitterness. So did the C.I.A.'s revived client Abdul Rashid Dostum, who accepted the surrender of several thousand Taliban and allied prisoners in November. Hundreds of those prisoners soon died from suffocation after being stuffed into shipping containers or shot by guards. Dostum said he was in Kunduz, did not order the actions that led to the deaths, and did not learn about them until a year later. In any event, the Bush administration did nothing to hold anyone accountable for the massacres; Dostum entered politics and soon held high office.[43]

The United States had no serious plan for Afghanistan after the war. The nearly uniform worldwide support for Hamid Karzai's interim government created a framework for massive reconstruction and for new politics. Yet the Bush administration had little appetite for nation building or peacekeeping. Osama Bin Laden and Mullah Mohammad Omar had escaped. Afghanistan's cities lay in the hands of strongmen, many of them C.I.A. clients, whose previous turns in office had been marked by abuse, internecine fighting, and incompetence. Thirty years of war—and now, after Operation Enduring Freedom, thousands of additional bombs dropped on the country—had left Afghanistan prostrate. Life expectancy and child mortality rates—to the extent they could be measured at all—stood at the very bottom of the U.N.'s worldwide human development tables. The country's only real equities were international goodwill and some collective memory of a multiethnic country that had once been peaceful.

Hamid Karzai invited Greg Vogle to his inauguration in Kabul on December 22. The new Afghan leader wore a lambskin hat and spoke in Pashto and Dari. Shouts and warm applause punctuated an emotional ceremony. From the ashes of September 11 a ruined country had won a new beginning. "We should put our hands together to forget the painful past," Karzai said.[44]

PART TWO

LOSING THE PEACE,

2002–2006

SIX

Small Change

R ich Blee flew to Bagram Airfield in mid-December 2001. Kabul's thin mountain air was smoky from cooking fires and winter was biting. He spent some of his first days in country arranging for turkeys to be acquired by Afghan staff and then deep-fried for Christmas dinner, to lift the morale of Kabul Station. Hank Crumpton and Cofer Black had asked him to serve as the new chief of station. He took a crammed, three-day refresher course in shooting M-16s and AK-47s and packed up. Kabul made Bangui, in the Central African Republic, the site of Blee's first C.I.A. posting, seem stable and well provisioned. The Taliban had unplugged the city. The international airport had no air traffic control systems to speak about. Only satellite phones could be relied upon for voice communication. Gasoline and diesel had to be flown in by the barrel. The Taliban had squatted inside ministry buildings. They cooked on the floor and slept in offices. Sections of the city destroyed by street-to-street tank and rocket battles during the civil war still lay in ruins. After Kabul fell to the Northern Alliance, the Panjshiris and their Uzbek and Hazara allies had rushed from building to building, reoccupying lost property or seizing abandoned compounds. The armed militias created an unstable patchwork of policing and checkpoints from block to block.

The C.I.A.'s redoubt, the old Ariana Hotel, was a wreck. Kabul

Station became a daily improvisation. The expatriates slept in shifts. The four-story hotel faced a traffic circle downtown, protected by a ten-foot wall. The C.I.A.'s staff built more walls and tried to push out the perimeter. The hotel had advantages: furnished rooms that could be used as bunks or as offices, and an Afghan staff seemingly eager to serve a reliable paymaster. Yet some of the staff had worked for the Taliban before the Americans arrived; their loyalties might be judged as uncertain. The dining room still functioned. The Ariana was close to the presidential palace, which made it easy for Blee to drop in on Karzai. Still, the hotel was truly decrepit. A Northern Alliance jet had dropped a bomb on it a few years back. C.I.A. officers chasing Al Qaeda into the White Mountains brought back a stray puppy and insisted that it be adopted; the dog slept on the hotel floors and crapped in hallways as it pleased. (Blee soon ordered the puppy banished, one of his more unpopular decisions.) Bearded special operators and case officers with Glock pistols strapped to their thighs tromped in and out. The atmosphere was a cross between a Central Asian organized crime clubhouse and a clapboard hotel on a muddy street in an old western.[1]

The C.I.A. had no institutional view about what should be done in Afghanistan after the Taliban. Blee and Hank Crumpton favored a major reconstruction program, to signal American commitment. Cofer Black thought the United States had a poor record of transforming countries like Afghanistan. He favored a light footprint and an unrelenting focus on Al Qaeda. In any event, the C.I.A. was supposed to offer presidents empirical intelligence and analysis and to steer clear of foreign policy advice. Yet agency operations created de facto policy in Afghanistan during 2002 by empowering strongmen with poor human rights records. The C.I.A.'s overall playbook that winter in Afghanistan was derived from its operations in Vietnam, Nicaragua, Angola, Somalia, and other Cold War proxy conflicts, in which many of the senior officers at the Counterterrorist Center had served. Station chiefs managed palace politics with cash, favors, and confidential advice to national leaders, while watching out for the influence of rival intelligence services. The Special Activities Division trained and paid rough militias as armed reconnaissance forces, to provide protection to expatriate case officers and to operate in contested areas or behind enemy lines. Career case officers recruited locals as reporting agents and vetted their information against satellite and Predator imagery or phone chatter picked up by the National Security Agency. To carry out such operations, the C.I.A. inevitably favored as political officeholders tough men independent of foreign intelligence services who would act reliably on American priorities. This client network would create a new landscape of winners in Afghanistan.

George W. Bush had given the C.I.A. one clear mandate: to attack Al Qaeda and its allies. As a practical matter, that meant Blee's operating directive for Kabul Station prioritized pursuit of the Arab, Chechen, and Uzbek volunteers who had followed Bin Laden east and then melted away after the bombing of Tora Bora. No one knew their numbers, but the best estimates were in the range of several hundred up to two thousand foreigners—that is, non-Afghans and non-Pakistanis. This was Al Qaeda's loose remnant army. Embedded within its ranks were the bomb experts, money men, and ex–Arab military officers who organized the cells that often conceived and backed the most ambitious overseas terror strikes.

By January 2002 some Al Qaeda foot soldiers and unit commanders had migrated into Pakistan. But others had gone to ground in eastern Afghanistan, along the mountainous border from Jalalabad south toward Paktia Province. As early as mid-December intelligence analysts at Task Force Dagger, the Special Forces command whose A-Teams had embedded with the Northern Alliance as they defeated the Taliban, had concluded that significant numbers of Al Qaeda were regrouping around Paktia and Gardez.[2]

Blee recruited Chris Wood as the incipient Kabul Station's chief of operations, in charge of the C.I.A.'s collaboration with U.S. Special Forces to the east. Wood had no military experience, but his Dari skills and his experience with the Panjshiris during the autumn campaign recommended him, as well as the fact that he had spent the previous four years in Islamabad, running Afghan agents. There were only about thirty or forty C.I.A. officers left in Afghanistan by the time of Karzai's inauguration, although the number would grow again during 2002. The Pentagon's Special Forces soldiers and officers now outnumbered case officers by about fivefold.[3]

The American-led units formed to push into eastern Afghanistan, to chase Al Qaeda remnants, comprised mixed teams of Special Forces—Green Berets, Delta Force, and Navy SEAL Team 6—plus C.I.A. officers and communications and intercept specialists. They were eventually referred to as Omega Teams. They might operate independently on reconnaissance missions, to identify Al Qaeda positions, or they might train and accompany Afghan militias of several hundred or more men. The C.I.A. officers on the teams included paramilitary specialists such as Greg Vogle, but also language and area specialists such as Chris Wood, who led a reconnaissance team that winter of 2002 that operated along the twisting highway between Khost and Gardez. Intelligence operations have a range, like radar or rifles, Wood told colleagues. C.I.A. tradecraft held that case officers should try to operate tens of miles from denied territory in order to run agents behind enemy lines.[4]

To recruit Afghan militias that could provide local support, the C.I.A. turned to Amrullah Saleh, and to Asadullah Khalid, a Pashtun from Ghazni Province, in the east. Khalid was then in his early thirties. His father had served in parliament during the pre-Communist era. Before 2001, as Sayyaf's intelligence aide, Asadullah had traveled to the United States and worked with the C.I.A. on programs to recover Stinger missiles and collect intelligence on Al Qaeda. Like Saleh, he was young, relatively independent, game for action, and implacably opposed to the Taliban.[5]

More senior and established commanders in the Northern Alliance such as Fahim Khan and Abdul Rashid Dostum controlled large armed forces, but they worked simultaneously with the C.I.A., Iranian intelligence, and Russian intelligence. Asadullah was less entangled in these relationships. By early 2002, he had become a partner of the C.I.A. for reasons of mutual advantage, as a European security officer put it: "In their weakness they became friends of the Americans, and gained strength."[6]

The Americans built up small forward bases to train and prepare their hastily recruited forces. Early in the New Year, they reinforced a forward operating base on the outskirts of Gardez, a provincial capital eighty miles due south from Kabul, in a fortress compound with twenty-five-foot mud-brick walls and a steel gate, located at about seven thousand feet above sea level.

Gardez became a hub of clandestine and unconventional warfare planning and intelligence collection. C.I.A. case officers and Green Berets rode out to local villages, met elders, offered food and medical aid, and sought out traveling Afghan agents who might be paid fifty or a hundred dollars to ride or walk into districts where Al Qaeda might be holed up. "It's a little like *Star Wars*," as an officer involved put it. "We would send these little agents all over the place to try to find where the rebel alliance was. And if the agents didn't come back, or they came back dead, or they couldn't get past roadblocks, we knew there was a problem." The essential questions plumbed by the C.I.A.'s agents were: Where are the Al Qaeda who fled Tora Bora but remained in Afghanistan? What weapons and defenses do they have? How many are there?

Michael Hurley, a senior C.I.A. case officer deployed at Gardez from December 2001 to May 2002, worked on "the big question after Tora Bora," which was "Where is the last redoubt in Afghanistan?" Yet it was difficult to sort rumor from fact. Paying impoverished locals for information created financial incentives for them to invent tantalizing false stories or settle vendettas by labeling a business or tribal rival as Al Qaeda. Even where multiple sources confirmed that foreign fighters were present, according to Hurley, "local agents weren't very good about sorting out foreigners' nationalities" or determining which leaders might be with them.[7]

In January, Major General Warren Edwards of Central Command flew into Kabul and met with Rich Blee. The station chief told him that he expected "the last battle" of the Afghan war to be fought soon around Gardez. Edwards took note; in his experience, Blee "had a much better feel for Afghanistan than most of the people I talked to." By late January, the "fire ants," as the human agents run by the C.I.A. mainly out of Gardez were known, reported with increasing credibility the existence of a large group of foreign Al Qaeda fighters in the Shah-i-Kot Valley, to the southeast of Gardez. The valley floor stood at 8,500 feet above sea level and the surrounding peaks rose as high as 14,000 feet. Shah-i-Kot had been an Al Qaeda sanctuary during the 1980s, as well as a base of the Haqqanis, a family-led network of Afghan Taliban allies. "We had estimates of 200 to 300 people, up to 1,200 to 1,400," Hurley recalled. Task Force Dagger's intelligence analysts assessed the foreigners as mainly from the Islamic Movement of Uzbekistan, an Al Qaeda ally. But the analysts could not confirm the numbers of enemy present through Predator photography, U2 surveillance planes, or satellite imagery. The weather was bad, the valley ridgelines had caves that were difficult to penetrate, and there was no sign of a large force in the open. Maybe they weren't there; maybe they had adopted strong measures to avoid detection. The C.I.A. "lost a couple" of reporting agents who were captured and executed and "we ran into a couple of roadblocks, and they were manned by Chechens and Uzbeks," according to an officer involved. "We knew that was bad" but "we didn't know how many."[8]

Major General Franklin "Buster" Hagenbeck, a West Point graduate who commanded the Tenth Mountain Division and who was then the highest-ranking officer commanding conventional forces in the country, organized planning exercises at Bagram Airfield for an attack on the Shah-i-Kot. His officers built a terrain model of the region on the floor of an old Soviet hangar; Hagenbeck and his men walked through it every day, war-gaming their plan. Among other things, Hagenbeck and his lieutenants sought to absorb the lessons of Tora Bora, to plan from the start for the deployment of reliable American and allied N.A.T.O. forces, led by the 101st Airborne Division, behind Al Qaeda's positions, to prevent the enemy's escape into Pakistan.[9]

Where were Osama Bin Laden and his deputy, Ayman Al Zawahiri? There were reports of his presence at Jalalabad, Peshawar, and Kandahar. None of these panned out, and increasingly there were no good leads. Yet there were plenty of false sightings of both men that had to be run down by Kabul Station. At one point, an Afghan Tajik vendor in Utah contacted his congressman and persuaded him to inform the Pentagon that the vendor knew where Bin Laden was hiding, near Gardez. The military spun up an operation to attack the site. It turned out that the F.B.I. had previously documented that the source was a fabricator. From Langley, Charles Allen circulated his daily Bin Laden hunt memo for about three months after Tora Bora, but he dropped it when the leads ran dry. Allen consulted case officers who had served in

Pakistan; they suggested regions where Allen might look around, such as the northern Pakistani border city of Chitral and the Swat Valley. He went into Langley headquarters on weekends to take a hard look at the satellite and other overhead imagery with analysts, but they found nothing. One hypothesis was that Bin Laden had actually died at Tora Bora, but when F.B.I. forensic teams, working with Special Forces, exhumed Al Qaeda grave sites there, they identified some of Bin Laden's bodyguards, but found no trace of the leader himself.[10]

Kabul Station became a destination for visitors from Washington, all of whom Blee and his deputy had to brief, protect, and entertain. Among the early arrivals was A. B. "Buzzy" Krongard, the C.I.A.'s executive director, a wealthy former investment banker from Baltimore whom Tenet had recruited a few years before to bring private sector management expertise to agency operations. A Princeton-educated lawyer and former Marine, Krongard lived in a hillside mansion outside Baltimore that had a private shooting range; he had a large gun collection. Like Tenet, he had an expansive personality. Krongard toured Kabul and Gardez. Tenet sent Jose Rodriguez of the Counterterrorist Center as an escort, "just to make sure Buzzy doesn't kill anybody," as Rodriguez told colleagues. The visit was another distraction, but it produced a momentous decision.[11]

Krongard was struck by how insecure Kabul Station seemed even though the war was supposedly won. Inside the Ariana Hotel, officers carried a weapon even to the bathroom. Krongard had known Blee when he worked on the Seventh Floor, as an aide to Tenet, and admired him. They discussed the Afghan guard force protecting the Ariana Hotel. Blee had to assume the C.I.A.'s address was no secret around Kabul. If they were attacked, Blee said, "you could have the whole hotel in a firing position, but we don't know if the Afghans will fight, leave, or lead the enemy in." At one point, the C.I.A. conducted an internal security review of Kabul Station and found the facility to be virtually indefensible; it was a hotel, and hotels are meant to be accessible. The guards' primary loyalty was to the Northern Alliance, not necessarily the C.I.A. Krongard pledged to do something when he got back to Langley.[12]

The C.I.A. contracted for training facilities with Blackwater USA, the

private firm run by Erik Prince, a former Navy SEAL. According to Krongard, he had never worked with Prince directly before early 2002, but
they knew of each other. After Krongard returned from Afghanistan to
Langley, Prince, who was in C.I.A. headquarters, made a cold call at
Krongard's office, seeking to identify how Blackwater could grow its business at the agency. Prince asked what needs the C.I.A. had. Krongard
mentioned his Kabul Station issue. "I've got a Rolodex," Prince said, meaning a network of former noncommissioned officers, Special Forces, and
retired SEALs.

"Go down to the contract office," Krongard told him. As Krongard
recalled it, "'Let's move' was the attitude." Blackwater's for-profit provision of bodyguards, shooters, spies, and other operatives in the global
war on terrorism was born. Weeks later, Kabul Station had an expatriate
protection force in place, organized by Prince.[13]

The militia and reconnaissance operations Chris Wood oversaw in
Afghanistan's east early in 2002 constituted one leg of the C.I.A.'s
counterterrorism strategy in post-Taliban Afghanistan. A second was to
fund the reconstruction of the National Directorate of Security, Afghanistan's intelligence and security service. The C.I.A. now had the opportunity to shape a friendly intelligence agency at the axis of Central and
South Asia. (The mandate of N.D.S. approximately combined those of
the F.B.I. and the C.I.A. in the United States.) After the Panjshiris took
Kabul, Engineer Arif returned to N.D.S. as de facto chief, on Fahim
Khan's orders. Karzai formally appointed Arif as his interim government's head of intelligence in late December 2001. As a practical matter, Karzai had no choice—the Panjshiris constituted the main armed
power in Kabul at the time, and he was in effect their international representative.

Arif was a problematic partner for the C.I.A. He had contacts with
Russians and Iranians dating back years. The N.D.S. still carried the influence of its years as a stepchild of the K.G.B. Also, before September
11, Massoud had entrusted Arif with selling the Panjshir's gemstones to
fund their war effort—emeralds, rubies, and lapis lazuli mined in North-

ern Alliance territory. Each year, Arif would load up trunks the size of coffee tables and fly to Las Vegas for the American Gem Trade Association exhibition. He would make $3 million to $4 million for the Northern Alliance cause, but along the way, he seemed to develop a taste for comfortable hotels and condominiums. He flew on the supersonic Concorde at least once—quite possibly the only Panjshiri ever to do so.[14]

At C.I.A. headquarters early that winter, the C.I.A.'s longtime South Asia hand Gary Schroen sat at a desk with a legal pad and a calculator and drew up an outline for funding the Afghan service, which he hoped to work through with Engineer Arif. He modeled the prospective service on the SAVAK, the shah's intelligence service before the Iranian Revolution, which Schroen had studied. In February, Schroen flew to Kabul. He was dismayed to learn that Arif wanted to move temporarily with his family to Washington, D.C., to seek medical attention. Arif had developed a sciatic nerve problem. He said his wife also needed counseling to work through the lingering effects of her traumatic experiences during the Soviet war. (His wife's father had been killed by the Soviets; as a teenager, she had then taken a position on the household staff of a Russian officer, shot him in revenge and fled, according to what Arif told the C.I.A.) Schroen agreed to support Arif; after all, the Panjshiris had gone to great lengths to accommodate the C.I.A. at the agency's hour of need in the autumn of 2001.

Arif and his family moved into a safe house in the Washington area. Schroen arranged medical appointments. Weeks passed and still Arif was in no hurry to return to Kabul. He was trying to run Afghan intelligence with a fax machine from his C.I.A. guesthouse. One rumor was that Arif might be reluctant to return because he had fallen under suspicion among some Panjshiris because of Massoud's assassination. Arif had cleared the Al Qaeda assassins for their "interview" with the commander, and then he had left the room before the suicide bombing took place. In fact, there was no sound basis for the suspicion, but as Arif put it, Massoud's death "had a negative psychological effect on the people and the leadership of the United Front." For his part, Schroen could understand why such suspicions might arise but he could not see why Arif would have any motive to collaborate in Massoud's death. Arif had been loyal to Massoud for years. In any event, whatever his reasons for remaining in the United States, after two months, Arif at last returned to Kabul. The suspicions about him subsided. "Everyone knew Arif was not a killer," as one of his Panjshiri colleagues put it.[15]

The larger question was what sort of intelligence and security service the C.I.A. would build in Afghanistan. N.D.S. had roots tracing to the nineteenth century. As the Afghan state grew more centralized, Kabul's kings built intelligence networks in villages and provincial capitals to ensure that the palace had early warning about political threats. These networks reported to a security bureau in the palace. The Soviet occupation converted this into K.H.A.D., a monstrosity constructed in the K.G.B.'s image and a feared instrument of political and social control. K.H.A.D. had 150,000 or more Afghans on its payroll at its peak, including paramilitaries. It had provincial offices and numbered directorates. The directorate names changed from time to time, but at the height of the Soviet era, Directorate 1 ran external operations, Directorate 5 was in charge of counterterrorism, Directorate 6 ran counterintelligence, and Directorate 7 was in charge of monitoring universities, madrassas, and political elites for their loyalty to the state.

When Engineer Arif ran N.D.S. in the early 1990s, he kept on some K.H.A.D. veterans. When the Taliban took power, they renamed the service and brought in former Communists from a different faction. This was the C.I.A.'s inheritance: a workforce of opaque subgroups that had operated torture chambers and prisons, intimidated citizens across the land, and owed its professional culture mainly to the K.G.B.[16]

The budget Engineer Arif worked with initially was about $15 million annually, and although this could support hundreds of intelligence officers and even more support staff, it was far short of what would be required to attempt to create a national police force or an F.B.I. equivalent for Afghanistan. In any event, that lay well beyond the ambitions of Bush administration policy that winter. The C.I.A.'s mission was Al Qaeda.[17]

Langley's hesitancy to fund N.D.S. aggressively only grew as C.I.A. officers noticed that the funds they did provide did not seem to be producing the kinds of results they would have expected, while Arif seemed to be living beyond the means of a civil servant. Arif said that any accusation of personal corruption was "unfair," but if the concern was organizational corruption within N.D.S., "there were some problems because of the war situation and [the] lack of control over N.D.S. personnel outside Kabul." Eventually, Arif would occupy an expansive compound in the Panjshir, a Kabul home, and a high-rise apartment in the United Arab Emirates.[18]

It was simpler for the C.I.A. to work directly with the individuals they knew and trusted best—Amrullah Saleh, Asadullah Khalid, and Hamid Karzai. Arif also accommodated the agency at first. Among his assignments, Saleh ran counterintelligence at N.D.S. as well as liaisons with foreign spy services. Arif named Khalid the head of Directorate 5, in charge of counterterrorism. "We wanted to rescue Afghanistan from the darkness, to take this country that had been imprisoned and free it, place it inside the normal international community," an Afghan official involved recalled. "But we did not control this change: It was controlled by the United States."[19]

Operation Anaconda, commanded by Major General Hagenbeck, opened on March 2. It would be the largest U.S. military operation since the Gulf War of early 1991, as well as the highest-altitude battle ever fought by a sizable U.S. force. In *Not a Good Day to Die*, the journalist Sean Naylor provides an independent-minded, well-sourced account of the operation. Special Forces, C.I.A. officers, and an Afghan militia loyal to Zia Lodin attempted the main attack across the valley floor but withdrew after an American Spectre gunship mistakenly shot up Lodin's men. Bombing and intrepid fighting at close quarters by American and allied forces killed dozens and perhaps hundreds of Al Qaeda holed up on high ridges. (Greg Vogle fought with Afghan militiamen and later received the C.I.A.'s equivalent of the Medal of Honor for battlefield valor, after he rallied Afghans who had been left behind back into the fight.) But Anaconda witnessed failures of planning and execution, the product of the fractured lines of command.

Defense Secretary Donald Rumsfeld had imposed a hard cap on the number of American soldiers allowed on the ground in Afghanistan. The total deployment would average 5,200 through the summer of 2002.[20] The great majority of those forces were immobile at the bases at Bagram and Kandahar. Even the roving target-hunting special operators were stretched thin, given the vast length of the Afghan-Pakistan border and the size of the remnant Al Qaeda force thought to have moved there. Britain, Australia, Denmark, Norway, Poland, New Zealand, Canada, and other allies had sent Special Forces units to Afghanistan, but organizing them to fight Al Qaeda required a unified command that did not exist. There were two Special Forces task forces—one headquartered in Uzbekistan, a second in Kandahar—that operated independently. Hagenbeck putatively commanded all U.S. forces in Afghanistan—yet he did not control the special operators. And the general did not have his full headquarters or division with him. The command design was a prescription for error.

The Tenth Mountain Division had originally been deployed to provide security at a transit base in Uzbekistan; its units were "not properly trained, manned or equipped" for the battle they were ordered to fight, a Naval War College assessment later found. The absence of a "fully functioning intelligence cell" made errors "inevitable."[21] According to Hagenbeck, there were several important intelligence failures. They expected Al Qaeda forces to retreat under fire, as they had at Tora Bora; instead, they fought to the death and summoned reinforcements. There were about three hundred more Al Qaeda volunteers in the valley than anticipated. There were four times as many caves as forecast, meaning the enemy had ample places to shelter. Central Command prohibited American forces from using artillery in Afghanistan at this time, for fear of civilian casualties that would evoke memories of brutal Soviet tactics. That meant close air support would be essential to protect soldiers if they were ambushed or encountered heavier Al Qaeda forces than expected. Yet the commander of the Combined Air Operations Center in Saudi Arabia, whose planes would provide that close air support, did not even learn of Operation Anaconda until five days before the scheduled launch. The blocking forces attempting to squeeze the enemy encountered much heavier Al Qaeda resistance on the ridges than had been expected. In the end U.S. forces suffered eight dead and about eighty wounded in four days of heavy fighting. That was a light toll compared with many past American battles. But it was more than half the number of dead suffered in all of Operation Enduring Freedom the previous fall. One death was especially shocking: Neil Roberts, a Navy SEAL, fell out of a helicopter as it attempted to land under fire. Roberts lay abandoned on the snow as Al Qaeda surrounded him. He fired back but was either captured and executed or killed in the firefight.

It remains difficult to assess Operation Anaconda's outcome because of uncertainty about how many Al Qaeda fighters were in the Shah-i-Kot Valley, how many were killed, and how many escaped to Pakistan. American generals estimated the number of Al Qaeda dead to be "as high as 800 publicly and over a thousand in private," Naylor reported. "However, they offered no evidence to back up their claims." Soldiers found only a small number of enemy corpses in the valley after the battle. "Some of this can be explained by good guerrilla tactics—no irregular army leaves its dead in the field of battle if it can help it," Naylor assessed. "But it is hard to imagine 600 or 700 bodies being spirited out of the Shah-i-Kot without anyone noticing." Naylor concluded that the best estimate was in the range of 150 to 300 Al Qaeda killed. That would imply that "at least as many" foreign fighters escaped to Pakistan. Hagenbeck insisted that a higher estimate was correct, that bombing obliterated many Al Qaeda dead.[22] What is certain is that a substantial influx of hard-core Uzbek fighters migrated to South Waziristan, in Pakistan's Federally Administered Tribal Areas, during this period. There they would embed in a sanctuary at least as formidable as Taliban-ruled Afghanistan had ever been. And they would add to the infusion of hardcore guerrillas flushed by American forces into Pakistan, for its army and I.S.I. to manage.

David Sedney flew into Kabul on a United Nations flight from Islamabad on March 8, as Operation Anaconda concluded. He was a former truck driver and factory worker who graduated from Princeton University, earned a law degree, and became a career State Department diplomat, now in his fifties, who had served in Central Asia and had volunteered for Afghanistan after September 11. He had been selected to serve as the Kabul embassy's number two, under Robert Finn, a scholar of Turkish literature, who would arrive to become ambassador later that month. The U.S. embassy compound, shuttered in early 1989, looked after by an Afghan gardener and a few watchmen, offered a time capsule of the late Cold War. It was situated on the edge of Wazir Akbar Khan, the wealthy neighborhood in north Kabul named for a nineteenth-century king. Dusty Volkswagens left in the embassy garage still had gas in the tanks and, in a testament to German engineering, started up and ran. Packets of old spaghetti and canned vegetables remained on the commissary shelves, welcome cuisine for expatriates sickened by local bacteria. During the civil war of the 1990s, the State Department had helped its Afghan watchmen build a concrete bunker to live in, fifteen feet underground, with six rooms and a bathroom. Sedney was now assigned a bed in that bunker. The chancery building was designed for about twenty-five people to work in but now accommodated about four hundred, including a U.S. Marine Expeditionary Unit guard force—not the typical, specialized Marine embassy guards, but a field combat unit. Diplomats slept on cots set up around the walls of the main conference room and held meetings there by day.[23]

They visited Karzai and his ministers frequently at the nearby Arg Palace. The palace had been constructed in the early twentieth century. The compound contained several buildings, lawns, courtyards, and tiled pools. Karzai lived in a residence to one side that was stuffed with heavy furniture and velvet curtains. He worked in the main palace. Beyond the front door a carved staircase ascended to a large reception room. The Taliban had defaced the staircase by whittling away decorative images of fish and horses.

The big room at the top of the stairs was swathed in marble. The palace had been the scene of bloody assassinations during the Communist period. Karzai and his aides remarked regularly on its ghosts. Karzai held formal meetings in the office earlier used by kings and presidents. He also maintained a more informal reception room. There was a fireplace, a desk, and bookshelves. The furniture was necessarily improvised.

There were two chairs at one side so that Karzai could sit to the left of a principal guest and talk. A small sofa and other chairs allowed ministers to crowd in. There they sat day after day discussing how to rebuild the country.

The Bush administration's initial plans for reconstruction in Afghanistan were designed to avoid burdensome American leadership. The assumption was that the United Nations would carry out what humanitarian and state-building projects international governments chose to fund. In January, the administration agreed to a plan under which the United States would train a new Afghan National Army, Germany would build up the police, Italy would rebuild a justice system, and Great Britain would work on counternarcotics. "None of these countries had the capacity, designated budget funds, or political commitment to do that work," David Sedney discovered upon arrival.[24]

In February 2002, the White House's Office of Management and Budget proposed to allocate only $151 million for all assistance to Afghanistan for the fiscal year beginning the following October, including only $1 million for training the new Afghan National Army—"laughable," as Dov Zakheim, a Bush appointee then at the Pentagon, put it. President Bush told a private meeting of House Republicans, "We are not fielding a nation-building military. We are a fighting military. We need to define the mission clearly." The administration had spent $4.5 billion on the 2001 war in Afghanistan, including $390 million just to replace a bomber, a tanker, two helicopters, and two unmanned aerial vehicles that crashed during operations. Yet the administration would not propose to spend even 10 percent of the war's cost on Afghanistan's recovery or to secure the peace with new Afghan forces. "You get what you pay for," Robert Finn observed later, "and we paid for war."[25]

In the upper-middle levels of the State Department and the Pentagon, there were some who had lived through the C.I.A.'s covert action program against the Soviet Union in Afghanistan during the 1980s, and the abandonment of Afghanistan to civil war in the 1990s. They regretted America's inconstancy. David Champagne, an Army analyst who had served in Afghanistan for the Peace Corps, and Barnett Rubin, a political scientist who specialized in the region, briefed Bush administration officials soon after the Taliban's fall. They emphasized the need to invest in reconstruction. When National Security Council staff objected, Champagne replied, "We did this to the Afghan people." He surveyed the meeting participants, locking eyes with several of them. "Nearly everyone here was involved. . . . We have a responsibility to assure that this never happens again."

"This is not serious," the State Department official coordinating Afghan aid wrote in an e-mail to colleagues when he saw the proposed budget figure that winter. Only State Department protests and congressional intervention forced the Bush administration to increase the reconstruction and humanitarian aid budget in 2002, to just under $1 billion. It was still probably about $500 million short of what was required initially, in the separate estimations of Zakheim and Finn. The tightfistedness "reflected not only the administration's preoccupation with Iraq but its seeming loss of interest in following through on support for the reconstruction of Afghanistan," Zakheim concluded. "The Administration squandered an opportunity to manage a post-conflict environment properly."[26]

That left Sedney and Finn, working long hours in their U.S. embassy squat in Kabul, to pursue "what in retrospect were pathetic attempts to help the Afghans set up a government," as Sedney put it. "There was no human capacity. There was no physical infrastructure. . . . We would have these media ceremonies to give a grant of thirty-five thousand dollars to new ministers to help start up their ministries, in which there was no paper, nothing. It makes me angry to think about it—thirty-five thousand dollars!"

Ministers appointed to the interim government worked and lived at the Hotel Intercontinental, a relic of the relative prosperity of the 1960s that commanded a view from a bluff in Karte Parwan. It had no telephones, no running water, no electricity, and no heat. Yet among the Afghans arriving from exile that winter "there was optimism that the U.S. could eliminate the Taliban once and for all and protect our country from Pakistan," as Sharif Fayez, one of the new cabinet members, put it. "There was incredible faith in their power to bring peace."

At Kabul University, the library's collection of 175,000 books, 3,500 manuscripts, and 2,500 rare books was gone, except for some books in Russian. There were no roofs, windowpanes, or pipes; the materials had been stripped out and sold in Pakistan in desperation. A few treasures had been hidden away from the Taliban and the looters. At the Arg Palace, staff discovered some 21,000 objects of Bactrian gold, dating to the time of Christ, stored in a hidden vault, safely protected from the Soviet-era war and the Taliban. Surviving family members of old royal retainers turned up from time to time with silver or gold decorative objects that had been hidden away in private homes.[27]

Hanging over the whole threadbare enterprise was the fear that the interim government's vice chairman and minister of defense, Fahim Khan, might be planning to murder its chairman, Hamid Karzai. Fahim had consolidated power within the Northern Alliance in the months since Massoud's death and he now commanded the most guns. He had no obvious incentive to assassinate Karzai but there was loose talk around Kabul that he might nonetheless order a hit, to claim Kabul for the Panjshiris he led.

Fahim's relations with Karzai remained shadowed by the former's arrest and rough interrogation of the latter less than a decade earlier. Fahim considered Karzai to be a playboy who had benefited from a rich father. In any event, Fahim had troops while Karzai had none. Karzai insisted years later that he and Fahim enjoyed a "very respectful relationship" once they joined government together, but it seemed to some of the Americans who met with him in this period that Karzai trusted very few people.[28]

In Washington, President Bush asked Zalmay Khalilzad, then the senior director for Afghanistan at the White House's National Security Council, whether he should take the rumors about an assassination threat from Fahim seriously. Khalilzad had been born and raised in Afghanistan before earning a doctoral degree in political science at the University of Chicago. He had served in previous Republican administrations and had become, after September 11, the most influential adviser on Afghanistan who enjoyed direct access to President Bush. He was a

self-invented man, gifted and adaptable, a natural Washington operator—
a phone juggler, a network builder, disorganized, charismatic. He was
tall, clean-shaven, with a head of receding graying hair. His manner was
all smiles and shoulder grabs. He had the sort of Oval Office style George
W. Bush enjoyed—jocular but respectful, quick with a story or an insider's detail about a foreign leader. He also offered something no other
White House adviser could. He had deep, personal knowledge of
Afghanistan.

"These guys are unpredictable," Khalilzad told the president. The
probability was low that Fahim would bump off Karzai, he judged, but
the impact would be high. Bush urged Khalilzad to persuade Hamid
Karzai to accept American bodyguards. The public symbolism would
not be great, but the loss of face could be endured; a coup d'état eliminating a conciliatory Pashtun leader might trigger a new civil war.

Khalilzad called Karzai from the White House and spoke in the code
they used when they assumed the call would be overheard by foreign
intelligence services. "I am calling you on behalf of your friend," Khalilzad said, referring to President Bush. Khalilzad said he recognized the
subject was "very sensitive" but he urged Karzai to give "due consider-
ation" to the recommendation. But Karzai hesitated. Fahim questioned
how it would look for an Afghan leader to so distrust his own security
forces that he would accept Americans in substitute. Yet other Panjshiris,
including Yunus Qanooni, the minister of interior, told Karzai that he
should accept the offer. He eventually said yes.

Karzai's greatest asset in Washington was his relationship with
George W. Bush. The president talked with Karzai as often as twice a
month by secure videoconference, once the infrastructure in Afghanistan was available. Karzai understood the effort Bush was making and
appreciated the respect and deference he showed. Their relationship
eventually came under strain but never broke down, and for a remarkable number of years after 2001, Bush's mentorship succeeded and Karzai stretched himself to cooperate with the United States.

To Americans who worked with him in Kabul, Karzai could seem a
lost and even lonely figure. According to reports that circulated at the

American embassy, the chairman would sometimes slip away from his personal protection detail and travel around the city anonymously. Some versions of the reporting held that Karzai kept a secret car for these journeys. Karzai later denied that there had been any such vehicle. In any case, he was in a searching mood. Interim leader of war-shattered Afghanistan was not a job he had campaigned to hold. It wasn't clear what his conception of being president really was. Ambassador Robert Finn thought of medieval France: Karzai was "the king, and he was in Paris, and everyone acknowledged that he was the king, but that did not mean that he told everybody what to do."[29]

That spring, the actual former king of Afghanistan, Zahir Shah, returned to Kabul. He had been forced from the throne in a 1973 coup d'état and had gone into exile in Rome. He was eighty-seven years old and frail. He brought a staff with him and moved into private quarters one floor above Karzai's office at the Arg Palace. The former king enjoyed rooms with twenty-foot ceilings and an outside patio with a view of the grounds. Zahir Shah's retainers clearly hoped for a royal restoration as Afghans finalized a new constitution. Karzai treated the former king respectfully but also maneuvered for power. The palace atmosphere overall was one of intrigue and hidden danger, but also hope and purpose.

Karzai's office became "like a late-night TV program," as Finn put it. "Guest number one came in and sat on the couch and got his fifteen or twenty minutes. And then he moved over to the couch, and guest number two came in. And this went on all day long. By the end of the day there would be ten or fifteen people in the room, and I would say, 'Who the hell is running this country?'"

Part of Karzai's instinct, Finn recognized, was to "keep your enemies where you can see them." The difficulty was that "he wouldn't make decisions." One talking circle led to the next.[30]

Many Afghan leaders before Karzai had died violently. The city was full of northern gunmen and it would take only one warlord with a bankroll to put out a hit contract. "We were trying to help him learn to be president," Sedney said. "The C.I.A. was worried about just trying to keep him alive."[31]

Donald Rumsfeld flew into Afghanistan that spring. He was not a popular figure at the Ariana Hotel, the embassy, or in the military barracks at Bagram. At one meeting, the secretary of defense pronounced, "The war is over in Afghanistan."

Rich Blee contradicted him. "No, sir, it's not." Rumsfeld responded profanely. The gap between how Rumsfeld saw Afghanistan and how career spies, diplomats, and military officers on the ground saw it was growing wider by the month. Rumsfeld told Lieutenant General Dan McNeill, the highest American military commander in the country, to "do two things—pursue terrorists to capture or kill and build an Afghan National Army." Yet Central Command had given McNeill no written campaign plan, and Rumsfeld provided no specifics about what size or shape of an army he wanted in Afghanistan.[32]

Rumsfeld believed that N.A.T.O. security forces in Bosnia and Kosovo had fostered dependency by the host country. "At the time, 13,000 troops seemed like the right amount," Bush recalled. "We had routed the Taliban with far fewer, and it seemed that the enemy was on the run. . . . We were all wary of repeating the experience of the Soviets and the British, who ended up looking like occupiers."[33]

Brigadier General Stanley McChrystal landed at Bagram in May as the chief of staff of Joint Task Force 180, the Central Command force devised to succeed Hagenbeck's command. (This was an American command distinct from N.A.T.O.'s security effort, then primarily focused on Kabul.) McChrystal's main job was to set up a headquarters unit at Bagram. Yet he wasn't sure whether the force's mission was going to be nation building or continuing the pursuit of remnants of Al Qaeda and the Taliban. A senior Army officer in Washington told him, "Don't build Bondsteels," referring to the N.A.T.O. base in Kosovo that Rumsfeld saw as a symbol of peacekeeping mission creep. The officer warned McChrystal against "anything here that looks permanent. . . . We are not staying long." As McChrystal took the lay of the land, "I felt like we were high-school students who had wandered into a Mafia-owned bar."[34]

His mission included training the Afghan National Army, but "we just weren't scoped when we got there, mentally or physically, to even contemplate that seriously. We were a very small headquarters that was pulling together disparate forces and there were very few." The Bonn Agreement had contemplated building an Afghan National Army of 70,000 soldiers, but the Pentagon was in no hurry to resource that program and Rumsfeld seemed to be wavering about whether a force of that size would ever be necessary. Hamid Karzai and Fahim Khan wanted something on the order of 250,000 soldiers, wildly beyond what the Americans had in mind (at least for now).[35]

In June 2002, McChrystal's superior, McNeill, attended a Central Command conference in Germany. When he came back he announced, "That meeting was all about invading Iraq." They were stunned. The planning for the next war created fresh incentives for officers and intelligence analysts in Afghanistan to downplay signs of trouble in that theater—if you wanted promotion and frontline battlefield assignments, you went on to the next war.[36]

That month, Taliban or Al Qaeda guerrillas attacked and blew up a C-130 transport plane while it was parked on the ground at an airstrip near Gardez, killing three American soldiers aboard, according to a senior military officer then at Bagram, who reviewed intelligence about the attack. "That really got the attention of a lot of people," the officer said, "because it was like, 'Hey, we didn't go in there to lose a lot of people.'" Yet the Pentagon put out a false story that the plane had crashed during takeoff and that there had been no enemy fire. Rumsfeld insisted that the Afghan war was won; his public affairs bureaucracy accommodated him.[37]

SEVEN

Taliban for Karzai

G ul Agha Sherzai, the C.I.A.'s man in Kandahar, or one of them, grew up around dog fighting. His father bred squat, fierce winners, organized tournaments, and oversaw gambling. In Sherzai's deft repertoire of public personas—tribal balancer, cash dispenser, business monopolist, reliable American client, land-grabber—the dog fighter was never far from summons. When agitated, he punched people. To demonstrate his prowess to his militia while fighting his way back into Kandahar, with Special Forces and C.I.A. officers alongside, he once jumped out of his car and shot dead several Arab fighters. He later suggested that he and Mullah Mohammad Omar should settle things with a knife fight, to see which "motherfucker" cried out first.[1]

Sherzai held court at the governor's headquarters in downtown Kandahar, an arched compound surrounded by dusty flowering gardens. Some days he appeared in the robes and turban befitting a Barakzai tribal leader. Other days he wore American-issued camouflage and Special Forces insignia. He and his brother, who ran security operations for him, were fans of the *Die Hard* movies, Steven Seagal, and Bollywood gangster musicals. A visitor recalled Gul Agha decamping once from his sport utility vehicle in a pin-striped suit, black shirt, and white tie. After a spate of rocket attacks on Kandahar Airfield, Sherzai's men captured a suspected insurgent, cut his throat, skinned him, and hung the corpse from a bridge on the main road to the city. They affixed a cardboard sign to the body: "DON'T FIRE ROCKETS AT THE CAMP."[2]

There were about four thousand American and allied soldiers at Kandahar Airfield. Their mission was not peacekeeping, but terrorist hunting. They needed reliable local security forces to protect their base and patrols. They had few proven allies in the Taliban heartland. The Sherzais filled the gap, for a fee. N.A.T.O. troops maintained an inner ring of security around the air base. The governor's militias maintained an outer perimeter under contract.

Some C.I.A. officers who worked with Sherzai found him to be a lovable rogue, an anachronism, perhaps, but a dependable and necessary one in post-Taliban Kandahar. State Department assessments were less generous. One described Sherzai as "a poor listener who always tries to dominate the conversation" and a "weak administrator" whose method of governance relied heavily on payoffs to tribal elders, journalists, and political office seekers. His lifestyle certainly challenged American sensibilities. He married at least four wives, who gave him ten sons and seven daughters. One of his wives was a former airline stewardess he had first seen as a twelve-year-old girl in Pakistan, and who he claimed had proposed to him "because she had heard so many good things" about him. Sherzai also followed the local practice of dressing up preadolescent boys as girls and apparently thought nothing of turning up before Western diplomats with such companions.[3]

The Taliban had taken power in Kandahar by challenging predatory corruption. Yet American policy in 2002 rested on the restoration of Sherzai's compromised rule in the Taliban's birthplace. The United States had transformed Afghanistan by overthrowing its government in a whirlwind but it had no political plan and few locally credible anti-Taliban allies to choose among, at least in Pashtun areas. Sherzai quickly seized upon the opportunity to enrich his family and rebuild tribal patronage. He took control of customs revenue at Spin Boldak, at the Pakistani border, a spigot of cash. He ran monopolies in water supplies, stone quarries, gasoline distribution, and taxi services. He opened a gravel and cement plant to service his American contracts. By one estimate, his take was about $1.5 million a month. Of the province's sixty heads of civil departments, Sherzai appointed fellow Barakzai tribe members to fifty-two, although he did allow other tribes some positions in the police and district administration. None of his lieutenants had the benefit of higher education.[4]

Haji Bashir Noorzai, an opium trafficker and former C.I.A. agent then about forty years old, was among the opportunists who met regularly with Governor Sherzai in 2002. Noorzai had come into contact with the C.I.A. a decade earlier, during the Afghan civil war, when the agency had run a clandestine program to buy back some of the more than two thousand heat-seeking, portable Stinger antiaircraft missiles the United States had distributed to mujaheddin guerrillas battling the Soviet occupation. After the Soviet withdrawal, the agency feared that terrorists might acquire Stingers to attack civilian airliners. Through I.S.I. officers and unilateral agents, C.I.A. officers working out of Islamabad Station paid about $80,000 for every missile returned for destruction.

Noorzai heard about the program through a friend in Pakistan and volunteered to locate and buy back Stingers in his home region of Kandahar. He met a C.I.A. officer at the start of each mission. The officer tore a ten-dollar bill in half, gave one half to Noorzai, and told him that if an American met him with the other half, that would authenticate their contact. Ultimately, Noorzai brokered the sale of about half a dozen Stingers to the C.I.A. and cleared a total of $50,000 in commissions.[5]

His family included leaders of the Noorzai tribe, who were large in number and controlled lands rich with opium crops, but did not enjoy great political influence. Taliban rule benefited the Noorzais. Bashir grew up in Maiwand, where Mullah Mohammad Omar had settled after the Soviet war. Bashir Noorzai provided cash and arms to the Taliban when they took power in Kandahar after 1994. In 2000, his father died and Bashir became "the Chief of the Noorzai," as he called himself. After September 11, he waited out the American invasion in Quetta. When Gul Agha Sherzai seized Kandahar, Noorzai sent word to him that he wanted to renew his help to the C.I.A. The governor invited him to Kandahar.[6]

He did not receive the welcome he expected. American military officers detained Noorzai for six days at Kandahar Airfield and interrogated him. They asked him about his relationship with the Taliban, which Noorzai admitted had been friendly. He told the various Americans who questioned him—military officers, C.I.A. officers, Drug Enforcement Administration agents—that America was already falling into the trap of allowing local Afghan allies around Kandahar to put down enemies by labeling them Taliban when they really weren't. "Many people take advantage of American friendship to harm their rivals," Noorzai explained.[7]

Noorzai eventually convinced them that he could once again help collect Stingers and other heavy weapons. The Americans released him. He purchased batches of old weapons the Taliban had left behind—Blowpipe missiles and caches of rocket-propelled grenades. He turned trucks full of arms in to the Americans at Kandahar Airfield.

By Noorzai's account, however, Gul Agha Sherzai's men hijacked the C.I.A.'s Stinger repurchase program and turned it into a racketeering venture. Noorzai said he identified five or six Stingers held by old commanders and paid for them, planning to sell them for a profit to the C.I.A. (The agency was now paying as much as $125,000 per returned missile.) But when Noorzai told Sherzai's aides about his deals, he said, the governor's men "beat up some of my people," stole Noorzai's money, and also stole the missiles so they could sell them back to the C.I.A. themselves. "He is just a crow," Noorzai said of Gul Agha, "but you have made him a hero."[8]

Noorzai said he traveled to the United Arab Emirates with Sherzai and Khalid Pashtun that spring, to help them obtain payments from U.A.E. sheikhs in exchange for allowing the Arabs to access Kandahar's desert hunting grounds, where they used falcons to hunt bustards, a migratory bird. The Taliban had run such a hunting program, and Sherzai had the idea that he could obtain fresh rental payments. Emirati go-betweens handed over a briefcase with two hundred thousand dirhams in cash and arranged for another payment of one million dirhams, or about $320,000 in total. "Everything is the money business in Afghanistan," as one of Noorzai's aides explained. "Politics is for money, fighting is for money, government [is] for money."[9]

Secretary of Defense Rumsfeld had ruled out amnesty for surrendering Taliban in late 2001. Yet by the spring of 2002 the context for his policy had changed. Al Qaeda had abandoned Afghanistan's cities. The Taliban had dissolved and disappeared. The country had quieted, apart from the eastern mountains. Karzai had started to lead a constitutional process outlined by the Bonn Agreement, to determine the form of national government. He remained open to negotiation with the Taliban, just as he had been in December.

At Kabul Station, Rich Blee shared Karzai's opinion that some Taliban might be corrigible. Taliban leaders held abhorrent ideas but at least they were not corrupt, Blee told colleagues. It would be valuable to win peaceful defectors to bolster Kabul's shaky new government. Besides, any student of military history knew that it was wise after victory in war to create reconciliation and pacification programs for the defeated enemy. The victor might hang a few enemy leaders and generals, but it could be dangerous to hold every official and military officer on the other side accountable—too much punishment was a prescription for future rebellion.

Credible Taliban leaders continued to reach out to both Karzai and the United States despite the rejections they had received in late 2001. Tayeb Agha, a political and press aide in Mullah Mohammad Omar's former office in Kandahar, and Mullah Abdul Ghani Baradar, a military deputy to Omar, approached Haji Mohammad Ibrahim Akhundzada, a leader in Uruzgan Province who was from Hamid Karzai's tribe. Although he was a youthful and obscure figure at the time, Tayeb Agha would prove to be a consequential figure in Washington's coming misadventures in Afghanistan. He was one of the few people who could reliably speak for Mullah Mohammad Omar, who had vanished. He provided a letter purportedly from the Taliban leader. The thrust of the note, according to an American official who later reviewed the matter, was "Look, the Bonn

Conference just happened. . . . We want to be part of Afghanistan's future and I'll let my Shura decide how to do this." Karzai wanted to pursue the opening, but the Bush administration refused.

Bashir Noorzai offered a second opportunity. Wakil Ahmad Mutawakil, the last Taliban foreign minister, came from Noorzai's home district. Mutawakil's father had been an imam at a local mosque. The deposed foreign minister had gone into hiding in Quetta, Pakistan. Noorzai reached him by telephone and "convinced him" to meet the Americans in Kandahar. Mutawakil traveled to Kandahar Airfield, where he was arrested.[10]

The C.I.A. had a base there, in a fenced-off area that also housed clandestine Special Forces, mainly Navy SEALs. Frank Archibald, a six-foot-two-inch former college rugby player and U.S. Marine, who had risen in the C.I.A.'s Special Activities Division, questioned Mutawakil.

They talked about creating a new political party allied with Karzai. "Let's bring him on board," Blee agreed. "Taliban for Karzai" was the general idea the C.I.A. explored—it offered a propaganda line, if nothing else. According to what Archibald later described to colleagues, the C.I.A. officer "was practically living in a tent" with Mutawakil, while working with him on "creating a legitimate Taliban political party to join the system." Mutawakil suggested that he could recruit other significant former Taliban to join.[11]

Archibald worked up a presentation about Taliban defectors and the future of Afghan politics, according to the account he later gave to colleagues. He flew back to Virginia and presented his ideas at C.I.A. headquarters. Vice President Dick Cheney attended. "We're not doing that," he declared after he heard the briefing. One American official involved in the discussions put it: "It's the same crap we saw in Iraq: 'All Baathists are bad. All Taliban are bad.' What American naïveté."

The message from Washington for Mutawakil was "He's going to be in a jumpsuit. He's going to Guantánamo." Archibald managed to prevent that, at least. The Afghan government imprisoned Mutawakil at Bagram Airfield for about six months, before he was released into house arrest in Kabul.[12]

Mutawakil's imprisonment "affected my prestige and discredited me with Mutawakil's family and many other people," Bashir Noorzai complained to the Americans. The Bush administration's harsh policy "would not encourage former Taliban leaders and militants to moderate their attitude and cooperate with the new government." For Noorzai, it got worse. He persuaded another Taliban ally, Haji Birqet Khan, to return to Kandahar, but someone passed a "false report" to the Americans that Noorzai and the commander were planning an attack. American helicopters swooped over Khan's home and opened fire. They killed Khan and also wounded his wife and one of his sons. The son lost the use of his legs. Two of the commander's "young grandchildren were killed when they jumped into a well in order to try and hide from the bombardment." The raid caused Khan's tribe "to go against the Americans," according to Noorzai.[13]

Noorzai gave up on the C.I.A. and fled to Quetta, where he returned to international opium and heroin smuggling. The Drug Enforcement Administration lured him to a meeting in New York several years later and arrested him. He was not the most unimpeachable of witnesses, but the essence of his testimony about Kandahar in 2002 was unarguable. The city had succumbed again to racketeering. Afghan allies passed false reports to the Americans for ulterior purposes. Violent Special Forces raids and intelligence errors alienated Pashtun families and tribes. "We in that stage started our process of killing all sorts of people" in poorly judged Special Forces raids and close air support operations, recalled a senior military officer then based in Afghanistan. A B-52 Stratofortress mistakenly killed dozens of Afghans at a wedding in Uruzgan that June, after reconnaissance officers confused their celebratory gunfire for hostile action. In Kandahar, Gul Agha's approach to opposing tribal factions in Maiwand was to tell the Americans they were all part of the Taliban, "and we believed him," the senior officer conceded. "And Maiwand has never been the same way since."[14]

Green Berets among the Army's Special Forces, trained to influence local populations through engagement and small development projects, traveled patiently and for the most part peaceably, but theirs was not the predominant mission. Terrorist hunting was. "Black" Special Forces focused on identifying and targeting insurgents. An Army Psychological

Operations officer accompanied a Special Forces raid on a Zabul village and watched Navy SEALs beat and threaten Pashtun villagers who weren't sufficiently cooperative, the officer told Army criminal investigators.

Q: When the three villagers were assaulted, how were they assaulted?
A: [Redacted] was kicked in the head, chest, back, stomach, punched in the neck and shoulders and head. . . . The second individual was being hit in the face with closed hands and open hands. . . . [Redacted] had taken the villager behind a wall in the village and I could hear the villager screaming as though he were in pain, and then I heard a gunshot. Later I heard [Redacted] say "I should have killed him!"

Q: What do you think [Redacted] meant by "He should have killed him"?
A: In my opinion, [Redacted] was getting angry and frustrated and meant exactly what he had said.[15]

After 2002, the C.I.A. and Special Forces discovered there weren't many Al Qaeda left in Afghanistan after all. They had migrated to Pakistan. So the American operators started attacking Taliban "because they are there," as Arturo Muñoz, a C.I.A. officer who served in the 2001 war, put it. Yet the political consequences of this shift were poorly considered, in his judgment: "If you start shipping people to Guantánamo who many other Pashtuns know are not terrorists—if you start confusing horse thieves with terrorists—then they come to see that your idea of terrorism is impossible to accommodate. By our words and our actions we destroyed the opportunity to take advantage of the Pashtun mechanisms for accommodation and reconciliation."[16]

Cheney and Rumsfeld had imposed the policy they preferred: to signal to former Taliban that they faced war without compromise because of their alliance with Al Qaeda. Yet for the most part, by mid-2002, the Bush administration had stopped thinking seriously about Afghanistan. Archibald's presentation about "Taliban for Karzai" was a rare instance when the issue of political pacification was even put up for discussion. The Bush administration's policy was: The Taliban had been defeated, they remained illegitimate, and stragglers should be hunted down, imprisoned, and interrogated about Al Qaeda. The Taliban did constitute a millenarian revolutionary movement with an uncompromising leader, although it was indigenous and had never attacked outside Afghanistan's borders. The movement's core leadership might have rejected political engagement in 2002, if that had been attempted. Yet with incentives, influential former Taliban might have come in from exile, just as Mutawakil had done. The Bush administration's message to the movement's survivors and their backers in I.S.I. was clear, however: The Taliban could expect no future in Afghan politics unless they fought for it. The Bush administration did not consider that they constituted a large part of Afghan society, legitimized by faith, ethnicity, and their fighting during the anti-Soviet war.

The first Taliban *shabnameh*, or night letters—typically handwritten death threats posted in mosques or slipped under doorways—appeared to the east of Kandahar late in 2002, near the Pakistani border. They made reference to the history of Afghan resistance against foreign invaders, great heroes of the past, and Islamic theology. They threatened death to anyone who worked with the United States or the government in Kabul. Taliban runners tacked them on mosque walls or private doorways, or demanded that local notables read them aloud.[17]

On September 5, 2002, Hamid Karzai toured Kandahar. An assassin opened fire on his vehicle from ten yards away, just missing him. American bodyguards gunned the shooter down, accidentally killing Afghan soldiers as well. The same day, a car bomb exploded in a downtown Kabul marketplace, killing fifteen shoppers and bystanders.

Larry Goodson, an American scholar of Afghanistan, interviewed Taliban leaders along the Pakistan border during this period and found that the movement benefited from "a perception that the Americans would leave, that reconstruction would not succeed, and that Afghanistan would return to chaos." Especially in areas such as the Kandahar heartland, the movement's leaders sought to exploit "popular dissatisfaction in the south over the gap between the expectations of western assistance and the reality that virtually none had arrived." Taliban units made up of twenty-five or thirty guerrillas crossed over from Pakistan to lob mortars and fire rockets at Kandahar in the night.[18]

As it prepared for war in Iraq, the Bush administration handed control of Afghan policy increasingly to Zalmay Khalilzad, now a roving envoy to Afghanistan. In April 2003, Khalilzad flew into Kabul to meet with Engineer Arif, the Afghan intelligence chief. Arif reported that I.S.I. clients were "working in Kandahar and Jalalabad . . . providing free passage to terror elements to cross into and out of Pakistan in vehicles loaded with arms." Arif warned the Bush administration that Pakistan was now "promoting instability in Afghanistan."[19]

Evidence that I.S.I. was back in the game was not difficult to find. That summer, the Pakistani journalist Ahmed Rashid traveled through Quetta and southern Afghanistan to document the Taliban's return. He found the family of Mullah Dadullah, the movement's vicious military leader, living openly in a village outside Quetta; in September, Dadullah staged a "family wedding in lavish style, inviting leading members of the Baluchistan government . . . and military officers." In Kandahar, Rashid met Ahmed Wali Karzai, who told him, "The Taliban are gathering in the same places where they started. It's like the rerun of an old movie."

The Afghans primarily blamed Pakistan. The sanctuary the Taliban enjoyed in Pakistan as they regrouped empowered them. Afghans wondered, reasonably: How could the United States fail to see that I.S.I. was up to its old tricks? In a land of conspiracy theories, Washington's apparent acceptance of Pakistan's policy created confusion and doubt.[20]

There was no grand American conspiracy, of course. The truth was more prosaic. In all of 2003, Bush's National Security Council met to discuss Afghanistan only twice, according to records kept by a former administration official. The invasion and occupation of Iraq, overconfidence about Afghanistan's postwar stability, and the cabinet's desire to avoid further commitment to reconstruction explained this complacency. It would have required energy and determination to confront and threaten President Musharraf and I.S.I. By 2003 I.S.I. seemed to be running a low-level, testing version of the same covert program it had run in Afghanistan for more than two continuous decades, probing what the

service could get away with while the Bush administration tried to subdue Iraq. And a new generation of Pakistan Army officers was rising
under Musharraf, schooling itself in the arts of "yes, but" with the United
States. Among them was Ashfaq Kayani, a mumbling, chain-smoking
general who, even more than Musharraf, would shape America's fate in
South Asia in the decade to come.[21]

EIGHT

The Enigma

T he Pakistan Army provided a means for poor, striving families to reach the middle class or higher. There were many ways to succeed as an aspiring general officer. Pervez Musharraf overcame inferior discipline through audacity on the battlefield. Ashfaq Parvez Kayani was a grinder, a classroom star. Kayani's father had been a noncommissioned army officer, the equivalent of a sergeant, who raised his boys in a Punjabi village and urged them to follow in his footsteps, but to aim for the top. Ashfaq attended a prestigious military high school before winning entry to the Pakistan Military Academy, the country's equivalent of West Point, located in the mountain town of Abbottabad. After early tours as a young officer, he earned a ticket toward generalship with a seat at the Command and Staff College in Quetta, the leadership-grooming school where the D.I.A.'s Dave Smith had developed his connections to future commanders.

In the early 1990s, the United States imposed sanctions on Pakistan over its clandestine nuclear program. I.S.I.'s support for the Taliban deepened Pakistan's estrangement from the United States. Officer exchanges and training programs between the two countries shriveled. Yet Kayani lived and trained in the United States several times. Dispatched to Fort Leavenworth, he studied strategy. He wrote a thesis analyzing how the Afghan resistance defeated the Soviet occupation and how

Pakistan played its hand in that war, managing the rebellion so that it was successful but did not provoke a total war with Moscow.

As he matured and rose in rank, Kayani positioned himself as an intellectual and a military strategist. After Fort Leavenworth, having reached the rank of brigadier, he studied for a year at the Asia-Pacific Center for Security Studies in Hawaii. There he befriended a U.S. Special Forces officer, Barry Shapiro. Stuck for hours in Hawaii's choking traffic as they shuttled in transport buses, Kayani educated Shapiro about Pakistan's mission to liberate Kashmir. Shapiro thought he was brilliant. Kayani was married, with a son and a daughter, and he brought his family to Hawaii. His son enrolled in Hawaii's public schools. Later, back in Islamabad, at the National Defense University, Kayani finished a master's degree and passed with the highest possible grade.[1]

He spoke softly, in an accented mumble, so that it was necessary to strain to follow him even if he was seated just a few feet away. As Kayani aged, the caramel skin on his face darkened and his eyes sank behind coal-hued hoods, which only added to his inscrutability. He worked hard and pursued conventional hobbies. He golfed enthusiastically, striding down the army's private fairways in Rawalpindi.

As Kayani rose, his family was positioned to exploit military connections for business ends, just as American military officers did in contracting firms around Washington. His brother Amjad retired as a brigadier and went into Pakistani defense contracting. His brother Babur retired as a major and went into construction. And his brother Kamran also retired as a major and went into real estate.[2] The Punjabi sergeant's sons had made good by the time of Musharraf's post–September 11 pivot toward the United States. As Kayani won promotion to two-star general, his family was placed to secure a fortune for a generation or more through military-enabled business ventures. The military-industrial complex was one of Pakistan's binding forces, alongside Islam, national pride, suspicion of India and America, and cricket. One common narrative about Pakistan held that its powerful army competed for power with civilian political families like the Bhuttos and the Sharifs. Certainly there was rivalry between civilians and the military, evidenced in periodic coups and "democratic" restorations. Yet Pakistan's informal system of shared control of the economy's commanding heights bound together families like the Kayanis and the Bhuttos as much as it divided them.

By 2002, Ashfaq Parvez Kayani had become one of Musharraf's most trusted generals. His billet at that time was director-general of military operations. Musharraf showed no signs of wanting to leave office anytime soon and he had arrogated extensive powers to himself. In effect, his key lieutenants were military princes, beholden to the boss. For now, Kayani diligently served his superiors.

In March 2003, on the eve of America's invasion of Iraq, Kayani traveled to the United States in a delegation led by Pakistan's vice chief of the army, Yusuf Khan. Dave Smith served as "conducting officer," part liaison, part tour guide, part intelligence collector. The U.S. Army installed the Pakistani generals in the distinguished visiting officers quarters at Fort Myer, a short walk from Quarters One, the official home of the American army chief, then General Eric Shinseki. One night, Shinseki hosted a dinner where an ensemble from the Army Band played classical music during the meal and a few Pakistani numbers afterward. At the Pentagon, the group met Chairman of the Joint Chiefs Richard Myers, Undersecretary for Policy Douglas Feith, and at the State Department, Richard Armitage. At the C.I.A., they met Director George Tenet.

The Pakistan officer corps "is completely reliable," Khan assured his American hosts, "liberal and moderate." He reported that a cousin of his served as a captain in an army field unit and had confided that alcohol consumption was more prevalent than just a couple of years before. (For some reason, American officials often measured the reliability of Pakistani military officers by their willingness to drink.) Khan outlined his priorities as one of the Pakistan Army's chief administrators. These included improved physical fitness, a plan to downsize the uniformed force by outsourcing to commercial contractors, and closing the income gap between junior and senior officers. He mentioned that he wanted to eliminate fifty thousand positions for "officer orderlies," or servants, to replace them with cash subsidies that would allow each Pakistani officer to hire private servants. Certain traditions died hard.[3]

Dave Smith led the generals on a tour of American bases and training facilities around the United States. They visited Fort Monroe in Virginia, Fort Knox in Kentucky, and Fort Irwin in Southern California. They took a weekend off in Los Angeles, where some of Yusuf Khan's relatives resided. They stayed in a hotel in Anaheim and made repeat visits to a local indoor mall. The generals and their wives carried shopping lists and plenty of cash. Smith procured V.I.P. passes to Disneyland. In civilian clothes, the travelers skipped the resort's lines and rode all the popular rides—It's a Small World, Space Mountain, Pirates of the Caribbean—and were out in just a couple of hours.

From the tour, Smith assessed Kayani to be "a very smart, intelligent guy, quiet, not boastful—someone Musharraf counted on." Six months after Kayani returned home, Musharraf promoted him to lieutenant general and handed him command of X Corps, the army's most politically sensitive force because it was headquartered near Islamabad and had enforced past army coups d'état, including Musharraf's, in 1999. Previous X Corps commanders had led I.S.I. The spy service was in Kayani's future, too. He would prove to be a natural.[4]

After the Taliban's collapse, I.S.I.-C.I.A. collaboration fell into a steady tempo. C.I.A.-controlled Predators flew out of a Pakistani air base, mainly on surveillance missions. During the weeks after Tora Bora, Pakistani security forces captured about 130 Arabs, Uzbeks, Chechens, and other foreign fighters fleeing from Afghanistan. They found the Al Qaeda stragglers in the country's western hills but also in Karachi, Rawalpindi, and Lahore. The Pakistanis transported the captives to Chaklala Airbase near Islamabad and handed them over to the United States. Air Force C-17 transport planes flew them to Bagram Airfield, then on to Kandahar Airfield, where the prisoners were held in outdoor cages.[5] Some were subjected to sleep deprivation and other harsh conditions. Many were sent on to Guantánamo, once the Bush administration opened that prison on January 11, 2002. Yet hundreds of other Al Qaeda volunteers escaped capture and hid in Pakistan's cities, sheltered by religious parties and networks that had collaborated with Bin Laden and his followers since the 1980s.

Musharraf found it tolerable to support the Americans as they hunted down Arabs. The Arab fighters were not decisive to Pakistan's guerrilla strategy against India in Kashmir or to its efforts to influence Pashtuns in Afghanistan. The bargain of targeting Arabs while leaving local Islamist guerrillas alone worked as long as the C.I.A. recognized that "any Pakistanis," including violent radicals fighting in Kashmir, should be "remanded to Pakistani law enforcement," as Islamabad station chief Grenier put it.[6]

Under the Bush administration's generous policy, in exchange for its arrests of Al Qaeda suspects, Pakistan received cash and armaments, as well as a veneer of legitimacy as an ally in Bush's global war on terrorism. The administration would eventually authorize the sale of thirty-six F-16 fighter jets to Pakistan, ending a long stalemate over Pakistan's access to America's high-performing aircraft. Also, under a program referred to as Coalition Support Funds, the Pentagon transferred hundreds of millions of dollars in cash each year to Pakistan, ostensibly to reimburse its military for its participation in counterterrorism operations that benefited the United States. In fact, the program was little more than an unaudited cash subsidy to the Pakistan Army, strengthening Musharraf's grip on the country's politics.

Barry Shapiro, the Special Forces colonel who had studied with Kayani in Hawaii, served during 2002 and 2003 in the U.S. embassy's swelling Office of the Defense Representative–Pakistan, where he channeled requests for reimbursements from Pakistan to Central Command. The Pakistanis presented itemized bills to Shapiro for all of the military activity they had supposedly conducted against terrorists in the previous month. Shapiro was unimpressed by the accounting: "It was amazing the crap they would try to tell us they were doing just so that we would reimburse them." The bills would list specific actions, such as "Seventeen T.O.W. antitank missiles fired at enemy targets in the Federally Administered Tribal Areas," accompanied by a price tag in the tens of thousands of dollars. The Pakistanis billed out air defense expenses such as radar tracking even though the Taliban and Al Qaeda had no air force. Judging by their invoices, they were expending ammunition at a rate that exceeded that of American combat units in Afghanistan, even though the Pakistani military was rarely in the fight against militants during this period.

Shapiro asked, "What did you fire the missiles at? What is your battle damage assessment?" Yet he never received documented answers. The Pakistan Navy would bill him on a per diem formula for sailors "on duty fighting the Global War on Terrorism." Shapiro thought that was laughable—what were these sailors doing to thwart Al Qaeda? (Supposedly, the Pakistan Navy conducted patrols to prevent Al Qaeda members from escaping by sea.) The most egregious cases concerned supposed road construction to support Pakistani military operations, especially in the country's western tribal areas. If Shapiro had sat down and counted all the roads they claimed to have built, he thought, Pakistan's tribal areas would have been "one big asphalt parking lot."[7]

Yet when Shapiro challenged the bills or demanded proof, word came down to him from superiors "to just stop asking questions and sign off on this stuff." The Pentagon was content with blanket subsidies. His orders were to pass on the requests for Coalition Support Funds "even though we knew all of this stuff was trumped up." The Coalition Support Funds provided a kind of legal bribery to Pakistan's generals. Musharraf and his lieutenants could use the cash for legitimate military purposes, or they could spread it around as they wished. Theoretically, if the Pakistani generals came to depend on the American largesse, they might moderate their conduct to align with the Bush administration's aims in the region, so as to avoid being cut off. The money did not buy love, but it did seem to purchase a certain level of cooperation and tolerance.[8]

Musharraf delivered by arresting Al Qaeda fugitives in Pakistan while evading accountability on Taliban or Kashmiri militants. The I.S.I. did betray a few highly visible Taliban leaders, such as Ambassador Mullah Zaeef. The Pakistanis arrested him and turned him over to the Americans, who shipped him to Guantánamo. Yet as many other high-ranking Taliban officeholders melted into Quetta, the I.S.I. ignored them or claimed they could not be located.

According to Hank Crumpton of the Counterterrorist Center, the C.I.A. suffered from "a lack of intelligence . . . lack of access and collection" in Quetta, now the Taliban's principal sanctuary. The agency accepted "dependence to some degree on the Pakistanis" to identify high-value Taliban suspects hiding there. In any event, after 2001, Mullah

Omar "was a secondary target" for the C.I.A. Cooperating I.S.I. officers were "chasing down key Al Qaeda targets and rendering them to us." The feeling at Langley was "Why push them, and why anger them" by harping about the defeated Taliban? Another motivation remained: to keep as close to I.S.I. as possible so that C.I.A. case officers in Islamabad or offshore could identify and recruit I.S.I. officers as unilateral American sources. The C.I.A. might not be able to recruit many important Al Qaeda defectors—that organization has proved to be a very hard target— but surely there were I.S.I. officers who might be willing to work with the C.I.A. and who knew or could find out where Osama Bin Laden had taken shelter.[9]

Robert Grenier and his I.S.I. counterparts set up a joint intelligence operations cell in a walled safe house in Islamabad, from where they targeted Al Qaeda fugitives. They pooled tips, directed surveillance, and planned raids on suspected compounds in Pakistani cities. Islamabad Station swelled with temporarily deployed C.I.A. officers, F.B.I. agents, eavesdroppers, and contractors—TDYers, as they were known in U.S. government jargon, referring to their short, temporary deployments. And just as the C.I.A. had infused the Afghan National Directorate of Security with cash, the agency now poured tens of millions of dollars into I.S.I.'s counterterrorism directorate. The payments took the form of reward money for the capture of specific Al Qaeda leaders as well as investments in new facilities, vehicles, technology, and training.

It did not require deep experience in Pakistan to understand that even though I.S.I.'s counterterrorism directorate found it agreeable to operate with the Americans against Al Qaeda, other I.S.I. directorates might simultaneously monitor and support Pakistan's indigenous jihadi clients, including the Taliban. The Bush administration and the C.I.A. accepted this arrangement as necessary, if chronically frustrating, during 2002 and 2003. As John McLaughlin, then the C.I.A.'s deputy director, put it: "We were getting traction on Al Qaeda. In a war situation, you're drawn to where you can succeed. . . . The attraction of going after Al Qaeda was just so great."[10] All along, it was clear what I.S.I. wanted from the United States, besides cash and arms: Pakistan sought greater influence in Kabul, to counter India's presumed influence over Hamid Karzai and the Northern Alliance. (India had funded the Northern Alliance before 2001 and Karzai had attended school in the country.)

During this period, the director of the Defense Intelligence Agency, Vice Admiral Thomas Wilson, visited headquarters. He met Director-General Ehsan ul-Haq. The I.S.I. chief opened the meeting with a thirty-minute monologue about what a terrible ally of Pakistan the United States had proved to be over the years. The Nixon administration had stood by as India dismembered Pakistan during the 1971 war, he noted. The first Bush administration and then the Clinton administration washed their hands of Pakistan after the Soviet withdrawal from Afghanistan, leaving Pakistan alone to bear the costs of refugees, heroin addiction, and loose guns.

"September 11 has provided another opportunity," the I.S.I. chief continued, but now, once again, the United States was neglecting Pakistan's legitimate desire to influence Afghanistan. "The interim government" in Kabul "is being led by the Three Musketeers of the Northern Alliance," Haq said bitterly. He meant Fahim Khan, Karzai's minister of defense; Yunus Qanooni, another former lieutenant of Ahmad Shah Massoud, who was the minister of interior; and Abdullah Abdullah, who was minister of foreign affairs. The Russians and Iranians had infiltrated Afghanistan through the Northern Alliance and were "in there with a vengeance," the I.S.I. director continued. "I'm speaking with my heart, but Pakistan has suffered as an ally of the United States."[11]

He summoned for Wilson two brigadiers from I.S.I.'s analysis directorate. They advanced their boss's talking points. "The ethnic composition of the government in Kabul is unbalanced," one of them complained. "As soon as the U.S. leaves, there will be a return to chaos." It was a forecast that could also be read as a threat.[12]

Since the 1970s, the Haqqani network had been a linchpin of I.S.I.'s covert policy. The network consisted of thousands of fighters along the Pakistan-Afghan border, relatively close to Kabul. The network drew funds and volunteers from a web of smuggling businesses, fund-raising operations in Saudi Arabia and elsewhere in the Gulf, and prestigious

Islamic schools. As with so many other nodes of influence in Pakistan and Afghanistan, at the network's heart lay an extended family empowered by war and instability. The family's home village lay in the Wazi Zadran district of Afghanistan's Paktia Province, close to the porous border between Afghanistan and Pakistan's tribal agency of North Waziristan. Before the Second World War, a family patriarch, Khwaja Muhammad Khan, owned land and traded on both sides of the border. His son Jalaluddin was born in 1939, followed by several other boys. Khan had means to enroll his boys at a conservative Deobandi madrassa in Pakistan's Northwest Frontier Province, known as Dar al-'Ulum Haqqaniyya. The Deobandi school of Islam, born in northern India, was a rule-prescribing sect that sought a purer faith. The madrassa also had ties to an Islamist political party in Pakistan, the Jamiat Ulema-e-Islam, or J.U.I. Jalaluddin graduated with an advanced education in 1970 and took his school's name as his own, as did his brothers. He dabbled in electoral politics before the spread of Communist ideology in Afghanistan drew him into the skirmishes of an incipient jihad against the Communists and secularists, as early as 1973. As Abdul Salam Rocketi, a former Taliban commander who met with Jalaluddin over the years, put it: "His background was in politics—he was a politician and also a religious scholar. He had plans. He always seemed to have some secret plans that I did not know about—this was his personality."[13]

Geography, above all, determined the family's rise to wealth and power during the anti-Soviet war of the 1980s. A key part of I.S.I.'s strategy in the war was to exploit the relatively short distance between its frontier in North Waziristan and the capital of Kabul to stage guerrilla strikes that harassed and punished Soviet forces around the capital. Pakistan's covert supply lines ran through the highlands of the two Waziristans, but especially through North Waziristan. By the account of a former I.S.I. officer who ran logistics during the covert war, the Haqqanis received as much as twelve thousand tons of supplies every year. Jalaluddin and his brothers poured their funds into the construction of religious schools on both sides of the Afghan-Pakistan border, an archipelago of influence, shelter, ideological support, and fresh student recruits. In 1980, they built an elaborate flagship madrassa in Danday

Darpakhel, outside Miranshah, the tribal agency's capital. Urban North Waziristan was an ideal base of operations. It lay beyond the reach of Soviet ground forces, beyond the writ of the Pakistani government, yet it was proximate to the battlefield and to supply lines fed by I.S.I. and the C.I.A. Just inside Afghanistan, in a natural citadel, Zhawara, the Haqqanis and I.S.I. constructed a massive base and training center, ultimately consisting of dozens of buildings and underground tunnels and arms depots. The project benefited from Osama Bin Laden's aid and participation. The Haqqanis did more than any other commander network in Afghanistan to nurture and support Arab volunteer fighters, seeding Al Qaeda's birth.[14]

During the late 1980s, the C.I.A. adopted a strategy of providing cash directly to anti-Soviet commanders, in addition to funneling the money through I.S.I. A case officer operating under nonofficial cover, outside the embassy, handled the Haqqani account and provided hundreds of thousands of dollars. The Haqqani family in turn was professional and efficient. It maintained representative offices in Peshawar, Islamabad, and Riyadh, for ease of doing business. During the early 1990s, the family used its control of an airstrip in Khost to export scrap metal gathered from the war's detritus, earning millions. It published magazines and ran a radio station.[15]

American and N.A.T.O. intelligence officers would come to spend long hours after 2001 trying to evaluate the Haqqanis' loyalties—to I.S.I., to the Taliban, to Al Qaeda. The record makes plain that the family valued its independence. The Haqqanis maintained alliances and client ties to I.S.I. but they were also estranged, at times, from the Pakistani service. Equally, the Haqqanis swore fealty to Mullah Mohammad Omar and the Taliban after they took power, and cooperated with the Taliban on the battlefield, but there were also strains from time to time. The Haqqanis differed with the Taliban's bans on music and women's access to education; the family allowed some charities to build coeducational schools in territory it controlled around Khost and in Pakistan.[16]

Musharraf's decision to back the United States in its war against the Taliban presented the Haqqanis with a profound dilemma. Jalaluddin visited Islamabad in October 2001 and held ambiguous meetings with

I.S.I. officers and American interlocutors. By one account, the Bush administration demanded only a form of unconditional surrender. The longtime Pakistan-based correspondent Kathy Gannon reported that Pakistan told the Haqqanis to hold firm against the Americans and await I.S.I. aid. In any event, Jalaluddin made his decision clear in an interview as he left the Pakistani capital: "We will retreat to the mountains and begin a long guerrilla war to claim our pure land from infidels and free our country like we did against the Soviets."[17]

Then in his early sixties, scarred by war injuries, Jalaluddin commanded the family enterprise. He relied on two of his younger brothers, Ibrahim and Khalil, both educated at the Haqqaniyya madrassa as he had been, to negotiate and mediate on the family's behalf. Ibrahim in particular evolved into a kind of ambassador.

After the fall of the Taliban, Ibrahim moved to Kabul. The Haqqanis did not reconcile formally with Hamid Karzai's administration, but Ibrahim's presence signaled that they were open to discussions. The Haqqanis had fought with Ahmad Shah Massoud during the 1980s and against him during the mid-1990s. They were masters of violent coexistence.

During 2002, Ibrahim Haqqani had even established contact with C.I.A. officers in Gardez and had been helpful. In November 2002, he visited the station at the Ariana Hotel to talk with C.I.A. officers. A senior officer named Mike, in Afghanistan on a second tour, was working on a plan with the agency's Paris station chief to persuade Ibrahim to arrange a meeting with Jalaluddin in the United Arab Emirates. Mike wanted to propose that the Haqqanis help the C.I.A. locate Osama Bin Laden. At the Ariana, speaking through a Pashtu translator, Mike warned Ibrahim that the United States would track down and kill his brother if he didn't cooperate. If the Haqqanis used intermediaries and distanced themselves from the betrayal of Bin Laden they might end up better off, enhancing their prestige and creating new conditions for their own influence. If not Bin Laden, perhaps they would help with Ayman Al Zawahiri or Mullah Mohammad Omar.[18]

The gambit fell apart before the hypothesis could be tested, a victim, as one C.I.A. officer involved saw it, of fraying trust and communication between the C.I.A. and Special Forces in Afghanistan. At Bagram Airfield, C.I.A. officers marked off their computer terminals with the equivalent of yellow police tape to prevent Defense Department personnel from looking at their screens, an almost comical expression of the agency's posture toward everyone else in the government. The C.I.A.'s clandestine service had long struggled to overcome its reputation for arrogance. The agency's élan and mythology of omniscience and power was a key aspect of its effectiveness in the field, in the same way that great salesmen drive expensive cars in order to influence clients with the shine of their success. Yet if a certain degree of constructed hubris was an aspect of spying tradecraft, it also invited self-delusion. The C.I.A. never stopped projecting its claim to be the elite of the elite. Yet while the Senior Intelligence Service certainly had star performers and jaw-dropping stories of bravery and daring to tell, it also had fools and screamers in its ranks who authored operational failures that colleagues elsewhere in U.S. intelligence and the military had no trouble learning about, if they had the right clearances.

Stan McChrystal, then on his way to lead Joint Special Operations Command, traveling in and out of Afghanistan, felt the C.I.A. had "a culture of insularity." The attitude they projected was "Nobody should tell us what to do. We got it. We are special." He thought the agency attracted strong talent but "they don't have very good leadership." There was no system for selecting and forging successful leaders over careers, as the military sought to do. Whether a C.I.A. station chief was an exemplary decision maker or a whacked-out freelancer seemed to McChrystal almost random, serendipitous, a matter of rotation schedules and internal politics. And the C.I.A. tended to regard military officers and units with barely disguised condescension. There were exceptions like Greg Vogle or Chris Wood, whom McChrystal latched on to as peers and collaborators, but in general, "They weren't as good as they thought they were and we weren't as bad as they thought," he believed. The C.I.A.'s assessment, in turn, was that the Pentagon special operators were shooters and door crashers who lacked regional expertise and situational awareness. McChrystal made it his mission to fix the working relationship, but it was a project that turned out to be measured in years.[19]

Even as Ibrahim Haqqani talked cooperatively with the C.I.A. through one channel, a special unit in Kabul Station targeted him for arrest. The unit was made up of a mix of C.I.A. officers and Special Forces personnel and its operations were heavily compartmented— meaning knowledge of its existence and work was restricted to those judged to have a need to know, even within the C.I.A. The C.I.A. and Special Forces kept their own lists of high-level Al Qaeda and allied targets; somehow, Ibrahim made a list, even though he was meeting with Mike and other officers in Kabul and elsewhere. The Kabul station chief, a successor to Rich Blee, knew that Ibrahim had been targeted but did not share this with Mike or others. On May 4, 2003, the black operations unit "basically jumped the guy" and arrested Ibrahim. As a C.I.A. document put it later, the agency at higher levels "judged that he did not merit detention by the C.I.A." Haqqani ended up in the custody of the National Directorate of Security and later U.S. military custody, according to the C.I.A. Haqqani told American interlocutors years later that he was tortured. His fate signaled the descent of American counterterrorism policy into black depths of systematic abuse.[20]

NINE

"His Rules Were Different
Than Our Rules"

By the late spring of 2003 the Omega Teams of Special Forces, C.I.A. officers and contractors, eavesdroppers, and Afghan armed reconnaissance militias had settled in a string of mud-fort bases along the Afghan side of the border with Pakistan. The clandestine bases ran from Asadabad in the north to Shkin in the south. The C.I.A.'s private army—Counterterrorist Pursuit Teams, in agency jargon—numbered about seven thousand men, the agency told counterpart services. The forward bases also supported smaller Tactical Humint Teams, or THTs. They consisted of expatriate case officers and Afghan interpreters, often Tajiks and Hazaras whose ethnicity could strain relations with local Pashtuns. All of them could access the national language of Dari but the locals preferred Pashto, which the Tajik and Hazara interpreters did not always speak fluently. The basic task was to talk to locals on what were called "local civil action" trips. "Who wants to cooperate?" the teams would ask, as a participant described it. "Who wants to be a human source? Talk to the tribal elders. It was tough. They were very hesitant to talk with us."

The priorities for collection were "Number One" (Bin Laden), "Number Two" (Zawahiri), or "A.Q.S.L." (Al Qaeda Senior Leadership). Some of the deployed case officers had long experience in the Middle East, if little acquaintance with Pakistan and Afghanistan. Some were retirees in their sixties back on contract. Increasingly, the rotators included very inexperienced case officers fresh out of career training in Virginia. They typically paid their human agents about five hundred dollars a month to wander the border area and report back. The American officers referred to their agents by their national file number, or NFN, which concluded in a number, so that reporting sounded like "NFN37 has departed for Khost and NFN113 is expected from Quetta." The more entrepreneurial Pashtun agents would take a salary from a C.I.A. case officer at Shkin, then walk to Gardez and link up with a D.I.A. Humint team for another thousand dollars. "They were wandering triple-dippers," the participant said. The local agents typically did not have bicycles or motorcycles. They walked. "I'll see you in a month," they would tell a case officer. "It will take a week to walk to my house, two weeks to do the surveillance, and another week to walk back to you."

Navy SEALs supported the THTs with direct raiding capability if a target could be identified. Increasingly the teams were drawn into local violence against the *mukhalafeen,* as they were referred to in Pashto, meaning "rivals" or "opposition." It was a suitably vague term. There were too many violent groups to describe accurately under any one label. They included the Hizb-i-Islami led by Gulbuddin Hekmatyar, known as "H.I.G.," in American jargon, pronounced like "pig," as well as Haqqani commanders, Taliban veterans, timber smugglers, tribal rivals, and local boys enlisted to fight for a salary. The Omega bases contained bored SEALs and Deltas working out every day for weeks at a time with nothing to do, "begging for villages to raid," as the participant put it. "They didn't want to spend too much time confirming the targets."[1]

It also became apparent that the very presence of forward-deployed Americans in the border bases provoked local attacks, almost reflexively. This was the case at Asadabad Firebase, which lay in a river basin in Kunar Province, a forbidding region of peaks and gorges stretching northwest from Jalalabad. Elements of the 82nd Airborne, a pair of Special Forces A-Teams, and a C.I.A. contingent shared a compound perhaps two hundred yards by two hundred yards. Its mud-brick walls were ten feet high and two feet thick. Kashmiri guerrillas had used the fort during

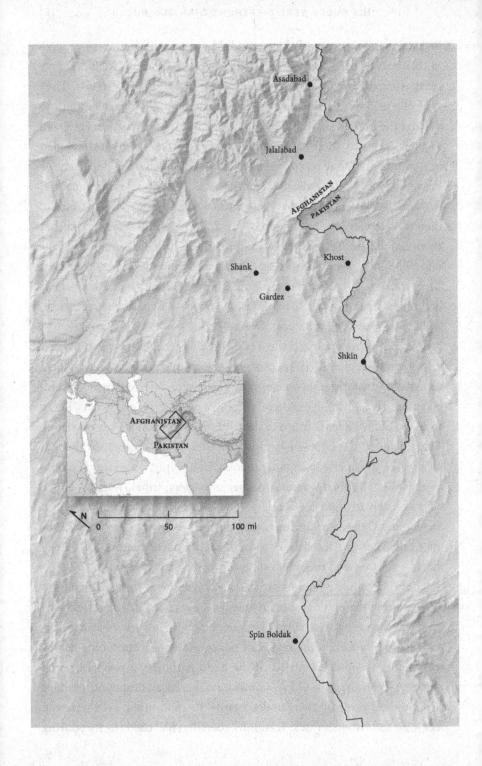

the 1990s, to train to fight against India's military. A dozen flat-roofed huts attached to the outer walls served as bunks, offices, storage depots, and detention centers. It was cold and muddy, a "Third World cesspool," in the words of Brian Halstead, a noncommissioned Special Forces officer who served there. At irregular intervals—sometimes several times daily—someone out there among the woods-shrouded *mukhalafeen* shot off artillery rockets at the firebase. The valley was quiet but for birds and the rustle of pines, so the Americans could hear the crack of a rocket launch and then count the seconds before it exploded nearby. The attacks were unnerving but usually poorly aimed.[2]

Halstead was the Special Forces intelligence officer in charge of force protection in Kunar. Every time a rocket smashed into or near the base he analyzed the crater, examined radar to trace the location from where it had been fired, and plotted the patterns on a map. He also talked to locals for insight. He had been serving on Special Forces A-Teams for two decades around the world and knew by now that it was essential to spend "a lot of time and effort building personal relationships. Last thing you want to do is go out there and get in the middle of somebody's tribal vendettas."[3]

Asadabad Firebase's principal local contact was Said Fazal Akbar, the governor of Kunar, who had been running a clothing store in Oakland on September 11. He served Hamid Karzai as a spokesman before the interim leader appointed him as his man in Asadabad. Akbar occupied the governor's mansion and brought along his son Hyder, then eighteen, who had been raised in California and spoke fluent American-accented English. (He would soon attend Yale University.) Their outpost of the Karzai regime was barely more rooted in Kunar society than the firebase's roving squads of bearded Americans.

At some point that spring, a C.I.A. colleague mentioned to Brian Halstead the name Abdul Wali as a suspected organizer of the rocketing they endured. The basis for this suspicion wasn't clear, but if the grounds for suspicion were adequate, one of Halstead's standard procedures was to try to "puck" the suspect, to conduct further questioning. "Puck" was an invented verb derived from "Person Under Control," or PUC, a category of prisoner status under post-2001 Pentagon policy. To puck someone at a firebase was to incarcerate them for a limited number of days for intelligence interrogation, to determine if the individual should be released or transferred to the larger detention facility at Bagram Airfield. That spring, Asadabad Firebase informed Governor Akbar about Abdul Wali and the word went out to local villages that he was a wanted man.[4]

One mid-June afternoon, Abdul Wali appeared at Governor Akbar's compound with his brother and some elders from his village. The governor's son Hyder joined the meeting. Abdul Wali told them he was afraid that an informer had ratted him out to the Americans as part of a tribal feud. The governor assured him that if he was innocent the Akbars would provide *zamanat* about the Americans, a kind of guarantee or personal backing under Islamic law. All Abdul Wali had to do was go talk to the Americans, to straighten things out.

Abdul Wali was frightened. He said he had heard rumors of torture at the American base, "everything from beating and sleep deprivation to disembowelment."

"That's nonsense," Governor Akbar assured his guest. "I know the Americans. I've been there myself. The Americans don't do things like that."

But Abdul Wali was still afraid to go to the base. Finally, the governor said, "My son is here from America. He's schooled in English and he'll go and escort you to the base and he'll be your translator."

That satisfied him. They drove to Asadabad Firebase in a pickup truck. On the way, Abdul Wali was shaking a little. Hyder tried to tell him to calm down.[5]

The Americans received them in an interview room near the gate. Brian Halstead opened the questioning calmly and took notes. Were you ever involved with the Taliban? Were you involved with Al Qaeda? Were you involved with H.I.G.? Abdul Wali answered no. Then Halstead asked if he had recently been to Pakistan. Abdul Wali admitted that he had, to settle some debts, but he couldn't remember how long he had stayed or what dates he had traveled.

Hyder Akbar thought this apparent forgetfulness reflected local understandings of time. Visiting his father in Kunar reminded him of a time travel movie he saw advertised as a kid in California where one of the characters in the film declares, "My father is stuck in the fourteenth century—I have to go get him back." When Hyder came to Kunar he felt he was "going to visit my dad in the fourteenth century." One of the time warp's characteristics was that nobody kept calendars or made specific appointments. "People don't know how old they are. They don't keep track of time." Yet he could tell in the interview room that Abdul Wali's vagueness about his trip to Pakistan was raising suspicion among some of his interrogators.[6]

David Passaro was one of two C.I.A. personnel in the room. He was a former policeman, twice divorced, who looked like an out-of-shape Sylvester Stallone, Hyder thought. He was a C.I.A. contractor, not a career officer. About 85 percent of the C.I.A. personnel who conducted interrogations after 2001 were contractors. Interrogation had never been a skill taught at "the Farm," the C.I.A.'s career training academy. David Passaro's boss, the Asadabad chief of base, went by the cover name Steven Jones. He was a career officer who, like Passaro, was a former police officer. The two C.I.A. men joined the questioning of Abdul Wali, but Jones seemed to become bored after ten or fifteen minutes and left, according to Hyder Akbar.[7]

Passaro became aggressive. He leaned into Abdul Wali, stared at him menacingly, spoke in a contemptuous tone, and threatened him. "If you are lying to me, you—your whole family, your kids—they could all get hurt from this." Hyder Akbar became upset and stopped translating. Another interpreter took over. Passaro only became angrier. Finally he announced that Abdul Wali would be pucked.

Passaro asked his prisoner, "Is there anything you want to give to your family" before you are taken away? Abdul Wali stuttered that there was nothing. He was almost in a state of shock, Hyder thought, because it sounded as if Passaro was saying, "We're taking you out back and shooting you."

Hyder was sickened. He had just finished high school. He was an American citizen who had returned to help the war-broken country of his family's origins, yet here he was watching an American-led version of "what the Soviets did in Afghanistan."

As Hyder departed, he put his hand on Abdul Wali's shoulder to reassure him. "Just tell the truth," he advised. "Just tell the truth."[8]

Soldiers handcuffed the prisoner, placed an empty sandbag over his
head, and led him to a detention cell, where he was shackled to the floor.
Enlisted soldiers guarded Abdul Wali on four-hour shifts. That night
David Passaro turned up at the cell while the soldier Matthew Johnson
was on duty. Passaro announced that Abdul Wali was a C.I.A. prisoner
and that he would be handling the interrogation. He warned Johnson
that his techniques might be harsher than what military guards were
used to seeing. "His rules were different than our rules" was the way
Johnson would remember Passaro's explanation. "He didn't fall under
the Geneva Convention, as we did. . . . His only rule was not to cause
permanent injury."[9]

Passaro entered an adjoining cell, "got a chair, made a lot of racket in
there, broke a chair apart, came out and said he was ready to go into the
room with Abdul Wali."

He kicked the cell door open and hurled in a two-by-four, striking
Abdul Wali. He slammed the prisoner's head against the wall and shoved
him onto the floor face-first, all while the prisoner was shackled, cuffed,
and still had a bag over his head. Passaro hoisted Abdul Wali into a stress
position, squatting with arms out, and questioned him. Dissatisfied, Passaro hit him, kicked him, and knocked him back onto the floor. "If you
don't give the answers I want," Passaro said, "it's going to get worse."[10]

David Passaro's belief that he operated by special C.I.A. rules traced
back to an initially ad hoc, confused response inside the Counterterrorist Center after September 11 to the problem of prisoner detention
and interrogation. President Bush's covert action Memorandum of Notification six days after the attacks gave the C.I.A. authority to kill terrorists, as well as to detain and question them. The agency was poorly
prepared to run prisons. On September 27, C.I.A. headquarters cabled
stations worldwide that any future agency prison would be designed to
meet "U.S. POW Standards." Official C.I.A. policy at the time held that
all direct interrogations carried out by agency personnel should follow

the U.S. Army Field Manual standards, which prohibited physical abuse. After initial discussions about detention planning that fall, as the Afghan war sped forward, Cofer Black wrote C.I.A director Tenet that having the Pentagon take charge of all detention facilities would be the "best option." If the C.I.A. maintained its own prisons, Black warned, "Captured terrorists may be held days, months or years [and] the likelihood of exposure will grow over time." Eventual press exposure of the operation "could inflame public opinion against a host government and the U.S." He urged Tenet to persuade Rumsfeld to take responsibility.[11]

As Al Qaeda prisoners fled Afghanistan after Tora Bora and fell into Pakistani custody, the question of whether the C.I.A. should adopt an independent detention program became more urgent. The agency had a dark history in this field, as career officers in C.T.C. and on the Seventh Floor well knew. During the Cold War, the agency had produced the KUBARK Counterintelligence Interrogation Manual, which provided for the use of techniques such as sensory deprivation, "threats and fear, debility, pain . . . and hypnosis." The agency brutally interrogated a Soviet defector, Yuri Nosenko, between 1964 and 1967, believing that he was an impostor. During the 1980s, some of those techniques found their way into the C.I.A.'s Human Resource Exploitation Training Manual, which was shared with liaison services in Latin America. During the 1990s, the agency had reversed policy to align with the Army's compliance with the Geneva Conventions. (One reason the military favored humane treatment of prisoners was the probability that its own uniformed personnel would be captured; the Pentagon had sought before 2001 to promote positive reciprocity.) Yet the Counterterrorist Center nonetheless managed a covert program that involved its officers, at least indirectly, with the torture of terrorism suspects, right up until September 11.

This was the counterterrorism practice known as "rendition" or "extraordinary rendition." If an Egyptian radical with ties to violence was arrested in Albania, the C.I.A. might take possession of the prisoner secretly and fly him on a private jet to Cairo to hand the suspect over to Egyptian authorities. American presidents since Ronald Reagan had approved the practice. The program allowed the Counterterrorist Center to work with allied intelligence and police services to keep terrorist suspects

in custody when there was not sufficient evidence to bring the suspects to
the United States to face American criminal charges.

Several of the countries that partnered with the C.I.A. in this way—
Egypt, Jordan, and Syria, among them—had documented records of extensive human rights abuses against prisoners. As a practical matter, in
those countries, it was common knowledge that the secret police routinely and often grotesquely tortured prisoners, including Islamist radicals. Human Rights Watch, Amnesty International, and even the State
Department had published libraries of documentary evidence. To evade
this stain, the C.I.A. officially required governments receiving suspects
under the rendition program to promise not to abuse them. But few involved were naïve enough to think this was anything but a face-saving
exchange of paper for the sake of lawyers and Congress.[12]

In addition to the moral problem, indirect interrogations by secret
police employing torture produced imperfect intelligence. The agency
had acknowledged in congressional briefings that torture produced false
testimony. Even where abusive questioning by Egyptian or Syrian police
might also produce reliable information, "We couldn't control interviews
done by others, had limited ability to ask time-urgent follow-on questions," and were constrained by whatever the liaison service wanted to
withhold or invent for its own reasons, as the Counterterrorist Center's
Jose Rodriguez put it. Even close allies didn't have the same interest in
prioritizing American security when conducting prisoner interrogations.
Still, during the late 1990s, the Clinton administration had embraced
rendition of terrorism prisoners to countries such as Egypt as an essential
tool in its campaign against Al Qaeda. About seventy prisoners were
shuttled from one country to another by the C.I.A. during the Clinton
years. The branch also carried out more straightforward renditions,
bringing indicted criminals to the United States to face trial.[13] The Rendition, Detention and Interrogation Group inside the Counterterrorist
Center contracted for Gulfstream jets, pilots, and security guards and
managed these transfers. Yet the renditions group was mainly a prisoner
transfer outfit. It operated no prisons of its own and had no cadre of expert interrogators.

The Counterterrorist Center had another connection to the black arts of torture. Its Psychological Operations group had ties to Special Forces counterparts at Fort Bragg. The base was home to the Survival, Evasion, Resistance and Escape program, or S.E.R.E., which sought to prepare pilots and other personnel for the possibility of capture. The program used psychologists to act as enemy interrogators and deliberately placed thousands of American trainees under intense physical and psychological pressure, to help them learn what they might have to endure in captivity. The Air Force and the Navy had used waterboarding on thousands of trainees as part of the curriculum. The C.I.A.'s Counterterrorist Center had several ties to the S.E.R.E. program. Ric Prado, one of Cofer Black's deputies, had gone through the training when he was an Air Force Special Operations rescue specialist, before he joined the C.I.A., although he had not been placed on a waterboard. The agency also maintained ties to James Mitchell, an Air Force psychologist who had worked in the S.E.R.E. program, and Bruce Jessen, who had also worked there. Mitchell retired from the military in mid-2001. That year the C.I.A. hired him as an adviser. By the following spring he was consulting for the Counterterrorist Center. Mitchell and Jessen were familiar with a document recovered in Manchester, England, that appeared to be a manual for Al Qaeda and allied volunteers, suggesting how they might resist interrogation. They wrote a paper for the C.I.A. about how to recognize when Al Qaeda prisoners might be resisting interrogation. They pointed out that the manual instructed Al Qaeda prisoners to "stick to a pre-coordinated cover story during interrogation, request legal council [sic], complain about treatment and conditions, ask for medical attention, and then report that they have been tortured and mistreated regardless of the actual events." At C.T.C., Mitchell joined a discussion about how to overcome such tactics through the application of various kinds of pressure on prisoners. Some C.I.A. officers threw around terms like "learned helplessness," an idea derived from experiments carried out on dogs by University of Pennsylvania psychologists during the 1960s. In the C.I.A.'s distorted adaptation of the work, it considered whether, if a prisoner concluded that he had lost control over his conditions, in addition to becoming passive and depressed, he might also cooperate with his jailers. A problem with this hypothesis was that "learned helplessness" actually describes conditions where the subject is so broken and discouraged that he won't even try to escape, given the opportunity. It was not a good way to encourage cooperation—that required the prisoner to have a sense of hope for improvement. Mitchell and Jessen later said that they tried to impress upon C.I.A. officers new to the field that the purpose of S.E.R.E. interrogation techniques was to induce the prisoner to cooperate.[14]

Early in 2002, an Al Qaeda operative named Abu Zubaydah, who was well known to the Counterterrorist Center, surfaced in telephone intercepts from Pakistan. He was a Palestinian who had been raised in Saudi Arabia and had been one of the few Al Qaeda suspects to speak openly on the telephone and use e-mail over a period of years. His visibility and his involvement in arranging travel and housing for Al Qaeda members heightened the C.I.A.'s interest in him. The early 2002 intercepts showed that Zubaydah was in Pakistan but not where. The C.T.C. formed a task force to hunt him down, with forward elements deployed to Islamabad Station.[15]

In late March, anticipating Zubaydah's capture, the agency renewed debate about its detention and interrogation options. On March 27, the C.I.A. produced a PowerPoint presentation, "Options for Incarcerating Abu Zubaydah." The presentation rejected putting the Pentagon in control "in large part because of the lack of security and the fact that Abu Zubaydah would have to be declared to the International Committee of the Red Cross," as Senate investigators later put it, summarizing the classified slide deck. The PowerPoint also raised doubts about Guantánamo Bay because of its "lack of secrecy" and the "possible loss of control to U.S. military and/or F.B.I."[16]

On March 28, Pakistani forces raided a house in Faisalabad, Pakistan, shot and wounded Abu Zubaydah, and placed him in custody at a Pakistani military hospital. George Tenet approved a proposal to approach Thailand about hosting a secret prison where Zubaydah could be held and questioned. Tenet discussed the plan with National Security Adviser Condoleezza Rice and her deputy, Stephen Hadley, so they could brief President Bush. On March 29, Bush approved the C.I.A.'s plan.[17]

The F.B.I. sent agents to question Zubaydah. The C.I.A. sent a career officer to run the base and also dispatched James Mitchell for advice. Abu Zubaydah was placed in an all-white room that was lit twenty-four hours a day. (Mitchell later defended the detention conditions as necessary to supervise the prisoner's wounds and medical care.) The C.I.A.'s team clashed with F.B.I. agents, including an Arabic-speaking agent named Ali H. Soufan, who sought to use the interrogation methods of law enforcement, which are designed to establish a close rapport with the prisoner, to draw him gradually into disclosures, and to build a legal case that would stand scrutiny in a court of law. The C.I.A.'s officers, still animated by fear of some unknown Al Qaeda nuclear plot, urgently sought information from the prisoner that would prevent future attacks. The C.I.A.'s officers and consulting psychologist acquired "tremendous influence," an F.B.I. agent reported to his headquarters.[18]

The C.I.A.'s prisons now departed from Army Field Manual and F.B.I. practices into a science fiction–tinged dystopia of intimidation and dominance over prisoners. A C.I.A. cable from April described Zubaydah's cell in Thailand as "white with no natural lighting or windows, but with four halogen lights pointed into the cell. An air conditioner was also in the room. A white curtain separated the interrogation room from the cell. . . . Security officers wore all black uniforms, including boots, gloves, balaclavas, and goggles," to protect the officers' identities, but also to prevent the prisoner "from seeing the security guards as individuals who he may attempt to establish a relationship or dialogue with."[19]

The stage was set for the most shockingly bureaucratized descent into the application of pseudoscience on human subjects by the C.I.A. since the agency's notorious MK Ultra Project, during the 1950s and 1960s, when the agency used L.S.D. and other drugs on involuntary subjects in an effort to develop techniques for mind control.

Early in May 2002, Tenet informed Cofer Black that he wanted to make a change in the Counterterrorist Center's leadership. Tenet said he was proud of Black's work before and after September 11, and retained confidence in him, but that it was time for a change. "I did not volunteer to leave," Black admitted later. "And of course, I will say that I was tired. No doubt about that."

His struggles to elevate the counterterrorism mission within the C.I.A. bureaucracy had placed Black in relentless conflict with colleagues over slots and budgets. These were "trying psychological circumstances because there was a lot of competition with other components in the Agency," as he put it. "So we were having to fight all the time." Tenet offered Black any job he wanted at C.I.A., but Black and his wife did not want to go overseas again and he certainly didn't want to run a part of the bureaucracy that had been resisting counterterrorism, as he saw it. He ended up accepting nomination as the State Department's global counterterrorism ambassador. Tenet's decision to replace Black was seen by some at C.T.C. as a revanchist victory by James Pavitt and the regional leaders in the mainstream Directorate of Operations.[20]

The Africa Division clan that had gathered around Black before and after September 11 now scattered. Rich Blee rotated out of Kabul Station that spring. The C.I.A. offered him a management position, but he wanted something closer to the action, so he contacted the F.B.I. and asked if they would take him on as a special C.I.A. adviser at the bureau, starting in the summer of 2002. Hank Crumpton took an academic sabbatical to study for a master's degree at the Johns Hopkins School of Advanced International Studies.

Tenet elevated Jose Rodriguez to replace Black as the Counterterrorist Center's director. "To many insiders," Rodriguez recognized, "it was quite a surprise." He had spent the great majority of his career in Latin America and had "only modest experience in counterterrorism," yet he was being handed a position where "you might expect to find the most seasoned Arabic-speaking Middle East hand." Rodriguez had grown up in South America and the Caribbean before arriving in the United States at about eighteen to attend the University of Florida. After finishing law school there, he joined the C.I.A. as an operative. He was a classmate of Cofer Black's at the Farm. He rose into the Senior Intelligence Service but had setbacks. At one point he was removed as Latin America Division chief in the Directorate of Operations after what he considered to

be "a very biased and unfair Inspector General investigation" of actions
he had taken to aid an imprisoned friend. Yet Rodriguez had suffered
no serious harm from that reprimand and went on to run the C.I.A. station in Mexico City. He was a hard-line but popular figure, humorous,
an attentive manager, but he was not known as a geopolitical thinker or
a sophisticated Washington hand. He avoided delivering congressional
briefings, sending more polished analysts in his stead. As evidenced by
his dustup with the C.I.A.'s inspector general, his antennae about what
might be regarded as controversial or unethical were not always reliable.[21]

Rodriguez was very close to Ric Prado, the S.E.R.E. graduate who
had worked on the front lines of the Contra guerrilla war against the
Sandinistas in Nicaragua. Prado had no role in decision making about
interrogation methods for C.I.A. prisoners, but he and Rodriguez both
regarded squeamishness about harsh interrogations as misplaced and
naïve, a symptom of "political correctness," in Rodriguez's phrase, that
had to be set aside given that "we were under the constant threat of new
and even more deadly attacks, and time was of the essence." Prado reminded him, referring to his own experience of S.E.R.E., alongside many
other Special Forces trainees, "I've been through this crap and so has every
G.I. Joe that ever wore a funny hat in the military. It's not plucking finger-
nails." Of course, the military men who endured S.E.R.E. were volunteers
and were given a safe word to exclaim if they felt in jeopardy. That would
not be true of C.I.A. prisoners.[22]

Rodriguez felt the F.B.I. had done what it could to interrogate Zubaydah but when the prisoner recovered his strength, he stopped cooperating. In July 2002, Rodriguez asked Mitchell how long it would take them
to put "more aggressive" pressure on the prisoner than the noise and
sleep deprivation that had already been employed, in order to determine
whether Zubaydah would break or was the sort of hard man to "take any
secrets with him to the grave." Mitchell and Rodriguez met often. On
July 8, they attended a meeting with C.I.A. officers from ALEC Station,
the Office of Medical Services, agency lawyers, an F.B.I. liaison, and others. Afterward, according to Mitchell, he drew up a list of possible techniques at the C.T.C. director's request. He said later that he was concerned
that, otherwise, the government would just proceed to beat Zubaydah

up, and that would produce, in his experience, no useful information. Mitchell's initial list of techniques did not include waterboarding, according to him. He added that technique later after reflecting upon how, in S.E.R.E. training, as he now told Rodriguez, "the thing that is rumored to [be] most effective on Navy fighter pilots is waterboarding." Mitchell "had no idea" if it was legal. He thought the C.I.A. would bring someone in to evaluate that. Rodriguez asked Mitchell to join the effort. A career C.I.A. officer would control the secret prison and was ultimately responsible, but Mitchell would be the lead subject matter expert. Mitchell speculated that they would know whether Zubaydah would break in "thirty days" if they were given permission to apply the new techniques.[23]

The F.B.I. withdrew its agents. Director Robert Mueller, a Princeton-educated former Marine and federal prosecutor, was a politically sophisticated Washington hand. Arriving at the bureau that summer, Rich Blee advocated for joint interrogations teams made up of bureau agents and C.I.A. officers, teams that would combine F.B.I. interrogation expertise with the C.I.A.'s worldwide intelligence collection. But Mueller could see where the C.I.A. was going in Thailand, with Tenet's full support, and he wanted no part of it. Tenet fronted for Jose Rodriguez with the Bush White House. John Rizzo, the C.I.A.'s general counsel, insisted that the Department of Justice write memos expressing an opinion about whether the harsh techniques Mitchell described were legal. By August 1, Jay S. Bybee, an assistant attorney general, had issued internal classified memoranda later infamous as "the torture memos." They ratified the legality of ten of the C.I.A.'s proposed "enhanced interrogation techniques," including waterboarding, but not "mock burial," a second severe technique that Mitchell had originally listed and that Rodriguez had proposed.[24]

Even though ten months had passed and there had been no follow-on attacks even approaching the scale of September 11, there remained "a hysteria" that more attacks were coming, as a senior intelligence official involved put it. "That was just the consensus." A second factor was that the C.I.A. and allied European intelligence services had developed scant insights into Al Qaeda's leadership despite a full year of effort. Bin Laden and Zawahiri had .disappeared. They and other leaders had curtailed electronic communications. Human agent reporting such as the "fire ant" program along the Afghanistan-Pakistan border had produced only fragmented and even counterproductive intelligence. Fresh Al Qaeda detainees looked more promising. Abu Zubaydah's knowledge of Al Qaeda operations would be recent enough to be helpful. If he could be made to disclose what he knew accurately, he could provide lifesaving insights not otherwise available, the thinking went. "We were flying blind," a former senior British intelligence officer recalled. "We didn't know who was where and what they were doing. Detainee debriefings were all we had." Robert Gates, a career C.I.A. analyst who later served as secretary of defense for both the Bush and Obama administrations, later blamed the "overload" of threat reporting arriving each day at the desks of cabinet and senior White House officials, with "all the filters" off and no sound way to determine which intelligence was reliable and which was not. "A lot of the measures, including the renditions, Guantánamo, the enhanced interrogation techniques—all were out of a sense of desperation to get information because we had so little." Rodriguez remained convinced that he had made the right decisions, sought the right approvals, and delivered results in fresh intelligence from prisoners subjected to waterboarding that justified his risk taking. Officers in the Bin Laden unit of C.T.C. and elsewhere at the agency, including in Tenet's office, backed him fully. If there were dissenters in the C.I.A. informed of the decisions and willing to risk their careers to stop the plan in the summer of 2002, their whistle-blowing remains unknown.

One basic problem was competence and experience. At the C.I.A. and MI6, its British counterpart, "Detainee interrogation is no part of a foreign intelligence officer's training," as the former British officer put it. So the C.I.A. "turned to contractors who claimed to know what they were doing."[25] The moral and strategic failures that flowed from the C.I.A. interrogation program born that summer, as well as similar programs in Iraq and Guantánamo (approved by Defense Secretary Donald Rumsfeld), had many consequences. One was to color the experience a significant number of Afghans had of the American intervention in their country.

Bagram served as the prisoner collection and transshipment point for the C.I.A. and the Pentagon. Record keeping by the C.I.A. was so poor that investigators later had difficulty piecing together which prisoners had been under the agency's control at Bagram and what had been done to them. Beatings, shouting, humiliation, and threats were commonplace. The prisoners were held in about half a dozen large cells wrapped in barbed wire, each named after an Al Qaeda attack: Nairobi, USS *Cole*, et cetera. Interrogators occasionally tried to convert prisoners to Christianity. Every Afghan who passed through Bagram—whether as a prisoner, an interpreter, or prison staff—became part of an ever denser network, spreading testimony to family, village, and tribe about the Americans.

At C.I.A. headquarters, desperation, fear, groupthink, pseudoscience, and misplaced faith in aggression and the humiliation of enemy prisoners shaped the agency's program as it grew. Forward in Afghanistan, managerial incompetence, stupidity, and cruelty were the more important factors. As Afghanistan looked more and more like a backwater without a significant Al Qaeda presence, and as the invasion of Iraq beckoned, the C.I.A. increasingly deployed rookies, lightly experienced officers, and officers with troubled records to Bagram, Kandahar, and the Omega bases. The agency's talent pool in the clandestine service was thin. Demographically, it looked like a barbell—a sizable cadre of experienced Senior Intelligence Service and colonel-level officers toward the ends of their careers, and a sizable influx of rookies inducted in a massive surge after 2001. Generally, the C.I.A.'s "A" team now deployed to Iraq, the wider Middle East, and Pakistan, some officers working on Afghanistan concluded. The "B" team too often went to Afghanistan, they believed.

Rich Blee's successor as Kabul station chief, who took charge in the summer of 2002, oversaw the construction of a new C.I.A. prison on the ten-acre grounds of a former brick factory north of Kabul, which became known as the "Salt Pit." It opened in September. The windows "were blacked out and detainees were kept in total darkness," investigators with access to classified C.I.A. cables from this period reported. "The guards monitored detainees using headlamps and loud music was played constantly.... While in their cells, detainees were shackled to the wall and given buckets for human waste."[26]

The new station chief's tour proved to be a disaster, in the estimation of some senior colleagues. He stopped counseling Karzai on the grounds that the interim leader was irrelevant compared with the warlords. He assigned a junior officer on his first assignment overseas to supervise the agency's prison. That junior officer's career was off to a troubled start. He "has issues with judgment and maturity [and his] potential behavior in the field is also worrisome," a supervisor wrote. In November, Bruce Jessen, the former S.E.R.E. psychologist, visited Afghanistan and assisted the inexperienced C.I.A. warden in an interrogation of an Afghan suspected of extremism named Gul Rahman. The prisoner endured two days of "sleep deprivation, auditory overload, total darkness, isolation, a cold shower, and rough treatment," according to a C.I.A. cable. Jessen later admitted to slapping Rahman once, to assess his reactions, but denied that he had been involved in more abusive action. He blamed the professional C.I.A. officer and his guards at the prison facility for using unauthorized rough techniques. A few days after Jessen departed, noting that Rahman was being held in "deplorable conditions," the junior C.I.A. warden, who has never been formally identified, ordered Gul Rahman shackled in a position that left him on a cold concrete floor in only a sweatshirt. The Afghan died overnight, probably of hypothermia.[27]

After that death, Jose Rodriguez directed the Counterterrorist Center's renditions group to take charge of the Detention and Interrogation Program. As Senate investigators later pointed out, however, "many of the same individuals within the C.I.A. . . . . remained key figures" in the program and "received no reprimand or sanction for Rahman's death."[28]

In Virginia, the targeting analysts at ALEC Station, including several of the analysts whose warnings had been overlooked before September 11, urged the use of harsh techniques on Al Qaeda suspects. They pressed colleagues in cables, attended interrogations in person, and urged harsh measures even when C.I.A. wardens felt it had become inhumane or useless to continue. The analysts at ALEC appear to have exercised an unusual kind of moral influence on the interrogation program at the C.I.A. Having issued warnings before September 11, they now insisted again, with higher credibility, that anyone who opposed their willingness to brutalize Al Qaeda detainees for insight into the next attack could wind up with blood on their hands.[29]

The effect of harsh interrogations on Afghanistan's post-Taliban environment received hardly any formal analysis. In fact, by late 2002 and early 2003, the C.I.A.'s senior leaders, including those at the Counterterrorist Center, had stopped paying much attention to Afghanistan at all. That winter, C.I.A. inspector general John Helgerson, a career analyst who regarded the detention and interrogation program as unsound, opened an investigation that would play a significant role in documenting the program's abuses and setting the stage for its eventual demise. Tenet told Helgerson he was "not very familiar" with what the C.I.A. was doing in Afghanistan or with "medium value" prisoners in general, a category assigned to many Afghan detainees. General Counsel Scott Muller said he had "no idea who is responsible" for the Salt Pit's detention site. Jose Rodriguez told Helgerson he did not focus on it because he had "other higher priorities." Yet the Senate's investigation later found that at least several dozen of the C.I.A. prisoners subjected to enhanced interrogation techniques experienced them in Afghanistan.[30]

The same harsh C.I.A. interrogation practices could be applied to agency prisoners held at Kandahar and the Omega firebases along the Pakistan border. In early December 2002, immediately after Gul Rahman's death, George Tenet sent a formal message to all C.I.A. stations and bases: "When C.I.A. officers are involved in interrogation of a detainee, the conduct of such interrogation should not encompass any physiological aspects. For example, direct physical contact, unusual mental duress, unusual physical restraints or deliberate environmental deprivation beyond those reasonably required to ensure the safety and security of our officers and to prevent the escape of the detainee without prior and specific headquarters advice." Yet even after this order, C.I.A. officers could strip a prisoner naked, keep him in a stress position for seventy-two hours, and douse him with cold water repeatedly without prior approval, if such approval was not "feasible." In practice, such abuse continued without significant review.

At Asadabad, the C.I.A.'s David Passaro had every reason to believe that his aggression toward Abdul Wali was consistent with agency norms in Kabul. Passaro would have passed through Bagram and seen how detention operated there. In Afghanistan, an atmosphere of impunity and neglect evolved during 2003. That year, Kabul Station acknowledged in a cable to headquarters, "We have made the unsettling discovery that we are holding a number of detainees about whom we know very little." The majority of these detainees "have not been debriefed for months and, in some cases for over a year."[31]

Certainly, Passaro showed no qualms about allowing military guards and an Afghan interpreter to observe him as he pummeled Abdul Wali. Steven Jones, the career officer who supervised Passaro, sanctioned sleep deprivation, at a minimum. On the evening after Abdul Wali was pucked, Jones wrote to his wife, "Our prisoner remains uncooperative, but we didn't let him sleep last night. We think it will take about four days before he wears down and starts to talk."[32]

After the beating he endured the first night, Abdul Wali gestured to his military guards, urging them to use their shotgun or pistols to kill him. Instead, on Passaro's instructions, the guards kept the prisoner in the "Iron Cross" position—knees bent halfway, back against the wall, arms out. They instructed Abdul Wali through an interpreter that whenever he was ready to talk about what he really knew about the rocketing of the firebase, he should say "Dave Dave Dave" to summon his interrogator.[33]

Sergeant Kevin Gatten was on duty on the night of June 20. When he came on shift, he said later, Abdul Wali had "been 24 hours with no sleep, no food, little water, no breaks." He had "some marks" on him from the beatings and "he was acting delirious, knocking his head up against the wall, talking to his shoes." He gripped his abdomen, apparently in pain.

After Gatten arrived, Abdul Wali called out, through the interpreter, "Dave Dave Dave."

"Are you sure you want him to come down?" the guards asked.[34]

Passaro drove up in a truck a little later, his lights on, in violation of the base's nighttime security protocols. Gatten was annoyed—it was typical of C.I.A. to disregard discipline the military tried to enforce on their shared base. Passaro climbed out holding a plastic cup of what smelled like bourbon or scotch. (Under General Order No. 1, the U.S. military banned alcohol for American troops in Afghanistan. The C.I.A. allowed booze on forward bases. At Asadabad, the agency kept beer, bourbon, and scotch.) "Hold this," Passaro said as he gave his drink to one of the sergeants. He gestured for Gatten to follow him into Abdul Wali's cell.

Passaro resumed his questioning. Who gave you your orders? Where are the weapons caches?

"I don't know," Abdul Wali answered repeatedly.[35]

Whenever he professed ignorance, Passaro turned off his flashlight. Gatten couldn't see in the blackness but he could hear smacks, "like a body being hit," and then Abdul Wali "groaning, crying . . . just making painful sounds."

"Why are you hitting me?" Abdul Wali asked at one point.

"Don't be saying or doing anything," Passaro answered. "You don't know if I'm hitting you." (The prisoner had a bag over his head.) "It could be my guard hitting you. It could be anybody." This upset Gatten further, since, as he said later, "I wasn't hitting him."

The questioning and beating went on for about ninety minutes. Then Passaro walked out.

"Keep him stressed," he instructed. "Make sure he doesn't sleep."[36]

Gatten returned to duty the next day, June 21. Abdul Wali now "looked like he had just gotten into a fight. . . . His face was covered in bruises. He had bruises on his hands. He was staggering. The guy couldn't move. [He] just kept talking—not to us, just talking to himself, to the wall, to his shoes."[37]

Steven Jones, the C.I.A. base chief, was in the office when one of the men watching Abdul Wali turned up to say that Jones should take a look at the prisoner. Jones found Abdul Wali lying on his side, groaning. "He looked white in color and obviously was in distress," Jones recalled. The base medics put him on oxygen and intravenous fluids. But Abdul Wali died an hour later.

Major Mark Miller, the base's Army commander, arrived soon after. He was "very angry," as Jones put it.[38] That afternoon they summoned Governor Akbar and his son Hyder back to the firebase. They sat on the floor of a meeting room.

"Unfortunately, we have some bad news," Miller began. "Unfortunately, Abdul Wali passed away."

The governor shook his head. "That's no good," he said in English.

Passaro described Abdul Wali's interrogation. He told the Afghans the prisoner had been fed PowerBars and had not been harmed. However, Passaro continued, the prisoner had sometimes tried to break out of his shackles and hit his head against the wall.[39]

The Afghans inspected the body. Miller explained that his military superiors wanted to perform an autopsy. The governor insisted this would only compound the crisis because, "to people in Kunar, an autopsy will merely serve as proof that the Americans are torturers."

After some effort, Governor Akbar persuaded the Americans not to touch Abdul Wali further. The prisoner's family arrived to receive his corpse. The Americans gave them about $2,000 for their loss.[40]

TEN

Mr. Big

By 2003, it was evident to many Afghans in Kabul that the Bush administration had turned its attention to Iraq and had handed the day-to-day management of their country's recovery to their native son, Zalmay Khalilzad, the unlikely Republican operative. In the White House, Khalilzad was seen as an immigrant success story and a regional specialist. In Kabul, he was also understood as the product of his family and ethnic history. His father came from the east of the country, from a tribe of the Gilzai federation, the less aristocratic of the two principal Pashtun tribal groupings. He had only an elementary-school education and worked as a midlevel clerk for the provincial finance department in Mazar-i-Sharif. Zalmay was his eldest son. Around 1965, the family moved to Kabul. In high school, Zalmay entered the American Field Service exchange program, by which Afghan teenagers studied at an American high school for a year while living with a local family. He flew off to New York and rode across America in a bus, struggling to make himself understood with his limited English, marveling at wonders: massive highway bridges, ubiquitous electricity, the prevalence of television. In Modesto he joined the Pera family of Ceres, California, in a region of the Central Valley known for the Gallo family's winery business.[1]

Later Khalilzad enrolled at the American University of Beirut, under a U.S. Agency for International Development program designed to educate future leaders. At the University of Chicago, he earned a doctoral degree under Albert Wohlstetter, the influential nuclear war strategist who also mentored Paul Wolfowitz and Richard Perle, who would become prominent neoconservatives. During the Reagan administration, Khalilzad worked at the Pentagon on nuclear war planning. After a few years he moved to the State Department to work on the Afghan war as well as Iran and Iraq. By now a committed Republican, Khalilzad spent the Clinton years in academia, business consulting, and think tanks.

In December 2000, after the United States Supreme Court awarded the presidency to George W. Bush, Dick Cheney appointed him head of the transition team at the Pentagon. But Khalilzad and Donald Rumsfeld didn't get along. Condoleezza Rice found a refuge for him at the National Security Council. After September 11, Khalilzad joined the Bonn negotiations that created the Karzai government as part of a broader plan of elections and the rewriting of the Afghan constitution. During 2002, he flew in and out of Kabul as a White House special envoy, to the chagrin of Ambassador Robert Finn, the Turkish linguist, who could not hope to compete with Khalilzad's influence among Afghan politicians or with his White House connections. Yet initially, Khalilzad's influence on post-Taliban Afghanistan was constrained. His N.S.C. portfolio also included Iraq and Iran, which distracted him. The key issues in American policy toward Afghanistan—troop levels, reconstruction, outreach to possible Taliban defectors, burden sharing with European allies— appeared to be settled by Rumsfeld's forceful advocacy of minimalism. Rumsfeld continued to believe that "we did not go there to try to bring prosperity to every corner of Afghanistan." Such a goal "would have amounted to a fool's errand." His skepticism won Bush's endorsement. Their convictions explained the parsimonious budgets and authorities Finn and David Sedney struggled with at the dusty, paraffin-fueled U.S. embassy in Kabul during 2002.[2]

By 2003, the political consequences of minimalism looked more and more disturbing. As Afghans wrote a new constitution that would bring presidential elections at the end of the following year, Hamid Karzai remained weak, certainly in comparison with Fahim, Dostum, Sherzai, Ismail Khan, and other strongmen backed by the C.I.A. during the Taliban's overthrow. Karzai was only an interim leader at the Arg Palace—the "chairman" of a provisional administration—sharing rooms and influence with Zahir Shah upstairs, receiving ministers more powerful than he was. As minister of defense, Fahim controlled the Northern Alliance's well-armed militias, including the incipient Afghan National Army. It wasn't at all clear that Fahim or other generals would follow Karzai's orders if he issued them. Dostum, Sherzai, and Ismail Khan operated their own regional militias and maintained independent liaisons with the C.I.A. President Bush favored Karzai's continuation in office. Yet how could Karzai run for and mobilize votes for the presidency from such a position?

In late April 2003, Rumsfeld flew into the capital and met Karzai on a Sunday in his office at the Arg Palace. Karzai said he needed U.S. bombers and Special Forces to force the strongmen around him to disarm their militias before any election. "Just hit them, and they'll all fall into line" was the essence of Karzai's message.

Rumsfeld said he was not about to do that, but he did promise to think about the dilemmas Karzai outlined.

When he returned to the Pentagon, Rumsfeld initiated a new planning exercise about Afghanistan. Around the same time, Bush asked to see Zalmay Khalilzad at the White House. Khalilzad had just lost a power struggle within the administration over how to manage Iraq after Saddam Hussein's overthrow. Khalilzad favored turning authority over to Iraqi politicians, on an interim basis, as they wrote a new constitution, as had been done in Afghanistan. Bush decided instead to impose an American occupation government, the Coalition Provisional Authority, a decision that left Khalilzad "sad and angry." As a salve, Bush now asked him to become the next U.S. ambassador to Afghanistan. Khalilzad hesitated but soon agreed.

The Pentagon's new planning offered Khalilzad a means to develop a more ambitious U.S. policy for Afghanistan, one that might commit to strengthening Afghan institutions. The scale of the Coalition Provisional Authority and related reconstruction projects planned for Iraq in

2003—in the tens of billions of dollars—belied all previous declarations by Rumsfeld and Bush that they eschewed nation building. Surely there could now be spared a billion or two more for Afghanistan, from which the September 11 attacks had actually originated. Afghanistan was also a vastly more impoverished country than lower-middle-income Iraq. Despite returning refugees, a relative peace, and some reconstruction work, Afghanistan remained among the three or four poorest countries in the world in 2003, alongside Somalia and Chad.

With help from Rumsfeld's policy staff, Khalilzad built out a classified thirty-slide PowerPoint deck titled "Accelerating Success." He sold the plan to the White House and the Pentagon during May and June. It was the administration's first formal program to invest purposefully in the Afghan state. The draft proposed speeding the buildup of the Afghan National Army; breaking Fahim's grip on the Ministry of Defense, to broaden the army's ethnic and geographical base; and reforming the National Directorate of Security, to diversify its ethnic makeup and make it more professional.

The plan also contemplated the use of American arms to challenge Karzai's warlord rivals. Since the Taliban's fall, Rumsfeld had refused to allow American forces to fight for Karzai or any other Afghan leader in "green-on-green," or intramural, conflicts. Now he relented, if tentatively. Khalilzad assured him and the cabinet that the warlords could be brought into peaceful politics primarily through pressure and negotiations, with only occasional shows of American force.

The deputies committee at the National Security Council approved the plan on June 18. The principals met two days later, with President Bush presiding. As Khalilzad clicked through his slides, Bush stopped him.

"Zal, I want you to turn Karzai into a great politician," he said. The entreaty was typical of how Bush thought about Karzai. During their video calls, he tried to build up his counterpart by treating him as a fellow professional pol. "You have your politics, I have mine," Bush would say when they struggled over divisive problems like Pakistan or civilian casualties.[3]

The president signed off on a final memorandum a few days later. The "Accelerating Success" PowerPoint deck became an action plan with tasks parceled out to cabinet departments. That August, Condoleezza Rice approved the formation of an interagency body, the Afghan Inter-Agency Operations Group, to follow through. An Army colonel, Tony Harriman, arrived from the Pentagon to run the effort at the N.S.C., from offices at the Eisenhower Executive Office Building.

Harriman discovered that the new White House plan for Afghanistan was better understood as a plan to write plans: "What's our plan to reform the judiciary? What's our plan to deal with people who had been captured on the field of battle, our reconciliation plan?" How would they build up the Army and reform the Ministry of Defense and professionalize the Afghan spy service under Engineer Arif? The Operations Group reviewed that autumn whether plans were complete or not complete. The problem was, as Harriman put it, "They were all 'not done.'"[4]

In early October, Major General David Barno, a West Point graduate, landed at Bagram Airfield to assume command of international conventional forces in Afghanistan, which then numbered about twelve thousand. Barno was appalled at the lack of organization and planning he inherited. He was allowed by the Pentagon to travel with half a dozen staff but had no headquarters team befitting such a large and dispersed force. Pentagon planners were so overwhelmed by the Iraq invasion and initial occupation that they seemed to manage Afghanistan from pieces of scrap paper. In his fifteen years of senior command, Barno had never seen a poorer transition from one general to the next. He found it "completely ad hoc" and discovered "there was not a campaign plan," indeed, "not a plan, period."[5]

Khalilzad had his PowerPoint slides and a signed presidential memorandum, but he was not one to be controlled by paperwork. He had secured what he needed from Washington: a new Bush-endorsed policy that promised bigger budgets and access to American troops to reinforce Hamid Karzai's authority. As a special envoy, Khalilzad had already established himself in Afghanistan as an improviser and local string puller. He would now become the most unconventional of ambassadors, less a diplomat than a kind of Afghan-American warlord, advertising benign intentions, wearing a smile and a suit.

On November 27, 2003, Thanksgiving Day, a convoy of American armed guards and diplomats packed into sport utility vehicles roared through Kabul toward the airport. One S.U.V. struck a pedestrian, a woman fully covered in a burqa. She fell; it wasn't clear how badly she might have been injured. The vehicles rolled on. The U.S. embassy's security protocols for Afghanistan forbade drivers from stopping for an accident, at least in some circumstances. There were about five thousand international peacekeepers in Kabul, yet the city remained insecure. If Americans attended to accidents, crowds might gather and grow excited, security planners feared. Security constraints shaped the lives of American diplomats and aid workers in Kabul. They endured long days inside heavily guarded buildings, forbidden from making spontaneous trips to markets or restaurants, their confinement relieved only by occasional outings in armed convoys, journeys that could be wondrous and terrifying in the space of a few hours. For Kay McGowan, a young embassy staffer in the convoy to the airport that Thanksgiving Day, who witnessed the collision with the anonymous Afghan woman, it was a heart-stopping way to begin what was to be a memorable day of V.I.P. duty.[6]

The convoy was headed to receive Hillary Clinton, a champion of women's rights in Afghanistan, who was completing her first year in office as a United States senator. Clinton deplaned that morning with Jack Reed, a West Point graduate who served with her on the Senate Armed Services Committee. The pair was making a lightning tour of Afghanistan and Iraq—Clinton's first battlefield tour as a senator. They had chosen to spend Thanksgiving with troops from the Tenth Mountain Division, which was based at Fort Drum, New York. Already it was apparent that Clinton might run for president eventually. She had just published a best-selling memoir, *Living History*, and the crowds that turned out for her book tour signaled her rise as a celebrity. Bush faced reelection in just a year. The Iraq war was deteriorating by the month. Democratic leaders saw an opening to argue that Bush had neglected Afghanistan and Al Qaeda and had failed to plan adequately for the invasion of Iraq. It was the first draft of a Democratic electoral strategy that would commit the party's candidates to the cause of Afghan security and development during the next two presidential cycles.

Between turkey helpings and photos with soldiers, Clinton affirmed that she favored sending more Western soldiers to Afghanistan, to prevent the Taliban's revival. She referred to American interests in the country much as the Bush administration did. Afghanistan was a frontline state in the war on terrorism. The Taliban were hardened terrorists. "The U.S. is resolved to stand as a strong partner and to ensure that the terrorists, whoever they are, wherever they come from, will be dealt with," she told reporters. "The message should be: The Taliban terrorists are fighting a losing battle."[7]

Zalmay Khalilzad flew into Kabul the same day aboard a U.S. military C-17 transport jet, to take up his post at the U.S. embassy. He sat strapped in the cargo hold beside a demining tractor and thirty thousand pounds of ammunition. At Bagram, he hustled onto a helicopter and landed outside the embassy. Khalilzad talked with Clinton and Reed and then accompanied them to the Arg. They talked with Karzai about Pakistan and the Taliban's resilience. Clinton would become an ally of Khalilzad's across the aisle as he sought budget increases for Afghan aid.

Khalilzad moved into a metal rambler on the embassy grounds, a kind of imitation house made of three trailers fitted together in an H shape. His corrugated home was not far from where he had attended high school. Generators and prefabricated buildings had eased some of the primitive conditions embassy staff had known early in 2002, but the embassy complex remained lightly resourced, reflecting White House policy and Office of Management and Budget priorities.

Not least to avoid spending long hours in his trailers, Khalilzad ingratiated himself at the Arg Palace and quickly became Hamid Karzai's chief *wazir* in residence. They had known each other since the anti-Soviet war, when Khalilzad visited Peshawar during the Reagan and Bush administrations and Karzai served as a political adviser. The pair spoke in a rapid-fire patois of Dari, Pashto, and English, sometimes dropping words from all three languages into a single sentence. That ensured they could maintain a two-way conversation that usually only a few other Afghans in the room could comprehend.

Khalilzad visited Karzai two or three times every day. He had dinner with him often. He helped Karzai prepare talking points for meetings with other ambassadors. They seemed to U.S. embassy staffers to get along like brothers, intimate but capable of intense squabbling. In Khalilzad's opinion, the squabbles "always ended cordially because I would explain what the facts are. We had a lot of information. He had a lot of rumors. . . . And he had enough confidence to say, 'Well, you are not gaming me.'" There was a sense that winter that the Bush administration had "abandoned us, but we get to do what we want," as McGowan, Khalilzad's chief of staff, put it. Khalilzad invented American policy from day to day during the long hours he spent huddling with Karzai, chattering in their patois. "*None* of us really knew what he was doing because we didn't have the language," McGowan said.[8]

DynCorp International, a military security contractor headquartered in Virginia, supplied bodyguards to both Karzai and the U.S. embassy during this period. The two teams assigned to keep Karzai and Khalilzad alive fell into a strange rivalry, arguing about which principal had the higher Al Qaeda or Taliban bounty on his head. Aware of the matter of appearances, Karzai accepted his bodyguard of burly men wearing wraparound sunglasses after "consultation with Afghans from [the] provinces." At the ceremonial opening of a road project, a DynCorp guard punched out Karzai's minister of transport because he did not recognize him and feared he might be rushing Karzai. To combat Karzai's palace fever, Khalilzad and his staff scheduled as many ribbon cuttings out of Kabul as they could, partly because DynCorp would agree that it was safe for Karzai to travel only if the destination was an American-run event.

Khalilzad attended cabinet meetings as if he were a member of the government, which, in effect, he was. A few days after an Afghan cabinet debate, the ambassador would read top secret C.I.A. cables reporting on what had transpired, based on reports from paid agents inside the Karzai administration. Reading the intelligence cables at his embassy desk, Khalilzad would snort, "That is not what so-and-so said, that is not what happened."[9]

Soon after Khalilzad arrived, Karzai asked him to help him remove Engineer Arif as chief of the Afghan spy service. From Karzai's perspective, the main problem involved ethnic politics. To build his political base as the presidential election approached, Karzai needed support from diverse Pashtun tribal leaders. These leaders inevitably included some with histories of accommodation of the Taliban during the 1990s. Karzai encouraged Pashtun leaders to visit him in Kabul to talk about reconciliation and post-Taliban politics. N.D.S. sometimes arrested, interrogated, and even beat up these prospective allies, suspecting them to be enemies of the state.

Khalilzad sympathized with Karzai's complaints about the N.D.S. He knew as well that the C.I.A. and the Afghan Ministry of Finance had found evidence of extensive corruption at the service. (According to Arif, accusations of personal corruption against him "are unfair," but "there were some problems" with "organizational corruption" because of the chaotic situation and the lack of supervision of N.D.S. staff in the provinces.) Arif did not speak English fluently and was not as sophisticated about international politics as some of his Panjshiri colleagues. But Khalilzad would have to go through the C.I.A. if he wanted to make a change. After 2001, Arif built out intelligence liaisons with Britain, Canada, France, Germany, Australia, and others. Yet the C.I.A. inevitably became his dominant partner. The agency supplied a stipend to N.D.S. in the budgetary year of 2002–3 of $6.5 million, as well as irregular support, in smaller amounts, for specific operations.[10] Yet this was only a fifth of the annual funding Arif sought as he rebuilt N.D.S. in every province. He argued with his C.I.A. advisers. He wanted to build a hospital for N.D.S. employees, for example, because Afghanistan lacked a formal health system of any quality. The C.I.A. pressed him instead to consolidate N.D.S.'s huge workforce.

Karzai had appointed Ashraf Ghani, a former World Bank official with a doctorate in anthropology from Columbia, as his minister of finance. Ghani happened as well to be an old acquaintance of Zalmay Khalilzad's.

They had played basketball in Kabul as teenagers and had even been in the same cohort of the American Field Service exchange program, traveling together from Kabul to America. (Ghani stayed with a family in Oregon.) With Khalilzad's encouragement, Ghani tried to strengthen and normalize the central government by assembling Afghan technocrats around him, and allocating budgets and finance from his ministry, as other countries did. Engineer Arif fell into Ghani's crosshairs.

At the end of 2003, the Ministry of Finance withheld salaries for fifteen thousand N.D.S. employees for three consecutive months. The freeze jeopardized Arif's credibility with his own men. Arif could tap Fahim from time to time for funds from the old Northern Alliance coffers, but it was becoming clear to both the C.I.A. and Karzai that Arif was "using the N.D.S. for the benefit of his own ethnic and personal interests, often working behind the scenes against Karzai and the government," as the C.I.A.'s Gary Schroen put it.[11]

Yet the C.I.A. station chief in Kabul that winter opposed firing Arif. Panjshiri gunmen still protected expatriate C.I.A. officers at the Ariana Hotel. It would not be wise to alienate them by removing their boss. And Arif cooperated well with C.I.A. militia operations at the Omega bases along the Pakistan border. Arif and his men recruited, vetted, and dispatched fighters to serve in the reconnaissance forces.

The station chief asked George Tenet to telephone Khalilzad at the embassy one evening to wave him off the plan to fire Arif. The ambassador stood firm, but Khalilzad and Karzai soon came up with a compromise they thought the C.I.A. might accept. Karzai would appoint Amrullah Saleh as Arif's successor as the country's top spy.

The clean-shaven, well-dressed Panjshiri occasionally interpreted during meetings at the Arg Palace. He was professional and had strong language skills. Khalilzad invited him to the embassy. Saleh came across as intelligent, a man who had lifted himself up through work and merit. He seemed to be a genuine Afghan nationalist, not a regional chauvinist. He was eager to take full charge of N.D.S.[12]

Finally the C.I.A. relented. In February, Karzai summoned Arif and told him that he was promoting him to "senior intelligence adviser." By offering him an advisory role, the departing chief's wealth would not be threatened and he would be eligible for other offices. (He later became an Afghan senator.) Arif had lost confidence in Karzai and believed that the interim president's advisers were spreading false accusations against him. For his part, Amrullah Saleh understood he had the C.I.A.'s backing but he also grasped why Karzai might have endorsed his appointment. He was almost a decade younger than Arif. "They thought, 'Let us put the youngest and least experienced of *them*,'" meaning the Panjshiris, in charge, "so that there is internal fighting between them."[13]

Saleh did seek to run N.D.S. on more modern principles. When he took office, he claimed to have identified and fired thirty-eight thousand ghost employees in one week. At his Kabul headquarters, he built up an organization chart very similar to the C.I.A.'s. He separated analysis from operations and produced regular intelligence papers and threat and analysis briefings for President Karzai. Even under Saleh's reform drive, N.D.S. remained too large, unruly, and penetrated by Iran and Russia to be a fully reliable partner in the most sensitive C.I.A. operations along the Pakistan border.

Saleh believed that "there were massive flaws in the American approach" to Afghan intelligence and security. The Bush administration starved N.D.S. of the capital it needed to preempt Pakistani interference and the Taliban's revival, he argued. Fifteen million dollars a year was nowhere near enough for an agency combining the functions of the C.I.A. and the F.B.I. in a country so sprawling and vulnerable to guerrilla incursions across an open 1,400-mile border with Pakistan. "Why does Afghanistan need a big organization?" his C.I.A. counterparts argued. "Let's bring it down to a couple of thousand collectors." The agency's mission was to locate, kill, or capture Al Qaeda leaders. Saleh's mission was to stabilize a war-scarred and impoverished unstable country. The C.I.A. "would argue with me over small issues—how many vehicles to buy."[14] It would be several years before they accepted his argument that defeating Al Qaeda and other transnational jihadists in the long run required much larger Afghan security forces. The N.D.S. example illustrated American investment in post-Taliban Afghanistan: deliberate minimalism, followed by tentative engagement, followed by massive investments only when it was very late to make a difference.

General David Barno, the commander of conventional forces in Afghanistan, kept an office at the embassy and lived fifty feet from Khalilzad in the compound's trailer park. Khalilzad and his aides regarded Barno as an effective, politically aware general. In fact, for the first time since the Taliban's fall, the ambassador, the military's commander, and the C.I.A. station were unified around a political agenda for Afghanistan, however quixotic it might look: to advance Afghan governance; to deliver visible reconstruction projects that would benefit Karzai's prestige, such as an asphalt ring road around Afghanistan; and to strengthen his government's control over the budget. At the heart of all these policies was a single bet, implicit in the "Accelerating Success" plan: to place Afghanistan's leadership in the hands of Hamid Karzai and to help him win election as president for a five-year term.

American policy under Khalilzad treaded a fine line. The United States would not interfere with or fix the eventual voting results, but it would prepare the ground for Karzai's candidacy by strengthening his writ in comparison with potential regional rivals. The goal was to "move warlords" into "being political figures," as Barno put it, so that they would no longer resort to violence but would become "part of the fabric of government."[15]

"What do you want to do, Mr. President?" Khalilzad asked Karzai, referring to the likes of Fahim, Dostum, and Ismail Khan. Those three warlords controlled tens of thousands of armed men between them across a vast swath of Afghanistan's north and west.

"They won't listen to me," Karzai said. "They will listen to you."[16]

Their first target was Abdul Rashid Dostum. In 2004, street protests and other agitation erupted against a Karzai-appointed governor in Faryab Province. Dostum claimed that he was not in control of the protesters but wanted their concerns addressed. Karzai dispatched an Afghan National Army unit to restore order. The A.N.A. unit had American trainers with it, and Khalilzad warned Dostum that if he attacked it, he would be going to war with the United States.

Khalilzad then joined Karzai at the Arg Palace. Dostum had called

Karzai to rant. Khalilzad listened as Dostum said, "We all thought Khalilzad was good, but he is the worst." Khalilzad called him again. "You will cross a bridge from which there is no return," Khalilzad said. Dostum slurred his words and seemed to be drunk. "It will be worse than Vietnam! It will be worse than Iraq!" he raged. Barno ordered a B-1 bomber to fly over Dostum's house and break the sound barrier. After a few more threats, Dostum relented.[17]

The next target was Ismail Khan, the governor of Herat. After the C.I.A. had helped to return him to power in the province, Khan had seized control of customs revenue from Afghanistan's border with Iran, restored a picaresque mini-emirate of marching bands and ceremonial palace patronage, and had then picked a fight with Amanullah Khan, a local Pashtun militia leader. Their skirmishes were the last straw, so far as Khalilzad was concerned. He asked General Barno to deploy helicopters to the American-controlled air base at Shindand, near Herat. They agreed it would be best to remove both Ismail Khan and Amanullah Khan. Khalilzad called Amanullah to tell him he was sending a C.I.A. plane and that he expected him to be on it. Khan cooperated. The ambassador then boarded a C-130 to Herat. Ismail Khan's ceremonial dancers greeted him. At one of the palaces of the emir (Khan's self-endowed title), Khalilzad asked to meet alone.

"I think the time has come for you to leave Herat," he said. "President Karzai is thinking of you becoming a minister."

"I would like to be minister of interior," Khan replied quickly.

Khalilzad said he didn't want to get into the details. Ismail Khan ended up as minister of water and energy.[18]

Karzai's most powerful rival remained Marshal Mohammed Fahim, the heir to Massoud's militias. Karzai's strategy was to hold his rival close. Initially, he decided to invite Fahim onto his election ticket as first vice president, to help pull in the Tajik vote. As 2004 passed and the election neared, however, Karzai wondered if he had made a mistake. He debated replacing Fahim with a less powerful Panjshiri, Ahmad Zia Massoud, one of the deceased commander's brothers, who had no armed following. General Barno opposed the idea. He worried that if Fahim was knocked off the ticket, he might stage a coup d'état.

Khalilzad was more sympathetic to Karzai's thinking. Barno felt that Khalilzad "counseled Karzai fairly even-handedly" on whether to dump Fahim, but eventually, he "kind of put his foot down" in favor of taking the risk.

Barno now organized a plan to break the news to Fahim in a way that might deter him from striking back violently against the Arg Palace. Quietly, Barno's command mobilized N.A.T.O. units with antitank weapons and stationed them in front of compounds holding Fahim's armored units. "We were ready to prevent a coup from happening that day, very explicitly," Barno said. In full uniform, Barno arrived at Fahim's residence to tell him that he was off the ticket. The marshal was unhappy but accepting. He gave Barno an extemporaneous lecture on the United States Constitution.[19]

I t was not only Zalmay Khalilzad's language and heritage that made him seem to Afghans like one of their own. He also had an entourage and kin network that looked familiar in the light of evolving post-Taliban Afghan politics. Khalilzad had at least two family members who held positions in the Karzai administration. A nephew, Wahid Monawar, served as an aide to Abdullah Abdullah, the minister of foreign affairs. Another relative held a diplomatic post. Like the Karzais, the Khalilzads straddled Afghanistan and America. Some of the ambassador's relatives sought to mix politics and business to cash in on reconstruction contracts, just as the Karzais and other newly empowered Afghan families did.

Lawrence Longhi, an American businessman, first met Khaled Monawar, another nephew of Ambassador Khalilzad's, at a tennis club in suburban New Jersey. Monawar worked there; Longhi was a member. A number of Khalilzad family members had settled around Livingston, New Jersey, including Zalmay's mother and his brother David, an investment banker. Khaled Monawar was a student at Seton Hall University. He had a receding hairline and an open face that bore a notable resemblance to his uncle's. After the September 11 attacks, he and Longhi talked about going into business together. From early on, Longhi regarded Zalmay Khalilzad as the "silent partner" in this enterprise. Khaled Monawar would ask him to set up meetings with U.S. government officials, "with contacts provided to him by his uncle." Longhi said he visited the White House to meet Khalilzad and Monawar. For his part, Khalilzad said later that he had a "vague memory" of Longhi visiting him when he worked at the National Security Council, before he became ambassador, but he said there were no meetings after he was assigned to Kabul. His nephew told him that Longhi "was his friend and was interested in Afghanistan." According to Khalilzad, he did not introduce Longhi "to anyone to get a contract or instruct anyone to give him a contract."

Khaled Monawar's ambition put Khalilzad in an awkward position. He could not ban his American relatives from going into business; they were free to do as they pleased. Yet Khalilzad knew enough about Afghan ways of business to fear that Monawar would use his connection to him to try to win business, even if Khalilzad did not want him to do so. As Khalilzad described it, Monawar "probably did try to trade on my name—but I never introduced him to anyone in the U.S. government or to help him get a contract. Never. When I heard that he was looking to do business in Afghanistan, I told my embassy assistant not to give anyone an appointment who was introduced by Khaled."[20]

In January 2003, Longhi and Monawar incorporated Afgamco Inc. in Delaware and soon formed a partnership with Michael Baker Corporation, a Pittsburgh-headquartered engineering firm with experience in construction projects abroad. Longhi's account is different from Khalilzad's. According to him, there were three meetings with Zalmay Khalilzad before and after he became the Bush administration's ambassador to Afghanistan, and at these sessions, "Discussions took place regarding the award of possible construction projects in Afghanistan and Iraq, including one to revitalize a quarry at the Kabul Airport," as well as "pipeline . . . and a major water resources project," according to a court document. At the meetings with Zalmay Khalilzad, however, "no confirmation was given" about specific contracts.[21]

The partners were not shy about advertising their connection to Zalmay Khalilzad when they presented their business plans. In the spring of

2003, Michael Baker developed a PowerPoint deck that included a slide titled "Who Is Afgamco?" One of the boxes underneath that question read "Mr. K Bush Admin. Afghan & Iraq." In later months, while trying to determine where to send a particular business proposal, the parties exchanged e-mails. In some of these e-mails, the ambassador was referred to as "Mr. Big."[22]

As the pursuit of U.S. government contracts went on, Longhi later complained, he was shut out of meetings and correspondence. He eventually sued Khaled Monawar because he believed he had been denied money he was entitled to. There is no evidence in the court documents that Khalilzad acted improperly. Still, the visibility of Khalilzad's family members in the Karzai government and in seeking contracts created an obvious problem of appearances. When American diplomats scolded the Karzai family or Fahim Khan or Engineer Arif for cronyism, or when the Americans called such family-connected contracting deals "corruption," the Afghans on the receiving end of such lectures had reason to cast a jaundiced eye.

ELEVEN

Ambassador vs. Ambassador

I n 2003 and 2004, Afghans witnessed remarkable political events—the adoption of a new constitution, mobilization for a presidential election, planning for a new parliament. Yet there were signs of trouble. Periodic insurgent attacks caused about fifty American casualties each year. Hamid Karzai and Amrullah Saleh became united in the conviction that I.S.I. was back in action, covertly deploying the Taliban to destabilize their fledgling government before it could consolidate. Zalmay Khalilzad heard again and again from Karzai about the dangers of I.S.I. He tried to intervene, despite resistance or indifference within the Bush administration.

Rich Blee had rotated to Pakistan as C.I.A. chief of station in Islamabad about the same time that Khalilzad arrived as ambassador. During 2004, Greg Vogle, the paramilitary officer who had traveled inside Afghanistan with Karzai, arrived as chief of Kabul Station. (He succeeded the officer who had opposed Engineer Arif's removal.) Vogle worked with Khalilzad and Barno to shore up Karzai, taking advantage of the trusting relationship he enjoyed. In Blee, Vogle, and Khalilzad, the Bush administration had now sent forward three men with long and unsentimental experience of I.S.I.'s covert support for the Taliban, dating back to well before the September 11 attacks.

The Joint Special Operations Command first collected concrete evidence of an organized Taliban revival early in 2004. The movement's

Shura Council produced an internal circular or strategy document to coordinate a plan for revival of military operations. The document was the rough equivalent of the campaign plans American war commanders wrote to ensure that frontline colonels and majors had a common understanding of strategy.

Khalilzad and many of his aides who had access to intelligence reporting were fully convinced that Musharraf had approved a policy of quiet support for the Taliban's comeback. Yet while they could point to circumstantial evidence—such as the fact that Taliban leaders were living openly in Pakistani cities, without harassment—they lacked hard proof of active Directorate S funding or training. Even so, Khalilzad believed it was obvious that the Pakistanis could do more to suppress the Taliban. In the Kabul embassy, the prevailing view was that "the Pakistanis were in complete and public denial," as David Sedney, then the deputy chief of mission, put it. Pakistani counterparts repeatedly denied the very existence of the Quetta Shura, yet the United States "knew from intelligence that they were there. All the Afghans knew they were there. All the Pakistanis knew they were there, for that matter." Still, in prolonged, face-to-face meetings, Pakistanis at the highest levels said otherwise.[1]

General Barno, who had access to all of the intelligence reporting, took a judicious position about Pakistani complicity. He never saw evidence "in any domain" indicating that the Pakistanis were "actively supporting" the Taliban's comeback. He could see that they "basically tolerated the Taliban in the tribal areas" but it was also obvious that the Pakistanis' "ability to control these areas was negligible." There were long stretches of the Afghan-Pakistan border where the Pakistani military had no presence at all. Where border posts existed, they were often unoccupied or commanded by paramilitary Frontier Corps soldiers. These were locally recruited tribesmen who were often influenced by the same preachers who fired up the Taliban. American forces deployed near the Pakistan border could see clearly that Frontier Corps soldiers waved small Taliban units into Afghanistan, or ignored them. Yet given the weakness of Pakistani institutions, Barno and his military intelligence analysts at I.S.A.F. assessed, this was not decisive evidence of Pakistani state policy. They thought, "Well, these guys are probably cousins."[2]

To Zalmay Khalilzad, the essential questions were Is a sanctuary being developed by the Taliban inside Pakistan and, if so, did this have
Musharraf's endorsement? He concluded that Pakistan's "double game
was undeniable." The raw intelligence he relied upon included N.D.S.
and C.I.A. agent reporting about training areas on Pakistani territory
and Taliban graduation ceremonies where I.S.I. officers were reportedly
present. Of course, particular agent reports could always be discounted
as unreliable. Khalilzad credited the intelligence overall, however, and
assumed Musharraf had to have endorsed such support. "Can this happen without his knowledge?" he asked. "Why is he doing it?"[3]

The U.S. ambassador in Islamabad, Nancy J. Powell, a career foreign
service officer who had served half a dozen tours in sub-Saharan Africa
and South Asia, argued that Khalilzad's pressure campaign against
Musharraf was misplaced. The struggle between the two ambassadors
played out in what became known to participants as "the war of the
No-Dis cables," meaning cables not to be distributed through wide channels. They exchanged a stream of invective—some of it in cables, more
of it in e-mails and direct phone conversations. Besides Powell, Khalilzad
also sometimes got into it with Deputy Secretary of State Richard Armitage. The essential subject was whether the United States was being
fooled by Pakistan. Powell's superiors at State had instructed her before
she departed for Islamabad not to get into cabling wars with the U.S.
embassies in Kabul and India over I.S.I.'s conduct or other sources of
controversy about Pakistan. But Khalilzad raised the temperature. In
one cable, Powell felt that he had attempted to question her "loyalty and
patriotism" simply because she had tried to describe Pakistan's position
of relative weakness in relation to the Taliban and the fact that the border between Pakistan and Afghanistan "has never ever been controlled."
She argued that Khalilzad "had exaggerated Musharraf's ability to control everything in Pakistan and everyone in it," especially in the Federally
Administered Tribal Areas. Khalilzad blamed her unfairly simply for reporting on Pakistan's outlook, she believed. Yet she did have a cautious
view of what the facts had established about Directorate S activity. To be
sure, Powell felt, there were military officers "with mixed loyalties," yet
there was "never a clear connection between the government of Pakistan

and support for those groups." She did not regard Musharraf as especially trustworthy, but the United States had other interests in Pakistan—if they went hard after I.S.I., especially without great evidence, it would disrupt her embassy's mission to try to work with Pakistan on controlling its nuclear weapons, reducing tensions with India over Kashmir, and supporting the country's economic and social development.[4]

For his part, Khalilzad thought he understood why Pakistan might be preparing the Taliban for a return to Afghanistan. Musharraf and his high command had concluded that the United States would leave the region. They had good reason: As it became mired in Iraq, the Bush administration signaled openly that it wanted European countries to take the lead in Afghanistan. Pakistan's generals assumed that without a U.S. military commitment, Afghanistan would fall apart again. Pakistani generals, including Musharraf, concluded, "They had better have some of their own horses."[5]

Musharraf seemed to confirm as much in an interview years later. As president of Pakistan, he said he would ask American visitors, "Are you leaving a stable Afghanistan or not?" If not, "then I have to think of my own security. If you leave without that, I am thinking of 1989 or 1996," two pivot points of civil war in Afghanistan. In both cases, I.S.I. backed Islamist Afghan factions aligned with Islamabad's interests and opposed to India.[6]

In December 2003, Al Qaeda–linked Pakistani assassins rammed two car bombs into Musharraf's convoy as he rode through Rawalpindi; he narrowly escaped death. It turned out that one of the suicide bombers was an I.S.I.-backed militant who had fought in Kashmir. A second bombing attempt by the same network followed in April. Musharraf fired an I.S.I. general in charge of the Kashmir cell of Directorate S and ordered Pakistani troops into South Waziristan to attack Al Qaeda and its local allies. He allowed C.I.A. officers and Special Forces to embed in Pakistani units and continued to cooperate with C.I.A. drone operations, including, for the first time, lethal strikes carried out against Taliban leaders in South Waziristan.

To President Bush and Secretary of State Colin Powell, that Al Qaeda tried to kill Musharraf and that the Pakistan Army moved into

Waziristan to retaliate seemed to make plain that Pakistan was on America's side. It did not compute for them that Musharraf might be simultaneously at war with Al Qaeda and promoting the Taliban.

To try to resolve the dispute between the embassies in Kabul and Islamabad, Stephen Hadley, Condoleezza Rice's deputy at the National Security Council, ordered an intelligence review of the Taliban's revival during 2003 and 2004. Yet the C.I.A. could not definitively resolve how the Taliban had constructed a sanctuary in Pakistan or the role of I.S.I. Paid agents run by N.D.S. would report something along the lines of "Mullah Dadullah's house is in the third street to the right off the main road in the old city of Quetta." But there were not many fixed street addresses in Quetta. The C.I.A. ordered satellite photography of the city. C.I.A. officers from Islamabad Station also visited Quetta with I.S.I. escorts to try to obtain a sense of its warrens firsthand. Even so, when imagery analysts looked at photos or Predator video to try to confirm specific N.D.S. reporting about Taliban addresses, they could discern little. Or it would turn out that a reported address was actually a mosque where Taliban turned up from time to time. The C.I.A. proved unable to place reliable unilateral American agents in Quetta to nail down addresses of senior Taliban leaders. Fugitive hunting in hostile "denied areas" was one of the most challenging tasks case officers undertook. Definitive proof of I.S.I. activity in such a scenario required matching signals intelligence, overhead photography, and agent reporting on the ground. The C.I.A "never got the complete triangulation of information, SIGINT, and everything," an official involved recalled. Quetta remained "a black hole."[7]

Zalmay Khalilzad just didn't believe Musharraf's claims. In Washington for consultations, he made headlines during a talk at a think tank by declaring openly that Pakistan was providing sanctuary to the Taliban.

In the Oval Office, President Bush told Khalilzad, "Musharraf denies all of what you are saying."

"Didn't they deny, Mr. President, for years that they had a nuclear program?"[8]

Bush said he would call Musharraf and arrange for the ambassador to meet with him, to discuss the accusations directly.

Khalilzad flew to Islamabad. Beforehand, he sent Musharraf a gift, a crate of Afghan pomegranates. When they sat down, Musharraf thanked him, but added that he hated pomegranates—too many seeds. They talked extensively about Musharraf's usual complaints about the Afghan government—too many Panjshiris in key security positions, too many Indian spies under diplomatic cover in Kabul and elsewhere.

Khalilzad proposed a joint intelligence investigation between the United States and Pakistan to document any covert Indian activity in Afghanistan.

"There are no Taliban here," Musharraf said blankly.[9]

Douglas Porch grew up in the South, served in the U.S. Army Reserves, and then, in the late 1960s, enrolled at Cambridge University, where he earned a doctoral degree in history. He wrote several books about France's expeditionary wars in Algeria, Indochina, and the Sahara. French officers were the first to identify counterinsurgency as a separate category of warfare. After 1840, to suppress the Algerian leader Abd al-Kadir, who, like Mullah Mohammad Omar, called himself the Commander of the Faithful, French forces under the command of Thomas Robert Bugeaud burned crops, orchards, and villages. They incinerated civilians who hid from them in caves. These horrors provoked opposition at home, and so gradually the military repackaged "counterinsurgency as a civilizing mission," as Porch put it. This included an assumption of Arab racial inferiority. Phrases like "hearts and minds" first arose in public discourse in the 1890s. The French called the strategy "peaceful penetration."

By the 1960s, counterinsurgency had evolved into a more technocratic "modernization theory" in some quarters of the West. Kennedy-era national security intellectuals argued that as the United States fought for free societies in the face of Soviet communism, it had "an obligation to protect emerging states as they evolve to become functional capitalist economies," in Porch's summary. That doctrine influenced America's fateful decision to accept France's legacy in Vietnam.[10]

In early 2004, Porch was teaching military history at the Naval War

College in Rhode Island. His students were captains, majors, and lieutenant commanders. Armed pacification campaigns by foreign forces
only rarely persuaded locals of the interveners' good intentions, he believed. (Porch later authored a book titled *Counterinsurgency: Exposing
the Myths of the New Way of War*.) Yet such campaigns did not always fail.
In 2004, the Afghan war looked to Porch as if it was going pretty well.
Perhaps this would be an exception to military history's general rule.[11]

That winter, he took a phone call from an officer at Joint Special
Operations Command. Major General Stanley McChrystal, J.S.O.C.'s
commander, now shuttled between two clandestine task force headquarters, one in Iraq and the other in Afghanistan. Every quarter he called his
commanding officers to a conference. The J.S.O.C. officer asked Porch if
he could talk to the group about Algeria, and specifically *The Battle of
Algiers*, the 1966 film depicting France's urban war against Algerian revolutionaries seeking independence. The film credibly showed both sides
of the conflict. Could Porch lecture on the movie and lead a discussion
about what French counterinsurgency history might imply for fighting
the American wars in Iraq and Afghanistan?

"Come to Fort Bragg," the J.S.O.C. officer added, "but bring things,
because the talk probably won't be in Fort Bragg." He did not mention an
alternative site, but he suggested, "Bring jeans and athletic shoes."

Porch was then fifty-nine years old. J.S.O.C. set him up for shots and
fitted him with a flak jacket. The next thing he knew he was at Bagram
Airfield. J.S.O.C. units lived and worked on Zulu, or Greenwich Mean
Time. They had breakfast at noon local time and went to bed at about
3:00 a.m., a strange rhythm for a visitor to follow. Bagram remained
primitive, covered with detritus from the Soviet war. The Americans
lived in tents and plywood shacks.

McChrystal summoned Porch after midnight. The general lived a
famously spartan existence, sharing a hutch with his sergeant major. He
explained that for his conference, in addition to screening *The Battle of
Algiers*, he had assigned his commanding officers to read *Modern Warfare*, a book written in 1964 by Roger Trinquier, a French officer who
served in Vietnam and Algeria.[12]

McChrystal was trying to provoke his commanders—door kickers,

shooters, terrorist hunters by training and vocation—to think more carefully about what kind of wars they had fallen into. He felt his operations
"were very tactical." The standard procedure was "Give me a list of the
bad guys and I'm going to go find them." Now culling alone looked insufficient. Iraq was falling apart and the violence in that theater was much
worse than anything his superiors in Washington were willing to acknowledge. In Afghanistan, McChrystal thought the Taliban had started
to get their feet under them, and there were "indications that they were
moving out."

He told Porch, "We don't know what the hell is going on out there,"
beyond the wire of their bases. "It's quiet."[13]

One problem, McChrystal believed, was that Special Operations
units lacked a common understanding of how to fight without making
the insurgencies worse. Again and again, he heard, "We have got to take
the gloves off." McChrystal asked, "What are you talking about? What
do we mean here?" He wanted his officers to reflect on experiences like
those the French had endured in Vietnam and Algeria, where they had
already documented "what works and what doesn't work."[14]

David Barno, McChrystal's West Point classmate and his counterpart
in command of conventional forces, harbored parallel worries. His forces
were on sprawling bases and routinely prepared for large two-week operations with names like Operation Mountain Thunder. They "would
tromp around in the nether regions," as Barno put it. "It was effectively
sticking your fist in a bucket of water and pulling it back out again." He
had read counterinsurgency literature, too, and wanted to apply its theories and lessons in Afghanistan, even though he commanded nowhere
near the number of troops that counterinsurgency doctrine dictated
would be necessary to suppress the enemy. Barno focused his effort on
small Provincial Reconstruction Teams "centered on the population" and
equipped to deliver aid and build local relationships.[15]

On a Friday night, about twenty J.S.O.C. commanders and an equal
number of senior noncommissioned officers assembled around plywood
tables arranged in a hollow square. Porch delivered a lecture about the
hard lessons of French expeditionary war and the Algerian war for
independence. One of his PowerPoint slides showed an old photo of

suspected terrorists kneeling on the ground, tied together at the neck with rope. "A portion of the French army lost its moral compass," Porch's headline noted. In the film, he previewed, the French counterinsurgency officer justifies "exceptional measures" in counterterrorism. "In your view, are his the arguments of a soldier?" Porch asked.

The next night they watched *The Battle of Algiers* and afterward Porch led a discussion. The film contained repulsive scenes of French forces torturing insurgent suspects, but it showed that brutality could destroy an uprising, even if the long-term goal of control and stability might be futile. As they talked, there were some J.S.O.C. operators who remained focused on the core mission, Al Qaeda: "We're going to get Bin Laden and hang him up by the balls," as Porch put it. But others, particularly the younger noncommissioned officers, picked up on the idea that there had to be more to success in this age of saturated media and global human rights consciousness than just capture and kill.[16]

Porch stayed on at Bagram for another ten days, waiting for a flight out. He befriended a military lawyer who took him over to the airfield's detention center, situated in old Soviet aircraft hangars. The interrogators Porch met complained that they had little good intelligence about the Taliban or Al Qaeda and that Tenth Mountain Division units detained Afghans for spurious reasons: "Well, he has new shoes—he must be an insurgent." To Porch, it all sounded like the French in Algeria and Vietnam: "You just pick up every military-aged male you can find."

The detention center was an enormous open space with balconies that ran around the top. On the second level were interrogation rooms. The detained men were held in a big cage at the bottom, exposed. A curtain shielded toilets. Many of the American guards were female. When they escorted prisoners to the interrogation rooms, they shackled, handcuffed, and hooded them. Porch reflected on the humiliation the Afghan prisoners must be experiencing.

Porch asked if he could visit Kabul. His hosts told him, "No, it's too dangerous." He flew home and returned to the classroom at the Naval War College. Over the next several years his students included young officers rotating back from Afghanistan and Iraq. Gradually it became obvious that both wars were deteriorating and that American forces struggled to win the loyalty of the populations they policed. An Army major told Porch, "You start out being nice to them, but as soon as we lose a couple of men, the gloves come off."[17]

By the spring of 2004 it was evident that the Iraq war's *casus belli* had been grounded in false intelligence reporting about Saddam Hussein's possession of biological and nuclear weapons. Press leaks from the White House fingered George Tenet's C.I.A. for this embarrassment. Press leaks from the C.I.A. emphasized that the Bush administration had interfered with prewar intelligence. Bush faced reelection in November. It was obvious who would win this fight. Tenet had by now run the C.I.A. for almost seven years, the second-longest tenure in the agency's history, after that of Allen Dulles during the 1950s. On June 3, 2004, he resigned.

His departure inaugurated two years of turmoil on the Seventh Floor. Bush appointed Porter Goss as his successor. He was a former C.I.A. case officer who led the House Permanent Select Committee on Intelligence as a Republican member of Congress. Even as one of the top congressional overseers of the agency, Goss had no idea that Tenet was about to go and was surprised when Bush asked him to take charge of Langley. To succeed Buzzy Krongard as executive director, Goss appointed Kyle "Dusty" Foggo. A year later, Foggo was indicted for his role in corrupt contracting deals carried out while he held office at the C.I.A. Mike Sulick and Steve Kappes, Senior Intelligence Service veterans who then ran the clandestine service, resigned in late 2004 after a fight with another Goss aide. The Goss team had arrived in a heavy-handed state of suspicion, they felt, asking for lists of officers who were acceptable, accusing senior officers of leaking unflattering stories and of being politicized. Sulick told one of Goss's aides, "You're not going to treat us the way you treated the Democrats on the Hill, like pukes." After the two quit on principle, Goss persuaded Jose Rodriguez, the architect of the interrogation black sites and enhanced interrogation techniques, to run clandestine operations. At C.T.C., Goss elevated Michael D'Andrea, a dark-tempered, chain-smoking convert to Shia Islam who had most recently served as chief of station in Cairo. This group portrait of leadership had some of the roughest edges yet.

Goss hadn't asked for the job; as he settled in on the Seventh Floor, he concluded that he had inherited a troubled agency. He knew for certain, from his own experience in the House of Representatives, that there was little trust between the C.I.A. and Capitol Hill, primarily because of the Iraq fiasco. Some Republican congressmen suspected Tenet of betraying Bush; Democrats opposed to the Iraq war were at the same time appalled and furious over the role of bad intelligence in the run-up to the invasion. Goss took it on himself to try to restore decent relations and win increases in funding from Congress, particularly to support expansion in the number of case officers and stations overseas. His "marching orders" from George W. Bush were to strengthen the C.I.A.'s ability to collect intelligence abroad and to adapt to the challenges of collecting insights on terrorists and guerrillas. Rebuilding a sense of confidence on the Hill "was a bitter pill" for some career C.I.A. officers to swallow. Goss's decision to bring Hill staff with him rather than draw his new executive team from C.I.A. career personnel redoubled his burdens. He felt that the agency had changed in unfortunate ways since his days as a case officer in the 1960s. Overall, there was a loss of discipline, he sensed, manifested in leaks to the press and a lack of accountability in the chain of command. He wanted to restore accountability, but he underestimated how difficult it would be for an outsider from Capitol Hill to succeed.[18]

Early in 2004, the C.I.A. produced a breakthrough about Al Qaeda's sanctuary in Pakistan's Federally Administered Tribal Areas. In January, Kurdish forces captured Hassan Ghul, an Al Qaeda–affiliated militant. They transferred him to C.I.A custody. He carried a notebook full of coded phone numbers and e-mail addresses. Ghul translated the codes for his captors. He explained that Al Qaeda had established safe houses around Wana and the Shkai Valley, in South Waziristan. Leaders of Al Qaeda and the Islamic Movement of Uzbekistan operated from both places. This was the same area from which the assassins who had attempted to blow up President Musharraf had emerged.

The Bush administration perceived a fresh opportunity to collaborate with Pakistan. Rather than following Zalmay Khalilzad's advice to pressure Musharraf over I.S.I.'s relationship with the Taliban, the administration adopted something like the opposite policy: It offered more financial aid to Pakistan's military regime. The White House announced that it would confer on Pakistan the status of "major non-NATO ally" and deliver $700 million in fresh assistance, more than half of it for the military. Musharraf ordered the Pakistan Army to step up its operations in South Waziristan, where he had already sent eight thousand troops.[19]

Musharraf and Bush agreed to quietly set up a Special Operations Task Force to attack militants in the tribal areas. The United States supplied helicopters "with precision weapons and night operating capability," in Musharraf's description. The campaign's tactics reflected Musharraf's neocolonial attitude toward Waziristan's Pashtuns: The only way to get their attention, he told the Americans repeatedly, was to hit the tribes ruthlessly.[20]

The C.I.A.'s main target that spring was a long-haired, charismatic militant leader of the Wazirs named Nek Mohammad. He ruled Wana and distrusted the Pakistan Army. He was a complicated figure—a tribal nationalist who consorted with international terrorists. He accepted Al Qaeda and Uzbek refugees. In Islamabad, C.I.A. station chief Rich Blee used the assassination attempts against Musharraf to try to motivate the president and I.S.I. to strike back: "You have to kill them or they're going to kill us." The C.I.A. and the Omega teams based just across the Afghan border, at Shkin and Khost, tracked Nek Mohammad to target him for a drone strike. They worked with Task Force Orange, a National Security Agency signals intelligence unit. The manhunt took place amid a wider, violent Pakistani campaign against Nek Mohammad's Wazir supporters.

The Omega base at Shkin lay less than two miles from the Pakistani border. At night, operators and case officers would sit up on a roof, smoke cigars, and watch Pakistani F-16s bomb Wana, often indiscriminately. The Pakistanis closed the town's bazaar, and refugees from what was already a deeply impoverished population began to walk into Afghanistan to escape the violence and beg for food. Case officers recruited agents from among the locals and sent them back into Waziristan to pinpoint Al

Qaeda facilities. These sorts of intelligence operations turned ugly and cost indigenous agents their lives. The C.I.A. "lost a lot of sources—to the Taliban, to a rival family," recalled a participant. Junior Pentagon and C.I.A. case officers under weak supervision would hand out Thuraya satellite phones and G.P.S. location loggers to local Pashtuns, to record the exact longitudinal and latitudinal coordinates of safe houses so the targets could be struck by drone missiles or smart bombs. But walking around with a G.P.S. logger in that region was itself "a death warrant."[21]

The Pakistan Army suffered similar agent losses. "The Taliban went witch-hunting" for American and I.S.I. spies, according to Major General Amir Faisal Alavi, who then commanded the Special Services Group, the commando unit that collaborated with the C.I.A. and Special Forces. Corpses of suspected spies began to turn up "all over Waziristan with their throats slit and a note in Pashto attached to their bodies explaining that the person had been caught, tried, proved to be a spy."[22]

That spring, Musharraf agreed to strike the hundreds of Al Qaeda–affiliated militants gathered in the Shkai Valley. Drone photography showed "training camps, people shooting," according to a senior intelligence official in the region. The C.I.A. briefed I.S.I. counterparts and placed small teams with Pakistani Special Forces in Waziristan. The C.I.A. officers carted around compact discs containing classified Predator footage approved for sharing with I.S.I. officers, to educate them about its potential to take out individuals and small groups with Hellfire missiles. From these discussions in the first half of 2004 arose the secret bargain on drone operations that would color U.S.-Pakistani relations for the next decade. Musharraf allowed the C.I.A. to operate drones armed with Hellfires in designated sections of the tribal areas. The C.I.A. agreed to deny that Musharraf had authorized any such thing.[23]

Musharraf argued, "Give the drones to Pakistan." But the C.I.A. refused him on this—the technology was too sensitive. Musharraf then proposed that the agency paint a couple of drones in Pakistan Air Force colors and go on operating as before, unilaterally. At least then he could more credibly claim that he was in charge. Again, the Americans refused.[24]

Both sides still agreed that they wanted Nek Mohammad dead. Not everyone on the American side thought this was a great idea. Assassinating a charismatic Wazir leader would mark a turn away from counter-terrorism operations against Al Qaeda into counterinsurgency against locally credible commanders, with unpredictable consequences. Perhaps it would be better to try to co-opt Mohammad to work with the Americans. Yet the predominant view among senior decision makers at the C.I.A. and in the American military was that the target was an Al Qaeda ally who posed a direct threat. Musharraf was delivering just the sort of risk taking conventional military operations in Waziristan that the Americans demanded. Nek Mohammad's tradecraft was poor. On July 17, 2004, as he talked on a satellite telephone, which he used to give radio interviews, and which could be easily traced by the likes of Task Force Orange, a C.I.A.-operated Predator launched a Hellfire missile from the skies above and killed him.[25]

Three months later, on October 9, more than eight million Afghans poured from their homes to cast ballots for president and dip their fingers in a pot of ink, to confirm their act of civic participation. The ink was supposed to be indelible, to prevent fraud, but it washed off easily. That glitch was not enough to call the election's legitimacy into serious question or to undermine the festival of national restoration the day of voting seemed to create. Seventy percent of registered voters turned out, more than in American presidential elections. Hamid Karzai prevailed against seventeen competitors, winning 55 percent of the reported vote. It was the first direct presidential election in Afghan history.

When the final tally was confirmed early in November, Karzai appeared in an illuminated garden at the presidential palace. "These votes are for stability," he said. "We hope with great love and friendship to help" the Afghan people. His magnanimity extended to the United States. Without the backing of the Bush administration and without Khalilzad's intense partnership during the previous two years the outcome might have been different. When Americans visited from Washington now, Karzai "made frequent reference to his fondness for the U.S. and Afghanistan's reliability as a partner in the war on terror," one note taker recorded. He spoke warmly about visiting his brother in Maryland

"and his pleasure driving himself (without an entourage and security) and enjoying coffee at Starbucks, as well as his enjoyment of country music in Nashville." As it turned out, this would be the high point of mutual regard between Karzai and America.[26]

Karzai and Khalilzad looked for factions of the Taliban and other armed opposition that might be persuaded to reconcile with the government. The election triumph created a new opportunity. Sections of Hizb-i-Islami, Gulbuddin Hekmatyar's party, had decided to enter politics. (Hekmatyar, who had taken refuge in Iran and then returned to Afghanistan and Pakistan, remained at large, operating an armed wing of his movement.) Hekmatyar's allies worked out a deal and entered parliament in Kabul.[27]

Zalmay Khalilzad sought new instructions from the Bush White House about terms for talking to the Taliban. The Afghan interagency group met to write an updated policy. American diplomats had talked with Taliban officials throughout the 1990s. The N.S.C. reviewed that history and now emphasized that any Taliban defector who wanted to avoid being sent to Guantánamo had to renounce Al Qaeda and be cleared of past involvement in terrorism. A few former Taliban did move to Kabul. In May 2005, however, Zalmay Khalilzad left to become ambassador to Iraq. Khalilzad was uniquely suited to defection talks with fellow Afghans. The momentum halted. Barno departed, too, a month later. He felt "there was a lost opportunity" after the election "to bring in larger numbers of the Taliban." Yet it did not seem a decisive failure at the time. When they left, he and Khalilzad both thought, "The Taliban are on the ropes, they were politically crushed by the election, this whole effort is on a success glide slope." They both "felt really, really good."[28]

The C.I.A., too, underestimated the Taliban's potential to regenerate. Partly this was because agency analysis concentrated on Al Qaeda. The C.I.A.'s analysts were also guilty in the first years after the Taliban's fall of a "kind of culture of self censorship," according to Paul Miller, an analyst at the Directorate of Intelligence, because they were reluctant to deliver bad news to the Bush White House. They feared that if their reporting on the early signs of the Taliban's revival was interpreted as criticism of Bush administration policy—its skepticism about Afghan nation building, for example—then the White House might stop listening to the C.I.A. Even when the evidence of trouble became harder to ignore, "there was a culture of optimism" about Afghanistan across the administration. Whenever somebody would say, "Things are getting worse," someone else would point out that the economy was growing, a new constitution was in place, they had just held a successful election, and, in any event, "Iraq is going much, much worse."[29]

TWELVE

Digging a Hole in the Ocean

Early in 2006, Ashfaq Kayani flew to Bagram Airfield on an unannounced visit. Kayani's place as Musharraf's most trusted and powerful lieutenant was by now ratified. He had been promoted to director-general of Inter-Services Intelligence. The sergeant's son and muddy-boots career officer now wore civilian suits at the whitewashed, manicured I.S.I. compound in Islamabad. His responsibilities encompassed the tribal areas, domestic politics, Baluch separatism, and I.S.I. platforms for anti-Indian operations such as Nepal, Sri Lanka, Bangladesh, and Thailand. Hardly a week passed without the Americans pressing onto his agenda. As a young officer, Kayani had smoked cigarettes, but he had given them up. The stress of running I.S.I. brought him back to the habit. He now chain-smoked, placing his Dunhills in a stemmed holder, which made him look like an eccentric British actor from the 1950s. Between his mumble and the clouds of smoke enshrouding him, he seemed well suited to the role of spymaster.

The C.I.A. sought to promote greater cooperation between I.S.I. and Afghanistan's National Directorate of Security. Rich Blee was one of the architects of the effort. He had a great fondness for both countries. He was among the Bush administration's South Asia hands who retained a hope that I.S.I. and N.D.S. had common interests in containing extremism and promoting stability. One problem was that Pakistan's generals regarded N.D.S. as a hostile force with a director, Amrullah Saleh, whom they judged to be an ally if not an agent of India. (Saleh regarded himself as an ardent Afghan nationalist and certainly not an agent of any foreign power; he worked with India, sometimes closely, among many other allies of an independent Afghanistan, including the United States.) Blee and others at C.I.A. respected Saleh and felt they could talk with him logically about anything—except I.S.I. Saleh would present a dossier of evidence that asserted something like "Colonel Mohammed is the Quetta Shura's contact at I.S.I." The C.I.A. would run it by their I.S.I. counterparts, who would reply, "We have a thousand Colonel Mohammeds." It was an objective fact that the Pakistani service had arrested and handed over hundreds of foreign Al Qaeda—many more than N.D.S. had collared. Wasn't that evidence of *some* good faith?

Saleh, however, had been accumulating files and addresses of Taliban and Al Qaeda leaders hiding in Pakistan. He placed Pashto-speaking agents into the Taliban's recruiting stream and chronicled changes in their salaries and training. He paid "watchers" to patrol the streets of Quetta and Peshawar, to map the homes, mosques, businesses, and families of exiled Taliban commanders. When N.D.S. caught would-be suicide attackers and assassins inside Afghanistan, the service exploited their cell phone records to trace support networks in Pakistan. Occasionally, Saleh would share with I.S.I. suspect cell phone numbers. Invariably, within a day or two, the numbers went dead, he told colleagues.

Saleh found the C.I.A.'s deference to I.S.I. and Musharraf highly frustrating. At one point during 2006, the United States had decided to build a new undeclared airstrip in Paktia Province, Afghanistan, near the Pakistan border, to facilitate reconnaissance operations. Crews hauled in bulldozers, metal sheeting, and other materials, but when Pakistan discovered the project, its generals demanded that it be shut down. The Americans complied. Because it was too much trouble to haul the equipment out, they bombed their own machinery so the Taliban could not steal it.[1]

At the Bagram conference, the idea was that Saleh and Kayani would exchange details about Al Qaeda and its allies. Detainees in N.D.S. custody had reported taking instructions in Mansehra, a mountain valley town in western Pakistan. Some even suggested Bin Laden might be hiding there. Saleh briefed Kayani on his intelligence.

"Which house?" the Pakistani spy chief asked.

"You'll have to do the last one hundred yards yourself," Saleh answered.

"This is unbelievable," Kayani said, meaning the N.D.S. reporting was not credible. Saleh said he would offer access to his source if Kayani agreed to work with the C.I.A. on the matter.

"Are you telling me you are spying in my country?"

"Yes."

Kayani was furious. "I don't need to be taught intelligence by someone the age of my son," he said, in Saleh's account.

The general went outside for a smoke. (The I.S.I. chief now struggled to last an hour in any meeting if smoking was not allowed.) He returned after he had cooled down. He said he hadn't meant his comment as an insult. He asked Saleh to invite him to his home in Panjshir. Saleh demurred. He was tired of hearing the Pakistanis always name him in reference to his home province—"that Panjshiri" seemed intended as a slur. He knew how hostile many Afghans were to I.S.I. "Mr. Director," he told Kayani, "you can't imagine how sensitive people are in regards to Pakistan."[2]

The Taliban were clearly on the march in 2006. The number of security incidents in Afghanistan documented by the United Nations grew tenfold between 2003 and the end of 2006. As the head of N.D.S., Saleh was obligated to investigate the Taliban's bases in Pakistan. Don't get caught, Saleh's colleagues at the C.I.A. urged him.

Saleh decided that spring to conduct a more formal study of the Taliban's resurgence, to inform Karzai, his cabinet, and allies of Afghanistan, including the Bush administration. He wanted to interview active Taliban field commanders personally. There were few impermeable lines in Afghanistan's internal conflicts. Saleh traveled to Zabul, Uruzgan, Helmand, Kandahar, and other provincial capitals. His colleagues in regional N.D.S. offices negotiated safe passage agreements with Taliban commanders, who came in to talk with him. This sometimes involved paying the Taliban for their time and insights. Saleh sat with enemy commanders for long hours. His classified paper, completed in May 2006, was titled "Strategy of the Taliban."[3]

Saleh regarded Pakistan as an "India-centric country," one that had never been "Afghanistan-centric." He concluded, based on the limited circumstantial and hard evidence available, that I.S.I. had made a decision in 2005 to support the Taliban more actively, with cash and other aid, backed by covert subsidies from Saudi Arabia. It was the 1980s and 1990s all over again. The consolidation of Karzai's government between 2003 and 2005 explained the timing of this Pakistani turn, Saleh judged.

"What made them switch?" he asked. "Parliamentary elections, presidential elections, Afghan consensus [that] we will make the new order work, and the growing, positive relationship of Afghanistan with India." In essence, Pakistan's generals feared that Karzai's legitimacy would steer Afghanistan toward a durable role as an Indian ally, with international backing, Saleh concluded. In a sense, both Pakistan and Afghanistan shared a dilemma: If they assumed the United States would not maintain a strong military commitment in the region for more than a few years, they had to maneuver now to construct alliances for a post–American scenario, recognizing that the region would almost certainly remain riven by the bitter conflict between India and Pakistan.[4]

Saleh's study predicted that the Taliban mobilization would intensify, and that by 2009, the guerrillas would be advancing from rural strongholds to threaten major cities like Kandahar. The paper forecast that the Taliban would mount a full-fledged insurgency that would bog down Afghan and international troops. This would turn out to be largely accurate, except that the Taliban drive on southern cities occurred even faster than that. "The pyramid of [the] Afghanistan government's legitimacy should not be brought down due to our inefficiency in knowing the enemy, knowing ourselves and applying resources efficiently," Saleh warned.[5]

Karzai was "extremely, extremely angry" about his findings. He ridiculed the predictions and asked him never again to call the Taliban "an insurgency."

Saleh told Karzai, "I hope time will prove me wrong. But this is a product of your intelligence service." It should be understood as an honest forecast based on independent field research.[6]

Condoleezza Rice, then secretary of state, was the first Bush cabinet member to grasp the seriousness of Afghanistan's deterioration. Although Iraq still overwhelmingly dominated the Bush administration's national security agenda, in the spring of 2006 Rice commissioned a study of the Afghan war similar to the one Saleh had initiated. She selected David Kilcullen, a former Australian Army officer who had earned a doctoral degree studying guerrilla warfare. He was a stocky, sandy-haired man then in his late thirties, with a bounce in his step and a gift for loose, entertaining expression. Kilcullen was well aware of Amrullah Saleh's view that "the Pakistanis are on the other side, and they're running the war" on the Taliban's behalf. Kilcullen dismissed this at the time as "a convenient excuse for" the N.D.S. chief and Karzai to evade responsibility for their government's corruption and inability to consolidate authority. His view was not an isolated one at the White House or the State Department. Any endorsement of Amrullah Saleh's assessment that officers within the I.S.I. commanded and controlled the Taliban's revival as part of official strategy endorsed by Musharraf remained an unpopular point of view in the Bush administration at the time.[7]

Kilcullen saw the Pakistani position as mainly one of weakness. He observed the awkward position the Pakistan Army had been forced into in Waziristan. Tribal uprisings had taught the British empire to maintain a light footprint there, to maintain control by providing cash subsidies from the relative safety of Peshawar. Independent Pakistan's generals were mostly ethnic Punjabis—effectively foreigners when they toured Waziristan. They had internalized Britain's lessons. Through a system of local political agents, and through I.S.I.'s construction of forward operating bases during the anti-Soviet Afghan war, Pakistan had developed its own Islamism-influenced system of light presence and heavy subsidies, with an implied guarantee of autonomy for local tribes. After 2002, however, the United States had pressured Musharraf to invade Waziristan with conventional, Punjabi-manned army forces. Musharraf had done so partly to assuage the Bush administration and partly to root out particular radical networks that had attempted to assassinate him. When local militants hammered the invading Pakistani troops, they forced the army into lock-down on scattered bases. Punjabi officers had to either fight or negotiate just to drive supplies down local roads. The Taliban and Waziri tribesmen had exposed the pretense of the Pakistan Army's invincibility.[8]

This left Musharraf in a complex mood by 2006: emotional about the tactical defeats and Pakistani casualties incurred in Waziristan, under American pressure; resentful of American imperiousness; cautious about further ground fighting in the tribal areas yet willing to at least consider more military action if the United States would equip the Pakistan Army for combat success.

Kilcullen traveled to Pakistan to study the war. His hosts provided him a "wish list" of upgraded defense and intelligence equipment they felt they needed. Some of the equipment Pakistan wanted the United States did not have—attack and transport helicopters, for example, which were in very short supply because of supply chain pressures created by the wars in Iraq and Afghanistan. Other equipment—night-vision goggles and infrared surveillance systems, for example—were judged too sensitive to hand over to Pakistan because they could leak to enemy guerrillas or be used against India.[9]

Kilcullen landed in Pakistan in May. He took briefings at the C.I.A. station. It remained a bastion of Counterterrorism Center personnel and funding. The station had evolved into an unusual forward interagency fusion center focused substantially on terrorism. There was a large room filled with cubicles occupied by officers from the National Security Agency, who ran signals intercept operations, and the National Geospatial Agency, which controlled satellite photography. The station still staffed traditional Near East/South Asia case officers who reported on local politics and counterproliferation specialists who followed Pakistan's nuclear program, but the Counterterrorism Center had a great many positions.[10]

With Musharraf's support, the C.I.A. had embedded officers on about half a dozen Pakistani military bases in the tribal areas. Case officers who rotated there found themselves trapped inside Pakistani facilities. Art Keller, a young case officer, rotated by helicopter to a Pakistan Army base in Waziristan during this period. An I.S.I. colonel and two I.S.I. majors were his liaison officers. They told him, "You can't come off this base because this is a secret base." Keller learned this was a polite fiction. The local Taliban knew the C.I.A. and American Special Forces were present; the real reason for their confinement was to prevent the Americans from trying to operate unilaterally and because of the genuine safety risks outside the base, where the Pakistan Army was vulnerable on the roads.

Running human agents outside base perimeters to collect intelligence about militants in Waziristan remained treacherous and difficult. Every few weeks another dead body turned up with "American spy" pinned to his chest. Most of the victims had nothing to do with the C.I.A., but case officers did lose agents. The atmosphere was deeply hostile to outsiders. Even Punjabi interpreters warned Keller that, because of their accents, they would themselves be killed if they tried to interview locals in markets or villages about sensitive subjects. That meant an effective reporting agent for the C.I.A. had to have the right vernacular, a plausible reason to be moving around a thinly populated region, and professional competence. They were not easy to find. The best a case officer could hope to do in many cases was to communicate by computer with agents who had access to militants. Recruiting new agents or meeting in person was difficult, and in the confines of Waziristan bases, all but impossible.[11]

During his study tour, Kilcullen heard the generalized doubts about Pakistan expressed by C.I.A. officers in the field. Yet Bush administration policy remained firmly rooted in partnership with Musharraf. Ryan Crocker, then the U.S. ambassador to Pakistan, feared that ramping up counterterrorism operations in Waziristan would blow back on Musharraf and destabilize Pakistan. And with reason: In March 2006, when a Pakistani Special Operations Task Force raided some Haqqani compounds in North Waziristan, killing Arabs and Chechens, local militants seized Pakistani government buildings in a furious and violent reaction. The operation "stirred up a hornet's nest that the military was unprepared for," the U.S. embassy in Islamabad reported. Now Kilcullen was studying how to equip and support the Pakistan Army to carry out more such operations. "Dave, I'm sitting on a powder keg here, and you're lighting matches," Crocker told Kilcullen.[12]

Which side was Musharraf on? Even after Amrullah Saleh's tetchy encounter with General Kayani, the C.I.A. continued to press Saleh to hand over evidence to I.S.I. so that Pakistan could round up suspected Al Qaeda and Taliban fugitives. The assumption was that the Pakistanis would make honest use of the N.D.S. intelligence. Kayani said so. Around the time of his study tour, N.D.S. and the C.I.A.'s Kabul Station jointly provided to I.S.I. "a list of known locations, addresses, fund details, last known position of a number of senior Taliban folks," as a senior Bush administration official involved described it. Some of the Taliban were under active surveillance. Within forty-eight hours, all of them moved. The Americans watched them disappear—they knew what had happened. Yet the Pakistanis just told them that their information was wrong.[13]

Kilcullen drove to Peshawar and then flew on a Pakistan Army helicopter to Waziristan. He traveled local roads in an armed convoy. His escorts included Frontier Corps paramilitaries drawn from local Pashtun families. When he returned, a C.I.A. officer called Kilcullen in. The officer showed him transcripts of intercepted phone calls his Frontier Corps escort had made to Al Qaeda leaders. "The American diplomat will be in your valley tomorrow if you want to kidnap them," his escort had reported.[14]

The Bush administration did not interpret the hostility of such local Pashtun enlisted men as evidence of high-level Pakistani collaboration with the Taliban, however. Because F.C. soldiers came from villages and tribes thoroughly infiltrated by the Taliban, their sympathies could not be relied upon—that was a historical problem that could not be fairly laid at Musharraf's feet, the thinking went. Indeed, the unreliability of the Frontier Corps was one reason Kilcullen wanted to equip Musharraf to increase regular Pakistan Army operations in the tribal areas.

Kilcullen's view of Pakistani complicity darkened, however. Even if one took the maximally generous view that Musharraf was merely a victim of his state's historical weakness in the tribal areas, the army's willingness to accept sanctuaries there and in Quetta was undeniable. Yet when Kilcullen first voiced concerns similar to Saleh's inside the administration, "People laughed at me." They thought he had gone native during his visits to Afghanistan, traveling out with Afghan security forces, absorbing their conspiracy theories about I.S.I. The conventional wisdom in the Bush administration remained that the Pakistani position was one of weakness and ineptitude, not malice toward the American project in Afghanistan.[15]

Т he way to defeat terrorism in the short run is to share intelligence and to take action." It was March 2, 2006, and President George W. Bush stood bathed in sunshine in the Moghul Garden of Hyderabad House in New Delhi, beside Indian prime minister Manmohan Singh. Bush had flown to India to ratify in public "a strategic partnership based on common values" that had emerged between the United States and India.[16]

The U.S.-India Civil Nuclear Agreement provided the clearest evidence that an alliance between America and India, one that might contain China's rise as a great power, had progressed beyond rhetoric. Under the accord, the Bush administration set aside objections to India's clandestine atomic bomb program and agreed to supply fuel and technology to support civilian nuclear power production. Bush signaled the end of any pretense of equivalence in American policies toward India and Pakistan. The latter would not be eligible for such nuclear assistance because "Pakistan and India are different countries," as a White House fact sheet put it, and "Pakistan does not have the same nonproliferation record as India," a reference to the Pakistani nuclear scientist A. Q. Khan's global nuclear smuggling enterprise.[17]

Bush flew from India to Islamabad, despite the threat of terrorist attacks. To fool assassins, the Secret Service sent a decoy motorcade down Islamabad's broad streets, with Bush's protocol director, Donald Ensenat, in the president's seat. Bush and his wife flew secretly by Black Hawk helicopter. The president's decision to trust Pakistani security at all signaled his genuine faith in Musharraf. Yet when he arrived, Bush pressured Musharraf to do more against terrorism and to accelerate a transition toward full democracy. Musharraf fumed over the Indian nuclear deal. Privately, he warned that it would alienate the generals in Pakistan's high command from the United States.[18]

"We understand your geostrategic relationship with India," Musharraf told Republican senator Chuck Hagel that spring. Yet the Indian nuclear accord was "vastly unpopular" inside the Pakistani military. Pakistan "would now be grappling with the prospect of a nuclear arms race," Musharraf complained, and this would inevitably affect his cooperation with the United States. He "cherished" his friendship with Bush: "I say he is a friend. He is sincere and open. . . . And we are together in fighting terror." Yet the India deal had created a strategic divide from Washington more significant than personal trust and affection.[19]

Musharraf also took note of the Bush administration's decision to hand peacekeeping operations in Afghanistan over to British, European, and Canadian forces. The plan dated to 2003 but was now being implemented. The International Security Assistance Force, or I.S.A.F., was a N.A.T.O.-deployed military distinct from America's terrorist-hunting task forces around Afghanistan. I.S.A.F. troops remained mostly confined to Kabul and cities in Afghanistan's north. The idea now was to spread out first to the north, then to the west, then to the south and east. If Afghanistan was a clock face, that is, the international forces would move from the top of the dial counterclockwise around, fully deploying in Helmand, Uruzgan, and Kandahar by mid-2006.[20]

Musharraf and Karzai reacted similarly to this transition. The handover only affirmed what they had feared and predicted. The United States, the world's most powerful military, would not stay the course in Afghanistan. None of the British, Canadian, or Dutch forces planned for aggressive combat against the Taliban. They would support peace and reconstruction in the manner of U.N. peacekeeping and peace enforcement operations in Africa or the Balkans.

The transition plan "makes us nervous and angry," Karzai told American visitors privately. Afghanistan's stability "is a journey still in progress."[21]

In Pakistan, Musharraf and the corps commanders concluded, "The

Americans . . . are out the door," as Colonel Tom Lynch, a special adviser at Central Command who served as a military assistant to Zalmay Khalilzad in Kabul during 2004, put it. Therefore, the thinking of Pakistani officers went, as Lynch summarized it, "We need our proxies," meaning the Taliban, "in as best condition we can [manage] without being fingered as state sponsors of terrorism."[22]

The blindness to Pakistan's intentions in Washington, London, Ottawa, and The Hague would have devastating consequences. The victims included British, Canadian, and Dutch soldiers who encountered fierce combat their politicians and intelligence services had not predicted. And they included many villagers in Helmand and Kandahar who were soon caught up in shocking, often indiscriminate trench and artillery battles from late 2006, a war sometimes fought at close quarters in thick marijuana, poppy, and grape fields, at other times by assassins, suicide bombers, and Taliban roadside bombing crews.

Just as Gul Agha Sherzai's self-enriching tour as Kandahar's governor after 2001 had set local conditions for the Taliban's revival there, Helmand's government of strongmen, narco-traffickers, and opportunists eased the Taliban's return. Karzai's appointed representatives in Helmand included some of the very thugs whose abuses had fueled the Taliban revolution in the first instance.

The provincial governor, Sher Mohammad Akhundzada, had ties to the opium trade. Dad Mohammad Khan, a local militia leader from the Alokozai tribe, ran the provincial National Directorate of Security forces. Abdul Rahman Jan, a warlord from the Noorzai tribe, ran the provincial police. They returned to their ways. The strongmen fought with one another and "attempted to fool U.S. Special Forces into targeting the others' militias as 'Taliban,' with some success." And they preyed on villagers. "Day by day, the situation got worse," as a member of a local Helmand council described it. "There was lots of extortion and stealing and people were killed." Gradually, "people got fed up with the Afghan government and welcomed the Taliban back into their districts."[23]

Through interviews and surveys with about 150 Taliban command-

ers and unaffiliated tribal elders in Helmand, the researchers Theo Farrell and Antonio Giustozzi constructed one of the most detailed portraits
of the Taliban comeback in southern Afghanistan between 2004 and
2006. The Taliban first infiltrated the area with "vanguard" teams of
two or three people who secretly contacted villagers and elders. As one
resident described it, "They told the people that they were coming back
to the district to fight against the government." The Taliban assassinated
Afghans holding government offices. By 2005 they had returned in
force to control rural areas, but they did not call attention to themselves
by seizing district centers. These Taliban forces included a heavy contingent of Punjabi speakers—that is, Pakistani nationals from that country's eastern and southern breadbasket. There were also Arabs and
Iranians.[24]

Since 2004, the United States had deployed barely one hundred soldiers to Helmand on counterterrorism and minor reconstruction missions. They had no orders or ability to collect intelligence on the Taliban
infiltration. They were "marauding companies of Alabama National
Guardsmen and Ranger Squads" who would "charge into villages all guns
blazing and AC/DC blasting out of the speakers on the PsyOps Hum-
mer," as Patrick Hennessey, a young British officer who served in Helmand on training missions during this period, put it acidly.[25]

In London, "there was little genuine intelligence available about how
benign or hostile an environment" Helmand might present when 3,300
British troops arrived there during 2006, according to a researcher who
interviewed army and intelligence officers, as well as cabinet officials.
MI6 and British military intelligence "seem to have" warned in classified
channels that Taliban leaders in Quetta had "decided to target the British in particular as they arrived in theater." Britain's history as an invader
of Afghanistan during the nineteenth century provided an obvious narrative for Taliban recruitment and mobilization. Yet Tony Blair's then
minister of defense, John Reid, said publicly in April 2006, "We would
be perfectly happy to leave in three years and without firing one shot."[26]

That spring, about two hundred thousand seasonal poppy harvesters
migrated into Helmand—many of them young men ripe for recruitment
against the British. Guns, drugs, and jihad: The essence of war against

international forces in southern Afghanistan had not changed much since the Soviet occupation.

Poppy production exploded in 2006—the area under cultivation in Helmand more than doubled compared with the year before, according to the United Nations. That upped local incentives to capture the opium trade. Around this time, Britain pressured Karzai to dump Governor Kahundzada. The deposed warlord's militia members soon "aligned with the Taliban" and attacked government posts. All this quickened the coming British fiasco.

Hamid Karzai and Akhundzada's successor, Mohammad Daoud, pressured Brigadier Ed Butler to rapidly send British forces to retake territory from the Taliban. "If the black flag of Mullah Omar flies over any of the district centers, you may as well go home," Daoud pleaded.[27]

Butler rapidly deployed small British units to isolated "platoon houses" in Now Zad, Sangin, Garmsir, and Musa Qala. By the end of May 2006 they were "fighting for their lives" in a "series of Alamos," as Lieutenant General Rob Fry put it. The British Gurkha forces in Now Zad held off Taliban who called out to one another in Urdu, Pakistan's national language.

"How the hell did we get ourselves into this position?" a British cabinet minister asked a colleague. "How did we go charging up the valley without it ever being put to the cabinet?"[28]

The answers included Butler's autonomy as field commander, poor coordination within N.A.T.O., and poor intelligence. The failures cascaded. Without enough men, armored vehicles, or helicopters for this unpredicted war, Butler relied on close air support—aerial bombing—to protect his stranded men from Taliban sieges. The British platoon house at Musa Qala called in 249 bombs onto enemy positions in a single ten-day period, just one example of a prolonged barrage that took civilian lives and property. The Taliban exploited the ensuing collateral damage—homes destroyed, women and children killed and wounded—to recruit local fighters.[29]

The forward element of Canada's commitment of more than two thousand soldiers to Kandahar Province, which arrived early in 2006, was called Task Force Orion, commanded by Lieutenant Colonel

Ian Hope. His domain covered twenty thousand square miles of jungle-like irrigated agricultural fields, mountains, stark deserts, mud-walled villages, and the smoky sprawl of Kandahar City. Hope was unprepared by intelligence or political reporting for the widespread Taliban infiltration he encountered.

"Where are they?" he would ask Afghan intelligence counterparts.

"Everywhere."

"What villages?"

"All of them."

"When?"

"Every day."

"What about the mountains?"

"In the mountains too."[30]

The only way to pinpoint Taliban positions was through reconnaissance by force, which meant driving around until "somebody shoots at you," as a Canadian officer put it. That spring Canadian patrols shot up small Taliban units. They found in abandoned encampments propaganda calling on all Afghans to wage jihad against the United States, Britain, and Canada. They also found concentrated opium paste so powerful "that if you touch it it'll absorb into your skin and really fuck you up."[31]

The Canadian plan emphasized "whole of government" approaches to assist Afghanistan, a "3-D" strategy of defense, diplomacy, and development. Canada's defense history included bloody combat at D-Day and in Korea, but since then the country had emphasized peacekeeping. Canada's development-first assumptions suffered on contact with the Taliban that spring. The guerrillas massed clandestinely in the lush, irrigated green zone to the west of Kandahar.

Brigadier General David Fraser, the top Canadian commander, judged that the Taliban intended to threaten Kandahar, "to demonstrate the weakness and the inability of the national Government to come after them with a conventional force. This also indicated to us that the Taliban were actually progressing . . . to the next stage where they thought they were capable enough to go and challenge the national government and coalition forces in a conventional manner." This was what Amrullah Saleh reported in his classified paper that spring.[32]

Fraser also thought that the Taliban wanted to draw Canadian troops into the green zone "in a battle of attrition" intended to inflict "as many casualties as possible" to weaken Canadian resolve and undermine public opinion at home. Fraser's commanders carried around dog-eared copies of Lester Grau's *The Bear Went over the Mountain*, a history of Soviet military experience in Afghanistan, which made clear that as the Taliban dug in during 2006 along the walled, vine-thickened fields beside the Arghandab River, they were only following a plan with a successful precedent.

Canadian forces launched Operation Mountain Thrust on May 15 "to defeat the Taliban in their traditional areas." Canadian forces took casualties but inflicted many more. Their officers interpreted the campaign as a decisive triumph. On June 4, the Canadian journalist Graeme Smith, who had moved to Kandahar, joined a convoy summoned by Canadian military public relations specialists to declare victory. Suicide bombers struck the convoy en route. "Charred pieces of human flesh stuck to the armor." The journalists assumed the victory ceremony would be canceled but it went ahead. "Four successive strikes against the Taliban broke the back of their insurgency here," Colonel Hope pronounced.[33]

By September the Canadians had come to realize that every time they pulled back from a firefight to refit on their bases, Taliban reinforcements slipped in to take up the positions vacated by their departed martyrs. It "was like digging a hole in the ocean," Fraser reflected.[34]

American Special Forces reconnaissance units patrolling the vast, unpopulated Registan Desert on the southern flanks of the Canadian deployments found evidence of why Taliban supply lines were so resilient. One patrol stopped a convoy of trucks manned by civilians in local dress who claimed they were gasoline smugglers trafficking with Iran. In fact, they were smuggling arms. The Americans found a current Pakistani military identification card that a driver had hidden under his truck's dashboard.[35]

Operation Medusa followed during the first seventeen days of September, the largest N.A.T.O. land battle in the alliance's sixty-year existence. Canadian forces rolled into the green zone and won violent dismounted firefights with Taliban fighters who were protected by vineyard structures and irrigation ditches.

Fraser estimated there were about five hundred Taliban fighters embedded in the green zone and that only two hundred of them were hard core. But a Special Forces linguist assigned to listen to Taliban radio chatter soon concluded that there were a thousand or more. Four Canadians died in the initial assault and casualties mounted in the withering heat.

Again, after Medusa, the Canadians and their Afghan allies declared victory. "The ability of the Taliban to stay and fight in groups is finished," Asadullah Khalid, the longtime C.I.A. ally and young confidant of Hamid Karzai, who was now Kandahar's governor, announced on September 17. "The enemy has been crushed."[36]

I t was not evident to senior American diplomats posted to Afghanistan during 2006 that the Taliban had acquired momentum. "The increased number of suicide attacks remains deeply disturbing," reported a Kabul embassy cable to Washington on April 24, 2006. The police needed more guns and ammunition. Afghan soldiers in Kandahar needed to form a quick reaction force to respond to pop-up Taliban attacks. Yet there was "noteworthy good news" from southern Afghanistan, the cable added. "So far this year, the Taliban do not appear to have the capability to recruit or field as many fighters as they did last year."[37]

To the extent that America's Iraq-distracted intelligence apparatus examined the Taliban threat closely, it focused across the border in Waziristan, where Al Qaeda had embedded and where American signals and overhead collection were expanding. There, too, in early September, the Bush administration received a shock. Musharraf's government announced a peace deal with tribal elders, Taliban commanders, and foreign fighters in North Waziristan. The Taliban said they would not cross into Afghanistan or mainland Pakistan to carry out attacks. The agreement had no enforcement mechanism. Pakistan released scores of jailed militants and promised never to prosecute the militants for past crimes.

The army dismantled recently established security checkpoints, promised to staff older checkpoints only with local tribal militias, returned previously seized weaponry and vehicles, stopped all military operations, and paid compensation for damage from past operations. The U.S. consulate in Peshawar noted that "many observers" were "skeptical" that the agreement would "effectively reduce cross-border attacks on coalition and Afghan forces" or halt the spread of Islamism in the long term. That would prove to be a considerable understatement.[38]

The Waziristan peace deal's architect was retired Pakistani lieutenant general Ali Muhammad Aurakzai. Musharraf had appointed him governor of Northwest Frontier Province earlier that year. The governor also oversaw the Federally Administered Tribal Areas. Aurakzai was a Pashtun; his family hailed from one of the smaller tribal agencies. The position of Pashtun Army officers who made up about 20 percent of the Pakistani military officer corps, the largest ethnic group after the dominant Punjabis, was complicated. General Aurakzai's local contacts and credibility among Pashto-speaking tribes struck Musharraf as an asset. For his part, Aurakzai urged Musharraf to give peace with his brethren a chance. The military incursions in the F.A.T.A. urged by the Americans had failed. Rather than attack the tribes, Aurakzai argued, Pakistan should negotiate to restore their autonomy in exchange for loyalty to Pakistan's core goals and interests. Once peace was established, Pakistan could provide jobs and services that would cement the tribes to the state.

Musharraf flew to Kabul on September 6. The Afghan government arranged for him to address about four hundred members of parliament and religious leaders. Hamid Karzai was reluctant to accompany Musharraf personally to the speech, for fear of being seen as soft on Pakistan, but the American and British ambassadors persuaded him to do so. In his remarks, Musharraf drew a line between Pakistani policy toward the Taliban before 2001 and now. He said Pakistan no longer "sees the Taliban as representing Pashtuns." His peace policy in Waziristan was designed to empower non-Taliban moderates through investment and development. In a rare concession, he acknowledged that Al Qaeda and the Taliban were active inside Pakistan, "as they are in Afghanistan," yet he took pains to make distinctions between good and bad Taliban. He argued that Afghan and Pakistani security were mutually dependent, and he concluded by reading a few lines of poetry: "Whenever there is trouble in Afghanistan, there is trouble in all of Asia."[39]

Musharraf and Karzai flew on to Washington. Bush greeted them in the Rose Garden. At dinner in the family quarters of the White House, Musharraf sold the North Waziristan peace deal as forcefully as he could. Give it a chance, he urged Bush. He spoke for more than thirty minutes, "sugarcoating the facts and overselling the potential benefits," as Condoleezza Rice put it. Karzai interrupted at last to say that Musharraf had cut a deal not with tribal leaders but "with the terrorists." Karzai theatrically pulled a translation of the agreement out of his cape and read from it at the table.

"Tell me where they are," Musharraf demanded of Karzai, referring to the Taliban's leaders.

"You know where they are!"

"If I did, I would get them."

"Go do it!"[40]

Later, it would become commonplace for American officials to describe Karzai as erratic, corrupt, ungrateful, or all three, off the record at first, then publicly. In late 2006, there was little basis for such an accusation. Tethered by his close personal relationship with Bush and still willing to bear the political fallout at home from American mistakes, Karzai spoke out publicly in defense of Bush administration policy, even though such advocacy risked reinforcing the Taliban's relentless propaganda that Karzai was nothing but a puppet of Western powers. Bush checked in with him regularly in order "to lift his spirits and assure him of our commitment." Yet while he offered advice and made requests, "I was careful not to give him orders." Years later, Karzai dated the first deterioration of his relations with Washington to 2005, when civilian casualties caused by American bombing first became untenable for him, yet even then, Karzai recalled, "I had a very good relationship with President Bush" and "we had not experienced what we experienced later" by way of stinging personal criticism of his rule. As late as the autumn of 2006, in television interviews, in speeches, Karzai's principal complaint was not

American arrogance or civilian casualties, but Pakistan. Musharraf was not doing enough to deprive the Taliban of a base of operations on its soil, and Afghanistan was paying the price.[41]

The Waziristan peace plan was now official Pakistan Army policy. Soon American military officers in Afghanistan encountered John Lennon's immortal plea in bold letters on PowerPoint slides presented by their Pakistani counterparts: "Give Peace a Chance." In the next slide the Pakistani officers would brief on Carl von Clausewitz's familiar observation about war as an extension of politics. Some of the American officers who endured these presentations could barely contain themselves.

Lieutenant General Karl Eikenberry commanded American forces in Afghanistan during 2006. He was in the midst of the second of what would prove to be three tours in the country. He was a West Point graduate who later earned graduate degrees at Harvard and Stanford. He had a reputation as a demanding character who could be difficult to work for, but who had a sharp and independent mind. When he arrived in Afghanistan, Eikenberry toured frontline bases and heard from diverse S-2s, the field military officers in charge of intelligence, about the enemy's infiltration routes and supply lines. The tactical picture was impressive in its specificity. His S-2s put up PowerPoint slides with red diamonds to mark cells and lines running into Pakistan.

"Where does this go to across the border?" Eikenberry asked.

"General, we really don't know" was the typical answer.[42]

Joint Special Operations Command and the C.I.A. "didn't want to be distracted by fights against the Taliban in the interior" of Afghanistan at this time, in Eikenberry's experience. They were focused on the borders and Al Qaeda. The tensions between C.I.A. officers based in Kabul and Islamabad that had flared during Zalmay Khalilzad's ambassadorship remained. Kabul Station felt Islamabad was naïve about I.S.I. complicity, while Islamabad defended the partnership. The fights were so intense that Eikenberry felt that "if two dear twin brothers were assigned respectively to serve the different station chiefs, they would hate each other within twenty-four hours."[43]

Eikenberry flew to Quetta and Rawalpindi with C.I.A. and intelligence officers to present classified briefings to Pakistani counterparts about Taliban sanctuaries inside Pakistan and the ease with which Taliban forces were flowing into Afghanistan. The Pakistanis would admit nothing and countered with briefings of their own about sanctuary Afghanistan provided to fugitive violent guerrillas from Pakistan's Baluchistan Province. On Al Qaeda, they could still do business, but on the Taliban, the C.I.A. and I.S.I. settled now into a dead embrace informed by accusation and denial.[44]

THIRTEEN

Radicals

I n May 2006, British security services asked Ashfaq Kayani at I.S.I. to
watch Abdulla Ahmed Ali, a Londoner traveling in Pakistan. It had
been less than a year since four British-born suicide bombers detonated themselves on London Underground trains and a double-decker
bus, killing 52 people. A second attempt three weeks later failed narrowly. The problem of violent extremism among British Muslims was
complex, but Pakistan was part of the story. About 825,000 people of
Pakistani origin lived in England; every year, at least a quarter of a million people traveled between Pakistan and Britain. Identifying violent
radicals within that flotsam became an urgent priority for British
intelligence after 2005. Cooperation from I.S.I.'s Directorate C, the
counterterrorism division, seemed essential, given the needle-in-a-
haystack dimensions of the problem.[1]

Abdulla Ahmed Ali was then twenty-five years old. He had been
born in Newham, a low-income borough of East London, to parents who
had emigrated from Pakistan's Punjab. He was one of four brothers. His
eldest brother was a technology consultant. Another worked part time
for the London Underground. The third was a probation officer at the
Home Office, which oversaw the British police. None of them had a
criminal record, nor did Ali. Yet Ali's frequent travel to Pakistan and his
contact with other Britons under surveillance as terrorism suspects had
led British services to request I.S.I.'s help.

A cousin picked Ali up at Islamabad's international airport and drove him toward the family's home village, Jhelum. Pakistani police stopped the car and searched it, but let the men go. In his village Ali learned from relations serving in the local police that I.S.I. was on his case.

The suspicions about him were well grounded, as it happened. Ali had entered into a conspiracy with Al Qaeda to carry out spectacular bombing attacks in Britain. His main contact was a fellow Briton, Rashid Rauf, who was now living as a fugitive in Pakistan. Rauf had left England in 2002 after falling under suspicion in the stabbing murder of an uncle. He had since joined up with an Al Qaeda bomb maker from Egypt known as Abu Ubaydah, who worked out of the Federally Administered Tribal Areas. By May 2006, when I.S.I. picked up Ali's trail, the conspirators had completed experiments on potent liquid explosives manufactured from hydrogen peroxide, hexamine, and citric acid. Their formula could disguise a powerful bomb as a colored sports drink, to be detonated by ordinary AA batteries. Initially, the group had planned to strike oil or gas refineries in England but by May they had discovered that their bombs might be smuggled aboard commercial airliners and detonated at altitude, bringing the planes down. Rauf and Abu Ubaydah had recruited Ali to lead a team of bombers that might destroy half a dozen or more packed airliners over the Atlantic as they flew from London to the United States. If the plan succeeded, it would be the most devastating Al Qaeda attack since September 11.[2]

After leaving his village, uncertain how closely he was being watched, Ali met Abu Ubaydah in Waziristan, studied the latest bomb design, and flew back to London carrying notes scribbled to himself:

Clean batteries. Perfect disguise. Drinks bottles, Lucozade, orange, red. Oasis, orange, red. Mouthwash, blue, red. Calculateexact drops of Tang, plus colour . . . Select date. Five days B4. Alllink up. Prepare. Dirty mag to distract. Condoms. One drink used, other keep in pocket maybe will not go through machine, putkeys and chewing gum on D in the elec device. Keep ciggies. Camera cases. The drinks that you drink should be dif flava. . . .[3]

The London Underground bombings of 2005 had appeared to be homegrown. The bombers' prerecorded martyrdom testaments emphasized their opposition to the Iraq war and Anglo-American occupation of Muslim lands. Their grievances suggested that the provocation of the U.S.-led Iraq invasion had led dispersed, isolated individuals to take action in the name of Al Qaeda or its ideology. In the absence of initial hard evidence about how the Underground bombers had made their relatively simple bombs, packed into lumpy backpacks, the British government was cautious about whether Al Qaeda had a role. A year later, however, surveillance of Ali and his conspirators, among other intelligence, had brought a revised picture into focus. Rauf and Al Qaeda bomb makers had in fact aided the Underground bombers decisively.[4] Between that case and this latest one, it was becoming clear that an evolving Al Qaeda consisted of both a new wave of dispersed angry Muslims inflamed by American and British foreign policy *and* the residual, skilled Arab terrorists who had fled Afghanistan to hide in Waziristan after 2001.

Following the U.S. invasion of Afghanistan, shocked by televised images of Afghan refugees seeking shelter from the American-led air war, Ali had volunteered at a London charity, the Islamic Medical Association. It ran an ambulance service in refugee camps near Chaman, the Pakistani town on the border with Afghanistan, to the south of Kandahar. Later, with one of his older brothers, Ali joined street protests against the invasion of Iraq. He attended the huge antiwar march in London on February 15, 2003. At the time, "It felt good . . . to know you're doing something, you're getting your voice heard," as he put it later. Soon after, he flew to Pakistan to volunteer as an ambulance driver around Chaman. He had never seen such suffering:

> It's so mucky, smelly, loads of kids running round crying, really like appalling conditions. Lots of arguing, kind of chaotic . . . I don't think anything can prepare you for something like that. . . . Emotionally it was very straining. . . . Some were maimed, some had their legs blown off, some had bits of their fingers missing, scars, burn marks, skinny, rugged, rough-looking faces. . . . There was lots of deaths in these camps, daily.

We have to come on funerals almost every day, but it's mostly kids that
were dying, children, young children . . . seeing the mothers going
through, pulling their hair out.

Ali blamed Britain and America for what he saw. The following spring
he wrote a will that suggested he was prepared for martyrdom. He became
"less enthusiastic and confident in things like protests and marches. . . . We
knew now the war was illegal in Iraq and it wasn't a secret no more. It was
a lie. It was just deceit. It was a criminal war. In my eyes that made the
government criminals. . . . The root problem was the foreign policy and
that's something that should be tackled."[5]

On several trips to Pakistan after 2004, Ali connected with Rauf and
Abu Ubaydah. In June 2006, after traveling under I.S.I. surveillance, he
flew back to Heathrow. British police secretly inspected his luggage. They
found AA batteries and many packets of powdered Tang. Unbeknownst
to Ali, the police then placed him under fuller surveillance, in the hope
that they could identify everyone Ali was working with in Britain, so that
all participants in the conspiracy could be arrested. Detaining Ali prematurely risked having his case dismissed for lack of evidence. It might also
leave other as yet unknown conspirators in Britain untouched.

The surveillance operation unfolded during a period of rising estrangement between the C.I.A. and British security services. In the
second-term Bush administration, some American policy makers had
come to think of the French as "really a more engaged ally than the
Brits," as one senior administration official put it. In Afghanistan, C.I.A.
officers from the paramilitary Special Activities Division dominated Kabul Station and the border bases. Their Omega Counterterrorist Pursuit
Teams operated on their own, without collaboration with the British.
Some of the paramilitary types from C.I.A. regarded MI6's Oxbridge
types as cerebral and even effete, or so it seemed to the estranged British
officials who dealt with Langley. In Afghanistan, the Americans dressed
in cargo pants and flak jackets and had beards and were "immensely cool
and carried a weapon," as one senior European official involved in the
war put it. "Most of the C.I.A. chiefs of station [in Kabul] came from
the sort of paramilitary wing." The Americans were "taking up all the

oxygen" in Afghanistan and Pakistan, as a senior British intelligence official described it. "The C.I.A. has always been very mission-driven and
they thought that we were a bit wimpy and weren't all that useful anymore. It was a difficult time."[6]

By August 2006, the C.I.A. had been drawn into the British surveillance operation involving Ali. American "clandestine technical resources"
had determined that "planning for the strike was coming from North
Waziristan," according to Jose Rodriguez, then the head of worldwide
C.I.A. operations. Rodriguez had only "a vague understanding that British authorities were hoping we would not move too rashly" against the
surveillance targets.[7]

That was an understatement. The Ali case was so sensitive that Prime
Minister Tony Blair spoke to President Bush about it, to obtain Bush's
agreement that the C.I.A. would move slowly so that British officers
could identify all the conspirators. The day Blair and Bush spoke, however, Rodriguez happened to be in Pakistan, meeting with Ashfaq Kayani at his home.

They had what was becoming a typically tense conversation about
whether Pakistan was succoring militants. "I'm tired of you Americans
saying we are not doing enough to fight the terrorists," Kayani declared.

As if to reinforce his grievance, the I.S.I. chief described an opportunity for joint counterterrorist action. He reported that surveillance officers following Rashid Rauf believed he was about to board a bus and
might be difficult to follow further. "We want to proceed with his capture," Kayani said. "Are you with us?"

"Let's get him," Rodriguez declared.

Rodriguez did not call back to Langley, which would have been "the
cautious thing" but also would have effectively refused Kayani, because
"Washington never responds instantly."[8]

I.S.I. officers seized Rauf on August 25. That sudden action forced
British police to arrest about two dozen people in and around London that
same night, before they could be tipped off. The British were furious.

The Al Qaeda plan to blow up half a dozen or more civilian airliners
flying to America from London remained weeks or months from being
attempted. British surveillance meant the plot would never likely have

succeeded. And yet the ambition and technical plausibility of the conspiracy shocked the Bush administration. As the C.I.A. documented the threat posed by British-born, Pakistani-trained radicals who could travel easily to the United States, the Americans started to push British counterparts for permission to run their own unilateral operations on U.K. soil. Eliza Manningham-Buller, then the director-general of MI5, the British equivalent of the F.B.I., had to warn C.I.A. counterparts at one point, "If we find you doing this, we'll arrest you."[9]

Six Britons, including Abdulla Ahmed Ali, recorded martyrdom videos before the arrests of August 25. Several others may have been prepared to blow up commercial airliners, according to a diary kept by Rauf. As with the testaments recorded by the Underground bombers, Ali's group described their terrorism as religiously sanctioned warfare.

During the 1990s, Bin Laden's writings and interviews describing Al Qaeda's ideology had included arguments for resistance to what he imagined to be American occupation of Saudi Arabia, as well as its military intervention in Somalia and support for Israel. Yet there had also been a millenarian, rambling quality to Bin Laden's thinking. By now the invasion of Iraq and the deteriorating Afghan war had broadened the appeal of Bin Laden's messages, attracting literate TV news-watching Muslims genuinely fed up with Western foreign policy and inclined to volunteer for the fight. As Ali put it in his martyrdom video that summer:

> We Muslim people have pride. . . . We are brave. We're not cowards. Enough is enough. We've warned you so many times to get out of our lands, leave us alone, but you have persisted in trying to humiliate us, kill us and destroy us. Sheikh Osama warned you many times to leave our lands or you will be destroyed.

Off camera, someone asked him, "What about innocent people? Surely, just because the *kuffar* kill our innocent does not mean that we should . . . kill theirs?"

Ali answered, "You show more care and concern for animals than you do for the Muslim *ummah*."[10]

The back-to-back American-led invasions of Afghanistan and Iraq had not only attracted new adherents to Al Qaeda, they had revived Bin Laden's own confidence in his ideas. After Tora Bora, it had taken about nine months for Bin Laden and Al Qaeda's operatives to reorganize public communication. In October 2002, Bin Laden released a "letter to America" seemingly written in reply to the many magazine covers and newspaper headlines in the West asking, *Why do they hate us?*

"Here we outline our reply to two questions addressing the Americans," Bin Laden wrote. "Why are we waging Jihad against you? What advice do we have for you and what do we want from you?" The answer to the first question, he continued, "is very simple: Because you attacked us. . . . You ransack our lands, stealing our treasures and oil."[11]

The next month, Al Jazeera released an audiotape from Bin Laden. He spoke about recent suicide and car bombings in Bali, Moscow, and Jordan. The C.I.A. confirmed Bin Laden's voice; for the first time since late 2001, there could be no doubt that Bin Laden was alive and restored to some sort of leadership role. The Iraq war brought forth a torrent of geopolitical messages from him. At one point, Bin Laden offered a truce to European nations if they withdrew from the Iraq coalition. Al Qaeda bombed train commuters in Madrid in retaliation for Spain's participation in Iraq.

Abu Musab al-Zarqawi, a squat Jordanian radical who had run a training camp in Afghanistan before 2001 but had never met Bin Laden, formed a vicious network inside Iraq to strike the United States and Iraqi Shiite allies. Zarqawi's grotesque beheadings on digital video worried Bin Laden and Ayman Al Zawahiri. They wrote to him to urge less sectarian, less ruthless tactics. Yet Bin Laden embraced Al Qaeda in Iraq, as Zarqawi's network became known, because it positioned Al Qaeda as a resistance force in the most violent war then taking place in the Islamic world. In June 2006, American warplanes killed Zarqawi outside Baghdad. Bin Laden eulogized him as a "knight, the lion of holy war," and urged that the fight continue.[12]

By 2006 Al Qaeda producers in Waziristan and elsewhere in Pakistan had also seized upon the digital revolution to launch a next-generation media arm, As-Sahab. From laptops and wireless hot spots its propagandists self-published mainly on Islamist Web sites. Bin Laden continued to communicate sporadically by audiotape and the occasional video. In the four years between 2002 and 2005 Al Qaeda released a total of forty-six messages, by one independent count. In 2006 alone it released fifty-eight, more than one per week.[13]

The Afghan Taliban and its ideological fellow travelers recovered their public voices in similar fashion. In 2005, a splinter group launched a Web magazine, *Tora Bora*. "Can anyone of you deny that Afghanistan is an American colony?" one of its writers asked. "Can any Afghan boast about the honor, respect and sacredness of his homeland without being humiliated and snubbed by the Americans? How is it possible for our young boys to introduce themselves as proud Afghans in the world? How can our women prove their chastity in the presence of the over-drunk Americans? Is there any other way than migration and suicides?"[14]

Tora Bora was more eclectic and less brutally strident than As-Sahab. It published essays on electric fish and gardening and offered disquisitions on Islamic history, law, and conduct. Yet the editors returned to certain themes of wartime propaganda. They offered a revisionist history of the fallen Islamic Emirate in Afghanistan, "a wonderful, peaceful system for the whole world," in which the "lives and property of all the people were safe." By comparison, "foreign masters" controlled Hamid Karzai's American-backed regime. The Karzai cabinet was "made by the C.I.A." and comprised formerly exiled Afghans who "don't know the geography of Afghanistan, nor do they know the culture and traditions of Afghans." These agents of America invited "occupying foreign forces" to intrude into Afghan homes "and do whatever they like; they kill some of them and kidnap others without telling any information about whether they are alive or dead."[15]

The authors repeatedly compared Karzai's regime to the Afghan quislings who collaborated with Soviet Communist occupiers in Kabul during the 1980s. "How can their conscience and morality accept it? They call the cruel America a friendly country and dance to that system which has been imposed by the Americans and call it a democratic gift.

Don't they see that without their permission the Americans conduct their operations underneath their noses and send their innocent sons to Bagram and Cuba?"[16]

In *Al Samood*, an official Taliban print magazine revived by 2006, the editors assured readers that the Afghan Taliban were "still united under the leadership of its Supreme Commander Mullah Mohammad Omar al-Mujahed. . . . The Amir supervises all the affairs of the movement through a number of employees who run the day to day work, and the Amir is the only person who takes decisions, after consulting with the Shura on all military, political and organizational affairs."[17]

Al Samood also promoted Al Qaeda figures such as Zarqawi, whom it eulogized as "one of the heroes of the Islamic *ummah* and a knight of the Islamic Emirate." The magazine published a guest essay from an Arab Al Qaeda prisoner in Bagram. In print as in police and intelligence files there had emerged by 2006 a clear connectivity among Taliban, Arab Al Qaeda, and radicalized individuals in the West, enabled by digital communication, centered on grievances around the twin wars in Iraq and Afghanistan.[18]

The C.I.A. had no counter for Al Qaeda's digital media strategy. Nor did the agency have a clue where Bin Laden or Zawahiri were hiding. The best-informed C.I.A. analysts had developed a generalized conviction that both Al Qaeda leaders were in Pakistan, but that was about as far as they could get. When Michael Waltz, an aide to Vice President Cheney, obtained clearance to read into the most restricted compartmented C.I.A. and other intelligence collection programs related to Al Qaeda, some so protected that they were listed on classified docket sheets only by their code names, he was surprised to find that some of the operations "were very basic and relatively new, a real disappointment."[19]

After the overthrow of the Taliban and the scattering of Al Qaeda, it had taken time for the C.I.A. to narrow the hunt to focus primarily on Pakistan. It was not until late 2002, six months after Operation

Anaconda, that the evidence from Kabul Station and Afghan bases led the Counterterrorist Center's Bin Laden unit, ALEC Station, to conclude that there was not much of Al Qaeda left inside Afghanistan at all. The leaders had migrated, to Pakistan or through Iran homeward toward Iraq and other Arab countries.

Chris Wood had taken charge of ALEC Station in mid-2002. The *Saturday Night Live* version of the hunt for Bin Laden assumed the Saudi was hiding in a cave, presumably in Afghanistan or along the Pakistani border. ALEC Station's analysts doubted that; it would be hard for someone like Bin Laden to live for long in the rough in such a barren region without becoming seriously ill. ALEC Station also concluded that other rumors—that Bin Laden had gone to Somalia by sea, or had returned to Saudi Arabia, or had found a refuge in his family's ancestral home, Yemen—were deeply implausible, although it was hard to rule out anything. Gradually, however, by 2004 or 2005, the unit's analysts mainly visualized Bin Laden in a Pakistani urban area, in a refuge comparable to the ones Khalid Sheikh Mohammed, Abu Zubaydah, and Ramzi bin al-Shibh had found after 2001 in Rawalpindi, Faisalabad, and Karachi, respectively, before they were each arrested.[20]

The Omega teams created in early 2002 by Wood and Rich Blee— the blended units of C.I.A. officers and American Special Forces, supported by clandestine Afghan militias—had been designed to carry out reconnaissance by force, to project intelligence collection inside Pakistan's tribal areas. The border base design worked reasonably well in 2002 and supported Operation Anaconda. When Al Qaeda–affiliated Uzbeks and some Arabs regrouped around Wana, in South Waziristan, local reporting agents run by the C.I.A. out of the Omega base in Shkin collected useful insights, according to participants. Yet the teams' overall record in reporting on Al Qaeda's two most senior leaders was spotty to poor. Nor did the embedding of C.I.A. officers inside Pakistani military forts in South and North Waziristan produce any breakthroughs in the search for Bin Laden and Zawahiri.

The border operations did produce false positives. Early in 2005, toward the end of Blee's tour in Islamabad, Blee and Ambassador Ryan Crocker fought to call off a Navy SEAL raid on a suspected Al Qaeda compound in the tribal areas, based on a single source, because the intelligence hadn't been vetted. The source had reported Zawahiri might be there. Secretary of Defense Donald Rumsfeld approved the strike and ordered strict secrecy so that neither Blee nor Crocker had been informed of the plan or the intelligence on which it was based. Blee's experience was that it was never wise to launch a high-risk, cross-border raid on the basis of human sources alone; half the time, agents are lying or confused.

"You might kill a couple of Al Qaeda guys, but it won't be worth it," Blee warned. "You're invading Pakistan. You're going to kill a bunch of women and children. It will be a fiasco. I'm not defending you."

Blee woke up Crocker, who called Deputy Secretary of State Richard Armitage. He laughed grimly. "We're fucked up here." Some of the planes were in the air when the order was finally issued to stand down.

In Afghanistan, the operators stranded on the tarmac or ordered back in flight were appalled. They believed that a Libyan Al Qaeda operative named Abu Faraj al-Libbi might have been meeting with Faqir Mohammed, a Pakistani Pashtun militant leader, and Zawahiri. After that abandoned attempt, a J.S.O.C. team manned by Army Rangers did clandestinely strike a suspected Al Qaeda compound in the tribal areas in early 2006 and made arrests, but did not capture significant leaders. The raid was neither detected by Pakistan nor announced by the United States. By coincidence, the undeclared American raid took place just as militants in Waziristan overran a Pakistani base, killing soldiers and distracting the army command.[21]

In 2005, in a paper titled "Inroads," a C.I.A. analyst at Langley tried to reframe the frustrating search for Bin Laden by identifying four pillars most likely to revive progress: the Saudi's courier network, his family, his communication with Al Qaeda operators like Abu Ubaydah, and his media statements. The analyst's paper would prove influential over time, but in the meanwhile, she and her colleagues wasted long hours studying the flora in outdoor videos where Bin Laden appeared or studying the crawl lines on Al Jazeera broadcasts for coded messages.[22]

The agency became distracted by bureaucratic and leadership problems after 2004. The Bush administration midwifed the birth of a new intelligence coordination agency, the Office of the Director of National Intelligence, a reform proposed by the 9/11 Commission, to address failures of intelligence sharing among diverse spy agencies. Inevitably, infighting over the new agency's prerogatives and budget role drew C.I.A. managers into prolonged interagency struggles. Congress also created a new National Counterterrorism Center, a second C.I.A. rival that focused on analysis but "inexorably" bled the C.I.A.'s parallel Counterterrorism Center "of vital resources," as Robert Grenier, the former Islamabad station chief, who was now back at Langley, put it. On the Seventh Floor, C.I.A. director Porter Goss never recovered from the high-level resignations of career officers soon after he arrived. The agency surrendered some of its political and operational crown jewels, such as the role of delivering the President's Daily Brief in person to the White House, which became the responsibility of D.N.I.[23]

Jose Rodriguez appointed Grenier to run the Counterterrorism Center. After he read into the failing hunt for Bin Laden, he concluded that ALEC Station itself was a serious problem. Long-serving analysts dominated the Bin Laden unit. They were "among the very best Al Qaeda experts we had," Grenier felt, and their devotion was "legendary." Yet the more senior among them had become "sometimes arrogant and obsessive and regularly alienated the geographic divisions on whose support we depended. . . . They were definitely a handful to manage." Several of them still had photos of Michael Scheuer, the unit's first leader, on the walls of their offices, "like shrines."[24]

The unit "had become an anachronism," Grenier concluded. It focused on the core Al Qaeda organization but after the invasion of Iraq Al Qaeda was metastasizing, forming new branches across the Middle East. The target's changing shape created fresh conflicts and confusion between the C.I.A.'s geographic divisions and the Counterterrorism Center. Grenier decided to "reorganize" ALEC "out of existence." He defended the changes by arguing that "the same people, in the same numbers, continued to pursue the same targets, very much to include Bin Laden, but in a more rational structure." Yet the reorganization of the core Al Qaeda mission team was one more disruption in a long season of them at Langley.[25]

The C.I.A. decided to work much more independently from I.S.I. as early as 2005, according to British counterparts. Joint Special Operations Command added Task Force Orange specialists in human source recruitment, analysts from the Army and Navy Reserves, and N.S.A. intercept teams to the Omega bases, despite the resource strain of the Iraq war. Since human agent recruiting had proved to be difficult, the push concentrated heavily on signals intelligence collection against cell phones and e-mail. There were few Predators available; the production line went straight to Iraq. A handful of serendipitous walk-in agents—Pakistani or other volunteers who approached the United States with information about Al Qaeda or the Taliban to sell—provided a baseline of phone numbers and locations in Waziristan and other parts of western Pakistan. During 2006, amid an interrogation at a J.S.O.C. prison in Afghanistan, an Uzbek prisoner directed his interrogators to a wheeled duffel bag he had been toting at the time of his arrest. The Americans found a false bottom with a folded-up paper containing coded information about Al Qaeda safe houses and contact numbers in North Waziristan. This and other C.I.A. mapping operations in Waziristan set the stage for a coming surge of unilateral lethal drone operations on Pakistani territory.[26]

Porter Goss resigned as C.I.A. director on May 5, 2006, after less than two years in the position. Bush named as his successor Air Force general Michael Hayden, a former National Security Agency director. Originally from Pittsburgh, Hayden was a balding, management-oriented leader who communicated well in meetings, understood bureaucracy, cooperated with reporters, and got along with diverse colleagues. His consensus-driven approach did not always succeed. While running N.S.A., relying on the judgments of his senior analysts, he had endorsed the inaccurate National Intelligence Estimate about Iraq's weapons of mass destruction. As a manager, Hayden's weakness was that he hated to fire people, so he addressed that by hiring tough deputies. For this and other reasons, he thought of persuading Steve Kappes, the senior operations officer and former Marine who had resigned in protest, to return as deputy C.I.A. director. As soon as Hayden learned that Bush was likely to appoint him, he tracked down Kappes, who was living in London. He called him while Kappes was standing on a platform at Waterloo Station.

"Steve, would you consider being the deputy?" Hayden asked.

"That would depend on who the director is," Kappes replied.

"I'm not at liberty to say, but I'm the one making this call," Hayden hinted. A couple of hours later, Kappes called back and said he was on board.[27]

Like many outsiders before him who had arrived in the director's suite on the Seventh Floor, Hayden had to adjust to the C.I.A.'s insular, loose, self-protecting, and hubristic culture. He was dismayed and a little upset the first time he entered a conference room and none of the C.I.A. officers assembled stood up; his N.S.A. colleagues had stood up for him. Hayden thought to himself, "Well, this will be different." At N.S.A., the image of Langley was "Old Yale and patch elbow sleeves and pipes," as a colleague put it. By contrast, the N.S.A. "was University of Maryland computer geeks . . . the worst sort of professional dressing— people in sweat suits, or even in sweat suits with torn pants."[28]

Soon after Hayden settled in on the Seventh Floor, senior C.I.A. officers complained to him about the Office of Inspector General, which was still led by John Helgerson, the career analyst who had written skeptically of the black sites and enhanced interrogation techniques in internal reports. The C.I.A. veterans told Hayden that Helgerson's internal investigations were "killing morale" around the agency. Hayden asked Robert Deitz, his general counsel, to look into the complaints. It was an awkward assignment. Congress had set up Helgerson's office as an internal watchdog at the C.I.A.; Hayden had no power to remove him. Deitz conducted interviews with senior intelligence officers and presented findings to Helgerson. Essentially, Deitz concluded, the conflict was between the analytical side of the C.I.A., which Helgerson represented, and the operational side, who took risks in the field and did not appreciate second-guessing. Ultimately, Deitz and Helgerson worked out a classified settlement agreement. It set up a new ombudsman for C.I.A. employees to complain to if they thought the inspector general was mistreating them and it required the I.G. to tape important interviews about alleged misconduct. This was not Hollywood's C.I.A.; it reflected the prosaic reality of office life in the federal government.

Another challenge involved the agency's hollowed-out workforce, "graybeards and all these goddamned kids," as the Hayden colleague put it.[29] At the C.I.A.'s Counterterrorism Center, still spread out in the bunker at New Headquarters, Hayden inherited Mike D'Andrea, the chain-smoking Muslim convert, as his director. D'Andrea had been promoted to run the center after Rodriguez removed Grenier early in 2006. The budget he oversaw ran into the billions of dollars annually; C.T.C. had become by far the largest organization at the agency. Its new overlord wore dark clothes, was physically unattractive, and treated colleagues harshly. He was regarded as a "brilliant operational thinker," as a colleague put it, but "if he thought you were his inferior, he'd just crush you. He had no tolerance. If you're really bright, he would nurture you, but he would crush you if you didn't run at his speed."[30]

D'Andrea huddled with a handful of fellow smokers outside New Headquarters, although he was constantly trying to quit, covering his arms with nicotine patches or chewing nicotine gum. Sometimes he smoked while wearing patches. He worked hard and was reliably at his desk at 8:00 p.m., flanked by equally devoted mentees. Colleagues compared him half facetiously to Darth Vader or, more ominously, as his power grew, to James Angleton, the long-serving, independently powerful counterintelligence chief at the C.I.A. during the Cold War, an intimidating power unto himself.

During his first months at Langley, Hayden internalized C.T.C.'s battle rhythms, the "responsibility to confront that external threat unceasingly, every minute of every hour," as he put it. At C.T.C., he told the operators and analysts, "Today's date is September 12, 2001." But when he got into his chauffeured C.I.A. car and drove "down the G.W. Parkway" to Washington, Hayden reflected, "It begins to feel like September 10th." The country was getting comfortable with the threat of terrorism, but anyone who read the threat reporting would worry that they were vulnerable to another big surprise.

It was a "true fact," Hayden admitted, that the misbegotten war in

Iraq had become "a cause célèbre for jihadist recruitment," making America, Britain, and other European allies unsafe. Hayden went so far as to describe the evolved, Iraq-inflamed conflict with Al Qaeda as a greater danger to Americans than the Cold War, when the United States faced a hair-trigger threat of nuclear annihilation. His logic was stretched but he meant that as a practical matter, Americans and Europeans who lived or worked in major cities now faced a realistic prospect of sudden violence, whereas the Cold War's nuclear threats had never materialized.

In public, Hayden adamantly defended the C.I.A.'s enhanced interrogation techniques, targeted killings, and secret renditions of terrorism suspects. Privately, after the journalist Dana Priest and others exposed the black sites and their treatment of prisoners, Hayden moved in tandem with Bush's second-term national security cabinet to empty the C.I.A.'s secret prisons and transfer the remaining prisoners to Guantánamo. He made no judgment about what his predecessors had done in the post–September 11 emergency. He recognized that the C.I.A. required a broad political consensus to sustain operations over a long period and that this required accommodating the opposition to torture expressed by influential Republicans like Senator John McCain, who had been tortured as a prisoner of war in Vietnam. Hayden tried to keep the C.I.A.'s options open—he declined to repudiate E.I.T.s and felt they should remain available in an emergency—but he also sought to assure Congress that C.I.A. operations were on a tighter leash. Still, Hayden insisted the country continued to face a grave emergency. "For us it's simply war," he said. At the C.I.A. and the Pentagon, "It's a word we use commonly, without ambiguity." He sought to lead "an expeditionary campaign" to "capture or kill those behind the threat." The C.I.A.'s leadership would be essential because this was largely "an intelligence war," Hayden said.

"Our primary adversary is easy to kill," he added. "He's just very hard to find."[31]

PART THREE

THE BEST INTENTIONS,

2006–2009

FOURTEEN

Suicide Detectives

I n the late summer of 2006, Brian Glyn Williams, an assistant professor of Islamic history at the University of Massachusetts, was sitting on the back porch of his Davis Square home in Somerville when a contractor for the C.I.A. telephoned. The caller said that analysts at the agency's Counterterrorism Center were seeking insights from scholars about a wave of suicide bombings remaking the battlefields in Iraq and Afghanistan. Williams agreed to talk further. The C.I.A.'s analysts, he soon learned, were puzzling over elemental questions. Why had the targets and use of suicide attacks changed so suddenly? Who were the recruiters, trainers, and financiers? What were the ages and backgrounds of those persuaded to kill themselves? Was there evidence of "diffusion" or "contagion" of suicide bombing from Iraq to Afghanistan? The agency wanted a large, multicountry study and hoped independent academics would participate.

Williams was intrigued. He had spent much of his earlier years in Florida and then made his way into Middle Eastern studies. He spent a semester in the Soviet Union during the 1980s and met soldiers returning from the war in Afghanistan; they told him that the war was "nothing but horror." Later he published histories of Chechnya and Central Asia. Since 2001, he had been drawn into analysis of the Chechen war and the upheavals in Afghanistan. He was forty years old but looked younger. He smiled often, displaying perfect white teeth that reflected upon the profession of his Turkish-born wife, a dental hygienist.

She was unenthused about the project. "Can't they send someone else?"

He agreed that field research for the C.I.A. in Afghanistan might be a little "beyond my pay grade." But he found suicide bombing to be repugnant. If he could help reduce it by studying it, he should.[1]

There could be no doubt that autumn that suicide bombers had become a newly destabilizing feature of Afghanistan's reviving war. Their increase also represented a departure from Afghanistan's recent military history. During the 1980s, across a long, bitter uprising against the Soviet Union, Afghan mujaheddin had not participated in suicide attacks. The mujaheddin's prideful, family-supported ethos of jihad emphasized individual bravery and, where possible, living to fight another day. When the Taliban conquered Afghanistan during the late 1990s, Mullah Mohammad Omar and his commanders did not employ suicide bombers, either. (The Arab volunteers who blew themselves up while assassinating Ahmad Shah Massoud belonged to Al Qaeda.) During the three years from December 2001 through December 2004, there had been eight suicide bombings in Afghanistan, all in Kabul. Yet by 2006 suicide bombers struck two or three times a week around the country, shattering public confidence and forcing Afghan and N.A.T.O. forces to hunker down behind walls and checkpoints manned by nervous pickets.

The Taliban announced their new plan in a policy editorial published in *Al Samood*, in January 2006:

> Let the Americans and their allies know that even though we lack equipment, our faith has been unshakable. And with the help of Allah the Almighty, we have created a weapon which you will not be able to face or escape, i.e. martyrdom operations. We will follow you everywhere and we will detonate everything in your face. We will make you terrified, even from vacant lands and silent walls. We know we are inevitably heading towards death, so let it be a glorious death by killing you with us, as we believe in the words of the Prophet (Peace Be Upon Him): "The heretic and his killer will be united in the fires of hell." We

have thus prepared many suicide operations that even will involve
women, and we will offer you the taste of perdition in the cities, villages, valleys and mountains with Allah's help.[2]

The most visible spokesman of the Afghan Taliban's initiatives was
Dadullah Lang, a one-legged Taliban military commander who bragged
about suicide operations on Al Jazeera. He called his young recruits
"Mullah Omar's missiles" and "our atomic bombs." He told another in-
terviewer in the summer of 2006, "We like the Al Qaeda organization.
We have close ties and constant contacts."[3]

The C.I.A. struggled to provide hard evidence to the national security cabinet about why this had evolved so suddenly. The agency offered
to buy out Williams's salary at UMass for a semester and to pay an additional $30,000 for his fieldwork and a research paper. He spent the
autumn and winter working with a student researcher to build a matrix
of suicide attacks in Afghanistan since 2001, to identify patterns and
questions that he could examine when he traveled to the country. On his
Excel spreadsheet, he recorded dates of suicide bombings, their locations, what category of target had been struck, the number of casualties,
and details about the strikes, if they were available from media or other
accounts.

As his grid of evidence morphed into color-coded patterns, two mysteries presented themselves initially. Williams realized that he was recording a surprising number of "zeros" in the casualty column, meaning
that the suicide attack had failed altogether. There were about a dozen
such cases in 2006, for example, about 9 percent of the total. Moreover,
the most common outcome of an Afghan suicide attack that year was a
single casualty—the bomber himself and no one else.

This was not what Williams had seen when he had previously studied
suicide bombings in Iraq. There, failures were abnormal and high death
tolls were common. This led to a second mystery about the Afghan pattern, concerning the bombers' targets. In Iraq, suicide bombers typically
struck crowds of civilians to sow terror by inflicting mass casualties, including women and children. The context for these attacks was often

sectarian: Al Qaeda–influenced Sunni suicide bombers struck Shiite civilian marketplaces or mosques, and vice versa. In Afghanistan, however,
suicide bombers most often struck military targets, such as heavily armed
American or N.A.T.O. convoys moving on roadways. Remarkably often,
only the bomber died. Williams and his researcher marveled morbidly
about how incompetent some of these suicide bombers seemed to be. One
had strapped on his vest, traveled to say goodbye to his parents, and accidentally detonated his device during the visit, taking his own life and
theirs. But when Williams reflected on it, the pattern seemed tragic. Presumably such failures indicated how many suicide bombers recruited to
die in Afghanistan might be coerced, naïve, illiterate, young, or disabled.[4]

The C.I.A.'s contractor and an analyst at the agency's Counterterrorism Center arranged for Williams to travel to Afghanistan. He departed
in the early spring of 2007. Williams connected with Hekmat Karzai, a
cousin of the Afghan president who ran a Kabul think tank. He provided
Williams with a base of operations. As to the risks he would take traveling to provinces to meet local police, investigate bombing case files, and
speak with affected Afghans, he was largely on his own. His C.I.A. supervisors told him, "If you get caught, we don't know you." He wasn't
sure how serious they were, but their instructions were clear: "We appreciate your service, but don't call us."[5]

The C.I.A.'s suicide bombing study coincided with a renewed stirring
of interest in the Afghan war at the White House. The Afghan
Inter-Agency Operations Group at the National Security Council remained the main vehicle for policy and budget decisions. The group
was bureaucratically weak and often ignored. John Gastright of the
State Department now cochaired the effort. His modest rank—deputy
assistant secretary of state—signaled his operation's low standing in the
Bush-Cheney-Rumsfeld hierarchy, an apparatus focused almost entirely
on the worsening war in Iraq. Yet at least Gastright's group was organized
across government to think about what American policy in Afghanistan
required, a change from several years before.

"We ought to take a look at where we are and what we're doing," Gastright announced one afternoon in mid-2006 at the State Department, where the Operations Group met. In Kabul, Ronald Neumann had succeeded Zalmay Khalilzad as U.S. ambassador. Gastright would typically arrive at Foggy Bottom around 6:30 a.m. and the first thing he did was call Neumann. They agreed that the levels of aid to the country were grossly inadequate and that the U.S. military needed to mount a bigger effort to prevent the war's further deterioration. They also knew that to persuade President Bush and the Office of Management and Budget to change course and spend more in the midst of the Treasury-draining fiasco in Iraq would require a formal policy review. Meghan O'Sullivan, the senior National Security Council adviser who worked mainly on Iraq but also kept track of Afghanistan, brought the idea for a review to Bush, who approved it.[6]

Neumann had tried with little success to persuade the State Department and the White House to radically increase investments in Afghanistan. He regarded the plan for a new policy review with skepticism. "Searching for a new strategy seems to be policymakers' recurring default reaction to problems," as he put it. Instead of properly resourcing the strategy the administration already possessed, it authorized a search "for a new idea. Certainly ideas are more easily come by than money and soldiers."[7]

In the autumn of 2006, Gastright and his cochair, Tony Harriman, the N.S.C. senior director for Afghanistan, commissioned classified study papers on every major policy subject that seemed relevant: the Afghan justice system, the police, narcotics, the Afghan National Army, and civilian aid. The final drafts of these papers contained recommendations. In essence, they identified the need for more resources, more spending. Harriman liked to point out to his colleagues that there were more combat aircraft controlled by the State Department operating in Colombia, to support the fight against coca growing and Marxist guerrillas there, than there were combat aircraft controlled by the Pentagon in Afghanistan.

"We cannot win in Afghanistan on the cheap," Neumann wrote to

Washington. Michael Waltz, the Special Forces officer, rotated from Afghanistan to a policy position at the Pentagon late that year. He was "pleased to find some growing awareness . . . of the worsening situation" in Afghanistan, yet many of the Afghan hands he encountered were "increasingly frustrated. Even though our senior leaders recognized the growing problem, the default response was to turn to the Europeans to do more."[8]

The American electorate soon came to the aid of their cause. In early November 2006, in mid-term elections, voters repudiated President Bush and handed control of Congress to the Democrats. Bush accepted Rumsfeld's resignation in the aftermath and appointed Robert Gates as secretary of defense. Gates had been at the C.I.A. and the White House when the United States abandoned Afghanistan in the early 1990s. He was determined not to preside over another failure in South Asia, yet he was skeptical that the United States could fix the war. His "historical perspective . . . screamed for caution" yet American generals in the field insisted they needed more forces and resources.

On November 13, 2006, the N.S.C. forwarded to President Bush a ten-page classified executive summary of "The Afghanistan Strategic Review." Bush approved its findings on December 10. The plan called for more money, a reenergized effort to improve security and governance, a new push to undermine the booming drug economy, and more American troops on the ground. The hypothesis of the paper promoted the need to "connect the Afghan people to their government." It proposed more schools, roads, and electricity. Of these recommendations, only the call for more American troops failed to materialize quickly. Early in 2007, Bush's decision to authorize a "surge" of troops into Baghdad under the command of General David Petraeus effectively used up all of the Pentagon's available personnel and then some. With about 150,000 American troops now in Iraq, there were no additional units available for Afghanistan. The Afghan review did reverse the administration's parsimony about reconstruction aid, however. Now the O.M.B. approved a supplemental allocation to Afghanistan of more than $1 billion, although to Neumann's disappointment, the White House split the funding across two fiscal years, diluting its impact. The ambassador "got pretty cranky," as Gastright put it, and cabled in protest, but the decision stood.[9]

The Bush administration's total spending on security in Afghanistan would nonetheless be greater during 2007 than during all previous years combined. The allocations included major new classified investments at Amrullah Saleh's N.D.S., for the Afghan National Army, and for the police. Paul Miller, the C.I.A. analyst who moved to the White House that year to work on Afghanistan, estimated that total security assistance, classified and unclassified, ballooned toward almost $8 billion a year, at least four times the levels of the "Mr. Big" era when Khalilzad was ambassador in Kabul.[10]

In February 2007, Bush appeared at the American Enterprise Institute in Washington to speak about the global war on terror. He gave over much of his speech to Iraq, but about halfway through his talk, he disclosed that his administration had just finished "a top-to-bottom review of our strategy" in Afghanistan. Bush laid out renewed aims: "To help the people of that country to defeat the terrorists and establish a stable, moderate, and democratic state that respects the rights of its citizens, governs its territory effectively, and is a reliable ally in this war against extremists and terrorists." He admitted, "Oh, for some that may seem like an impossible task. But it's not impossible."[11]

In fact, the war on the ground was deteriorating by the month. Its challenges had at last attracted the White House's attention. Yet the Bush administration's new strategy remained informed by undue optimism, not least because Afghanistan still looked much better than Iraq. Bush was defensive about the comparison. He told the Joint Chiefs, "Many in Congress don't understand the military. 'Afghanistan is good. Iraq is bad.' Bullshit."[12]

I n the parking lot of the Kabul International Airport, Brian Williams met Humayun, the tall driver-cum-bodyguard with whom he would work for the next two months. He was from Kandahar. He mentioned that he had not told his family about his work with the Karzai regime in

Kabul, as this would only attract the Taliban's ire. He kept a pistol in his car. He told Williams that he appreciated what the United States was trying to do in Afghanistan. "The day you leave, the Taliban will be back," he predicted.[13]

Williams settled into a room in Hekmat Karzai's walled compound. Each morning he descended to the common area for tea, naan, and cheese, and to check for news of the latest suicide bombings. If possible, he and Humayun would drive out to crime scenes. Sometimes they arrived when there was still blood on the ground.

Five days after he arrived, Williams drove to meet U.S. Army officers at Bagram Airfield. He was stunned by the self-imposed isolation of the American soldiers and military intelligence officers he met. By 2006 Bagram had acquired some of the amenities common on other American military bases worldwide. There was a bowling alley, a Burger King, and an Orange Julius, Williams discovered. He learned nothing from his meetings except that the American officers knew nothing about why the rise of suicide warfare had occurred or where it was heading. The officers he met seemed to consider "everything beyond their barrier to be a red zone."[14]

At N.D.S. headquarters, Williams met Amrullah Saleh's staff and several of his senior officers. They were better informed. They had a theory of how suicide bombings had accelerated. Their insights were derived mainly from arrests and interrogations. The Iraq war was one factor, they told Williams. Arab technicians fashioning suicide vests and vehicle bombs in Iraq were highly sophisticated, in comparison with the typically illiterate Pashtun commanders of the Taliban. The international jihadists were trying to export their suicide bomb technology to Afghanistan, but with mixed results. In Nimruz, a large province in the southwest, N.D.S. had arrested several Arabs crossing from Iran who were transporting prefabricated suicide belts for the Taliban. N.D.S. believed the majority of bombers striking inside Afghanistan were Pashtuns from the Federally Administered Tribal Areas of Pakistan.

Security officers at the United Nations, who were responsible for the safety of development and political officers scattered around Afghanistan, handed Williams a PowerPoint deck showing about fifty photographs of the severed heads of deceased bombers. There could have been a touch of dubious phrenology in the United Nations analysis of the pictures of the heads—a confidence about what the contours of the faces showed about the bomber's ethnic or national origins that would not pass as science. But the photos did make clear that the bombers were all very young. To Williams, they appeared to be Pashtuns, not Arabs.

Williams slowly developed a composite picture of a typical suicide bomber in Afghanistan. The Taliban bombers were often young, as young as twelve or thirteen. They typically had little experience at driving, never mind at speed racing along roads in a battered, bomb-rigged Toyota Corolla. Under pressure, in the last seconds of their immature lives, they failed. Police officers summarizing interrogations of detainees in N.D.S. custody explained that the Taliban paid the families of suicide bombers in the range of two thousand dollars to ten thousand dollars, a small fortune in Waziristan or the rural south and east of Afghanistan. The boys were recruited from madrassas where they had been enrolled for years in a curriculum of suffocating political-religious instruction.[15]

I n Pakistan, during the first half of 2007, separately from Williams's inquiries, Pakistan Army officers, psychologists, and social scientists confronted a parallel rise in suicide bombings against Pakistani targets. These attacks, too, emanated from Waziristan. Al Qaeda, Afghan Taliban, Pakistani Taliban, and Punjabi radicals had turned against the Pakistani state and I.S.I. itself on the grounds that it had betrayed Islam through alliance with the United States.

Abu Bakr Amin Bajwa, a Pakistani brigadier posted to Waziristan, stumbled into an abandoned Taliban suicide bomber school while on patrol. In Razmak, a district of North Waziristan near the Afghan border where Arab Al Qaeda units had embedded, he visited a *jannat*, or paradise facility for suicide bombers in the final stages of preparations. The recruits studied in concrete rooms whose walls were painted with murals of the afterlife, "channels of milk and honey, fruit trees, green mountains, street lights, and animals like camels and horses." Another room depicted paintings of virgin girls. One of the young women was shown filling a water jug at a pond. The faces of the virgins and the animals had been crudely brushed out in keeping with Taliban proscriptions against living figures in art. On the walls of the final room, Bajwa saw the names of suicide bombers who had fulfilled their missions, "written in blood." Across the way he found a water tank "where the Taliban used to execute or torture the people who would oppose them or spy on them." Family finances, enticements of paradise, and torture created an environment that no thirteen-year-old boy was likely to withstand independently.[16]

Bajwa discovered further that the boys were injected daily with the antianxiety medicines Valium and Xanax and weekly with Penzocine, an analgesic. Trainers preferred boys who were either seriously ill, "mentally challenged," or else had a reason for revenge, such as a family member killed in military operations. Bombers typically operated in pairs, monitored by their trainers. Those known to be suffering from mental illness or paralysis could be remotely detonated.[17]

Shazadi Beg, a British barrister who worked on programs to rehabilitate such boys in Pakistan after they were captured by authorities, encountered a fourteen-year-old in a Pakistani jail. He had been arrested after a failed suicide attack. The boy was shackled by the ankles and handcuffed. His eyes darted around the room. Beg asked what he was looking at. "I'm trying to see if there is something I can kill you with," he answered.

The boy had been recruited from his family in South Waziristan but said he did not want to see them again. He had been arrested at an army checkpoint, wearing a suicide jacket, just two hours from his home; it was the first time he had ever left his village. "I am in dishonor. I failed in what I was supposed to do." He said that if he was released he would complete his mission. His eyes brimmed with tears when Beg asked if he missed his mother, but he tried very hard not to show emotion and said that his mission was to kill unbelievers. He refused to watch television because he believed it was the devil's instrument and designed to deceive him. He had memorized the Koran yet could not translate the meaning of any verses from Arabic to Urdu or Pashto.[18]

Psychiatrists who counseled former suicide bomber recruits in

Pakistan found that the kids were bullied, assigned menial tasks, and beaten if they did not accomplish them. They were provided marijuana as a reward. They adapted. They had no alternative.[19]

The images of afterlife at the bomber school in Razmak—horses and virgins filling water pots from a pond—suggested how Taliban commanders had refined Al Qaeda's ideology to communicate with rural Pashtun communities. To Brian Williams this helped to explain why so many Afghan Taliban suicide operations targeted armored military convoys or armed guards at the perimeter of walled security bases, rather than marketplaces, mosques, or other soft targets, where they might kill many more people and sow terror, even if their victims were civilians. During 2006 and 2007, Taliban suicide bombers did attack civilians in settings such as dog fights where gambling took place, but they did not often follow the Iraqi or Pakistani sectarian pattern of killing large numbers of civilians deliberately. To maintain legitimacy among Pashtun families sacrificing sons, the suicide operations had to be honorable. It was acceptable to die in an attempted military attack on a U.N. convoy, even if the attack was difficult. It was not as honorable to blow up pious Afghan Muslims in a bazaar. This pattern would dissolve in the years to come, particularly as I.S.I. and the Haqqani network sought to destabilize Kabul, and as sectarian feeling hardened in the intensifying war, but at the beginning of the suicide bombing wave, Williams's research showed, the recruits and their families seemed to require a traditional military purpose.

As Williams completed his research, the number of Afghan suicide bombers who changed their minds at the last minute also impressed him. Afghan police showed him suicide vests that boys had torn off, dropped, and run away from. By now Williams empathized with the bombers and felt he understood their ambivalence. They really believed in the righteousness of their struggle. The attacks of September 11 meant nothing to them or their families; they did not even have televisions. The families that accepted payment for their sacrifice and glorified their martyrdom "really believe in the Taliban and believe in the war and the goodness of it," Williams reflected.[20]

Yet suicide bombing should not be understood as an indigenous aspect of the Taliban's revival, he concluded. In Gardez, he found D.V.D.s stacked for sale in a market. They were designed to inspire suicide bombers. The programs were Iraqi productions, originally produced in Arabic but dubbed in Pashto for the Afghan market. They presented calls to martyrdom amid *naheeds*, or Islamic vocal works. This was the clearest evidence Williams had yet encountered of "the Iraq effect."

In fact, the number of suicide bombings in Afghanistan declined in the years after Williams's study, while the number of land mine or improvised explosive device attacks increased more than sixfold. As N.A.T.O. and the U.N. imported armored vehicles and took greater precautions, powerful land mines were a more effective tactical counter for the Taliban. Suicide bombings constituted about 4 percent of all Taliban bombings in 2007; three years later, they constituted less than 1 percent, although the number of assassinations and mass casualty attacks against civilians increased.

Williams felt more convinced than ever before "of the rightness of the U.S. going into Afghanistan, that the U.S. needed to be there to fight off the Taliban," as he put it. Yet his support was tempered by his shock at how badly the war was going. Back home, he wrote up classified and unclassified versions of his findings. (Because he did not yet have a top secret security clearance, once he turned in the classified paper, he wasn't allowed to look at it again.) Williams presented his findings to analysts at the C.I.A.'s Counterterrorism Center. The contractor who had recruited him to do the study also asked him to a conference at a Virginia hotel, to present his work to about eighty C.I.A., military, and other intelligence analysts.

"I don't think this is organic" to Afghanistan, Williams told them. The C.I.A. analysts he encountered accepted that, but those from the Defense Intelligence Agency challenged him. The back-and-forth went on for ten minutes. How do you know suicide bombing did not evolve intrinsically from Afghan culture? the more skeptical analysts asked.

Well, Williams said, all he could say was that the pattern of attacks he had documented showed that Taliban suicide squads were made up of poorly qualified, often coerced youngsters. Many in his audience "didn't like" his overall conclusion, which was: "The Iraq war had destabilized the Afghan war."[21]

FIFTEEN

Plan Afghanistan

During the first few years after the Taliban's fall from power, opium poppy cultivation in Afghanistan rose by about a quarter. During 2006, it boomed. Afghan farmers planted just over four hundred thousand acres in poppy, the most ever measured, enough to manufacture just over 90 percent of the world's annual heroin supply. More than three million Afghans—about 14 percent of the population—by now participated in the drug economy, according to the United Nations. Afghan farmers might earn just over $30 planting an acre of wheat, but more than $500 for poppy. The total export value of opium and derived products like morphine was about $4 billion, or just over half the size of the legal Afghan economy. It was hard to say how many Afghans participated in those export profits, yet they certainly benefited from the "farm gate" price for poppy of about $1 billion, which was more than 10 percent of the economy.[1]

More than half of the poppy crop grew in the irrigated river belts of Helmand and Kandahar, the Taliban heartland. George W. Bush had served eight years as a border state governor in Texas and knew how drug syndicates had destabilized Mexico and Colombia. The fact that the Taliban's revival as a fighting force in 2006 coincided with an opium boom attracted Bush's attention. The National Security Council had earlier asked the Drug Enforcement Administration's intelligence division to produce a study comparing the Taliban with the Revolutionary Armed Forces of Colombia, or F.A.R.C., a leftist insurgent movement funded in part by Colombia's cocaine economy.[2] In the circumstances, this was the sort of intelligence study where both the commissioning party—the White House—and the analysts assigned knew roughly what the findings would be. It would have been surprising if the D.E.A. had reported back to the White House that the Taliban were not like the F.A.R.C. or that drugs figured little in their military resurgence.

Supervision of the assignment had fallen to Michael Braun, a career D.E.A. officer and administrator who had built up the agency's presence in Afghanistan. He served as director of the D.E.A.'s Office of Special Intelligence until early 2005, when he became chief of operations. Earlier in his career, Braun had been deployed abroad for seven years in Operation Snowcap, the Reagan-era paramilitary program in which Special Forces–trained D.E.A. agents embedded with Bolivian, Peruvian, and Colombian police and military forces to attack Andean coca labs and traffickers. In the early 1990s, he had seen up close how the F.A.R.C. and Peru's Shining Path Marxist guerrillas operated.[3]

The D.E.A. study about Afghanistan took note of recent academic work on the causes of civil wars. The Stanford University political scientists James Fearon and David D. Laitin had published influential studies in 2003 and 2004. They coded and analyzed scores of civil wars fought between 1945 and 1999. One of their most striking findings was that civil wars were getting longer. In the late 1940s, many internal conflicts lasted only two years, whereas by 1999, they lasted sixteen years on average. Fearon's analysis also showed that self-funding guerrilla groups with direct access to drug profits fight for unusually long periods, up to thirty or forty years. The F.A.R.C., for example, had been battling the Colombian state since 1964.[4]

Now the Taliban were "going down the same path," Braun concluded. Reporting from the D.E.A. office in Kabul showed that Taliban commanders had shifted from providing protection services to morphine labs in Afghanistan to actually running labs. To Braun, that made sense because it was similar to what Marxist groups in Latin America had done after they lost Soviet subsidies. Here the Taliban were also adapting to the loss of official subsidies. During the 1990s, the Taliban had received open support from Pakistan and Gulf States. Now the pressure on Pakistan not to get caught providing aid to the Taliban had forced the movement into greater financial self-reliance. Heroin was part of the Taliban's solution, Braun believed. And since infidels in Europe consumed most of Afghanistan's heroin, Taliban ideologists could rationalize their participation in the trade.[5]

The Bush administration had not previously linked war strategy in Afghanistan with drug policy. Mary Beth Long, an attorney, was the top Pentagon official in charge of counternarcotics policy. When she arrived in 2004, she discovered that the Pentagon's leadership, military and civilian, were "not interested" in suppressing opium poppy planting in Afghanistan. Some Pentagon officials asserted that they did not have authority under American law to conduct aggressive antidrug campaigns outside Colombia, even if they wished to do so. Long developed a plan to clarify that the Army could indeed "use our authorities, like the authorities that we have in Colombia," in Helmand and Kandahar. But it wasn't clear to her that anyone outside of the D.E.A. wanted to militarize the fight against opium in Afghanistan. A staffer for General David Barno, the commander in Afghanistan during Zalmay Khalilzad's tour as ambassador, accused Long of "trying to do a Cheney on them" by using argumentative intelligence to expand the war's scope. In addition, it hardly needed pointing out that American policy after 2002 empowered warlords with ties to the drug trade, from north to south. The Pentagon and the C.I.A. worked with "the worst of the worst, and they didn't care what these guys did on the side," as Doug Wankel, a D.E.A. agent who served in the U.S. embassy in Kabul, put it. "That's just a fact."[6]

A fierce argument erupted among U.S. intelligence agencies about whether opium and heroin were, in fact, a significant aspect of the Taliban's insurgency. The argument would go on inside classified conference rooms for several years. Analysts at D.I.A. discounted Braun's initial study comparing the Taliban with the F.A.R.C. There was no consensus on a basic question, namely, whether opium money was an indispensable, growing source of finance for the Taliban. Data about drugs and Taliban finance was inherently sketchy and often inferred from scattered criminal cases and detainee testimony. A few key points were well established. The Taliban imposed two religious taxes, *ushr* and *zakat*, on the opium economy. The taxes hit farmers, truckers, morphine makers, and smugglers. The tax rates were 10 and 20 percent, prescribed by the Koran, and so not subject to change. Therefore, as opium growing boomed in the south in 2006 and 2007, it was logical to conclude that the Taliban's coffers had also swelled. But how much money did the Taliban really earn? The movement did not have Swiss bank accounts that could be hacked and analyzed.

If the Taliban imposed *ushr* and *zakat* taxes on the $4 billion estimated export value of the 2006 opium crop, then it might earn upwards of $500 million annually from drug trafficking, D.E.A. studies estimated. That would be a huge sum for a guerrilla force of the Taliban's scale. But what evidence was there that the Taliban could tax the full $4 billion in revenue? Wasn't it more likely that they could access only the "farm gate" crop of about $1 billion? In that case their take might be $100 million. When the D.E.A.'s analysts first circulated its $500 million estimate, D.I.A. analysts challenged their assumptions.

The debates frustrated those like John Walters, the White House drug czar, who felt the agencies were deliberately shading analysis to support their preferred policies. Those analysts who doubted the D.E.A. emphasized that the Taliban had many other sources of income besides drug taxes: They also taxed other forms of smuggling, and they had long-standing business and preaching networks in Saudi Arabia, the United Arab Emirates, and other Gulf countries. And of course they enjoyed sanctuary in Pakistan. Why should the United States distort its already overstretched war strategy to attack one source of Taliban and Al Qaeda finance without making an equal effort to choke off the other income sources, or to eliminate the Pakistani sanctuary?

At the Pentagon, Mary Beth Long fought back by producing dossiers of evidence showing that American troops were tripping across narcotics in the same places where they were finding weapons caches in Taliban strongholds. Analysts at D.I.A. told her she was factually wrong; C.I.A. analysts were less vocal, but made their opposition clear. The main push back came from the Army and Central Command. Long wasn't sure why the uniformed services were so adamant, but she concluded that they just did not want to see a linkage between drug revenue and the Taliban's return because it would complicate their mission.[7]

Long created more dossiers of evidence showing caches of narcotics discovered on the Afghan battlefield alongside rocket-propelled grenades and improvised explosive devices. She briefed members of Congress and was eventually able to present to President Bush and the Principals Committee in the Situation Room. She tried to convince them "about the perils of allowing the opium trade to run unaddressed."[8]

At the White House, Long was pushing on an open door. With her evidence, along with the analysis of Braun and others at D.E.A. and at the State Department, the idea took hold in the Bush administration that the model for fixing Afghanistan was in Colombia. The long American effort there to strengthen the state, defeat drug traffickers, and isolate Marxist guerrillas was known as Plan Colombia. The Clinton administration had conceived Plan Colombia in 1998. The Bush administration had embraced and advanced it, aligning closely with President Álvaro Uribe Vélez, a conservative. The plan's elements included aerial spraying of coca fields, crop eradication by Colombian forces on the ground, American security and intelligence support for military and police, exports of helicopters, aircraft, weapons, eavesdropping equipment, and other gear, and staunch political backing for the elected government in Bogotá.

As with all things in Afghanistan, however, ambition outstripped means. On January 24, 2007, General Dan McNeill, the newly appointed commander of N.A.T.O. forces battling the Taliban, met George W. Bush in the Oval Office. After a few minutes of picture taking and question shouting from journalists, the two men were alone. "Tell me what you think you can do," Bush said.

"First on my list is to get the Europeans outside the wire and into the fight," McNeill answered.

"You need to do this," Bush agreed. He told McNeill that they would speak regularly and that the president would ask from time to time what equipment or additional troops the general needed to fulfill his mission. "And you have to tell me," Bush said. "Don't worry what anyone else thinks." He warned McNeill, however, "I've got to take care of this Iraq thing first."

That same week, Bush convened a National Security Council meeting about the exploding poppy problem in Afghanistan. The president wanted more effort on eradication. He appointed a new ambassador-level State Department coordinator on drugs and corruption in Afghanistan, Tom Schweich, and he directed the White House drug policy czar, John Walters, to get more involved. The Pentagon, State, D.E.A., and C.I.A. were all to be part of a new counternarcotics and poppy eradication effort, even though each of these agencies harbored different views about the wisdom of poppy eradication in Afghanistan. Before their differences were resolved, money began to flow. Congress allocated more than $1 billion to overt counternarcotics policy in Afghanistan for the two years between October 2006 and October 2008.[9]

Bush's adaptation of Plan Colombia for Afghanistan constituted the most significant change in U.S. policy in the war since 2002. Yet in early 2007, the Iraq war dominated media coverage, and the change was not clearly visible to the public. Bush's intentions were hardly disguised, however. As the new ambassador to Kabul, the president nominated William Wood, a career foreign officer who had served as the U.S. ambassador to Colombia since 2003. As the new ambassador to Pakistan, Bush nominated Anne Patterson, who had been Wood's predecessor in Bogotá. For the next several years the two most important American diplomats in South Asia would be career officers who had spent years fighting Colombia's cocaine cartels and Marxist insurgents under the premises of Plan Colombia.

The most dramatic aspect of Plan Colombia was the aerial spraying of coca crops with herbicide. In late 2006 and early 2007, for Afghanistan, Bush advocated strongly for spraying poppy crops from airplanes in the heart of Taliban country. He repeatedly told John Walters, "You have got to spray. I'm a spray guy."[10]

One reason there was little debate in Washington about Bush's turn in Afghan policy was that leading Democrats backed the president's new priorities. On January 28, 2007, the same week as the "urgent" cabinet meeting on the opium problem, newly elected Speaker of the House of Representatives Nancy Pelosi led a Democratic congressional delegation to Kabul to meet Karzai. They talked mainly about Pakistan and poppy. On drug eradication, the Democrats told Karzai flatly, "Future U.S. aid to Afghanistan could erode if poppy cultivation was not brought under control." Karzai admitted it was "a deep problem" and promised that his government would "eradicate as much poppy as it could."[11]

William Wood landed in Kabul that spring. No longer did American ambassadors live in cramped trailer parks. The same construction boom that had brought Orange Julius to Bagram Airfield had delivered a new high-rise apartment building for diplomats. It rose next to a large, barricaded, modernized embassy building. As Condoleezza Rice put it, "The big, ugly building . . . sent the message that, for better or worse, we were in Afghanistan for the long run." The ambassador's residence now constituted a penthouse on the high-rise's top floor, with an outdoor veranda offering dramatic views of the Kabul skyline.[12]

Wood was a tall man who fired off one-liners and enjoyed "the occasional cigarette and Scotch on the rocks," as the ambassador's British counterpart, Sherard Cowper-Coles, put it. He enjoyed history and English literature, especially P. G. Wodehouse. Wood arrived in Kabul with every reason to believe that the White House's plan to spray Afghanistan's poppy fields would work. During 2006, his final year as ambassador to Colombia, aerial coca crop eradication had reached its apex. American-supplied aircraft sprayed glyphosate, a herbicide sold commercially under the brand name Roundup, on 400,000 acres of Colombian coca, the most ever destroyed from above. The Colombian government declared a triumph.[13]

Wood's message was "It worked okay in Colombia, but it should work really well in Afghanistan" because the terrain in Kandahar and Helmand was flat and the poppy crop was tightly packed in a few green belts irrigated by rivers. A few spray planes and armed helicopters could swoop north to south over the Helmand Valley, wiping out hundreds of millions of dollars' worth of poppy. "If people would just come to their senses, we could eliminate this problem in three weeks," Wood told Tom Schweich, who agreed with him.[14]

Spraying would affect British forces deployed to Helmand. Wood sought an ally in the new British ambassador to Kabul, Cowper-Coles. He invited him one evening for drinks on his veranda. Looking over the parapet "through the dust-filled night at the uncertain flickering of Kabul's lights," Wood laid out his vision. To Cowper-Coles, it conjured up the Robert Duvall scenes in *Apocalypse Now*. Wood hoped to wipe out poppy fields in Helmand and Kandahar before the end of 2007. Cowper-Coles feared crop dusting in the Taliban heartland "might risk turning an insurgency into an insurrection." The British ambassador dubbed Wood "Chemical Bill," a moniker that stuck.[15]

There was another way to consider the problem of drugs and the Taliban. Perhaps it was not that opium caused war. Perhaps it was war that caused opium. Afghan farmers had grown poppy crops for centuries. But it was not until the Soviet invasion and the scorched-earth civil wars that followed that the opium economy grew to such scale. The fighting destroyed irrigation systems, "leveled the cities, cratered the roads, blasted the schools," as a British-funded report written for the Karzai government put it. Half of all farms were abandoned. The state collapsed in many rural areas. In these dire conditions Afghan farmers turned to opium production to survive. The returns per acre were higher, the crop was unusually weatherproof, and it did not require elaborate storage or marketing. An opium crop could be raised in just six months and stored as a form of savings. This was also Karzai's explanation about the spread of poppy across his native Kandahar. After the Soviet invasion, "there was complete despair," he told an American television audience in 2006. "No Afghan family was sure if they were going to have their house the next day." They needed ready cash, "so poppy came to Afghanistan out of an extreme desperation."[16]

Since the 1980s, there had been a self-reinforcing cycle in the opium belt: War created desperation, which made opium attractive for poor farmers, which created profits for warlords, who then used those

resources to fight for greater wealth and power, which created more desperation for poor farmers.

Britain had agreed to become the "lead nation" on narcotics policy
after 2002 because Afghan heroin was sold on British streets and Prime
Minister Tony Blair was personally enthusiastic about the drugs portfolio. British and Australian Special Forces formed a clandestine paramilitary force, Task Force 333, to raid labs in Helmand and Kandahar and to
mentor Afghan special police. Yet British development specialists opposed militarized poppy eradication and aerial spraying—they thought it
was counterproductive, unfair, and unsustainable, a view shared in much
of the British military, whose generals concluded they had enough of a
fight on their hands in Helmand without aggravating farmers and itinerant laborers. The British developed an integrated policy emphasizing
public education, demand reduction, and the development of alternative
livelihoods for farmers that might compete with the allure of poppy
prices. The approach made sense on paper but it was obvious by 2006
that it was having little to no impact on crop production.

Britain's Foreign Office also allocated tens of millions of dollars to
pay Afghan farmers to eradicate their own poppy fields. The money
yielded corruption, agricultural market distortions, and confusion. Career MI6 officers assigned to work on Afghanistan, who were drawn into
these antidrug schemes, concluded that the British narcotics brief was a
waste of time and effort. The C.I.A. had been blinded to Afghanistan's
political deterioration and the Taliban's revival by the distractions of Iraq
and the agency's relentless, narrow focus on Al Qaeda, these British officers felt. But they were willing to concede that MI6 had been similarly
blinded by opium.[17]

Faizullah Kakar, Afghanistan's deputy minister of public health, was
the member of Karzai's cabinet best qualified to evaluate the risks
that might be posed to the Afghan people by aerial spraying. He had
grown up in Kabul but earned a bachelor's degree in biology from Earl-
ham College in Indiana, a master's degree in toxicology from Indiana
University, and a doctoral degree in epidemiology from the University of

Washington. He had later worked for the World Health Organization in Pakistan. Kakar understood that glyphosate was widely used by American gardeners and farmers, who poured about one hundred million pounds of the stuff on their lawns and fields every year. The Environmental Protection Agency judged that glyphosate had "low toxicity" for humans, "slight toxicity" for birds, and was harmless to fish and bees. Apart from requiring a warning label, the E.P.A. did not restrict the chemical giant Monsanto from manufacturing or selling Roundup to Americans. Yet Kakar seriously doubted that it made sense to douse Afghan fields with the stuff.

"You are telling us about how safe it is," he told Doug Wankel, the D.E.A. official in the Kabul embassy. "Remember D.D.T.?"[18]

He was referring to dichloro-diphenyl-trichloroethane, a synthetic insecticide developed in the 1940s. Initially popular and believed to be safe, D.D.T. turned out to be highly persistent in the environment and was ultimately classified by the E.P.A. as a probable human carcinogen. Kakar pointed out that Afghanistan had "a much more agricultural economy" than the United States, that runoff from fields went straight to local water supplies, and that many Afghans were "totally dependent" on farming. The country could not afford a massive spraying campaign based on current scientific assessments, only to discover later that glyphosate was not as safe as advertised. Kakar propounded his views before Karzai and the full Afghan cabinet. He said that while the Americans "used thousands of pounds of the same spray safely in California," the United States did much better at protecting its water sources, whereas Afghans "drink from open watercourses."[19]

"This is the most popular chemical in the world," Bill Wood pointed out. Yet Wood and other advocates for spraying underestimated the asymmetries of power in these arguments with Afghans. Most Afghan decision makers (and for that matter, many Colombians) were not in a position to independently judge the long-term public health risks of glyphosate. And why should they accept E.P.A. judgments as gospel, given America's own history of regulatory failures involving chemicals and public health?[20]

Amrullah Saleh and other cabinet ministers objected to the spraying plan on the grounds that "Taliban propaganda would profit greatly from any spraying." Karzai's instinctive sense was that if farmers and itinerant poppy pickers in Helmand and Kandahar looked up and saw American helicopters thundering over the horizon as dusters poured chemicals onto their fields, they would recall the atrocities of Soviet aerial warfare and blame Hamid Karzai. Gradually during 2007, while remaining cautious about offending President Bush, but with the unified support of his cabinet, Karzai made his position clear to the Americans: He opposed aerial spraying. He also opposed any role for the U.S. military in fighting drug production.

Karzai battled within his cabinet to impose his view. In September 2007, Vice President Ahmad Zia Massoud, a brother of the late guerrilla leader, published an opinion piece in Britain's *Telegraph* newspaper arguing in favor of aerial spraying. Karzai blew up at him at a cabinet meeting the next day, by Massoud's account.

"You wrote on your own will or did the foreigners tell you to write it?"

"I don't have any contact with any foreigners but I know you do," Massoud answered.

"Oh, brother, those years have long gone in which you could print out your own money and do and say whatever you want," Karzai said, referring to the years of the early 1990s when Massoud's brother was Kabul's leading power.

"Mr. President . . . we all know the foreigners brought you to Uruzgan in U.S. helicopters."

"If you want to resign, you can resign right now," Karzai said.[21]

The problem was, for the advocates of Plan Colombia in the Bush administration, without aerial spraying in Helmand and Kandahar, there was no realistic path to reduce opium production enough to hurt the Taliban. The State Department contracted with DynCorp, a private security firm, to train Afghan forces to eradicate poppy fields one by one, on the ground. Taliban and armed drug gangs attacked the Afghan forces. Without the efficiencies of aerial spraying, all the ground eradication programs combined never eliminated more than 10 percent of the national poppy crop. "Ground eradication will never work," the D.E.A.'s Mike Braun argued. "You are going to have to hit it hard from the air."[22]

The British encouraged and supported Karzai's conclusion that aerial spraying was dangerous. Schweich raised the possibility that the United States could spray in Helmand and Kandahar even without Karzai's direct permission. His opponents in Washington replied with classified memos arguing that if the United States proceeded on its own, "you would be conducting chemical warfare" in violation of international law.[23]

The fights dragged on for so long because everyone involved on the American side knew that President Bush had a conviction about spraying. He mentioned the issue to almost everyone who visited him to talk about Afghanistan. Yet he could not make it happen. Bush would not act without Karzai's approval. And because neither the Pentagon nor the C.I.A. agreed that aerial spraying was wise, the two American security agencies with the greatest leverage over Karzai made little effort to change his mind.

The prolonged stalemate over Plan Afghanistan during 2007 wasted American money and effort. It also opened a breach of trust between Hamid Karzai and the United States—an early episode of mutual suspicion in what would soon become a cascade. Understandably, Karzai was losing faith in the conception and conduct of American and British policy in the Taliban heartland. He had long harbored suspicions that the British favored Pakistan over Afghanistan, at the expense of his government's authority. Implausible and even outrageous as it might sound to American officials, Karzai was open to the theory, whispered to him by some of his palace advisers, that the Americans and British might be working a secret plan to bring the Taliban back in southern Afghanistan in concert with Pakistan. He remained irritated that the British and Americans had forced him to remove Sher Mohammad Akhundzada as Helmand's governor on the grounds that he profited from the opium economy.

"The question is, why do we have Taliban controlling those areas now, when two years ago I had control of Helmand?" Karzai asked State Department visitors. "When Sher Mohammad was governor there, we had girls in schools and only 160 foreign troops. The international community pushed me to remove him and now look where we are. . . .

My question is, do you want a bad guy on your side or working for the Taliban? When Afghans are in charge, drugs are less, but where the international community is in charge, drugs are up."

The suspicion flowed both ways. In 2006, *Newsweek* published stories naming Karzai's half brother Ahmed Wali, based in Kandahar, as a narcotics trafficker. Karzai asked "both U.S. and British intelligence whether they had any evidence to back that up," but Washington and London admitted that they had only "numerous rumors and allegations," not the kind of evidence to support a criminal indictment. Karzai fumed and threatened libel actions. But to Schweich and other enthusiasts of aerial spraying, it was hard to ignore the hypothesis that Karzai might be protecting Ahmed Wali and other political allies profiting from opium, particularly in the south, Karzai's political base.[24]

Even though the debate about drugs and the Taliban was never resolved, the Plan Colombia model created a rationale for one of the most significant American military pivots of the war: the decision during 2008 and 2009 to send thousands of U.S. Marines to Helmand, the heartland of the poppy economy, despite the province's small population and isolated geography.

There remained those at the D.E.A. and the White House who believed fervently that if Karzai had permitted aerial spraying, it would have weakened the Taliban profoundly. Those who doubted Plan Afghanistan broadened their examinations of Taliban finance. Only after the production of new intelligence studies did the evidence become clearer, at least to some decision makers at the White House, that Afghanistan's opium economy was so decentralized that while the Taliban did indeed access funds, as a National Security Council official involved put it, "There certainly would be a Taliban insurgency without drugs."[25]

The drug policy argument became the latest *if only* thread of the classified Afghan war debate in Washington as the Bush administration expired. If only the Taliban did not make money from opium. If only the Pakistan sanctuary could be eliminated. If only reconstruction aid would deliver a credible alternative to the Taliban's coercive politics. In any event, for all the budget allocated, for all the fields burned and labs raided, Plan Afghanistan achieved little before it was largely aborted during the Obama administration. In 2007, the value of Afghan opium cultivation at the farm gate was one of the largest ever, according to the United Nations. The area under poppy reached a new record, at 476,000 acres. In the years to come, the Afghan opium economy would fluctuate, but ultimately reach new records still.[26]

SIXTEEN

Murder and the Deep State

By 2007, Dave Smith, the retired colonel deployed by the Defense Intelligence Agency, had moved to the Pentagon's policy office to work on Pakistan. Part of his job still included staying in touch with his network of friends in the Pakistan Army and I.S.I. to listen in private to their assessments. That spring, he sought out his old Command and Staff College friend, Mahmud Ahmed, the former I.S.I. director fired by Musharraf in October 2001. He now lived in Lahore, the tattered but entrancing former Moghul city in the heart of Punjab, near the border with India. The previous summer, General Mahmud had spent a month or so with friends in the Tablighi, or the Proselytizing Group, a worldwide network of Deobandi Muslims devoted to deepening the faith of Sunnis. At I.S.I., Mahmud had worn aviator glasses and kept a brush mustache. Now he wore a trim white beard. He padded around his comfortable home in a salwar kameez. Analysts at the U.S. embassy had told Smith that he would find his friend changed by faith, but Smith found him to be much the same.

He arrived at Mahmud's house on May 27, 2007. Pakistan was sinking into crisis, shaken by the very radicals the general had once protected. Encouraged by Al Qaeda, Islamist groups long nurtured by I.S.I. had turned on the Pakistani state. They mounted dozens of suicide bombings that would take more than six hundred Pakistani lives that year. In the capital, armed revolutionaries had barricaded themselves inside the Lal Masjid, or Red Mosque, from which they threatened the government and carried out vigilante assaults to enforce religious morals. Plainly, Pervez Musharraf had lost his grip on power after eight years in office. In March, he had rashly fired the chief justice of Pakistan's Supreme Court, touching off a mass revolt known as the Lawyers' Movement. He was under pressure from both liberals and Islamists.

The old friends settled in Mahmud's living room and took tea. Lahore was a bastion of the Lawyers' Movement. "He has shot himself in the foot, the ankle, the leg, the knee, and the thigh—and all of it unnecessarily," Mahmud said of Musharraf. Musharraf had held the high ground when he first seized power but had made one political mistake after another, Mahmud continued. Holding a phony referendum on his rule made him look like a tin pot dictator, and then he had built a political party run by traditional, thuggish pols who belied his promises of modernization. The question now was whether Musharraf would resign from the army and try to run for president again as a civilian, or whether he would do something rash such as to impose a national state of emergency to remain a dictator.

Musharraf was afraid of anything that threatened his grip on power, Mahmud went on, and would do anything to retain it. "He will keep his uniform on, because it is his source of power, and he will use the I.S.I. to manipulate the outcome of the next election if he thinks it's necessary." He spoke about that with an insider's confidence.

They talked at length about religion. If Islam was truth, then a messy state like Pakistan was a flawed vessel for its revelations. "Splits in Islam have always been caused by politics and politicians," Mahmud said. "Musharraf has no standing to advocate for enlightened moderation in Islam because he is not a moral man, and the people know it."[1]

About the prospects for security in Pakistan and Afghanistan, and for the success of American ambitions, he remained doubtful. "Religious extremism is spreading," he said. "Military force won't work. Military force won't work in Afghanistan, either," he continued. "If the intent is to stabilize Afghanistan, the Taliban were and are the best solution."

"What *is* the solution?" Smith asked him. It was clear that the Taliban was not an answer acceptable to the United States.

"Withdraw your legions," Mahmud answered with a smile, quoting a line from the movie *Ben-Hur*. "The U.S. military campaign is not working. You're creating more enemies than you're killing. You don't need a large military force to go after Al Qaeda. And what is Al Qaeda these days, anyway? It's more of an idea than a force in being."[2]

Smith took his leave and pledged to stay in touch. He wrote up his notes for the Pentagon's leadership. Mahmud's arguments would read to some there like the same I.S.I. talking points the United States had endured for a decade or more. In time, it would become clear that the general's views of the American military campaign in Afghanistan, if irritating to hear, had a basis in fact. That spring, however, withdrawal was not a recommendation Secretary of Defense Robert Gates or his Central Command uniformed leadership was in a mood to consider. Their instinct, shared at the C.I.A.'s highest levels and among many of the agency's operators on the front lines in South Asia, was something like the opposite: The United States had not yet applied *enough* military force to quell Al Qaeda and the Taliban.

Benazir Bhutto, the glamorous, Harvard- and Oxford-educated daughter of an executed former Pakistani prime minister, had served two terms as prime minister, between 1988 and 1990 and again between 1993 and 1996, before she was forced into exile in Dubai, pressured by corruption investigations focused on her family, particularly her husband, Asif Zardari, a rakish businessman who played polo and had bought a multimillion-dollar estate in England. Between her glaring sense of entitlement and a tireless use of the media, Benazir Bhutto could seem like "a machine that operates solely in the mode of victimization," as her estranged niece Fatima Bhutto put it. Yet she remained in 2007 "a symbol of reform in Pakistan and had generally liberal political impulses," in Secretary of State Condoleezza Rice's judgment. If the big idea shaping American policy toward Afghanistan in 2007 was Plan Colombia, in Pakistan it was the effort to bring Benazir Bhutto back home, to share power with Musharraf. Quietly but persistently, the State Department and the British Foreign Office worked to broker a deal between the two liberal leaders.[3]

Rice was aware that power-sharing arrangements are difficult to carry out because "in general, the parties don't really *want* to share power." Bhutto and Musharraf both tended to see themselves as indispensable saviors of Pakistan, a role that was inherently difficult to share. Yet Rice and her British counterparts hoped nonetheless that a deal might unite the country's liberal-minded forces against violent Islamists. Ashfaq Kayani, Musharraf's enigmatic protégé, now the director-general of I.S.I., led an initial round of discussions. In January 2007 Bhutto flew by helicopter to a palace in Abu Dhabi to meet secretly with Musharraf. To her surprise, the meeting was long and friendly. They exchanged cell phone numbers, talked periodically afterward, and met again privately in July. By then Bhutto had decided that she could return home and reenter politics, even though her negotiations with Musharraf were incomplete.[4]

In September, on the eve of her journey back to Pakistan, Bhutto met an American journalist in the lounge of the Ritz-Carlton Hotel in Washington. She had invited reporters to join her when she flew from exile into Karachi. She sat at a table near a jazz pianist. Her husband dropped by at one point, wearing a leisure suit and a gold chain and carrying shopping bags. Bhutto was fifty-four, with pale and youthful skin. She was in a giddy mood. She had the ability, honed when she was president of the Oxford Union, to transform informal conversation into oratory, a feat that made her seem at once impressive and untrustworthy. She spoke with particular conviction about the need to curtail Pakistan's intelligence services. "The security apparatus must be reformed," she said. "Unless that is done, it is going to be very difficult for us to dismantle the terrorist networks and the militant networks, and today they're a threat not only to other countries but to the unity and survival of Pakistan." She added that she wanted to bring the tribal areas "into the modern world, the twenty-first century. The people there do not have fundamental human rights."[5]

This was vintage Bhutto: perfect-pitch liberalism and, at the same time, a formulation barely distinguishable from the American foreign policy of the moment. The exception to her accommodation of the Bush administration's agenda lay in her jaundiced attitude toward the army and the I.S.I., institutions to which the administration had given more than $10 billion in financial aid. "General Musharraf's team has relied on the principle that to catch a thief, you send a thief," she said, speaking of the peace deals he had forged with militants in North and South Waziristan. "They've said, 'These are "reformed Taliban," or "reformed militants," and let's use them.' It hasn't worked. . . . And we must really pause and think, Where do they get their food from, after all, to feed and look after irregular armies that have thousands of people? And to clothe them, and to heal their wounds when they get wounded in battle? It requires a huge apparatus—so it requires a real breakdown in governance for such forces to continue to prosper and grow. That's what we're seeing in Pakistan, a breakdown in governance."[6]

That was in some respects the Bush administration's hypothesis as well. Its policy remained to train and equip Pakistani security forces and to provide extensive development aid. In the summer of 2007, the U.S. embassy in Islamabad produced a PowerPoint deck, "Strategy for Pakistan's Federally Administered Tribal Areas," that summarized the latest plan to fix the country. Its "strategic objective" was to "permanently render F.A.T.A. inhospitable to terrorists and extremists." This would be accomplished by enhancing "the legitimacy and writ" of the Pakistan government, improving "economic, security and social conditions," and supporting "permanent, sustainable change." These were buzzwords, but at least the clichés came with a well-funded five-year budget. In the tribal areas alone, where only a few million people lived scattered across a vast area, the Bush administration planned to spend $100 million a year on jobs, health services, water supply, and other development. It would add an average of about $25 million a year on road construction, to connect the region to the heartland of Pakistan, and tens of millions more annually on the Frontier Corps, "Special Ops," "intelligence," and "advanced training." The tribal areas "will not be transformed overnight," the embassy plan conceded, "but there are few missions more critical to U.S. national security, or more deserving of our considered patience. . . .

Force is a necessary component of an overall strategy, but not sufficient alone."[7]

The Bush administration placed a major bet during 2007 on the Frontier Corps, the locally raised paramilitary force. Its officers and soldiers were Pashtuns. They sometimes balked at assaulting fellow Pashtuns among the Taliban. The Pakistani Taliban and Al Qaeda exploited their weakness and recruited traitors. Compromised Frontier Corps soldiers faced court-martial proceedings and imprisonment in trials the Musharraf government never publicized. Mullahs in the tribal areas refused to preside over proper burials for fallen soldiers because the dead fought a mercenary campaign for Washington and did not perish righteously. "We know that you have become America's slave and are serving infidel Musharraf and have become a traitor to your religion for food, clothes and shelter," pamphlets tacked up on walls in North Waziristan warned. A soldier in a Frontier Corps uniform shot dead an American Army officer as he departed a "Border Flag" meeting that spring. The assassination was "most unfortunate," the Pakistan Army vice chief Ahsan Hyat told a State Department official. Pakistan, he said, had "investigated the assailant's personal history, family, and the state of the Frontier Corps generally" and remained "convinced the incident was the result of an individual disgruntled soldier, not part of any kind of trend or broader problem."[8]

Neither Musharraf nor the Punjabi-dominated army leadership wanted to mount an invasion of the tribal areas with regular Pakistan Army forces, since that might only provoke more revenge-seeking suicide bombings and violence in the Pakistani heartland. Musharraf's sense was that to have any chance of success in the tribal areas, the army needed at least one political ally among Waziristan's major tribal groupings. The Mehsuds, from their stronghold in South Waziristan, did not look like candidates. Baitullah Mehsud, a plump, black-bearded radical in his early thirties, had organized an armed force of several thousand militia fighters. He gave interviews threatening revolutionary war against the Pakistani state. Among the historical rivals of the Mehsuds were the Wazirs. They had been influenced by radical ideology as well, but their leaders saw less cause to act in overt hostility to Pakistan, at least for now. Musharraf adapted the British colonial strategy of playing one tribal network against the other. The Pakistani military's lines of communication to Afghanistan had long run through Wazir territory in North Waziristan. Musharraf and his corps commanders "thought we should play ball with the Wazirs," as Musharraf put it. When American officials protested, he told them, "Leave the tactical matters to us. We know our people."[9]

Musharraf's top generals backed his strategy to accommodate some militants in Waziristan. "Shock and awe is fine for you if you fly in from the U.S. or Canada," Musharraf's defense secretary, retired Lieutenant General Tariq Waseem Ghazi, told the Pentagon. "Shock and awe is no good for us when we have to live with the tribal areas as part and parcel of Pakistan."[10]

Ghazi increasingly found the Pentagon to be unsympathetic. In fact, U.S. commanders had concluded that American and N.A.T.O. soldiers across the border in Afghanistan were dying as a result of the Pakistan Army's accommodations in Waziristan. Pentagon delegations arrived in Pakistan with "fancy graphs about attacks going up" in Afghanistan as a result of Musharraf's approach but Ghazi and his colleagues found the statistics unconvincing. As more and more suicide bombers out of Waziristan attacked Pakistani government compounds and killed scores of innocent civilians in Pakistani cities, he found the American allegations that I.S.I. was complicit with such killers irresponsible. Was it not obvious that Pakistan had lost control of these groups and was just trying to quiet them? "If that's what you want to believe, believe it," Ghazi told his Pentagon counterparts. "There's nothing we can do about it."[11]

Besides Dave Smith, there was perhaps a basketball team's worth of senior intelligence officers in the American system with a deep, street-level feel for Pakistan's regional diversity, national resilience, kaleidoscopic Islamist militancy, and party politics. Like Smith, most of these specialists had lived and worked in the country in an earlier era, when informal travel was easier and safer. The embassy security protocols that kicked in after 2001 only tightened as suicide and truck bombings spread across Pakistan after 2006. That left American diplomats and spies often trapped behind the walls and razor wire of the embassy compound in Islamabad and the consulates in Peshawar, Lahore, and Karachi.

In the summer of 2007, the Bush administration recruited Peter Lavoy as the new national intelligence officer for South Asia—the government's chief intelligence analyst for the region. In several roles over the next eight years, Lavoy would become one of the most influential Pakistan experts at the White House—an Oval Office briefer, a supervisor of classified National Intelligence Estimates, the expert in the Situation Room who stood before maps to try to succinctly describe the nuances of Pakistani ethnography or party politics. He was in some ways an unlikely intelligence bureaucrat. As an undergraduate, he had studied government and international relations at crunchy Oberlin College, and then enrolled in the political science doctoral program at the University of California at Berkeley. California suited him. He was about six feet tall, athletic-looking, and had the manner of a surfer-bartender. He took great care with the martinis he decanted at dinner parties and he typically traveled with a humidor of cigars. He was a natural organizer and master of ceremonies, quick with a joke, difficult to rattle. As a graduate student, after a false start in Soviet studies, Lavoy took a research position in India, where he decided to write his doctoral dissertation on the Indian nuclear program. To deepen his language skills, he enrolled in the Berkeley Urdu program in Lahore, Pakistan. (Spoken Urdu, the national language of Pakistan, is similar to Hindi, India's predominant national language.) Between 1989 and 1990, Lavoy lived with a Pakistani family near Punjab University. He traveled widely—to the Karakorum mountain range along the border with China, the Federally Administered Tribal Areas, and the deserts of Baluchistan. He developed a genuine fondness for Pakistan and encountered its diversity as few of its own citizens have a chance to do.[12]

After graduate school he worked in Lawrence Livermore Laboratory's C-Division, the nuclear lab's center for proliferation analysis. Then he won appointment to the faculty of the Naval Postgraduate School in Monterey, the fog-shrouded beach town to the north of Carmel and Big Sur. At Monterey, Lavoy became well known in South Asia scholarship and policy networks for the conferences he hosted, which brought together Pakistani and Indian military officers, journalists, and civilian government officials. The events usually climaxed with a beach bonfire and barbecue where Lavoy presided as the Indian and Pakistani visitors talked over the pounding surf, in an atmosphere as far from enmity as it was possible for Americans to create. During the Clinton administration's second term, Lavoy joined the Pentagon's counterproliferation office, whose missions included the containment of Pakistan's nuclear program. In 2007, when the Bush administration searched for a new national intelligence officer to help the cabinet make sense of Pakistan's worsening implosion, it turned to Lavoy, and he took up his position on the C.I.A.'s campus that summer.

Once inside the government's classified bubble, Lavoy could see in vivid detail what he had discerned in broad strokes from outside, namely, how badly the relationship between the United States and Pakistan was going. A recent National Intelligence Estimate about terrorism had described Pakistan as a "safe haven" for Al Qaeda. It was a phrase that, to Musharraf at least, suggested that the Americans now believed Pakistan was collaborating with the authors of September 11. "'Hideouts' would be a better description," Musharraf complained privately. Trust had eroded to the bone. At the White House, the main question debated by Bush's advisers was "How can we navigate this increasingly impure relationship with Pakistan to pursue our urgent objectives against Al Qaeda?"[13]

As he began sitting in on national security meetings presided over by Bush, or, more often, National Security Adviser Stephen Hadley, Lavoy felt duty-bound to brief the material provided by the intelligence bureaucracy. But he could tell how frustrated cabinet members and deputies were with a lot of these prepackaged briefs and PowerPoints; they seemed loaded with a lot of information but did not provide a lot of insight. Hardly anyone among the secretaries or deputy secretaries managing policy had long, direct experience with Pakistan. They might have gotten to know their counterparts in the Pakistan Army or the Foreign Ministry and formed a few impressions from these relationships and from reading. Yet their responsibilities at State, the Pentagon, or the C.I.A. spanned the world, and it was impossible for most of them to untangle complexities within complexities involving the Wazirs, the Mehsuds, or the structure of the Afghan Taliban's revival. Principals and deputies in Washington tended to reach a judgment—"I.S.I. is the problem," for example, because of the operations of Directorate S—and then never change their minds. It wasn't as if such a judgment lacked a factual basis. The problem was that it did not account for what had become, in 2007, a very dynamic situation—the birth of a serious, violent domestic rebellion against the Pakistani state carried out by some of the Islamist forces the state had long nurtured.

On Directorate S and the revival of the Afghan Taliban, during 2007 and 2008, American and N.A.T.O. intelligence did become clearer, informed by harder evidence. It showed that Musharraf and Kayani had authorized deniable support to the movement, stopping short of weapons supply—the reporting showed that they were very cautious about directly providing money and weapons to the Taliban because they feared they could get caught and pay a price in the international system. Retired I.S.I. officers, nongovernmental organizations, and other cutouts supplied the Taliban to reduce this risk. American intelligence reporting on individual, serving I.S.I. case officers, who managed contacts with the Quetta Shura or the Haqqanis or Lashkar-e-Taiba, which fought in Kashmir, also showed that they were clearly in the Pakistan Army's chain of command. This reporting belied any "rogue I.S.I." hypothesis. Overall, it was very difficult to reach a judgment that "Pakistan" did this or that or even that there was such a thing as "Pakistan's policy," when there were so many actors and when Directorate S was engaging diverse militant groups for different purposes at different times. In the tribal areas, I.S.I. sometimes made deals with violent radicals for defensive, tactical reasons—to forestall attacks on themselves or to get military supplies through to isolated bases. Other times the I.S.I. made deals for strategic reasons—to encourage the groups to enlarge their influence inside Afghanistan or to attack Indian targets there. Still other times the army attacked these same groups in retaliation for attacks inside Pakistan.

Each major American intelligence agency had its own reporting stream about I.S.I. and Directorate S and each had its own emphasis. At the C.I.A., the most sophisticated analytical products about I.S.I. were distributed by the Near East and South Asia office of the Directorate of Intelligence, a warren of offices and pods in the New Headquarters Building at Langley. Some of the Afghan and Pakistan specialists there had moved to C.I.A. from intelligence positions in the military, while others had graduate degrees in political science or international relations. In considering I.S.I.'s relationship with the Haqqanis or the Afghan Taliban, the C.I.A. group would ask whether Directorate S or its contractors had "cognizance, influence, or control" of a particular guerrilla or terrorist unit—a sliding scale of culpability. Clearly I.S.I. influenced the Haqqanis and the Quetta Shura, but to say the service controlled these organizations was doubtful, according to this analysis. In Waziristan, the Pakistan Army was clearly weaker than the militants. The C.I.A.'s analysts also tried to convey the limits of I.S.I.'s competence. From experience tracing to the 1980s, agency operators and former chiefs of station knew that while some I.S.I. officers were highly professional and capable, others were venal, corrupt, and passive. In Washington, it was increasingly common for policy makers and members of Congress to talk of I.S.I. as an omnipotent, malign, highly effective force, when in fact the rise of domestic terrorism in Pakistan could be just as well understood as profound evidence of I.S.I.'s incompetence. Overall, the United States began to collect large amounts of evidence that Musharraf and Kayani were directing the Taliban's revival, but the Americans did not want to reveal this information because it would expose sources and methods that they wanted to continue to exploit. At the same time, the intelligence showed that at the lower levels of I.S.I., in the field, officers pursued their own plans without necessarily informing the army brass in advance of every operation. In the Situation Room, Lavoy learned, the best that might be realistically hoped for from overwhelmed decision makers, up to and including the president, was a willingness to avoid cartoonish, stubborn, black-and-white judgments, and to accept "It's complicated."

I do not believe that any true Muslim will make an attack on me because Islam forbids attacks on women, and Muslims know that if they attack a woman they will burn in hell," Benazir Bhutto told the journalists who had assembled in Dubai to accompany her on an Emirates Airlines flight to Karachi. "Secondly, Islam forbids suicide bombing."[14]

She boarded on the morning of October 18, 2007. Party workers in custom-made Benazir T-shirts chanted slogans as the jet reached cruising altitude, defying the pleadings of stewardesses in red pillbox hats to remain seated with their seat belts fastened. Bhutto agreed to a press scrum mid-flight. "I am not scared," she said. "I am thinking of my mission. This is a movement for democracy because we are under threat from extremists and militants."

Her plane skidded onto the tarmac and taxied to a V.I.P. terminal. The journalists descended first, to be in position to record her descent onto Pakistani asphalt. She had been away from Pakistan for almost a decade. Wearing a white head scarf and clutching prayer beads, she tilted her head to the sky operatically, summoned tears, and declared, "It's great to be back home. It's a dream come true."

The stronghold of Bhutto's Pakistan Peoples Party lies in rural Sindh Province, near Karachi. The party includes an undemocratic patronage machine that can mobilize large turnouts on order. At least a million loyalists packed the streets around the airport that afternoon. They waved red, black, and green P.P.P. flags, wore red, black, and green P.P.P. baseball hats, blew noisemakers, and pounded drums. By nightfall, the procession had advanced only a few hundred yards through the crowds toward the tomb of Mohammed Ali Jinnah, Pakistan's founder, where Bhutto planned to speak to a rally. She rode in a tall truck with a custom Plexiglas crow's nest on top, from which she could wave and orate through loudspeakers.

Near midnight two bombs—a smaller one, then one much larger—ripped through the throngs around her. They killed 139 people and wounded another 400 but left Bhutto unhurt. Her aides pulled her away from her truck as her parade descended into mayhem—body parts strewn about, ambulances pushing through the crowds, and rescue workers treating the wounded or carrying them away on stretchers. At Bhutto's truck, party workers lifted reporters up a ladder into the crow's nest, to examine the crime scene firsthand. She had left behind speech notes.

A few days later, at her Karachi home, Bhutto said she remained determined to campaign for office. Few targets of political murder attempts have contemplated the possibility of their demise in advance as thoroughly as she had. She had returned after half reconciling with Musharraf but did not know whether she trusted him. "You know, what is trust?" she asked. "You can't see into people's hearts. I don't know him, so I can't say."[15]

The intelligence service of the United Arab Emirates, perhaps informed by intelligence relayed from Britain or the United States, had warned Bhutto before she flew to Karachi that suicide-bombing squads had been dispatched from Waziristan to attack her. Because of her family's long history of intense, even fatal conflict with I.S.I. and the army, Bhutto was inclined to see the threat as rooted in Pakistan's deep state, not merely attributable to martyrdom-seeking independent radicals from the tribal areas. Two days before she flew to Karachi, Bhutto had written to Musharraf. She named at least one former and two serving Pakistani officials as likely suspects if there was an attempt on her life. One of the names on her list was Lieutenant General Hamid Gul, who had been director-general of I.S.I. during her first term as prime minister, until she dismissed him from the post. A second was Brigadier Ijaz Shah, the director-general of the Intelligence Bureau, the country's equivalent of the F.B.I. The third was Chaudhry Pervez Elahi, a civilian politician allied with Musharraf and then the chief minister of Punjab. Bhutto felt these three "would go to any length to stop me," as she put it. Yet she did not appear to possess—or, at least, she did not cite—specific evidence that any of them might be involved in a conspiracy to kill her.

Bhutto interpreted the bombing of her convoy in Karachi as confirmation that parts of the government were involved—at least on the periphery—in active plots to kill her. Her thinking was not irrational:

The police teams sent to protect her homecoming were inadequate, and in the area where the attack occurred the streetlights had been turned off—perhaps owing to one of the city's chronic power failures, but perhaps not. Anne Patterson, the American ambassador, flew to Karachi. Bhutto presented a written request to meet with U.S. embassy experts to evaluate her security. That night, Patterson cabled Washington urging that the Bush administration refuse her, because an audit "will inevitably expose performance gaps" in Bhutto's arrangements "that would not meet American standards of training and equipment. Responsibility for security belongs with the Government of Pakistan." This was a global policy, with only the rarest of exceptions, as with Karzai when he was first installed; the United States could not get into the business of managing security for officeholders and opposition leaders in foreign countries.[16]

Yet Bhutto insisted that Musharraf's protection was inadequate. Patterson urged that while the embassy might refer Bhutto to qualified Pakistani security contractors who could evaluate her security, the embassy should not help directly. The Bush administration "should either undertake full responsibility for Bhutto's personal security"—a nonstarter in nationalist Pakistan during an election campaign—"or not."[17]

In early November, Musharraf imposed a state of emergency, in what would prove to be his final effort to hold on to power. Even then, Bhutto never broke with him entirely, and when Musharraf eventually confirmed that elections would go forward in January, Bhutto decided that the Peoples Party would compete. Later that month, Musharraf at last resigned as chief of the army staff, to stand for reelection as president as a civilian. He elevated Ashfaq Kayani as his successor in command of the military, handing over to him the most powerful office in Pakistan. At I.S.I. Musharraf simultaneously installed a man with family and personal loyalties to him, General Nadeem Taj.

Once Bhutto committed herself to the election, the question of her personal security took on renewed significance. Her competitors on Election Day would be Musharraf's political followers, and they controlled the local governments and police forces whose services Bhutto required for her safety. Yet increasingly, amid the swirl of events, Bhutto and Musharraf no longer saw themselves as potential allies. Bhutto moved instead toward a political détente with Nawaz Sharif, the leader of the center-right Muslim League, who had also returned from exile to compete in the election.

Bhutto decided to hold a rally at Liaquat Bagh, a park in Rawalpindi. When the day arrived, December 27, Nadeem Taj, the new I.S.I. director close to Musharraf, visited her in the early hours, just after midnight. They talked for two hours about the campaigning as well as about threats on Bhutto's life. A few days earlier, the Pakistani Interior Ministry had received a report that Osama Bin Laden had ordered the assassination of Bhutto, Musharraf, and a third Pakistani politician. Taj warned Bhutto to take precautions.[18]

Hamid Karzai happened to be visiting Islamabad. After the I.S.I. meeting, Bhutto drove to see him in his fourth-floor suite at the Serena Hotel. She admired his cape and they laughed as he recounted how he had acquired it—an improbable tale that involved a visit to the exiled king of Afghanistan. They sipped tea and coffee and discussed the region's gathering political violence. Militant Islamic leaders had by now named both of them as targets for assassinations. "I am not afraid of death," Bhutto told Karzai.[19]

At the rally, Bhutto sat on the platform and listened to the opening speeches. Her aides' cell phones began to ring. Sherry Rehman, a senior political and media adviser, leaned over to relay some news: Elsewhere in the city, gunmen had killed some of Nawaz Sharif's election workers.

"Okay," Bhutto said. "We must phone him" to offer sympathy and support. She asked Rehman to remind her to make the call. She was hoarse from campaigning, but delivered a rousing speech.

"Long live Bhutto!" the crowd chanted as she descended from the platform at around 5:00 p.m. She got into a white Toyota Land Cruiser with a sunroof. As the vehicle left the park, the driver crossed a median to turn east. Another crowd of chanting supporters swarmed toward her. The vehicle stopped; Bhutto's aides unrolled the sunroof and stood up to wave to them. A clean-shaven man wearing sunglasses and a black vest moved toward her, raised a pistol, and fired three times. Then he tucked down his head and detonated a suicide vest filled with ball bearings. Bhutto died instantly. The blast killed twenty-four others.[20]

Bhutto's aides released to the press the various warnings she had written down, to be publicized in the event of her death. On January 3, Musharraf held a press conference in Islamabad to defend himself against Bhutto's accusatory ghost. His government announced it had obtained phone intercepts indicating that Baitullah Mehsud, emir of the newly declared Pakistani Taliban movement, had organized Bhutto's assassination. Musharraf wore a suit and tie and sat at a table by himself. "I have been brought up in a very educated and civilized family, which believes in values, which believes in principles, which believes in character," he said. "My family is not a family that believes in killing people."

Musharraf said Bhutto had ignored warnings that campaign rallies had become too dangerous, and he blamed her for standing recklessly in the open air to greet her supporters. As for Bhutto's suspicions that Pakistan's deep state might have been involved, Musharraf dismissed such thinking as a "joke." With apparent sincerity, he added, "No intelligence organization of Pakistan is capable of indoctrinating a man to blow himself up."[21]

In February, the Peoples Party swept to power and Asif Zardari, Bhutto's erratic widower, became Pakistan's president, at the time perhaps the world's most unlikely leader of a nuclear-armed nation outside of North Korea. He told Patterson that the United States was Pakistan's "safety blanket" and assured her that he believed there was no such thing as a "moderate Taliban." He added, "I am not Benazir, and I know it."[22]

Although it was not yet obvious to everyone in the Bush administration, Musharraf was finished politically. He would cling to the office of president for a few more months before resigning. He later went into exile. The twin pillars of the Bush administration's reformed policy in Pakistan—Musharraf and Bhutto—were gone.

SEVENTEEN

Hard Data

Toward the end of 2007, a team of career C.I.A. analysts at the Directorate of Intelligence, who specialized in assessing wars, carried a set of highly classified, color-coded maps of Afghanistan to the White House, to unfurl them for decision makers at the National Security Council. The map project was called the District Assessments. It attempted to describe political control and security in each of Afghanistan's 398 official administrative districts. The C.I.A. unit collected and aggregated about three dozen independent indicators for each district. Some of the data could be objectively counted—the number of roadside bombings or assassinations during the last six months, for example. Other judgments, such as the extent of Taliban influence on a rural population, might require more qualitative measurement, but these assessments could still be informed by data such as whether the Taliban operated checkpoints on the roads or were reliably reported to run informal courts in local mosques. After all the intelligence was organized, the C.I.A. team gave each Afghan administrative district one of four ratings. The spectrum ranged from districts controlled by the Karzai government to districts controlled or contested by the Taliban. There was also a category (and a distinct color on the map) for districts judged to be under "local control," meaning that they were run by independent warlords or drug barons not aligned with either side—or were controlled by nobody at all, essentially ungoverned.

In the closed world of secret intelligence, most analytical products wound up in locked cabinets, having had little impact. But every now and then a bestseller broke through. The C.I.A.'s District Assessment maps of Afghanistan proved to be such a blockbuster, one of the most popular top secret analytical products the agency had ever distributed. Tony Schinella, a courteous academic with a black mustache, would soon rotate in to supervise the project; he would work on it for almost a decade, becoming one of the most influential analysts of the Afghan war in the government. Schinella had analyzed the Balkan conflicts of the 1990s, and then, after September 11, the wars in Afghanistan and Iraq. He had earned a doctoral degree at the Center for International Studies at the Massachusetts Institute of Technology. Political scientists at M.I.T. had advanced the use of data and mathematical modeling in search of insights into war and peace. The Afghan maps Schinella and his colleagues created followed this methodology.[1]

The impetus for the maps' initial creation was a new focus on the Afghan war within the Bush administration, following the late 2006 strategic review carried out at the White House. In mid-2007, Bush and his national security adviser, Stephen Hadley, had recruited Major General Douglas Lute to the White House to coordinate support for the dual American war efforts in Iraq and Afghanistan. In time, Lute would become Washington's most important policy adviser on Afghanistan, but in his early days at the White House, he spent at least 90 percent of his time managing the fiasco in Iraq. Lute was among those at the White House who were enthusiastic about the District Assessments project. Rare is the general who does not love a map, and with the distractions of Iraq, here was a concise way to track progress or the lack of it in Afghanistan. Intelligence consumers in diverse agencies seemed to appreciate the C.I.A. maps' mesmerizing colors, unfurled in cascades of red and green.

In the emerging era of Big Data, the C.I.A. maps were an exemplar of the power of data visualization. They also provided a way to capture changes in the war's progress empirically. American military commanders in Afghanistan often rotated annually and ambassadors moved on every two or three years. In 2007, Condoleezza Rice hired Eliot Cohen to become her counselor at State. He was a Harvard-educated political

scientist who favored bow ties. Rice asked him to spend as much time
in the field as possible to offer independent assessments. He found in
Afghanistan that there was a pattern of briefings at military headquarters, whether at Kabul or in the regions. The commanders starting a
rotation would say, "This is going to be difficult." Six months later,
they'd say, "We might be turning a corner." At the end of their rotation,
they would say, "We have achieved irreversible momentum." Then the
next command group coming in would pronounce, "This is going to be
difficult. . . ."

At the U.S. embassy in Kabul, State Department reporting seemed
to some of Rice's advisers to have become detached from reality. Bill
Wood, the ambassador, was more optimistic than her senior analysts.
David Gordon, a political scientist who served as Rice's director of policy
planning, considered Wood "a solid citizen" but noted that he "was of the
view that things were becoming stabilized" when the evidence was hard
to find. Eliot Cohen commissioned memos objecting to an oft-quoted
claim, usually emanating from I.S.A.F. commanders, that more than 75
percent of the war's violence occurred in just 10 percent of Afghan districts, mainly in Helmand and Kandahar. He didn't think the United
States knew enough about what was happening in all of Afghanistan's
398 districts to be so precise.

The C.I.A. District Assessments purported to let numbers tell the
war's story, but it did not require access to secret information to see the
trends. Early on after his arrival at State, before the District Assessments
became popular, Cohen used unclassified United Nations maps dating
back to 2002 to try to shock Rice and other principals into recognizing
how badly Afghanistan was deteriorating. The U.N. maps depicted
Afghan districts as green if they were safe for aid workers. (On the C.I.A.
maps, green depicted government control but did not necessarily indicate that the area was safe for international travelers.) Cohen unfurled
annual maps that showed Afghanistan's green zone was shrinking fast.[2]

The indicators reflected on the C.I.A. maps came from all sources,
including military field reports, C.I.A. agent reporting, diplomatic reporting, allied governments, the United Nations, and published journalism. The C.I.A. took final responsibility for each district's rating, but the

team's analysts solicited data and dissents from other intelligence agencies. There were reasons for competing analysts to be skeptical. Paul Miller, the former C.I.A. analyst who moved to the National Security Council to work on Afghanistan just as the maps were being produced, noted that the color-coded scheme didn't have a category for "unknown." He thought the agency didn't own up to its intelligence gaps; he would have guessed that a large portion of the map should have been painted as "unknown." The officers who produced the maps heard this criticism regularly; they argued that it was misplaced because as troop and civilian deployments to Afghanistan rose after 2007, the United States had more reach in its field reporting than at any time since the Taliban's fall.[3]

The District Assessments had an antecedent in the Vietnam War, a project known as the Hamlet Evaluation System, undertaken by the Pentagon, starting in 1967. Civil Operations and Revolutionary Development Support, or C.O.R.D.S., oversaw that work. American provincial and district advisers working on the pacification campaign for C.O.R.D.S. filled out monthly questionnaires about all the hamlets in their areas, grading security indicators on a scale of "A" (most aligned with the South Vietnamese government) to "E" (heavily influenced by the Viet Cong) to "V" (totally under Viet Cong control). Later they also tried to measure development and governance indicators such as health care and education. The problem was that it was unrealistic to expect the Americans—mainly military officers—who were scattered around violent sections of South Vietnam to accurately collect such metrics. One issue was that "you know what your boss wants to hear . . . that we were winning the war," as Ron Milam, an adviser who worked on the project, put it. To make the scores look better, hamlets under Viet Cong control were sometimes removed from the calculations or blended with hamlets with better scores to make the picture look more encouraging.[4]

As part of the Pentagon's effort to convince the American public that the Vietnam War was going well, U.S. briefers created sanitized, unclassified versions of maps derived from the Hamlet Evaluation System. They used them in Saigon to impress visiting members of Congress, European ambassadors, newspaper columnists, and other opinion makers. The maps became a symbol of "the inclination of successive administrations in

Washington to manipulate information about the war for political advantage," as the historian David Elliott put it.[5]

The C.I.A. analysts who worked on the District Assessments forty years later were post-Vietnam skeptics well aware of that history of delusion and public dishonesty. If anything, in the judgment of Pentagon commanders and some White House aides, the C.I.A.'s analysts were inclined toward overwrought pessimism about the war in Afghanistan and the deterioration of Pakistan after 2007. In any event, the C.I.A. maps showed starkly that the Taliban were marching toward control or the ability to contest control of about half of the country, district by district. They did not provide a basis for official optimism.[6]

That did not prevent generals in Kabul from being optimistic. During a 2007 secure videoconference with General Dan McNeill, then top American commander in Afghanistan, Robert Gates, Rumsfeld's recently arrived successor as secretary of defense, asked, "Dan, I'm trying to get a sense if we are making progress. Are we making gains in quelling the insurgency? If we are winning, by what measure?"

McNeill defended the war effort. Since arriving in Afghanistan, he had repeatedly heard dark forecasts about the war's slide from C.I.A. analysts and others at State and D.I.A. He thought the pessimists were overstating the evidence. The general's take was that the war effort in the south had almost collapsed late in 2006, but that fight-back by the Canadians and more aggressive tactics by N.A.T.O. had stabilized the situation. Fundamentally, McNeill argued, the war hadn't changed. They had to be patient. Privately, McNeill figured it would take up to two decades to put Afghan forces in a position where they could defend the country adequately on their own.

When the general signed off, Gates turned to his aides, incredulous. As a former director of analysis of the C.I.A., he knew "a thing or two about taking the Agency with a grain of salt," he told them. Yet the C.I.A. analysts' "assessments that the situation is dramatically declining doesn't comport with what I'm hearing" from McNeill or the U.S. embassy in Kabul. "My sense is that we are not getting this right and that the situation is going sideways on us."[7] The C.I.A. maps revived a dilemma familiar from Vietnam: Could verifiable facts about a deteriorat-

ing war lead policy makers to understand the futility of the country's
policies?

Throughout 2007, the U.S. government's classified information systems were replete with candid reports about rising violence in Afghanistan and failing governance by the Karzai administration. The
problem was not a paucity of information; it was Washington's ability to
recognize the pattern. Provincial Reconstruction Teams scattered around
Afghanistan regularly sent to Washington lengthy written assessments,
drawing on their access to local conditions. The P.R.T. report from Kandahar, the Taliban's birthplace, was particularly bleak. The Canadian
military offensive late in 2006 had raised the local population's expectations, but N.A.T.O.'s "failure to consolidate victory" had proven to be
"costly." The inability of the United States to crack down on the Taliban's
sanctuaries in Pakistan had given rise to conspiracy thinking among Kandaharis. American passivity toward Pakistan was interpreted as "proof of
a plot to prolong instability in Afghanistan, or in the most extreme version, proof of a secret alliance between the West and the Taliban."[8]

The major political challenge "is the lack of good governance," the
report warned. Exploitative since 2002, the Karzai regime was sinking
into systematic racketeering across the south. "Real power is wielded by
a select few and standard practices would be considered corrupt in the
West. Ahmed Wali Karzai, brother of President Karzai, exercises far
more power than his position as head of the (advisory) Provincial Council should convey." Fifty thousand students were forced out of schools by
violence during 2006 and virtually all schools in the province had by
now closed. The rise of suicide bombing attacks against rolling convoys
had caused American and N.A.T.O. forces to ease their rules of engagement so that they now fired rounds into vehicles suspected of an attack.
Inevitably, the snap judgments of exposed soldiers on the front lines led
to mistakes and innocent deaths. "These deaths, while not easy to avoid,
do much to undermine our credibility with the population."[9]

"Corruption by police and government officials is having a corrosive
impact on government credibility while boosting that of the Taliban,"

noted a separate report about Kandahar from the U.S. embassy in Kabul that summer. Despite the killing of hundreds of Taliban volunteers, "insurgents have increased their presence in many districts." The Taliban struck soft targets such as the Afghan police, a force that was "very weak, poorly controlled, and virtually unsupported" by N.A.T.O. or the United States. Afghan police earned just $70 per month in Kandahar for work that was "high risk and low reward." Taliban night letters and assassinations intimidated villagers, farmers, and mullahs preaching publicly about the war; they increasingly adopted a stance of neutrality to avoid death, and, if they happened to work for Canada or the United Nations, they hid such information from their neighbors.[10]

There were also "strong indications that some district leaders and Chiefs of Police are engaged in supporting the trafficking of narcotics," the U.S. embassy in Kabul reported. "These same officials have extracted bribes from farmers to keep them off the list of fields to be targeted under the governor-led eradication program." There were also "strong indications" that Abdul Raziq, the local ruler and prized American ally in Spin Boldak, on the road to Quetta, "controls large-scale narcotics trafficking."[11]

Graeme Smith, the Canadian journalist who lived in Kandahar during this period, worked with Afghan colleagues to conduct an informal survey of Taliban fighters in the region. Thirty-seven of the forty-two Taliban they reached belonged to tribes that had lost out during the reigns of the Karzais and Gul Agha Sherzai. These Taliban also had only the thinnest understanding of their international enemies. They did tend to grasp that the United States was a world power, "a direct equivalent of past empires that sent crusaders to the Middle East." Canada puzzled them, however. Some did not even understand that it was a country: "It might be an old and destroyed city," one respondent said. This was not an aspect of the war's asymmetries that could be coded easily onto a data map.[12]

Regular travel to Afghanistan and Pakistan, sometimes in bow tie and flak jacket, left Eliot Cohen with the impression that Rice and Bush were getting "an awful lot of happy talk from people who should know better." The Afghan war might be better than Iraq, but there were many signs that things were not well.

On one of his field surveys, Cohen flew with a colonel over a contested Afghan valley. "Tell me the mechanics of this war," Cohen asked.

"Clear the valley," the colonel replied.

"What do you mean?"

"You walk through a valley until you get into a firefight and then you keep shooting until it stops."

"That's a little troubling," Cohen said.

"It's a valley-by-valley war, sir."[13]

Between 2002 and 2006, the C.I.A.'s operations in Afghanistan had concentrated largely on the secret Afghan militias built up by the Omega teams along the Pakistan border to hunt for Al Qaeda members, cooperation with Karzai and a few key governors such as Sherzai and Asadullah Khalid, and support for the N.D.S. The demands of the Iraq war, instability on the Seventh Floor at Langley, and short tours by Kabul station chiefs of erratic quality limited the agency's effectiveness. In 2007, as the Bush administration authorized much larger aid budgets for Afghanistan, the C.I.A.'s engagement expanded. The agency's financial support for N.D.S. increased. The agency operated about a dozen bases outside Kabul Station and commanded a private air force of planes and helicopters. Its two main priorities remained locating Al Qaeda cells operating across the border in Pakistan's tribal areas and the hunt for senior Al Qaeda leaders, particularly Bin Laden and Zawahiri. It was baffling and not an advertisement for C.I.A. capabilities and focus that the pair remained at large. Yet the agency was now drawn increasingly into the conflict against the Taliban as well.[14]

The American military and espionage machine, hardened by four years of brutal combat in Iraq, could find it difficult to share space with European counterparts in Afghanistan. An American two-star officer deployed to the I.S.A.F. headquarters in Kabul in 2007 found "a typical N.A.T.O. billet—appalling in many ways." Officers worked from 9:00 a.m.

to 2:00 p.m. and then retired to the pub. At night half the command was drunk. He "kept waiting for an attack to penetrate the grounds." Yet the Bush administration had sold Canada and European governments on the Afghan mission on the premise that it would resemble peacekeeping, not all-out combat.[15]

Early in February 2008, Condoleezza Rice flew to London to discuss the Afghan war with her counterpart, David Miliband, as well as other British analysts. The Foreign Office organized a seminar. It sometimes contributed to the Bush administration by functioning as a kind of think tank, generating classified white papers and hosting crisp meetings where British experts presented their analyses. To influence the Bush administration, they had to offer ideas within the scope of what the Americans would accept, and yet ideas that were fresh and interesting enough to warrant attention. In the case of Afghanistan, British experts emphasized the importance of political and development strategy in Afghanistan to complement military operations. But what kind of political strategy would defeat or co-opt or at least slow down the Taliban?[16]

Rice and other key figures in the Bush administration had reached a heightened state of enthusiasm about counterinsurgency doctrine, as advocated for by General David Petraeus. He had commanded Bush's risk-taking "surge" of fresh American troops into Baghdad in 2007 and by early 2008 the effort was showing success. Eliot Cohen, Rice's influential new counselor, had worked with Petraeus on counterinsurgency doctrine. Rice came to London "very focused on roads and economy and policing" for Afghanistan, staples of Petraeus's approach to quelling insurgents. The British were groping for an alternative to counterinsurgency theory for Afghanistan—a more sophisticated political strategy—but were not yet prepared to recommend a radical change of course, such as negotiating with the Taliban directly. In London, they agreed privately on a plan to promote a modest intensification of current policy, while publicly committing to stay the course to show resolve. There were now about 55,000 foreign troops in Afghanistan from thirty-nine countries, four fifths of them under N.A.T.O. command. The rest were American troops that operated independently on counterterrorism missions. Rice and Miliband agreed that the United States and Britain would call on N.A.T.O. to find 1,000 more troops to support the fight against the Taliban in southern Afghanistan, while the United States would rotate about 3,200 more Marines into the country later that year. The Iraq war meant the United States had no more troops to offer, and squeezing even 1,000 soldiers out of European governments looked difficult.[17]

On February 7, Rice and Miliband flew together into Kabul. Hamid Karzai took Miliband to point out a hill in the capital where British troops had fought in their second unsuccessful war in Afghanistan during the nineteenth century. Karzai mentioned that his presidential palace had been built on the site of a British camp; he seemed increasingly to enjoy reflecting on the history of Western failures in his country. He remained an Anglophile suspicious of British motives, particularly its supposed favoritism toward Pakistan.

"Either you know what's going on or your people aren't telling you what they're doing," he told Miliband. When Rice tried to speak up for Britain, Karzai would have none of it. "America doesn't have anything to do with this treachery," he said. Rice was stunned.[18]

Karzai complained as well about rising civilian casualties caused by the heavy fighting and aerial bombardment in Kandahar and Helmand. This was a complaint Karzai had been voicing regularly to American and British visitors for more than a year, with rising dismay. Bill Wood and his British counterpart in Kabul, Sherard Cowper-Coles both sympathized with Karzai and thought he was essentially correct about the problem of civilian casualties, even if there was little to be done, as the Taliban had to be challenged militarily. But visitors from London and Washington came away with an increasingly bitter taste, receiving Karzai's dissents as ingratitude.

With Wood and Cowper-Coles, Rice and Miliband flew to Kandahar. "This isn't a kind of blinding flash of success," Rice told reporters, assessing the war. "What you have is milestones along the way that you try to reach." At Kandahar Airfield, she thanked a multinational audience of soldiers, assuring them, "You are contributing not only to the security and future of the Afghan people, but to the security and the future of your own countries, your own people, and indeed, the security and the future of the world."[19]

In private, she was more skeptical. "We are winning, Madam Secretary, but it doesn't feel like it," Wood said at one point during a session with American briefers.

"Mr. Ambassador," Rice replied, "in counterinsurgency, if it doesn't seem like you're winning, you're not winning." She added, "This war isn't working."[20]

Two weeks after Rice departed, Senators Joe Biden, John Kerry, and Chuck Hagel flew in to Kabul. They were friends, bound by long years in the Senate and on its foreign relations committee. Biden then chaired the Senate Foreign Relations Committee; his campaign to win the Democratic Party's nomination for the presidency had just ended, leaving two other Senate colleagues, Barack Obama and Hillary Clinton, to slog it out.

Major General David Rodriguez, commanding 82nd Airborne units in eastern Afghanistan, escorted the three senators on a helicopter tour of his sector. They flew in an armed Black Hawk with their staff trailing in a second helicopter. They visited soldiers at a forward operating base in Kunar Province. On the flight back to Bagram, Rodriguez pointed out the window at the snowy, cragged peaks and said that Tora Bora was just a few miles away. They decided to fly over to take a look.

By now Hagel and Kerry were flying together in the lead helicopter and Biden was in the one behind them. Hagel, who had also served in Vietnam, where he was twice wounded, doubted the wisdom of the Tora Bora tour. "Christ, we've got blizzards coming up. We're running low on fuel. . . . I don't think you should do it."

As committee chair, Biden led the delegation. "Let's do it, but quick," he decided.[21]

The snow squall around them intensified and they couldn't see a thing. The pilot banked suddenly, jockeying in a fierce wind. Over his headset, Biden heard that his helicopter's pilot had lost sight of the Black Hawk in front of them and believed it had gone "down." They shortly discovered that it had successfully made an emergency landing on a high ridge above Bagram. They ended up stranded in the snow for hours, watching unknown armed men watching them from a nearby ridge. Soldiers escorting them set up perimeter defenses on both ends of the ridge and they took turns warming up outside by standing in front of the helicopter's air exhaust. They hadn't dressed for the cold. I.S.A.F. ordered F-16s above them, flying circles. Finally they hiked about a mile to the far end of the ridge, where a military convoy arrived to take them down to Bagram in predawn darkness.

They joined Karzai for dinner at the Arg that night. As he had been with Miliband, the Afghan president was in a foul mood. Biden sat directly across from him, next to Hagel. Karzai started "popping off," saying the United States didn't care about Afghanistan. He rankled all three senators.

Biden started talking back. He was "getting very pissed off." Hagel tried to catch Biden's eye and gestured to suggest that he lower the temperature. Biden ignored him.

"Your country hasn't done anything" to help Afghanistan, Karzai continued. Biden slammed his hand down on the table so hard that every plate jumped and rattled. Then he jolted back his chair and declared, "This conversation, this dinner, is over." He stormed out of the dining room. Hagel and Kerry followed Biden, but Kerry, who was farthest from the door, hung back a bit.

He pulled Karzai aside. He told him that he had to understand that Biden had a son about to deploy to Afghanistan, that this was personal to him. All three of us believe in the alliance with Afghanistan, Kerry went on, but those kinds of comments about the United States serve no one's interests. Karzai expressed appreciation. It was the beginning of what would become Kerry's run as America's Karzai whisperer. The work was about to get much harder.[22]

EIGHTEEN

Tough Love

On July 7, 2008, in Kabul, just after 8:00 a.m., a twenty-two-year-old Pakistani named Hamza Shahkoor steered a Toyota Camry through the morning rush. Near the Interior Ministry, he fell in behind two cars with Indian diplomatic plates. They inched toward the iron gates of the Indian embassy. Scores of civilians stood in line along the compound walls, waiting to apply for visas. Shahkoor detonated two hundred pounds of explosives. The blast could be heard miles away; fifty-eight people died, including the bomber and Brigadier Ravi Datt Mehta, the Indian defense attaché in Afghanistan.[1]

Afghan N.D.S. investigations into Shahkoor's history, as well as U.S. National Security Agency intercepts, appeared to show that I.S.I. officers had coordinated the attack on the Indian embassy in Kabul by working with commanders of the Haqqani network in North Waziristan. The Haqqanis had inserted the bomber and his vehicle into the Afghan capital. Shahkoor had also been trained by Lashkar-i-Taiba, the I.S.I.-managed insurgent force in Kashmir. The investigation was still developing, but American, British, and other allied intelligence services would eventually conclude that a special Haqqani unit had carried out the attack under I.S.I. orders to hit hostile targets in Afghanistan, including Indian ones. I.S.I. officers knew they were under surveillance, so limited their direct involvement with daily operations, but the intelligence analysis held that they were fully culpable nonetheless. The strike was effectively an act of guerrilla war by the Pakistan Army against the Indian military.[2]

The Indian bombing infuriated Bush; to that point, no single attack had more hardened the president's attitude against the I.S.I. The intelligence case against I.S.I. had shifted from ambiguous and debated to definitive—the embassy attack provided one dossier of evidence, but there were others accumulating against I.S.I. that spring as well. The National Security Council met in the Situation Room on July 11 and reviewed the matter. Bush dispatched deputy C.I.A. director Kappes and Admiral Mike Mullen, the new chairman of the Joint Chiefs, to challenge Ashfaq Kayani, now the army chief. Among other things, they were to demand concrete "reform" at the Pakistani spy service.[3]

Kappes flew into Islamabad aboard an Air Force transport five days after the attack. By now Kappes and C.I.A. director Mike Hayden all but operated a secret shuttle service to Pakistan, flying stretched out in the back of C-17s on overnight routes, hauling briefing books so thick they could serve as ballast. Typically Kappes spent time with Kayani alone, one-on-one. The reception party awaiting him included Frank Archibald, now the Islamabad station chief. Archibald was the veteran operations officer who had tried, while serving in Kandahar during 2002, to convert remnant Taliban into a Karzai-tolerant political party, only to have his plan overruled by Washington. Six years later the C.I.A. was still puzzling over how to contain the I.S.I.'s influence inside Afghanistan.[4]

Kappes was best known at Langley and at the White House for his service at Moscow Station and for his role in negotiating Libya's surrender of its nuclear and chemical weapons programs during the first Bush term. His connections to Pakistan were less well known. Early in his career, after five years in the Marine Corps, Kappes had served as a C.I.A. case officer in the country, reporting on politics at a time when it was possible to travel freely. His son had arrived in Pakistan at the age of five weeks and spent his early years there. Kappes had also served in India, reveling as a young operations officer in the openness and occasional hilarity of expatriate life in the subcontinent. Now in his fifties, he was bald, bespectacled, and wore a cropped salt-and-pepper beard. He remained fit and muscled, although, in late middle age, his large shoulders had expanded above his narrow midsection, making him appear slightly misshaped, in the manner of a tall, retired football player.

At the meeting, Kayani smoked from his long-stemmed holder. He did not admit to culpability for the deaths in Kabul but neither did he deny communication with Haqqani commanders. He was reticent, professional, a listener, but his method was to never really say yes and never really say no. "You see, any intelligence agency—if they're going to do their job—you have to have contacts," Kayani said. "Every intelligence agency has contacts. The C.I.A. has contacts. The I.S.I. has contacts. If I tell the I.S.I. not to have contacts, they will be blind. Contacts are maintained with the worst of the lot. It's a compulsion of intelligence that you will have contacts with the worst kind of people. But the question is, how do you use these contacts? Do you use them positively or negatively?"[5]

I.S.I.'s leadership that summer of 2008 was in disarray. The I.S.I. officer in charge of Directorate S was Major General Asif Akhtar. He reported to the spy service's director-general, Nadeem Taj, who in turn reported to Kayani. Yet Taj had not been Kayani's choice for the job; it was an awkward fit. Taj was a general notable mainly for his personal loyalties to Musharraf, now out of power. He had worked as a military secretary with Musharraf during the period when the president faced assassination attempts. The Americans didn't think much of him. He immersed himself in "political machinations," the embassy reported, and "never seemed comfortable in his role as intelligence chief and was reluctant to engage with his U.S. counterparts." A senior American officer who worked with Taj and read sensitive intelligence about him that year put it more directly: "He was just a bag man for Musharraf . . . a guy nobody trusted." That presumably included Kayani, who owed his power to Musharraf but now had to free himself from his mentor's influence and promote his own lieutenants inside I.S.I.[6]

Kappes flew home. The Principals Committee and then the National Security Council met in late July. They had before them new C.I.A. plans to address Waziristan. Hayden and Mike D'Andrea at the agency's

Counterterrorism Center proposed to ramp up Predator and Reaper drone attacks and other intelligence collection in the tribal areas. The plan called for an end to the practice of seeking "concurrence" from I.S.I. about suspected terrorists targeted for death in drone attacks. The C.I.A. also sought to loosen top secret targeting rules for its operations by introducing for the first time practices that would become known as "signature strikes," meaning that a suspected militant might be killed even if his identity was unknown, as long as his observed behavior showed threatening hostility. They also expanded the target list to include "more Al Qaeda as well as the Taliban and Haqqani leadership." Altogether, the C.I.A. plans marked a departure from the consultation and restraint that had governed the agency's drone operations in Pakistan after 2002. Since the killing of Nek Mohammad in June 2004, the C.I.A. had conducted only fourteen lethal drone attacks in Pakistan's tribal areas over four years.[7]

Hayden argued that escalation and the new targeting rules would shorten the time required to strike a fleeting, dangerous target—an Al Qaeda bomb maker with a confirmed cell phone riding away from Miranshah, for example. The changes would also prevent I.S.I. from warning targets. In addition, the C.I.A. and the Pentagon proposed expanding authorities for U.S. Special Operations and Omega Team forces to raid compounds inside Pakistan from bases in Afghanistan.

In Kabul, Greg Vogle arrived as C.I.A. station chief to try to salve America's fraying relationship with Karzai, drawing on their battlefield comradeship during late 2001, and to improve coordination between the C.I.A. and McChrystal's special operators. Vogle supported more aggressive ground raids into Waziristan.

"After the next attack, knowing what we know now, there's no explaining it if we don't do something," Hayden argued at the White House. Bush heard as well from Pentagon officers who had recently served in Afghanistan as waves of Taliban fighters crossed from Waziristan to strike American troops. Mick Nicholson, then a brigadier general running the Afghanistan-Pakistan cell at the Joint Chiefs of Staff, had recently returned from a tour in eastern Afghanistan, where his forces had suffered thirty-five killed in action and another thirty wounded because of the Haqqanis, he told colleagues. "We're going to stop playing the game," Bush declared. "These sons of bitches are killing Americans. I've had enough."[8]

Yet even at this turning point, the Bush administration did not wish to break with the Pakistan Army. In essence, the National Security Council decided to confront General Kayani as he took control of the army, and yet, simultaneously, to embrace him more closely, with aid and closer consultation. A major reason was Pakistan's nuclear arsenal. The administration had "regular reports" of Al Qaeda and other groups plotting to steal nuclear weapons. They did not want to do anything that would destabilize Pakistani command and control. As Michael Waltz, an aide to Vice President Cheney, put it: "If we began to retaliate for Pakistan's support of the Taliban, how far were we prepared to go? Could we really afford to make Pakistan an enemy? Were we prepared to . . . fight the Pakistani Army's tanks and artillery on the way in and out? Were we prepared to shoot down its Air Force, planes the United States had supplied?" Whenever the cabinet contemplated "such dark scenarios," it backed away.[9]

And it was plain that the Pakistan Army was in trouble that summer. Domestic insurgents had seized Swat, a mountainous district about 150 miles to the northwest of Islamabad, and now threatened the Pakistani capital. The Pakistan Army fought back strongly and seemed to gradually contain the threat, yet the durability of this military achievement—Pakistanis fighting Pakistanis, for the most part—was questionable. The Americans wanted to reinforce the tentative progress the army had made in Swat. Kayani had been in charge of the military for less than a year. He had enough history with the United States—at Fort Leavenworth, in Hawaii, on base tours, and line skipping through Disneyland with Dave Smith—to be seen as a potentially constructive partner.

Steve Kappes and Peter Lavoy, the administration's two most senior intelligence experts on Pakistan, advocated for engagement. After a long career in C.I.A. espionage operations, Kappes had developed an operating philosophy about challenges such as Directorate S. All national security services were loyal to their own sovereign governments, he reminded C.I.A. colleagues and the National Security Council. I.S.I. represented itself, the Pakistan Army, and, to a lesser extent, the civilian-led Pakistani state. One American ambassador and C.I.A. station chief after another had tried across many years to convince I.S.I. that it did not need the Taliban to influence Afghanistan and that it did not require militant Islamists in Kashmir to pressure India. Yet those entreaties had failed. The situation now called for realism. The I.S.I. was not motivated to challenge America's enemies in the tribal areas. That justified more drone strikes. It did not imply that it would be wise to sanction Kayani or I.S.I. or that such pressure would succeed, this line of thinking went. The expiring Bush administration was divided between those "who saw Pakistan as totally lost," as the State Department's David Gordon put it, and those "who had the view that they're complicit, but there's a chance this could turn out better."

Sanctions imposed by the United States on Pakistan during the 1990s had had limited American influence as the threat from Al Qaeda metastasized, Kappes, Lavoy, and other Pakistan specialists believed. They recognized that the United States had conflicting interests with Pakistan but argued that Washington would get further through engagement. On the other side of the debate, C.I.A. officers such as Chris Wood argued that Washington had not gone *far enough* to pressure I.S.I. during the 1990s or after September 11. Wood and his allies believed that if I.S.I. did not stop tolerating and supporting the Taliban, the United States should threaten to impose sanctions that would stigmatize senior Pakistani generals, restricting their travel or personal access to international banking, as if they were equivalent to Sudanese war criminals or North Korean totalitarians. Wood argued that generals like Kayani so valued their legitimacy, travel, and freedom to bank and send children to universities abroad that they would bend to such pressure before sanctions ever had to be imposed.[10]

When he spoke privately to Kayani about the turn in American policy after the summer of 2008, Kappes tried to talk as one professional intelligence officer to another. To Kappes, engagement was the essence of intelligence work—without contact and continual discussion there was no chance to influence behavior. Kappes warned that if the C.I.A. located Osama Bin Laden or Ayman Al Zawahiri hiding on Pakistani soil, the agency would recommend direct action inside Pakistan and that any American president would likely order an attack. He emphasized that the C.I.A. prided itself on never closing a communications channel. Kayani could always contact Langley if he wanted to get a message through to the White House, no matter how bad things got.

Kappes and Admiral Mike Mullen sweetened this tough messaging with new offers: What new military or counterterrorism equipment did Kayani need as he reevaluated the Pakistan Army? What was on his wish list? Could the United States and Pakistan restart a conversation at the highest levels about strategy and about how the United States might help Kayani modernize Pakistan's forces?[11]

In the long history of schizophrenia involving Washington and Rawalpindi, a new chapter had opened.

That summer, Senator Barack Obama landed at Bagram Airfield. The presumptive Democratic presidential nominee was on a tour of the wars he might inherit in Iraq and Afghanistan. He traveled with Senators Jack Reid of Rhode Island and Chuck Hagel of Nebraska, both military veterans. At Bagram, Obama spoke to troops and posed for selfies. Helicopters lifted the three senators to an American base in Jalalabad.

Leading the Afghan delegation to greet Obama was Gul Agha Sherzai, the dog fighter's son who had returned to power with C.I.A. backing after the Taliban's fall. Following his dystopian tour as Kandahar's governor, he had moved on to become the governor of Nangarhar Province, an important and relatively prosperous region near Pakistan. This day, the governor wore a striped western shirt over his large, soft belly and sported a trimmed black beard. Obama pumped Sherzai's hand warmly and put his arm around his shoulder. At a hollow square table, across from American generals and colonels in camouflage uniform, Sherzai occupied the place of honor to Obama's right and held forth about his accomplishments in eastern Afghanistan.[12]

Why the U.S. embassy in Kabul would select Sherzai as Obama's huggable first interlocutor in Afghanistan was a mystery some of Obama's aides would puzzle over in the years ahead. Among other things, the decision insulted Hamid Karzai before Obama had ever met him by elevating a rival and subordinate ahead of the Afghan president in highly visible protocol.

Obama was new to Afghanistan but he had personal connections to Pakistan. As a college sophomore in Los Angeles, he had shared an apartment with a Pakistani friend, Hasan Chandoo, a business-minded Shiite from a prosperous Karachi family. Obama visited Pakistan with Chandoo and made other Pakistani friends as he came of age and later entered Harvard Law School. Years later, this small Pakistani-American network helped raise some money for Obama's political campaigns in Illinois and celebrated him in Washington when he reached the United States Senate in 2004. These friends provided Obama with informal insights about Pakistan. Gul Agha Sherzai might be familiar in that he resembled a Chicago ward boss of the Prohibition era, but the local mysteries of tribe, profiteering, landgrabbing, and influence peddling the governor presided over from Jalalabad were opaque even to the Americans who studied him up close. All Obama could really hope for as he prepared for the possibility of command of the Afghan war was an instinctual sense of direction.[13]

Hamid Karzai received Obama for a working lunch at the Arg Palace the next day. Amrullah Saleh of N.D.S. joined the discussion, as did other members of the national security cabinet. Karzai's war advisers did not always work coherently, but this time they and their president had settled on a firm plan: They would seize this opportunity to try to educate Barack Obama about the treachery of I.S.I.

Saleh saw the coming Kayani era in Pakistan ominously. Saleh told American counterparts in 2008 that General Kayani would become more active "as he realizes the breadth of his power" as army chief, and that he would encourage the Taliban and allied radicals to concentrate on fighting in Afghanistan for as long as possible, while the army tried to restore order at home.[14]

At lunch, Karzai described Pakistan "as the source of increasing instability in Afghanistan." His remedy included "U.S. military operations in

Pakistan." Pakistan's civilian leaders, such as the late Benazir Bhutto and Asif Zardari, had good intentions, Karzai emphasized, but the problem was "I.S.I. and the Pakistani military."

Chuck Hagel asked if Zardari could control the army and I.S.I.

"No, not without the help of the U.S.," Karzai said.

The United States had to insist that Pakistan stop "using radical Islam as an instrument of policy" and issue an ultimatum as Bush had done in 2001, namely, that Pakistan choose whether it was with the United States or against it. "Softly, softly won't work," Karzai said.

Obama asked if Zardari's problem was a "lack of capacity."

"The problem is I.S.I.," Karzai repeated, "which runs the country."

Obama already knew enough to take Pakistan blaming by Afghan officials with a grain of salt. He told Karzai that the United States was committed to his country for the long run, but that U.S. support would be much more durable if Afghans started taking credible action on drugs and corruption. Obviously, too, the Taliban's message was getting through to Afghans, regardless of Pakistan's covert warfare. Were Afghans susceptible to Islamist messages? Obama asked gently.

Karzai insisted that without Pakistan's intervention, the Taliban message would never have influenced Afghans. "Over three decades, thousands of Afghan boys were indoctrinated into hatefulness disguised as Islam." The Taliban were now killing off older Afghan clergy and replacing them with "younger, Pakistani-trained mullahs."

"We still have a lot of work to do," Obama noted.[15]

B y 2008, evidence to support the C.I.A.'s assessment that Al Qaeda was fusing with the Afghan and Pakistani Taliban in the Federally Administered Tribal Areas was openly available on YouTube. The digital, laptop-enabled output of Al Qaeda's media arm in Pakistan, As-Sahab, surged. Between 2002 and 2005, Al Qaeda released messages or videos once a month; between 2006 and 2008, it released fresh content more than once a week.[16] Its videos, war documentaries, and digital magazines were diverse and global in concern but they bore down increasingly on the cause of the American war in Afghanistan.

Mustafa Abu al-Yazid, a then-fifty-two-year-old Egyptian with a thin, long face, had been convicted as a young man in the successful conspiracy to assassinate Anwar Sadat and had gone into exile with Ayman Al Zawahiri, the Al Qaeda deputy emir. In 2007, he emerged as the spokesman for Al Qaeda's commitment to the Afghan Taliban cause. He called himself the leader of "Al Qaeda in Khurasan and Afghanistan," a name referring to historical territory overlapping with Afghanistan and Pakistan, "under Mullah Omar," who remained at large and recognized as the Taliban emir. Yazid's exact rank in the Al Qaeda hierarchy was hard to specify but he was the latest in a succession of visible senior frontline commanders, just below Zawahiri, and he evidently operated from Waziristan.[17]

In June 2008, a Toyota bearing Pakistan-issued diplomatic plates blew up in front of the Danish embassy in Islamabad, killing about half a dozen Pakistanis. Yazid surfaced through As-Sahab to claim responsibility, saying the attack was revenge for the cartoons depicting the Prophet Muhammad published the previous winter in a Danish newspaper. The Egyptian felt secure enough the following month to invite a reporter from Pakistan's freewheeling, independent satellite channel, GEO, to interview him. Yazid wore a white turban and owlish plastic-framed eyeglasses.

"The U.S. claims that it has successfully occupied Afghanistan and brought the resistance under control," the GEO reporter observed.

That is "a total lie," Yazid said mildly. Within the limits of Islamist propaganda idioms, he spoke crisply and coherently. "By the grace of Allah the killing of US soldiers is continuing and the mujaheddin are fighting against the Americans and their slaves with steadfastness," he continued. The United States had "tried to assemble some tribal militias and use them against the mujaheddin," he observed, apparently referring to the C.I.A.'s Omega border units. "And their failure in Afghanistan is even more evident. The proof of this is after every few days they hold an emergency meeting of NATO and request each other with great pleading to increase their forces in Afghanistan. But very few are ready for this great sacrifice." He added that of all the compromised Muslim regimes in the world, none had more betrayed the Muslim faith than Pakistan under Pervez Musharraf.[18]

Because the United States, Afghanistan, and Pakistan did have common enemies, the Americans persisted in the belief that Kayani and the army would make common cause with Washington. But the closer Kayani moved Pakistan toward the United States, the more it brought violence down on his country from Al Qaeda and its allies.

The C.I.A.'s plan to step up its war in the tribal areas had two prongs: more drone strikes and more direct Special Operations raids by helicopter against Al Qaeda and affiliated compounds on Pakistani territory. A few weeks after Yazid's interview with GEO, on August 28, Bush's National Security Council met to authorize a ground strike in Angoor Adda, in South Waziristan, a town of ramshackle shops and bus depots that lay across a flat mud plain from Shkin, the long-standing site of a joint C.I.A.–Special Operations base. Uzbeks and other foreigners still infested the region. Around 2:00 a.m. on September 3, Navy SEALs borne by Chinook helicopters, flanked by Apache attack helicopters, struck three homes in Musa Nika, near Angoor Adda. Ten local tribesmen, one ninety years old, five women, and two children died in the firefight. A man from one of the targeted families drove a taxi and had recently carried an Arab passenger; the local assumption was that an informant had told the Americans that a senior Al Qaeda leader was staying at his house. The Pentagon insisted that all the victims were militants, but a Pakistani brigadier serving in South Waziristan later published a convincing roster of the women and children he said had died.[19]

Kayani dispatched Foreign Secretary Salman Bashir to inform U.S. ambassador Anne Patterson that Pakistan would issue a statement denouncing the strike but, as a courtesy, would not name the United States as the culprit. Bashir was a circumspect professional diplomat. He told Patterson that bilateral intelligence and military cooperation was "good" overall, but that this raid had occurred "without regard to the high-level understanding between the two military commands" that Pakistan would be taken "into confidence" about covert action on its soil. A week later, *The New York Times* reported what few beyond Kayani understood: The attack was a signal of the increased willingness of the United States to take unilateral action inside Pakistan. President Bush had directly approved the raid. Kayani issued an unusual statement declaring that "the sovereignty and territorial integrity of the country would be defended at all costs, and no external force is allowed to conduct operations inside Pakistan." An army spokesman added that if it happened again, Pakistan would "retaliate" against the attacking force. Twin headlines in Pakistan's *Daily News* captured the army's public ultimatum: BOOTS ON THE GROUND: BUSH and NO WAY: KAYANI.[20]

The White House and Special Operations Command had over-reached. But Al Qaeda was becoming even bolder. On September 20, 2008, a Pakistani citizen drove a dump truck onto the grounds of the Marriott Hotel in Islamabad, a center of international diplomatic and expatriate life in the capital. The truck carried perhaps six times the explosive load of the car bomb deployed against the Indian embassy in July. The detonation and fire that followed killed fifty-four people, the great majority of them Pakistanis, and injured more than two hundred others. Two Americans died, one a Navy cryptologist on assignment in Pakistan for the National Security Agency.[21] The attack allegedly was the brainchild of a Kenyan Al Qaeda operator who used the nom de guerre Usama al-Kini and who had been indicted in Al Qaeda's 1998 embassy bombings in Africa. Al Qaeda celebrated, but killing privileged Pakistani civilians en masse was a miscalculation; it hardened Pakistani and media opinion against foreign terrorists and the Taliban, as well as against the United States.

Kappes and Mullen flew back to Islamabad to again press their request for "I.S.I. reform" on Kayani. The C.I.A. had drawn up and vetted with the White House a list of concrete steps the general could take to demonstrate that he was sincere about cleaning up I.S.I. Kappes conveyed that he was speaking for President Bush. One proposed step was to appoint more reliable officers to run I.S.I. and Directorate S. The protocol in such messaging was to leave out the names of individuals, but the implication was clear: Kayani should fire Nadeem Taj and remove Asif Akhtar from Directorate S.

Kayani assured them he planned to act. To minimize embarrassment, he would reveal a shakeup at I.S.I. as part of a regular announcement about promotions, reassignments, and up-or-out forced retirements. Kayani had his own motivations: Moving Musharraf's "bag man" out of

I.S.I. would allow him to appoint a successor loyal to him. On September 29, Kayani announced that Taj would rotate to a division command. Asif Akhtar rotated from Directorate S and was assigned to the National Guard. As to the rest of Kappes's confidence-building proposals—which included demonstrative steps to break ties with Taliban and Kashmiri militants—Kayani was noncommittal. The Islamabad embassy nonetheless remained optimistic. "Kayani has taken a critical first step," it reported.[22]

Kayani had made his objections to American helicopter raids inside Pakistan crystal clear. Kappes made clear that the United States intended to attack Al Qaeda directly with armed drones, given that the Pakistan Army was unable (or unwilling or both) to clear out North Waziristan. These positions did not preclude cooperation on some shared interests. Kayani indicated that summer and autumn that he wanted Baitullah Mehsud dead. In this the general had the full support of the civilian government of the Pakistan Peoples Party. They held Mehsud at least partly responsible for Benazir Bhutto's assassination, along with the Pakistani security services.

The targeting discussions did not change the fact that Pakistan still distinguished between good militants and bad militants, however; it was merely Mehsud's misfortune to have crossed the line. Even after the Marriott bombing, during an in camera session of parliament that autumn, I.S.I. officers briefing Pakistani lawmakers tried to explain "the virtues of some Taliban elements versus 'the real militants.'" The I.S.I. briefers "reasoned small numbers from some of the militant groups could be useful in future operations in Kashmir or elsewhere." Anyone in Washington reading the U.S. government's own cable traffic would have reason to regard I.S.I. reform as an unlikely prospect.[23]

Mike Mullen doubted that Kayani would follow through on the C.I.A.'s proposed reform list. His relationship with Kayani was just months old but it was becoming deeper. By protocol, as America's most senior military officer, Mullen was Kayani's counterpart. The admiral intended his willingness to devote more and more time to Kayani as a signal of respect and seriousness. Over the next three years, Mullen would be the good cop with Kayani, in tandem with a rotating cast of American bad cops.

Mullen had the least likely upbringing of anyone wearing four stars in the American military. His mother had worked as an assistant to Jimmy Durante, the comedian. She met his father in the publicity department of Republic Pictures. Jack Mullen struck out on his own as a Hollywood press agent whose clients included Gene Autry, Roy Rogers, Peter Graves, Ann-Margret, Anthony Quinn, and Julie Andrews. His son Mike, one of four brothers, grew up in North Hollywood and the San Fernando Valley among actors, vaudevillians, comedians, and gossip columnists. Except for one uncle who was a veteran, his family had little military heritage. Mullen was tall and athletic and enrolled at the Naval Academy as a basketball recruit in 1964. He rose in the Navy as an operations manager and collaborative, people-centric leader. Congenial, self-effacing, curious, he was a natural for staff command, liaison with foreign militaries, and Pentagon process—a sailor-diplomat who placed his faith in relationships, made himself accessible, and did not seek to bend the world to his will. The Democrats had taken control of Congress and looked, with Obama, to be in a strong position for the 2008 presidential vote. Mullen was an ideal figure to communicate across the aisle.[24]

The admiral resided in the chairman's residence on Twenty-third Street, across from the State Department. He and his wife were Broadway enthusiasts and covered their home's walls with framed playbills from the musicals and plays they had seen. Learning about Afghanistan, he was enthralled by Greg Mortenson's book *Three Cups of Tea*, the national bestseller about schools and culture. He read copiously, hired advisers to connect him to think tanks and humanitarian organizations like Doctors Without Borders, and tried to get out of Washington as often as possible. He visited Iraq, Pakistan, and Afghanistan at least once a quarter. The Navy regularly produced leaders with some of Mullen's characteristics—Army and Marine generals did not require much prompting to joke about admirals with their feet up on a ship's bridge, cruising the open seas, smoking cigars, and thinking great thoughts about world order. But even for a Navy man, Mullen was ambassadorial. The question was whether he had a sharp enough mind of his own to shape the disastrous conflicts he had inherited.

Mullen's relationship with Kayani was "the most difficult, intense" of the liaisons with world military leaders worldwide. Between early 2008 and the summer of 2011, Mullen would travel to Pakistan twenty-seven times to visit with Kayani. He met the general many other times in Washington, Europe, and elsewhere and they spoke frequently by secure telephone. Mullen had no experience in Pakistan. That summer of 2008 he relayed to Kayani in their early meetings talking points developed by his Afghanistan-Pakistan staff, the C.I.A., and the White House—"Nadeem Taj at I.S.I. must go" was one such talking point—but mainly he tried to connect the lengthy classified memos in his briefing books to what he observed and heard during long, open-ended conversations with the general.[25]

By the fall of 2008 Mullen was forming a hypothesis about Directorate S, one aligned with intelligence reporting. At the very top of its hierarchy, I.S.I. was a black-and-white organization, fully subject to discipline and accountability, Mullen told colleagues. In the middle the organization started to go gray, fading into heavily compartmented operations that drew upon mid-level officers, civilians, contractors, and retirees. Then there were retired I.S.I. director-generals or senior brigadiers with their own followings among militants.[26]

At their first conference in Islamabad, Kayani presented a list of seven counterterrorism and surveillance technologies that he said Pakistan needed urgently. He emphasized that Pakistan needed its own signals intelligence intercept ability. Kayani's list included technology to intercept and listen to satellite telephone conversations, digital or GSM cell phones, mobile platforms that would allow Pakistan to locate cell phones quickly, and aerial collection platforms for Pakistani aircraft that could intercept low-powered military radio transmissions. He said he was not interested in acquiring and operating Predator drones, but he wondered if there were smaller, less expensive tactical drones that the United States could grant or lend to Pakistan for surveillance in Waziristan. Kayani's other great need was helicopters—Cobra or Apache gunships to strike militant compounds and more Chinook transports to quickly lift Special

Forces to and from attacks. Waziristan's vast terrain and muddy roads had trapped Pakistan's infantry-heavy army into a lumbering, defensive position, holed up on bases.[27]

Helicopters were a tough ask, Mullen warned Kayani. Everybody in N.A.T.O. seemed to need more; the supply chain remained stressed. The admiral pledged to send a team of National Security Agency and other experts out to Pakistan to study the army's SIGINT capabilities and needs, to see what the United States might be able to do.

From the start, Kayani's requests for state-of-the-art surveillance technology strained the trust Mullen sought to build. Cell phone intercept equipment, night-vision goggles, and aerial SIGINT platforms could be used to thwart the Taliban or enable them. If the United States supplied such gear, would it make I.S.I. and the Special Services Group more dangerous?

Kayani told Mullen that his army had to focus on the "fundamentals" of Pakistan's internal security. By this he meant public opinion and the fighting morale of his soldiers when forced to kill fellow citizens preaching revolution in the name of Islam. Kayani feared that too many of the army's rank and file doubted the righteousness of the fight in alliance with the United States.

"What is fundamentalism? What is extremism?" Kayani asked as he traveled from cantonment to cantonment that year, speaking to officers and enlisted men. To his generals, he emphasized: "We have to define extremism so that it's the 98 percent against the 2 percent. We can't define it so that it's 50-50 or 60-40—then we'll be fighting a civil war. Different opinions don't make someone an extremist. It's when they take no one's advice, when they arrogate to themselves the right to define who is a Muslim or who is legitimate. When this person picks up the gun, he becomes a terrorist. This is how you make it 98 to 2."

Four decades of promoting faith as a source of morale in the Pakistan Army had made it necessary to distinguish between "fundamentalism and extremism" in order to hold the army together, Kayani believed. That meant tolerating the conservative practice of individual faith while waging a counterrevolutionary campaign against those who challenged the state's legitimacy. It was necessary to accept a rising tide of Islamism in the military and public life in order to maintain unity against Al Qaeda and Pakistani Sunni extremists.

"The army has to detach itself" from America, Kayani told his corps commanders. "This is our fight, our war. This is not a U.S. war."[28]

Kayani suggested to Mullen that they convene a conference with senior commanders from both countries about joint strategy in Afghanistan and Pakistan. "Let's have a very open discussion," he proposed.

Mullen jumped at the suggestion. In late August, Kayani flew secretly across the Arabian Sea to the USS *Abraham Lincoln*, an American aircraft carrier. In addition to Mullen, the U.S. delegation included David Petraeus, who had just been appointed to lead Central Command, Admiral Eric Olson of Joint Special Operations Command, and General Martin Dempsey, then acting head of Central Command. Kayani brought along Major General Ahmed Shuja Pasha, then director-general of military operations.

They talked for at least eight hours over two days, trading PowerPoint decks and maps. Kayani pledged to be "transparent" about his campaign plan in the tribal areas over the next two years. The army was in the midst of an undeclared surge of troops into Waziristan, Kayani said. He did not want to inflame the locals further by announcing the troop deployments but he had rotated in tens of thousands of infantry from mainland Pakistan or the Indian border. Kayani presented charts of "major operations" carried out by brigade-size units. With Musharraf gone, he had removed Aurakzai and abandoned the failed negotiations with Taliban and tribal leaders, yet there could be no purely "military solution" in the region.

"We're carrying out operations against our own people," Kayani emphasized. "It has to be done subtly."[29]

All Kayani had to do was read the newspapers to understand that many in Washington—probably many of the commanders on the *Abraham Lincoln*—believed that he was "hedging his bets" in Afghanistan by covertly enabling the Taliban's revival. He tried once more to convince them that it wasn't so. No outside power had ever controlled Afghanistan, Kayani often pointed out. Pakistan had a vitally important relationship with the West at stake. "We can't be controlling Afghanistan," he said. "That would mean we haven't learned anything."[30]

He warned Mullen and the generals, however: "Don't expect too much because I can't do everything." Major ground operations in North Waziristan would have to wait as he built up forces, morale, and political support from civilian politicians. He needed help—technology, equipment, and patience. "If your expectation is here," he said, gesturing at eye level, "and our abilities are there," he said, dropping his hand, "the gap will be frustrating."[31]

About that he was prescient. The American commanders on the *Abraham Lincoln* generally respected Kayani. He cared about soldiering. He was reticent and professional, if also hard to comprehend—literally, when he spoke, and more broadly, as a mystery of intentions. The conference also gave Mullen, Petraeus, and the others their first sustained look at Kayani's trusted lieutenant, Ahmed Shuja Pasha. About five feet eight, clean-shaven, with a glint of gray in his eyes, Pasha displayed little of Kayani's reticence. He was energetic, openly emotional. He clearly had the army chief's confidence. Like Kayani, Pasha was the self-made product of a modest Punjabi middle-class family and had grown up without access to wealth or social privilege. Five weeks after the conference, Kayani named Pasha the next director-general of I.S.I. It would prove to be a momentous choice.

NINETEEN

Terror and the Deep State

The new I.S.I. chief's family had come originally from India, in the Punjab, and had migrated to what was now Pakistan before Partition. Ahmed Shuja Pasha's father attended Government College in Lahore and then moved his family to a village about forty miles from Islamabad. He taught high school there. He had three daughters and four sons; Ahmed was the youngest boy. They were not poor but it was a strain to raise seven children on a teacher's salary. By the time Ahmed came of age the family had fallen under financial pressure. One of his brothers had enlisted in the air force; the other two brothers had joined the Pakistan Army. His father urged him to become a scholar, but Ahmed wanted to follow his brothers. He passed the admission exam for the Pakistan Military Academy in Abbottabad, equivalent to West Point. He enrolled there during the spring of 1972. This was less than a year after Pakistan's devastating defeat in its third war with India, a military and political catastrophe that led to the dismembering of the country and the birth of independent Bangladesh on the former territory of East Pakistan. The humiliation left many young Pakistani military officers thirsting for revenge against India.

Pasha graduated as a second lieutenant assigned to the infantry. Two of his brothers left the military after relatively short periods, one after falling ill, and the other following disciplinary infractions. (The third brother eventually became a brigadier.) Ahmed rose steadily. His assignments included a tour on the Line of Control in Kashmir, the militarized de facto border where Pakistani and Indian troops routinely skirmished and shelled one another. He was also selected for advanced military education abroad, at the German Staff College in Hamburg, where he learned German. He married and raised a family but was tested by tragedy just as his professional success seemed assured. His eldest son died in a car accident that took place on Pasha's birthday. It was a wound so deep that it would surface unexpectedly and emotionally in conversation, even with American counterparts with whom he had complicated relations.

Pasha never studied in the United States. He did not send his surviving children abroad for college or graduate education, as many elite Pakistani families and generals did. By the time he reached his fifties and won promotion to general, Pasha's decision to school his children in Pakistan had become a part of his identity. He seemed increasingly to define himself in opposition to the globalized salons of Karachi, Islamabad, and Lahore, and he expressed contempt for their cosmopolitanism.[1]

"Your problem," he once announced to a Pakistani journalist with whom he had become annoyed, "is that you're an elitist, whereas I began my life as a son of a schoolteacher. I sat on a mat on the floor and learned to read and write. . . . We are homespun. We are nationalists. We are not like your Sandhurst friends. Not like Musharraf."[2]

He saw the army as a kind of Spartan force defending—even as it was undermined by—Pakistan's dissipated, privileged, landed families. "Why is the Army different from the rest of society?" he once asked a visitor. "Training is part of the answer, but there is more. It comes, in the end, from a feeling of responsibility. Young men pick this up, in good schools or in the Army. A lieutenant will say that he wants to repay what he has been given, that he wants to serve. The Army is very different from the rest of the country."[3]

On September 11, Pasha was posted to a U.N. peacekeeping mission in Sierra Leone. After he returned to Pakistan as a two-star general, he seethed at Musharraf's accession to American demands. On security policy, Pasha was essentially in the Mahmud Ahmed camp. He believed that if the United States negotiated with the Taliban, with Pakistan serving as an intermediary, the region might be stabilized and even Bin Laden could be located with the Taliban's assistance. At private commanders' conferences, Pasha made a habit of challenging Musharraf, to such an extent that he wondered if he would be fired. But he wasn't. Instead he made a favorable impression on Kayani, who shared some of Pasha's views but did not make such a display of them.[4]

Pasha had not worked closely with American generals or spies until 2006, when he became director-general of military operations. The United States had fine intentions for Pakistan, Pasha said repeatedly, and he appreciated all that American aid had done to support the country's economy. Yet he also thought that American diplomats in Islamabad trapped themselves by overreliance on Pakistan's debased elites. A relatively small circle of politicians, corrupt businessmen, and journalists misled the United States about Pakistan's true character and assumptions, Pasha told his American interlocutors. In the years to come, some of the Americans who worked with Pasha would come to think of him as an extreme nationalist, overly emotional and prickly, a man who seemed to take everything personally. Pasha certainly made no apologies for his nationalism; he embraced it.[5]

Pasha stated his politics plainly and in line with the views of many educated, urbanized Pakistanis, in uniform and out: "I want to live in a country where my kids don't have to choose between a Bhutto and a Sharif." The Americans wanted Pasha to embrace Pakistan's counterterrorism alliance with the United States more or less as Musharraf had done. Going further in 2008, they wanted him to recognize that I.S.I.'s tolerance of domestic militants and the Afghan Taliban was unsustainable and unacceptable. Pasha bristled at such talking points.

"Of course we have links with these guys," Pasha would tell American counterparts when they pressed him about I.S.I.'s relations with the Haqqani network. "Of course we influence them. Of course you can have phone taps of us talking with them. We talk to them, I imagine, the way the F.B.I. talks to the Mafia. That doesn't mean they do what we say."

He came to understand that virtually every American he met with professionally believed that he was a liar and assumed that any particular claim he made about I.S.I.'s operations could be a lie. The suspicion galled him.[6]

One hundred fifty-five Americans lost their lives in the Afghan war during 2008, an increase of about a third from the previous year. British, Canadian, and other N.A.T.O. casualties also rose to their highest levels since the war began. It seemed all but guaranteed that 2009 would be worse. The Taliban had improved their fighting tactics. They had stopped investing great effort in ineffectual suicide bombers, reserving those dark networks more often for strategic assassinations of Afghan officeholders. They had learned to avoid massed infantry fighting that invited N.A.T.O. to call in its airpower on defenseless Taliban positions. They had ramped up their manufacture and use of improvised explosive devices detonated by pressure or remote control—roadside bombs, mines on footpaths, bicycle bombs, even the occasional donkey bomb. The Taliban mounted some 3,867 improvised explosive attacks during 2008, an increase of almost 50 percent over the previous year. Just as had been the case for Soviet forces during the 1980s, the improvised bombs and mines forced N.A.T.O. to restrict its movements, tempted forward commanders to hunker down on bases, and left platoons to struggle with the random devastation the bombs inflicted on comrades who lost legs, arms, and lives.[7]

David Kilcullen, the unconventional warfare specialist advising Condoleezza Rice, returned to Pakistan and Afghanistan that year. The Taliban clearly had professional help, he could now see. Their indirect fire from mortars and rockets had become more accurate. They had acquired heavy sniper weapons and optics, which demand training. Some units even had uniforms with badges of rank. He and other American analysts also started to grasp that the Taliban forces operated a formal rotation system—training in Pakistan, field deployment, and then rest and recuperation back in Pakistan. Pakistan Army and Frontier Corps troops along the Pakistani border were firing on American border posts to provide covering fire for the Taliban to infiltrate into Afghanistan and return—the same tactics Pakistani forces employed for Kashmiri militants along the Line of Control.[8]

In Washington, Kilcullen's latest report reinforced the case that the Afghan war was spiraling in the wrong direction. At the White House, about once a quarter, National Security Adviser Steve Hadley invited the N.S.C.'s Afghanistan staff to his office for an informal roundtable discussion. Doug Lute, the two-star general and "war czar" coordinating both Iraq and Afghan policy, would attend these sessions, along with John Wood, the senior N.S.C. director for Afghanistan, and his colleagues, including Paul Miller, Christa Skerry, and Marie Richards. Pakistan was a perennial topic. So was Afghan governance. Hadley would throw out a question, such as "How do you build a police force in a country as broken as this?" The conversation would range widely. Hadley listened but rarely revealed his own opinion.[9]

Since Doug Lute's arrival at the White House in mid-2007, Iraq had consumed almost all of his attention. President Bush was committed to the primacy of Iraq; he was more personally invested. In the interagency committees, while trying to turn the Iraq war around, Lute had developed a circle of confidants, civilians with an analytical bent, including David Gordon and Eliot Cohen, and, at the Pentagon, Jim Shinn, who had made a fortune in the software industry before joining government, and Mary Beth Long, the international lawyer who worked on counternarcotics. They had bonded over Iraq's unrelenting crises. By mid-2008, however, the surge of troops into Baghdad that Bush had authorized eighteen months earlier under Petraeus's command had reduced the violence there. There was now greater space to consider Afghanistan.[10]

Lute was a large, affable, humorously skeptical general who had risen high because of his facility for operations and process. He had grown up in Michigan City, Indiana, an Eagle Scout and president of his high school class. He won acceptance to West Point one year behind the class Petraeus dominated (marrying the superintendent's daughter, among other achievements). Lute chose the armored cavalry upon graduation in 1975. He spent much of his early career with a cavalry regiment in Germany tasked to hold off the Soviets at the outbreak of World War Three. He took a master's degree at Harvard, taught international politics at

West Point, fought in a cavalry unit during the first Gulf War, worked on the Balkans during the 1990s, and landed as a military assistant to Chairman of the Joint Chiefs Hugh Shelton in 2000.

General John Abizaid, then leading Central Command, recruited Lute as his J-3, or chief operations officer, just as the Iraq war turned into a bloody grind. Of Lebanese descent, Abizaid was the first Arab American to wear four stars. Lute traveled continually with him to both Iraq and Afghanistan. If Petraeus increasingly led the school of generalship in the Army that advocated for counterinsurgency, a doctrine that typically required long time lines and state building, Abizaid was the most credible voice of an opposing school of thought. He believed counterinsurgency carried out by large numbers of highly visible American forces in Muslim societies, over an extended period of time, was unlikely to succeed because locals would revolt before there was time for the United States to achieve the expansive political and economic objectives that counterinsurgency theory promoted. Repeatedly, Abizaid warned colleagues about Iraq and Afghanistan: *The clock is ticking on the American presence.* The Petraeus network within the Army sometimes dismissed such thinking as defeatism. Abizaid considered his warning to be realism. He had burned his convictions into Doug Lute's head by the time the Bush White House recruited Lute as war czar—or, as he was sometimes referred to less provocatively, a senior coordinator.[11]

In May 2008, Lute arranged for a Gulfstream V jet to carry him, Cohen, Gordon, Shinn, and Long to Afghanistan. They heard much to be discouraged about. Road building was behind schedule and the roads that had been completed weren't being defended successfully. Battlefield intelligence collection seemed disconnected from strategy—the system was a massive vacuum cleaner of stray facts, feeding into conclusions that were "not rigorous," as Long put it. The chain of command was a fractured mess. As an operations man, Lute was especially appalled by the incoherent command structure that had grown up in Afghanistan as a result of ad hoc compromises with N.A.T.O. and within the American military.

In Kandahar, the group spent hours poring over battle maps of Kandahar and Helmand as local N.A.T.O. commanders inventoried all the units deployed in their areas. These included American "black" or covert Special Operations units, "white" or Green Beret–style American Special Forces, British forces, Dutch forces, U.S. Marines, and multinational Provincial Reconstruction Teams. There were also small international training units embedded with the Afghan army; these officers reported through their own chain of command to Kabul. By the time they were done, they had identified more than half a dozen distinct N.A.T.O. or American armed forces operating in southern Afghanistan—only one of which the top N.A.T.O. general on the scene in Kandahar commanded. This patchwork was the legacy of Rumsfeld's reluctance to deploy in Afghanistan, N.A.T.O.'s fractured system of military federalism, and the insistence of U.S. Special Operations Command and the U.S. Marines that they operate independently, which Rumsfeld and then Gates had accepted.[12]

American officers told them about a soldier wounded in the foot near Herat, in western Afghanistan. If he had been struck above the waist, he likely would have bled out and died because of the lengthy time required for Spanish commanders, who were deployed in the region, to request permission from the N.A.T.O. chain of command to dispatch a rescue helicopter. That episode became a touchstone for Gates. The "bleed out" time in Afghanistan—the time a wounded soldier had to wait for specialized help to arrive—was about two hours, on average. Gates pushed to reduce it to one hour.

The study team spent long hours on the flight home, over wine and baguettes, discussing what they had seen. They agreed that Afghanistan and Pakistan had to be understood as a unified theater and set of problems. Back in Washington, Lute briefed the interagency deputies committee about the command problem. Besides the half a dozen overt military commands, "No one in this room has good visibility on the C.I.A. with partnered Afghan intelligence units," Lute said. That summer, Lute sent a memo to Bush warning that the Afghan war could fall apart during the next six months, as the president departed office. Bush wrote back almost immediately. He wanted to work on the problems even though the time was short. Hadley told Lute, "I want to launch a very deliberate look at this."

The National Security Council met on September 17. Bush told his war cabinet he wanted a review similar to the one that had produced the recommendation for a troop surge into Baghdad, a decision in which Bush took pride. That launched the last and most ambitious of his administration's strategy reviews on Afghanistan.

During the next two months, Lute convened sixteen sessions lasting a total of more than forty hours in Room 445 of the Eisenhower Executive Office Building, a secure conference room. Deputies of roughly Lute's rank in the national security bureaucracy staffed the study from the Pentagon, the State Department, C.I.A., the Office of the Director of National Intelligence, the Office of the Vice President, and other agencies. Typically there were about two dozen people in the room. The review went topic by topic—poppy and heroin, corruption, Afghan security force training, N.A.T.O.'s command structure, Pakistani sanctuaries. Typically, an intelligence analyst such as Peter Lavoy of the National Intelligence Council or Tony Schinella of the C.I.A.'s military analysis unit would open a session with an in-depth presentation. Schinella's team updated the C.I.A.'s top secret District Assessment maps for the review; in the years ahead, the agency would revise the maps every six months, in part because they were so popular. After their briefings, the intelligence analysts would usually leave and the political appointees and generals from the Pentagon would debate what should be done.[13]

The N.S.C. staff under Lute also produced memos concerning basic questions about the war, ones that might seem worrying to be asking after seven years of involvement: Why was the United States still in Afghanistan? What did it want to achieve? Was it necessary to crack down on corruption to achieve America's strategic goals? Was it necessary to invest in reconstruction and governance to succeed at counterterrorism?

The apparent success of the Baghdad surge, skillfully promoted in the media by Petraeus, had created a kind of intellectual bubble in Washington around his ideas. Diplomats, generals, and aid workers toted thumbed copies of *Learning to Eat Soup with a Knife*, a history of counterinsurgency by an Oxford-educated protégé of Petraeus's, Lieutenant Colonel John Nagl. Philip Zelikow, a historian and counselor to the State

Department, while working on the Iraq war, had coined a phrase that now became a kind of mantra in Room 445: Clear, hold, build. Zelikow meant that a counterinsurgency campaign should seek to clear enemy-held areas by military force, hold them, and build popular consent through reconstruction and better governance. Zelikow was no longer in government. He did not actually believe that the formula he had developed for Iraq policy would work in Afghanistan, because of the problems of Pakistan sanctuaries, weak governance, and poverty. Yet the consensus in Room 445 was that the United States needed to resource a more full-bodied counterinsurgency strategy in Afghanistan, which would involve more reconstruction aid and training of Afghan security forces. They believed the central government in Afghanistan still had a chance to establish itself. The Taliban were on the upswing but did not threaten a takeover of Kabul or the overthrow of Karzai's regime. The idea was to carry out counterinsurgency primarily through Afghan security forces, but to give the forty thousand or so Western soldiers then in the country a new focus.[14]

The support for a larger counterinsurgency mission in Afghanistan—more money, more troops, and more diplomats—introduced a logic problem that would bedevil American strategy in the war for the next several years. The purpose of the American intervention in Afghanistan was to defeat Al Qaeda, which remained dangerous, everyone at the table agreed. However, Al Qaeda was primarily in Pakistan. So why carry out counterinsurgency against the Taliban in Afghanistan? The answer the review arrived at was that only by creating conditions in Afghanistan that precluded a full Taliban comeback and takeover could Al Qaeda be prevented from restoring itself in a sanctuary similar to what it had enjoyed in Afghanistan on the eve of September 11.

"Al Qaeda is more disrupted than at any time since October 2001, but the organization is damaged, not broken," as Peter Lavoy summarized some of the thinking at a N.A.T.O. briefing that autumn. "The international community cannot afford to let pressure off al Qaeda because it has demonstrated an ability to reconstitute itself in the past, and could easily reverse-migrate back to Afghanistan if the Taliban were to regain control. . . . The consequences of failing in Afghanistan and permitting al

Qaeda to shift its center of gravity to Afghanistan would pose a threat to all nations inside their borders."[15]

The argument made sense, but as a rationale for putting tens of thousands more American and European soldiers in harm's way it had an indirect, speculative quality. Al Qaeda had established itself in Pakistan and had no need of Afghanistan. And seeking to defeat the Taliban in a counterinsurgency campaign was a much different kind of war from the C.I.A. and Special Operations covert campaign against Al Qaeda or the supposed peace enforcement operations sold to N.A.T.O. governments as their militaries rotated to the south. The C.I.A.'s operating directives still tasked operators and analysts to focus on Al Qaeda; they had no orders from the White House to help defeat the Taliban, according to what agency leaders told their British counterparts at the time, to the latter's dismay, given the rate that British soldiers were taking casualties in Helmand inflicted by the Taliban.[16]

On October 15, Lute, Cohen, and Shinn flew back on their Gulfstream jet to Afghanistan and Pakistan to conduct a week of field interviews before writing up the strategy review. They traveled to the border between Pakistan and Afghanistan at Torkham. Lute's Marine aide arranged for a kosher TV dinner to be brought along for Cohen, who was fairly certain he consumed the first kosher meal ever transported there. The big questions were, first, were N.A.T.O. and the United States winning or losing? A second was trying to figure out what the enemy's game plan was. The intelligence remained poor; Cohen concluded that American analysts were much better at counting things than extracting strategic insights. A third big question was what to do about Pakistan, at a time when "everyone was getting a darker and darker view of Pakistan," as Cohen put it.

At the embassy in Kabul, they realized there had been a major turnover in personnel even in the months since their spring visit. The delegation from Washington knew more than the people briefing them. After one desultory session, Cohen and Lute headed to the men's room. Standing at the urinals, they remarked simultaneously, "We're fucked."[17]

Lute facilitated the final discussions in Room 445 and also weighed in with his own analysis of the Afghan war's fractured command structure.

He created a PowerPoint deck with a slide titled "Ten Wars," referring to what his final count had determined were ten distinctly commanded military forces in Afghanistan. How could they bring greater coherence to the effort? What if they adopted a more complete counterinsurgency approach inspired by their experience in Iraq?

The core intelligence resource for the review was a National Intelligence Estimate on Afghanistan and Pakistan that Peter Lavoy had overseen across the summer and autumn. It acknowledged that the security situation in Afghanistan looked "bleak," as a classified summary for N.A.T.O. governments put it. "The Afghan government has failed to consistently deliver services in rural areas. This has created a void that the Taliban and other insurgent groups have begun to fill in the southern, eastern and some western provinces. The Taliban is mediating local disputes in some areas, for example, offering the population at least an elementary level of access to justice. . . . The Taliban have effectively manipulated the grievances of disgruntled, disenfranchised tribes."

The N.I.E. endorsed Kilcullen's assessment of rising professionalism in Taliban guerrilla operations, presumably aided by the Pakistan Army. The guerrillas were "demonstrating more sophisticated infantry, communications and command and control techniques. Their marksmanship is more precise, and their explosives more lethal than in previous years."

The N.I.E. predicted that even if the Afghan National Army and the Afghan National Police could be funded and trained into a professional force of several hundred thousand men, that project "would be insufficient if Pakistan remains a safe haven for insurgents." Equally, solving the problem of the Pakistani sanctuary abetted by I.S.I. was "necessary but insufficient" to win in Afghanistan—that would require "addressing the severe governance, development and access to justice gaps."

The estimate rendered a split verdict on I.S.I.'s culpability and Kayani's role. "Pakistan now identifies both al Qaeda and the Taliban as existential threats," the estimate concluded, but the Taliban that bothered Kayani was the Pakistani branch, not the Afghan one. To influence Afghanistan, I.S.I.'s Directorate S still "provides intelligence and financial support to insurgent groups" attacking N.A.T.O. and Indian targets inside Afghanistan.[18]

Briefing the findings to N.A.T.O., Peter Lavoy said that I.S.I.'s aid to the Taliban was explained by three factors. First, "Pakistan believes the Taliban will prevail in the long term, at least in the Pashtun belt most proximate to the Pakistani border." Second, Pakistan "continues to define India as the number one threat" and "insists" that India seeks to undermine Pakistani security through covert operations inside Afghanistan. Third, Pakistan's high command believes "that if militant groups were not attacking in Afghanistan, they would seek out Pakistani targets."[19]

The world outside Room 445 changed dramatically during the two months that the review went on. The study began as Lehman Brothers failed, touching off the worst financial crisis and recession since the Great Depression. The collapsing economy lifted Obama's presidential prospects, and by October it seemed likely that the deputies would hand off their findings to a Democratic administration. Before the election, members of Lute's staff met advisers to both the Obama and McCain campaigns informally at the Army-Navy Club. They discussed with them the Afghan war's deterioration and the policy questions it raised. Obama had made clear during his campaign that he favored more effort in Afghanistan, but his specific views about troop levels and military doctrine were unclear.

Lute completed the final top secret report, about forty pages in length, about ten days after Obama was elected president. "The United States is not losing in Afghanistan, but it is not winning either, and that is not good enough," read the first sentence. The report made ten recommendations about fighting the Taliban, including the dispatch of more troops, a more ambitious effort to train and equip Afghan forces, tackling corruption and finding an approach to counter drug operations that would starve the Taliban of finance without alienating farmers—a form of drug policy for which N.A.T.O. had been searching without success for at least four years. At the Pentagon, Gates authorized preparations to send two more American brigades to Afghanistan, if the next president chose to do so. The review also urged that Afghanistan and Pakistan be organized as a single theater. A theme of the review, at least for some of the analysts involved, was the "need to re-Americanize the effort," as

Eliot Cohen put it. It had become a N.A.T.O. war, but it was not going to succeed that way.[20]

Bush also prepared to hand off to Obama the expanding C.I.A. drone campaign in the tribal areas that he had approved in July. In the four months between that decision and the completion of Lute's strategy review, the C.I.A. had carried out twenty-three drone strikes on Pakistani soil, more than in the previous four years combined. Mike D'Andrea now oversaw what amounted to an undeclared air war in the Federally Administered Tribal Areas waged from the Global Response Center on the Langley campus. C.I.A. mission leaders tracked drone feeds on the Response Center's big screens while Air Force pilots and sensor operators flew the missions more than two thousand miles away at Creech Air Force Base in Indian Springs, Nevada. The first strike under the new rules killed seven foreigners in Azam Warsak village in South Waziristan, according to a ledger of attacks kept by the F.A.T.A. government. In North Waziristan, the C.I.A. fired missiles at a dozen Haqqani-linked targets, some of them long ago mapped and surveyed in Miranshah and contiguous Dandey Darpa Khel, where the Haqqanis ran their large madrassa. The first two dozen strikes killed 40 foreigners but also 178 "locals," according to the Pakistani government count. On September 8, 2008, missiles demolished a North Waziristan home belonging to Jalaluddin Haqqani. He was absent, but Al Qaeda's latest chief in Pakistan, Abu Haris, was reportedly killed. Eight women and five children also died, according to the F.A.T.A. records. They record ten other cases of civilian casualties between September and December of 2008. In all of 2008, at least one child was killed in a third of all C.I.A. drone strikes, according to the available figures—a shocking percentage, if accurate.[21]

It would require C.I.A. mission managers several more years of intensive drone operations in the tribal areas before they reduced such mistakes to rarities. Because drones could dwell above a target for hours or days, multiple analysts usually had time to confirm that a target was appropriate. Yet the available record suggests that D'Andrea oversaw a relatively indiscriminate first season of strikes in F.A.T.A. before experience and improved technology reduced child and civilian deaths. The essential problem was that without reliable human agents reporting in real time on the ground from a village or town under surveillance, video imagery and fragmentary phone intercepts could not in every instance clarify the identities of the individuals being surveyed for death. And because the C.I.A.'s targeting rules had deliberately been loosened to allow drone strikes that more resembled conventional Air Force bombing, the risk of error expanded. Just as had been the case during the botched Mullah Mohammad Omar drone operation in the fall of 2001, secrecy rules meant pilots and sensor operators at Creech had no access to the details of C.I.A. intelligence. That left the pilots as trigger pullers following orders. The pilots could certainly object and hold off if they saw women and children in the target area, but where the imagery might be ambiguous they had to rely on superiors' understanding of secret intelligence they could not access.[22]

The larger question involved the strategic impact of ramped-up Predator attacks. Steve Kappes and other C.I.A. operations veterans referred to armed drones as a "homeland security weapon." They meant it could be effective as a tactic against terrorists identified as active plotters against American targets. They pointed out, however, that Predator strikes did not constitute a strategy to stop the sweep of terrorism or the attraction of dangerous numbers of young men to a jihadist cause larger than themselves.

In Pakistan, it soon became evident that the tactical punch of the C.I.A.'s secret air war had to be weighed against the boomerang effect on Pakistani political and public opinion. As evidence of civilian casualties mounted, Pakistani media publicized the strikes critically, perhaps encouraged by I.S.I.'s media wing. Of course, any country with free media would protest attacks on its territory that killed innocents, and when the attacking country was the United States—a hyperpower, seemingly unaccountable—the outrage and resistance within Pakistan was hardly surprising. The American attitude was We are not asking for permission. Patterson and the C.I.A. station briefed diverse Pakistani officials about the new American "strike policy." The briefings were declarations—not requests for acquiescence—sweetened with pledges of cooperation and expressions of appreciation for Pakistan's partnership.[23]

On November 19, C.I.A. drone operators strayed outside the Federally Administered Tribal Areas and the authorized flight corridors previously agreed with Kayani to unleash missiles on a compound in Bannu, in the "settled areas" of Pakistan. The strike reportedly killed a Saudi leader of Al Qaeda, another Arab, two Turkmen, and a local militant. Like the September Special Operations raid on Angoor Adda, the attack on mainland Pakistan visibly challenged the government's sovereignty and stretched the tolerance even of sympathetic civilian Pakistani politicians, never mind nationalists like Pasha. GIVE U.S. AN INCH AND IT'LL TAKE A MILE blared a typical headline after the dead and wounded were hauled from the rubble. Zardari, normally cooperative, told visiting American generals that month that he "did not mind paying the price for high-value targets, but it did not appear that Osama Bin Laden had been in your sights lately." The United States had never scored well in public opinion surveys in Pakistan, but its favorability ratings were sinking toward new lows, in the single digits, below India's.[24]

L ute presented the Afghan review's findings to Bush and the National Security Council in late November, before Thanksgiving.

"Putting counterinsurgency in front of counterterrorism as a priority is a significant shift," Gates observed. "That's an entirely different ball game in terms of resources." He worried that if too many U.S. troops poured into Afghanistan now, they would be seen as the Soviets were, provoking deeper resistance. "The Afghan Army must gain the ability and numbers" to do the job, he said.

"Is that realistic?" Bush asked.

"The Afghan Army is getting there," Lute advised, "but the police are a long way off."

Bush returned to the central logic problem: The review proposed new investments of American blood and treasure to stabilize Afghanistan, yet Al Qaeda was in Pakistan, as was the Taliban's leadership.

"Targeting is ongoing in Waziristan," Lute said, referring to the

C.I.A.'s stepped-up drone program, but Quetta, where the Taliban leadership resided, "is going untouched."

"Is Quetta a realistic goal?" Bush asked.

"We need to get Pakistani concurrence," C.I.A. director Michael Hayden argued. "Quetta is considered part of Pakistan proper. What goes on in Waziristan and the other tribal areas is much more of a gray area. I make no apologies for them, but for the Pak Army, the Quetta Shura is a strategic hedge against our withdrawal from Afghanistan, and they aren't likely to go after them anytime soon."

"Can't we get after them unilaterally?" Bush pressed.

"Sir, buildings blowing up in the midst of one of Pakistan's major cities is a lot different than an isolated mud hut getting struck out in the mountains somewhere," Hayden answered.

For American forces to go into Quetta on the ground, even with Pakistani cooperation, if it could somehow be obtained, "will be like taking on the Mafia on their home turf. Everyone will know you're coming, and it won't be pretty," Hayden continued. They would have to accept that outside the F.A.T.A., they were dependent on Pakistan.[25]

Bush approved the report but told his cabinet that he wanted to identify only those recommendations that required immediate action. Steve Hadley checked with the incoming Obama team, and they signaled that they "preferred that we pass along our report quietly." Lute briefed Obama's transition team, but they were noncommittal about the recommendations for more troops and money. Of course, Lute did not expect Obama's advisers to exclaim, "Thank God, Bush just gave us the answers."[26]

P eace be upon you."

"How are you?" Sajid Mir, a commander in Lashkar-e-Taiba, the I.S.I.-nurtured force that sought the liberation of Kashmir from India, spoke by telephone from Karachi to a terrorist in the midst of a two-day assault on Mumbai, India's financial capital. Sajid had grown up in Karachi. His father worked in Saudi Arabia, where he visited frequently. He was a worldly man who had traveled to Dubai, Qatar, Syria, Thailand, and Canada; he carried multiple passports and used several aliases.

"Doing well," the commander's fighter in Mumbai said.

"What are the conditions, brother?"

"It's *normal* at our end for the time being."

"Is there any firing?"

"No, not towards us . . ."

"Should they keep the hostages or kill them?" Sajid appeared to pose the question to a colleague with him in the Karachi command center.

"Kill them," the colleague instructed.

"Okay, listen," Sajid continued.

"Yes, yes."

"Uh, get rid of them right now. Rid yourself of them, friend. . . . Do it, do it. I said, I'm listening, do it."

"Should we open *fire*?"

"Yeah, do it. Make him sit, have him face the front and place it on the *back side* of his head, then shoot."[27]

Ten heavily armed Pakistani citizens landed after dark on Mumbai's Nariman Point on November 23, 2008, only hours after Bush approved the new Afghan war strategy review. The terrorists had been trained for three months at two Lashkar camps, one in Karachi and the other near Thatta, in Sindh Province. Trainers told the volunteers initially that they would fight their way to escape following their raid on Mumbai. Later, in September 2008, the plan changed. Now they would fight to the death. A Lashkar commander "thought this plan was better because it would cause the boys to fight harder."

Hafez Saeed, the spiritual and political leader of Lashkar, which he had founded in the 1980s as the armed wing of a proselytizing movement, delivered motivational lectures to the ten boys, alongside Zaki ur-Rehman Lakhvi, Lashkar's military commander. Lakhvi's black beard fell to his chest; he had at least eight children by three wives, and one of his sons had died fighting in Kashmir. Saeed assured the boys "that being shot would feel like a pin prick, blood stains would be like rose petals, and that angels would come down to take their souls."[28]

After two failed attempts, the squad departed Karachi by boat on November 22, hijacked an Indian fishing vessel, murdered four of the crew, and ordered the captain to navigate to Mumbai. Four miles

offshore, they murdered the captain and loaded weapons into their dinghy. Onshore they split into five teams of two. Their initial targets included a synagogue, a café, a large railway station, and two seaside luxury
hotels, the Oberoi-Trident Hotel and the Taj Mahal Hotel. They terror-
ized hostages before murdering them. The siege lasted more than forty-
eight hours, the most dramatic and sophisticated televised terrorist
attack worldwide since September 11. The raiding team killed at least
166 people, the great majority civilians, including 6 Americans, one of
them a thirteen-year-old girl. Nine of the 10 terrorists died; Indian police arrested the survivor, Ajmal Kasab, whom they soon identified as a
Pakistani from the Punjab.

American and allied spy services had run intercept coverage of
the communications between the attackers and their handlers in Karachi. An international team of intelligence leaders specializing in South
Asia, including the acting C.I.A. station chief in Islamabad, arranged a
meeting at I.S.I. and drove to the Pakistani service's headquarters carrying maps and link charts depicting the calls between the attackers and
phone numbers in Pakistan. The charts included some numbers associated with known I.S.I. officers. They met the major general who ran
I.S.I.'s analysis directorate.[29]

The exchange unfolded along familiar lines. The I.S.I. general opened
with denial and defensive accusations that India was inventing lies about
the Mumbai evidence to besmirch Pakistan. "I'm surprised and disap-
pointed that you believe this Indian propaganda" was the thrust of
his initial argument. Then the visitors laid out their evidence. The
general backed up to a secondary defense: "We will both have to investigate this."[30]

Anne Patterson, the U.S. ambassador to Pakistan, was away. Gerry
Feierstein, her deputy, and the acting C.I.A. station chief soon met Kayani and Pasha. Kayani said that the government of Pakistan "had nothing
to do with the matter." He denounced India's "rush to judgment about
the details of the case" and said that as a former intelligence chief, "he
would never have suggested that he could offer up an analysis of the
events so quickly after they concluded."[31]

Yet the evidence made it all but certain that Lashkar had been responsible, and Lashkar was effectively a paramilitary arm of the Pakistani state. It had been officially banned in 2002, under U.S. pressure, and had reorganized under a new name, but although some of its ranks had become so radical that they had joined violent jihad against Pakistan, the group remained cooperative with I.S.I. It had collaborated closely with Directorate S on training and cross-border attacks for more than a decade. Indian counterintelligence files in Kashmir brimmed with transcripts of cross-border communications during violent attacks. Lashkar had tens of thousands of members in Pakistan and its infrastructure in the country was open and unmolested—its successor after the ban maintained a large campus just outside Lahore, ran schools and hospitals, and maintained bank accounts as if it were a legitimate nongovernmental organization. The sophistication of the Mumbai assault required planning and resources that Lashkar possessed.

Pasha arrested Lakhvi, the Lashkar military chief, and interrogated him about the attack's history. The Americans asked for direct access to the prisoner. Pasha held them at bay. Eventually, the F.B.I. and C.I.A. would document that several retired or active I.S.I. officers had planned and funded the Mumbai operation. They learned this primarily through the confessions of David Headley, a Pakistani American involved in the plot. He was arrested in the United States and cooperated.

Born Daood Gilani in Washington, D.C., Headley grew up in Pakistan and joined Lashkar after the September 11 attacks. At a mosque, he met Abdur Rehman Hashim Syed, a retired Pakistani major. Syed, who went by "Pasha," had once been active with Lashkar but disagreed with what he regarded as its relatively soft approach to jihad. He regarded Lakhvi as an I.S.I. puppet, and he joined debates among Lashkar cadres about whether it was permissible to assassinate Pervez Musharraf. Lakhvi told them that their loose talk had reached I.S.I., which was "annoyed." Eventually, Pasha joined a more independent jihadi group led by Ilyas Kashmiri, an ambitious radical who operated out of the tribal areas. During this period, the Pakistani cells surveyed diverse targets inside India. Lakhvi plotted an extravagant attack on the Indian Military Academy at Dehradun. One squad would attack cadets during morning exercises and a second would go inside and recover the pistol surrendered to

India by Pakistan's commanding general at the end of the 1971 war. It was the terrorist equivalent of a fraternity raid, but Lakhvi thought it would thrill I.S.I. The plan fell apart when local conspirators were arrested.

In 2006, Headley traveled with his friend Pasha to Khyber Agency in the Federally Administered Tribal Areas. He was stopped and interrogated by a Pakistani officer who identified himself as Major Ali. Headley explained to Ali that Lashkar had trained him for action. Ali asked for his cell phone number. Several days later, another officer, who described himself as Major Iqbal, telephoned. Headley became Iqbal's espionage agent, on behalf of I.S.I. Iqbal gave Headley a total of about $30,000 for expenses and trained him in intelligence tradecraft, "including spotting and assessing people, recognizing Indian military insignia and movements, dead drops and pick up points, and clandestine photography." Under Iqbal's direction, Headley used his American passport to travel to Mumbai five times to survey targets by videotape and to mark potential landing zones with G.P.S. equipment. Headley eventually identified an I.S.I. colonel and an I.S.I. brigadier who worked the account out of Muzzafarabad, the capital of the section of Kashmir occupied by Pakistan.[32]

Even as it became fully evident that I.S.I. officers had cooked up the Mumbai attack, the scale of its provocation presented a puzzle. Directorate S's strike on the Indian embassy in Kabul the previous summer might be rationalized as a warning or reprisal shot against an Indian government target. The Mumbai attack was a Hollywood-inspired terrorist extravaganza that would delegitimize Pakistan abroad and risked igniting a nuclear war. Who in the Pakistani establishment or in active command at I.S.I. could have thought that was a winning idea? Kayani was clearly responsible for the broad contours of I.S.I. covert policy in Afghanistan and Kashmir, but it was not easy to believe that he would have sat down, ticked through military and political calculations, and ordered an attack of this scale and character.

Kayani and Pasha had replaced General Akhtar at Directorate S just weeks before the Mumbai attack. The scale of the covert and militant networks I.S.I. sought to manage or influence was mind-boggling. American intelligence reporting put the total number of armed militants in

Pakistan at about 100,000 and estimated that I.S.I. ran 128 different training camps and facilities.

London and Washington continued to hopefully regard Pasha as the "broom," as British foreign secretary David Miliband put it that December, a modernizing leader who would sweep in reform at the spy service. The American hypothesis, too, was that Mumbai offered a perhaps constructive shock to the system Pasha had inherited. Zardari encouraged such thinking: The overreach of the Mumbai attack offered his civilian government a rare opportunity to seize control of I.S.I. and "strike at my enemies," he told the Americans.[33]

An intelligence study of the Mumbai attack carried out by the United States and allied services concluded that the cabal of retired officers working with the Lashkar units and Hafez Saeed believed they had been given strategic direction from the top to pressure India. The purpose of such pressure, Indian officials firmly believed, was to undermine their booming economy, which was leading India to separate from Pakistan year by year in wealth and power. The Mumbai attack would make it appear to the world that India was not a rising power but a fragile state. Yet the retired I.S.I. officers had not cleared the audacious scale of the Mumbai operation with superiors, the analysis concluded. "The clearance rules have changed" was the sardonic line C.I.A. and British operations officers used with one another to explain what happens when a semiauthorized covert action goes wrong. That is, actions that might have been authorized if they had succeeded become unauthorized when they don't.[34]

I.S.I. may have also sought a perverse sort of credibility through the Mumbai assault—to prove to its own restive clients that it was not going soft, and that it should not be considered the enemy. After I.S.I. lost control of important sections of its militant clients in 2007, not only were its offices targeted in suicide bombings, its legitimacy was increasingly ridiculed within radical Islamist circles. There was "I.S.I. jihad," the dissenters argued, meaning pinprick strikes in Kashmir, and there was "the real jihad," carried out by Taliban militias and allies against Western occupation forces in Afghanistan. I.S.I. officers could point to the Mumbai attack as evidence of their credentials: *We are still with you, bolder than ever.*

A few weeks after the attack, a new C.I.A. station chief arrived in Islamabad. John Bennett had graduated from Harvard University in 1975, served five years as a U.S. Marine officer, and then joined the C.I.A. In between management roles at Langley, he had served seventeen years abroad, mainly in the Africa division, including several previous tours as station chief.[35]

The U.S. embassy's strategy after Mumbai was to present Pakistan's government with as detailed evidence about the attack as could be released to such a poorly trusted foreign ally. Anne Patterson and the F.B.I. handed over copious amounts of "tearline information"—intelligence cleared for sharing with a foreign government, sometimes written in sanitized form below the "tear line" of a fuller classified cable—about the Pakistani company that had sold the outboard motor used on the dinghy bearing the terrorists to Nariman Point, as well as information from the surviving attacker, Kasab, who was now undergoing interrogation in Indian custody. Bennett presented to I.S.I. dossiers of evidence about the attack that India had distributed to international diplomats. The Americans again sought direct access to Lashkar commanders in I.S.I. custody. Pasha now said the F.B.I. and C.I.A. could submit written questions quietly and he would see what could be done. Pasha told Bennett "that the detainees refused to sign their confessions," leaving I.S.I. to work with Pakistani police "to develop an evidentiary trail that would allow prosecution." A familiar I.S.I. rope-a-dope to protect clients had begun.

The U.S. embassy hypothesized that Pakistan was "struggling to come to grips with the consequences of an attack that exposed I.S.I.'s decades-old policy." Yet the best evidence was that Pakistan sought to minimize the fallout from Mumbai, not reverse I.S.I. policy. As ever, the default American approach remained engagement and hope for change, a hope based on the attraction of new leadership personalities in the army and at I.S.I. In the final days of the Bush administration, as the South Asia hands departed, they took with them a darker view, with Mumbai as the last straw in a seven-year journey from counterterrorism partnership to disillusionment. After Mumbai, Eliot Cohen concluded, "I think in some ways we were actually fighting the I.S.I."[36]

Bush wanted to visit Afghanistan one last time. Despite the war's deterioration on his watch, he remained proud of the Taliban's initial defeat and the elections that had brought in Karzai and a diverse parliament. He found it difficult to grasp that the Taliban were rooted in rural Pashtun society. In Bush's mind, the Taliban were merely the promoters of "a fanatical, barbaric brand of Islam" characterized by the oppression of women and the denial of "the simplest pleasures—singing, clapping, and flying kites." The National Intelligence Estimate of 2008, issued as Bush prepared for his farewell visit, tried to explain the Taliban's comeback as partly the result of its perceived growing legitimacy, as an alternative to Karzai's predatory government. In the Oval Office, before Bush departed for his final visit, Peter Lavoy presented these findings.[37]

"The Taliban? Legitimate?" Bush asked. "These same guys who are hanging people on soccer fields?" He rejected the conclusion. He could afford to stand firm; the war was no longer his to solve.

Flying by Black Hawk helicopter from Bagram to Kabul, Bush detected an acrid smell and realized it was coming from burning tires, "sadly, an Afghan way of keeping warm." After meetings at the palace, Bush and Karzai shook hands and hugged. Bush made one pointed concession to the Afghan president. About I.S.I., he told Karzai, "You were right."[38]

TWENTY

The New Big Dogs

S ince the 1970s, the vice president of the United States has lived in a white nineteenth-century home on the grounds of the Naval Observatory, a tree-lined campus on a rise between Massachusetts and Wisconsin avenues. Dick Cheney, who had made a fortune in the oil industry, had furnished the home from his own resources. When he moved out, he took his furniture with him. Joe Biden had been living on a senator's salary for thirty-six years. He commuted to Washington by train from his family home in Delaware. He had no spare sofas and beds grand enough for such a place when he moved in early in 2009. Navy personnel rummaged around some warehouses and pulled together a loosely coordinated, classical-looking assortment. In its air of improvisation, the house reflected its newest occupant.

Biden was sixty-six years old that winter, still vigorous and handsome with a full head of silver hair and an uncannily white smile. Obama had only arrived in Washington in 2005. It made sense for him to choose a running mate with Biden's experience. The vice president–elect had served for a dozen years as chairman or ranking member of the Senate Foreign Relations Committee, traveling widely and meeting many world leaders. Yet Biden could be a frustrating source of counsel. He talked a lot and seemed to revel in the sound of his own voice. "I'm here to listen," he would say to open a meeting and then he would hold forth for twenty minutes. He was not mean-spirited but he could be defensive and

combative, as Hamid Karzai had discovered the previous January over
dinner in Kabul. Because Biden spoke in such an undisciplined fashion
and made a display of his vanity, he was also easy to underestimate.
Over the decades he had rejected conventional Washington opinion on
some important foreign policy dilemmas, such as whether Iraq could
survive as a unified, multiethnic state after the Bush administration's
invasion (he did not think so) or the threats of leakage posed by Pakistan's growing nuclear program (which Biden called out well before
A. Q. Khan's smuggling network was revealed). On those issues he had
been lonely and right. Yet his judgment was hardly infallible. He had
endorsed George W. Bush's invasion of Iraq.

Well before Inauguration Day, Obama asked Biden to investigate the
time-sensitive choices he would face about the Afghan war. George W.
Bush's final strategy review had passed along a recommendation from
the American field commander in Kabul, now General David McKiernan, that the United States dispatch thirty thousand additional troops to
help provide security for the Afghan presidential election scheduled for
the summer of 2009. Bush had deferred the general's request so that
Obama could decide. The president-elect had said during the campaign
that he supported sending at least seven thousand additional American
soldiers. The request for thirty thousand was a large demand. And Central Command's generals said they needed an answer quickly, to deliver
the troops to Afghanistan before summer.

"What do I need to put into Afghanistan now, so that when the summer arrives, we are not losing ground to the Taliban?" Obama asked
Biden privately.[1]

Biden flew to Pakistan and Afghanistan. He invited Lindsey Graham, the Republican senator from South Carolina, a vocal supporter of
the war in Afghanistan, to come along. It was tempting for Biden to
think that the problems the Obama administration would inherit were
due in large measure to Bush's coddling of Karzai and Pakistan's generals, and that what was required was greater toughness. In the Senate,
during 2008, Biden had coauthored a plan, eventually enacted, to deliver
billions of dollars in additional aid to Pakistan's civilian government, in
an effort to stabilize the country and strengthen civilian rule over the

army. He was well acquainted with I.S.I. leaders' long record of unreliability. As vice president, he would be in a position to play enforcer to Obama's statesman.

In Islamabad, on January 9, he and Graham met Ashfaq Kayani and Ahmed Pasha. Biden told them that he "wanted to be sure the U.S. and Pakistan had the same enemy" as they moved ahead, meaning the Taliban. "What kind of Afghanistan would represent success for Pakistan?" Biden asked.

Kayani assured him that "Pakistan and the United States have a convergence of interests" in the Afghan war. Kayani's goal was "a peaceful, friendly and stable Afghanistan. I have no desire to control Afghanistan. Anyone who wants to control Afghanistan is ignorant of history, since no one has ever controlled it."

That phrase—"a peaceful, friendly and stable Afghanistan"—had become Kayani's stock answer to international leaders inquiring about the Pakistan Army's aims amid the Taliban's revival. Kayani thought the phrase conveyed a neutral, cooperative approach that identified shared stability as the main goal. Yet Americans and Afghans heard his search for a "friendly" Afghanistan as a subtle demand for I.S.I. influence through the Taliban, an interpretation also well grounded in recent history.

Kayani told Biden that there had certainly been some "confusion" about I.S.I.'s pursuit of "strategic depth" in Afghanistan since the Soviet war. "Strategic depth" was the phrase a previous army chief had used to describe Pakistan's pursuit of a friendly regime in Kabul. In fact, what it meant, Kayani said, was merely the search for a peaceful neighbor where Afghan Pashtuns were adequately accommodated in Afghan politics.

"The Taliban are a reality," Kayani also said, using another of his stock phrases. Yet Pakistan did not want to go back to the 1990s or restore the Islamic Emirate in Kabul. The Taliban government of that era "had had a negative effect on Pakistan," Kayani said.

Biden made clear that the C.I.A. did not trust the I.S.I. and held it partly responsible for the Taliban's resurgence. Pasha said he was "hurt" by Biden's inference. After his appointment to I.S.I. three months earlier, he assured Biden, he had enjoyed a "frank talk" with C.I.A. director

Michael Hayden, and he had "sought the advice" of the Islamabad Station repeatedly, he added.

"I'm not going to revisit the past," Biden said.

There is no reason for I.S.I. to be protecting "these people," meaning the Taliban and its allies, Pasha insisted, and he had no interest in saving them.

"I need to know the situation has changed," Biden said. He understood that the Pakistan Army had limited capacity, but if the Obama administration provided more aid, would anything really change?

"It's important to know if we have the same enemy," Biden repeated.[2]

In Kabul, Biden met Karzai at the palace and told him the Obama administration would offer a "new contract" to Afghanistan but that it would have conditions: Karzai *had* to address corruption and the opium problem.

Biden said these problems could be managed privately, without resort to public criticism or pressure. Karzai should stop publicly calling out the United States over civilian casualties caused by American forces and the White House would express its concerns about graft and drugs discreetly, too.

"Mr. President, if you will keep the volume down about civilian casualties, you won't hear about corruption or the drug problem," as Karzai recounted the exchange to aides. Yet the discussion was tense. Biden's insulting theater of the previous year remained in Karzai's mind.

"Mr. Vice President, we should do more about Pakistan, the sanctuaries," Karzai argued.

"Mr. President, Pakistan is *fifty* times more important than Afghanistan for the United States." Karzai received this analysis in stunned silence. Biden also told him, "The golden time of the Bush administration is gone." The essence of his message, as Karzai summarized it after the meeting, was: "The Taliban is your problem, Al Qaeda is our problem."[3]

No sooner had Biden departed for Washington than Karzai read anonymous quotes in the media, attributed to senior Obama administration officials, that America would "expect more" from Karzai on corruption. He also heard reports that Secretary of State Hillary Clinton had called Afghanistan a narco-state. So much for discretion, it seemed.

In private, Karzai now expressed resentment toward Washington continually. He struck his own cabinet as unstable. At an Afghan cabinet meeting on January 17, some ministers remarked to Karzai that the Afghan people were facing real difficulties.

"Are you with me or against me?" Karzai raved. "The U.S. can leave. What they are talking about is unacceptable. I will declare jihad and go to the mountains!"

The meeting broke up and the ministers asked one another what had just happened. Several made discreet calls to Washington: Someone should try to talk to Karzai and calm him down.

A few days later, an Afghan aide spoke to Karzai for two and a half hours. The president denied saying that he would "go to the mountains" but he complained that the United States "is not listening to us." Karzai seemed enormously insecure about how the Obama administration would view him. He was on the eve of seeking reelection as president. His family's security and financial interests were at stake in that election. Improbably enough, Obama seemed to favor Gul Agha Sherzai, his rival, whom Obama had met the previous summer and who claimed to be invited to his inauguration, according to Karzai's information.[4]

Karzai summoned to the palace Kai Eide, a Norwegian diplomat who was the United Nations special representative to Afghanistan. Karzai told him, "They are after the two of us, the Americans. They are after you and I."[5]

Several weeks later, back in Washington, Biden invited half a dozen specialists on Afghanistan to dinner at the Naval Observatory residence. He was still ruminating over what the Obama administration should do. The issue he was most qualified to assess, he said, was domestic politics, and he knew one thing for certain: The American people were not going to sustain the Afghan war for very long. They were already weary. "This is not the beginning," he said. "We're already seven years in."

The American economy was collapsing that winter, shedding jobs by the hundreds of thousands. Every morning, President Obama received two dark briefings: one about international threats from the director of national intelligence, and a second about the collapsing financial system. Seventy-five percent of American banks were underwater, Biden remarked. And here come hubristic generals from Central Command with polished stars on their shoulders, demanding the president's signature on a costly troop escalation in Afghanistan, graveyard of empires. Obama's position was like Kennedy's in 1961, Biden thought, when Kennedy was pressed in his first months to endorse a C.I.A. invasion of Cuba. Obama reacted to the pressure coolly and deliberately. The president, Biden remarked, "has balls like pool cues."[6]

Biden instinctively resisted the counterinsurgency doctrine General David Petraeus promoted around Washington that winter. He wondered if using the American military to stabilize Afghanistan made sense when the real problems lay in Pakistan. He leaned back in his chair and asked, at length, "what if" the United States poured all the new money it was being asked to direct toward Afghanistan into Pakistan, coupled with a push for regional diplomacy, to include bringing in the Chinese and the Saudis to put pressure on I.S.I. to change course once and for all? It was a radical notion, certainly unconventional. Of course, Biden's idea would leave the Kabul government to fend for itself, which it could not do. A few weeks later, Obama settled on a seemingly safer course: He cut the Pentagon's request for thirty thousand troops to seventeen thousand and approved sending them forward to try to hold a successful election.[7]

On February 13, 2009, in the director's conference room at Old Headquarters, Steve Kappes swore in Leon Panetta as C.I.A. director. Panetta, like Biden, was a seasoned Washington hand. He had served in Congress for sixteen years and another six in Bill Clinton's White House, ultimately as chief of staff. He was a charming, profane first-generation Italian American who owned a small ranch outside

Carmel, California. He had scant experience of intelligence. He barely knew Obama and considered his appointment to C.I.A. as "odd" and "not necessarily a great fit."[8]

As with all outsiders arriving on the Seventh Floor, Panetta's first challenge was to establish authority over a permanent C.I.A. workforce that had long ago learned to distrust and outlast political appointees. The task was complicated in his case by the reluctance of his predecessor, Mike Hayden, to leave. Hayden had hoped that his credentials as a non-partisan career military officer might prompt Obama to leave him in place for a year or so, to oversee a transition in C.I.A. operations. But Hayden was an advocate for waterboarding and other enhanced interrogation techniques that Obama intended to end. Hayden had pressured the incoming national security team to reconsider its position on interrogation. It was futile. Obama called Hayden early in the New Year and told him, euphemistically, "I don't want to look back," referring to the years of enhanced interrogation techniques. The new White House team wanted only Hayden's departure as a symbolic change; they worked hard to keep Kappes and D'Andrea, at the Counterterrorism Center, in place. On his third day as president, January 22, Obama signed executive orders banning harsh interrogation techniques, which he called "torture," to the consternation of many career C.I.A. officers who had convinced themselves over the previous eight years that they had engaged in no such thing.

Obama accepted Hayden's advice on drone operations in Pakistan, however. The next day, while presiding over his first National Security Council meeting, the president approved C.I.A. proposals to continue lethal strikes against Al Qaeda targets under the same rules Bush had approved the previous summer. Hayden remained in charge of the C.I.A. for several weeks as Panetta awaited confirmation. He briefed Obama on targets in Waziristan under active surveillance. Two C.I.A. drones fired missiles at suspected Al Qaeda operatives that same day, January 23— one in South Waziristan and one in North Waziristan. Both attacks reportedly killed civilians. The strike in North Waziristan hit a private home in the village of Zeraki. According to an affidavit from two witnesses, the dead included an eighth-grade boy and schoolteachers. The

South Waziristan strike killed a pro-government peace negotiator who was a tribal leader and four of his family members, entirely in error. When John Brennan, the former C.I.A. leader who had joined the White House as a senior counterterrorism adviser, briefed Obama about the civilian deaths, the president was incredulous, but ordered no immediate changes in C.I.A. procedures.[9]

Leon Panetta might not know what a dead drop was, but he knew how to maneuver among Washington's big dogs. He met with Kappes, D'Andrea, and other top agency career officers to assure them that he would have their backs. After two lengthy conversations, Panetta asked Kappes to stay on as the C.I.A.'s deputy director. When Kappes agreed, his endorsement influenced other career veterans.[10]

Panetta empowered the leadership he inherited at the C.I.A. He found D'Andrea's Counterterrorism Center to be "a very effective, well-run, well-resourced, well-managed" unit, "an incredibly useful, effective weapon in the effort against Al Qaeda," as a former senior intelligence official put it. For their part, the more sophisticated career officers at the agency recognized that Panetta could deliver on two of the Seventh Floor's essential functions: protecting the C.I.A. at the White House and in Congress. Moreover, the new director was seventy years old. His wife Sylvia had remained at their California ranch and Panetta intended to commute home as often as possible, which meant that he regularly flew off from Washington for long weekends. He was not going to microman-age C.I.A. field operations.[11]

Panetta flew secretly to India, Pakistan, and Afghanistan on his first trip abroad. In India, he heard an earful from Research and Analysis Wing officers and police about I.S.I.'s role in Mumbai's carnage the previous November. The R.A.W. officers urged Panetta to pressure I.S.I. to tear down Lashkar-e-Taiba and its branches.

In Islamabad, Panetta drove past the Marriott Hotel, bombed and burned the previous September, now reopened. John Bennett, the station chief, and other C.I.A. officers briefed him on the search for Fahid Mohammed Ally Msalam, who went by the nom de guerre Usama al-Kini. He was the suspected organizer of the hotel attack. The briefers inventoried the large number of American dead and wounded. Their message came through clearly: This is an American war.

Panetta dined with Pasha and Asif Zardari, Benazir Bhutto's widow, who shared authority uneasily with the army. Zardari made jokes about I.S.I.'s pervasive surveillance of him—jokes that sounded paranoid but were grounded in fact.

"Ahmed knows everything I think and everything I say," Zardari remarked of the I.S.I. chief sitting near him. "I walk into my office every morning and say, 'Hello, Ahmed!'"

Zardari mentioned that once, his presidential plane wasn't airworthy and he had an urgent trip to make. "The only person I could call was I.S.I. And I said, 'Ahmed, I'm going to ask for your airplane, but only on one condition, which is that you have to fly with me.'"

Pasha laughed along but the scene was awkward. It seemed to the C.I.A. delegation that Zardari might employ a food taster. After Musharraf, the Bush administration had bet on democracy, but with Benazir Bhutto eliminated, they had ended up with a widower of erratic temperament who was seen by few of his countrymen as effective. Zardari did little to reduce his reputation for loose financial dealings when he gave American officials in Islamabad sophisticated advice about buying real estate on the luxurious Upper East Side of Manhattan. Don't buy in Sutton Place, Zardari advised—too far from the action.

For his part, Pasha at least offered "a voice of moderation" that evening, as a participant put it. Throughout western Pakistan, the I.S.I. chief explained to Panetta, Taliban mullahs had replaced traditional tribal *maliks* "and a religiosity has taken hold." Tens of thousands of madrassas had sprung up and young Pakistani men and women were not being properly educated.[12]

At the U.S. embassy, Panetta walked the third floor and addressed the C.I.A. station. He typically carried bottles of high-quality California wine as gifts, which made him seem more charming still.

But Panetta and John Bennett fell into conflict over the C.I.A.'s counterterrorism assistance to Pakistani forces. The Islamabad station supplied geolocation information to Pakistani counterparts, to help them arrest the targeted militants. Sometimes, the Pakistanis shot the suspects dead, rather than process them for trial. Bennett received a message that he and his officers might be held liable for murder if they did not stop supplying the information to the Pakistanis. The station chief demanded that Langley obtain approval from the Justice Department. "Fuck you, John," Panetta said at one point. "Just get it done." Bennett answered, "Then you'll have to get a new station chief."[13]

The issue was soon resolved but Bennett put in his retirement papers and left the C.I.A. that summer. Later, when Panetta needed to find a new chief of the entire clandestine service, he recalled the exchange. Panetta saw himself as a leader who felt "an obligation" to tell the boss the truth, "no matter how uncomfortable." He concluded that Bennett had done the same. He persuaded him to unretire and appointed him to lead C.I.A. espionage operations worldwide. It remained axiomatic that profane men should lead the agency.[14]

The essential question facing Panetta in Pakistan was how to assess I.S.I. He had tried to make sense of Pasha over dinner, but it wasn't easy. Briefings from Bennett and other career officers emphasized both I.S.I.'s unreliability and its vital partnership in capturing Al Qaeda leaders like Khalid Sheikh Mohammed, the architect of September 11.

In Kabul, Panetta met Amrullah Saleh, who had reported to American interlocutors that spring that Saudi Arabia was paying the Pakistan Army directly, to supplement American aid and to win influence. Pasha was telling people that he "can be rogue," Saleh said, and follow whatever path was best for Pakistan. He was protecting the Quetta Shura from C.I.A. Predator operations. The United States had to "find a way not to be a cash cow for Pakistan," Saleh emphasized, and it had to "end the Pakistani veto" over the conduct of the war.

To strengthen the Afghan government's position, Karzai should hang criminals and corrupt strongmen to show he was serious, he added. The Taliban were more corrupt than the Afghan government, he said, but they were accessible to the people and had rebuilt their credibility.[15]

C.I.A. leaders like Kappes in Langley nonetheless continued to feel that they could not afford to isolate the Pakistan Army when it was battling domestic insurgents and cooperating with drone strikes against Al

Qaeda. Gradually, Panetta would come to think that I.S.I.'s new boss, Ahmed Pasha, was "as good a partner from Pakistan as he was going to find," as a colleague put it.[16]

On a Saturday morning that winter, Panetta arrived at the director's conference room to receive Richard Holbrooke. At Hillary Clinton's urging, Obama had appointed Holbrooke as special representative for Afghanistan or Pakistan, or "S-rap," as the inevitable acronym was usually pronounced. Holbrooke had been Clinton's leading foreign policy adviser during the often-bitter campaign against Obama. As a young Foreign Service officer, he had worked in the Mekong Delta and Saigon during the Vietnam War. During the Clinton administration, he led negotiations to end the Bosnian war and served as the U.S. ambassador to the United Nations. He was a man of legendary appetites and ambition, bold and restive, "a giant among Pygmies," as Sherard Cowper-Coles, his British counterpart on Afghanistan, put it.[17] His grandiosity both charmed and grated. He had hoped to become secretary of state if Hillary Clinton defeated Obama for president. Instead he had accepted what he described as the hardest task the Obama administration faced overseas, resolving or at least stabilizing the Afghan conflict. If he succeeded, he might yet become secretary.

That Saturday, he wanted the C.I.A. to brief him about the secrets that would shape his chances for success. Steve Kappes joined the meeting, as did analysts and aides. Holbrooke sought Kappes out. "I hear you are the go-to person on Pakistan over here," he said.

Kappes chuckled. Flattery was a case officer's tradecraft, and here was Holbrooke trying to practice it on him.

Holbrooke took a chair at the middle of the long table. Kappes and Panetta sat across from him. Teams of analysts rotated in to present to Holbrooke. One group briefed him on the status of David Rohde, a *New York Times* reporter who had been kidnapped by the Taliban. During the Balkans war, Bosnian Serbs had kidnapped Rohde while the reporter was investigating war crimes, and Holbrooke had negotiated for his freedom. He wanted to do it again.

Another C.I.A. team briefed him about the I.S.I., including what was known and unknown about Directorate S. A third group of analysts briefed him about the Afghan army and police. Unsustainably high desertion rates, corruption, and drug use plagued the police especially. Holbrooke asked question after question. Lunch arrived. Holbrooke kept going.

Kappes thought Holbrooke was sincere about wanting their insights and advice, but that he was also probing to determine if the C.I.A. would be on his side. The agency was not about to hand over highly compartmented details about which Afghan or Pakistani political and military figures were or had been on the C.I.A.'s payroll, and they were not going to be trapped into taking sides in policy arguments at the White House. Holbrooke understood the basic picture: In Afghanistan, the C.I.A. had installed men like Karzai, Sherzai, and the Panjshiris formerly loyal to Ahmad Shah Massoud in 2001 and had maintained ties with leading personalities ever since, for counterterrorism and political access.

Holbrooke argued that the C.I.A.'s web of strongmen in Afghanistan, including Ahmed Wali Karzai in Kandahar, was part of the problem in the war. They provided a mirage of security but governed as predators, exacerbating popular grievances. But Kappes rejected Holbrooke's argument. The United States was at war with Al Qaeda, the C.I.A. was on the front lines in Afghanistan, and its assets among the country's power brokers were vital. The security of the United States trumped any concerns about the moral qualities of its Afghan interlocutors. "Kappes fought tooth and nail," Holbrooke told staff later.[18]

Kappes told C.I.A. colleagues that Holbrooke was there to drain the agency's vaults of all its analysis about Afghanistan and Pakistan, dispute the C.I.A.'s conclusions, and find the agency's weak points for future interagency policy debates. Holbrooke wanted to end the drone program and make counterterrorism operations against Al Qaeda more transparent, with a greater role for the military and the F.B.I., the C.I.A. leaders feared.

Holbrooke pressed the C.I.A. for help in bringing Pasha and Amrullah Saleh together in a new cooperative intelligence effort. This would

Cofer Black (*left*) and Rich Blee in January 2002 in eastern Afghanistan on Al Qaeda counterterrorist operations.

From left: General (ret.) Muhammad Yusaf Khan, the first vice chief of army staff under Musharraf; Colonel Dave Smith; and Lieutenant General Ashfaq Kayani, Director-General of I.S.I., in April 2005, at the centennial celebration of the Pakistan Army Command and Staff College in Quetta, Pakistan.

Wendy Chamberlin,
U.S. ambassador to Pakistan
on September 11, 2001,
in May 2003.

Head of Pakistani intelligence
lieutenant general Mahmud
Ahmed on Pakistan's
Independence Day in
August 2000.

Hamid Karzai, then-
chairman of Afghanistan's
interim government, with
General Abdur Rashid
Dostum, then-deputy
defense minister, at the
Arg Palace in Kabul in
December 2001.

Pakistani president Pervez Musharraf with President George W. Bush in the Oval Office in September 2006.

Amrullah Saleh in Berlin in 2011.

Former U.S. ambassador to Afghanistan Zalmay Khalilzad in Kabul in October 2011.

Deputy C.I.A. director Stephen Kappes at C.I.A. headquarters in February 2009.

Lieutenant General Ahmed Shuja Pasha, head of Pakistan's Inter-Services Intelligence, in Islamabad in July 2011.

U.S. secretary of state John Kerry and Pakistani chief of army staff general Ashfaq Kayani in Brussels, Belgium, on April 24, 2013, after a trilateral meeting with Afghan president Hamid Karzai.

Peter Lavoy working in the national airborne operations center while traveling to the Asia-Pacific in October 2011 with then-secretary of defense Leon Panetta.

A Canadian soldier on patrol in a field of marijuana plants in Kandahar, Afghanistan, in June 2011.

Then-first lieutenant Timothy Hopper near COP Stout, in Kandahar's Arghandab River Valley, in spring 2011.

U.S. secretary of state Hillary Clinton and Afghan president Hamid Karzai in a meeting at the Arg Palace in Kabul in October 2011.

From left: President Barack Obama, "war czar" Lieutenant General Doug Lute, Deputy National Security Adviser Denis McDonough, and National Security Adviser Tom Donilon in the Situation Room in March 2011.

Richard Holbrooke (*left*) and Barnett Rubin at the
Arg Palace in Kabul in January 2010.

Darin and Holly Loftis
with their daughters,
Alison and Camille,
in 2008.

Marc Sageman in
Afghanistan
in 2012.

Ahmad Massoud, son of the
late Ahmad Shah Massoud,
in Bazarak, Afghanistan,
in September 2016.

A framed picture of Ahmad Shah
Massoud in Bazarak, Afghanistan,
in September 2016.

be part of a wider push for cooperation between the Pakistani and Afghan governments, he said.

The discussions went on. One C.I.A. official looked at the clock: It was now 4:30 p.m.

Kappes's instincts about Holbrooke were mostly right. Holbrooke aimed to shape Obama's priorities through interagency decision making, and to outflank the C.I.A. and the Pentagon, even as he appeared to embrace them. The C.I.A. leadership's view was that Holbrooke was Holbrooke. He was going to fly around the world and try to make something happen. "We didn't know what it was," as a C.I.A. official at the meeting put it. Holbrooke was going to talk to the Russians and talk to the Chinese about Afghanistan and Pakistan. Every other day he was talking to someone else. He was "irrepressible."[19]

Holbrooke set up his operations in a suite of windowless offices on the ground floor of the State Department. The setting was unglamorous and crowded. There were about forty staff. Holbrooke's approach was to replicate the interagency process at the National Security Council under his own leadership at State by bringing in liaisons and seconded officials from the Pentagon, Central Command, the F.B.I., the C.I.A., and even the Department of Agriculture, which he saw as key to reviving Afghanistan's rural economy. He was building a mini–American government in his own office. Holbrooke's construction of a shadow N.S.C. annoyed staff at the actual N.S.C. Yet it seemed wiser to get inside his tent than to stand outside. The C.I.A. sent over Frank Archibald, the former Kandahar case officer and Islamabad station chief. Archibald provided Holbrooke continuous access to Langley and also a way for Panetta and Kappes to keep track of what he was doing. Holbrooke also urged N.A.T.O. governments worldwide to appoint their own special representatives so that he could coordinate global action through them—his own mini–United Nations. British and Australian liaisons moved into his suite.

Holbrooke was a terrific subordinate and an exciting boss but a terrible colleague, a diplomat who worked with him once remarked. He compared diplomacy to jazz improvisation. He riffed at the frenetic tempo of a bebopper. He was often on his BlackBerry and thought nothing of getting up in the middle of a solemn meeting to take a personal call. His behavior struck some of the civil servants around him as arrogant and rude. But Holbrooke seemed to regard self-dramatization as essential to his art.[20]

When Holbrooke visited Cowper-Coles in London, the British representative arranged a briefing on Afghanistan and Pakistan for him at the Vauxhall Cross headquarters of MI6. Holbrooke agreed only reluctantly because he had theater tickets that evening with George Soros. He stayed for hours, asking questions. At the end, he pulled out several mobile phones, all turned on, in total violation of counterintelligence rules.[21]

Pasha flew in to Washington toward the end of winter. He met Holbrooke at the Pakistan embassy, off Connecticut Avenue, in the ambassador's office. Holbrooke brought a map that he unfolded, to go over areas on the Pakistan-Afghanistan border.

"Don't think this part of the world is like Serbia," the I.S.I. chief advised. "Don't come here with an idea that what you did in the Balkans will work in Pakistan or Afghanistan. They're just not the same kind of places."[22]

The Pakistani state looked to be more fragile that winter than at any time since September 11. Pakistani Taliban insurgents bolstered by hardened Uzbek volunteers swept out of Swat and took the district of Buner to its east, just over one hundred miles from Islamabad. They enforced harsh Sharia law. This was the challenge Ashfaq Kayani feared—if the war became about Islamic legitimacy, it might split the country and the army, evolving from insurgency to civil war.

By spring, the American and Saudi governments were in full panic about the possible entry of the Taliban into Islamabad. Kayani told Anne Patterson he was "desperate" for helicopters and had only five airworthy Mi-17s to fly. Holbrooke flew secretly to Abu Dhabi to meet Zardari, under cover of a visit to the ruler of the United Arab Emirates, to discuss how the United States might do more. Adel Al-Jubeir, the American-accented foreign policy adviser to Saudi king Abdullah, told Holbrooke that the kingdom, too, was trying to shore up the Pakistan Army. The "greatest issue is the collapse of the Pakistani state," Jubeir warned.[23]

On March 27, 2009, in Room 450 of the Eisenhower Executive Office Building beside the White House, President Obama announced to the public "a comprehensive, new strategy for Afghanistan and Pakistan." General David Petraeus, among other advisers, sat before the president in full uniform. "The situation is increasingly perilous," Obama said. He continued:

> Many people in the United States—and many in partner countries that have sacrificed so much—have a simple question: What is our purpose in Afghanistan? After so many years, they ask, why do our men and women still fight and die there? And they deserve a straightforward answer. So let me be clear: Al Qaeda and its allies—the terrorists who planned and supported the 9/11 attacks—are in Pakistan and Afghanistan. Multiple intelligence estimates have warned that al Qaeda is actively planning attacks on the United States homeland from its safe haven in Pakistan. And if the Afghan government falls to the Taliban— or allows al Qaeda to go unchallenged—that country will again be a base for terrorists who want to kill as many of our people as they possibly can.
>
> The future of Afghanistan is inextricably linked to the future of its neighbor, Pakistan.[24]

A few hours later, one floor below, in a high-ceilinged conference room with parquet floors, Richard Holbrooke joined a private meeting about how President Obama's goals might be achieved. Beside him at a hollow square table sat General Doug Lute, who had led the Bush administration's last war strategy review and had stayed on as the National Security Council senior director for the region. Also at the table sat Bruce Riedel, a former C.I.A. officer who had worked at the agency for almost three decades and had also served as a National Security Council staffer during the Clinton administration. Obama's speech that morning had endorsed the findings of what had become known as the "Riedel review," a fifteen- to twenty-page top secret paper defining the new administration's strategy. The paper had a classified annex with sensitive analysis of terrorism in Pakistan, drone strikes, and Pakistan's nuclear weapons.

Holbrooke could not sit still. He slumped in his chair and announced that he had to leave early to get home to his wife, the journalist and author Kati Marton. He took several cell phone calls. He mentioned that he had received a call earlier from Hamid Karzai, who was effusive about Obama's speech. Of course, the Afghan president's flattery might just be designed to curry political favor, Holbrooke acknowledged, but Karzai had to be forgiven—under Obama, he had lost his lifeline to the White House, the videoconferences he had held with his "former best friend," George W. Bush.

"How often did they do those?" Holbrooke asked Lute.

"Often," Lute mumbled. He thought the conferences were valuable; he had seen Bush get a lot done in them over the previous eighteen months, but he could tell that the Obama team wanted to send a different message to Karzai.

"It was a cable station," Riedel added skeptically.

The newcomers made no effort to disguise their contempt for Bush's close cultivation of Karzai and the mutual dependency they believed it had created.

Holbrooke's phone rang again. "It's Zardari," he confided. He walked out of the meeting, returned, and said he'd told the Pakistani president that he would call him back.

The conversation turned to Obama's dilemmas in managing the Pentagon and Petraeus. "This is not 1965," Holbrooke pronounced. "I would know. I was there."

He was referring to President Lyndon B. Johnson's escalation of the Vietnam War, based on ad hoc tactical decisions. Instead, Obama had commissioned the Riedel review to identify vital interests and goals.

Yet the Riedel review they were celebrating was merely a light blueprint, Holbrooke acknowledged, not a full-blown military or diplomatic or intelligence plan. He had met Petraeus the night before, he said, to start to "operationalize" the review's principles.[25]

In fact, the review was an unusual, deadline-pressured exercise. It was odd for a new president to commission an outside consultant to study an inherited war. Riedel was a think tank scholar who had advised the Obama campaign but had no desire to enter the administration. Obama valued him and knew Riedel better than he knew James Jones, the tall former Marine general fluent in French whom Obama had appointed as national security adviser. Jones was not interested in running the Afghan review, he told Obama's aides, because he had to oversee other foreign policy reviews, such as about Iraq.[26]

Riedel was a well-informed, direct-speaking analyst, particularly on the subject of Pakistan. He was an ardent I.S.I. skeptic. He wrote well. All of the new team had read Lute's longer, researched top secret review from the expiring Bush administration. That document made clear that the war wasn't going well. The general policy direction of escalation in Afghanistan and renewed attention to Pakistan and I.S.I. seemed clear. Riedel offered a convenient solution to Jones's deflection of responsibility.

A week after Obama's inauguration, Riedel had chaired a meeting in Room 445 of E.E.O.B., the same secure conference room where Lute had run the final Bush review, to announce his study process. "We'll have a draft in a week," he said. That seemed insanely fast. But Obama had declared that he wanted the review finished before he attended his first N.A.T.O. summit in early April. Another context for the work was that the White House had already defined "the big challenge" as "how to keep Holbrooke out" of the strategy formation, as a participant put it. This had not to do with policy differences but reflected a view that he was disruptive and hard to control. "The whole thing was weird and awkward and ugly, unsavory," the participant said. Lute and others at the White House were pleased with Riedel's work, but Robert Gates, who had stayed on as secretary of defense, thought the draft had "no new ideas."[27]

The review team sneakily arranged to brief the report to President Obama on a domestic Air Force One flight to Los Angeles when they knew Holbrooke would not be present. It was already becoming common for the White House to schedule meetings on Afghanistan on dates they knew Holbrooke could not make. The president made no fuss about this maneuver; his staff understood that Holbrooke's theatrics put Obama off, and the more contact the two men had, the more alienated the president seemed to become.

The Riedel review mattered because its findings would be distributed as binding presidential guidance to every agency involved in the Afghan war and policy toward Pakistan. Riedel's final draft found that the United States had only one truly "vital" interest in the region: to defeat Al Qaeda. The highly classified annex identified another high priority, to prevent extremists from acquiring Pakistani nuclear weapons, but this was not something Obama's advisers wanted him to highlight in public, because it was sensitive and might sound provocative or alarmist. America had other interests in the war, such as stability in South Asia and the reduction of heroin trafficking, but Al Qaeda trumped all others.

On Al Qaeda, Riedel had proposed that America seek to "disrupt, dismantle and destroy" the organization "and its affiliates" in Pakistan and Afghanistan. The classified paper used that language. On the morning Obama was to deliver his speech announcing the findings, Mike Mullen and Bob Gates from the Pentagon joined him. Twenty minutes before the president took the lectern, Mullen took him aside. Speaking for Gates as well, he said, "We don't like the term 'destroy.' It's a really high bar." Obama agreed to change the word to "defeat," a somewhat looser benchmark. Riedel, who was standing behind the president as this drive-by editing of his work concluded, thought to himself, "The U.S. military doesn't destroy things anymore?"

The hard focus on Al Qaeda and its allies raised another question: Did Al Qaeda's "affiliates" include the Afghan Taliban? This was undefined. From the beginning, Obama felt very strongly that the United States should *not* set an objective of defeating the Taliban, and he authorized background briefings to the press during Riedel's study emphasizing that his Afghan war would focus on Al Qaeda. That frustrated some at the Pentagon who wanted to take on the Taliban fully. Riedel himself saw no daylight between the Taliban and Al Qaeda. Indeed, Riedel's final draft endorsed a "fully resourced counterinsurgency

strategy" at least in southern Afghanistan. Yet this did not necessarily equate to a war aim of fully defeating the Taliban; it might be
enough, for example, to keep the Taliban at bay in the countryside
while eradicating Al Qaeda and its transnational terrorist allies. Because there was disagreement on the point the paper left it vague,
deliberately.[28]

What did "fully resourced counterinsurgency" war mean? This was
also undefined. Defense strategists often cited a ratio of 20 soldiers and
police to every 1,000 local inhabitants in estimating the requirements of
full counterinsurgency war. In that case Afghanistan might require as
many as 600,000 troops and police, an unrealistic number anytime soon.
The review elided this problem by defining the Afghan population base
to be secured and subdued—in Kandahar, Helmand, and areas of the
east—more narrowly. For example, it was not necessary to dispatch
counterinsurgency forces to the Panjshir Valley, which was calm and
whose population and leaders seemed firmly allied with N.A.T.O.

The vagueness suited Petraeus. Just before the president's public
speech, the Principals Committee approved a decision to send 4,000
more troops to Afghanistan, in addition to the 17,000 approved in February. Only Biden opposed this escalation, arguing that it was politically
unsustainable. Obama's top aides at the White House and Gates at the
Pentagon did not anticipate at the time they announced the Riedel review that Petraeus and Mullen would recommend sending yet tens of
thousands more troops in just a matter of months. They assumed the
commanders in the field would work with what they had. They were
wrong.[29]

Gates and Mullen decided they needed to replace General Dave
McKiernan, the American commander in Afghanistan. Obama
had now endorsed a counterinsurgency strategy, however undefined.
McKiernan was a conventional armored officer who had fought in Desert Storm. Like many of his generation in the Army, he had no experience with implementing counterinsurgency doctrine. He was a reserved

man, unaccustomed to interagency meetings, and he had never been to Afghanistan before his assignment to lead the war. Gates flew to Kabul and relieved him of command over dinner.[30]

Gates and Mullen had already settled on Stan McChrystal as Mc-Kiernan's successor. McChrystal's résumé as a hunter-killer in Special Operations left many colleagues doubtful about his ability to lead a strategy centered on winning hearts and minds. Yet McChrystal had served years in Afghanistan and his recent tour in Mullen's office at the Pentagon had exposed him to the ideas he would be expected to implement. Watching two policy reviews up close, he had found the process "awkward at best" and he "saw little enthusiasm" for what he sensed was going to be needed to succeed in Afghanistan. During a brief meeting at the White House, Obama offered no specific guidance, but thanked him for taking on the responsibility. On Capitol Hill, the longtime chair of the House Armed Services Committee, Representative Ike Skelton, told him, "All you have to do is win."

McChrystal flew to Brussels to meet Ashfaq Kayani. N.A.T.O. had invited Kayani to talk to the alliance's military leadership about his plans to win back control of Pakistani territory and to support N.A.T.O.'s effort in Afghanistan. Pakistan still provided N.A.T.O.'s principal land supply route to Afghan bases. As more American troops poured into Afghanistan after 2008, more supply ships arrived at Karachi ports carrying weapons, ammunition, fuel, food, and construction equipment. Pakistani trucks carried the goods hundreds of miles by road to U.S. bases.

Kayani asked the room of European generals, "What should be the measure of success?" He offered an answer: "Are we winning the public opinion or not?"

He urged N.A.T.O. to "look at the fundamental issues." If N.A.T.O. sent more troops to escalate the war in Afghanistan, while adhering to assumptions that turned out to be wrong, there would be serious consequences, not least for Pakistan's stability. What if the Bonn constitution's approach to centralized government concentrated in Kabul turned out to be wrong, and Afghanistan needed a much more decentralized system? What if the assumption that the Afghan National Army could be built rapidly into an effective fighting force turned out to be wrong? This is not like maneuvering a speedboat, Kayani said. The core assumptions of N.A.T.O. strategy had to hold up over four or five years.[31]

"The number of troops that you have—you won't be able to do it," Kayani said. "You have to control population centers and the roads that link them. But given the number of troops you have and the time constraints, you won't be able to do it."

Outside of Brussels, Kayani met separately with McChrystal, Mullen, and Petraeus. He wanted McChrystal to redirect the new American forces to the east, along the Pakistan border. "I'm in the F.A.T.A. already," Kayani said. "I can't pull out anytime soon. Go to eastern Afghanistan first, then go south." That would squeeze the militants in Waziristan who were rocking Pakistani cities.

McChrystal countered that Kandahar and Helmand were the "center of gravity" in the war, the Taliban's birthplace. "We have limited time. We have to hit the center of gravity."

"You don't identify the center of gravity for the purpose of attacking it," Kayani said, according to one participant. "You find ways to unbalance it without going straight at it." He might have been describing I.S.I.'s twenty-year strategy against Kabul. "This will become a revolving door in the south—you'll go in and out, the Taliban will go in and out."

The Americans were in no mood to take military advice from Kayani. Petraeus became aggravated. The last person he wanted advice from about the war in eastern Afghanistan was a general whose refusal to tear down the Taliban leadership in Quetta or to clean their militias out of North Waziristan was itself undermining N.A.T.O. strategy enormously. Pakistani sanctuaries were probably the biggest vulnerability in their military plan. The decision to go big in southern Afghanistan could not be undone, in any event. The Marines were in Helmand and Army task forces were headed to Kandahar. Petraeus made his irritation plain and Kayani went outside to cool off with a smoke.[32]

Kayani had to accommodate multiple American policies—Central Command's ambitious counterinsurgency against the Taliban, the C.I.A.'s lethal targeting of Al Qaeda by drones on Pakistani soil, the S-rap's improvisational diplomacy, Biden's blunt talk on behalf of the White House, and a push by the Defense Department's office in Islamabad to train Pakistani troops. "Ten Wars," Doug Lute's damning classified slide deck about N.A.T.O.'s fractured chain of command in Afghanistan, might easily be adapted to describe American policy in Pakistan. Bruce Riedel had written an abstract of unified strategy for Obama. But every American agency still ran its own war on the ground.

TWENTY-ONE

Losing Karzai

By 2009, the Arg Palace near Wazir Akbar Khan, where President Hamid Karzai lived, had recovered some of its grace from the degraded years of Taliban occupation. Palace staff tended the eighty-three-acre grounds, which held gardens, a pond, a mosque, and a parade ground. The staircase up from the main entrance displayed polished calligraphy inscribing "Allah" in gold script, ninety-nine different ways. The complex still contained a private residence for Karzai and his family. It also had to accommodate his official office, other offices for aides, and scores of security personnel. Karzai remained subject to a benign form of house arrest because of the risks of traveling outside. Kabul had evolved into a smoky, militarized city hunkered behind blast walls and razor wire. Tajiks in diverse hats wearing perpetual five o'clock shadows waved cars through checkpoints with the muzzles of their assault rifles. From his gardens Karzai could hear car horns, helicopter rotors, and the occasional distant thud of a suicide bomber.[1]

In his private quarters, the greatest change in Karzai's life was the arrival of his first son, Mirwais, born in 2007 to his wife, Zeenat. She was his first and only wife; Karzai had married her relatively late in life. Mirwais plainly brought joy to Karzai. Yet the president increasingly seemed a man who suffered. He was often ill with colds and sinus ailments. He kept vials of pills and vitamins nearby during his endless meetings. He struggled to eat enough, sometimes ordering cakes that he would finish off eagerly.[2]

Karzai had a soft, sentimental side. He read poetry. His British interlocutors catered to his fondness for an imagined England of warm beer and immaculate cricket pitches. The British ambassador once delivered a boxed set of Karzai's favorite television series, *Last of the Summer Wine*, a long-running middlebrow comedy about three friends in an English town.[3]

To relieve stress, Karzai would spend hours walking in the Arg gardens. It was little wonder that he displayed signs of agitation, given his constricted circumstances. Yet by 2009 Karzai's mood swings had become so visible and intense that it was no longer plausible to explain them merely as manifestations of cabin fever. The British government circulated reports that Karzai had been treated for psychological issues in Quetta and India earlier in his life, but the State Department could not document these accounts. In any event, there was no need for a medical record to confirm Karzai's volatility.

The president's inner circle by now consisted mainly of Pashtun technocrats dependent upon his patronage, men with no substantial popular constituencies of their own. They included Rangin Spanta, who had fled to Germany during the Soviet war, where he became a professor of political science and an activist in the Green Party before returning after 2001. There was Zalmai Rassoul, another foreign affairs adviser, who had become a medical doctor in France during his years of exile, before joining Karzai. There was Hanif Atmar, a capable administrator who had connections with the Communist regime during the Cold War and later worked at a Norwegian nongovernmental organization. Rahim Wardak, a general who defected to the mujaheddin during the Soviet war, served as Karzai's minister of defense. Umer Daudzai, a former administrator at the United Nations Development program, was his chief of staff. The Panjshiris who were still in Karzai's orbit, such as Amrullah Saleh at N.D.S. and Ahmad Zia Massoud, the first vice president of Afghanistan, saw the president less frequently, in formalized cabinet meetings or at national security briefings. The sense among them was that U.S. ambassador Zalmay Khalilzad's project to consolidate power for Karzai in

2004 had turned out to be a kind of ethnic putsch, reducing Tajik influence and elevating dependent Pashtuns around the president. Among the endless parade of foreign ambassadors and generals seeking Karzai's time, he often favored the Indians and the Turks, although he had little choice but to accommodate the relentless Americans.

Karzai raged openly at his aides, even in the presence of foreign visitors. His behavior became so bad that his aides and ministers arranged to discuss the problem at the compound of Kai Eide, the Norwegian diplomat who was the U.N. representative to Afghanistan. They were concerned that Karzai was sabotaging Afghanistan's relationship with the United States at a time when the country needed the alliance to survive and advance. In the garden, they asked, "What can we do with the President? We must stop this."[4]

They urged Eide to help. He wasn't sure he could. Eide counseled Karzai to raise his concerns about American conduct of the war in a less confrontational way, but as Karzai came to fear treachery by the Obama administration during the first half of 2009, he grew angrier and angrier.[5]

The president's aides were sympathetic, up to a point. They agreed that the international media and the United States had mistreated Karzai. As one minister put it, Karzai went "from an Afghan Mandela" in 2002 to "an Afghan Mugabe" in 2007. That was not fair. But during 2009, Karzai's own conduct crossed new lines.

"If we can't run the government, we should bring the Taliban back—to punish both the Americans and the Panjshiris," Karzai declared one day to this minister, as he recalled it.

Mirwais happened to be with them. "Do you want this boy to grow up under a Taliban regime?" the minister asked. "I don't want that for my son."

They took a walk in the palace gardens. "Mr. President," the minister said, "yes, I believe the United States was not fair to you. But they bring some good things. We should take some responsibility, too, for the things we have done wrong."

If the Kabul government collapses, he continued, "the U.S. will not be threatened, but we will be wiped out."[6]

In the first half of 2009, Karzai's principal goal was to be reelected president. The best evidence of his sanity was his tactical skill in service of this ambition. He maneuvered deftly to sideline potential rivals, one by one, without revealing his own designs until it was absolutely necessary. He seemed particularly worried about Gul Agha Sherzai, whom he feared Obama had anointed.

That spring, Karzai summoned Sherzai to the palace and demanded he withdraw from the presidential contest. Karzai's "tone changed from diplomatic to angry to desperate to threatening," as a U.S. embassy report put it. "The suddenness of his mood swings reportedly left most guests silent." Sherzai resisted Karzai's demand at first but then relented because he calculated "that Karzai's extreme behavior foreshadowed the lengths to which he would bully his competition."[7]

The American government increasingly regarded Karzai's psychology as a subject for all-source intelligence analysis. Greg Vogle, the reticent C.I.A. paramilitary fighter who had accompanied Karzai into Afghanistan in 2001, argued that the matter was not overly complicated: Karzai was a proud Afghan loyal to family, tribe, and country who felt profoundly disrespected. The National Intelligence Council circulated more elaborate analysis drawing on the work of Jennifer Lerner, a psychologist at Harvard's Kennedy School of Government who specialized in "decision science," and particularly the effect of stress and emotion on judgment. She documented that anger on the job may cause leaders to make riskier decisions. In Karzai's case, stress interacted with the president's increasingly independent-minded beliefs about Afghan history and regional geopolitics, the N.I.C. analysis held.[8]

Taliban propaganda constantly compared Karzai to Shah Shuja Durrani, a nineteenth-century Afghan king installed on the throne by imperial Britain. After the British withdrew from Afghanistan, Shuja was assassinated. There was also the example of President Najibullah, the Soviet client of the 1980s who had been hanged by the Taliban in the streets of Kabul after the Soviet Union collapsed. Particularly after 2008, Karzai worried acutely that civilian casualties caused by American air strikes and the deaths and arrests that took place during American Special Forces night raids would leave him badly exposed before the Afghan people, particularly before his own southern Pashtuns—another Shuja or Najibullah, complicit with the United States, the imperial power of his day. Karzai criticized the Pentagon about civilian casualties and night raids in public to establish credibility in an election year. He sometimes told American diplomats that this was all he was doing, that they should not take his rhetoric too seriously. This led some American policy makers at a remove from Kabul to conclude that Karzai was entirely in control of what he was doing, that his volatile moods were merely political theater. He was "not off his meds," as one senior Obama administration official put it, noting the consistency of Karzai's complaints about civilian casualties. "He was on his three-by-five card," repeating talking points.[9] But many Afghan aides and international diplomats who knew Karzai more intimately in Kabul thought that he was both tactically savvy *and* emotionally unstable.

Karzai believed that the United States might be an unreliable ally, even as Obama dispatched tens of thousands more soldiers to fight and possibly die on his behalf. In Karzai's thinking, Afghanistan was an essential prize in a new Great Game, as the nineteenth-century struggle by imperial powers for influence in South Asia was called. Afghanistan, Karzai thought, had now become a vital part of American schemes of worldwide power projection, a foothold for the United States to challenge Russia and China in the twenty-first century. This was an inflated, inaccurate understanding of Afghanistan's importance to the United States. In fact, although bipartisan elites in Washington believed in 2009 that it was both morally right and in the national interest to try to suppress the Taliban and establish stability and security in Afghanistan, they did not see a vital geostrategic interest in Afghan geography, beyond counterterrorism. The United States had more stable, accommodating allies of long standing in the Persian Gulf, particularly Bahrain, Qatar, and the United Arab Emirates, which provided air and naval bases. Having a few bases in Afghanistan would allow the United States to launch helicopter or drone attacks inside Pakistan, which was not possible from the Gulf, but it was not clear how important that would be over decades. Karzai, however, interpreted the continuing American intervention in his country as evidence of the latest imperial landgrab in Central Asia.

He was trapped by his position as the head of a weak client state, unwilling to be a stooge in an American colony but unable to stand on his own. He also believed by the spring of 2009 that the United States had tired of him and wanted to remove him from power. On this point he was on firmer ground.[10]

I t was in late 2008, as Zalmay Khalilzad served as the expiring Bush administration's ambassador to the United Nations, that G.C.H.Q., the British eavesdropping agency, first began to document calls Khalilzad was making to warlords and politicians around Afghanistan. Khalilzad was sizing up who might be interested in running for president in the summer of 2009, besides Karzai. It seemed unmistakable from the intercept transcripts that the former American ambassador to Kabul was exploring whether to run himself.

As an intelligence matter, it was an awkward situation. Under U.S. law, the National Security Agency was not supposed to seek out or report on the communications of "U.S. persons," meaning citizens or permanent residents, unless there was specific evidence of the person's connection to terrorism, espionage, or the like. The British were under no such restrictions. To defer to U.S. rules, however, when Britain shared intercepts involving Americans, the reports would typically leave out the overheard person's name, substituting "[U.S. Person]" instead. In this case, however, it was obvious from the context of the intercepts that the speaker was a high-ranking American diplomat based in New York with rich connections in Afghanistan. Just about everyone with access to such compartmented intelligence who was following Afghanistan knew Zalmay Khalilzad personally or by reputation. They could readily guess that he might be exploring a presidential run. If the United States wanted to dump Karzai and install a successor more firmly allied with American priorities, why not choose Khalilzad, who had already served successfully as a kind of viceroy in Kabul between 2003 and 2005?[11]

Karzai knew, too, about Khalilzad's telephone conversations. Many of the ministers and aides with whom Khalilzad spoke reported to the president about them, to protect themselves from allegations of treachery. When confronted privately, Khalilzad insisted that his probes were being misunderstood. He wasn't going to run. He had become an informal counselor to Doug Lute at the National Security Council. Khalilzad's exclusive back-channel reporting during visits to Kabul and over the telephone about who was in or out of the presidential sweepstakes provided unique insight to the White House. Even so, it was quite possible, many who knew Zal agreed, that the purpose of his calls was not just to feed the White House timely analysis but also to try to decide whether to throw his hat in.

"Watching Khalilzad," as a headline in a cable from the U.S. embassy in Kabul that spring put it, became an awkward subdivision of the intrigue surrounding Karzai's reelection bid. "Despite former U.S. Ambassador Zalmay Khalilzad's statements that he will not run, his activities and those of his supporters are watched carefully by the political class" in Afghanistan, the cable noted. While meeting with Afghan political figures, Khalilzad seemed to be trying "to persuade opposition figures to withdraw their candidacy to unite behind one candidate" to take on Karzai. Who did Khalilzad have in mind? He did not say.[12]

He was such an operator, had such a transparent love of political games, that he did not necessarily require a master plan—it would be enough to be in the mix, talking and playing the politics forward, to see where it all led. Karzai, for his part, believed that such a well-known representative of the United States would never consider running for president in Afghanistan without at least the tacit support of the U.S. leadership. By late spring, the situation was becoming clearer. The Obama administration—or, more precisely, Richard Holbrooke—clearly wanted Karzai out. He was neither for nor against Khalilzad. Holbrooke's attitude, recalled an adviser, was "the more people who challenge Karzai the better."[13]

David Miliband, the British foreign minister, and Sherard Cowper-Coles, now his special representative on Afghanistan, tried to convince Holbrooke early in 2009 that the presidential election should be postponed indefinitely and perhaps scrubbed altogether in favor of a new *loya jirga*, or traditional grand assembly. They argued that they were fighting a counterinsurgency campaign on behalf of a president who did not appear to have an adequate democratic mandate. The British advisers involved had divided views, but the most radical strain of thought held that the Bonn constitution ratified five years earlier should be reconsidered, to reduce the power of the presidency and strengthen the parliamentary and executive function of the cabinet, among other changes. This might allow Karzai to evolve into a symbolic and unifying role, akin to the former king of Afghanistan or the current queen of England or the president of India. That might in turn provide a face-saving way to remove Karzai from his position as the linchpin of N.A.T.O. ambitions in Afghanistan and allow more capable technocrats to run the government.

Holbrooke didn't want Karzai to return either and he appeared intrigued by the British proposal, but Hillary Clinton ruled the idea out. She did not want to be seen as interfering with the Afghan constitution. Beyond that, Clinton never fully bought the British argument that Karzai wasn't the right man and seemed to have a soft spot for him. She was always trying to understand his point of view. The British ended up in the "worst of all worlds," as one official involved put it, where their government was known privately to want Karzai gone (Holbrooke told Karzai as much, they believed), causing him to harbor even more of a grudge and more of a fantasy about perfidious Britain than he held already. Yet London lacked a plausible path to remove Karzai without American partnership.[14]

Holbrooke seemed to believe he could find a candidate who could defeat Karzai in the summer election, or at least use the specter of such a candidate to pressure Karzai to improve his governance. Holbrooke's methodology—diplomacy as jazz improvisation—in this instance threatened only to alienate Karzai and motivate his network of allies to generate fraudulent votes as a defense against any American scheme to overthrow him by ballot. In fact, Holbrooke had no rigorous plan for a successful electoral coup d'état. Nor did he have formal White House backing for his improvisations or any interagency plan to try to promote an opposition figure in the election. Some of the officials working with Holbrooke thought that he might have tacit backing from the White House, but Jim Jones, the national security adviser, thought it was clear that Obama opposed such maneuvering. Whatever his reasoning, Holbrooke repeatedly and indiscreetly told journalists in Washington that Karzai was "incompetent," that aides such as Ashraf Ghani or Hanif Atmar would govern the country much more effectively. Karzai said at one point that he had obtained accounts of a meeting between Holbrooke and Ghani during which Holbrooke said there "should be a change" in Afghan leadership, that the new president should be someone "with experience," and that Ghani should run.

"Before we took office everything was Bush's fault, but since we've been in government, everything is Karzai's fault," Barnett Rubin, a political scientist specializing in Afghanistan whom Holbrooke brought in as an adviser, remarked half jokingly that spring.

"You're learning," Holbrooke answered.[15]

In Kabul, Holbrooke asked Kai Eide, "Can we live with Karzai for another five years? Who would be the best candidate to replace Karzai?" Holbrooke answered his own question by mentioning Hanif Atmar as a possibility. He said that he intended to speak with Atmar about getting in the race. Atmar declined, and Eide guessed that Karzai learned about the solicitation before the day was out.

A little later, Eide ran into Ahmad Zia Massoud, the late commander's brother. "I must be the only person in Kabul whom Holbrooke has not invited to challenge Karzai for the presidency," Massoud remarked.[16]

Early in April, Holbrooke flew in to Kabul again and made an appointment to see Karzai at the Arg. Holbrooke asked the reception room to be cleared of Karzai's aides. He raised the issue of Karzai's half brother in Kandahar, Ahmed Wali, the notorious C.I.A. ally, typically referred to as "A.W.K.," who was "widely understood to be corrupt and a narcotics trafficker," as U.S. embassy reporting put it.

He had to go, Holbrooke insisted. "He's hurting you," he said. "He's holding you back" because of his visible involvement in racketeering.

"Everybody always says this," Karzai answered, "but nobody ever shows me evidence." He refused to budge.[17]

Despite his disillusioning early experiences in Vietnam, Holbrooke embraced an essential premise of counterinsurgency doctrine as applied to Afghanistan in 2009: It should be possible to reduce corruption and improve the effectiveness of the Karzai government in a matter of five years and, by doing so, suppress the Taliban's appeal and stabilize the country. Removing A.W.K. was just one plank in that campaign. Holbrooke's engagement with counterinsurgency doctrine that spring was complex. He was confident from experience that the war could not be won militarily. He believed, as he once told aides, that the military escalation David Petraeus and Stan McChrystal were promoting constituted "a national goal that we cannot achieve but that people will die for."[18] Yet he did not have President Obama's ear. Within the national security cabinet that spring, Petraeus, running all American military forces from Pakistan to Egypt, from Central Command, was the dominant figure. Holbrooke did not have the clout to successfully oppose a four-star general-hero's promotion of counterinsurgency doctrine, so he rode along, seeking to create space for himself as a notional Petraeus ally. His boss, Hillary Clinton, obviously retained presidential ambitions; for that reason alone, she was unlikely to defy Petraeus at a time when his ideas seemed triumphant and his popularity looked unassailable. Besides, the emerging plans for counterinsurgency in Afghanistan included a call for a "civilian surge" from the State Department in parallel to a military escalation, a form of diplomatic activism that Clinton favored. Given his constrained mandate as special representative, tackling the Karzai problem seemed to Holbrooke a way to make concrete progress and establish his own authority within "his lane," as Washington phraseology put it.

Over breakfast with Eide at one point, Holbrooke insisted, "I know how to handle Karzai."[19]

Yet as summer arrived Holbrooke's encouragement of opposition candidates remained unconnected to any plan by which one of them could win. It did not require secret information to discern that Karzai's backers were preparing to commit fraud to reelect him. Taliban violence all but assured that voting in Karzai's southern and eastern strongholds would be suppressed compared with the north of the country, where

Karzai's last-standing, most plausible rival, Dr. Abdullah Abdullah, drew
his greatest strength. Abdullah was of mixed ethnic heritage, and although he was associated with the factionalism of the Northern Alliance, he was educated, dignified, and able to speak to a wider narrative
of Afghan nationalism. Between his general appeal and the fact that his
strongholds were more peaceful, and therefore easier to vote in, than
Karzai's, the president's allies faced a problem. The situation was clearly
tempting southern and eastern governors loyal to Karzai to boost his
position through fraud and manipulation. As early as February 2009,
Martine van Bijlert of the nongovernmental Afghanistan Analysts Network published an extensive white paper reporting that an updated voter
registration drive might have produced up to three million duplicate voting cards ripe for abuse. In addition, she described how the strange system of "proxy" registration of female voters in Pashtun districts, designed
to protect the modesty of local women, was vulnerable to large-scale
fraud. There were many other reports signaling preparations for fraud in
open sources.[20]

Holbrooke backed the appointment of Peter Galbraith, who had
served as ambassador to Croatia during the Clinton administration, as
Kai Eide's deputy at the U.N. political office in Kabul. Galbraith took up
the fraud issue vigorously as Election Day neared. He and Holbrooke
believed that if they brought international pressure to bear, they could
disqualify fraudulent ballots and enforce a "clean" result, one that might
allow the winner—presumably Karzai—to enjoy legitimacy. Galbraith
insisted that the point was not to lift Abdullah to victory, but to prevent
Karzai from undermining himself by rigging an election he could win
cleanly. Holbrooke had gone looking for alternatives to Karzai in the
spring, it was true, but by June he and Galbraith had concluded that
their aspiration was fanciful. The mantra was to prevent Karzai from
"pulling a Nixon," that is, trying to steal an election he would still have
won if he had played it straight.

Abdullah mounted a spirited campaign. He held rallies in Kandahar
and sought to project a panethnic case for his election, to overcome his
history as a Panjshiri partisan. But in July, the International Republican
Institute and other American nongovernmental organizations released

polls showing Karzai with a commanding lead. Karzai had to win 50 percent of all votes cast to avoid a second round and the polls showed him close to that threshold.

On August 20, Election Day, the Taliban unleashed attacks around the country, killing two dozen Afghans and several N.A.T.O. soldiers deployed to provide security. Millions of Afghans braved the violence to cast ballots, yet turnout was a disappointing 35 to 40 percent, just over half of the turnout in the presidential election of 2004.[21]

Holbrooke flew to Kabul to monitor the voting. It was clear that the announced count would be compromised by fraud allegations. In an extreme case, Abdullah might mobilize supporters to riot in Kabul and powerful northern leaders such as Atta Mohammad Noor, the former Massoud ally who now governed Balkh Province, might back an armed coup d'état, Holbrooke warned. Intercepts showed that Iranian officials had told Abdullah that there should be "no unrest"; Tehran did not want chaos on its border any more than the United States wanted its project in Afghanistan to collapse. The "top priority," Holbrooke advised colleagues, should be that "no one goes to the streets." He had a proposal: Abdullah should decide to stay out of government, lead a peaceful opposition, and cede victory to Karzai.

The most remarkable aspect of Holbrooke's involvement in the election remained his indiscretion. On August 21, before any preliminary results had been released, but after Karzai had already claimed victory, Holbrooke organized a conference call with special representatives for Afghanistan from other N.A.T.O. and international governments. He held the call over open lines. From an intelligence collection perspective, Holbrooke might as well have stood in the middle of Kabul streets and spoken with a megaphone. Operatives from N.D.S. listened in and took notes. Karzai soon learned of the details.

Holbrooke laid blame for the mess on the Bush administration, because it had effectively forced the Obama administration to support a presidential election in this summer that was destined to make things worse. He emphasized that his fellow envoys should use their influence to make sure that no frustrated candidates or allied militias took their protests into the streets. "We have to respect the process," Holbrooke said. The outcome of the vote "will be disputed" because of fraud allegations already being voiced by Abdullah, Ashraf Ghani, and other trailing candidates. The envoys' common position should be to wait for a certified outcome, which might well include a second round of voting.

Only Abdullah had a prayer of winning in a second round, and even his prospects looked dim. Ghani, who had received less than 5 percent of the vote, urged Holbrooke into action, arguing that the election had been "entirely illegal."[22]

The next day, Holbrooke returned to the Arg to meet Karzai. Citing the conference call they had just listened to, Karzai's aides had informed the president that Washington and London were "pushing" for a second round. This may have been a distortion of Holbrooke's comments but it reinforced what Karzai already believed. Furious, Karzai had already tried to telephone world leaders, including Obama, to protest outside interference in the election. His advisers assured him that he had crossed the 50 percent threshold and had been reelected—any effort to suggest otherwise was an American conspiracy to unseat him.

Karzai's face darkened. He declared to Holbrooke, "I will not accept fake facts based on foreign interference."[23]

It required two months and countless meetings and threats to resolve the election. The essential problem was simple in form but very difficult to fix. Even setting aside the massive fraud carried out by Karzai's allies, the president had won close to half the vote. In a second-round face-off with Abdullah, Karzai would almost certainly prevail. Yet if the two election commissions overseeing the vote certified that Karzai had won outright in the first round, Abdullah and others "will say he stole it," as Holbrooke put it.

Karzai held firm, telling just about every diplomat who met him that the West was "trying to defeat him." Gradually, through September, the Obama administration came to accept reluctantly that Karzai would likely be president for another five years, and an even unhappier partner than before. "One way or another Karzai is going to be president of

Afghanistan," Holbrooke told a private meeting of former Clinton administration foreign policy officials and other specialists on Afghanistan
on September 12. "It's a fact."[24] The truth was that Holbrooke's improvisations during the election had not removed Karzai and only destabilized
further Karzai's strained relationship with the Obama administration.

Karzai was also suspicious of Karl Eikenberry, the retired general
who became U.S. ambassador to Kabul in the spring of 2009, succeeding
Bill Wood. Eikenberry knew Afghanistan from his three tours in uniform but in meetings with Karzai as ambassador he was stiff and formal,
marching through structured agendas and taking it upon himself to educate Karzai about how he should conduct himself as a statesman. Eikenberry had a well-grounded skepticism about Karzai but he was too much
a general to manage such an insecure and moody client.

Senator Chuck Hagel and Vice President Joe Biden recalled the role
John Kerry, now Biden's successor as chairman of the Senate Foreign
Relations Committee, had played in mollifying Karzai during their difficult dinner in the Arg early in 2008. Kerry flew in to Kabul in October.
The plan was to persuade Karzai to accept the recount; if he could
achieve that, he was confident that Abdullah would forgo a second vote,
to spare the country the risk of violence and instability.

Karzai was under enormous pressure. His standoff with Abdullah
revived the tension with the Panjshiris going back to 2002. Karzai's Pashtun aides worried that the Panjshiri groups backing Abdullah might act
rashly. Karzai's closest bodyguards included two Panjshiris who walked
beside him with loaded rifles. Panjshiri snipers manned positions on the
palace rooftops. They could take him out in an instant. The situation
recalled Indian prime minister Indira Gandhi's vulnerability after she
ordered a violent raid on a Sikh temple to root out armed separatists.
Two of Gandhi's Sikh bodyguards assassinated her. Karzai asked Rahmatullah Nabil, the trusted Pashtun who oversaw his personal protection, whether he should be worried. "Mr. President," Nabil told him,
"there are more than seventy Panjshiris around you. They are snipers,
drivers, they are manning the I.D. checkpoints." If he removed Panjshiris in the inner circle, he would "create a trust deficit" with all the
others. That would only make things worse. In fact, to signal trust and

his faith in the bodyguards' professionalism, Nabil *added* Panjshiris to Karzai's inner protection force. But the tension remained. Few presidential transitions in Afghanistan during the past century had occurred bloodlessly.[25]

Kerry walked with Karzai in the Arg gardens to try to resolve the stalemate. He discovered, however, that Zal Khalilzad was staying in the palace, dining with Karzai and counseling him as a friend. Khalilzad was now a private citizen, and he was in Afghanistan to work on a foundation to support education in the country. He always stayed at the palace as Karzai's guest, because of their friendship and for the sake of security. Yet the situation bordered on the absurd: Both Kerry and Khalilzad had access to Karzai at a decisive moment of crisis. Kerry told aides that he was unhappy about Khalilzad's presence because of the risk that it would create multiple channels of communication and confusion about who was talking to whom. He feared that whatever arguments he made to Karzai during his five-day marathon of garden walks, Khalilzad would unpack them over dinner and complicate Karzai's thinking.

Khalilzad met with Karl Eikenberry, who told him that the policy of the Obama administration was that no one had won the first round of the election; that there should not be a second round; and that, instead, Karzai should remain as president of Afghanistan and should appoint Abdullah as chief executive, with powers that would be negotiated with the help of the United States and the United Nations.

Kerry asked to meet Khalilzad at the U.S. ambassador's residence. They went out on the roof and talked. Kerry said his mission was to persuade Karzai to agree that he had not won the first round, to skip the second round, and to work out a power-sharing deal with Abdullah. Khalilzad advised against this strategy. He did not think Kerry could possibly persuade Karzai to go along.

Kerry said that President Obama had approved his approach. Then you should reengage with the White House and get new marching orders, Khalilzad insisted. Kerry said that would be difficult and asked Khalilzad to help him with the plan he had. Khalilzad declined. They agreed to remain in touch, but recognizing that Kerry was not receptive to his advice, Khalilzad left Kabul.

Kerry had always believed that Karzai was a nationalist at heart, and that the best course would be to appeal to his sense of Afghanistan's national interest. During their walks, he cited his own decision to accept his close defeat in the 2004 American presidential election, when some supporters had urged him to challenge electoral snafus in the decisive state of Ohio. "Look, we've all had some tough decisions to make about the outcome of elections," Kerry said. In the end, Karzai agreed to concede that he had not won the first round, and to allow the Obama administration to persuade Abdullah to stand aside, to avoid the violence and chaos of a second round. He would not consider the power-sharing plan Kerry had in mind.[26]

Despite their outrage at Karzai, Abdullah and other opposition powers such as Governor Noor had little incentive to attempt a coup. The Obama administration and N.A.T.O. and other allied governments had promised a major escalation of aid and military support if the election could be sorted out, a massive infusion of funds, manpower, and technology that might improve security and would certainly create economic opportunity for Kabul's elites. Twelve days after Kerry persuaded Karzai to agree to a second round of voting, Abdullah withdrew and declared in a press conference in his Kabul garden that he would lead the opposition to Karzai's second-term government peacefully.

To try to repair the damage with Karzai, the C.I.A. dispatched Greg Vogle for another tour as Kabul station chief soon after the election was settled. Vogle remained close to McChrystal, the new American war commander. Karzai might be a maddening partner, but any objective reading of his performance in 2009 had to account for the fact that he had outwitted his American doubters, including Holbrooke. He would be president for five more years. His half brother remained in power in Kandahar. His supporters in the south and east had gotten away with fraud. He had established himself with N.A.T.O. governments as intractable and independent minded, no longer pliant or passive, with new room to maneuver in Afghan domestic politics. The U.S. embassy, the State Department, and the White House might be frustrated and even disgusted with Karzai, but through his personal relationships with Vogle and McChrystal, he had also renewed private channels to the C.I.A. and the Pentagon, legendarily the true centers of American power. It was an outcome that other South Asian politicians with a bent toward conspiratorial thinking about America could only envy.

Holbrooke understood his own marginalization in Kabul. The State Department would be a "backseat driver in Afghanistan," he told his aides. American policy in the country was becoming a "runaway car" steered mainly by the Pentagon, under Petraeus's sway. He still saw room for diplomacy. With Mike Mullen, he could work to change the American relationship with Pakistan. And on his own, protected by compartmented secrecy, he could try to negotiate a way out of the war directly with the Taliban.[27]

TWENTY-TWO

A War to Give People a Chance

I n June 2009, Major General Michael Flynn arrived in Kabul as Stan McChrystal's J-2, or chief intelligence officer, in the Afghan war command. Flynn was a dark-haired, wiry, direct-speaking Rhode Islander who had grown up in a roughhousing family of Irish American brothers. He had been at McChrystal's side since 2004, largely engaged in door-kicking special operations in Iraq and Afghanistan. Those hard experiences had schooled Flynn about tactical intelligence for counterterrorist and counterguerrilla operations—tracing insurgents, managing interrogations, the surveillance of routes for attack or patrol, and looking out for enemy infiltrators.

Sunni and Shiite militias in Iraq, like the Taliban in Afghanistan, had bled American forces by embedding in local populations, deploying suicide bombers, and implanting improvised explosives where soldiers patrolled. By 2008, in much of Baghdad, at least, McChrystal and Flynn, along with Petraeus and his theater high command, had stitched together "I.S.R." systems—for intelligence, surveillance, and reconnaissance—that allowed commanders on secure bases to watch on television screens as guerrillas in nearby neighborhoods buried mines or maneuvered for ambushes. The surveillance systems included drones, blimps with digital cameras tethered to ground stations, blimps tethered to patrolling armored vehicles, and more traditional reconnaissance aircraft. Their

continuous video feeds shone on flat screens in "fusion centers" filled
with targeting analysts. The setup resembled the Global Response Center at C.I.A. headquarters in Langley or the joint intelligence operations center at Central Command in Tampa. The analysts in Iraq had
developed what McChrystal termed an "unblinking stare" at active battlefields or risky neighborhoods. On the inside, the facilities looked every bit as high tech and spookily omniscient as the imagined versions
conjured up in Hollywood thrillers like the *Mission: Impossible* series.
The I.S.R. systems had not provided a decisive answer to Al Qaeda
in Iraq or Shiite militias but they had certainly helped improve the
safety and offensive lethality of American and allied Iraqi forces in
Baghdad.

In Kabul, as he set up shop around the rose gardens and hammered-
together trailer parks of I.S.A.F. headquarters in the summer of 2009,
Flynn was stunned to discover how comparatively weak the Afghan
battlefield's I.S.R. systems were. American soldiers and Marines, as well
as British, Canadian, Dutch, and other European soldiers, were dying
and suffering catastrophic injuries in I.E.D. strikes because they could
not see from hour to hour what was happening around their bases or on
the roads they were ordered to patrol.

In Kabul that summer, a single, highly visible, $20 million aerostat
blimp hovered above Bala Hissar, a fourth-century fortress. Drifting on
a white line over crumbling mud-rock parapets, the blimp presented an
ominous image of N.A.T.O. technology, something from science fiction.
In fact it was a fairly straightforward aerial surveillance machine. Its
cameras were linked to a ground station that fed the imagery to I.S.A.F.
operations centers, providing live coverage of Kabul streets around the
clock, much like security cameras in office buildings or subways in New
York or London. But elsewhere in Afghanistan, there was not a single
blimp in operation. In addition, that summer, I.S.A.F. had but one or
two "lines" of drones, meaning pairs of machines and linked ground stations that could provide continuous, twenty-four-hour surveillance
wherever the drones were directed to fly. And, of course, in comparison
with Iraq, the Afghan battlefield was much larger and more dispersed.

Flynn's first advice to McChrystal was "We are blind on the battlefield and we had better move fast."

Flynn worked his classified e-mail and phones to call in favors from colleagues scattered worldwide. He tried to speed up the Pentagon's procurement and supply lines. He had an ally in Robert Gates, the defense secretary, who had ordered a crash increase in drone and other I.S.R. production when he arrived at the Pentagon in 2007. Yet it had taken time for manufacturing to catch up with his orders, and two years later supply was still inadequate.

Like a manic project manager building a secret television network, Flynn ultimately imported about 175 fixed and mobile aerostat blimps to Afghanistan. He became partial to the smaller aerostats that could be tied to patrolling armored vehicles and toted across the vast stretches of southern Afghanistan, providing over-the-horizon reconnaissance. (The blimps were visible, tempting targets for the Taliban and other Afghans with guns. Small rounds from assault rifles generally didn't damage the aerostats severely, but a rocket-propelled grenade could. Once, Flynn's team was visiting Kandahar when an intelligence unit reeled down a blimp for maintenance and found an arrow stuck in its skin.)

Flynn also created secret flat-screen-filled fusion centers packed with targeting analysts in Kandahar, Mazar-i-Sharif, and Herat. Simultaneously, I.S.A.F. and the C.I.A. expanded the number of Omega bases along the Pakistan border to about eight and linked them to drone and other surveillance and cell phone intercept systems. When Flynn and McChrystal first arrived in June, American forces had perhaps two full "strike packages" for offensive raids against Taliban commanders or units. (A strike package was a sizable integrated unit that included not just the men and helicopters to carry out lethal raids or searches but dedicated helicopter support, artillery units, interpreters, and intelligence.) They soon increased the number of strike packages to about fourteen.[1]

Yet as Flynn and his intelligence aides flew about Afghanistan building out infrastructure to support ramped-up kill-or-capture operations against the Taliban, they also became increasingly disquieted by I.S.A.F.'s lack of political and social insights about the enemy. Since 2002, for all the captains and Green Berets who had taken tea and chatted about tribes and development with local elders, the I.S.A.F. intelligence collection and analysis system remained overwhelmingly focused on tactical events—a shoot-out here, a bombing there, or reports on the component parts of the latest I.E.D. that had blown up. As Flynn put it starkly in a paper he coauthored in 2010, criticizing not only Pentagon intelligence but the C.I.A. and National Security Agency as well:

> Eight years into the war in Afghanistan, the U.S. intelligence community is only marginally relevant to the overall strategy. Having focused the overwhelming majority of its collection efforts and analytical brainpower on insurgent groups, the vast intelligence apparatus is unable to answer fundamental questions about the environment in which U.S. and allied forces operate and the people they seek to persuade. Ignorant of local economics and landowners, hazy about who the power-brokers are and how they might be influenced, incurious about the correlations between various development projects and the levels of co-operation among villagers . . . U.S. intelligence officers and analysts can do little but shrug in response to high level decision-makers seeking the knowledge, analysis, and information they need to wage a successful counterinsurgency.[2]

It was a stark, impolitic, even shocking summary of the American position in Afghanistan. The paper's boldness was characteristic of Flynn, a man not prone to self-censorship. It raised at least three fundamental questions about the Obama administration's incipient war strategy. If kill-or-capture operations were inadequate by themselves and if I.S.A.F. lacked basic insights into how those raids affected the social and political landscape, why was the United States doubling down on lethal operations? Was I.S.A.F. actually capable of acquiring the subtle insights Flynn listed concerning a society as complex and opaque to outsiders as Afghanistan's? And what *were* the most important insights about the Afghan public's likely reaction to a surge of U.S. forces? Nobody had

ever asked them whether they wanted so many ground troops in the
first place.

It did not require an expeditionary battalion of anthropologists and
political scientists to discover much of what was at issue. Daily reading
of *The New York Times*, *The Washington Post*, and *The Wall Street Journal*
alone would provide any Obama cabinet member a directionally reliable
sense of rising Afghan anger over civilian casualties and intrusive night
raids, at least in Pashtun areas of the country; popular disgust at the
predatory Afghan government and police; and declining faith that
American-led troops could defeat the Taliban.

If policy makers discounted journalism, they could read raw field
reporting from the State Department, C.I.A., and D.I.A. that documented the same attitudes. In Zabul, Special Forces raids and casualties
brought so many protesters into the streets at one point that the local
governor feared public outrage might tip the balance and hand the
Pashtun-dominated province to the Taliban. N.A.T.O. convoys following
safety protocols continued to flee the scene when they ran over Afghan
pedestrians or crashed into civilian taxis. Their lack of accountability
provoked angry Afghan mobs to gather and sack the next foreign vehicle
through.[3]

The same files documented the growing influence of the Taliban's
shadow governments around Afghanistan. Across the south, Taliban
commanders ordered commercial Afghan cell phone providers backed
by N.A.T.O. to shut down certain cell towers so that the guerrillas could
infiltrate for attacks without being tracked by their phone signals. The
Taliban destroyed switching stations if the carriers disobeyed.[4]

That summer in Helmand, as the Marines settled in, a State Department political officer touring the province described in a classified cable
the residue of British occupation in New Zad, once Helmand's second-
largest city, now "Fallujah-like," with packs of dogs roaming the streets,
dead trees in the fields, and buildings abandoned "amid piles of rubble."
The officer met with elders and mullahs on the town's outskirts and recorded the local Afghans' advice. They wanted security, strongly preferred Afghan forces to American Marines, noted the absence of any

Afghan government presence, and reported on the closure of all local schools, as well as the resilient influence of the Taliban. "We are like rocks here," one man said. "You kick us, the Taliban kick us, no one listens to us."[5]

From Tampa, Petraeus commissioned Marine Major General Douglas Stone to study Afghan prisons. In July, as Flynn and McChrystal settled in, Stone produced a seven-hundred-page classified report that shocked some of those in the Obama administration who read it. It found that Taliban commanders had effectively taken control of major Afghan prisons and were running sections of the war by cell phones from inside. (Hundreds of Taliban broke out of Sarposa Prison in Kandahar in the summer of 2008, the first of two mass escapes from that facility.)[6]

In July 2009, the National Security Council also reviewed intelligence reporting on "threat finance," meaning the Taliban's budget. The latest reporting listed the Taliban's key financial sources as fund-raising in the Persian Gulf emirates, including Saudi Arabia and the United Arab Emirates, which brought in an estimated $100 million annually, and then drug dealing, protection rackets, local taxation, extortion, and kidnapping. Doug Lute noted to an interagency meeting that the Taliban appeared to be succeeding with very lean operating funds: "We spend $60 billion a year," Lute remarked. "They need $60 million a year."[7]

Gates had formally tasked McChrystal to conduct an assessment of the war by the end of August. Mike Mullen, the chairman of the Joint Chiefs, asked Jeff Eggers, a Navy SEAL who had completed graduate studies at Oxford University, to join the command team as his strategic adviser. McChrystal also recruited Christopher Kolenda, a West Pointer who had graduate degrees in national security studies, to his Kabul headquarters. They flew around Afghanistan for three weeks of interviews and fact-finding. Stone's alarming prison study folded into their research. Following a model Petraeus pioneered in Iraq, McChrystal also invited sympathetic think tank specialists to Kabul to kibbitz about the study. It was a way to take outside advice but also to implant McChrystal's ideas with influential op-ed writers whose work might shape American public opinion.

McChrystal's effort constituted the third review of American strategy in the war in less than twelve months. As with the previous two, it suffered from a lack of clarity about the plausibility of counterinsurgency doctrine in Afghanistan. McChrystal was not necessarily advocating for a big war in Afghanistan. He was assessing the mission he had been given, in the form of the Riedel review. McChrystal knew he could not "defeat" the Taliban with the troops available, although it was not clear at this point whether that was truly America's objective. Taking into account the typical requirements of counterinsurgency, it would be impossible to provide enough capable troops—international and Afghan—to secure the entire Afghan population anytime soon. McChrystal solved this by identifying eighty "key terrain districts" out of the four hundred administrative districts in Afghanistan. These included many with urban populations in the south and east. There were an additional forty-one "Areas of Interest." Most of the territory in question lay in Helmand and Kandahar, as well as around Kabul and along the Pakistan border. The districts constituted a map of "ink spots" that might be secured and then linked together gradually through governance, aid, and security. Within this map the United States would now resource a new counterinsurgency campaign of a classical clear-hold-build-transfer type.

The eighty "key terrain districts" formulation, once accepted by the Pentagon and the White House, soon became an overdetermined engineering diagram. The plan birthed a jargon-filled language of acronyms and "District Stability Frameworks." Pentagon briefers would exclaim slogans such as "It's great to make sure the population is attached to the government." The plan also suffered from the decision made before McChrystal's arrival to deploy the Marines to Helmand. The entire province held just 4 percent of Afghanistan's population yet it contained half a dozen key terrain districts that would absorb a large share of the new American military resources. The Marines were in Helmand by order of McChrystal's predecessor and largely because their generals had demanded independence, or, as one of McChrystal's aides put it, "We need our own science project." The Marines were not even under McChrystal's command at this point; they reported directly to Marine leadership at Central Command in Tampa, Florida. The problem of fractured command identified in the last Bush administration review remained almost a year later.[8]

At least the key terrain districts formulation solved the counterinsurgency math problem—by reducing the geographical scope of the campaign, enough American, N.A.T.O., and Afghan troops might be identified to carry it out, in rough line with traditional troop-to-population ratios. What the plan could not solve was the absence of an Afghan government capable of receiving the "transfer" of security and governance once N.A.T.O. cleared, held, and built.

"Afghan capacity is an illusion," Sherard Cowper-Coles, the British envoy with two years of hard experience in Kabul, told Richard Holbrooke bluntly during a July 2009 meeting. The entire sequence of hold-build-transfer was "based on wishful thinking."[9]

"Mr. President," Lute advised Obama during this same period, "you can send a battalion of U.S. Marines, not only anywhere in Afghanistan, but literally anywhere in the world, and they will clear an area. Anywhere in South-Central Asia, a battalion of Marines is going to be so tactically dominant that they can clear that area. And as long as you are willing to keep them there, they can hold it. . . . The problem is handing the cleared area to the Afghans and doing something with it."[10]

McChrystal and Flynn and their allies had two ideas about how to prove the doubters wrong. One was to attack corruption in Afghanistan and promote good governance. Their other idea was less conventional: McChrystal would listen to Hamid Karzai's advice and make a concerted effort to reduce civilian Afghan casualties in the war, to try to make the American military presence more welcome and sustainable. "What is it that we don't understand?" McChrystal asked colleagues at I.S.A.F. that summer. "We're going to lose this fucking war if we don't stop killing civilians."[11]

As a career door kicker, McChrystal had the credibility to promote what he called "courageous restraint" in Afghanistan, even if it occasionally meant walking away from a firefight with the enemy. He hosted dinners with Afghan human rights advocates and European civil society groups to listen to their ideas about how to find a better balance between the use of force and the protection of civilians. Yet McChrystal endured grumbling and skepticism from the start within his own I.S.A.F. command, particularly from the Marines. Their doctrine emphasized merciless combat; they worried that the Taliban would exploit any new tactical rules promoting battlefield restraint. It was doubtful that there *was* a form of just-violent-enough warfare carried out by foreign armies and air forces that could inspire confidence among beleaguered, rural Afghan Pashtuns.

On August 30, McChrystal submitted his "Commander's Initial Assessment" to Gates. An unclassified version of the report ran sixty-six pages. "Many indicators suggest the overall situation is deteriorating," the commander acknowledged. "We face not only a resilient and growing insurgency; there is also a crisis of confidence among Afghans." A "new strategy" was now required, one that would rapidly train Afghan forces to take the lead from N.A.T.O. while foreign forces, during the transition, carried out "classic counterinsurgency operations" in which "our objective must be the population."

"Success is achievable," McChrystal assured his superiors. It would require recognizing civilian casualties as a strategic issue, addressing Flynn's insights about the failures of intelligence, and refusing to accept any longer "abuse of power, corruption or marginalization."[12]

Karzai warmed to McChrystal that summer, even as he raged at Holbrooke over the envoy's scheming to dump him. Yet as McChrystal sent his analysis to Washington, he discovered that Hamid Karzai's vision of the Afghan war was fundamentally at odds with the precepts of his campaign plan.

During the last week of August, McChrystal, Greg Vogle, Ambassador Karl Eikenberry, and a few of their aides arrived at the Arg Palace to brief Karzai on McChrystal's completed assessment of the war. They assembled around a table in Karzai's small conference room next to the main cabinet room. McChrystal had distilled his study into about twenty PowerPoint slides. He presented them for about ninety minutes.

Eikenberry watched Karzai. At first, the president's facial expression suggested that he might be thinking, "Why don't I have a staff that puts up slides that look this good?" The president took out a notebook and started scribbling.

"Mr. President, do you have any questions?" McChrystal asked at last.

"Two, general. You say the situation is bad and getting worse. I disagree. You say the situation is 'dire.' Are you going to make the briefing public?"

McChrystal said he was, in summary form.

"We have to think about this," Karzai continued. "We don't want the Afghan public to panic. Is there another word for 'dire'?" This inaugurated a search for euphemisms.

Karzai went on to a more fundamental observation. "You call this an insurgency," he said. "This is not an insurgency. An insurgency, as I understand the meaning, suggests there are citizens of a country who are fighting against their government because they think the government is illegitimate. Now, we are a conservative, simple Muslim people. If they are fighting against an illegitimate government, then who are you, the United States? You are propping up an illegitimate government. No. There is no insurgency. There is a problem of international terrorism. We are allies in a battle against international terrorism."[13]

Karzai believed, like many other Afghans, that the true story of the war—the essential problem—was not his own legitimacy but the mysterious unwillingness of the United States to challenge I.S.I. and Pakistan. Karzai did not seem to see himself as Afghanistan's commander in chief. He eschewed the martial symbols of a wartime head of state. He didn't seem sure that the Taliban and other fellow Afghans his security forces fought were truly enemies; they were merely the misguided hired hands of Pakistan.

Perhaps the boldest of McChrystal's promises in his Commander's Initial Assessment concerned Pakistan. The report's key sentence was convoluted: "While the existence of safe havens in Pakistan does not guarantee I.S.A.F. failure, Afghanistan does require Pakistani cooperation." Essentially, McChrystal asserted that the United States could achieve its goals even if the I.S.I. continued to provide the Taliban sanctuary.

Karzai believed that Pakistan should be the main effort of the American war. As Eikenberry once put it to him, "If you had a choice about where to deploy thirty thousand new American troops, you would put five thousand into training Afghan forces, five thousand along the border with Pakistan, and twenty thousand in the Federally Administered Tribal Areas," inside Pakistan.

"That's exactly the point," Karzai answered. "You're fighting a second-best strategy. You're fighting Taliban foot soldiers in Afghanistan and destabilizing the country. You can't play the game of saying Pakistan is your ally and telling me in private that they're not."[14]

For his part, Eikenberry doubted that McChrystal's strategy could succeed. Along with Doug Lute and Joe Biden at the White House, he was a well-placed and increasingly vocal skeptic of the premises of counterinsurgency in Afghanistan. Among other things, the ambassador agreed with the C.I.A.'s Vogle and Wood that the Taliban insurgency could not be defeated unless the movement's sanctuary in Pakistan was eliminated or at least badly disrupted.

Immediately after the meeting with Karzai in late August, Eikenberry wrote a series of three highly classified cables laying out his concerns. They were pursuing a war strategy that Karzai did not endorse. (Unlike a later cable Eikenberry wrote that fall containing similar analysis, this one did not leak.) McChrystal's war strategy was premised on Karzai's reliability, but the ambassador worried that Karzai's growing waywardness did not seem to be registering with Obama's cabinet and White House advisers. He tried to address this by inviting note takers to his meetings with the Afghan president. Eikenberry instructed the aides to write down Karzai's extemporaneous remarks verbatim. Then he ensured that the classified cables contained long paragraphs of Karzai's raw speech. He hoped it would shock Washington into recognition. He certainly got McChrystal's attention. The commanding general reacted furiously to Eikenberry's analysis and took the criticism personally. But Eikenberry and colleagues at the embassy felt the military wasn't taking their views seriously. Karzai was playing the Americans by always scheduling separate one-on-one meetings with the ambassador, Greg Vogle, and McChrystal. One view at the highest levels of the U.S. embassy in Kabul by summer's end was that Karzai "was a very clever madman—just because he was insane doesn't mean he was stupid."[15]

Every Monday at 5:00 p.m., Holbrooke assembled five dozen or so aides and outsiders at a "shura" meeting in Hillary Clinton's principal conference room at the State Department. The purpose was to drive policy execution about Afghanistan and Pakistan across the government. On other days, Holbrooke ran smaller shuras to discuss sensitive subjects. Senator John Kerry attended one Wednesday that summer and asked Frank Archibald, the C.I.A. liaison to Holbrooke's office, about the "'humint' situation in Afghanistan," meaning human intelligence collection. Archibald said Kabul Station was "good" on counterterrorism, palace and electoral politics, and was "working on" Iran's activity in the country. An "increased number" of analysts and officers were now "looking at the Taliban," Archibald added.[16]

Mike Flynn wanted 360-degree intelligence collection about Afghanistan's society and economy, from subtribal loyalties to graft networks that alienated the public. Holbrooke was curious about all that too but he was more interested in finding deeper insights into the Taliban's leadership. Like Flynn, Holbrooke could see that battlefield intelligence produced reams of information about Taliban commanders and tactics but hardly any insight about the movement's Pakistan-based leaders or their political and military strategy. Pakistan was no help on this score. Its army officers continued to inform American counterparts that autumn "that the Quetta Shura is a fiction," as one Pakistani brigadier put it, nothing more than an "unsubstantiated fabrication." Unfortunately, the United States had "fallen victim to rumors" that the Taliban's leaders had a base in Pakistan, the brigadier said. Holbrooke chuckled at the denials but noted that, "on analysis, what they really deny is the word 'Quetta.'" That was a fair point because many Taliban leaders appeared to live in Karachi, where they were even harder to trace. Pakistani generals had been lying to American counterparts about their support for the Taliban since the movement's birth in 1994. It was evidently a hard habit to break.[17]

I t was not until they received McChrystal's dire assessment of the war that Lute and other aides to Obama understood that their field commander and Petraeus intended to recommend that tens of thousands *more* American troops be dispatched to Afghanistan to carry out the "key terrain districts" counterinsurgency strategy. Until then, the White House had thought the troops Obama ordered forward in February and March were all that would be required. At the time of the Riedel review in April, neither Gates nor Petraeus had said they would be looking for more soldiers. Petraeus, however, had been careful to make no promises. Informally, McChrystal now let the White House know that he might request up to eighty thousand more American troops. To Biden, Lute, and other skeptics in the White House, the news was stunning. Robert Gates, too, at the Pentagon, was surprised by the request.[18]

Amid rising mistrust among his key war advisers, Obama ordered, through Jim Jones, yet another interagency review of strategy in September to digest McChrystal's report from the field and to decide the question of more troops. Lute directed the process from his cramped office in the West Wing, fifty feet from the entrance to the Situation Room, between a men's restroom and the White House mess. He drew support from the N.S.C.'s Afghanistan-Pakistan directorate next door in the Eisenhower Executive Office Building.

To prepare, Hillary Clinton convened a lengthy meeting at Foggy Bottom with her senior advisers to hash out the State Department's positions. Deputy Secretary of State James Steinberg, Deputy Secretary Jack Lew, Policy Planning director Jake Sullivan, Holbrooke, and several of his aides joined a half-day summit. Eikenberry connected by secure video from Kabul, Anne Patterson from Islamabad. Almost all of them agreed that military pressure was necessary to roll back the Taliban, but they also agreed that McChrystal's plan alone was insufficient. Clinton would propose a complementary plan of regional diplomacy, including efforts to talk to and pacify the Taliban. She would push as well for a much stronger focus on the alliance with Pakistan—a "new partnership," as Clinton would put it, with more civilian aid, more military aid and training. Her draft plan was essentially a less militarized expansion of the Plan Colombia–inspired strategy for Pakistan conceived by the Bush administration in its final years.[19]

On September 30, Obama presided over the first formal war strategy review session in the Situation Room. The president declared at the outset that the United States would not abandon Afghanistan. Peter Lavoy, now running analysis in the Office of the Director of National Intelligence, presented an intelligence briefing derived in part from the C.I.A.'s updated District Assessments maps. The Taliban controlled or contested between one fourth and one third of Afghan territory and controlled or. influenced about a third of the Afghan population, Lavoy said. The intelligence community's best judgment was that there was no chance the Taliban could take over all of Afghanistan anytime soon, but the guerrillas could gain enough influence in Kandahar, the Taliban's birthplace, to establish a refuge and create strong new momentum for their insurgency.

Lavoy tried to lead the principals and their key deputies—Obama, Biden, Clinton, Gates, James Jones, Panetta, Mullen, U.N. ambassador Susan Rice, Holbrooke, Lute, and others, along with Petraeus and McChrystal from Central Command—through a kind of seminar. At its heart lay the problem of war aims. The purpose of the war in Afghanistan was to disrupt, dismantle, and defeat Al Qaeda and its affiliates. But what did this stated resolve about "affiliates" imply, exactly, about the war against the Taliban? The Pentagon presented a PowerPoint slide displaying numerous American statements and policy declarations over the years showing that, whether they wanted to admit it or not, United States policy had long been to defeat the Taliban. That gave the group in the Situation Room pause because they knew the goal was implausible. Gates, who had served at the C.I.A. and the White House as the Soviet war in Afghanistan faltered, worried that it was too ambitious to try to defeat the Taliban. The movement was "part of Afghanistan," he said at one point. He led the cabinet toward an agreement that while they should continue to try to defeat Al Qaeda, with the Taliban, the objective should be to "degrade" the movement and "reverse its momentum."

Several times over the next few weeks, Lavoy spread out the C.I.A. maps and walked the group through the history and fundamentals of Islamist political violence in South Asia. He reviewed the demographics of "Pashtunistan," the overlapping areas of Afghanistan and Pakistan where tribally organized Pashtuns lived. Two thirds of Pashtuns were in Pakistan, not in Afghanistan, he reminded the group.

Millions of Afghan refugees from the Soviet war had married and settled in Pakistan, some sending their sons to work in the Persian Gulf. After their rise in the 1990s, the Taliban built networks and found sympathy or support within this diaspora, from Dubai to Karachi to Quetta to Kandahar. The Taliban's "sanctuary" involved more than just training camps and safe houses in Baluchistan or Waziristan. They had depth. They were also not the same as Al Qaeda, Lavoy reminded them. They might have provided sanctuary to Al Qaeda but they had not joined in the September 11 attack and they did not promote war outside Afghanistan.

The maps and Lavoy's demographic and historical briefings made plain to almost everyone—although Petraeus and McChrystal seemed to be exceptions—that there was no way to defeat the Taliban militarily, to eradicate them or force their surrender, unless the United States was prepared to invade Pakistan, an unstable nuclear weapons state. Obama ruled that out. That implied that the goals of the Afghan war had to be reduced to something less than the Taliban's full military defeat. Either that or Pakistan's army had to finally take on the Taliban, to wipe them out.[20]

Obama scrutinized the puzzle diligently. He hauled away fat briefing books to the White House residence and came back with notes indicating that he had read them carefully. He detected some of the contradictions. The briefing books reported, for example, that General Ashfaq

Kayani and the Pakistan Army would take the United States seriously only if Obama showed staying power. Yet the same books reported that Kayani and his high command did not want the United States to send yet more combat troops into Afghanistan. How was this to be squared? Obama tried to focus several sessions of the review on Pakistan and India. He was frustrated that he kept getting back analysis that as long as Pakistan's strategic focus was on India, the army would never end support for the Taliban or allied groups. No one predicted that the relationship with India and Pakistan was going to improve quickly, yet no one had new ideas about how to manage that problem in Afghanistan.

They all agreed that Pakistan required another huge infusion of American aid to help the country defeat its own Taliban insurgents. Anne Patterson, the ambassador in Islamabad, warned against putting too much faith in Pakistan's civilian government. "Let's not fool ourselves that we have a democracy" to work with in Islamabad. The United States had to work with the Pakistan Army. More money would not purchase the generals' love, however. "We can't buy our way out on the core goal," she said.[21]

Here were more contradictions to consider, dating back to the early 1980s and the anti-Soviet jihad in Afghanistan. The United States judged Pakistan's army to be its essential partner, to be resourced above all other Pakistani institutions, yet the United States also wished for a more effective civilian government in Islamabad. As in earlier eras, Obama's advisers had convinced themselves that Kayani and Pasha were with them, at least to an adequate extent, or else, if they weren't, that the United States had no choice but to forge ahead and achieve what might be possible. Jim Jones had grown steadily convinced that I.S.I. was not an American ally, but he reported to the principals that autumn that he also saw "real progress with I.S.I." Biden said that when he spoke with Pasha, the I.S.I. chief had told him, "Let's kill Mullah Omar and move on Haqqani too."

On September 28, Kayani told Mullen over a secure telephone line that he might be willing to go after the Haqqanis. This was progress, Mullen felt. The Pakistan Army was still reeling from its war against domestic insurgents. At last, Pakistan "fears Mullah Omar," Biden thought.[22]

If the National Security Council had taken a ride up Connecticut Avenue to the embassy of Pakistan, and had gone for a leisurely walk with the Pakistani ambassador, away from the listening devices he feared were implanted in his office by I.S.I., they would have heard a different analysis. Husain Haqqani, the ambassador, was a former journalist and a persistent critic of the Pakistan Army who had landed in Washington after Asif Zardari's election.

One day in October, as the White House review went on, Haqqani received a visitor in his office. He handed over an old newspaper clipping about the "shadow games" within Pakistan's deep state—for instance, the bugging of rivals' offices in Islamabad.

Haqqani pointed to the ceiling, to indicate the presence of listening devices.

"Pakistan's army is determined to fight the Pakistani Taliban," he said loudly, as if speaking to the microphones. Then he mouthed Kayani's name silently and patted his shoulders, like a charades player trying to mime "epaulets." Haqqani silently mouthed words to make clear that Kayani would not fight the Afghan Taliban. The Obama administration had to understand that "shadow games" persisted.[23]

On October 8, General McChrystal formally presented to the National Security Council three options for more American troops in Afghanistan. In the most aggressive plan, he would require about eighty thousand additional soldiers. In the middle case, he would use forty thousand to secure the eighty key districts he had identified in the east and south. At the low end, in a plan put forward by Joint Chiefs vice chairman James Cartwright, he could try to deploy about ten thousand to resource fewer key districts, although the chances of success would be lower. From then on, the strategy review often devolved into discussions about troop deployments, "critical districts," and numbers.

Holbrooke raged privately at McChrystal's Goldilocks-inspired proposal, telling aides it was "one of the shabbiest intellectual presentations of all time." Clinton, however, leaned toward recommending forty thousand more soldiers, the middle course. She seemed reluctant to break with the Pentagon as she also advocated for complementary diplomacy and a "civilian surge." Following on the Bush administration's late interest in accelerating Afghan reconstruction, the Obama administration pushed through $4 billion in fresh funds for the fiscal year beginning that October. Clinton seemed careful about the record she was creating at such a critical juncture of war-or-peace decision making.

Petraeus yielded little. "We can't wait one day," he insisted at one session, urging more troops. Without them the war would fall into "a death spiral."

They all agreed that something had to be done about corruption in the Karzai government. Yet the cabinet did not examine in any depth how billions of dollars in international aid or C.I.A. covert counterterrorism armies or the massive numbers of security and Western transport contractors flying back and forth each day between Kabul and Dubai might be incentivizing and creating corruption. "So much nonsense," Holbrooke fumed.[24]

The war review meetings in the Situation Room dragged on—there were eventually ten of them, totaling about thirty hours. By October's end, Clinton had grown frustrated by the review's drift away from diplomacy and the challenge of Pakistan. She directed Holbrooke's office to produce a bound volume of every paper she had submitted to the White House that fall, as well as supplementary memos and slide decks. She said she wanted to ensure there was a record that at least her department had attempted to discuss issues other than troop numbers. An aide hand-delivered the volume to the West Wing office of Jim Jones. The White House never responded.[25]

In November, Jones flew to Pakistan bearing a letter from Obama to President Asif Zardari. Protocol required an exchange between counterparts, but the real audience for Obama's correspondence was Kayani. The letter's essence, as Holbrooke summarized it, was "We want to listen to your strategic terms" for a peaceful settlement in Afghanistan. "Tell us what they are."

Holbrooke flew to Pakistan next. He dined for four hours with Kayani and Pasha. They delivered the first draft of an answer: "It was all India all the time," Holbrooke recounted. "The Pakistanis see everything through the prism of India." The specifics included Kashmir, their access to water from Indian glaciers, and whether Afghanistan would be governed by the likes of Amrullah Saleh and other perceived Indian allies. Kayani's goal, Holbrooke thought, was to "get us to lean on the Indians. Fool us a little. Play us against ourselves. The usual game." Holbrooke's solution was to "concentrate on one issue," the fact that "the Pakistanis believe that if we leave [Afghanistan], the Indians are going to move in."[26]

Kayani told McChrystal privately in the midst of the autumn review that the most important issue in the Afghan war was whether there was a "perception that the U.S. was winning." Without that perception the Taliban would never give up violence or consider a political compromise. He might as well have been speaking about the I.S.I. as well. Yet at the end of his review, Obama reached a decision that made clear that the United States did not intend to "win" the war in a conventional military sense.[27]

The final written documents and orders to come out of the review redefined America's objectives so as to eschew victory over the Taliban. The goal instead would be to "reverse the Taliban's momentum" and deny the guerrillas access to major cities and highways. Outside the key terrain districts, the goal would be merely to "disrupt" the Taliban and prevent Al Qaeda from recreating a sanctuary on Afghan soil. It was explicitly not the objective of the United States to "defeat" the Taliban. That would be left to the Afghan National Army after the bulk of American troops began to withdraw, starting in 2011. Therefore, another key objective of American troops surging into Afghanistan would be to train and prepare the Afghans to carry on the long war to a successful conclusion, largely on their own.

The Obama war cabinet had concluded more or less by consensus that there was no purely military solution to the problem of the Taliban. The ambivalence of the president and his most senior White House advisers exacerbated the gap between them and the uniformed commanders they relied on. Obama felt fully committed to the destruction of Al Qaeda and he supported efforts to give the Afghan government and security forces a chance to take charge. Yet Obama was simply not invested in a military mission designed to defeat the Taliban. His aides saw the Pentagon's uniformed commanders—Petraeus above all—as hubristic about what they had accomplished in Iraq and unrealistic about Afghanistan. Every time the generals would brief him in detail about how counterinsurgency would work, step by step, in Afghanistan, Obama would become more skeptical, particularly about the amount of resources that would be required to make sustainable progress. Petraeus's view was: *I'm the only one in this room who has been to war. What do you want to do? Quit? We have a mission. What are your ideas to achieve it?* The more the back-and-forth went on, the more Petraeus and his command came to see Obama and his aides as indecisive naysayers, carpers from the sidelines with no constructive alternatives to the war they were charged to fight.

In late November, Obama made an additional decision: He would announce in advance that American troops would start to withdraw in 2011. It was odd on its face for a president to order American soldiers into harm's way for an urgent national security cause while simultaneously naming a date when those interests would be achieved sufficiently for the troops to start to go home. Obama's rationale was twofold. He wanted to force the Afghans into recognition that they had to prepare quickly to take responsibility for the war against the Taliban and for successful governance. He also wanted to ensure that the generals could not maneuver the White House into extensions of time or further increases in troop numbers. The United States remained in the grip of its worst economic crisis since the 1930s. Democrats in Congress were increasingly restive about the Afghan war. Obama derived the 2011 date from the Pentagon's own internal documents, which stated that adequate progress should unfold by then if a troop surge was approved. Gates, too, had advised that if the surge of troops was not making progress by mid-2011, two years after the first Marines went in, then that would be a good indicator that the plan was not working. Obama decided to bind the military to its own predictions.[28]

The problem with announcing a withdrawal date was the effect it would have on Kayani and his corps commanders. They already believed that the American project in Afghanistan was destined for failure, and that its collapse might saddle Pakistan with yet another wave of turmoil. By making clear that the United States was going home, Obama would affirm the I.S.I.'s convictions and redouble the service's incentive to aid the Taliban as a means of Pakistani influence in post-American Afghanistan.

Obama chose to keep his own counsel on his decision to announce a date for the start of withdrawal. At the final review session in the Situation Room, on November 23, the subject never arose. The main question remained how many more troops to dispatch. The range of proposals on the table had by now narrowed to between twenty thousand and forty thousand.

On Sunday, November 29, Obama held a secure videoconference with Eikenberry and McChrystal. They sat in Kabul, in the U.S. embassy's classified conference room, as Obama's face appeared alone on a flat-screen monitor. The "feeling was strangely intimate," as McChrystal put it. Obama explained that he had decided to send thirty thousand more American troops to the war. His administration would also try to round up as many as ten thousand more from N.A.T.O. allies, to come closer to McChrystal's forty-thousand-troop option. Obama now also disclosed his intention to announce publicly that American troops would start heading home in July 2011.

McChrystal told him that such an announcement "would give the Taliban the sense that if they survived until that date, they could prevail" and it "might decrease confidence" among Afghan allies.

Obama asked McChrystal point-blank if he could live with the decision as outlined. McChrystal said yes. He wrote later that if he had felt that an announcement of a withdrawal date "would have been fatal to the success of our mission, I'd have said so."[29]

At around 5:00 p.m. that same afternoon in Washington, Obama summoned Gates, Mullen, Petraeus, Biden, Lute, and a few others to the Oval Office. He handed out draft orders. He said his strategy did not constitute fully resourced counterinsurgency or open-ended nation building. He asked each of them directly if they could carry out the strategy as described, including his intention to announce July 2011 as the start of a withdrawal. Petraeus was stunned by the figure of just thirty thousand more troops; it seemed to him to have been plucked from thin air. They all said yes. Petraeus thought it was not a choice. It was either take the thirty thousand or nothing at all.[30]

Obama told his advisers, "I think I have to do this," because the war was deteriorating so badly that if he didn't "do something to at least create some space, this whole thing could collapse." The troop surge was a holding mission necessary to allow the counterterrorism mission—drone strikes, primarily—to decimate Al Qaeda and to give Afghan security forces a chance to succeed. The Pentagon's commanders had bigger ideas. They had been trained at West Point and elsewhere to win large conventional wars, not manage expeditionary counterterrorism missions rife with contradictions and subtleties. They also knew that fighting wars successfully required confidence, momentum, sacrifice, and ambition— a rallying cause. They chafed at constraints.

The next day, Obama spoke to Karzai by secure video. Karzai's inauguration to a second term as president had lately reduced his state of aggravation. He had won power for five more years. As a practical matter, he needed the United States to survive, however distasteful and irritating that dependency might be to him. He now told Obama he was ready to publicly support the American troop surge, or, at least, this was how Obama's aides understood him. He repeated once more, however, according to a contemporary record, that the "military and political dimensions of achieving peace in Afghanistan can't be addressed unless the issue of sanctuary in Pakistan is made explicit and is a priority in the new strategy." (Years later, Karzai would ascribe a different emphasis to his views about the Obama troop increase. His goal, he recalled, was to reduce the American military "footprint," garrison the American troops on bases, and ensure that there were "no troops in our villages or towns."

In any event, he was out of sync with Washington; the counterinsurgency doctrine Obama had partially endorsed turned on pushing troops into villages, towns, and urban neighborhoods.)[31]

McChrystal flew that day to Rawalpindi to brief Kayani on Obama's decisions. The Pakistani general said once more that the United States "lacked the time to accomplish all that was necessary." Kayani also said again that he did not think the United States could build up effective Afghan security forces to carry on the fight against the Taliban after N.A.T.O. departed. McChrystal left thinking that "our chances were better than he believed."[32]

On December 1, on prime-time television, Obama delivered a solemn speech at West Point. He announced, "As Commander-in-Chief, I have determined that it is in our vital interest to send an additional 30,000 U.S. troops to Afghanistan." In the very next sentence, without any prologue or clarification, he added, "After 18 months, our troops will begin to come home."

He spent the next several minutes emphasizing how agonizing his choices had been. Obama's going-in-while-going-out decision reflected his temperamental search for middle ground and consensus, his reading of domestic politics, and his painstaking study of the Pentagon's claims and plans for the war, about which he retained skepticism.

"He made an amazing decision," Holbrooke explained to a visitor soon afterward. "To send thirty thousand troops and announce the withdrawals would start in eighteen months—no one's ever done something like that." In Holbrooke's judgment, "The Taliban was not the audience. The primary audience was the American public and the Congress. The secondary audience was the Afghans, to tell them they had to really focus on Afghan National Security Force training. The more complicated audience was the rest of the world, starting with the Pakistanis and the Iranians, who were of course thoroughly befuddled. . . . It was, all things considered, the best course to take . . . a very interesting idea. So far as I can tell it came directly from the president."[33]

In Kabul, on the morning after the West Point address, in the classified command center of I.S.A.F., McChrystal spoke to his high command. He sat in a secure briefing room filled with screens showing the faces of regional commanders around Afghanistan. Other generals and colonels sat with him around tables set as a hollow square.

"I think we're at an inflection point," McChrystal declared. "We have a new clarity in our mission." That mission was to "provide our Afghan partners time, space, and resources" to defeat the Taliban eventually. "The success of this operation will be determined by the minds of the Afghan people," McChrystal added. "It's a war to give people a chance."[34]

PART FOUR

THE END OF ILLUSION,
2010–2014

TWENTY-THREE

The One-man C.I.A.

During the first week of August 2009, while on vacation in the south of France, Barnett "Barney" Rubin took a call from a Saudi lawyer he had met. His contact occasionally did odd jobs for Saudi intelligence. The Saudi said that Rubin should travel to Dubai. Rubin was a political scientist with a doctoral degree from the University of Chicago who specialized in Afghanistan as well as conflict prevention and resolution. He now worked at the State Department as a senior adviser to Richard Holbrooke. Rubin called Holbrooke and asked what he should do. By all means go, Holbrooke said. Just don't tell anyone what you are doing.

Rubin drove to Nice and flew to Dubai, arriving in the early hours of August 9. He took a cab to a comfortable hotel. His contact received him in his rooms a few hours before dawn. Rubin, then fifty-nine, was a stout man with thinning white hair and a bushy white beard. He had an "alarming physical resemblance to Leon Trotsky," Holbrooke once noted, which was "not a big asset" at the Pentagon or the C.I.A. Holbrooke valued him because he offered "a level of intellectual quality you almost never see in the U.S. government." Rubin had been traveling through Saudi Arabia and the smaller Gulf States for many years, while going in and out of Afghanistan and Pakistan. The leading South Asia specialists in the U.S. intelligence community generally acknowledged that Rubin was the premier scholarly American expert on Afghan politics. He spoke Dari haltingly as well as Hindi and Urdu, and had studied literary Arabic. As an undergraduate at Yale, he had majored in history and joined the Students for a Democratic Society, a leftist youth movement involved in the civil rights movement and the opposition to the Vietnam War. During the 1980s, as an assistant professor at Yale, he had been drawn to human rights issues in Afghanistan during the Soviet occupation. This led him to write an influential book, *The Fragmentation of Afghanistan*, about Afghan elites and the modern Afghan state. He was a liberal with a strong interest in peacemaking, an outlook that was in the mainstream on the Upper West Side of Manhattan, where he lived.[1]

He had gotten to know his Saudi friend recently, while trying to probe for Holbrooke the possibilities for dialogue between the United States and the Taliban. His contact had fought in the anti-Soviet jihad of the 1980s as a volunteer, aligned at the time with Saudi and American policy. He had known Osama Bin Laden. Later he gave up war and became a professional in the kingdom. Because of his credibility with Islamists, Prince Muqrin bin Abdulaziz, the head of Saudi intelligence since 2005, had asked him to play a liaison role between Saudi Arabia and the Taliban.

In his hotel rooms, as the multicolored lights of Dubai blinked outside, the Saudi revealed that in recent days, he had received a letter and two telephone calls from well-known Taliban representatives who said they were in direct contact with Mullah Mohammad Omar. They wanted to convey privately to Saudi Arabia and the United States that Omar had appointed a new, exclusive representative for political negotiations. The man's name was Tayeb Agha. He was visiting Jeddah, the Saudi city on the Red Sea.

"There is one channel" for talking to the Taliban, the Saudi explained to Rubin, and "it should be protected and strengthened." He said that he had told the Taliban that the Americans were ready to stay in Afghanistan for twenty years if that's what it took. Yet there were nonetheless possibilities for negotiation, to separate the Taliban from Al Qaeda and coax them into power sharing and Afghan politics. "The U.S. does not want to lose, and the Taliban do not want to lose," the Saudi interlocutor observed. "Both want a way out in which they do not lose."[2]

He said he was about to fly to Morocco, where Prince Muqrin maintained a summer palace, to tell the spy chief about this new development. As for next steps, he said, the Saudis were wary about becoming too exposed in a peace negotiation with the Taliban. The kingdom considered itself at war with Al Qaeda, which had staged terrorist attacks inside Saudi Arabia. The royal family, he went on, wanted a letter "plus a voice cassette from Mullah Omar" making clear that the Taliban do not support terrorist activities anywhere in the world and that the Taliban have had no contact with Al Qaeda for the past seven years. That was a tall order. Yet Saudi Arabia had been damaged by allegations that its royal family officially supported Al Qaeda and other terrorists; the kingdom would not broker talks with the Taliban if there was any risk that it would be accused again of such complicity. How could this anxiety be squared with the Saudis' acknowledgment that Tayeb Agha, an official Taliban envoy, in his account, was resting comfortably in Jeddah? Officially, the royal family took the position that, as custodians of the Two Holy Mosques in Mecca and Medina, they could not refuse entry to any Muslim seeking pilgrimage. Unofficially, the policy allowed the kingdom to maintain contacts with Islamist groups, to convince them that Saudi Arabia meant them no harm.[3]

Rubin flew back to France. He did not know it then, but his meeting had inaugurated what would become a four-year project of secret diplomacy between the United States and the Taliban, aimed at finding a political settlement to end the Afghan war or at least reduce its violence. The project would ultimately draw in President Obama, who would invest long hours of personal effort. Not since Vietnam had the United States undertaken a comparable effort to negotiate with its enemy secretly while in the midst of war.

On August 11, Rubin wrote privately to Holbrooke that Tayeb Agha "is the chief of finance for the Taliban Leadership Shura and frequently travels to Saudi Arabia to collect funds" from individuals, businesses, and charities. The United States faced a dilemma. It seemed apparent that the same Taliban envoy who traveled outside Afghanistan and Pakistan to raise funds for the movement was also a potential channel for diplomatic contact. If they sanctioned him for fund-raising, they would lose him as a potential point of entry to Taliban leadership. A few days later, at Holbrooke's invitation, Rubin penned a second memo formally urging that any sanctions decision be postponed while they assessed this opening for engagement with Mullah Omar.[4]

Holbrooke did not share Rubin's reports widely, if at all, in Washington. If Holbrooke surfaced the news about Mullah Mohammad Omar's appointment of Tayeb Agha as a special envoy, he risked further isolation. Rubin had been reporting to Holbrooke periodically about all sorts of putative channels to the Taliban leadership. He was confident about Tayeb Agha's probable legitimacy, but the overall picture of who represented whom and what Mullah Omar or the rest of the Taliban's leadership wanted in possible talks was confusing. The best course was to wait and probe.

Holbrooke warned Rubin to be discreet and patient. Proposing talks for a "political settlement" with the Taliban was much too incendiary an idea for the Obama administration to digest right now. "Remember," Holbrooke told his adviser, "your problem is not with the Taliban. Your problem is with Denis McDonough and the C.I.A."[5]

On Saturday, September 12, at a meeting at the Brookings Institution, Holbrooke disclosed that the C.I.A. had recently completed its latest update of the District Assessments. A superficial examination of the colored maps showed that more of the country was under Taliban control than under government control, Holbrooke remarked, but a deeper look, accounting for areas that were contested or controlled by neither side, presented a less dire picture of the war. There was time to turn this conflict around.

Yet it frustrated Holbrooke that so much analysis of the war looked at the Taliban from the outside in. Where was Mullah Omar? With whom was he consulting about Taliban strategy? What did diverse members of the Quetta Shura think about the Obama administration's escalation of the war? Recent intelligence reporting suggested that

Mullah Omar had threatened to kill anyone who tried to reach out for political talks with the United States without his personal authorization, Holbrooke disclosed. If this was accurate, what was Mullah Omar worried about? Were splits emerging in the leadership?[6]

On Monday, September 14, Holbrooke met with Steve Kappes of the C.I.A. to discuss how the agency could probe the Taliban's political outlook more deeply. Until now, the C.I.A. had been given no formal tasking from the White House to collect intelligence on political debates within the Taliban leadership or how the movement might think about peace negotiations with Karzai, Saudi Arabia, or the Obama administration. It seemed evident from military reporting that the Taliban had suffered heavy casualties in Kandahar and Helmand after 2006 but the impact of these losses on the movement was also a mystery. The C.I.A.'s mission in Afghanistan still prioritized counterterrorism and Karzai watching. Holbrooke and Kappes agreed that the agency would now undertake "more collection on the Quetta Shura and political views" within the Taliban leadership. It was not a brand-new tasking, but Kappes wanted to be fair to Holbrooke and the C.I.A. was in business to take deeper looks at such difficult targets.[7]

The C.I.A. responded that autumn by circulating intelligence reports derived from secret interviews its field officers conducted with Taliban leaders, current and former. Yet even as this intelligence seeped into the American system, the possibility of direct talks with the Taliban leadership was not on the table during the long review of Afghan war strategy that Obama oversaw in the Situation Room that autumn of 2009. General Petraeus, extrapolating from his successes in Iraq turning Sunni tribesmen against Al Qaeda, advocated for trying to induce battlefield defections of Taliban commanders and soldiers—a program he called "reintegration" of enemy fighters, from the bottom up, as opposed to "reconciliation" with Taliban leaders, from the top down, which might come later. Petraeus did not actually believe Holbrooke's vision of reconciliation was viable because there was no way for the United States to threaten the Taliban leadership, who felt safe in Pakistan. Without such coercion, why would the Taliban negotiate seriously? Drawing on Bush administration policy, the White House did seek to give space for Afghans to talk among themselves about peace. The president's West Point speech therefore contained only a single sentence about seeking accommodation with the Taliban: "We will support efforts by the Afghan government to open the door to those Taliban who abandon violence and respect the human rights of their fellow citizens."[8]

In the absence of presidential support, Holbrooke used Barney Rubin as the forward probe of his own diplomatic operation, to identify and test Taliban negotiating channels. Rubin was an unconventional choice. He had never worked in government before Holbrooke drafted him, never mind on top secret, compartmented national security matters. Yet Doug Lute, the general who ran Afghanistan and Pakistan policy at the National Security Council, remained friendly with Rubin and protected him. As Rubin provoked the national security bureaucracy with his travel and discussions with Taliban interlocutors, Lute made sure the White House and the Pentagon did not cut him off.

On December 11, 2009, ten days after Obama's West Point speech, Rubin arrived at the Foreign Office in London to talk about his project with British counterparts. A Taliban specialist from MI6 joined the discussion. "Change is in the air," the British intelligence officer reported. A "substantial part" of the Taliban senior leadership "is interested in reconciliation" talks. Their motives were not benign—they wanted to divide the N.A.T.O. coalition in Afghanistan by demonstrating willingness to compromise. Yet it remained hard to read who within the Taliban high command was behind these gestures or where Mullah Mohammad Omar stood.

In a separate meeting during this period, a senior Foreign Office official asked an MI6 counterpart: If we wanted to pass a private message to Mullah Omar, do we have a reliable channel to do so? Not really was the reply.

Foreign Secretary David Miliband sought to push the Obama administration toward negotiations. Yet Prime Minister Gordon Brown's government did not think having Barney Rubin fly around the Gulf looking for Taliban intermediaries was the best approach. Drawing on experience in Northern Ireland and elsewhere, the British argued that the

C.I.A. should open up initial direct contacts with the Taliban, to probe, collect insights, and build confidence in the event that serious negotiations evolved. The C.I.A. had cachet. Enemies of the United States often preferred to deal with the spy service directly. Also, Langley managed the American relationship with I.S.I., the Taliban's historical patron.

As Steve Kappes, the C.I.A.'s deputy director, put it during one discussion, "You don't think the I.S.I. doesn't have the Taliban penetrated and will find out everything that is going on anyway? Why not collaborate with I.S.I. and guard our interests at the same time?" Rubin and other interlocutors heard repeatedly from Taliban leaders that they wanted to speak directly to the United States, free from I.S.I. interference. Yet it was likely that Kappes was correct about the penetration issue—the Taliban could not travel easily outside Pakistan without passports I.S.I. approved, unless they resorted to forged documents.

Holbrooke, however, didn't want to lose control of any talks that might lead to negotiations to end the Afghan war—that was his turf, his potential legacy. He merely wanted the C.I.A. to collect intelligence about the Taliban's leadership and internal politics. He preferred Rubin, whom he could control, more or less, and he feared that the C.I.A. had become imprisoned intellectually about Afghanistan by wartime and counterterrorism dogma.[9]

After the New Year, Rubin flew to Saudi Arabia, where he met Holbrooke in Riyadh, the capital. Prince Muqrin received them in his small and dark office at the General Intelligence Department. He introduced them to a general who had worked for Prince Turki bin Faisal, the Saudi intelligence chief during the anti-Soviet war of the 1980s. "The Taliban is still controlled by Pakistan," the general said. Some Taliban leaders wanted to break free of Pakistan but they were weak and would need support to act independently. Also, if the United States and Saudi Arabia negotiated with the Quetta Shura, they would have to reassure Pakistan that any settlement of the war would not harm its interests. Otherwise, the I.S.I. would surely act as spoilers.

Muqrin seemed hesitant to proceed. He "won't lift a finger," Holbrooke complained. The Saudis seemed reluctant to become entangled in the triangle among the United States, Hamid Karzai, and the I.S.I. They needed good relations with the I.S.I. for their own reasons—Pakistan had nuclear know-how and infantry muscle that the kingdom might require in future crises. The inertia was typical of Saudi statecraft: The kingdom had high-level contacts across the Muslim world, it had wealth to buy influence, but its octogenarian royal family rarely took bold risks and lacked capacity to follow through. King Abdullah, Muqrin's boss, was then eighty-five years old.[10]

They traveled next to Abu Dhabi, where Holbrooke had convened a conference of special representatives to Afghanistan from governments worldwide—his mini–United Nations of counterparts. The plenary, hosted by the Foreign Ministry of the United Arab Emirates, was largely cere-monial, designed to signal unity about Afghanistan to weary publics in Europe and Asia.

Bernd Mützelburg, the German representative, asked for a private audience with Holbrooke. When they were alone, Mützelburg disclosed that two months earlier, while visiting Kabul, he had met with Mullah Zaeef, the former Taliban ambassador to Pakistan, a founder of the movement, and later a prisoner at Guantánamo. After his release, Zaeef had settled in Kabul. Zaeef asked Mützelburg if he would sound out the possibility of direct contact between Germany and the Taliban leader-ship. Mützelburg had consulted with Hamid Karzai, who encouraged him to go ahead. So the envoy flew to Dubai to meet a man he now de-scribed as "the head of the political commission of the Quetta Shura."

They had talked twice. Mützelburg had some trouble remembering the Taliban envoy's name, but said that he had once served as number two in the Taliban embassy in Islamabad and also as Mullah Mohammad Omar's private secretary. Soon it became clear that the negotiator was Tayeb Agha, the same representative identified to Rubin the previous summer.

What did the Taliban want? The "paramount" issue, Mützelburg said, was for the Taliban to find some sort of independence from I.S.I., as well as relief from international sanctions and blacklists. Once free to negoti-ate without I.S.I. coercion, the Taliban and N.A.T.O. could try to build mutual confidence. "Pakistan is playing its own games," trying to ma-nipulate the Taliban, the German said. Taliban leaders and their families depended on I.S.I. for identity cards, subsidies, and the right to live freely and earn a living. They wanted to negotiate directly with the Obama administration, not through I.S.I.[11]

Again, Holbrooke kept this startling disclosure largely to himself. Tayeb Agha's bona fides remained uncertain. When Holbrooke did start to introduce what he had learned from the Germans to colleagues in Washington, he said that Tayeb Agha's outreach merely represented "a thread" of contact with the Taliban high command. There were other "threads," such as Zaeef and separate Taliban contacts the Karzai family had developed without American involvement. The prudent course was to pull on each thread to discover what might be promising. Meanwhile, Holbrooke promoted Rubin's role within the administration. At I.S.A.F. headquarters in Kabul, a few days after the meeting with Mützelburg, Holbrooke enthusiastically introduced the professor as "a one-man C.I.A." This did even less than his Trotskyite beard to endear Rubin to Langley or the Pentagon.

On January 22, 2010, Doug Lute convened a National Security Council subgroup meeting to talk about talking to the Taliban. Present were Deputy National Security Adviser Tom Donilon, Rubin, Holbrooke, the Pentagon's Michèle Flournoy, Marine General James Cartwright, who was the vice chairman of the Joint Chiefs, White House counterterrorism czar John Brennan, and Chris Wood, the former Kabul station chief. Wood had lately been sent by the C.I.A. to the Office of the Director of National Intelligence, to work on Afghanistan and Pakistan.

Lute asked Holbrooke to open the discussion. Any negotiation would be "tougher than Vietnam or Bosnia," Holbrooke said, because the Afghan war had "so many actors." They were at the beginning of the beginning, he estimated. "There is no secret negotiation with the Taliban," he said, in case they feared otherwise.

They reviewed the policy on Taliban talks they had inherited from the Bush administration. It dated to 2004, when Zalmay Khalilzad had worked successfully with Karzai to bring some former Taliban ministers and diplomats into Kabul from Pakistan, as defectors. The Bush administration policy, which had been revised in 2007, concerned what the

United States thought was acceptable for the Karzai government to do by itself when it talked to the enemy. It did not contemplate direct U.S. talks with the Taliban. The policy's main provision was a blacklist of thirty-one names. These were senior Taliban leaders that Karzai should not talk with under any circumstances, at least according to the United States. Mullah Mohammad Omar was at the top of the list. Several Haqqanis were listed, as were Gulbuddin Hekmatyar and some of his commanders. Tayeb Agha was also banned. He was described as a "former aide to Mullah Omar" who "continues as an aide to Omar." Lute asked one of his deputies, Jeff Hayes, a Defense Intelligence Agency analyst on loan to the White House, to "review the bidding" and see how they should handle the blacklist if serious talks now developed, through Tayeb Agha or otherwise.[12]

I n Hamid Karzai's growing alienation from the Obama administration, Generals Kayani and Pasha saw an opening for Pakistan. N.A.T.O. governments had strong intercept coverage of at least some of the telephones Kayani and Pasha used. After Obama's West Point speech, the eavesdroppers heard Kayani express fears that a U.S. pullout would leave Pakistan vulnerable to more domestic violence as Afghanistan fell into chaos again. The army chief decided to see if he might lessen this risk by persuading Karzai to reach a political deal with Pakistan that might cut out the United States, at least partially. That winter, Pasha sent messages to the Arg Palace to indicate that Pakistan wanted "to break the ice" about a new alignment between Karzai and Pakistan.

The Afghan president summoned Amrullah Saleh. "I want to invest in peace," Karzai told him. "I want to invest in friendship in Pakistan." Karzai invited Pasha to Kabul, unannounced, on January 18, 2010. Karzai did not mention the visit to Saleh until Pasha was already at the Arg Palace. As it happened, that day, the sounds of gunfire and grenade explosions had Kabul in a panic. As the I.S.I. chief settled in at the palace, small squads of Taliban raiders attacked the Central Bank, near the palace, as well as a hotel and a cinema. The timing was apparently coincidental.[13]

Karzai summoned Saleh, who was helping to direct the day's counterattack. Saleh greeted the I.S.I. chief and provided a situation report. Karzai then asked him to leave the room. The implication was unsubtle: I don't trust my spy chief, and neither do you, General Pasha, so let us talk without him.

"You are more independent of the U.S." now that you have been re-elected, the I.S.I. chief told Karzai. Pakistan, Pasha emphasized, was pleased to hear Karzai talk publicly from time to time about a broad-based, inclusive government in Afghanistan, one that might accommodate elements of the Taliban. The United States was on its way out, even as its forces flowed in for their temporary "surge." Pakistan and Afghanistan could shape the region's future separately, without the burdens of American interference or hubris. Pasha invited Karzai to Islamabad for deeper talks with Kayani.

As the conversation went on, Saleh waited in a reception area. Explosions echoed in the distance. He worked his cell phone as Afghan counterterrorism police tracked down and eventually subdued the Taliban attackers, who had disguised themselves in Afghan police uniforms.

Karzai and Pasha emerged. The president asked Saleh to escort Pasha to the airport safely.

"Do you have any leads as to who is doing this?" Pasha asked him in their sport utility vehicle as they wove toward Kabul International.

"Yes, if you want, I can share with you—the attack is not finished, Mr. Director. The people inside the bank are communicating with a number in Pakistan. They are taking instructions. Right now, while you are with me."

"Brother, give it to me," Pasha said.

Saleh wrote down the number. "I will get back to you," Pasha promised. A week later, according to an Afghan account of the episode, Pasha called Saleh to report that he was right, but that, after the attack, the number was switched off and there was nothing more to be done. According to a Pakistani version of the same episode, the army followed up on the number, arrested seven Afghans, and handed them over to N.D.S. without publicity, only to have Saleh go public with a statement that he had proof the whole thing had been an I.S.I. operation. The Pakistanis swallowed their frustration, according to this account, and the Pakistani security services concluded that Saleh was more interested in anti-Pakistan propaganda than cooperation.[14]

Toward the Americans, on the subject of talking to the Taliban about peace, Pasha adopted a posture of passive aggression. That winter, he summoned a Pakistani journalist and told him that Obama's "surge" into Afghanistan would inevitably fail. There were not enough Pashtuns in the Afghan army and police; the Taliban were popular and had the moral high ground as resisters to occupation, he went on. He denied outright that his service was supporting the Quetta Shura or the Haqqani network yet indicated that only Pakistan could deliver the Taliban away from war and into politics—not the Saudis, not the Americans on their own. I.S.I. did not regard a Kabul government controlled by the Taliban as the only acceptable outcome, Pasha said. "No, no, not at all. Our national interests have to be protected, that is our main concern." Pasha's message was clearly intended to reach the Obama administration, to signal that I.S.I. was indispensable to any negotiation and that it did not seek a maximalist outcome.

The morning after Pasha departed Kabul, Karzai summoned Saleh to breakfast. The Afghan spy chief did not know what had gone on between the president and the I.S.I. director in his absence. He was insulted by the exclusion, but he tried to be cordial. "Mr. President," he said, "whatever your purpose in pushing me out of the meeting, in my opinion, it didn't give a good signal to the Pakistanis." It showed I.S.I. that the Afghan government lacked unity, that there was friction at the highest levels.

Karzai said he wanted to accept the invitation to meet with Kayani and Pasha again in Islamabad, to advance the discussions. He assured Saleh that he would participate fully. In fact, Karzai would again exclude Saleh from some meetings with Pasha, which fueled Saleh's suspicion that Karzai was discussing removing him or making other compromises for the sake of improved relations between the two countries.

They flew to the Pakistani capital on March 11. Karzai met with his civilian counterparts, President Asif Zardari and Prime Minister Yousaf

Gillani. At the Serena Hotel, a fourteen-acre compound of gardens with touches of Islamic architecture, Karzai met with Kayani and Pasha in a V.I.P. suite. As promised, this time, Saleh was there.

Kayani's message was "Talk to us, not the Americans." If there was to be peace, it had to come through Pakistan. The door is open. The support of I.S.I. is essential to any workable resolution of the war, Kayani emphasized.

If they were going to talk about a new relationship, Saleh said, they had to be honest about what Pakistan was trying to achieve. "Mr. Kayani, please don't tell me you are not supporting the Taliban," Saleh ventured. "Please tell me *why* you are supporting the Taliban. What is it that they do for Pakistan that we do not do?"

Kayani demurred. Saleh pressed the point several times. Finally Kayani said, addressing Karzai, "Mr. President, if you want us to trust you, let us create a strategic framework for our relationship, to define it." They agreed to move forward.

"Will the Northern Alliance comply if you agree with us?" Kayani asked.

Karzai turned to Saleh, putting him on the spot. "Mr. President, I am not Northern Alliance," Saleh said. "I'm serving you. And I tell my Pakistani brothers, there is no 'Northern Alliance.' It will be Pakistani pressure that will recreate the Northern Alliance—it doesn't exist now. And if it does, it is entirely in support of Karzai as the legitimate president of Afghanistan. President Karzai is representing Afghanistan."

The heart of Kayani's offer to Karzai was "We can help you sort out the insurgency—we can turn it off," as a N.A.T.O. diplomat briefed on the discussion soon after described it. In exchange, Pakistan would expect Karzai to "end"—that was the word Kayani used, according to these accounts—Indian influence in Afghanistan.[15]

How would Kayani define the "end" of India's presence? As the clandestine contacts between I.S.I. and the Arg Palace evolved in 2010, reportedly including face-to-face meetings and encrypted digital messages, Kayani and Pasha pressed to be provided a detailed map of the Indian footprint in Afghanistan—lists of companies, contracts, and personnel.

They pressed for access to the Afghan National Army, through the Pakistani military attaché in Kabul, to understand the army's development and leading personalities. They proposed training dozens of Afghan army officers in Islamabad, which would create a channel of long-term influence. They sought an end to public rhetoric from Afghanistan bashing Pakistan. In exchange, the Pakistanis dangled the possibility of peace in Kabul, negotiations on strategic issues such as water and borders, and delivering the Taliban to a political settlement that might include Karzai continuing.

Kayani and Pasha were particularly aggravated that N.D.S. was protecting armed Baluch separatists from the Bugti tribe who were fighting the Pakistan Army in Pakistan's Baluchistan Province. One Bugti leader lived in a safe house on Street 13 in Kabul under N.D.S. protection. Baluch fighters trained in Kandahar, Kayani and Pasha reported, citing intelligence collected in part by the Pakistani embassy in Kabul. Pakistani diplomats lived near the Kabul safe house and documented the Bugti leader's take-out orders from a local Lebanese taverna: The man was wanted for terrorism in Pakistan, yet he was enjoying kebab and shelter with N.D.S. connivance, the Pakistanis claimed. Karzai should make sure that India's diplomatic, business, and humanitarian projects around Afghanistan did not become covert launching pads for destabilizing Pakistan. It seemed to them obvious that Afghanistan remained an essential aspect of India's strategy of containing Pakistan. With its booming economy and expanding defense budget, India was a kind of irreversible tide, gathering influence in the region, including in Afghanistan. The Pakistanis saw India's spy service, the Research and Analysis Wing, or R.A.W., behind every rock, Indian officials complained. True, this was unfair; India carried out reconstruction and humanitarian projects in Afghanistan in the same way many other countries did. There were about four thousand Indians in the country but more than half of those were cooks and maintenance workers on N.A.T.O. bases who were recruited from labor contractors in the Persian Gulf—they never left the bases. Yet in fairness to Kayani, it was not as if R.A.W. had dropped out of covert action specifically designed to undermine Pakistani stability.[16]

After the meeting at the Serena in Islamabad, Pasha and Saleh met secretly several times, in Ankara and elsewhere, to work on a draft strategic framework agreement. Pasha flew back to Kabul and met privately again with Karzai.

Yet Karzai seemed to change his mind from day to day about whether he should pursue a separate peace with the I.S.I. He seemed rattled. Some of his aides advised him that Pasha and Kayani were right—Afghanistan would be better off dealing with Pakistan directly. "Don't you think there's too much Indian influence on Afghanistan?" Karzai asked several American visitors privately in the weeks after his trip to Islamabad.

"My first choice would be a strategic alignment of the United States, India, and Afghanistan against Pakistan," Karzai explained to a senior American official. "But I don't think that's what you're pursuing. I think you're cutting a separate deal with Pakistan, leaving me out. If that's the case, I need to cut my own deal with Pakistan."

"It's actually a lot less conspiratorial than you think," the American tried to argue. "We're trying to forge a moderate, balanced policy among all these parties." But Karzai wasn't buying it. He was clearly toying with a deal with I.S.I., but he also recognized that it would be a great risk.

In Washington, Barnett Rubin warned Holbrooke that it was not just Karzai who had lost confidence in American strategy. The United States, he wrote on March 18, "is in danger once again of allowing its policy in the region to be manipulated by the deception of the Pakistan military," which would result in granting "Pakistan an outsized role in Afghanistan." The perception that the United States "is positioning itself for a deal with Pakistan at Afghanistan's expense" is "widespread in the Afghan political elite and is not confined to President Karzai." The fear that Washington was prepared to sell out to I.S.I. or was too naïve to see that it was being had "is a major factor driving the Afghan government's precipitous efforts" to find a line to talk with the Taliban or a separate deal with Pasha and Kayani. "Afghans believe that if their country is to be sold to Pakistan they would prefer to bargain over the price directly rather than rely on an agent," meaning the United States, Rubin wrote.[17]

One Saturday late that winter of 2010, Richard Holbrooke met a reporter privately for lunch at the Four Seasons Hotel in Georgetown. The dining room was almost empty. Holbrooke juggled a cell phone and a BlackBerry restlessly.

Before he even looked at a menu, he admitted that he wasn't at all sure that the Afghan war would succeed. "The military clears areas out but if they can't transfer security and governance to civilians, it won't matter," he said. "McChrystal doesn't know if it will work and neither do I. Petraeus is the best four-star general I've ever seen, but he's spinning all the time. . . . Unlike David Petraeus, I'm willing to tell you . . . that I don't know if it's going to work or not. And neither does Stan McChrystal or Karl Eikenberry or Hillary Clinton. Or, I think, the president."

"There's a very clear definition of midterm success," he continued, "and that is a policy that allows our combat troops to start leaving in the summer of next year, at a pace, and a size and configuration to be determined—but which, when it occurs, does not collapse the country. That's what Nixon and Kissinger and Abrams tried to do in Vietnam. They called it 'Vietnamization.' We have avoided the word 'Afghanization' because it didn't feel right and would evoke Vietnam . . . which people *hate*, by the way. But they should be less scared of history."

He was feeling his way toward a negotiation with the Taliban. Mullah Mohammad Omar had defended his ties to Al Qaeda at every critical moment, even though it cost him the Islamic Emirate in 2001. "I think Mullah Omar is incredibly important," Holbrooke said. "The more I look at this thing the more I think he is a driving, inspirational force whose capture or elimination would have a material effect. . . . That's why I think eliminating Mullah Omar is so critical. Right now, if you could choose between Mullah Omar and Osama Bin Laden, I personally would lean toward Mullah Omar."

"Do you assume that I.S.I. could deliver Mullah Omar if they wished to do so?"

"I don't know. If I had an answer to that, I would act on it."

Holbrooke continued, "There are three countries here—Pakistan,

Afghanistan, and India—with vastly different stages of political, social, and economic development. They share a common strategic space. As has happened so many times in history, the weak state is the one that sucks in the others. That's the history of Afghanistan and now the Great Game is being played with different players. The India-Pakistan relationship is an absolutely critical driver."

Holbrooke was preparing a secret memo for Hillary Clinton, which he would deliver in about two weeks. The draft had a despairing tone. He wrote it under the slightly anachronistic heading "Private and Most Confidential." The title was "How Does This Thing End?: In Search of a Policy."

It began, "Since last August, I have been trying, unsuccessfully, to get a serious and sustained process in the interagency on policy toward what we call, somewhat euphemistically, reconciliation—by which we really mean contacts with the Taliban. . . . We cannot defer this issue any longer." Based on his extensive discussions with Petraeus, McChrystal, Mullen, and Gates, as well as private comments from senior White House officials, "I believe it is quite likely that there will be significant differences of opinion within the Executive Branch, and even inside the military, on these issues. The differences can be ironed out, but only with the President's personal involvement." He went on to inventory the disagreements. His memo surveyed the underexamined assumptions of the Obama administration's expeditionary war:

PREMISE ONE: The war will not end in a pure military victory.

Everyone says they agree with this premise.

But upon closer examination, even this truism produces some disagreement. For Petraeus, it means that the war will follow the Iraq model—a slow reduction of violence as reintegration "works its way upward." David does not foresee, and so far opposes, any real discussion with the leadership of the Taliban. He feels it would show weakness, might if and when it became public demoralize people, and would be unnecessary. He appears to believe completely that the current offensive will succeed to such a degree that the enemy will simply switch sides in increasing numbers, as they did in Iraq. . . .

Of course, we all know where Hamid Karzai stands on the issue. He simply does not believe our counter-insurgency policy will succeed—hence his constant outreach, in private and public, to the enemy. . . .

ISSUE ONE: What is an "acceptable and achievable" end state for the U.S.?

It is a difficult question, fraught with strategic, political and even moral implications. Our stated goal is to destroy Al Qaeda. Suppose we were to achieve just that—would we then leave Afghanistan once again, or simply remove our combat forces? . . . In the end, there is this: Even if the Taliban maintains a very hard line position, the American public and our Allies will not accept an open-ended commitment that involves continual combat and casualties, nor is it likely the Afghan people will, either. Most Afghans may not want the Taliban to return, but there is an old adage: If the guerillas do not lose, they ultimately win. . . .

PREMISE TWO: Whatever else is decided, we should maximize our military pressure.

This is a fundamental point, although often disputed by well-intentioned but misguided members of the European and American left. The chances of success of any reintegration or reconciliation policy will be significantly increased by battlefield success. . . . But Karzai's support for this is less clear. His constant public requests for an end to night raids, an end to all Afghans held by the United States, and his vocal public exploitation of the civilian casualties issue are all warning signs that he might turn on us one day if it would help him negotiate a deal. . . .

PREMISE THREE: Timing is critically important.

Integrating the military and diplomatic track is essential for success. . . . Nixon and Kissinger encountered this problem, and were defeated by it; when they began negotiating with Hanoi in 1969 there were 550,000 American troops in Vietnam, but under domestic pressure, Nixon unilaterally drew down to about 135,000 while Kissinger negotiated for almost five years. By the time they cut the final deal in later 1973, the two men were like the losers in a strip poker game, naked. They had no chips—or clothes—left with which to bargain; the result was a communist takeover of our South Vietnamese ally less than two years later. Roughly the same thing happened to the Soviets in Afghanistan, without even the negotiating.

This argues for a simple proposition: If we are going to explore the options for any sort of settlement, it should be done while U.S. troop levels are increasing, not flat or declining. . . .

It was Holbrooke at his strongest—at once an outsider and an insider in his thinking, bold and clarifying. The problem was, within the Obama administration, beyond Hillary Clinton, he had lost his audience. The president could not abide Holbrooke's mannerisms and undisguised ambition and tried to avoid meeting him. In January 2010, Obama instructed Jones to suggest to Clinton that it was time for Holbrooke to depart. Holbrooke's relations with the ambassadors in Kabul, Islamabad, and New Delhi had deteriorated. The election fiasco with Karzai lingered. Holbrooke was in regular conflict with Doug Lute at the N.S.C. They shared skepticism about the military surge in Afghanistan but disagreed about how to pursue diplomacy. Holbrooke wanted to talk to the Taliban himself, but Lute argued that they needed a non-American in the lead; he suggested Lakhdar Brahimi, the Algerian-born diplomat and troubleshooter. In any event, Clinton was unwilling to fire Holbrooke and she had enough influence with Obama to prevail. The result, however, was less a team of rivals than a system of parallel policies and priorities running on diverse premises.[18]

As diplomatic and intelligence reporting about Karzai's unmoored musings and flirtations with I.S.I. came in, the White House recognized it had to make an effort to reel Afghanistan's president back. British intelligence officials warned American counterparts that the "Pakistanis are confident in their strategy" and at the same time "confused" about what the United States wants. There was a reason, as Holbrooke had outlined in his memo: The administration remained divided and "in search of a policy" that could produce an acceptable outcome.

"The U.S. government seems utterly focused on secondary or trivial issues," Rubin wrote to Holbrooke on April 13, "and remains virtually clueless about and unengaged with the rapid and deep political shifts taking place in the region." These included "the degradation of the U.S.-Afghanistan bilateral relationship," as well as "the perception that the U.S. and N.A.T.O. are on a fast glide path out of the region" while the Pakistan military displayed "increased confidence and assertiveness."

Kayani sought a separate understanding with Karzai but he also wanted to explore whether it might be possible to change Pakistan's relationship with the United States. Early that year National Security Adviser Jim Jones flew to Islamabad to meet with the army chief. Kayani handed him a 106-page document describing Pakistan's views on a range of issues. The document came to be known at the National Security Council as "Kayani 1.0." When intelligence and State Department analysts pored over it, they noticed that it seemed to have been drafted by the Pakistani Foreign Office and contained a lot of familiar boilerplate. It described five key areas of Pakistani security interests: nuclear deterrence, Kashmir, access to water, the future of Afghanistan, and the search for a "nonhegemonic South Asia," meaning one in which India had less influence. Islamic extremism wasn't on the list. From his reading of the paper and his discussions with Kayani, Holbrooke boiled down the position of I.S.I. and the army: They believe the United States wants to take away Pakistan's nuclear weapons. They see the Afghan National Army and N.D.S. as pro-Indian forces commanded by the remnants of the Northern Alliance. They want the U.S. to mediate on Kashmir. It would take a great deal of effort to change that mind-set.[19]

Jones and Doug Lute worked on a plan to invite Karzai to Washington. In mid-March, Obama and Karzai held their first secure video teleconference in months. It seemed plain that an enormous effort would be required to break the alienation between the White House and the Arg Palace. In a gesture of respect, Obama would fly to Kabul to formalize the invitation for a state visit to Karzai in person. The president landed at Bagram on March 28, just over two weeks after Karzai returned from Islamabad.

Wearing a flight jacket, Obama flew by helicopter to the Arg, where

Karzai received him upstairs. They spoke one-on-one and then joined a table of Karzai's cabinet members and advisers. Obama's message—to Karzai, the Afghan cabinet, and American troops he addressed—was one of unwavering commitment: "The United States does not quit once it starts on something," he said. "We keep at it. We persevere. And together with our partners, we will prevail. I am absolutely confident of that."[20]

Each Afghan minister said a few words to Obama. When Amrullah Saleh's turn came, he spoke bluntly. He wanted to be sure Obama heard what he believed to be the unvarnished truth.

"Pakistanis believe the West has lost" the war against the Taliban already, Saleh said. The Pakistani view is that it is just a matter of time before the United States and Europe acknowledge their defeat. The West, on the other hand, thinks that Pakistan is losing because its economy is weak, it can't produce enough energy to light its houses and factories, and its politicians are corrupt and ineffectual. "But that is not how they see it," Saleh insisted. "They see you are losing. They see division between Europe and the United States. . . . They see these mild approaches to talk to the Taliban."

He continued, "We have to change their perception, to say, 'We have not lost and you are too weak to defeat us.' If we do not do that, we lose. We lose to whom? Al Qaeda, Pakistan, Taliban . . . It is our joint mission. We don't need to compliment each other every day. This effort needs such intense cooperation. And remember, a failure here means some time of trouble in more than sixty countries" as extremist movements find space for revival.[21]

Obama listened, stone-faced. He said nothing in reply.

Amrullah Saleh understood that he was working on borrowed time as the N.D.S. director. For one thing, he had a reliable sense of what Karzai was discussing with Pasha, even when Saleh wasn't present. He had been head of N.D.S. for six years. He had survived many iterations of palace intrigue. He had the C.I.A.'s confidence, but to many of Karzai's aides and Pashtun allies, he remained a symbol of undue Panjshiri influence over the government. He was well aware that his removal from office would please Kayani and Pasha at a time when Karzai was exploring a new partnership with Pakistan.

The N.D.S.'s tree-shaded compound in downtown Kabul had been renovated since 2004 by infusions of C.I.A. and European budgetary support, but it lacked the high sheen and washed marble look of the I.S.I.'s new headquarters in Islamabad. Saleh furnished a musty room just off the main entrance to receive foreign visitors. He remained clean-shaven and typically wore a dark suit. He was a hard man and oversaw a network of prisons and interrogation centers where torture and brutality remained common, according to human rights groups.

Saleh knew that talking to the Taliban about peace was in the air. Barnett Rubin had discussed the project with him. He opposed such talks because they would inevitably empower I.S.I. He felt that Karzai was pursuing not a national agenda, but a Pashtun ethnic agenda, evident by the president's regular remarks, in private, along the lines that the Taliban were his "cousins" and that "we can't keep fighting them forever."

"The Taliban, all of a sudden, once again, have become the bargaining tool for the Pakistanis," he told an international visitor during this period. "Talks with the Taliban, in the eyes of I.S.I., must be under the control of the Pakistani military. Regardless of how much we kill the outer circle of Taliban soldiers or influence the middle circle of Taliban commanders, they can create massive numbers of infiltrators from our refugee population in Pakistan, train them again, send them back to fight in Afghanistan. And they will keep the Taliban leadership hibernating somewhere in Pakistani territory, with some degree of deniability."

In Saleh's analysis, the strategy of I.S.I. and Kayani was now to help N.A.T.O. leave Afghanistan with dignity, preserving as much stability and access to Western finance and defense supplies for Pakistan as possible, before I.S.I. again asserted political control over Afghanistan. The Obama administration could reach out to the Taliban all it wished. Its grasp of its enemy would prove elusive.

"They are masters of this," Saleh said, referring to the I.S.I. and the

Pakistan Army. "They developed their nuclear bomb under the watchful eyes and smelling nose of the West. Keeping twenty-five guys roaming around Quetta is far easier than developing a nuclear bomb. The West has to ask itself: How many times in its history with Pakistan have they been deceived?"[22]

TWENTY-FOUR

The Conflict Resolution Cell

D uring the first months of 2010, the Obama administration pursued three strategies in Afghanistan and Pakistan. From I.S.A.F. headquarters, Stanley McChrystal commanded an intensifying ground war based on the clear-hold-build-transfer principles of counterinsurgency. His campaign plan posited that the Afghan war could be handed off successfully to Afghans even if the problem of Taliban sanctuaries in Pakistan was not addressed. From the Global Response Center in Langley, the C.I.A. independently ran a secret drone air war against Al Qaeda and the Taliban holed up in Waziristan. The rate of strikes reached an unprecedented tempo during 2010, about two per week. Simultaneously, from the ground floor of the State Department, Richard Holbrooke and his aides, who were largely shut out of the first two lines of war strategy, pursued a third: trying to talk to Mullah Mohammad Omar's lieutenants about peace. Holbrooke's team also moved to persuade Kayani and Pasha to abandon Pakistan's historic pursuit of influence in Afghanistan through the promotion of violent Islamists.

On paper, Obama's National Security Council supported all three policies. But it would require feats of mental gymnastics to call these lines of action synchronized.

That spring, under the rubric of "strategic dialogue," Holbrooke showed Kayani and Pasha around Washington and tried to give them the intimate, high-level attention afforded to leaders of Britain or France or

China—flags and flowers by day, fireside chats by night. The more Kayani and Pasha felt welcomed to informal conversation with high-level
American counterparts at Blair House, the guest home across from the
White House, or at Admiral Mullen's residence, the more likely the generals were to finally move past the stiff formulations of the Kayani 1.0
white paper and toward some honest discussion of the I.S.I.'s tangled
relationship with the Taliban, Al Qaeda, and Afghanistan's violence. At
least, this was the theory.[1]

Holbrooke and Mullen also encouraged Kayani to repair I.S.I.'s battered image in Washington by talking more openly about how Pakistani soldiers and spies had suffered their own casualties from terrorist
and insurgent attacks inside Pakistan, particularly since 2007. *Tell your
story*, the Americans urged Kayani. It was not his strong suit, but he
agreed.

Black Suburban S.U.V.s with red police lights on the dashboards
whisked the army chief down L Street one weekday morning in late
March. Kayani traveled with a minimum of aides. He gripped a laptop
containing a PowerPoint slide deck. At a think tank where he was to
present, he ducked into the stairwell for a cigarette. He was wearing his
army greens, but he wished to appear onstage in civilian clothes, so he
stripped to his undershirt in a conference room, pulled on and half but-
toned up a dress shirt, and then ducked out for another smoke. A few
minutes later, his eyes hooded and his hair lightly combed, Kayani sat
folded up in an armchair before a crowd of former American policy makers, journalists, and intelligence analysts. He spoke in sentence frag-
ments, barely audible. Over his shoulder his PowerPoint slides flashed on
a small movie screen.[2]

"PAK ARMY'S CONTRIBUTIONS—SILENT SURGE" read the
title of one slide. Its bar graph showed that the number of Pakistani soldiers and paramilitaries deployed to the Federally Administered Tribal
Areas had grown from just under 40,000 after the September 11 attacks
to more than 140,000 by 2009. The "silent" part of the surge reflected
Kayani's reluctance to trumpet these figures in Pakistan, which might
aggravate the Pakistani Taliban and other local insurgents by disclosing
the scale of the army's "occupation" of the tribal areas.

"PAK ARMY'S CONTRIBUTIONS—MILITARY CASUALTIES" flashed next. The slide reported that terrorist attacks and fighting in the tribal areas had killed more than 2,300 Pakistani soldiers through early 2010 and injured another 6,800. Nearly all of the casualties had occurred after 2006. A third slide showed that during the same period, there had been more "major terrorist incidents" inside Pakistan than in Afghanistan or Iraq. Kayani refrained from saying what he, Pasha, and many other Pakistani generals believed: Pakistan had paid a higher price than the United States for joining the post–September 11 alliance against the Taliban, and now it was being rocked by the spillover of America's failed invasion of Afghanistan, against which Pakistan had warned. The I.S.I.'s support for the Afghan Taliban's revival, if the generals acknowledged it at all, should be understood as a defensive measure— an effort to push the violence caused by America back across the border, into Afghanistan—rather than as a covert offensive aimed at retaking Kabul.[3]

Kayani flashed a slide showing a blown-up building in Lahore. It was a regional office of I.S.I. bombed by former allies of the spy service who had turned against the Pakistani state. The casualties endured inside Pakistan since 2006 included dozens of I.S.I. officers, Kayani said. I.S.I. could not possibly be fomenting terrorism if its officers were also victims of terrorism, he argued. Eighty percent of I.S.I. officers came from the army. "I know how I.S.I. functions and how I.S.I. operates," Kayani said. The service is "aligned with army policy."

He displayed a slide showing Tiger Woods at the top of his golf swing, in his signature red shirt. Kayani went into his thesis, by now familiar to Admiral Mullen and other American interlocutors, about the "fundamentals." He compared the pursuit of stability in Afghanistan to a sound golf game. One fundamental was the internal discipline and morale of the Pakistan Army. A second was public opinion in the region and America. He concluded by defining what the army and I.S.I. sought across their western border: "a peaceful and stable Afghanistan, a friendly Afghanistan." Given the I.S.I.'s history, it was hard to avoid hearing this formulation as code, once again, for "Pakistani influence, through the Taliban."[4]

Mullah Abdul Salam Zaeef, the former Taliban ambassador to Pakistan, who had helped select Mullah Mohammad Omar as the movement's emir, lived in a two-story concrete home at the end of a muddy road in the Khushal Khan neighborhood of Kabul. He had painted his house green. Pashtuns dominated his neighborhood. A small shack occupied by armed N.D.S. soldiers guarded Zaeef's front door.

One morning during the first week of April, one of the former ambassador's sons greeted an American visitor and showed him to an upstairs sitting room. As tea was prepared, young children and teenagers wandered in and out, practicing their English. The house was cold and modestly furnished. There were green curtains and green light fixtures with ornamental shades designed as tulips. The bookshelves held leatherbound copies of the Koran, the Sunnah, a Webster's English dictionary, and a French translation of Zaeef's recently completed memoir, *Prisonnier à Guantánamo*.[5]

It was Zaeef who had put the Germans in contact with Tayeb Agha, Omar's envoy. After the Germans reported their secret meetings with Tayeb Agha to Holbrooke, Zaeef organized an unpublicized nighttime meeting at Kabul University that brought together former Taliban officeholders and Mike Flynn, the I.S.A.F. intelligence chief, to explore the possibilities of negotiations.[6]

Zaeef understood from the Americans and Europeans he met that the C.I.A. and the Pentagon presented the greatest obstacle to developing peace talks. "I think the European countries are interested in stopping war and finding an alternative," he said after the tea arrived that April morning. He was a large, soft man. His untamed beard was jet black. "It's just the Americans. . . . They are ready to fight and they seek to defeat the Taliban by force."

He outlined his version of the Taliban's negotiating position. Foreign troops had to leave Afghanistan. The Taliban should be removed from blacklists and given an address—a safe office—from which to negotiate. The movement did not seek the overthrow of the Karzai government, but would seek amendments to the constitution that would bring the country into line with the Taliban's understanding of Islamic law. This would not require a return to all the old social rules of the 1990s, when Afghan women and girls were deprived of education, he emphasized. The Taliban would negotiate with fellow Afghans and Muslim scholars to define a new era of women's access to work and education, in concert with Islamic law. "The people of Afghanistan, they are Muslims, and nobody is rejecting Islam here," he said. "This is very easy for the people of Afghanistan to come together and solve this. America came here for what? They came for women? No. They came for education? No. They came because they were attacked from Afghanistan and they sought security. This is their right. But they should not occupy or interfere with Afghanistan."[7]

The Taliban had perhaps twenty-five thousand or more men under arms that spring, concentrated in the south and east of Afghanistan. Many high-ranking leaders lived with their families in Pakistan. There they operated training camps. Some of them traveled to the Gulf on Pakistani passports, operated businesses and hospitals, or smuggled war materials to the battle lines inside Afghanistan. The revived Taliban could be described as decentralized because commanders exercised considerable autonomy. These fighters included many young men who had no memory of the Islamic Emirate of the 1990s as well as some opportunists who engaged in racketeering and other crime. The movement could also be described as centralized because its *rahbari shura*, commonly referred to as the Quetta Shura and headed at least notionally by Mullah Mohammad Omar, appointed and removed governors, supervised the war through a military commission, and issued written policies on everything from smoking to the avoidance of civilian casualties.

It was not easy to gauge opinion among frontline Taliban commanders, but by 2010, independent scholars, journalists, and researchers, as well as N.A.T.O. military analysts, had conducted extensive interviews with some of them. In a classified report, "The State of the Taliban 2009," an American military task force interviewed Taliban prisoners about their motivations and beliefs. In essence, the survey found, the prisoners opposed all foreigners in Afghanistan, including Pakistanis. The Taliban believed they were winning the war, that they had not been defeated in 2001, and that they were thrown out of power illegitimately. Obama read this document in the winter of 2010 and told his aides it was "one of the most interesting and useful things" he had seen "in a long time."[8]

The Taliban of 2010 differed from the movement of the 1990s. Alex Strick van Linschoten, a British scholar who had lived in Kandahar after 2001 and interviewed many Taliban, emphasized that the resistance to American occupation occurred because of the restoration of corrupt, predatory pre-Taliban strongmen such as Gul Agha Sherzai and newer figures such as Ahmed Wali Karzai. The Taliban saw themselves as heirs to Afghan resistance to the British empire, followed by the Soviet occupation, and now followed by the American intervention. In the context of the American invasion of Iraq, the narrative of Islamist resistance to American occupation of Muslim lands offered a fresh international context for the Taliban's resistance. Also, Taliban leaders forced into exile in Pakistan after 2001 were exposed to diverse strains of Islamist politics they had previously ignored or disdained when they were mired in the Islamic Emirate's obscurantism. These Taliban leaders joined a wider international discourse after 2001 about the strategies of Islamist revolution. They absorbed the examples of negotiation and proselytizing advocated by the Muslim Brotherhood and the case of Hezbollah's tactical power sharing in Lebanon. The expansion of the movement's political imagination after 2001—and the openness of at least some leaders to negotiations with the United States—was "partly due to the embracing of information technology and the free media," as one Taliban leader put it, which led to "the circulation of the diverse ideas." Another factor was a lesson learned from the Islamic Emirate's overthrow: If the movement came back to power, it would be better if it was not sanctioned or illegitimate in the international system.[9]

Barnett Rubin argued that there was clear evidence that the Taliban were open to political compromise. The position of some C.I.A. operators in the region, including Chris Wood, was that the Taliban saw negotiations as merely a diplomatic annex to their military campaign. The purpose of talks, from the Taliban's perspective, might include dividing European governments from Washington or hastening an American withdrawal. But Mullah Mohammad Omar would never accept the compromises necessary for a political agreement to end the war, these skeptics argued.[10]

The possibility of direct talks with Tayeb Agha at least offered a path to clarify the puzzle of Mullah Omar's position in the war. In shadowy exile, he had been portrayed by Taliban and Western media as a kind of fire-breathing, screen-projected figure, heard from in periodic statements, never seen.

An arrest in Karachi in the winter of 2010 further scrambled the picture. The C.I.A. base in Karachi had expanded to include about three dozen case officers and assignees from the N.S.A., Special Operations Command, and other agencies, under an agreement worked out with President Asif Zardari and Pasha at I.S.I. In February the base traced a phone call to a house in Baldia Town, a neighborhood in the city's Pashtun-dominated western reaches. Pakistani forces raided the home and arrested Mullah Abdul Ghani Baradar, whom the Taliban described as Mullah Omar's principal deputy. American targeting information led Pakistani police to the address, but the Pakistanis did not know who they had arrested until the Americans informed them. The U.S. side emphasized that they were certain of Baradar's identity and pressed the Pakistanis to keep the Taliban leader alive: "If you kill him, we won't understand."[11]

The I.S.I. transferred Baradar to a prison. The service's media wing told the local press that they would not allow the C.I.A. direct access to the prisoner, an assertion of nationalist prerogatives. In fact, Pasha soon allowed C.I.A. officers from the Islamabad Station to speak with Baradar, but only "under I.S.I. guard," as an officer involved described it. "The 'truths' Baradar could tell about I.S.I., not to mention other Pakistani notables," a cable from the U.S. embassy in Kabul noted, made Baradar a dangerous prisoner for Pakistan.[12]

I.S.I. pressured and even tortured significant Afghan Taliban leaders. On March 5, 2010, Obaidullah Akhund, a former defense minister for the Islamic Emirate and a field commander after 2001, died in Pakistani custody, reportedly of heart disease. Former Taliban leaders believed it was almost certain he was beaten or tortured to death. The I.S.I. also arrested Gul Agha Ishakzai, a former head of Taliban finance that had been placed on sanctions lists by the U.S. Treasury. When they released him in December 2009, Ishakzai flew from Karachi to Mecca, where he entered a Saudi hospital with life-threatening injuries inflicted during beatings in I.S.I. custody, according to reports relayed by the Saudis. For Afghan Taliban who fell in I.S.I.'s crosshairs, "Pakistani prisons are worse than Bagram or Pul-i-Charkhi," meaning the dungeons run by the N.D.S., as Wakil Ahmad Mutawakil, the former foreign minister, explained to N.A.T.O. interlocutors.

It was almost impossible for the United States to discern which I.S.I. arrests of Taliban leaders were designed to give the appearance of cooperation with Washington and which were carried out to punish Taliban clients who had fallen out of I.S.I.'s favor. The two categories were not mutually exclusive. "We have eleven offices that are with you and one that's against you, so be careful," I.S.I. officers explained to Taliban commanders, according to a N.A.T.O. intelligence collector.[13]

It took months, but N.A.T.O.'s intelligence services gradually documented the leadership succession at the Taliban's highest levels that followed Baradar's arrest. Mullah Abdul Qayyum Zakir ran the Taliban's war as the head of its military commission. He was a Helmandi who had been sent to Guantánamo early in 2002 but assumed a false identity and fooled American authorities into releasing him late in 2007, after which he returned to the Afghan battlefield to seek retribution. As Baradar's successor as deputy emir, the Taliban promoted Mullah Akhtar Mansour. During the 1990s, Mansour had held positions in Taliban aviation, including at the state-owned Ariana Airlines. This placed him at the center of Taliban finance because Ariana was the Islamic Emirate's supply lifeline, operating shuttle flights to the United Arab Emirates and Saudi Arabia. (Those governments, with Pakistan's, were the only ones in the world to recognize the Islamic Emirate as Afghanistan's legitimate regime.) Mansour, an ample-bellied man in his late forties, traveled more frequently than other Taliban leaders to the Gulf and may have had business or financial interests there as well as in Pakistan.[14]

According to what the Obama administration pieced together, money was another factor in Mullah Mansour's rise to prominence during 2010. Previously, a Taliban aide named Agha Jan Motasim had carried out Taliban fund-raising in Saudi Arabia and the U.A.E. He was close to Baradar. During the summer of 2009, Mullah Mohammad Omar, or someone acting in his name, removed Motasim from this role. There were rumors that Motasim had not accounted properly for every riyal he had collected. Later, when he was campaigning to replace Mullah Omar, gunmen ambushed and wounded Motasim in Karachi. He fled to Afghanistan and then to Turkey, to recover in a hospital there. It was around the time of Motasim's removal that Taliban leaders had informed Saudi intelligence that Tayeb Agha would be their new international and fund-raising envoy. Tayeb Agha told his European interlocutors that he was in direct touch with Mullah Mansour. All that could be said for certain was that Motasim and Baradar were out, and Tayeb Agha and Mullah Mansour were in.[15]

Tayeb Agha was a relatively young man, believed to be in his thirties or early forties. He said he was from a family of Syeds, or descendants of the Prophet, from around Kandahar. He was related by marriage to Mullah Omar. During the last years of Taliban rule, Tayeb Agha had been visible in Kandahar as a personal secretary to Omar, as well as a translator and press spokesman. He spoke English and Arabic and occasionally spoke for the Taliban to the BBC. He had also played a liaison role with Arab fighters then in Afghanistan. Because of his youth and lack of battlefield credentials, Tayeb Agha lacked gravitas, but he had a documented record of proximity to Mullah Omar. As the Obama administration collected these biographical details early in 2010, the National Security Council designated Tayeb Agha as one of several "threads" of possible contact with senior Taliban leaders. At some point, it also became clear that the Taliban had formed a committee to handle liaison and possible political negotiations with the I.S.I., a committee headed by Mullah Mohammad Abbas Akhund. The underground senior leadership of the movement was organized enough to establish separate diplomatic strategies for the United States and Pakistan.[16]

Pasha flew to Washington in April. At Langley, the I.S.I. chief met Leon Panetta in the director's dining room on the seventh floor of Old Headquarters. Steve Kappes, the C.I.A.'s number two, had informed Panetta and the White House that he planned to retire in May. It was a personal decision; his first grandchild was about to be born, and he wanted to leave the C.I.A. before he started to lose a step. His departure meant the Seventh Floor would lose its most experienced Pakistan specialist. (Panetta had, however, decided to recruit John Bennett, the former Islamabad station chief he had cursed out in 2009, to run the National Clandestine Service.)

"You really ought to be thinking about talking to the Taliban, because you guys are leaving," Pasha now advised them. "You should cut a deal now. We need to be part of that deal."[17]

Panetta was skeptical about talking to the Taliban through any channel. But after the White House digested the German reports on Tayeb Agha, President Obama authorized a classified initiative to explore what might be possible. On April 20, 2010, Doug Lute convened the Conflict Resolution Cell, a highly compartmented interagency group designed to evaluate and coordinate possible political negotiations with the Taliban. The White House wanted strict secrecy because they weren't confident about their plan and didn't want to raise expectations before they made progress. Lute chaired the cell's weekly meetings in a secure conference room. Holbrooke, Chris Wood, Michèle Flournoy, who was the policy chief at the Pentagon, and David Sedney, now one of Flournoy's deputies, attended the meetings. Rubin and a few others on Holbrooke's staff also attended often.[18]

There would be "four cornerstones" to the administration's approach to peace talks, Lute announced at the first meeting. Any talks had to be Afghan led. To encourage that, the cell quickly abolished the Bush administration's restrictions that theoretically prevented Hamid Karzai's government from talking to thirty-one named, blacklisted Taliban and other armed opposition leaders. They also adjusted the positions the Bush administration had set for any negotiations. Under Bush, as a precondition to any talks, the Taliban had to break from Al Qaeda. It could not be incorporated into Afghan politics under arms. And the Taliban had to accept the Afghan constitution. The Conflict Resolution Cell changed these from preconditions for talks to goals of a successful peace negotiation and political settlement. Clinton added a phrase about all Afghans enjoying equal human rights, an indirect reference to the status of women; this would be part of the goal of Taliban acceptance of the constitution. Potentially, Holbrooke said, the work ahead could be "historically important."

An immediate question was what to tell Hamid Karzai about the administration's willingness to talk to the Taliban. The Afghan president was due to visit Washington in May. His trip offered an opportunity to repair the damage done by the 2009 election fiasco. The Conflict Resolution Cell had glimpses of I.S.I.'s campaign to reel Karzai in that spring. They believed Karzai favored talks with the Taliban. Offering support for talks might help to steer Karzai back to the American camp.

Holbrooke told his aides that he favored "small steps. We get in trouble when we say we want a peace deal with Mullah Omar." Petraeus advocated waiting until 2011 to consider talks so that American forces could batter the Taliban and win defections.

Rubin quipped, "Negotiating when leverage is at the maximum is like selling your stocks at the top of the market—it's desirable, but not easy to do. Negotiating takes a long time. We are already late if you want to be negotiating at top leverage."

Tom Donilon, the deputy national security adviser, appeared at the next meeting, on April 27, and again two days later, when the cell reassembled. What should they tell Karzai? Holbrooke objected to Petraeus's timetable. "We will be lame ducks by the beginning of 2011," he said. "The real issue is, should we accelerate? This schedule is too slow. It will take a long time."

"The Taliban want to talk to the United States," Rubin emphasized.

Chris Wood agreed. He had met with Taliban commanders through the C.I.A.'s channels and "they want to hear it from an American. We can provide safe passage" to organized talks "and not confuse that with a ceasefire."

"Pakistan wants to control this," Holbrooke reiterated.

Yet the cost of any political deal with the Taliban that was influenced by Pakistan, said Sedney, would be the risk of "civil war in Afghanistan." The former Northern Alliance leaders and large sections of the Afghan population would convulse if they believed I.S.I. had authored a peace deal that returned the Taliban even partially to power. The United States was in a difficult position, Sedney continued. I.S.I. believed the United States had aligned with India and the Northern Alliance, to win a military victory that would leave Afghanistan hostile to Pakistan. Simultaneously, Hamid Karzai interpreted Holbrooke's embrace of Kayani and Pasha—the "strategic dialogue" and the flags-and-flowers tours of Washington that spring—as just the latest evidence that the United States planned to sell Karzai's government out and cut a secret deal with Pakistan to exit the war. If they could not somehow resolve this chronic, triangular mistrust, they were unlikely to succeed—at war or at secret diplomacy.[19]

TWENTY-FIVE

Kayani 2.0

aisal Shahzad, the son of an air force vice marshal, enjoyed the privileges and mobility common to families of senior Pakistani military officers. He studied at English-language schools in Karachi. He earned a master's of business administration in the United States, married, fathered two children, and took a succession of corporate jobs in Connecticut, including one with Elizabeth Arden. Around the time he became a naturalized American citizen, at the age of twenty-nine, in 2009, Shahzad had grown disillusioned with the United States. He had suffered personal setbacks. He borrowed to buy a house but lost it to his bank during the Great Recession. Increasingly, he felt called to jihad against his adopted country. He decided to wage war, he explained later, "until the hour the U.S. pulls its forces from Iraq and Afghanistan and stops the drone strikes in Somalia and Yemen and Pakistan and stops the occupation of Muslim lands."[1]

Late in 2009, Shahzad contacted the Tehrik-i-Taliban, the Pakistani Taliban—the confederation that had murdered Benazir Bhutto. He traveled to Waziristan, stayed about six weeks, learned to build bombs, and accepted $5,000 in cash to cover expenses for an attack inside the United States. He flew back to America on February 2. His family left for Pakistan.

In late April, Shahzad bought a used Nissan Pathfinder, a sport utility vehicle. He packed its rear gun cabinet with white plastic bags of explosive fertilizer. He also installed two five-gallon canisters filled with gasoline, three canisters filled with propane, and 152 M-88 fireworks. He fused his vehicle bomb to a pair of alarm clocks.

On the afternoon of May 1, 2010, Shahzad drove to New York City. He brought along a 9mm Kel-Tec rifle folded up in a laptop case, in the event he had to fight the police. Around 6:00 p.m., Shahzad parked near the corner of Forty-fifth Street and Seventh Avenue, in the heart of Times Square. It was a warm evening. Revlon had sponsored its annual Run/Walk for Breast Cancer earlier that day, drawing tens of thousands for an opening ceremony that had featured Jimmy Fallon. Run/Walk volunteers still mingled with thick crowds of tourists as the sun fell behind the Hudson River. Shahzad kept the Pathfinder's engine running, grabbed the bag holding his rifle, and walked toward Grand Central Terminal, listening for an explosion.

It didn't come. He was a poor bomb maker. The car smoked, drawing the police, who quickly ordered an evacuation. When the bomb squad eventually broke into the vehicle, officers found an incriminating car key Shahzad had left behind. The police traced him in two days. On May 3, the F.B.I. discovered his name on the manifest of an Emirates Airlines flight from New York to Dubai. They stopped the plane as it taxied toward a runway at John F. Kennedy International Airport. Shahzad soon pleaded guilty and was sentenced to life in prison.[2]

The near miss jolted the Obama administration. The previous Christmas Day, a Nigerian jihadi loyal to Al Qaeda in the Arabian Peninsula, in Yemen, had tried to blow up a Northwest Airlines passenger jet as it landed in Detroit. The suicide attacker's bomb, stuffed in his underwear, had fizzled. Now again, just five months later, the White House found itself one mediocre terrorist away from a bloody made-for-TV crisis.

If Shahzad's bomb had gone off, the fact that his attack had been prepared and funded in Waziristan could have forced the Obama administration into an escalating military confrontation with Pakistan. Republicans in Congress, seeking to take back the House of Representatives during an angry midterm election year, would likely have demanded action—heavier bombing inside Pakistani territory, Special Forces raids, or even an American ground invasion to clear out Taliban and Al Qaeda training camps. Shahzad's fusing failure reduced the pressure but did not eliminate it. How should they convert this crisis into an opportunity? Perhaps if Kayani and Pasha truly understood that another terrorist attempt on American ground might lead the United States to war against Pakistan, they might at last reconsider I.S.I.'s position. This was perhaps the best leverage they had, short of breaking relations. Some of the Pakistan hands in the administration thought of it this way: They wanted Kayani to wake up every morning concerned that this was the day the United States had lost patience and decided to come after Pakistan.

Stan McChrystal and Karl Eikenberry worked closely with Hamid Karzai to prepare for his state visit to Washington, scheduled for May 10. Holbrooke flew out to Kabul to join the preparations. Throughout, Karzai failed to mention that he was in private contact with Pasha and I.S.I.

On May 9, Pasha flew secretly to Kabul and rode to the Arg Palace for what Karzai described to the Obama administration, a few days later, as a "twelve-minute" one-on-one discussion. To some of Karzai's aides, who later briefed American counterparts, the visit seemed to be Pasha's latest opaque effort to recruit the wobbly Karzai to I.S.I.'s priorities. It isn't fully clear what Pasha and Karzai discussed. Pakistan wanted peace and stability in Afghanistan, Pasha assured Karzai again, according to one account. Pakistan would not submit to "pressure by others," meaning the United States. You are the president of Afghanistan and we support you, Pasha said.[3]

The next morning, Karzai boarded a U.S. military transport for the long flight to Andrews Air Force Base. That evening, at Blair House, Hillary Clinton hosted a state dinner. Only then did Karzai mention Pasha's latest visit and entreaties.

As Vikram Singh, one of Holbrooke's aides, put it, I.S.I.'s plan was to recruit Karzai to work with Pakistan exclusively and then bring the United States in after a peace settlement with the Taliban had been forged. The Obama administration's plan, on the other hand, was to talk to the Taliban in secret about a settlement, then bring I.S.I. into the picture afterward. In this tug-of-war, Karzai looked like a kind of floppy rag doll, holding the middle of the rope.

Pasha had another agenda during his briefly secret visit to Kabul. The I.S.I. worried, because of the Times Square bombing attempt, that Karzai would defame Pakistan repeatedly during his state visit and perhaps rally Obama into action against Islamabad. To preempt that, Pasha offered Karzai "partnership without conditions." It was an effort to persuade him to bite his tongue while in Washington, Karzai's chief of staff, Umer Daudzai, thought.[4]

On May 11, Karzai joined Clinton, Lute, Holbrooke, and other American officials at the State Department. It seemed clear that Karzai imagined he had great leverage and was cleverly using his indecision to extract concessions from the United States. He seemed unaware that what he was really doing was driving the Obama administration mad, undermining the president's faith in the cause of an independent, democratic Afghanistan. Karzai's tone was both friendly and threatening. "Afghanistan needs to rally people against extremism and for partnership with the U.S.," he said. "We will pay a price and work with the U.S.," but only if Washington was invested in Afghanistan for more than just a war on terrorism.

"It's not just the war on terrorism," Clinton assured him.

Karzai repeated his point: "If the U.S. is only in Afghanistan for the War on Terror," then he needed to partner with Pakistan. "If the U.S. has a broader purpose, we will be with you." He added, "Pakistan wants you out."[5]

Lute asked Karzai what he thought Pasha's latest offer of "unconditional support" to Afghanistan really meant.

Two months ago, Karzai answered, Pasha had said there were two preconditions for an agreement: Reduce or eliminate India's presence in Afghanistan and create political accommodations for Pashtuns. The latter goal was implausible, Karzai had concluded, he said. It would be "suicide" for any Afghan leader to compromise on some of the political issues most important to Pakistan, such as the future of the Afghan-Pakistan border.

"Maybe Pakistan is not capable of changing," Clinton said. "Maybe it needs enemies" so that the army and I.S.I. could retain power.

Karzai leaned in to the secretary of state. "What is your objective?" he asked. "Either you are with us forever, or I make a deal with Pakistan."

By "forever," Karzai explained, "we want the same relationship as Israel," or at least the same as Egypt and South Korea. Those American allies enjoyed long-term defense guarantees and robust arms sales. Republicans and Democrats alike accepted those countries as essential allies. Was Afghanistan in the same category?[6]

There was no way for Clinton to answer Karzai's questions directly. It would have been awkward to explain, in any event, that the policy reviews undergirding Obama's dispatch of tens of thousands more U.S. troops to Afghanistan had actually concluded that the security of Pakistan's nuclear weapons and the elimination of Al Qaeda on Pakistani soil were America's only truly "vital interests" in the region. The United States had declared publicly, again and again, its enduring commitment to Afghanistan, yet it was doubtful whether Obama and bipartisan leaders in Congress regarded Afghanistan's importance as comparable to South Korea or Israel.

They discussed the prospects for talking to the Taliban. "How do we fight and die while also pursuing peace talks?" Clinton asked.

There were Taliban determined to be "inclusive and take manpower away from the I.S.I.," Karzai answered. These Taliban were "all for peace without Al Qaeda."[7]

With the Conflict Resolution Cell now formed secretly at the White House, Richard Holbrooke's objective was to persuade Karzai to "authorize direct contacts" between the United States and the Taliban, as he now put it. But Karzai refused. Pakistan controlled the Taliban. Peace talks had to involve the I.S.I., Karzai believed. There was no other way because the Pakistani service controlled the Taliban.

He reached out to a tray before him. "Picking up Mullah Omar for them is like picking up this cookie," Karzai said. The Taliban were just a bunch of "country bumpkins," of no consequence without their Pakistani patrons, he added at another point.[8]

Holbrooke met separately during the visit with Hanif Atmar, the Afghan interior minister, whom Holbrooke had unsuccessfully promoted as an alternative to Karzai the previous year. The I.S.I. believes "that without Massoud, the Taliban will sweep through" to power and take Kabul when the time is ripe, Atmar said.

Holbrooke said that the problem was that in order to turn off the Taliban insurgency, Kayani probably wanted a civilian nuclear deal comparable to the one the Bush administration granted India, and also a major free trade agreement to lift Pakistan's economy. Yet these demands were politically unrealistic in Washington. To give Islamabad what it wanted is a "deep impossibility," Holbrooke said.

The Times Square attack was "important," he went on, because the case history showed that the Pakistani Taliban now posed a direct threat to the U.S. homeland. The Afghan Taliban did not. "Faisal Shahzad's phone numbers all led to the T.T.P.," the Pakistani Taliban, "not Al Qaeda."

Holbrooke asked Atmar a question that had been on his mind all year. "Would the elimination of Mullah Omar change anything?"

"No," Atmar predicted. The I.S.I. would find a way to manage a leadership succession within the Taliban, he implied.[9]

After all the hours of preparation, after all the flags and flowers and one-on-one time with Karzai, the Afghan president's state visit left Clinton frustrated and sarcastic. Obama, Lute, and the National Security Council had displayed a "mania" for process—"threads," "resolution cells," and the like, Clinton complained to aides. "I wouldn't do it this way if I were president," she declared pointedly.

What was the "end-state vision" that the United States sought in Afghanistan? Clinton asked. That was perhaps why Karzai pressed so hard for Israel-like guarantees—perhaps he sensed correctly that the Obama administration did not know the answer. "Pakistan knows what end state they want," Clinton said. "They've gotten more threatening to

Afghanistan recently. They are letting loose the Haqqani network. But we don't know our end-state vision because we don't have one. We don't have a Pakistan strategy or a reconciliation strategy. Just words and process."[10]

Ashfaq Kayani asserted that he was being misunderstood. His efforts to recruit Karzai into a separate peace negotiation might be competitive with Washington but, in fact, American and Pakistani interests were compatible, he believed. To prove it, after Karzai's Washington visit, he said he was willing to talk to Karzai openly, with the United States in the room.

McChrystal invited Kayani to Kabul on May 26 to spend time with Karzai alone, with the American general standing by to facilitate or mediate. By this time McChrystal had warmed to the possibility of ending the war through a negotiated settlement. "They didn't give me enough to win outright," he told an aide that spring, referring to troop levels, and Karzai's government "is not going to win the battle of legitimacy." McChrystal did not think that the United States could settle the war but he thought he might be able to set conditions for an agreement between Kayani and Karzai.

Kayani flew in bearing a concession. The general said that he would no longer describe Pakistan's goal as the establishment of a "friendly" government in Kabul. Pakistan would merely seek a "stable, secure" Afghanistan. Kayani regretted that his earlier statements about seeking a "friendly" Afghanistan had been heard as code for the Taliban's restoration. That wasn't his goal, he insisted.[11]

The army chief sold Karzai, who was "glowing" afterward, Ambassador Eikenberry reported to Washington. McChrystal's view was that Karzai and Kayani were moving ahead as a pair to find an understanding despite serious doubts among their advisers. Amrullah Saleh and Rangin Spanta were among those in Karzai's cabinet who opposed seeking a deal with Pakistan. Spanta felt that such an agreement had to be grounded in equality and that Pakistan wanted to dictate its conditions to Kabul. In Islamabad, Pasha and I.S.I. had their own doubts. Yet Kayani and Karzai "showed that they want a relationship," in McChrystal's estimation. The C.I.A. circulated analysis that month reporting that "Kayani has been pushing for reconciliation" with Afghanistan since 2004, but that Musharraf had overruled him. Kayani was probing now for what kind of agreement might be possible. "Pakistan doesn't know what its red lines are" in pursuit of a deal, according to the C.I.A.'s take. If Pakistan's army could achieve by negotiations what it had tried and failed since the late 1980s to achieve by force—a stable Afghanistan that was not regarded by the corps commanders as an ally of India—it might welcome all kinds of unlikely bedfellows in a political settlement, including the Panjshiris.[12]

Yet it was obvious that Kayani and Pasha remained hostile to some of the key figures in Karzai's security cabinet, particularly Amrullah Saleh. Karzai's own doubts were growing about Saleh, partly because of Saleh's close ties to the C.I.A.[13]

The Loya Jirga Tent on the flowered grounds of Kabul Polytechnic University had become a symbol of a revived Afghanistan. The tent covered an area the size of a soccer field, serviced by a generator and equipped with Internet connections. That spring, Karzai organized a National Consultative Peace Jirga at the tent complex, to symbolically engage more than 1,500 delegates around the possibility of negotiating with the Taliban. As with so much else, Karzai's approach was instinctive, tactical, and erratic, but also deft and hard to derail. He had fashioned international support for his peace initiative. The United Nations, Great Britain, and other European Union governments openly backed Karzai's search for a political solution to the war, even if they lacked faith in his ability to find one.

On Wednesday, June 2, members of parliament, tribal leaders, businessmen, and activists streamed into the Loya Jirga Tent. The men wore turbans, robes, and vests. Hundreds of women had also been named as delegates. Soon after they found their seats, explosions rang out. Taliban infiltrators fired rockets, inaccurately but loudly, at the Polytechnic campus. Four suicide bombers attempted to reach the assembly. Afghan police took heavy casualties but shot several attackers dead before they could harm anyone and later chased down other suspected conspirators. None of the peace delegates was injured. Yet the attack embarrassed and infuriated Karzai. The assembly went forward, nonetheless. Karzai asked for a mandate for negotiations. He referred to the insurgents as "brother Taliban-*jan*," a suffix indicating affection. He urged the Taliban to stop fighting and promised to push for peace "step by step."[14]

On Sunday, June 6, Karzai summoned Amrullah Saleh and Hanif Atmar, the interior minister, to the Arg Palace. Both men knew Karzai was furious about the failure of security, even though, in their opinion, the police and counterterrorist squads they commanded had responded bravely and effectively. They both resented Karzai's public appeasement of the Taliban and his failure to celebrate the sacrifices of his own security forces.

Atmar carried a resignation letter in his pocket. Ever since Holbrooke and Biden had promoted him as a possible presidential candidate, Karzai's insecurities had made Atmar's position as chief of Afghanistan's police and internal security less and less tenable. Saleh was in a mood similar to Atmar's. He was ambivalent about resigning, however, because he knew his departure from office was precisely what I.S.I. wanted. That angered Saleh and made him more determined to stay.

After they settled into their chairs, Karzai stunned them by declaring that he believed the attack on the peace *jirga* had been organized by the United States, to undermine his search for a political settlement. He knew this, he continued, because during the hunt for fugitives involved in the attack, he had called McChrystal. The American commander had assured him that if he decided to continue with the *jirga* for two more days, McChrystal would make sure that the assembly would be secure.

"Where did he get that confidence?" Karzai asked. "Because they were behind it! And as they saw that the *jirga* was not proceeding against their interests, they stopped the second episode of the attack," and allowed the delegates to finish their work. Karzai added that he suspected Saleh and Atmar were part of the American conspiracy.[15]

Saleh told him he was wrong. They had enough evidence to be sure this was a Taliban operation, like many other suicide strikes in Kabul before. McChrystal's forces had chased down and arrested conspirators in Khost.

"Do you think I'm stupid?" Karzai asked.

"No, you are the president of the country," Saleh said.

"Mr. President, you are going too far," Atmar intervened at one point. "First, this was not the Americans. Second, I am not complicit in this. I would not turn a blind eye." But when Atmar tried to say more, Karzai told him to shut up.

At that, Atmar tossed his letter of resignation on the table. "You are not my commander-in-chief," he said. "I cannot serve you."

Karzai turned to Saleh. "If Atmar is resigning, you should do the same."

Saleh let a few seconds go by in silence. Then he agreed. "I don't have a written resignation," he said, "but for me it's also enough."[16]

The two men left together. Saleh had concluded that Karzai had lost trust in N.A.T.O. and sought to undermine the American military mission. This much seemed unarguable as the news of his resignation spread around Kabul that night: The Afghan cabinet's most hawk-eyed foe of I.S.I. had been neutralized.

O n July 14, 2010, about ten weeks after Faisal Shahzad's Pathfinder fizzled in Times Square, the Pakistani Taliban released a video. It showed Shahzad training with a machine gun and speaking to the camera while gripping a Koran. "I have been trying to join my brothers in jihad ever since 9/11 happened," he announced, somewhat implausibly. "I also want to inform my brother Muslims living abroad that it is not difficult at all to wage an attack on the West, and specifically in the U.S., and completely defeat them."[17]

The video inflamed again American anger at Pakistan. This was turning out to be less than a congenial summer for "strategic dialogue" about a new American-Pakistani partnership. Yet Kayani persisted. He decided to write something more definitive and honest than the sterile Foreign Office white paper he had delivered to the White House earlier in the year. The general now drafted a second paper about Pakistan's requirements and strategic goals, a paper more in Kayani's own voice. It ran more than one hundred pages. This became known as "Kayani 2.0." It was fashioned as a "think paper," as Holbrooke called it, providing a "road map for the next five years." Kayani delivered it to the Obama administration on July 18.[18]

Between the paper and Pasha's conversations with C.I.A. counterparts, the Pakistanis advanced a more candid position than the deny-deny-deny lines of Musharraf vintage, such as "The Quetta Shura is a fiction." On counterterrorism, Kayani and Pasha offered a nuanced if self-interested argument. The C.I.A.'s drone war was driving the Afghan Taliban, the Pakistani Taliban, Al Qaeda, and the Haqqanis into closer cooperation, particularly in North Waziristan, the I.S.I. feared. This was dangerous for both Pakistan and the United States. Yes, Kayani and Pasha said repeatedly, the I.S.I. had contacts with the Haqqanis, but this was to gain influence and information, as surely fellow professional spies could understand. Pasha repeatedly pointed out to his C.I.A. counterparts that the agency, too, maintained direct and indirect contacts with violent militias around the world, to collect intelligence and develop influence. As for Lashkar-e-Taiba, the Kashmiri militant group that had struck Mumbai so devastatingly in 2008, it would be a mistake for I.S.I. to break ties and drive it further underground. Pasha said he could have prevented Mumbai if I.S.I. had maintained closer contacts with Lashkar and the Directorate S officers involved had kept him, as the new chief, in the loop. (The United States and India had no evidence that Pasha had personally known about Mumbai in advance.)

If the Obama administration wanted to change the calculus of the Pakistani public and elites, it would have to make bold bets on the country's independence, prosperity, and security. As one reader of the Kayani 2.0 paper summarized the general's evolving line of argument: *You Americans are just focused on the military and counterterrorism. You are running up against the hard limits of how far our relationship will go in these fields, and you are getting frustrated, and I'm sorry about that. But I have my realities too. If you don't visibly address the big deficits in our economy, energy supplies, and water supplies, this relationship is just going to continue to be a muddle.*[19]

On July 19, as she began to digest Kayani's "2.0" white paper, Hillary Clinton gave a roundtable interview to Pakistani journalists. Her main purpose was to reinforce the strategic dialogue by talking about energy, water, Afghanistan, India, and the possibilities for mutual understanding. Yet when the questions turned to terrorism, Clinton laid out the risk of a total breach between America and Pakistan—perhaps war—if another attack such as the one at Times Square took place. "If an attack is traced back to Pakistan, people in America will be devastated—devastated," Clinton said. "I cannot predict what the consequences would be because there would be many people in the United States who would say, 'Why did this happen? Why are we investing so much in our partnership?'"[20]

Kayani received this just as it was intended: as a threat. At the end of the month, he composed an anxious letter to Admiral Mullen, the chairman of the Joint Chiefs. "I write to you at a critical juncture of our history," the August 2, 2010, typed confidential letter on Kayani's embroidered stationery began. "For Pakistan, these are defining moments." He referred to the litany of recent statements "made by the United States' leadership suggesting that any act of terror in the United States or anywhere else against the United States' interests having links with terrorists in Pakistan will warrant a direct action by the United States against Pakistan." The letter continued,

> These are very dangerous thoughts. . . . I am sure you realize that any such action will jeopardize the very basis of our cooperation. It will push the Pakistan Army to the wall and force me to take a position which may nullify our joint efforts of years, made at such enormous costs. The consequences of such a scenario for overall security in the region are not difficult to predict. We must do anything and everything possible to avoid such a catastrophe. . . .

His reference to "a scenario for overall security in the region" carried an implied threat of his own. In the event of an American attack on Pakistan, his forces might abandon all constraint in backing the Taliban against American troops in Afghanistan. Kayani also seemed to interpret the

American threats after Times Square as a kind of public pressure campaign designed to force him into pushing his army into action in North Waziristan. He wrote that he could not give in to this pressure, because he lacked the political support in Pakistan to attack in Waziristan. If the United States broke with Pakistan or escalated its bombing in the country, he warned, there would be no return:

> We are fully aware of the United States' concerns. We also know that terrorists cannot be allowed to attack anywhere across the borders. . . . However, we cannot design operations, the fallout of which can destabilize Pakistan as a country. Pakistan's Army draws its strength from the bedrock of popular support. Come what may, we shall have to guard this vital fundamental on which we based our campaign right from the beginning. . . . I can feel we are running out of both time and patience. . . . If the people of Pakistan feel let down once again, their alienation with the United States will be complete, and perhaps forever.[21]

TWENTY-SIX

Lives and Limbs

*June 16, 2010: We are at KAF [Kandahar Airfield] now, complete with
the poo pond, dust storms, and rocket attacks. We heard the alarms go off
last night around dusk. They said it happens about once every three days
during morning, night or limited visibility. They target our barracks and
the boardwalk. Five civilians were killed in the last few attacks and there
is shrapnel on the side of the building we are staying at. It isn't really as
scary as I thought it was going to be. KAF is huge, with 25,000 people on
it from multiple nations including Romania, Netherlands, UK, France, US
and others I haven't seen yet. . . . There are seven [military cafeterias] here
and TGIF as well [as] multiple gyms. It's pretty crazy. I can't wait to be
done here and get up to where we are going to operate. . . .*

*We had a briefing on COIN and some of the directives from Gen.
McChrystal. It was the standard stuff that we have been talking about
since we knew we were coming to Afghanistan. I didn't know how
dangerous the rocket attacks are, though. The Taliban have conducted 80
rocket attacks since January and one of their attacks killed or injured 14
civilians. They take 107mm Chinese rockets and place them on a berm or
stakes connected to a timer or a bucket of water with a hole in the bottom,
so when the water drains, the rocket fires. . . . The Brigade CSM
[Command Sergeant Major] and [a] few other field grade officers from
Brigade were injured in a RPG [rocket propelled grenade] attack down in*

*Zhari. . . . It is pretty crazy. Coming back from counter-I.E.D. trainer we
saw some Afghans outside the wire and they flicked us off or shook their
fists at us. Some hearts and mind campaign, huh?*

—Journal of Lieutenant Timothy J. Hopper, First Battalion,
320th Field Artillery Regiment, Second Combat Brigade Team,
101st Airborne Division, Combined Task Force "Strike"¹

Highway 1 runs west from Kandahar toward Helmand Province,
through or near four districts—Arghandab, Panjwai, Zhari, and
Maiwand—that were the Taliban's birthplace. Since 2006, the area had
provided the movement an important military redoubt. To the highway's
south lay the irrigated green zone watered by the Arghandab River. It
contained tributaries, canals, wheat fields, opium fields, pomegranate
orchards, and marijuana crops that sometimes grew ten feet tall. From a
soldier's perspective, grapes were the most significant crop. Kandahar's
vines grew in rows on mud berms or walls. The rows presented staggered
obstacles—and protection—comparable to the hedgerows of Normandy.
Grape farmers built concrete drying houses that could be used as bunkers or rigged with improvised explosive devices. The region's lush vegetation varied in thickness by the season. During the late autumn and
winter the fields could be brown and denuded. During the peak growing
seasons of spring and summer, the zone could feel as wet and thick as a
tropical jungle. The foliage was so dense during the high season that Taliban guerrillas hiding in one pomegranate orchard beside a walled American combat outpost could sneak through the trees and toss grenades over
the outpost walls without being seen. On foot patrol, every fifteen feet
there seemed to be a ten-foot grape berm or a wet five-foot-tall grove
blocking the way.

By 2010 the Taliban used their base in the green zone to menace traffic on Highway 1 and to infiltrate Kandahar City. It was obvious that the
guerrillas had a significant presence in the zone but neither American
nor N.A.T.O. intelligence had a clear picture of how large the Taliban
force might be or how it had prepared its defenses. Canopies of trees and
vines allowed the Taliban to hide from aerial surveillance. By early 2010,

the American military's tactical rules forbade helicopters from flying south of Highway 1, over the irrigated areas, because of the likelihood that the helicopters would be shot down. An exception might be granted only if the helicopters tracked directly overhead of a maneuvering ground combat patrol strong enough to prevent the capture of pilots if they were downed.[2]

McChrystal's campaign plan, devised in the summer of 2009, identified Kandahar as the war's most important geography, the "center of gravity" for Obama's surge. Kandahar was the Taliban's first capital and the Karzais' home region. If the guerrillas regained control there, the movement would enjoy the kind of unmolested supply lines to Pakistan that had fueled its national conquest during the 1990s. It would signal clearly to southern Afghans that the Taliban was again on the march. In the early execution of his war plan, McChrystal had been diverted by the Marines' insistence on having their own combat theater in underpopulated Helmand. Early in 2010, the Marines mounted a kind of demonstration assault on Marjah District in Helmand, a hub of the opium trade. The campaign required great effort and had produced debatable results by the spring. McChrystal had infamously promised to roll out "government in a box" in Marjah. He meant the Afghan government would deploy a mobile phalanx of civil servants to deliver services and establish the Karzai government's legitimacy. The idea seemed almost implausible on its face. British officers commanding on the front lines in Helmand saw virtually no evidence of the Afghan government. Taliban forces enjoyed complete freedom of movement. Villagers had little faith that the government could deliver. In any event, the significance of the early American-led action in Helmand paled in comparison to the coming fight in Kandahar. If McChrystal's "ink spot" strategy of securing critical districts in the south was to succeed even partially, the Taliban had to be cleared out of the green zone. The area connected Helmand and Kandahar. The clearance operation was also necessary to secure Kandahar City.

American generals sometimes sniffed at the Canadian forces as insufficiently aggressive, yet prior American rotations through Kandahar had not reduced the Taliban's influence, either, and in some respects the most recent American units deployed there had made things worse. In 2009, Colonel Harry Tunnell commanded Task Force Stryker in Kandahar. Tunnell rejected Petraeus's population-friendly counterinsurgency doctrine as "musings from amateurs, contractors, plagiarized journal articles, etc.," as he put it acidly in a dissenting memorandum to the secretary of the army.[3] Yet during Tunnell's command, undisciplined, out-of-control "kill teams" had rampaged against Afghan civilians. Five soldiers from a battalion in Tunnell's task force were later charged with murdering Afghans for fun and keeping their fingers as mementos. It was hardly surprising that the Stryker tour had left some Kandaharis shaking their fists as Tim Hopper's men from the 101st Airborne arrived.

After Obama's West Point speech, McChrystal, Mike Mullen, and Secretary of Defense Robert Gates selected the Second Combat Brigade of the 101st Airborne Division to fight what they conceived of as the war's most decisive battle. The brigade had been formed for the invasion of Normandy and had shouldered three rotations to Iraq since 2003. It contained about 3,400 personnel, plus the 101st Combat Aviation Brigade, which fielded Apache attack helicopters, Chinook helicopters for air assault and casualty evacuation, and other aircraft. The Second Combat Brigade was ordered to Kandahar as Combined Task Force "Strike," made up of about 4,800 soldiers, to carry out close-quarters counterinsurgency warfare from small outposts in the green zone. "You're the main effort of the war," McChrystal told Colonel Art Kandarian, the brigade's commander.[4]

In February 2010, Kandarian arrived in Kandahar for a predeployment site survey, to ready for full deployment in May. He discovered there were only two small battalion bases and half a dozen platoon-size observation posts in the zone that he was supposed to conquer. In Baghdad, Petraeus had built up small combat outposts shared by American and Iraqi forces almost block by block to enforce security. This would be the model for these agricultural fields, too. There were local villages to pacify but the area was not heavily populated, except by Taliban. The landlords who owned the zone's orchards, grape, and marijuana fields lived mainly in Kandahar. They hired day laborers and sharecroppers to tend their crops.

Colonel Kandarian, a balding man in his midforties with extensive combat experience in Iraq, rolled through the area with an armed escort. He sent his Afghan interpreter to talk to some children he saw hanging around, watching him.

"What did those kids say to you?" Kandarian asked when the interpreter returned.

"They said, 'You can build your fort anywhere, because when the gardens grow, the Taliban will run at you."

Kandarian thought, If that's what an eight-year-old understands, what do the local adults know?

"How far do you get on patrol?" Kandarian asked a forward American officer he met.

"About a kilometer."

"What happens after that?"

"After that, they think we're Russians."[5]

As they planned, Kandarian and his lieutenants studied the history of Soviet operations in the green zone during the 1980s. It was not encouraging. The Soviets had sent two armored regiments into the Arghandab Valley and still had not been able to hold it. Those were the battles that had taken Mullah Mohammad Omar's eye.

The first elements of the "Strike" task force landing at Kandahar Airfield included engineering units that worked at a furious tempo to site and build new walled combat outposts along and south of Highway 1. By June, foot patrols began at an aggressive tempo. Strike soldiers discovered the unknown one walk at a time. One of Kandarian's early decisions was to combine all bases into joint U.S. and Afghan facilities, to improve the Afghan forces and to give American soldiers greater access to local knowledge while on patrol.

The First Battalion, 502nd Infantry Regiment, or "First Strike," deployed early on in Zhari District. The regiment's Bravo Company called themselves the "Bull Dogs." On June 18, one of Bravo's platoons marched on a routine patrol to a village. Staff Sergeant James Hunter, twenty-five, an Army journalist and photographer whose family lived in Kentucky, joined the maneuver. As he walked down a sandy lane holding his camera, a massive I.E.D. detonated, badly wounding him. The platoon radioed for evacuation and a helicopter soon appeared. Private First Class Benjamin Park, also twenty-five, of Fairfax Station, Virginia, just outside Washington, D.C., lifted Hunter's body and carried him toward the chopper. A second I.E.D. detonated. Both men died.[6]

With that "double tap" land mine strike, the Second Combat Brigade's war of attrition in the green zone—a fight that would become, alongside some of the Marines' engagements in Helmand, the costliest in lives and limbs of the entire American war in Afghanistan—had opened.

June 19, 2010: Last night we went to a ceremony for two soldiers [Hunter and Park] that were killed from 1-502. It was all the units from 101st that were still at KAF and some other foreign units. It was a long-ass walk to the airfield where we waited around for about 30 minutes and then we marched out to the rear of the airplane and had 8 ranks lined up on each side, to form a corridor for them to bring the bodies into the plane. . . . Not that I didn't know we were going into the shit of it but damn its different seeing a casket with an American flag wrapped around it being carried by you, while they play taps, and you have hundreds of other soldiers doing a ceremonial salute. I really don't want to go home like that.

Some of the soldiers were a little freaked but I was surprised that so far everyone seems pretty resilient. I mean, we are only in second week though and still sitting around at KAF with not much to worry about except rocket attacks. I haven't really gotten much of a chance to call Jenny. I'm starting to miss her a lot. It is just weird to not really have the ability to just call conveniently. . . . It was much different in Korea. The information flow is still just a drip from the faucet. So the guys that were killed were on a dismounted mission and hit a pressure plate I.E.D. One was the PAO [public affairs officer] who actually took our battalion photo.

—Journal of Lieutenant Tim Hopper

Art Kandarian had joined the Army in 1986, out of R.O.T.C. at Washington and Lee University in Virginia. He had gotten to know McChrystal on the battlefield in Iraq. Kandarian's most difficult tour there was in Diyala Province, as a battalion commander in the Second Combat Brigade. The brigade rotated home in 2008. Kandarian took command in

March 2009 and was told they would be headed back to Iraq after rest and refitting. Only in December were they told, no, they were headed to Afghanistan for a combat mission. Normally they would have a year to prepare; this time, it would be less than six months. Some of the brigade forces trained in dry mountainous terrain near Yuma, Arizona. Platoon leaders arriving in Kandahar were stunned to discover they had to ford muddy canals and Arghandab tributaries with their carbines held above their heads, as in iconic Vietnam photographs. This was a step-by-step battlefield where visibility was extremely poor and hidden I.E.D.s were the main danger. The basic tactical plan was to provoke contact with embedded Taliban forces and then destroy them or force them to flee the region. The patrolling conditions would test the acumen of even the most experienced infantrymen. There were, in fact, many such infantrymen in the Second Combat Brigade: soldiers, sergeants, and captains schooled the hard way about I.E.D.s in Iraq and elsewhere in Afghanistan, who knew how the enemy booby-trapped footpaths and the best ways to walk safely. Often, the Taliban rigged the easiest and most obvious pathways with trip wires and pressure plates. To survive, the veterans knew, you had to patrol down the least likely, most arduous routes. Never walk through an obvious opening in a grape wall, for example, when it was possible to climb over the highest point of the wall, however difficult. The easy openings were where the Taliban placed trip wires.

Yet not everyone in Kandarian's task force had been trained for such yard-by-yard, life-or-death decision making. Because of the strains on the Army's combat readiness after nearly a decade of continuous war, Kandarian had to fill out his green zone force by converting an artillery unit, the First Battalion, 320th Field Artillery Regiment, to an infantry role. Many of the officers and soldiers of the 1/320th had spent their careers learning how to fire big guns at the enemy from distant points, often from secure bases. They did not train routinely to conduct harrowing foot patrols. The 1/320th was Lieutenant Tim Hopper's battalion, which partly explained the butterflies he recorded in his journal. He was taking command of platoon-level infantry operations he had never experienced; the lives and limbs of his men depended on his eyesight and judgment. Hopper was in his midtwenties. He had grown up in

Lunenburg, Massachusetts, a town of ten thousand to the west of Boston. He enrolled in R.O.T.C. at Northeastern University. After college, he had served a year in South Korea before moving to become a medical platoon leader at the 1/320th at Fort Campbell. The idea that he should lead a platoon through the most difficult terrain of the Afghan war struck him as strange. When he enlisted in the Army, he listed infantry duty as fourteenth out of fourteen choices in declaring his preference for assignment. But he was accepting of his duty. This was not the only place in Iraq or Afghanistan where the Army had been forced to convert artillery to infantry. It was, however, an especially difficult place to try.

June 22, 2010: So the latest word is that we are going to this town Jazah to the north of the Shuyens, which is where Bravo is going. It is a town where no one has really been so it could be really good or really bad, we don't know. . . . Well, I'm sure the plan will change a few more times, though. I got an intel dump from the S-2 the other day. . . . It was pretty good but worrying at the same time. I mean, it is about 80 percent I.E.D.s and some of them have fucked up these vehicles we have a lot. They have these new I.E.D.s called D.F.F.C. [Directionally Focused Fragmentary Charge] which are basically a big shotgun shell that shoots out a concentrated blast instead of buck spray. So they pack an old artillery round case with shrapnel and charge and cover the end with enamel to shape the charge a bit along with some HME [Home Made Explosives]. It blew the turret off the same type of vehicle I'll be riding in about 75 [meters] away from the vehicle itself and the engine block about 50 [meters] . . . holy shitake.
                                                   —*Journal of Lieutenant Tim Hopper*

"We will be unable to succeed in the governance in Kandahar if we cannot eliminate a vast majority of the corruption there and set up a legitimate government structure—period," Admiral Mullen told reporters traveling with him to Afghanistan early in 2010. He added, "We're not going to keep risking the lives of our soldiers if the will is not there to address these issues."[7]

"Sending troops into Kandahar is like sending them to Chicago in the

1920s," Holbrooke remarked to his staff in Washington. "The city administration is controlled by Al Capone," that is, Ahmed Wali Karzai, or A.W.K., the longtime C.I.A. ally and a security contractor whose gunmen protected U.S. fuel and supply trucks. Ahmed Wali described himself privately to Frank Ruggiero, Holbrooke's deputy, as "the most powerful official in Kandahar," who could "deliver whatever is needed." In reply to accusations that he was a drug runner, he volunteered to take a polygraph to prove his innocence. His protestations worked. Across the Obama administration and within N.A.T.O., opinion varied widely about how dangerous Ahmed Wali Karzai was, whether he really trafficked opium or not, and whether he should be engaged as a necessary evil or removed from power. The British commander of RC-South, Major General Nick Carter, favored tough love as the only practical course. McChrystal's intelligence chief, Mike Flynn, and a civilian adviser, Sarah Chayes, who had lived and founded a nongovernmental organization in Kandahar, advocated ousting Ahmed Wali, although it was not clear how this might be done. McChrystal concluded reluctantly that without Hamid Karzai's cooperation, he had few options.[8]

In mid-March, Flynn met Ahmed Wali at his Kandahar compound and told him that if the C.I.A. or I.S.A.F. intelligence units acquired any evidence that Karzai was collaborating with the Taliban or engaged in major criminal activity, Flynn would place Ahmed Wali's name on the Joint Priority Effects List. This was the classified capture-kill list of enemy leaders and facilitators on the Afghan battlefield. American or N.A.T.O. forces could strike anyone on the list without warning.

"You're threatening me," Ahmed Wali observed.

"Yes, it's a threat, but you're threatening us by standing in the way of our success."[9]

Still, I.S.A.F. never acted. American generals and diplomats tried to work with Ahmed Wali, as the Canadians had also tried, to persuade him to adopt the good-government tenets of counterinsurgency. He was dealt with as a "sort of unfortunate fact that was wished away or left to the C.I.A. to deal with," as a senior N.A.T.O. official involved put it. McChrystal and Flynn settled on a policy by which they identified "red lines" that Ahmed Wali must not cross, such as providing material aid to the Taliban. The implication was that they would not arrest or attack Karzai for routine bribery or racketeering. The "red lines" strategy, reported a classified State Department cable, would at least mean that American "intelligence collectors will have a focus" and could gather evidence on the kinds of drug crimes and massive corruption that might trigger more decisive U.S. intervention.[10]

The uncomfortable truth was that the Obama administration did not have the means or will to remove Ahmed Wali Karzai or other strongmen in Kandahar. Hamid Karzai would have to act, and he had chosen to leave his allies in place. In any event, some of the Americans involved feared that if they decapitated a mob boss like Ahmed Wali, they might touch off a free-for-all to control his abandoned rackets.

June 26, 2010: Last night a [Specialist] from C/2-508 was killed [by an] IED followed by a complex attack from five different directions. They came up to a canal and were conducting a deliberate crossing and clearing it when they hit what they believe was a pressure plate IED followed up by small arms fire. . . . All this stuff has me really thinking about what's going to happen up there. Not to mention that General McChrystal, the I.S.A.F. Commander, was relieved of command for contempt of the President. General Petraeus the CENTCOM commander is stepping down from his position to take over. Every day Kandahar is on the headlines and all the issues surrounding the war. We are really in the middle of history here and it probably is not going to be a good thing. . . .

Damn . . . what did I get myself into here? I am not a tactical genius. I'm smart but this doesn't come naturally to me. I keep trying to put myself in the mindset of the Taliban but I can't seem to wrap my head around it. . . . Regardless of whether I feel like I'm ready or not I am being thrust into this and do not have a choice. My life is going to be on the line in the next month or so. . . . I've decided I am going to write a death letter for my parents, Jenny and my brother. I know it is morbid but I think it is probably a good thing to do just in case anything happens.

—Journal of Lieutenant Tim Hopper

On June 22, 2010, *Rolling Stone* published "The Runaway General," a profile of McChrystal in which unnamed aides to the commanding general were quoted making loose, disparaging remarks to an embedded reporter about Vice President Biden and the French, among other subjects. The article made it sound as if the officers commanding the Afghan war held Obama and other civilian leaders in contempt. Stan McChrystal was a disciplined individual but retained something of a fraternity boy's imperviousness to political risk. He did understand immediately the scale of his error. On Tuesday, June 22, 2010, the day the story appeared, McChrystal was supposed to appear by secure video for an interagency meeting about negotiating with the Taliban to end the Afghan war. The session was postponed. The general boarded a long flight to Andrews Air Force Base to meet the president.

The White House had previously scheduled a National Security Council meeting on Afghanistan in the Situation Room for Thursday, June 24. Upstairs in the Oval Office, Obama accepted McChrystal's resignation after what the general described as "a short, professional" exchange. David Petraeus was already in the West Wing, waiting for the N.S.C. meeting on Afghanistan and Pakistan. Reggie Love, the president's personal aide, turned up in the hallways asking if Petraeus was around. Petraeus had no idea that Obama had accepted McChrystal's resignation. The general followed Love upstairs; he passed the White House national security team coming out, refusing to make eye contact with him. He sat down with Obama and waited for a White House photographer to record the moment and leave.

"I'm asking you as your president and commander-in-chief to take command in Afghanistan," Obama said.

Petraeus knew the only answer was yes. He tried to introduce his thinking about the planned drawdown of surge forces, that his recommendations would all be based on "facts on the ground," as well as an awareness of the realities of politics in Washington and N.A.T.O.

The assignment was a step down in authority, as Petraeus oversaw the entire Central Command area of operations, from Cairo to Islamabad. (McChrystal had reported to him.) As it happened, although he had backed McChrystal fully during the first half of 2010, Petraeus had somewhat different ideas about how to prosecute the Afghan war on Obama's time line. His arrival in Kabul that summer would lead to a reinterpretation of counterinsurgency, from Kandahar's green zone to the Pakistani borderlands.[11]

> *June 28, 2010: So we are leaving KAF tonight. We are taking a Chinook up to FOB Jelawur. Four guys from my platoon went up yesterday. I was on the boardwalk getting some ice cream with Doc and my FO [Forward Observer] when we saw a couple guys from the 82nd [Airborne]. They came up and asked who we were relieving and we said we were going up to the Arghandab. The were telling us about it and man I'm not going to lie but it scares the shit out of me and kind of depresses me. They were telling me that it is really bad up there. . . . There is a shitload of I.E.D.s and they travel in a file with a dog team up front and a mine detector and that they are still losing guys. . . . He said they [the Taliban] are using kids as spotters and that when you see them get down and book it get ready for something to go down. Same thing with the farmers—when you see them leave, something is going to happen. He also said these guys are not your regular Taliban. They are the Pakistani I.S.I.-trained guys and that they will ambush you and not break contact until rotary wing [American attack helicopters] is called in. . . .*
>
> *This is going to be crazy. The trip wires are not only down at the foot or leg level but head level too. People get so focused on the ground that they forget to look up so we need to look up as well as down. The orchards are super fucking thick and you basically have to bear-crawl through them. The number one thing he said was that every operation needs to be incredibly deliberate and take everything slow. . . .*
>
> *Well I am going to go relax and enjoy having two arms and two legs while I still have them.*
>
> —*Journal of Lieutenant Tim Hopper*

The initial phase of Colonel Art Kandarian's campaign in the green zone wasn't much different from that of the U.S. Army in the American West during the nineteenth century: Build forts in Indian Country and poke around. The task force's engineering units designed a crude combat outpost—a C.O.P. or "Cop" as it was rendered in jargon—that could be erected in ten to fourteen days. The outposts were usually about 200 meters by 250 meters in area. The outer walls were made of HESCO gabions—manufactured blast walls of dirt held together by mesh wire, 11 feet high and 7 feet thick. The standard outpost design included Rapid Aerostat Initial Deployment, or R.A.I.D., cameras with infrared capabilities that allowed soldiers to watch their perimeter from behind the HESCO walls. The larger forward operating bases in the zone also installed big aerostat blimps of the sort General Mike Flynn had ordered in large numbers, starting in 2009. These blimps were known as Persistent Threat Detection Systems. They allowed intelligence officers in secure quarters below to see for miles. "From six kilometers away, I could see a guy holding an AK and tell you what color his beard was," as Lieutenant Colonel Brian Spears, who deployed to the green zone that summer, put it. Spears used the blimps to watch small Taliban groups as they shot at supply convoys on Highway 1. He could then order aircraft to drop a bomb on them.[12]

Combat engineers also erected tall observation towers where soldiers on watch could look out directly at the foliage. It was sometimes easier for the Taliban to spot the Americans in the towers than vice versa, however. In June, a Taliban sniper killed Brandon King, of the 1/320th, shooting him square in the face as he stood on watch in a tower.

Forward American units detained suspected insurgents and used retinal scanners to log them in classified databases. But interrogations and human intelligence collection in Kandahar that summer rarely produced insights beyond the known fact that many Taliban fighters were from or trained in Pakistan. More useful tactical intelligence about Taliban positions and movements came from listening to their radio communication. The enemy had no means to encrypt their chatter, which was easily intercepted and translated. That monitoring allowed American platoons to anticipate ambush attempts and to stay ahead of the Taliban's reactions during combat.

By far the most urgent intelligence requirements were to map the enemy inside the green zone and avoid I.E.D.s. The blimps and R.A.I.D.

cameras could spot Taliban if they moved in open areas but were less helpful in identifying enemy infrastructure and supply lines underneath the vines and orchard canopies. As the fighting intensified that summer the Combat Aviation Brigade's S-2, or chief intelligence officer, undertook an elaborate mapping exercise to try to infer hidden Taliban positions from the sources of their firing. She plotted every engagement with the Taliban—air-to-ground, ground-to-ground, and ground-to-air—as well as trajectories of fire. The map lines were all color-coded. As the colors thickened over time, she hypothesized that the Taliban must be moving through the green zone underground, in a tunnel network. Guerrillas would pop up, fire, disappear, and then reappear across the map in a pattern that only tunnels seemed to explain. Kandarian sent platoons to the places she identified and, sure enough, they found tunnels, some running almost the length of a football field. Engineers blew the tunnels up with high explosives. This became part of what Colonel William Gayler, the aviation brigade commander, dubbed the Enemy Tactical Infrastructure Reduction Campaign, which went on well into the autumn.[13]

A problem, it turned out, was that some of the tunnels were part of an ancient irrigation system called the *karez*, an informal network of sediment tunnels managed by local Afghan communities for vital water supplies. Some *karez* tunnels had been watering fields in Kandahar Province for centuries. There were similar systems throughout South Asia, the Middle East, and China. The tunnels were not on the maps the Americans had brought to battle, however. After commanders realized what they might be destroying, the Army Research Office hired Rolfe Mandel, a University of Kansas archaeologist, to map Kandahar's *karez* system, in order to protect it. American forces "had inadvertently destroyed some or contaminated some and really irritated the people," Mandel noted. The Americans destroyed some of the tunnels; the Taliban blew up others and blamed the Americans.[14]

July 3, 2010: So we ended up pushing out today. It was definitely strange being out there for the first time. I thought it was going to be much more

*high strung and that everyone would be more stressed out, including
myself. Instead it was more like a Sunday stroll, granted it was with about
70 pounds worth of gear and it was 110 degrees . . . almost like a maze of
mud walls ranging from six to twelve feet high. CPT Shaffer stopped off
and spoke with the Mullah while we hung out on the street and talked with
some kids. I gave this one kid some Sour Warheads and his face was
priceless when he tried it. I offered him sweet or sour. He proceeded to
chuck it over a wall.*

Platoons depended on their most experienced sergeants to survive.
Sergeant Josh Strickland had served two tours in Iraq and one in Afghanistan before joining Third Platoon, A Battery, of the 1/320th, the
artillery misfits. During his first couple of weeks at Combat Outpost
Nolan, Strickland's patrols could not walk a hundred yards without hitting an I.E.D. or getting lit up by Taliban from several sides. Listening to
enemy radio talk, they learned the enemy knew they were artillery, not
infantry. The Taliban said, "These are not real warfighters." They were
wrong, but it took time and heavy losses for the 1/320th to prove it. The
first time Strickland's platoon got hit, he saw a young artilleryman burst
out crying. The soldier screamed again and again, "I didn't sign up for
this shit!"[15]

In general, Strickland thought, the lowest-ranking first-time soldiers
adjusted to the stress better than the more experienced artillerymen
because the rookies had no expectations from prior deployments. Because of Strickland's experience and uncanny ability to avoid I.E.D.s,
soldiers continually asked him to walk point on their patrols. He chose
to walk ten to fifteen feet ahead of everyone else so that he could carefully identify the best route, and so that, if he did make a mistake, it
would cost one life instead of several. He was ultimately wounded and
medevaced to Kandahar Airfield four times. Each time, as he recovered
in the hospital, a doctor would ask Strickland if he wanted to go back or
go home. "What am I going to say?" he thought. He went back. Day after
day, in platoon after platoon, they shouldered their loads, stepped out on
"presence patrols," and hoped for the best. They walked past villagers

near their outposts who were neither helpful nor hostile. One elder near Strickland's base kept a pigeon that he would let fly every time a platoon departed, apparently to let Taliban know they were on the march.[16]

By July, the I.E.D.s and the escalating casualties had rattled even the most experienced infantrymen. In Zhari, the four companies of the 1/502—Alpha, aka "Hard Rock," the "Bull Dogs" of Bravo, Charlie or "Cobra," and Delta or the "War Dogs"—stepped down paths that the Taliban had been implanting with I.E.D.s for at least a month before the battalion arrived. Every soldier carried seventy to ninety pounds of gear, water, and ammunition. They patrolled at night to avoid the sun or drank water continually to stave off dehydration in heat that soared daily above 100 degrees. The I.E.D.s were so thick around the Bull Dogs' encampment that they had to clear a hundred yards at a time from the HESCO walls out. A lot of soldiers struggled with the stress. The First Platoon of the 1/320th started out with nineteen men; after three patrols, they had six remaining. Eighty percent of Bravo Company's personnel had to be replaced during Strickland's tour because of combat deaths, severed limbs, concussions, and other injuries.[17]

July 12, 2010: It was much better moving around at night, although it was pretty eerie at 3:30 a.m. when we were walking through the village and all of [a] sudden the call for prayer came on. I felt like I was in Call of Modern Duty Warfare. We walked in the canal down to the fields we were going to move towards the 2nd canal and we had SPC Spalding using the Gizmo which is our metal detector. Spalding is usually an iffy soldier but he was pretty on it with this thing. I guess death is a good motivator as everyone says. We got set up in the field and held it for an hour or so and right as we were about to leave we got PID [Positive ID] on one insurgent firing towards Bravo's position. We all cracked off some shots and then we ended up being there for another few hours. . . . So we came back from that 7-hour mission, racked out for like 2 hours, and then woke up and kicked back out for another mission that ended up being 12 hours. . . . I don't even know what we did but I do remember it sucking and there being a huge fucking I.E.D. that went off about 200 meters away from us, right where our original plan had us cutting across the river. Second time we've been lucky.

—Journal of Lieutenant Tim Hopper

Major Kevin Moyer commanded the Second Combat Brigade's engineering company, about one hundred specialists in construction, breaching walls, bridging rivers, and blowing things up. He talked with Kandarian's operations and intelligence officers about the I.E.D. problem. A lot of antimine equipment deployed previously in Kandahar had been designed to clear roads. This included *Mad Max*–inspired bulldozers rigged with armored plates. Those wouldn't work on the narrow footpaths in the green zone now claiming so many.

Moyer and Lieutenant Colonel Clint Cox, the brigade's operations officer, fell into conversation about a Cold War–era antimine weapon called the Mine Clearing Line Charge, or MICLIC, referred to as a "micklick." As a concept, the system dated back to the First World War. A modern MICLIC resembled a two-hundred-foot fire hose packed with explosives. A rocket was fitted to one end of the hose. When fired, the rocket shot out and laid the hose in a straight line on the ground. Then the rocket set off all the explosives in the hose. That massive detonation in turn set off any buried I.E.D.s across a fifteen-foot-wide path—a cascade of thunderous booms. When the dust cleared, presto, infantrymen had a reliably safe path one hundred yards long and fifteen feet wide to walk. MICLIC systems had been sent out in small numbers to Afghanistan but they had never been used because they were considered too destructive for wars where hearts and minds figured.[18]

Art Kandarian was ready to bear that risk. The problem was, because of the length of its explosive hose, a MICLIC had to be moved around on a wheeled trailer, which made it unwieldy in the dense green zone. Moyer was talking to other engineers when one mentioned a portable mini-MICLIC called the Anti-Personnel Obstacle Breaching System, or APOBS. An APOBS consisted of two twenty-five-foot explosive hoses that soldiers could carry in backpacks, fit together, and then detonate to

clear out a fifty-yard walkway. It turned out there were ten APOBS
stored at Kandahar Airfield. Special Operations Forces had brought
them out thinking they might need them someday, but they had never
been used. Moyer thought this was "the coolest thing ever." They tried
them out. It was fun to set off such huge explosions and the systems offered the closest thing to a guaranteed safe walking path as there could
be in that terrain, even if the path was only forty yards long. And as the
APOBS came in, engineers also started to clear road sections with the
larger Mine Clearing Line Charges. The weapons were not panaceas—
they were heavy and awkward to deploy, they did not detonate every
single buried I.E.D., and the Taliban could implant new explosives overnight. But they were a lot better than the grappling hooks and improvised booby-trap detectors platoons had been given at the start.[19]

When Art Kandarian learned how effective the explosive hose
systems might be, and how they raised troop morale, he tried to order as
many as he could find. But the Pentagon balked. Army lawyers responsible for enforcing the battlefield's rules of engagement worried the explosive force was too great and too indiscriminate—there might be
farmers hidden in the orchards who would be killed inadvertently. Kandarian created a PowerPoint deck arguing that the need was urgent and
that more lives and limbs would be lost needlessly if the Army did not
move fast. Petraeus endorsed Kandarian's position and peppered the
Pentagon with e-mails to get the systems moving to Afghanistan. They
found some lying in storage in Kuwait and had them shipped in. When
Defense Secretary Robert Gates visited Kandahar in late summer, Kandarian used his time with the secretary to persuade him to speed up
shipments, which Gates did. But it still took months to receive the approximately 250 APOBS and 100 MICLICs that Kandarian wanted. By
the end of its tour the Second Combat Brigade had detonated 207 explosive I.E.D.-clearing hoses in order to fan out through the green zone.
They also used highly flammable white phosphorus to burn out dense
vegetation. They destroyed acres and acres of farmland but slowly, over
months, the brigade moved from desperation to tentative offense.[20]

Kandarian also begged Petraeus and Gates for help in obtaining more

bomb-sniffing military working dogs; they had only six at the start. After MICLICs, dogs were the most popular anti-I.E.D. system at platoon
level. The dogs' effectiveness in identifying buried explosives was debated. The extreme heat took a toll on the animals. Also, a bomb-sniffing
dog's effectiveness depended on his training and human handler, which
meant that quality varied. Still, the dogs' companionship was comforting
and helped with the stress, and there were sergeants like Strickland who
saw the dogs point out I.E.D.s and save lives. Kandarian sent through to
his companies as many working dogs as he could obtain. They, too, were
frustratingly slow to arrive.

> *July 17, 2010: I am getting pretty sick of these walk-around-Jelawur
> patrols and SLEs [Street Level Engagements]. I am starting to feel like this
> is pointless. . . . We just walk around and talk to people. It is just starting
> to turn into a grind. Well, coming up on the 25th there is a big security/
> clear operation so we'll see what that does. . . . I am so thankful that Jenny
> is such a faithful, loving and good wife. Two of my soldiers and my P.S.G.'s
> [wives] are leaving them. I can't imagine doing all this with that weight
> hanging on my soldiers. Well, I am exhausted today since we spent all day
> dicking around. I'm going to go get some sleep.*
>
> *—Journal of Lieutenant Tim Hopper*

"Secure the People . . . Connect the Government to the People . . .
Improve Quality of Life." The "lines of operation" on Art Kandarian's
PowerPoint decks seemed increasingly at odds with the sheer amount of
explosives and white phosphorus deployed to rip the Taliban out of the
Arghandab's foliage. Before arriving in Afghanistan, some of the brigade
had trained at "Freedom Town" at Fort Sill in Oklahoma. Freedom Town
was a training village set up to imitate conditions in Afghanistan. The
soldiers practiced rudimentary Pashto and studied Islam and Afghan culture. Their scenarios had not touched upon how to convince Afghans
that blowing up orchards one hundred yards at a time would contribute
to their well-being.[21]
Counterinsurgency doctrine had a solution: cash payments. After the

1/320th managed to clear at least some of the nests of I.E.D.s around Combat Outpost Nolan, officers initiated a "cash for work" program to employ local villagers to clean up canals and fields. The 1/320th was largely responsible for destroying the area; now they paid the locals by the hundreds not to fight back. Officers had backpacks with one to two million Afghanis to fund these improvised payrolls. (The exchange rate was about forty Afghanis to one dollar at the time.) Villagers turned up at the outpost gate each morning for assignments. The soldiers used R.A.I.D. cameras to watch them from behind their HESCO walls, to make sure the Afghans performed the work. Then they handed over cash at day's end.

The brigade laid out larger sums as compensation for property destroyed by American operations—tens of thousands of dollars at a time, sizable fortunes locally. Army lawyers at Kandahar Airfield ran a kind of arbitration court to consider claims. The Second Combat Brigade had bricks of cash to pay successful applicants. The brigade's officers were scammed, initially, at least by the standards of American law. Sharecroppers and day laborers in the green zone presented claims for damaged fields and buildings as if they were the owners. They accepted the biggest paydays of their lives and then disappeared. Only gradually did the Americans come to understand that the real landowners were in Kandahar City or Quetta. At one point, Karzai sent a commission to the province to investigate whom the brigade was paying. Karzai suspected an American conspiracy to undermine him politically; ignorance was the reality.[22]

July 26, 2010: So last night . . . it was super-eerie when we were walking through an open field with loose dirt and hearing the insurgents out there talking about us. Last night was the first time I prayed. I was really nervous going through those fields. The fields had been flooded so we were walking through tomato fields [where] the dirt was the consistency of thick chocolate pudding. So here we are, 100 men strong, sludging through fields of chocolate pudding with half the people not having NODs [Night Optical Devices] or speaking the same language while the enemy watches us as we approach the area where they plant all sorts of I.E.D.s . . . very comforting. So we were the platoon to push across the 2nd Canal to set up security

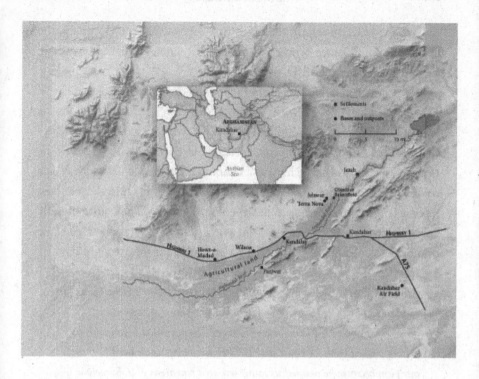

around the compound we were supposed to seize. . . . I had waterproofed
my stuff but apparently not well enough because the water was up to my
chest at points as we crossed. All my stuff got soaked and I almost fell over
because the current was so strong.

—*Journal of Lieutenant Tim Hopper*

Objective Bakersfield was a four-way intersection of raised road controlled by the Taliban, naturally fortified by a large canal on one side.
Beside the intersection was a compound of thick mud walls three to
eight feet high. Along the roads near the intersection were other heavily
armed Taliban compounds. According to the Second Combat Brigade's
study, during the 1980s, the C.I.A.-backed mujaheddin had managed to
hold the intersection throughout their combat with Soviet forces. The
Canadians and the American Stryker units deployed in 2009 had failed
to take it. Whoever controlled the intersection could influence traffic
between Kandahar and Zabul Province. In late July, Kandarian prepared

to have the 1/320th assault the objective. Captain Venkat Motupalli, the battalion's intelligence officer, estimated that, on average, there was one hidden antipersonnel I.E.D. every six meters.[23]

The platoons, including Hopper's, opened the Battle of Bakersfield on July 30. Hopper moved with a team leader he called his "war dog," a young Texan named Kyle Stout. They had played golf a few times before the Afghan tour and had become friends. Stout had two big blue stars tattooed over his nipples; he was a character, but also squared away as a soldier. The assault on Bakersfield was by orders of magnitude the most intense combat either of them had ever experienced. "They quite literally charged across an open field into enemy fire, straight out of a video game or movie," as Motupalli put it. "They kept going for four straight days."[24]

August 4, 2010: Sergeant Stout is dead. Objective Baker's Field 1 was [a] goddamned hellhole that was rigged to kill everything that went in there. . . . I don't even know where to start. The operation began with us getting pushed back 24 hours and LTC Flynn telling us we need to change our plan because he wanted us to tighten up a few areas of it. Somehow we still ended up rushed and didn't have enough time to plan out things well and rehearse them. . . .

Next thing I know we are entering right at the middle of the first field of the west part of the compound. Ok, well we made it up to that point alright and then an ANA soldier stepped on a small I.E.D., but he was fine, since only the blasting cap went off. He said his foot hurt a little bit. Ok . . . pretty good indicator of how much this place is going to suck. We moved our security positions into place and then we began going into the compound and clearing. Now I should have supervised SGT Stout more and forced him to be more thorough. We "cleared" the first field and Building One. So then he continued to clear Building Two. . . .

SGT Stout had torn up his pants just like mine . . . but his were much worse than mine were. . . . SGT Stout just happened to not be wearing boxers. One of my last memories of SGT Stout was him standing there with everything hanging out. He was exhausted as we all were so I gave him my 5 hour energy drink. . . . He was real pumped up about it. At that

point we had gotten to about Building Four and it was slow going. . . .
Right as I got into the first courtyard of the east side I saw Stansberry
walking towards the west and then there was a huge explosion. No one
knew what had happened. I looked around the corner and I saw half of a
body laying in the middle of the intersection. . . . His head was back and
not moving [and] he did not have any legs at all. . . . We started moving
up that way and then all of a sudden there was an explosion right in the
middle of the group of us. It was SGT Stout, SGT Hubbard, SGT Hatton,
Alec, me. . . .

As the dust cleared I saw someone on their back with their helmet
blown off and they were missing both legs from what I could see. I looked
around at first, a little stunned and didn't know what to do. I was scared
to go up because of secondaries. I ended up just running up and pulled out
a CAT and began putting it on SGT Stout's left leg. . . . I saw his face as
he looked down all confused and then he saw his legs and just let his head
fall back. . . . When I got closer I saw that his left arm had been blown off
as well. . . .

[They stayed in the fight for three more days.] The last night I was
there I ended up sleeping in a body bag because it was so cold and we had
nothing else. We all felt like gypsies. I think SGT Stout was fucking with us
and looking out for us because a dud—the only one in the three days we
were mortared—landed right in the middle of the platoon. . . .

We all had to sit down with CPT Stone to talk about everything. We
had to say where we were and how we felt when it happened. It was really
hard and there was a lot of tears let out and a lot of anger. There are a few
guys that are psych casualties and are going to KAF. . . .

We have been here for two months [and] 5 days and I don't know how
we are all going to make it another 10 months. One of the worst parts was
when I had to go back over with [the bomb disposal squad] to be their local
security. I didn't want to send my men back over there. I was scared
shitless, to be honest. I had to see the crater from the IED that hit SGT
Stout. There were pieces of his flesh all over the area and bees were eating
it. . . . It was horrifying. I felt compelled to pick them up and bury them in
the crater. I know it is disgusting but it just didn't feel right. . . .

I can't remember what I have said and what I haven't. I guess I'll go
back and edit later if I get around to it. Life is too fragile and short to
worry [about] all this inconsequential shit. Things really get put into
perspective out here. I never want to leave on a bad note with anyone
back home.

—*Journal of Lieutenant Tim Hopper*

In Kabul, among N.A.T.O. ambassadors and the generals and colonels
at I.S.A.F.'s command headquarters that summer, it was regarded as an
open secret that President Obama's heart wasn't in fighting the Afghan
war to the last Taliban. It was equally well understood that many of
Obama's advisers on Afghan strategy at the White House, including
Doug Lute and his deputy, the former Navy SEAL Jeff Eggers, did not
believe the surge of American troops into Kandahar and Herat and the
plans to connect the Afghan people to a reforming Karzai government
would produce durable success. At best, the doubters in Kabul and at the
White House thought, the sacrifices made by the likes of Kyle Stout
would buy the equivalent of what Henry Kissinger, speaking to Richard
Nixon about withdrawal from Vietnam, once cynically described as
"some formula that holds the thing together a year or two, after which . . .
no one will give a damn."[25]

Yet Petraeus was revered by some of Obama's most forceful foreign
policy critics in Congress, such as Republican senators John McCain and
Lindsey Graham. Whatever Obama thought privately about Petraeus's
prospects in Afghanistan, the president had clearly handed the war to
the most qualified general available. Yet all the skepticism, ambivalence,
and signaling of withdrawal plans from the White House frustrated Petraeus. Of course there was no purely military solution in Afghanistan,
he argued, but there was a military context, and unless they seized the
time they had to change facts on the ground, to discourage and set back
the Taliban significantly, there would be no hope for diplomacy, either.
Obama's reelection and legacy were at risk in Afghanistan. Why give the
enemy hope?[26]

Petraeus had no on-the-ground experience of Afghanistan. He had served two tours in Iraq before leading the Baghdad surge of 2007. He had developed an informed understanding of Iraqi politics, particularly the critical position of the country's Sunni minority, whose grievances had fired the anti-American insurgency after 2004 and opened space for the rise of Al Qaeda in Iraq. Petraeus had no comparable knowledge of the Taliban or the grievances the movement had exploited while reviving itself with I.S.I. support. Instead, in talking about the problem of political legitimacy after he arrived in Kabul, Petraeus often reduced the Karzai problem to "corruption," which he vowed to eradicate through investigations and prosecutions, as if the war-bloated Afghan political economy could be quickly reshaped by technocratic or judicial effort.

After Petraeus arrived at I.S.A.F. headquarters, the general often said he understood that Afghanistan was different from Iraq. He had produced papers spelling out the differences—the absence of resources in Afghanistan, the lack of infrastructure, the massive problems of corruption and drugs. Yet he couldn't help himself—he spoke repeatedly to Afghans, N.A.T.O. generals, and his command team about how he had succeeded in Baghdad. He made Freudian slips, saying "Iraq" when he meant to say "Afghanistan." His references to Iraq deeply irritated European colleagues in Kabul, as well as Afghan counterparts.[27]

By now counterinsurgency theory, which had thrilled so much of Washington in 2007 and 2008, had lost its varnish. An anonymous wag at the U.S. embassy in Kabul dispatched a mocking "Sensitive But Unclassified" cable to Washington titled "A KEY STRATEGIC TIPPING-POINT GAME-CHANGER." It posited:

> The primary challenge in Afghanistan has become the ability to get fidelity on the problem set. Secondarily, we need to shape the battlefield and dial it in. Whether or not we can add this to a stairway to heaven remains to be seen, but the importance of double tapping it cannot be overlooked. After getting smart so that we do not lose the bubble, the long pole in the tent needs to be identified. Once we have pinned the rose on someone, then we must send them downrange. Then we

must define the delta so it can be lashed up. This can be difficult, as there are a lot of moving parts; in the end, it is all about delivery.

To some American generals and colonels who worked with Petraeus that summer of 2010, he seemed tired and worn out. He had been going hard since 2003; this was his fourth overseas command in seven years. He had endured radiation treatment for early-stage prostate cancer the previous year. In addition to seeming run down, he also seemed impatient. Petraeus seemed to have an unshakable theory of the case in Afghanistan, namely, that he could recreate in the country a version of the "Sunni awakening" in Iraq, in which the United States had supported and paid Sunni tribes as they turned against Al Qaeda. Petraeus pressured Hamid Karzai to back his plan to rapidly arm and pay village levies around Afghanistan. Karzai feared creating more fragmented militias beyond anyone's control but reluctantly gave in. His and his cabinet's ambivalence slowed the program. In any event, relatively few Taliban took the offer to "reintegrate," certainly not enough to change the war's contours. If Taliban soldiers or units wanted to leave the battlefield, they mainly just retreated to Pakistan and settled there.

The PowerPoint slides displayed by the general's counterinsurgency advisory team, describing the structure of the Taliban insurgency, showed big red lines emanating from Pakistan. There was not a counterinsurgency campaign on record that succeeded when the guerrillas enjoyed a deep cross-border sanctuary, the team's briefers conceded; they would have to hope this would be an exception. Petraeus's strategy included energizing Special Operations Forces that conducted night raids and direct assaults on Taliban commanders. He sought to dramatically increase military pressure on the Taliban in a short time; the clock was ticking, as the first surge forces would start to leave in a year. To Petraeus, this was the war's biggest factor: that Obama had imposed a deadline and seemed determined to follow it, no matter the facts on the ground. To do something fast about corruption, Petraeus appointed a charismatic one-star general he had worked with in Iraq, H. R. McMaster, to run a kind of organized crime strike force in Kabul. Somehow, when all this pressure and effort came together, Petraeus believed, enough Taliban field commanders and fighters would change sides, from the grass roots, to swing momentum in the Kabul government's favor and buy time for the buildup of Afghan security forces. When officers held over from McChrystal's tour questioned his assumptions, Petraeus could be direct: He was tired of debating his strategy, he was going to prosecute the war violently on the short time line available, and he needed people around him who would execute and not create distractions.[28]

At a hollow square table in a secure inner room at I.S.A.F. headquarters, with regional commanders around Afghanistan piped in by video, Petraeus presided each morning over an update briefing. European generals in attendance that summer, as well as some of McChrystal's holdover American command, were shocked by how Petraeus proceeded. The general seemed much more interested in body counts and Special Operations night raids than they had expected, given his reputation as a politics-and-people-minded general. Petraeus went out of his way at the morning updates to praise news of midlevel Taliban commanders killed or detained. When J.S.O.C. presented its overnight body counts, Petraeus "was all huzzahs," as a senior participant put it.[29]

Petraeus remained a multidimensional general interested in such matters as economic development, the future of Afghan mining, regional diplomacy, and counternarcotics. Yet night raids by American Special Forces grew fivefold between 2009 and the end of 2010. Between early May and early August 2010 alone, by I.S.A.F.'s count, American Special Forces killed 365 Taliban "commanders" and captured some 1,400 Taliban foot soldiers in nighttime operations. Petraeus felt that he had inherited a crisis of confidence among the troops under his command because of the way McChrystal's euphemism of "courageous restraint" had played with the rank and file. He was determined to use all the forces he had as aggressively as he could, to take back districts from the Taliban and hand them over to the government, which Petraeus was trying with equal speed to clean up.[30]

The general regarded Kandarian's campaign in the Taliban heartland as central. "The Taliban are now losing infrastructure, in Panjwei and Arghandab. It's really very impressive," he said as the fighting in the green zone raged. That area constituted the Taliban's "most important sanctuaries in Afghanistan," he continued. "They've lost their infrastructure. They've lost massive amounts of weapons and I.E.D. materials. They can't go back—not easily."[31]

> *September 9, 2010: The last month has been a blur of shittiness.*
> *Today LT Weaver the new platoon leader for 1st Platoon was killed by a*
> *pressure-plate I.E.D. They were out setting [an] ambush and while he was*
> *emplacing a security position he hit the I.E.D. He was a triple amputee*
> *and had a large laceration on his neck. He was done by the time Shannon*
> *(Doc) got there. . . . These are people's lives that we are playing with here.*
> *The entirety of that did not hit me until I got letters from SGT Stout's*
> *family and saw his memorial DVD. This shit is fucking with me. When I*
> *go home I am going to break down bad. . . . I am going to need Jenny in a*
> *bad way. When someone is killed out here it is not just an NCO, soldier,*
> *leader, etc. . . . It is someone's uncle brother cousin friend boyfriend*
> *husband son father etc. . . . LT Weaver was 26 years old and his daughter*
> *just turned one a couple of weeks ago.*
>
> *—Journal of Lieutenant Tim Hopper*

Combined Task Force Strike's Operation Dragon Strike opened early in September, in the midst of Ramadan. After a summer of walking probes and hard learning, Kandarian launched a systematic campaign of air assaults by helicopter and infantry backed by air support to clear out Taliban and push the area of American control toward the Arghandab River. The Combat Aviation Brigade eventually mounted 863 air assaults in the green zone, or just under three a day. These included everything from operations that lifted a platoon by Chinook behind Taliban positions to full-on rocket and bombing assaults by Apaches and fighter-bombers. On the ground, every hundred yards remained a slog. Operation Dragon Wrath followed and then Operation Dragon Descent. Eventually Kandarian built a huge ten-foot concrete wall in the green zone, similar to Israel's security wall in the West Bank, to make it harder for the Taliban on the southern side to creep back up toward Highway 1. By November, as the foliage browned and thinned, the Combat Aviation Brigade could fly with greater freedom, mapping and attacking Taliban positions. By the time they had finished, there could be no doubt that Kandarian had won the tactical battle in the green zone, killing or removing Taliban from large sections south of Highway 1. It would require two more years to fully clear the zone, however. The question remained: Would the territorial gains endure, and even if they did, was such sacrifice in lives and limbs necessary to protect vital American interests?

The purpose of the assault on the green zone in 2010 was to strengthen the "transfer" phase of the troop surge plan, to partner with Afghan forces that would soon take the lead. Yet unbeknownst to Kandarian and his lieutenants fighting through the "blur of shittiness" on the front lines, Hamid Karzai had lost faith in the American military's ability to achieve shared objectives.

During Ramadan that September, Zalmay Khalilzad was in Kabul sharing *iftar*, or fast-breaking dinners, with Karzai. The former ambassador had maintained his relationship with Karzai despite the strains of 2009. Khalilzad tried to make himself useful to the Obama administration by reporting on what he heard privately from Karzai. His reports from the *iftar* dinners in the middle of Operation Dragon Strike were stark.

Karzai "thinks the United States is undermining him," Khalilzad relayed. "He does not believe in Petraeus's strategy." He believes there is "too much American face on the war" and that he has been treated with "total disrespect." Karzai told Khalilzad that he wanted "the U.S. to stay for a hundred years, but this can't succeed, the way [counterinsurgency] is being carried out. The real war is in Pakistan."

Alarmed at his alienation, Khalilzad told Karzai in reply, "You can't destroy the whole country for a personal vendetta."[32]

At the platoon level, increasingly the estrangement was mutual. There was no way to generalize about relations among American and Afghan soldiers under the pressure of the green zone's intense combat. They often fought hard together, sacrificed for one another, took extraordinary risks, and chased off Taliban in tandem. I.S.A.F. statistics showed that joint patrols were attacked less often than when Americans went out alone. Yet there was rampant indiscipline among the Afghans and it was no small problem among the Americans. One of Sergeant Josh Strickland's soldiers made a bong out of an apple and got his whole squad stoned before battle, a practice inspired by routine prebattle smoking by their Afghan counterparts. ("When I smoke hashish, I fight and I'm brave," one Afghan soldier explained to Hopper. "When I don't smoke hashish, I hide behind a rock.") The more serious issue was an atmosphere in which both sides knew that intramural violence—what I.S.A.F. would later label the "insider threat" to American troops—could erupt at any moment. Strickland alone counted four serious incidents. An American sergeant asked an Afghan counterpart carrying a loaded weapon on base to put the safety on and the Afghan sergeant responded by putting the barrel of his gun in the American's mouth. (He did not fire.) Another time, Strickland joined colleagues in a weapons-drawn standoff with about twenty Afghan National Army allies before reason prevailed. An A.N.A. unit once shot at Strickland while he was maneuvering with a small "kill team" against the Taliban. On another patrol, the A.N.A. appeared to tip the Taliban to where Strickland's platoon would arrive; the enemy had three or four snipers in position. By late 2010 I.S.A.F. command's "shoulder-to-shoulder" slogans sounded increasingly strained to soldiers on the front lines.[33]

It would be the following spring before the Second Combat Brigade could go home. Its platoons endured 116 Taliban I.E.D. detonations while on foot patrol in the green zone over eleven months—in the toughest period of the summer and early autumn of 2010, they took an average of about one booby-trapped or pressure-plate strike every other day. Sixty-five of their soldiers died. Four hundred seventy-seven were wounded, 60 percent of those so badly that they had to be medically retired for life. The wounded included thirty-three single, double, or triple amputees.[34]

Among those who survived intact was Lieutenant Tim Hopper. Between patrols, he relieved stress by playing *Call of Duty: Black Ops* on a

PlayStation. He listened to music and tried to keep his platoon safe. Outside his tent hung a welded sign that had been sent in a care package by the father of one of his men. The sign memorialized informally I.S.A.F.'s naming of a newly built combat outpost on the frontier of American control in the green zone, near Objective Bakersfield: C.O.P. STOUT.[35]

Kayani 3.0

On Monday, September 13, 2010, a warm and cloudy late summer's day in Washington, President Obama descended to the White House Situation Room for a National Security Council meeting. Corruption in Afghanistan was on the agenda. Defense Secretary Robert Gates, C.I.A. director Leon Panetta, and Secretary of State Hillary Clinton took their places. Their briefing books contained a classified white paper from Richard Holbrooke's office. It sought to distinguish among three categories of Afghan graft. There was "high-level" theft, meaning by Hamid Karzai's relatives. There was "predatory" theft by cabinet officeholders and presidential appointees who depended on the Karzai family's patronage. These were referred to as criminal patronage networks, or C.P.N.s. One prominent C.P.N. included the executives and borrowers at Kabul Bank, where, it had been discovered, about $800 million in depositor funds had been distributed to influential politicians and power brokers, who had made no effort to pay back interest or principal. And finally, there was "functional" corruption, which might range from routine payoffs demanded by a traffic cop to the marketplace of bribery required to land jobs in the Afghan bureaucracy, from which the purchaser of a position could pursue further rake-offs to recoup the price of office.

What did this taxonomy of corruption imply for American war strategy? The paper had been commissioned in part to address a bitter conflict within the U.S. embassy and I.S.A.F. headquarters in Kabul. The dispute had drawn in the C.I.A. and the Department of Justice, among other agencies. It concerned how much immunity should be granted to longtime C.I.A. allies suspected of graft. Some officials held that the Obama administration should accept some corruption as endemic and concentrate on a "kingpin" strategy, to make an example of high-level offenders. The paper at least allowed the administration to "decide what matters and what doesn't," as Holbrooke put it.[1]

Robert Gates and Karl Eikenberry, the ambassador in Kabul, who appeared at the N.S.C. meeting by secure video, pointed out that Karzai had become "obsessed" with the "denigration" of Afghan sovereignty, partly because of the American anticorruption drive targeting Karzai's family. Gates said he thought Karzai's resentment was "legitimate," all things considered. The defense secretary, a former career C.I.A. analyst, proceeded to attack the agency for having so many Afghan officials on its payroll.

"We do it all over the world," Panetta retorted.

"We are the principal source of corruption" in Afghanistan, Gates went on. American contracting in Afghanistan had become larger than the opium and heroin trade, he pointed out.[2]

"We have to step back and reassess," Obama said. If Karzai "can paint us as occupiers, violators of sovereignty, how can we possibly work with him?" If the administration did not figure out how to successfully cut back aid and military involvement in Afghanistan, the president added, Congress would do it for them.

Petraeus championed the anticorruption drive. His command had studied the problem and although there were "no good answers," he said via video, "if we can't win on anticorruption," N.A.T.O. could not succeed in handing off the war as planned to Afghan forces loyal to Karzai. A problem was that building up the legitimacy of the Afghan government required routing massive sums of aid money through a Kabul bureaucracy that stole systematically. Yet the more traditional strategy, allowing U.S.A.I.D. to independently vaccinate children or clean up water supplies, meant money went to Beltway contractors, exacerbating the appearance that Karzai was a figurehead.[3]

The reach of official theft and racketeering was breathtaking,

Petraeus's investigators had discovered that summer in Kabul. I.S.A.F's anticorruption task force headed by Brigadier General H. R. McMaster had opened an investigation into Kabul Bank; it appeared that many of the hundreds of millions of dollars missing from the institution had been siphoned offshore, to the benefit of diverse Afghan officeholders. There were now several American task forces investigating corruption in Kabul, in addition to McMaster's. They found crimes everywhere they looked. A police chief in eastern Afghanistan ran a kidnapping operation out of his Kabul office. Afghan soldiers died of starvation at the National Military Hospital because pervasive bribery left the facility stripped of supplies. Petraeus pushed Karzai to fire the country's surgeon general and the hospital commander. A former Afghan watermelon salesman ran a trucking firm, Host Nation, with contracts worth about $360 million from the Pentagon, in concert with Ahmed Wali Karzai's racketeering operations in Kandahar.[4]

Petraeus funded an investigations unit at the Afghan Central Bank. It started to report on million-dollar deposits and other transactions in real time, exposing diverse Afghan officials and businessmen moving inexplicably large sums. When investigators questioned those Afghans, they claimed, sometimes plausibly, that unknown criminals had hijacked their identities. Forensic accountants traced hundreds of millions of dollars to banks in Bahrain, Germany, Canada, the United States, and Dubai. Investigators at the Department of Justice in Washington employed civil forfeiture laws to seize illicit funds or else imposed sanctions to freeze assets in place. Sometimes, if there was evidence that Taliban commanders benefited from particular schemes, the American anticorruption task forces even handed over classified case files to I.S.A.F. for the inclusion of accused individuals on the Joint Priorities Effects List, the "kill or capture" targeting dossier.[5]

Yet American policy remained laced with contradictions, as the exchange between Gates and Panetta in the Situation Room highlighted. The C.I.A. put warlords and Karzai aides on its payroll for information, security, and stability. Simultaneously, Petraeus's command, Justice prosecutors, and Treasury investigators tried to put some of the same men in jail.

"If we can't tell our story on metrics of progress, there will be tough months ahead," Petraeus told the National Security Council meeting. He said that I.S.A.F. had "broken Taliban momentum" and would soon take and hold the villages west of Kandahar occupied at such high cost by the Second Combat Brigade.

In the weeks following, the White House and the State Department distilled a refined anticorruption doctrine. It was tempting but unrealistic to jail members of the Karzai family in the middle of a war designed to convince Afghans of Hamid Karzai's legitimacy. If theft by an Afghan official violated U.S. law directly, the Justice Department would take action. But this was plausible only if the accused was a dual Afghan and American national or if the scheme touched American banking or passed through American territory. If not, the United States would brief Karzai about the facts and encourage him to prosecute. Ultimately, however, Karzai would decide. Unfortunately, his record was well established.

"Afghans liberated this country, not the U.S.," Karzai told a visitor to the Arg Palace that autumn. "Now the U.S. blames us for its failures. They have failed to win over the country." The Obama administration "is feeding the U.S. press about these so-called scandals. The U.S. screwed up our elections deliberately" and now "the Americans are trying to weaken me again." Karzai added, "I do believe in conspiracies. There have been major conspiracies against me, so do you blame me if I believe in them?"[6]

Those at I.S.A.F. headquarters who regarded the defeat of corruption as a cause that could not be compromised found Obama's search for balance deeply frustrating. At the White House, the doctrine became a pillar of emerging policy designed as realism but which could sound like condescension or worse: "Afghan-good-enough."

By that September, five months after its formation, the N.S.C.'s secret Conflict Resolution Cell had reached a turning point on another track of exit strategy from Afghanistan: talking directly to the Taliban about peace.

Doug Lute and the cell's interagency membership prepared to make a formal recommendation to the president that he authorize direct talks with the enemy. Over the summer, the cell had identified three "threads" of possible negotiation with Taliban leaders. One was through Tayeb Agha, the young aide to Mullah Mohammad Omar who had been talking to the German government. A second was with Mullah Akhtar Mansour, the former Taliban aviation minister who had become the Taliban's number two. British intelligence had made contact with a man claiming to be Mansour, although the man's identity was questionable. Petraeus had provided the man safe passage to Kabul, where he had met Karzai and accepted tens of thousands of dollars in cash as an incentive to keep talking. A third "thread" had been developed by the C.I.A. Its operatives had made contact with a son-in-law of Gulbuddin Hekmatyar, the former C.I.A. and I.S.I. client in the war against the Soviet Union now aligned with the Taliban.

Three days after the N.S.C. meeting, the cell met to approve a top secret decision memo for Obama's signature. The memo authorized direct American talks with the Taliban for the first time. The State Department, and in particular Holbrooke, would liaise with German diplomats to develop the talks with Tayeb Agha. Because Petraeus had supervised the contact with Mullah Mansour, I.S.A.F. would own that negotiation. And the C.I.A. would pursue its track with the Hekmatyar family. The overall premise of the Taliban talks at this stage, as Lute described it, began with a recognition "that the war will not end without a political settlement (the nature of which was still very unclear); that while the Afghan government should lead, it cannot deliver a settlement by itself; that to be durable any agreement had to be rooted in a broader regional process . . . and that any Afghan political process [needed] to be broader than just the government and the insurgents, in order to avoid turning an insurgency into an ethnic civil war."

National Security Adviser Tom Donilon delivered the decision memo to President Obama on September 17. After Obama signed it, instructions were distributed as a formal order to those few at the Pentagon, C.I.A., and State then aware of the policy.[7]

In late September, speaking to reporters outside Kabul, Petraeus disclosed that there were "very high-level Taliban leaders who have sought to reach out to the highest levels of the Afghan government." Petraeus cast the negotiation as one in which the United States supported an initiative by Hamid Karzai, as "we did in Iraq, as the U.K. did in Northern Ireland." The American involvement reflected a recognition that "you are not going to kill or capture your way out of an industrial-strength insurgency." The general's indiscretion made headlines and roiled Holbrooke's office and the White House. It also put a powerful and popular general on record in support of talking to the Taliban, in alignment with Obama's newly enacted but still-secret memo. Petraeus's gifts had always included knowing how to manage superiors.[8]

Ahmed Pasha was furious about the American engagement with the Taliban, which he knew about in a fragmentary way. That September, the I.S.I. director met with Jonathan Bank, the C.I.A. station chief in Islamabad, to vent about American perfidy. Bank had no reason to be surprised at Pasha's anger. The National Security Agency listened to the I.S.I. director's phone conversations. Recent intercepts documented the Pakistani spy chief ranting about being excluded from N.A.T.O. contacts with the Taliban. Of course, it was hard to evaluate such signals intelligence. Pasha and Kayani were well aware of American intercept capabilities; they themselves lobbied to obtain the technologies. So they might use their phone conversations to broadcast manipulative positions, knowing that the Americans might be inclined to interpret such overheard conversations as authentic.

"You guys are arrogant to think you can have repeated conversations with the Taliban without our knowledge," Pasha told Bank. "We know about your meetings in Germany. If you don't include us we will be forced to act in the interest of Pakistan." Pasha even showed Bank copies of travel records for Tayeb Agha and the supposed Mullah Mansour.

Direct talks between the United States and Tayeb Agha hadn't actually started yet—Pasha was confused about that. But Germany, Britain, and Norway were all in secret discussions with Taliban leaders. Pasha will "push Haqqani," the I.S.I.'s most reliable client in the Taliban coalition, as Pakistan's preferred representative for peace negotiations, Jonathan

Bank reported. I.S.I. hoped that the Haqqani network could "deliver eastern Afghanistan" to Pakistani influence in any possible settlement.

Only a handful of senior C.I.A. officials happened to know that autumn of 2010 that C.I.A. analysts had recently opened an investigation of a house in Abbottabad, Pakistan, where Osama Bin Laden might be hiding. The house had suspicious characteristics. C.I.A. analysts had no idea whether I.S.I. was protecting this possible hideout. This would be a season of games within games between the C.I.A. and I.S.I. More contact with Pasha was better than less contact.

Ashfaq Kayani arrived in Washington on October 19. The army chief's itinerary included a meeting with Secretary of State Clinton. They gathered in the Deputies Conference Room on the State Department's seventh floor. Kayani opened his briefcase and took out a dog-eared copy of Bob Woodward's recently published book, *Obama's Wars*. Kayani had underlined many passages. The book had provided him with useful insights about how the Obama administration made decisions. Its disclosures of sensitive high-level discussions about Kayani and his cooperation with the United States had embarrassed him. Following on the publication of State Department cables by WikiLeaks, Kayani felt exposed, at risk of being painted as an American lackey within his own high command, whose generals typically had less exposure to the United States than he had enjoyed at Leavenworth and in Hawaii. "How is it that such sensitive discussions are leaked in great detail?" he asked Clinton.[9]

When he met Mullen, Kayani returned to a delicate subject they had been reviewing privately for months. Should Kayani engineer and accept a three-year extension as chief of army staff and de facto head of state? Mullen wanted him to extend but talked with him gently about the pros and cons. In public, the Obama administration emphasized the importance of Pakistani democracy and civilian rule; in private, it negotiated for the continuation of favorable military control. The rigid promotion and retirement system in the Pakistan Army meant that if Kayani stayed on, he would effectively cap the promotion opportunities of colleagues and force their retirements. That could stir resentment. Kayani's credibility in the army arose from his sergeant's son persona, after the egoism of Musharraf. If he extended his time in power, it would look as if he was putting himself and his family's business interests ahead of institutional norms. On the other hand, Pakistan was in the middle of a low-grade civil war. The Pakistani Taliban were threatening major cities; Karachi was a mess, even by the measures of its recent violent history. Asif Zardari was a weak civilian leader. Kayani offered continuity. If he stayed, he could ensure that the next election would go off as planned, to determine a successor to Zardari, whom Kayani by now viewed with undisguised contempt. "I want Pakistan to emerge as a normal democracy," he insisted to Mullen repeatedly.

Mullen enjoyed the closest relationship with Kayani, but the admiral's natural congeniality caused him to pull too many punches, some Pakistan watchers at the White House, Pentagon, and C.I.A. felt. Mullen was well aware that some colleagues saw him as too credulous about Kayani. In fact, he was coming to think of his Pakistani friend as I.S.I. personified—a man of layers and deflections, comfortable in command of both Directorate C and Directorate S. On balance, Mullen told the Obama cabinet, it was better to keep going with Kayani.

At the White House that October, Kayani met with national security staff in the Roosevelt Room. By design, Obama dropped by, feigning surprise to find Kayani. (Because the Pakistani general was not a head of state or government, Obama did not want to violate protocol or undermine civilian rule in Pakistan by setting up a formal meeting.) Kayani handed Obama an updated version of his July white paper on the future of U.S.-Pakistani relations, a ten- to fifteen-page paper that would become known as "Kayani 3.0."

The Americans had been expecting this. Intelligence collection before Kayani's visit showed that the army chief had been working long hours to refine his latest memorandum. Kayani told White House officials that he had written this latest version himself. He hoped the document would shape a joint American and Pakistani strategy to stabilize Afghanistan. Among other things, he had refined his demands about ending India's presence in Afghanistan, acknowledging that India could have an economic role.

Kayani addressed the paper to Obama, Mullen, Marine General James

Mattis, who was Petraeus's successor at Central Command, Doug Lute, and Colin Powell, the retired secretary of state. It was like a war college thesis, one person who read it remarked. The document had five parts, titled "Afghanistan," "Pakistan-Afghanistan Relations," "The Federally Administered Tribal Areas," "Pakistan-Indian Relations," and "Pakistan's Concerns." The essence of Kayani's argument was: You can't win your war; we know Afghanistan. "They beat the Russians, they beat the British, they are beating you," as he told one senior State Department official. Could they now find a way to talk honestly about what would follow? And he had requests: We will also require your help in settling Kashmir and other strategic problems between Pakistan and India, he wrote.[10]

"Pakistan is quite adequately aware of U.S. concerns regarding Pakistan," Kayani wrote. His sense of grievance was transparent: "Pakistan has transitioned from 'most sanctioned ally' to 'most bullied ally.'"

Yet he wanted Obama to cooperate on a plan for joint negotiations with the Taliban. I.S.I. had now been promoting such talks for a decade. "Peace in Pakistan will only be possible if Afghanistan is peaceful," Kayani wrote. "An early end to conflict in Afghanistan is one of Pakistan's key strategic interests. . . . This is a defining moment, time for political process to take the lead and enable people of Afghanistan to take charge of their destiny. . . . The United States and Pakistan wish to see Afghanistan free of extremist and radical forces. . . . It is the political strategy which should provide a focus for military strategy."

Kayani advocated first reducing the war's violence through ceasefires, then isolating Al Qaeda, and then developing a new consensus about the Afghan constitution that the Taliban might accept. The measure of success, Kayani reiterated, could not be how many guerrilla commanders were captured or killed or how much territory the Karzai government or the Taliban controlled at any one time. The measure of success was "Are we gaining or losing public support?"

Obama's initiative to explore a deeper strategic partnership with Pakistan was "very important," Kayani wrote, but the administration's ambition had to be grounded in "the relationship between the people of the two countries." Yet the Obama administration was undermining such a possibility. "The impression that we are constantly under pressure to do more does not help," he argued. He went through America's assumptions about the army and I.S.I. You think we are in bed with the Haqqani network, he wrote. That is false. You think we are accommodating the Quetta Shura. That is completely false. He wanted to play a role in any negotiations with the Taliban.

Pakistan "would like to remain a part of the solution and not the problem," Kayani wrote.[11]

Obama's advisers had diverse reactions to Kayani's paper. At the White House, Lute saw Kayani's personal investment in the document as a rare opportunity to align with Pakistan, perhaps the most promising opening since September 11. At the Pentagon, skeptics of I.S.I. read the paper as a kind of coercive ultimatum: You are doomed without us, and if you don't manage Afghanistan while accommodating our core interests, you will fail.

On October 28, a month after Petraeus had spoken publicly about negotiations with "very high level leaders" of the Taliban, the C.I.A. confirmed that the Mullah Mansour feted in Kabul was a fake. "We're sending him a bill for $150,000," one of the president's aides quipped. The C.I.A.'s line to Hekmatyar also looked unpromising. That left Holbrooke where he wanted to be, in position to pursue a war-altering deal with the Taliban's leadership, through Tayeb Agha. Holbrooke insisted on referring to the envoy by the code name "A-Rod," the nickname of Alex Rodriguez, the Yankees slugger.

Holbrooke called his deputy Frank Ruggiero to inform him that he would be the initial negotiator with the Taliban. The administration told Kayani and Karzai of the outline of their negotiating plan, but withheld details. Since the disclosure of Tayeb Agha's position the previous winter, Saudi Arabia had dropped out of the talks. Tayeb Agha had in the meantime reset his refuge in the Persian Gulf by deepening his ties to Hamad bin Khalifa Al-Thani, the emir of Qatar. The emir was an American ally who allowed the Pentagon to operate a massive air base in his kingdom, yet he also maintained ties with Islamist movements and tried to position Qatar as a neutral facilitator.

Early in November, Michael Steiner, the German special representative for Afghanistan and Pakistan, passed to Holbrooke a Taliban position paper about talks with America. The paper was on Islamic Emirate of Afghanistan stationery, dated 23 Ramadan, or early September 2010, but it bore no signature. It was what diplomats call a "nonpaper," or deniable negotiating memo. It stated that the Taliban agreed to talks with the Americans on two conditions: that there be no arrests, and that negotiations take place in total secrecy. Steiner proposed that they hold the first meeting in a safe house in a suburb of Munich, his hometown. The paper also said the Taliban wanted German officials in the room and had selected a "Muslim brother," Qatar, to participate as well. Steiner noted that the Taliban leaders had previously been tricked into attending meetings, only to be arrested by the C.I.A. or I.S.A.F. and shipped off to Guantánamo. How could Tayeb Agha be sure that this was not another American sting operation?

Lute approached Obama. The president said that they should convey his personal word through Steiner that the United States would not interfere with Tayeb Agha's travel to or from Munich. Lute decided not to tell the C.I.A. about the meeting, out of fear that the information might trigger some kind of snatch operation down in the bureaucracy that the White House wouldn't know about in time to stop it. The German government would fly Tayeb Agha in one of its own planes; surely the C.I.A. would not mess with the Taliban envoy on German soil, even if it did detect what was going on.

The Qatari emir informed the Americans that he judged Tayeb Agha to be authentic. The Taliban could not afford to alienate Qatar, a source of refuge and finance. "They might fool you," Al-Thani said, "but with all due respect, the Taliban are not in a position to trick me."[12]

On November 26, the German intelligence service arranged a plane to pick Tayeb Agha up in Doha and fly him. Worried about Pakistani surveillance, Agha dressed in Western street clothes as the Germans drove him to a safe house. Once inside, he changed into a shalwar kameez and jacket.

Jeff Hayes, the Defense Intelligence Agency analyst working for Lute, and Colonel Christopher Kolenda, a West Point graduate and former aide to McChrystal who had served four tours in Afghanistan and now worked on regional policy at the Pentagon, flew to Germany with Ruggiero. Hayes and Ruggiero were not happy about Kolenda's role, but the Pentagon had insisted on having its own member of the negotiating mission. Hayes would accompany Ruggiero to the meeting; Kolenda would stay in a nearby hotel. They went over some icebreaker talking points. Ruggiero had served in Kandahar and knew the Arghandab, where Tayeb Agha had grown up. That might be a good subject for casual chat.

On November 28, Tayeb Agha appeared alone to meet with the Americans, his hair closely trimmed and his black beard cropped short. He said he was thirty-five years old but he looked younger. His manner was reticent, calm. He spoke English well but not fluently. In addition to Steiner, who happened to be celebrating his sixty-second birthday that day, a German diplomat and a B.N.D. intelligence officer joined the meeting, as well as a Qatari prince.[13]

Steiner proposed a three-part agenda. First, they would introduce themselves to one another. Then they would talk about confidence-building measures, including the possibility of prisoner exchanges. Finally, they would agree on next steps.

Tayeb Agha said he wanted to read an opening statement, which he unfolded before him. You won't like this, he warned Ruggiero and Hayes, but I must read it aloud. The essence of it was: America invaded Afghanistan unjustly, falsely accusing the Taliban of terrorism, martyring thousands of innocent Afghans. Now the United States carried out an unjust occupation and continued to kill innocents. "The Taliban [have] been unjustly accused of responsibility for 9/11 and labeled as terrorists," Tayeb Agha said. "There [is] no point in talking to other Afghans if the U.S. considered [the] Taliban a terrorist organization like Al Qaeda."

When Ruggiero's turn came, he delivered a long statement on why the Americans had intervened in Afghanistan, and why the world's nations had joined in the effort to rebuild the country. The instructions worked up for Ruggiero at the White House included an admission that it did not look like either N.A.T.O. or the Taliban would win on the battlefield, so the United States was looking to develop a form of political talks that would allow Afghans to talk to Afghans, to settle the war.

Ruggiero also said, in essence, "You know who we are—we work for the American government. You know who our boss is, President Obama. But we're not sure who you are—or where you stand with the Taliban." The United States needed evidence that Tayeb Agha had authority. At one point, the Americans asked a question they had rehearsed: "Who knows you are here today?"

Tayeb Agha answered that everything he did was under the authority of Mullah Mohammad Omar, but that Omar did not know about this specific meeting. "I see him and will see him again," he added.

Mullah Akhtar Mansour, the Taliban number two, did know about today's meeting, however, he continued. Ruggiero asked if Mullah Abdul Qayyum Zakir, who commanded the Taliban's military campaign, knew about the meeting. No, Tayeb Agha said, Zakir had no need to know. They asked about I.S.I.'s knowledge. Although Tayeb Agha traveled on a Pakistani passport, he said he doubted that the Pakistani spy service knew exactly what he was doing because he "travels a lot."[14]

The discussions lasted six hours over a day and a half. Tayeb Agha seemed unaware of the Obama administration's announced plan to dramatically reduce U.S. forces in Afghanistan between 2011 and 2014 and hand off the war to Afghan forces. At one point he said the problem between the United States and the Taliban was the presence of foreign forces, but that the international troops should withdraw gradually. But his priorities were the development of a prisoner exchange, improved treatment for Taliban prisoners in Afghan custody, the abolishment of sanctions against the Taliban, and the opening of a Taliban political office in the Gulf.

The full negotiation over prisoners would take months to develop, but it seemed to some of the Americans involved to be Tayeb Agha's first priority. He had won support from the Taliban's political commission, the Taliban envoy said, for confidence-building measures that would begin with the release from Guantánamo of six Taliban detainees and the reciprocal release by the Taliban of Sergeant Robert "Bowe" Bergdahl, held by the Haqqani network. Bergdahl had wandered off a base in eastern Afghanistan in the summer of 2009 and had ended up in the hands of the Haqqanis. The detainees Tayeb Agha sought were Mohammad Fazl, a former deputy minister of defense and army commander in the Taliban government; Abdul Haq Wasiq, a former deputy minister of intelligence; Mullah Norullah Noori, a former commander and governor; Khairullah Khairkhwa, a former minister of interior; Mohammad Nabi Omari, a former security chief; and Awal Gul, whom the Pentagon described as a former military commander. As they studied the files of these men, Khairkhwa intrigued some of the Americans involved because he looked as if he might have the potential to become a valuable political negotiator. (Gul died in custody on February 11, 2011, leaving five others to be considered. The Conflict Resolution Cell began to refer to these prisoners as the "Varsity Five," to distinguish them from a second list of lower-ranking Guantánamo prisoners Tayeb Agha also wanted released. They were referred to as the "Junior Varsity Seven.")

None of the six Taliban leaders at Guantánamo were captured on the battlefield fighting the United States, Tayeb Agha pointed out. They had all either surrendered to the Afghan government or offered their cooperation to the United States. (Nabi Omari reportedly said in an interrogation that he accepted $500 from a C.I.A. operative to help track down Mullah Mohammad Omar and Al Qaeda figures in Afghanistan.) "The charges that some had been involved in the killing of Americans were false," Tayeb Agha said. He said that a prisoner exchange would be a way for the United States to demonstrate good faith to skeptical Taliban fighters and commanders, opening the way to a more comprehensive negotiation that could lead to cease-fires and political agreements.

A prisoner exchange could empower those in the Taliban who valued peaceful politics. "Many in the Taliban questioned the utility of talks with the Americans, but all agreed it was a sacred Islamic duty to rescue prisoners," he said. If the Taliban political commission that had appointed him "could deliver the release of these detainees, it would enable the leadership to gain the support of the fighters for a political process."

Ruggiero said the Obama administration would consider all of these issues but could not agree to anything now. He had instructions from Holbrooke not to respond positively to anything Tayeb Agha proposed in the first meeting. "Have a second meeting," Holbrooke had told him. On America's highest priority, the isolation and destruction of Al Qaeda, Tayeb Agha said this could be resolved "at the end of the process." On his ability to deliver the Haqqani network's commitments as part of a negotiation, he said the idea that there was a split between the Taliban and the Haqqanis "exists only in media."

They talked about how Tayeb Agha could prove that he had authorization from the Taliban leadership. One possibility was to agree in secret on an unusual statement or reference to a foreign event, such as the war in Somalia, to be inserted into a public communiqué in the name of Mullah Mohammad Omar, to be released through official Taliban media. They would agree on the event and the comment and Tayeb Agha would show them a draft three days in advance of its release. That would show that Tayeb Agha had the juice at least to produce statements under Omar's name. That would be an item for future discussion.[15]

At sixty-nine, Richard Holbrooke extended himself as if he were in his thirties. He often exuded great energy, but he could also appear exhausted. At Army House, in Pakistan, during meetings with Pasha and Kayani, he sometimes fell asleep from jet lag. British or French diplomats visiting him in his ground-floor suite at State that autumn would find him on the phone to his wife Kati Marton, recounting his plans for a new trip to London and Dubai while also finalizing a dinner party in New York for the coming weekend.

The truth was that Holbrooke was deeply discouraged about the Obama administration's prospects and his own "AFPAK" project. "Our current strategy will not succeed," he wrote to Clinton in the second half of 2010. "Even though everyone paid lip service to the proposition that 'counter-insurgency' required a mixed civilian-military strategy, last year the military dominated and defined the choices. And even though everyone agreed the war would not end in a purely military outcome, State was never able to make a detailed presentation to the full N.S.C. on the civilian-political process or the possibility of a political solution to the war."

He had been deprived of a chance to convince the president personally, despite the enormous stakes in the war. "Unlike the military, the civilians never had a meeting alone with the President, with the important exception of your weekly private meeting with the President, which I attended once." Petraeus was selling "tempered optimism," he continued, but "I have my doubts. . . . There is a fundamental flaw in our strategy: the mismatch between our stated objectives and the time and resources allocated to achieve them."

At this point, he continued, "The best that can be hoped for is a bloody stalemate. Moreover, as far as I can tell, one constant about counterinsurgency: It does not work against an enemy with a safe sanctuary—and I do not believe we can get Pakistan to see its strategic interests as being symmetrical with ours." He had been working on these problems since he took office; it sounded as if he was giving up.

On Thursday, December 9, Holbrooke lunched with one journalist, Susan Glasser, the editor of *Foreign Policy* magazine, and dined with a second, Michael Abramowitz, a longtime *Washington Post* reporter and editor who had recently taken up a senior position at the Holocaust Museum. Holbrooke met Abramowitz at 1789, an expensive Georgetown restaurant. (Holbrooke complained that while in government service, his expenses were outrunning his income by hundreds of thousands of dollars a year.) They talked for two and a half hours about family and journalism. Holbrooke lamented the passing of "fact-based" reporters and the rise of bloggers who trafficked in drivel.[16]

The next morning, at 7:30 a.m., Holbrooke called Ruggiero to prepare for a briefing later that morning with Hillary Clinton. The White House had scheduled a Principals Committee meeting for Saturday,

December 11, to review drafted assessments by the national security staff that reviewed how the Afghan war was going a year after Obama's West Point speech.

Holbrooke arrived late on State's seventh floor and found Clinton with her aides, including Jake Sullivan. He joined the discussion but suddenly turned very red.

"Richard, what is the matter?" Clinton asked.

"Something horrible is happening," he answered.[17]

Clinton told him to seek treatment from State's medical unit at once. Soon Holbrooke lay prone in an ambulance racing to George Washington University Hospital. Doctors found a tear in his aorta. They operated for twenty-one hours but did not emerge optimistic.

Clinton attended the Principals meeting on Saturday with Ruggiero to discuss the Munich meeting with Tayeb Agha. Everyone was in casual weekend clothes. Clinton and Defense Secretary Robert Gates were in a pitched battle with Doug Lute and his national security staff over the staff's judgments about progress—or the lack of it—in Afghanistan.

Gates argued that the N.S.C.'s paper understated military gains on the Afghan battlefield. Clinton argued that State's diplomatic and civilian efforts in Afghanistan were going better than the N.S.C. paper described. The pair was "furious" at Lute's pessimism about the war, in Gates's characterization. Gates argued that Lute "appeared to question the strategy itself rather than identify how to make it work better."[18]

Yet to Lute and his staff, the facts were stubborn: The war was not going well. Why shoot the messenger? Since the late 2009 West Point speech, the I.S.A.F. command had expanded the number of "key terrain districts" to ninety-six, effectively enlarging the size of the battlefield N.A.T.O. was supposed to subdue. Lute and others at the White House were digging in against any effort by Petraeus and Gates to prolong a counterinsurgency war that they believed was not sustainable. Lute's position, backed by his N.S.C. staff, was that the color-coded metrics on the C.I.A.'s District Assessment maps of Afghanistan, updated late in 2010, had not changed much—the hard data described a stalemate that might slightly favor the United States, although it wasn't clear for how long. The most recent National Intelligence Estimate, a product of the entire intelligence community, was pessimistic. Petraeus, Gates, and Clinton might "feel" progress being made, but where was the objective evidence? Moreover, Lute argued, whatever territorial gains might be made in Kandahar and Helmand, on what basis did anyone think the gains would be held once American forces departed?

The December review's outcome, after so much contention, was incoherent. The review ratified—but did not prioritize—five American "lines of effort" in Afghanistan. One was to continue to degrade the Taliban militarily and build Afghan capacity to fight the war. The second was to execute a transition to place Afghan forces in the lead combat role. A third was to negotiate a long-term strategic and security agreement with Afghanistan that might allow some American forces to stay behind after 2014. The fourth was to try to stabilize Afghanistan through regional diplomacy. And the fifth was to pursue political reconciliation with the Taliban, through direct talks.[19]

These lines of policy were not integrated into a single plan. Petraeus could fight his hard war of night raids as aggressively as he saw fit, and the State Department could try to negotiate a peace deal through Tayeb Agha, but there would be no effort to unify those strategies. Petraeus rejected Holbrooke's premise that there was a deal worth pursuing with Tayeb Agha; Holbrooke rejected Petraeus's premise that counterinsurgency doctrine could succeed.

Holbrooke died in the hospital on the evening of Monday, December 13. Three days later, Obama appeared with Gates and Clinton in the White House briefing room to present summary findings of the president's latest Afghan war review. Obama acknowledged Holbrooke, "whose memory we honor and whose work we'll continue."

Obama delivered the positive spin about Afghanistan promoted in the Situation Room by Petraeus, Gates, and Clinton. "This continues to be a very difficult endeavor," the president admitted, yet "we are on track to achieve our goals." He detected "considerable gains toward our military objectives" on the ground in Afghanistan, although the progress was "fragile and reversible." As for Pakistan, Obama was pleased that its government increasingly "recognizes that terrorist networks in its border regions are a threat to all our countries," and he hoped to "deepen trust and cooperation."[20]

All in all, it was an assessment that might have been delivered—and sometimes was—in 2006 or 2007. Whatever Obama's private doubts about the Afghan war he had escalated, in public, at least, he was willing to speak optimistically. It was a practice soon to expire. The gossamer illusions of American partnership with Pakistan and with Hamid Karzai would be exposed in the coming year as never before.

TWENTY-EIGHT

Hostages

B y late 2010, the estrangement between the C.I.A. and I.S.I. had become so deep that officers on both sides resorted to dismal metaphors to describe its descent. The liaison was like a bitter marriage that neither party had the will to break. It was like a fingernail on a dead man's hand that kept growing when all other life had ceased. The more the C.I.A. and the Pentagon worked with Ahmed Pasha, and the more they eavesdropped on his conversations, the less they thought of his capabilities. Pasha texted Ruggiero and others on open cell phones; Ruggiero gave him a code name, "The Shoe." He seemed more emotional and sensitive than ever.

The new American ambassador to Islamabad was Cameron Munter, a Ph.D. historian and career foreign service officer who had previously served in Iraq. As he settled into the embassy, he took a more sympathetic view of the I.S.I. chief. He saw Pasha's outlook as the product of genuine feelings of betrayal. The I.S.I. chief had taken considerable professional risks to forge a closer relationship with the C.I.A., including putting up with unilateral drone operations that killed Pakistani citizens. Yet despite such cooperation, Pasha had often been treated as an incorrigible enemy. They had to deal with him as he was, a strong nationalist who might be cooperative from time to time. For holding these views, Munter was accused by C.I.A. counterparts of being soft on Pakistan.[1]

For his part, although he maintained and valued personal friendships with American counterparts in Islamabad, Pasha had more than wearied of the pressure and stubbornness of official visitors. One after another they arrived at I.S.I. headquarters or Army House with their diplomatic démarches, their complaints and their requests for more visas, more military offensives against Pakistani citizens, more access to Taliban prisoners. They constituted a diverse bureaucratic parade: ambassadors, special envoys, deputy secretaries, assistant secretaries, deputy assistant secretaries, generals, C.I.A. directors, C.I.A. deputy directors, I.S.A.F. commanders, Central Command generals. Pasha and Kayani found these formalized meetings repetitive at best, offensive at worst, and, overall, less and less useful. They felt that most of their American visitors understood Pakistan and Afghanistan poorly. Yet the Americans' cloak of global power made them hubristic, rarely inclined to listen sincerely to local knowledge.[2]

Around this time, U.S. intelligence distributed to allied spy services a memo laying out the Pakistani spy service's day-to-day priorities, based on U.S. collection of intelligence about I.S.I. The document offered a snapshot of what I.S.I. really cared about. The service's number one priority was collecting information about Pakistani president Asif Zardari—his scheduled meetings, his conversations, his political activities. A second priority involved suppressing the Pakistani Taliban. A third was to monitor and assess a medley of militant groups active against India, including indigenous Maoists operating in poor areas of India's interior. The list of priorities did not include Al Qaeda or the Afghan Taliban, the enemies that animated the Obama administration. The United States might still have a few overlapping interests with the Pakistan Army, but not many.[3]

In mid-November 2010, American relatives of victims of the Mumbai terrorist attack named Pasha as a defendant in a lawsuit seeking compensation for the families' losses. Pasha blew up in private about the suit. The Americans tried to assure him that he would not be subject to arrest when he next traveled to the United States. This was a civil case in a court outside the control of the Obama administration, they explained.

Pasha didn't buy it. If you really thought of me as a friend, this wouldn't happen, he said. Pasha's young adult children warned him to be careful about traveling to the United States ever again—this looked like a trick, one that could end with his arrest. The Pentagon and the C.I.A. assured Pasha he would not be bothered when he next flew to Washington, to attend Richard Holbrooke's memorial service, where Pasha felt a personal need to be present. Yet he remained on guard.[4]

A month later, an Islamabad human rights lawyer, Shahzad Akbar, who had previously worked on army-backed investigations into Bhutto family corruption, filed a lawsuit against the United States on behalf of victims of C.I.A. drone attacks. The court papers named as a defendant the C.I.A.'s Jonathan Bank, breaking Bank's cover as station chief. Akbar said he had obtained the name through local journalists and had developed his case without any contact with I.S.I. The C.I.A. doubted that. This was Pasha's revenge for the Mumbai lawsuit, some at the agency concluded. Pasha pleaded innocence; the C.I.A. station chief in Islamabad was as much diplomat as spy and enjoyed hardly any cover. In any event, Bank received death threats. Akbar's car and office were mysteriously trashed. C.I.A. deputy director Michael Morell flew to Pakistan. At the end of his scheduled visit, Bank followed his boss onto his unmarked jet and departed the country, without telling Pasha he was pulling out.[5]

The bad voodoo spread to street-level operations. By the end of 2010 there were 285 American military personnel in the country. More than half were Special Operations forces. They were notionally on a training mission but they had effectively created a forward operating base that neither Kayani nor Pasha could monitor or control. The goal in some sections of the Pentagon was to eventually persuade the Pakistanis to grant the United States "Title 10" authority, a reference to the section of federal law that governs American armed forces. This authority would allow the U.S. military to operate on Pakistani soil as it did in Afghanistan, which would be unprecedented in Pakistani history. There were also dozens of C.I.A. case officers, temporary duty officers, and security personnel in Pakistan. The C.I.A. and Pentagon personnel often applied for visas as "diplomats" but then arrived at Islamabad International in cargo pants and T-shirts, inked with tattoos.[6]

"Do you think we're stupid?" a Pakistani official asked a State Department intelligence analyst over lunch one day during this period. "Do you think we think those three hundred visas are for first and second secretaries?"[7]

American intelligence officers and diplomats with long experience in Pakistan were appalled by the rough arrogance of contractors and street surveillance specialists rotating through. The old hands were used to floating around Pakistan on their own, but now, whenever they wanted to visit carpet shops or bookstores, even in placid Islamabad shopping centers, they had to bring along personal security detail officers to keep them safe. Children would run up to shine the Americans' shoes or beg for a few rupees and the contractors would shove the kids out of the way—conduct no American diplomat would have countenanced a decade before. The contractors drove around aggressively in S.U.V.s, talking on their Motorola radios as if they were deep in enemy territory, sideswiping or threatening Pakistani drivers who bothered them, calling them "monkeys" or "niggers" and getting spun up about any offense. The contractors and TDY types didn't know anything about Pakistan or care. For the few Obama administration Urdu-conversant hands who had known the country before September 11 and were supposed to be fashioning a durable relationship in difficult circumstances, it all seemed embarrassing and ugly. The C.I.A. station was as infected as the Pentagon's mission, some of them felt. These diplomats and intelligence analysts wondered: What happened to the agency's elegant, light touch of old?[8]

American policy toward Pakistan remained on expansive automatic pilot. The State Department embarked on a massive building project on the Islamabad embassy grounds. The project called for every existing building to be replaced. The compound would grow from 60,000 square feet of office space to more than 600,000 square feet. Two Brutalist-inspired residential towers would ensure that American personnel would never have to travel outside the walls unless they wished. The design was a metaphor for misguided policy, Dave Smith, the D.I.A. veteran remarked: They were building Fort Apache.

When he went over the building plans, Munter cabled the office for the undersecretary of state for management, warning, "This is going to be a white elephant. It is going to be half-empty." In reply, the office said it was expensive to change plans. He would need hard facts about the projected U.S. presence in 2016 or beyond in order to scale back. "I have no hard facts," Munter admitted. "I have only trends." They were bad and about to get worse.[9]

The safe house from which Raymond Davis operated early in 2011 lay in Scotch Corner, an upscale Lahore neighborhood of flowering bushes and vine-draped brick-walled homes. Davis was typical of the new militarized American cadres in Pakistan. He had grown up in Big Stone Gap, in rural Virginia, wrestled and played football in high school, joined the Army, migrated to the Special Forces, and then retired and joined Blackwater, which sent him as a security contractor to Iraq. At the time of his Pakistan tour, Davis was thirty-six years old and working exclusively for the C.I.A. He was a barrel-chested, clean-shaven street operator whose agency contract involved setting up and providing security for career case officers when they held "hostile meets" with paid reporting agents in cars or cafés. He also conducted photographic surveillance of Pakistani targets and may have done the odd black-bag job, judging by the gear he carried. Since Mumbai, the C.I.A. base in Lahore had been assigned to watch and document Lashkar-i-Taiba, the Kashmir militants whose cadres had carried out that mass murder. C.I.A. contractors photographed and helped N.S.A. colleagues eavesdrop on the homes of I.S.I. and Pakistan Army officers who met with Lashkar leaders.[10]

On Thursday, January 27, 2011, at midday, Raymond Davis drove out from Scotch Corner by himself, steering through Lahore's smoky traffic in an unmarked Honda VTI. He had a digital camera, a Motorola radio linked to the C.I.A. base in Lahore, a G.P.S. device, a 9mm Glock pistol, five magazines of ammunition, a mobile phone, a small telescope, an infrared lighting device, wire cutters, a flashlight attached to headgear, another flashlight, cigarettes, a passport, various bank documents, a little over 5,000 Pakistani rupees, and 126 U.S. dollars. He was conducting a routine surveillance check of routes to and from meeting points for reporting Pakistani agents. At a traffic light on Jail Road, a ten-lane divided expanse lined by stores and auto dealers, Davis noticed two men on a motorcycle behind him who appeared to be following him. He pulled out his pistol and set it on the passenger seat. He drove on toward Qartaba Chowk, a massive roundabout where five main roads converge. As he idled at a red light, the motorcycle pulled up. The passenger flashed a 30-bore pistol. Davis picked up his Glock and fired five times through his windshield, killing one of the two men, Mohammed Fahim, who was nineteen. The second man, Faizan Haider, fled on foot. Davis got out of his car, followed for about ten yards and shot Haider dead.[11]

Calmly, he retrieved his camera and took five photographs of the dead men, apparently to document that one of the victims had a gun. A crowd gathered. Davis's picture taking inflamed them and they began to shout. Davis radioed C.I.A. colleagues for help but decided to drive away. He steered past the crowd. Outraged Pakistani bystanders jumped in cars and onto motorcycles to trail him.[12]

The C.I.A. base chief in Lahore had been stationed at the American consulate since the previous summer. The consulate was on Davis Road, so named during the British colonial period. The chief knew the city well by now. He ordered two armed colleagues on a rescue mission. They roared down Jail Road in a Land Cruiser with tinted windows and phony license plates.[13]

Ibad ur Rehman, thirty-two, steered his motorcycle in the opposite direction, toward the Mall. He owned a small shop in the wealthy Gulberg area of Lahore, where he sold cosmetics, handbags, and upscale accessories; two of his brothers, who lived in Britain, had invested in his business. The Rehman brothers had grown up in the Punjab's precarious middle class; their father edited an Urdu children's magazine called *Uncle Moon*. Ibad was to marry in a month.[14]

The driver of the C.I.A.'s Land Cruiser saw congestion where the crowd had formed a few minutes earlier around Raymond Davis and the two dead men, who still lay in pools of blood. The driver decided to jump the median strip and speed against traffic. As he hopped the median he struck Ibad Rehman's motorcycle; the shopkeeper flew skyward and landed on the asphalt. He died. His bike lodged in the S.U.V.'s grill. The C.I.A. driver backed his vehicle into a wall as he tried to discard the motorcycle. A traffic warden threatened to stop the vehicle, but one of the Americans opened the door and brandished a weapon. The C.I.A. team fled back to the U.S. consulate without Raymond Davis. The men tossed live ammunition, a pair of gloves, and a black mask out of their vehicle.[15]

Pakistani police arrested Raymond Davis near Old Anarkali Square, about a mile and a half from where he had killed Fahim and Haider. The victims turned out to have long records of petty crime and armed robbery. Their possessions included Pakistani rupees, Japanese yen, Omani rials, five mobile phones, and a pistol pouch. Zulfiqar Hameed, the senior superintendent of police for Lahore, took charge of the case that afternoon. He was a well-educated career police officer who spoke English fluently and enjoyed cordial relations with the American consulate. Hameed sealed off the several crime scenes, bagged physical evidence, and ordered witnesses interviewed. He was afraid that an angry mob might break into the police station where Davis was being held, so he moved the American to an unmarked safe house used by the police to store sensitive witnesses and prisoners.

"Seeing the situation, I shot at them in self-defense," Davis told one of Hameed's colleagues.

Davis intimated that he was afraid that I.S.I. would frame him for unjustifiable murder.

"This is not a witch hunt," Hameed assured him. "We're not after anyone. We're trying to investigate this as police professionals."[16]

Carmela Conroy, a former prosecutor from eastern Washington State who had traded law for the Foreign Service, was the consul general in Lahore. She was an attractive, fashion-forward woman who, as part of her public diplomacy efforts, joined haute couture shows for Lahore's wealthy elite and sat for glamour spreads in the local papers. She had extensive contacts in the city. Her staff dialed police officers and politicians frantically that Thursday to try to assure that Davis was kept safe.

As soon as the C.I.A. team that had run over Rehman in the Land Cruiser returned to the consulate, Conroy huddled with the base chief to discuss what to do with them. They considered whether it was right to evacuate the two colleagues immediately. Jonathan Bank's experience was fresh in their minds. His successor as Islamabad station chief, Mark Kelton, had arrived in Islamabad only a few days earlier. He had joined the C.I.A. in 1981 and spent a dozen years initially overseas, including in Africa. From 1999, he had worked periodically in and on Russia and had rotated to Islamabad from Moscow. That was a posting that required operating under the nose of a hostile service, where mistakes with agents or sources were matters of life and death. Kelton knew about the ongoing assessment of a house in Abbottabad, Pakistan, where it was possible that Osama Bin Laden was hiding. He had to supervise that surveillance operation from Islamabad Station that winter while keeping the secret from virtually everyone else at the embassy and also managing I.S.I. on the assumption that its officers or leadership might be knowledgeable about Bin Laden's sanctuary.

"Don't give an inch," he told Munter when the news about Davis broke. "Don't tell them anything." Pakistan was a dangerous place; so far as Kelton could tell, Davis had acted properly. He was on a mission that was designed to keep American soldiers in Afghanistan safe; he deserved full support.

The assessment about the matter on the Seventh Floor at Langley was similar: It wasn't as if Raymond Davis got drunk and killed people on a rampage. He was doing his job. He was assaulted by armed men and responded. The fatal accident caused by the rescue mission was unfortunate but not an egregious crime. At the Lahore consulate, Conroy could not see a reason to delay evacuation. Davis had diplomatic status, as did the two men in the rescue vehicle, she firmly believed. "We don't want three Raymond Davises" in Pakistani custody, she and the C.I.A. agreed.

They arranged for the two hit-and-run men to fly out of Lahore that night. They were out of the country before Pakistan's government could object.[17]

Zulfiqar Hameed, the Pakistani police superintendent, went through the evidence collected from Davis's car. Hameed was a skilled detective, but it did not require the deductive powers of Sherlock Holmes to figure out that Davis was C.I.A. The detainee's papers included documents from a bank account in the United States that listed the agency as his employer. The thirty or so photos in his digital camera included tourist-style shots from when Davis had been stationed in Peshawar but also surveillance-type photos of a few Pakistani military facilities, including some near Punjab's border with India, as well as private homes in Lahore. The sloppiness in tradecraft reflected how little the station worried about being held to account by I.S.I.[18]

In Washington, Husain Haqqani, the Pakistani ambassador, called his contacts at the C.I.A. to ask if Davis was one of theirs. "I want a categorical yes or no," he said.

"No," his C.I.A. contact said emphatically.

A few days later, the I.S.I. sent Haqqani a memo documenting everything the service and the police had learned about Davis—his bank information, his wife's name, much of his career history. The contractor's tradecraft was laughable, Haqqani thought. The ambassador was a political figure and author of penetrating books about the Pakistani Army who nonetheless had little power other than that derived from his close relationship with President Zardari. He was a complicated man but cooperated with the C.I.A. and State Department. *They don't know how to have friends*, he thought, reflecting on the C.I.A.'s lie to him. *They only know how to buy out friends or bully them.*[19]

At I.S.I. headquarters, Pasha learned quickly that Davis worked for the C.I.A. He decided to test the quality of his relationship with Panetta by feigning ignorance.

"Is he your boy? If he is, we'll help you get him out."

No, Panetta told him.

All right, then, Pasha said, fuming privately. We will let the law take its course.[20]

That week, Panetta was reviewing the latest evidence that Osama Bin Laden might be hiding near Pakistan's leading military academy. The C.I.A. director was preparing to brief the case to a wider circle in Obama's national security cabinet and at the White House. If Bin Laden was at the house in Abbottabad, someone in I.S.I. had to know about it, Panetta was inclined to think.[21] By now the mentality that I.S.I. was an enemy of America—despite Pakistan's status as an officially designated major non-N.A.T.O. ally receiving hundreds of millions of dollars in American aid each year—was so embedded around the C.I.A. and the Pentagon that it was a kind of reflex, a safe zone of conventional wisdom. Richard Holbrooke had hoped that 2010 might be the year the United States changed the Pakistan Army's strategic calculus toward Afghanistan. It had turned out to be the year the Obama administration changed its calculus about Pakistan.

Kayani's "3.0" memo to President Obama and his generals remained unanswered. The administration just did not seem to know what to say. Admiral Mullen's staff drafted a reply and passed it to the White House, but Lute's aides thought it was too accommodating. A paralyzing debate ensued over who should author the reply letter. Kayani was the true leader of Pakistan yet he was notionally subservient to the democratically elected president, Zardari. Would it be bad form, a violation of democracy promotion principles, for Obama to write back to Kayani directly? This went around and around. In the end, Lute supervised a drafting process led by his aide Shamila Chaudhary. An interagency review produced an authorized, classified reply letter in late January 2011, just as the Raymond Davis mess unfolded.

They debated whether to share with Kayani the C.I.A.'s analysis of which leaders of the Taliban might be most receptive to peace negotiations, but then decided not to provide that intelligence. State Department analysts proposed a reply promising deeper engagement, but those at C.I.A. and some sections of the Pentagon wanted more threatening language about I.S.I.'s conduct. The final reply was tough. It repeated the American assessment that Pakistan had accommodated Afghan Taliban on its soil for too long, that I.S.I. was not moving adequately. The letter posed some questions for Kayani to consider: Could he help bring Saudi Arabia into a more constructive role in persuading the Taliban to forsake war for politics? Could he help bring the Iranians into a more constructive posture? But the overall attitude from Obama down was hardening. When Cameron Munter encountered the president occasionally at the White House early that year, Obama would grab his arm and say, "We have to stay tough with these guys."[22]

On February 5, at the Munich Security Conference, an annual Davos-like affair for defense officials, Hillary Clinton met privately with Kayani and handed him the reply to his "3.0" memo. The subject of Raymond Davis hijacked most of their discussion. We have important issues like reconciliation with the Taliban to discuss, Clinton told Kayani, but we can't do that while we have this distraction unresolved.

A second secret meeting with Tayeb Agha was arranged for February 15 in Qatar. Chris Wood briefed the Conflict Resolution Cell from Kabul, where he had rotated again as station chief. The agency now targeted Taliban decision making for intelligence collection, to gain insights about what the other side was thinking as negotiations unfolded. They had obtained a draft text in Pashto that apparently originated from the Quetta Shura. The text reportedly came from a leadership meeting in Karachi. The Taliban leaders agreed that Al Qaeda was "out of control" and brought them trouble. The C.I.A. collection effort found no evidence that Tayeb Agha was sending e-mails or otherwise communicating with I.S.I. officers.[23]

Frank Ruggiero and Jeff Hayes flew to Doha with the Pentagon's Chris Kolenda. Ruggiero and Hayes met Tayeb Agha at a private compound arranged by the Qatari emir. The Taliban envoy reported that Mullah Omar was aware of this meeting, unlike the one in Munich. So was Mullah Mansour.

The Americans raised the possibility of including Karzai's administration in future negotiations. Tayeb Agha rejected the idea emphatically. "We will not deal with the Afghan government," he said. There was no point in even discussing it. The Americans tried to push him off this talking point over dinner, but made no progress.[24]

Ruggiero said that they needed proof of Tayeb Agha's standing to go any further. They proposed two ways that the Taliban envoy could demonstrate his authority. One was to publish an unusual statement about an international event under Mullah Omar's name that they would agree on in advance. The other was to deliver proof that Bowe Bergdahl, the Taliban prisoner, was alive. If Tayeb Agha could prove that he was all right, this would further show that the Taliban controlled the Haqqanis as Tayeb Agha claimed. Tayeb Agha said he would work on it.

Three days later, speaking at the Asia Society, Hillary Clinton went semipublic about the talks. She described the administration's strategy as including "an Afghan-led political process to split the weakened Taliban off from Al Qaeda and reconcile those who will renounce violence and accept the Afghan constitution." To the Taliban, she said, "Break ties with Al Qaeda, renounce violence, and abide by the Afghan constitution, and you can rejoin Afghan society; refuse and you will continue to face the consequences of being tied to Al Qaeda as an enemy of the international community." The Taliban "cannot wait us out," she declared. "They cannot defeat us. And they cannot escape this choice."[25]

The Conflict Resolution Cell was prepared to deceive I.S.I. about the Taliban talks but the White House team concluded they could not afford to keep Hamid Karzai in the dark. They had enough problems with him. Ruggiero and Hayes flew to Kabul and briefed Karzai at the palace.

Obama held another secure video call with Karzai on March 2, 2011. It was again a difficult conversation, punctuated by Karzai's complaints about civilian casualties and Obama's about the corruption at Kabul Bank. Obama said the purpose of talking to Tayeb Agha was to develop "an Afghan process."

"I know Tayeb Agha," Karzai said. "He is very close to Mullah Omar and Pakistan." His role "shows Pakistan is serious."

"Pakistan is not fully on board," Obama acknowledged. "Without

Pakistan, we can't enforce this" if the negotiation got anywhere, Obama added.

"Afghanistan is a client state, not a partner" of the United States, Karzai complained.

"We want the smallest footprint possible," Obama said. "We want you to be an ally, not a client."

"Afghanistan will support you if you want us to be a partner," Karzai repeated, and yet he made clear his opposition to Petraeus's military strategy. Karzai said he wanted American "troops on bases, not villages." That was just about the opposite of counterinsurgency.[26]

As Obama had asked before: How could the United States fight a war with such an ally?

A few days later, Leon Panetta arrived at the White House with a scale model of the Abbottabad compound the C.I.A. had been studying. He reviewed the evidence about Osama Bin Laden's possible presence with Donilon, Mullen, Vice Chairman of the Joint Chiefs James Cartwright, McDonough, and James Clapper, the director of national intelligence. The C.I.A. was not certain Bin Laden was there, Panetta said, and yet "there was a real chance" they had found him. Panetta and Admiral William McRaven, the commander of Special Operations Command, had developed half a dozen options if Obama decided to act. One was a bomber strike to destroy the compound and all those inside. Another was a more limited bombing strike that might spare some civilians but could make it difficult to know whether Bin Laden had been killed. Another was a helicopter assault by Special Forces. There were two options that would involve cooperating with I.S.I. and the Pakistan Army. One was a joint raid with Pakistani forces. Another was to "simply tell the Pakistanis what we knew about the compound and urge them to act," as Panetta summarized it. When Panetta returned to Langley that day, Donilon called to say that Obama "believes we need to move very quickly."[27]

That increased the pressure to somehow extract Raymond Davis from Pakistani custody. If the United States attacked the Abbottabad house on its own and Davis was still in prison, he might well be killed. In late February, *The Guardian* disclosed that Davis was C.I.A., further exposing the lies Panetta and agency officials had told Pasha and Husain Haqqani. The day-to-day diplomatic efforts to free Davis, meanwhile, as one participant remarked, suffered from the worst of the American system: C.I.A. testosterone and State Department lawyering. Cameron Munter, the ambassador in Islamabad, was among those who thought the situation was salvageable, but only if the United States came clean with Pasha and respectfully sought his cooperation.

Munter called on Kayani and Pasha in Rawalpindi. "We know who this guy is," they told him. Why on Earth would you persist in treating us as if we don't know the truth?

Yes, of course, Munter answered, confirming Davis's role privately, but what are we going to do? The Obama administration held that Davis had diplomatic immunity and should be released on those grounds. The Pakistani government—not least I.S.I.—had whipped up such a media frenzy about Raymond Davis that it was now politically implausible in Pakistan to simply release him on the terms demanded by Washington.

There were potential self-inflicted problems with the American claim about Davis's immunity—minor problems, but enough to create room for Pakistani resistance. Under the Vienna Convention, which governs immunity for diplomats, and to which both the United States and Pakistan were parties, immunity is established by a two-part test. First, the individual obtains a diplomatic visa. Davis did so; he traveled to Pakistan on a diplomatic passport. Second, notice is given by the embassy to the host government. The Americans believed adequate notice had been given, but in one updated list sent to the Foreign Ministry long after Davis had arrived, his name was not present. Munter described this as a bookkeeping error and sent an updated list after Davis's arrest. If Pakistan were a friendly ally, it might have been enough. It wasn't. Another problem was that when Davis was arrested, he said he was a contractor with the consulate. He should have asserted that he was a diplomat at the embassy. Consular protection is more limited than diplomatic immunity and might not protect him from a murder prosecution.

In Washington, Tom Donilon summoned Husain Haqqani, the

Pakistani ambassador, to the West Wing. Donilon said that Davis's immunity was unarguable. "I'm a lawyer. I know this."

"It's not documented," Haqqani answered. He wanted to help but they would have to find some other solution than Pakistan capitulating. Haqqani felt that Donilon was trying to cajole him into backdating Davis's registration as a diplomat, if that's what was necessary.

Panetta invited Haqqani to the Seventh Floor at Old Headquarters. By now a new idea had been identified by both American and Pakistani negotiators, one that might save face. The United States could pay "blood money" to the families of Davis's two victims and the families could choose to forgive him. (The Rehman family would be left out of such a deal because the United States had never acknowledged that one of its citizens was driving the vehicle that killed him.) C.I.A. lawyers had determined there was nothing illegal about the proposal, but it did smack of paying ransom to release a hostage.

"Leon, you always say that you're on the side of whatever solves the problem," Haqqani said. "There's only one way to solve the problem," and that was blood money.

Haqqani added that he had "a bone to pick" with Panetta. "You lied." He added, "If you're going to send a Jason Bourne to our country, make sure he has the skills to get out like Jason Bourne," Haqqani added.

Panetta apologized for the deception, but said, "If we're going to do complaints, we can do that, too."[28]

Pasha remained aggrieved by what the Davis case had exposed, namely, that the C.I.A. was running extensive unilateral operations in Pakistan, belying the agency's frequent statements to Pasha's face that it considered I.S.I. to be a friendly service.

It was not easy to parse Pasha's resentments. I.S.I. directors knew that the C.I.A. ran unilateral operations in Pakistan and had done so for years; there was nothing new about that. I.S.I. ran unilateral operations inside the United States, too, trying to influence American policy toward Kashmir and monitoring or harassing expatriates. Yet the scale and character of the recent C.I.A. activity—the dozens of officers and contractors riding around with Glocks, infrared lamps, and wire cutters—was a departure. The United States would never accept such activity from a foreign intelligence service in Washington or New York. Why would it expect Pakistan to do so uncomplainingly? Given Pakistani nationalism, Cameron Munter reflected, Pasha was about as pro-American as was realistic to expect at the top of the army. If it weren't for him, Davis would never have a chance to get out of prison. And yet his C.I.A. counterparts fumed, "What a bastard."

In Lahore that February, the police at first held Raymond Davis at their safe house. Conroy visited regularly and consulate officers brought in snacks, magazines, and changes of clothes. The Pakistani police shuttled burgers from a nearby Hardee's franchise. After fourteen days in police custody, however, Pakistani law required that Davis be transferred to prison. Someone in the Pakistani system decided that there was a risk that the United States would deliberately poison Davis, and then blame Pakistan for the death. Davis was arraigned for trial on criminal charges of murder and was transferred to the high-security wing of teeming Kot Lakhpat prison on the outskirts of Lahore. Conroy was ordered to cease bringing Davis food. The American prisoner was restricted to lentils and other Punjabi staples cleared as edible by his jailers. The warden arranged for his food to be tasted before it reached him. As the weeks dragged on Conroy continued to visit, but the conditions were rougher and the prisoner's anxiety levels rose.[29]

I.S.I. hired Raja Irshad, an Islamabad lawyer in his sixties who kept a long dyed beard, to negotiate the blood money deal that might end the stalemate. Irshad met with more than a dozen family members related to the two robbers Davis had killed. He persuaded them, with the intimidating power of I.S.I. behind him, to accept a pool of compensation of 200 million rupees, or about $2.3 million, to be divided equally between the two clans. Widows, mothers, brothers, and sisters would receive shares according to the precepts of Islamic inheritance law. They would all be enriched. An arm of the Pakistani government would disburse the funds.[30]

On March 16, 2011, Davis arrived in court for what he believed to be a hearing on procedural motions. Police escorted him to a courtroom cage, where he was shackled. When the lawyers were settled, Irshad stood. Davis's local lawyers objected to Irshad's intervention, having no idea why the I.S.I. lawyer was present. A prolonged cacophony in Urdu erupted.

"What's all the noise and shouting about?" Davis asked.[31]

The judge carefully interrogated each of the blood money recipients, to make a record of their forgiveness and to tally the amounts each would receive. The judge also required Davis to plead guilty to illegal possession of weapons, an admission that undermined his claim to diplomatic immunity. Davis pleaded guilty; the judge declared him free. An S.U.V. surrounded by police escorts whisked him to the airport. He flew out of Pakistani airspace before midnight.

TWENTY-NINE

Dragon's Breath

Datta Khel, a town in North Waziristan, lies about twenty-five miles southwest of Miranshah, toward the border with Afghanistan. Near its market and bus depot is an open area suitable for an assembly. On the morning of March 17, 2011, the day after Raymond Davis flew home, about thirty-five *maliks*—tribal leaders approved and subsidized by the government of Pakistan—had gathered for a *jirga*, to resolve a feud over a chromite mine. Two tribes, the Manzarkhel and Maddakhel, were removing chromite, but there was a question of who owned what. *Khasadars*, or local police, paid by the Pakistani government, were in attendance. On the other side of the world, in the C.I.A.'s Global Response Center, targeting analysts watched the meeting on video transmitted from armed drones above. The agency's unmanned air force had been unusually active over North Waziristan in recent days. On March 11, drones struck a "suspected vehicle boarded by militants," as a ledger of drone strikes kept by the local government recorded. Two days later, a strike blew up a "state car" traveling across North Waziristan. On March 16, the day I.S.I. arranged for Davis to be released, a drone destroyed a target near Datta Khel, reportedly killing up to five people. The next morning, from the evidence available, it appears that C.I.A. analysts watching from Langley tracked a Taliban suspect to the *jirga* and then decided to kill everyone present.[1]

Malik Jalal, a wealthy tribal leader in the region, was about two miles away from Datta Khel that morning, but he could see drones in the air. Watching the machines hover and unleash death suddenly was a feature of daily life in Waziristan by 2011. Being attacked by a drone is not the same as being bombed by a jet. With drones, there is typically a much longer prelude to violence. Above Miranshah and its neighboring towns, drones circled for hours, or even days, before striking. People looked up to watch them, hovering at about twenty thousand feet, capable of unleashing fire at any moment, like dragon's breath. Predator and Reaper drones emit what, on the ground, sounds like a flat, gnawing buzz. (Locals sometimes refer to a drone as a *bangana*, a Pashto word for "wasp.") Their missiles make a *whoosh*-like sound when released, then streak off their rails to Earth to explode. That morning, Jalal watched missiles fly and heard several explosions. He drove to the site and saw many body parts scattered on the ground as ambulances rushed to and fro, tending to survivors.[2]

Angry protests erupted across Pakistan after TV networks headlined the attack and portrayed it as an atrocity against civilians. A few Taliban may have been present at the assembly, Pakistani officials told reporters, but the majority were not anti-American fighters. Kayani issued a rare public statement condemning the C.I.A.: "It is highly regrettable that a *jirga* of peaceful citizens, including elders of the area, was carelessly and callously targeted with complete disregard to human life."[3]

Cameron Munter, the U.S. ambassador in Islamabad, challenged Mark Kelton, his station chief. Yes, I.S.I. whipped up anti-American feeling after drone strikes and spread false reports of civilian deaths, but this one looked indiscriminate on its face. The *jirga* "had all the signatures" of a terrorist meeting, Kelton assured him. Since 2008, the C.I.A. had increasingly relied on "pattern of life" analysis to identify targets inside Pakistan. If visibly armed individuals behaved and spoke on cell phones in ways that confirmed their participation in groups carrying out terrorism or cross-border attacks against N.A.T.O., they might be struck, even if their identities as individuals were unknown.

"It was the timing that mattered," Munter argued. Pasha had just gone to great lengths to release Raymond Davis. Now it looked as if the C.I.A. was humiliating the I.S.I. director. "When you kick somebody in the teeth a day after they have done something for you, you are going to pay a price."

Kelton was unmoved. Davis did not enter into his calculations, he said. The United States was at war and the enemy was on the battlefield. If you can find the enemy, you strike them.[4]

The number of drone strikes on Pakistani soil more than doubled during 2010 from the previous year, from an estimated 54 to 122, or more than 2 per week.[5] To suppress the Haqqani network as U.S. forces poured into Afghanistan, the agency conducted an air war against Afghan Taliban sanctuaries in North Waziristan. This expansion beyond Al Qaeda broadened the target set.

The drone program stretched Kayani's already fraying tolerance of the Plan Colombia–inspired model for U.S. counterterrorism in Pakistan. During 2010, while Holbrooke had dangled the promise of a transformational "strategic dialogue," Kayani was willing to put up with the C.I.A.'s attacks on his own citizens. The general was realistic. He knew drone technology was too sensitive for the United States to transfer to Pakistan, and in any event, his country lacked the satellite networks to operate unmanned aerial vehicles. The C.I.A. killed Haqqani and other militants who generally accommodated the Pakistani state and therefore were not high on the general's list of internal enemies. Yet the agency also killed militants like the Mehsud brothers of the Pakistani Taliban that threatened Pakistan's stability. Kayani could accept this mixed picture, or he could try to challenge the C.I.A. and reduce its presence in Pakistan, at the risk of damaging or breaking the alliance and its financial aid flows. By the time of the strike on the chromite *jirga*, he was moving toward change. He wasn't looking to eliminate all drone strikes inside Pakistan or go to war with the C.I.A. Kayani *did* want to regain control of counterterrorism strategy from the C.I.A. and reduce domestic resentment toward the Pakistan Army over its cooperation with America. There was hardly a member of the national parliament, even from the secular-leaning Pakistan Peoples Party, who would vote publicly in favor of the current high-tempo C.I.A. drone war. Under Kayani's theory of working from the "fundamentals," above all public and political opinion, it seemed obvious that something had to give.[6]

Cameron Munter did not oppose the drone program, particularly when it targeted international Al Qaeda leaders, but by the spring of 2011 he led a faction within the Obama administration that questioned whether D'Andrea and Panetta had lost perspective. The strikes in Waziristan were too visible, too indiscriminate, and had created a dangerous political dynamic within Pakistan, Munter argued by secure video from Islamabad whenever the principals met to discuss the program.

Panetta, a genial man with a sharp tongue, hammered Munter in these meetings. The C.I.A. director argued that signature strikes had eliminated important Al Qaeda figures. Also, the agency needed to strike Taliban targets while they were inside Pakistan because once militants crossed over into Afghanistan they dispersed and operated more stealthily. In Waziristan they were easier to identify.

Munter countered that the C.I.A. had moved beyond targeted counterterrorism and was now running the world's most expensive artillery system. The agency could lob missiles at Haqqani formations in Waziristan a couple of times a week, but those attacks couldn't possibly be decisive in the Afghan war. What they were guaranteed to do was to mobilize yet more Pakistani volunteers to the fight and undermine the Pakistan Army in the eyes of the public. Munter felt isolated. He recognized that his arguments were dismissed by some in Washington as clientitis—too much sympathy for Pakistani viewpoints. "This is a never-ending war," the C.I.A. officers he butted heads with told him. "Whose side are you on?"

When Munter's interventions blocked a particular strike, C.I.A. colleagues would turn the knife: "Those sixteen Uzbeks you saved yesterday? They're going to try to kill American troops." Yet Munter was also more convinced than ever that he was on the right side.[7]

After the mess at Datta Khel, Obama ordered a suspension of C.I.A. drone strikes. None took place in Pakistan for a month. Obama did authorize an exception to his freeze if the C.I.A. located a "high-value target." When drones struck South Waziristan in mid-April, a debate erupted in the White House about whether the C.I.A. had violated Obama's order.[8]

As the agency's operations in Waziristan came to resemble an air war, they changed life on the ground. The strikes spurred militants to try to identify spies who might have betrayed them. Around North Waziristan's main towns, Miranshah and Mir Ali, which took the brunt of the C.I.A. attacks, paranoia spread. The Taliban blamed local *maliks* who had long presided over the area's economy—smuggling, arms dealing, mining, and government contracting. Taliban gunmen seeking control of local rackets executed *maliks* and their family members in the hundreds. In local bazaars, the Taliban distributed D.V.D.s of their socially superior victims confessing that they had spied for C.I.A. drone operators. The confessions included elaborate narratives about how the agency supposedly distributed "chips," or homing beacons, to local spies. The spy would toss a chip over a neighbor's wall or into a Taliban jeep to guide drone missiles to it. The men also confessed that the C.I.A. had given out special pens with invisible ink, which were used to mark Taliban vehicles for destruction. The Taliban tortured their prisoners, so the confessions could hardly be taken at face value. The Taliban also had a powerful motive to force the *maliks* to admit to spying, because that would complicate the position of the victim's tribe and family as they considered revenge, as spying for the United States was widely regarded as criminal. No chips were ever discovered or photographed by local journalists. Although homing beacons are common in police and espionage, and may well have been used by some paid C.I.A. agents in Waziristan, there was an air of dark hysteria in the torture-induced confessions of the Taliban's victims and the rumors they spawned.[9]

Kayani had tolerated the C.I.A.'s drone program not only because it eliminated declared enemies of the Pakistani state, but also because Pakistan Army officers deployed to Waziristan informed him that the strikes were for the most part popular among *maliks* and tribes opposed to the Taliban. The missile strikes encouraged fence-sitters to stay away from the militants, his generals reported, which made it easier for the army to establish some control as it set up permanent bases across the Federally Administered Tribal Areas for the first time in Pakistani history.

That spring of 2011, a Pakistani brigadier deployed to South Waziristan, where drone strikes were "almost a daily routine" around the capital of Wana, surveyed locals about the C.I.A. operations. They told him, "People were fed up [with] Taliban atrocities and wanted them to be eliminated." One elder said, "Local people wish that drones can carry more missiles." During the brigadier's two-year tour, he investigated four strikes and found only one case of a civilian death, involving a man who was "guiding the Taliban about the routes that were safe to travel."[10]

The C.I.A. reduced the number of mistakes it made gradually after the rough start of its escalation in 2008 and 2009. In the last year of the Bush administration, by one independent count, children died a third of the time in drone attacks. In Obama's first year in office, the figure was 20 percent. By 2012, it would be 5 percent. Smaller drone missiles, more precise targeting technology, more experienced operators, and greater emphasis from the Obama White House on preventing innocent deaths caused civilian casualties to drop. Yet all it took was one mass casualty attack like the one at Datta Khel to revive the imagery of callous atrocity.[11]

The video feeds transmitted from above North Waziristan documented one problem clearly: Pakistani forces still could not or would not stop Haqqani fighters from crossing into Afghanistan. It was not unusual for C.I.A. targeting analysts to watch from above as Taliban commanders loaded vehicles in Miranshah or its environs with men and weapons and then drove right through several Pakistani military checkpoints. C.I.A. officers at the embassy in Islamabad would occasionally show these videos to Kayani and Pasha, to reinforce the point that the border was open, American troops were being hit as a result, and that something had to change. The Pakistanis typically counterpunched by providing coordinates inside Afghanistan where anti-Pakistani militants operated, challenging the Americans to do something about *that* problem.[12]

The American leadership in Kabul—Chris Wood, the C.I.A. station chief; Ryan Crocker, the ambassador; and Petraeus, at I.S.A.F. headquarters—were united in advocating that disrupting the Haqqanis and the Taliban's sanctuary in Quetta and Karachi was essential if the troop surge was to be successful. To execute his war of attrition against the Taliban in the time Obama had provided, Petraeus regarded drones as a tool to decimate the Haqqani network while the 101st's Second Combat Brigade hit Taliban infrastructure in the green zone and the Marines cleared Helmand. The Haqqanis had about four thousand fighters, according to American estimates. Drones might be provocative but they were more effective than Pakistani ground forces and less provocative than a U.S. invasion or conventional air war would be.

Hamid Karzai egged them on. "I'm not asking you to go to war in Pakistan, but there's no pressure on them," he pleaded to the Americans he met. "You are getting played on this." Another time, Karzai confided, "Do you know why I'm always blowing up in public about civilian casualties, night raids? I'm trying to push you off your flawed approach. I'm trying to shock you into changing your policy on Pakistan."

When congressional delegations visited Kabul, they usually took a briefing from the C.I.A. station chief. Wood delivered what he jokingly called the "Chris Wood Power Hour," in which he argued that Pakistani sanctuary was the single most important problem in the war.

"We either address the sanctuary and we win the war, or we don't and we lose the war," Wood told visitors repeatedly during his 2011 tour in Kabul. "It's that simple." He had run operations in Islamabad, knew Pakistani officers and the military well. He did not buy the arguments that I.S.I. had rogue officers or retirees operating independently—an I.S.I. colonel was no more likely to go rogue than an American colonel commanding a tank unit. Nor did he believe the army was so weak or domestic politics so fragile that Pakistan could not withstand the backlash if it carried out a decisive crackdown on militants in Waziristan, Quetta, and Karachi.[13]

Wood believed that greater pressure on Kayani and Pasha—perhaps private threats of personalized travel sanctions against the generals, or threats to delegitimize the Pakistan Army internationally, as a sponsor of terrorism—might succeed. Yet Wood's views never attracted a critical mass of cabinet-level allies. For one thing, Pakistan controlled supply lines to the Afghan war. They could squeeze the Americans if pressed too far. Recognizing this vulnerability, Petraeus ordered planning for air bridges to Bagram and Kandahar from Qatar and Central Asia that could resupply I.S.A.F. adequately in case an all-out confrontation with

Pakistan closed the land routes. The secret planning for a raid on the house in Abbottabad, Pakistan, where Osama Bin Laden might be holed up, and the uncertainty of what backlash might result if an attack there went ahead, and potentially went wrong, added urgency to the planning for alternative routes. But full independence from Pakistani supply lines would take time and involve huge expense, at least until the number of American troops that needed to be fed and watered fell back toward fifty thousand. This was a legacy of the logistics bargain struck with Musharraf amid the shock of September 2001.[14]

After John Podesta declined the position, Hillary Clinton selected Marc Grossman as Richard Holbrooke's successor. Initially she asked him if he would prefer to be ambassador to Kabul or the special representative to Afghanistan and Pakistan. Grossman said that was up to her. When Ryan Crocker, formerly ambassador to Iraq and Pakistan, emerged as a candidate for Kabul, Grossman accepted Holbrooke's position. Obama asked Crocker to try to repair the frayed relationship with Karzai and to negotiate a long-term strategic partnership agreement with Afghanistan. Grossman would handle the secret talks with the Taliban. He was a career foreign service officer who had risen to become ambassador to Turkey during the 1990s. He also served as assistant secretary of state for Europe during the Kosovo crisis, the last war Bill Clinton had to manage. After George W. Bush took office, Grossman worked closely with Colin Powell and his deputy, Richard Armitage, as undersecretary of state for political affairs. Then he retired and went into business as a Beltway consultant. He was a tall man who wore wire-rimmed glasses and dressed like a civil servant. He had credibility with both Democrats and Republicans. In marked contrast to Holbrooke, he was quiet, methodical, a planner, not a jazz-inspired improviser.

"I can't be Dick," he told Clinton. "Dick was Dick. I do things more modestly, systematically."

There were those at the White House who wondered if he really wanted the job or if he had accepted it merely from a sense of duty. Grossman bristled at any such suggestion. He might not be flashy but he was dedicated, and he had put his own reputation on the line in a project fraught with political risk. At the Obama White House, it was certainly a relief to have someone less freewheeling than Holbrooke in charge of the sensitive matter of probing the Taliban in negotiations. Grossman did understand that his mandate was ambitious, whatever its probability of success. He was to finish what Holbrooke had started. He might help end the war.

"The time has come to jump over the inter-agency's hesitation, which will be never-ending," Grossman wrote to Clinton on March 24, 2011, in a memo titled "A-Rod on Deck," which adopted Holbrooke's code name for Tayeb Agha. They had come to the point where they had to "see what A-Rod can do in a real negotiation," Grossman wrote.[15]

Grossman hoped to agree with Tayeb Agha on a series of confidence-building measures that, once finalized, would lead to peace negotiations including Karzai's government, perhaps in the summer of 2012. Grossman's hope was that the Taliban would initially issue a statement denouncing terrorism, and then they would agree on a political office for the movement, and then the United States and the Taliban would exchange prisoners. In the meantime, Grossman would organize commitments of support to Afghanistan from international allies at a series of conferences. That diplomacy would provide a basis for U.S. support to Kabul if talks with the Taliban failed. If the talks succeeded, countries such as Pakistan, Qatar, and Turkey could provide a circle of support for the peace negotiations. There was also the possibility that the Taliban would raise the subject of U.S. troop withdrawals from Afghanistan as part of the negotiation. The White House signaled that it would be open to putting that question on the table in the right circumstances, as part of a larger discussion of postsettlement security arrangements in Afghanistan.[16]

Now that the Obama administration had briefed Karzai on the discussions with Tayeb Agha, Karzai shared his own information. His sketch of Tayeb Agha was intriguing. There seemed to be no question that Tayeb Agha was close to Mullah Mohammad Omar's extended family. There was also agreement that Agha had emerged as chief negotiator because of the split within the Taliban's leadership that followed Mullah Baradar's arrest in Pakistan, early in 2010. According to one account,

Tayeb Agha shared an office in Kyrgyzstan, the Central Asian republic, with two Taliban colleagues. Also, the Americans reviewed Saudi-sourced claims about Tayeb Agha's relations with Iran. These included an account that the envoy had traveled to Iran and another that Iran was paying Mullah Mansour, the Taliban number two, as much as $800,000 a month to back the movement's insurgency against N.A.T.O. In geopolitical terms, all these unconfirmed reports made sense: *Everyone* in the region, not just I.S.I., wanted the United States to fail militarily in Afghanistan, out of fear that if N.A.T.O. succeeded, America would be able to position forces in the region for decades, on air bases from Bagram to Shindand, near Iran's border. Yet because of Saudi Arabia's endless slander campaign against Iran, it was difficult to evaluate the credibility of the reports tying Mansour and Tayeb Agha to Tehran. The envoy had aligned himself more transparently with the Qataris.

On April 1, Hillary Clinton delivered to the White House an updated plan to advance the Taliban talks, based on Grossman's mid-March memo. Grossman also worked up a sixteen-page paper, an outline for the next meeting with Tayeb Agha, which Frank Ruggiero would again conduct. On Tom Donilon's advice, the document went straight to Obama, without the burden of another round of interagency argument. Increasingly, the president personally monitored the peace negotiations.[17]

The United States had its own extremists. In late March in Gainesville, Florida, the Reverend Terry Jones of the Dove World Outreach Center staged a "trial" of the Koran, found it guilty, and burned a volume in his sanctuary. The act sparked violent protests in Pakistan and Afghanistan.

Early in April, Obama spoke to Karzai again by secure video. His agenda included corruption at Kabul Bank and Tayeb Agha, but he felt compelled to say something about the Florida minister's incitement. "I condemn Pastor Jones," Obama said. "There is no room for bigotry. But no one should direct their anger at innocent people."

Karzai reminded him, "Eight years ago we were talking about cooperation among civilizations." That seemed a distant memory.

"We're planning a third meeting with Tayeb Agha," Obama informed Karzai. To build confidence, they planned to offer the Taliban representative the possibility of a political office for the movement. The Obama administration would prefer the office to be in Kabul, but if he refused, they would insist that Karzai's representatives join in future talks, wherever they were held.

Karzai remained deeply worried that the United States would sell him out by talking separately to the Taliban and Pakistan. He asked about planning under way for a conference on Afghanistan in Bonn, Germany, in December 2011, to mark the tenth anniversary of the agreement that had brought Karzai to power. "Is Bonn a peace conference?" Karzai asked. He meant, Would it be the forum where the Americans tried to finalize a deal with the Taliban?

Obama answered that they would all try to work together on an agenda for Bonn. He reminded Karzai that the U.S. troop withdrawal from Afghanistan would commence soon, in July. This was a time for political creativity. There was some discussion under way about whether the Taliban should be invited to Bonn, Obama acknowledged.

Karzai was adamant: "Afghanistan should be represented only by the government of the state." It was a warning. The Obama administration was prepared to talk directly to the Taliban, without Karzai, as the Taliban demanded. Yet the administration maintained a pretense that negotiations would be "Afghan led." Karzai had leverage over Washington and he knew it.[18]

Pasha flew in to Washington in mid-April. He met with Panetta to deliver a message: The C.I.A. needed to shrink its presence in Pakistan. He and Kayani wanted dozens of case officers in the country to leave. They would not be granting visas for replacements. The relationship between the C.I.A. and I.S.I. should be "reset," Pasha said. The same was true for the Pentagon. The Pakistanis would cut the number of U.S. military personnel stationed in Pakistan roughly in half. They would allow contractors who maintained military equipment purchased from the United States, such as F-16 fighter-bombers, but they would send the counterinsurgency trainers and special operators home. The C.I.A. should rely on I.S.I.'s intelligence and stop collecting intelligence on its own.[19]

The timing was awkward and so was the discussion. Pasha said later that he got into a "shouting match" with Panetta. In any event, the meeting took place amid high tension. Obama was that week considering two options for striking the house in Abbottabad occupied by "the Pacer," the tall bearded man who walked daily in the courtyard. In one scenario, two stealth B-2 bombers would drop sixteen precision-guided, two-thousand-pound bombs on the site—a massive amount of ordnance that would guarantee everyone inside was killed. In the second plan, SEALs would conduct a helicopter-borne assault. Obama had been leaning toward bombing but hadn't decided.

The president had reached one decision about Pakistan's involvement in any operation, however. There would be none. There was too much danger that I.S.I. would leak the information and allow Bin Laden to escape. Also, what if the C.I.A. shared its intelligence but Kayani and Pasha refused to act? As Panetta summarized Obama's position, "There was simply too much risk at stake to trust an untrustworthy partner."[20]

Pasha and Kayani continued to try to recruit Karzai into a separate bargain. That April, the generals again flew to Kabul. They reemphasized what they had been telling Karzai since the previous year. *The Americans are leaving. Don't rely on them. They use us and then they throw us out. Your future is with Pakistan, China, and Saudi Arabia. If you want peace, if you want the Taliban to make a deal, only we can deliver it.*

A few weeks later, Marc Grossman flew to Kabul and met Karzai at the Arg Palace. Karzai told him that he might have to choose Pakistan, not the United States.

"At least we know now what Pakistan wants," Karzai said. "They told us, like Bush, 'Either you are with us or against us. But if you are against us, the U.S. and Europe will not save you.'"[21]

Karzai went into one of his soliloquies. "I have been the most vicious critic of Pakistan and its policy toward Afghanistan, long before 9/11," he said. "Records of your embassies will show it. They killed my father and I have stood against them for that reason." Yet for "three years," Karzai continued, he had not "spoken a word against Pakistan" in public because he had "lost hope" in America's ability to manage I.S.I.

"Can you find a way to bring stability to Afghanistan without the cooperation of Pakistan?" Karzai demanded. "If you can find that way, I can give you everything else. If you can't, then we have to humbly accept a deal with honor," meaning with Islamabad. "Pakistan has Islam in their hands, madrassas, suicide bombs." To make matters worse, the United States and N.A.T.O. had "attacked Afghan patriotism," humiliating the country.

"Even the Communists showed more patriotism than us," Karzai continued. "This is a government on contract. It is not a government for a patriot. Either we make a deal with Pakistan, or the U.S. must work for Afghanistan's protection, rather than undermine Afghanistan's patriots. You tell me, Mr. Grossman, are you ready?"

"There is nobody in the U.S. that fears a strong and self-confident Afghanistan," Grossman assured him. He tried to steer the conversation back to the subject of negotiating with the Taliban. He was hoping to win Karzai's support for the next round of talks with Tayeb Agha. But Karzai went on. He would not sign a strategic partnership agreement with the United States if it was to be a "partnership in war" without a change in Pakistan's conduct, because "that means failure."

In the end, Karzai said, "It's easier to be friendly with Pakistan. . . . Pasha knows where Mullah Omar is. We know what goes on there in Quetta. . . . Nothing will change unless we make a deal with Pakistan— or stop Pakistan."[22]

Grossman returned to the embassy's residential skyscraper to sleep. His job was extremely difficult, but it was his habit of mind after decades in diplomacy to press on, one step at a time. There was no eliding the intractability of the parties he was supposed to corral through negotiation. One was a radical militia movement whose leader hadn't been seen in a decade. Another was an increasingly hostile military and intelligence service that controlled about one hundred nuclear weapons. A third was Karzai, who had lost confidence in the United States, and who sometimes spoke about the future like an unhinged street preacher.

It was Sunday, May 1, 2011, in Afghanistan, ten hours ahead of Washington. The next morning, Grossman woke to the news from Abbottabad.

THIRTY

Martyrs Day

Martyrs Day was the Pakistani military's annual remembrance of fallen soldiers and officers. Five thousand people crowded into a parade ground at General Headquarters in Rawalpindi on the evening of April 30. A mournful procession of hundreds of children, widows, and parents shuffled in to inaugurate the formal ceremony. Ashfaq Kayani stood at attention in a dress uniform, the brim of his hat pulled low over his forehead, his chest draped with ribbons and medals. Then he took his seat as two presenters addressed the crowd from podiums on a marble rise. One was an attractive woman whose uncovered hair blew in the hot breeze. A second woman dressed like a Karachi model belted out a song of remembrance. Images depicting army heroism flashed by on two large outdoor screens—officers teaching destitute children, rescuing civilians from floods, delivering aid to earthquake victims. The presenters told stories of the fallen and interviewed a widow onstage. Finally an honor guard goose-stepped forward. Kayani tucked a swagger stick under his left arm, laid a wreath at a marble memorial, stood to fold his hands in prayer, and then ascended the stage to read out a ten-minute speech.

He said that Pakistan "is an Islamic and ideological country, the foundations of which are based on the blood of hundreds of thousands of martyrs" who had sacrificed their lives to realize "the dream of a prosperous and strong" nation. The country was passing through a "critical juncture of its history," Kayani continued. Its military carried out its responsibilities, whether in the "fight against terror, services in flood and earthquake-affected areas, or safeguarding the borders." He quoted Mohammed Ali Jinnah, Pakistan's founder: "We have to make future generations secure and not let disappointments dominate us."[1]

The following night, at home at Army House, Kayani was still awake, smoking Dunhills, when an orderly interrupted. It was about 1:00 a.m. Major General Ishfaq Nadeem, the director-general of military operations, was on the line.

A helicopter has crashed at Abbottabad, Nadeem reported.

Is it one of ours? Kayani asked. It would be highly unusual for a Pakistani helicopter to be flying in that area at night. It was much more likely that Pakistan was under foreign attack. Kayani's first thought was that someone was staging a strike on one of Pakistan's nuclear facilities. There were several in the region.

In the flurry of telephone calls that followed, Kayani spoke to Air Chief Marshal Rao Qamar Suleman. They discussed ordering two F-16 fighter-bombers into the air. Exactly what transpired on this call is not clear. The commanders did agree to scramble the jets from a base some five hundred miles from Abbottabad. It also seems likely that by the time they made this decision, Kayani knew from I.S.I. and the police in Abbottabad that the helicopter raiders were Americans and that the house they had attacked had been a hiding place for Osama Bin Laden. By one account, provided afterward to Pakistani journalists by senior military officers, Air Marshal Suleman asked Kayani if he should order the F-16s to shoot down the intruding helicopters if they could locate them, an admittedly doubtful proposition. After a long pause, Kayani reportedly said yes. Kayani later gave local reporters a contradictory account, saying that such an order would have been pointless because "you can't shoot down an American helicopter with an American plane." He meant that the Pentagon would know how to interfere with the F-16's systems to prevent it from successfully operating air-to-air missiles. In any event, by the time the Pakistani F-16s reached the skies, the

Chinooks bearing U.S. Navy SEALs had crossed out of Pakistan and into Afghanistan. There was no opportunity to retaliate.[2]

About half an hour after the first call, the American embassy rang. Admiral Mullen wished to speak to Kayani. It took about ninety minutes for embassy technicians to set up a secure telephone at Army House. In the meantime Kayani learned the full story. Police and I.S.I. officers in Abbottabad had by now found several dead bodies at the site, as well as Osama Bin Laden's wailing widows. The widows had described the SEAL raid and explained that the Americans had shot Bin Laden dead and then taken his corpse away.

"Congratulations," Kayani said when Mullen finally came on the phone. "This is good for you, but there will be issues here."

Mullen reminded him that he had told Kayani more than once that if the United States ever located "Number One or Number Two," meaning Bin Laden or Ayman Al Zawahiri, any American president would have to act unilaterally. In seeking justice for the nearly three thousand people killed on September 11, the mission was in a category of its own.

Kayani had earlier said he understood. The problem was that this raid exposed the myths he so regularly promoted at events like Martyrs Day. The army hyped itself as a mighty institution yet it could not defend the country's borders. This had obvious implications for Indian military planners. "There will be no love lost for Osama" in the Pakistani public's reaction, Kayani predicted, but the military and his leadership would come under withering fire.

"It will forever remain a very deep scar in our national memory and our military's memory, that we failed to detect the raid," he told Mullen. "By the same token, it will never fade from our national memory that you guys did it."

Mullen disclosed that President Obama had not yet decided whether to announce the raid or Bin Laden's death. Although it seemed clear that the SEALs had killed Bin Laden, the C.I.A. was still working through a final confirmation of the corpse's identity. Kayani was appalled that Obama might be considering delay. Pakistanis were lighting up Facebook and Twitter with news of the attack—including posts of photos of a damaged American helicopter abandoned by the SEALs. There was no way Kayani would be able to contain media reporting and confused speculation about who the target had been. "Our people need to understand what happened here," he pleaded. "We're not going to be able to manage the Pakistani media without you confirming this. You can explain it to them. They need to understand that this was Bin Laden and not just some ordinary U.S. operation." In fact, as Mullen and Kayani talked, the White House was moving to disclose the news publicly, and quickly.

Kayani returned to the themes of the secret warning letter he had written to Mullen the previous August, when there was loose talk in America of bombing Pakistan. Direct American military action in the country would only turn public opinion against the United States and fortify extremists, Kayani had written. Privately, he was aggravated. He would have been prepared to put a Pakistani face on a raid on the Abbottabad compound. He knew there was mistrust, but I.S.I. and the police had arrested Khalid Sheikh Mohammed, the mastermind of September 11, Ramzi bin al-Shibh, and other high-value Al Qaeda leaders, in joint operations where there had been no leaks. The Americans had the drones and satellites necessary to watch overhead at Abbottabad, to make sure the Pakistanis did exactly what was required and that Bin Laden did not escape. If the Obama administration had wanted to be good partners, they could have worked out a way. Instead, they had humiliated the Pakistani military and him. Kayani and Pasha had already moved to reset the relationship after the Raymond Davis matter, to reduce the American presence in their country, but this event would change public opinion and stir emotions in the army's officer class. It was the end of an era between the United States and Pakistan.[3]

The full story of Osama Bin Laden's long fugitive exile in Pakistan may never be known. He appears to have lived in about four different houses in towns in the northwest of the country before moving to Abbottabad in August 2005, where he remained until his death. Kayani had been I.S.I. director for less than a year when Bin Laden set up in

Abbottabad. The Al Qaeda emir and his family enjoyed support from a sizable, complex network inside Pakistan—document manufacturers, fund-raisers, bankers, couriers, and guards. His youngest wife, Amal, gave birth to four children in Pakistani hospitals or clinics after 2002. Bin Laden limited his movements, rarely leaving his homes, but he did travel on Pakistani roads numerous times without getting caught, as did his sons and wives. Amal traveled at least once on an internal flight. In one case a man dressed as a policeman accompanied Bin Laden, according to one of the women who traveled with him. It is entirely plausible that I.S.I. ran a highly compartmented, cautious support operation involving a small number of case officers or contractors who could maintain deniability. Yet there remains no authoritative evidence—on-the-record testimony, letters, or documents—of knowing complicity by I.S.I. or the Pakistani state. Indeed, passages from Bin Laden's letters suggest that he did not have reliable or regular contact with the Pakistani state. In one 2010 letter he warned against allowing his sons to pass through the custody of a contact in Baluchistan because "people that he knows work for the Pakistani intelligence." In another letter that year Bin Laden asked an Al Qaeda correspondent to bring a "card" for his son Khalid, who was living with him, and another for himself. He appears to be referring to a forged Pakistani identity card, suggesting he did not have one already. In other correspondence about smuggling his son Hamzah and Hamzah's mother to Abbottabad, Bin Laden again worries about encounters with Pakistani police and makes clear that he must rely on forged identity cards provided by a contact in Baluchistan.

If I.S.I. did run a compartmented support operation, perhaps in the hope that it would encourage Al Qaeda not to target Pakistan, the service's incentive would have been to work as indirectly as possible and to urge Bin Laden to lie low. The Americans had publicized a $25 million reward for Bin Laden's capture. There was so much corruption in the Pakistani police forces and I.S.I. itself that even if the service had been ordered by Musharraf or Kayani to keep Bin Laden safe, there could be no guarantee against some enterprising officer in the know walking into the U.S. embassy or one of the American consulates and arranging to be resettled in Arizona with reward money and a new identity, as had happened with previous informers aiding American fugitive hunts in Pakistan.[4]

C.I.A. and other Obama administration officials have said they possess no evidence—no intercepts, no unreleased documents from Abbottabad—that Kayani or Pasha or any other I.S.I. officer knew where Bin Laden was hiding. Given the hostility toward Pakistan prevalent in the American national security bureaucracy by 2011, if the United States possessed such hard evidence, it almost certainly would have leaked.

However, the Abbottabad letters do contain references to negotiations between Al Qaeda and Pakistan about a kind of mutual nonaggression pact. Bin Laden wrote to Al Qaeda colleagues about the position they should take in such talks, but the letters provide no proof of who was negotiating on the Pakistani side, if anyone. "Our stance was essentially: We are ready to quit the fight with you, as our battle is primarily with the Americans; however, you entered into it with them," Atiyah Abd al-Rahman, a Libyan-born Al Qaeda operator who wrote regularly to Bin Laden, reported in July 2010, referring to apparent contacts with the Pakistani state. "If you leave us alone, then we will leave you alone."[5]

This passage and others suggest that Al Qaeda was making an appeal for a truce, not that one had been reached. And there are numerous indications in the letters that Bin Laden and his family members had no easy way to travel on Pakistani roads at this time and that they and other Al Qaeda figures regarded such travel as very risky.

The fuzziest period in the available chronology of Bin Laden's exile after 2001 involves the first months after he escaped from Tora Bora. There is some detainee testimony that he moved north to Kunar Province, inside Afghanistan, and other testimony that he hid inside Pakistan. None of this information appears as credible as the testimony of Amal, Bin Laden's young Yemeni wife. Her account picks up in mid-2002, when she said she was reunited with Bin Laden in Peshawar. By then Osama had connected with a man known within Al Qaeda as Abu Ahmed al-Kuwaiti, who was in his midtwenties, and his wife, Maryam, who was then fifteen years old. Al-Kuwaiti's real name was Ibrahim Saeed Ahmed. He was well suited to take charge of Bin Laden's personal security inside Pakistan. He was an ethnic Pashtun whose family came from northwestern Pakistan, yet he had grown up in Kuwait. He could therefore communicate with Al Qaeda operators in fluent Arabic while appearing to locals in western Pakistan to be a native.

Late in 2002, Bin Laden, his wife Amal, Ibrahim, and his wife, Maryam, traveled by "coach"—a bus or a minibus—in the company of a man dressed as a police officer. They rode to the Shangla District of Swat, about one hundred fifty miles northwest of Islamabad, a mountain resort long influenced by conservative Islamist preachers. The foursome stayed in the region for eight or nine months, in two different houses, according to Amal. Maryam remembered a stay in just one home for six to nine months, a house in "a beautiful area" with a "river behind it."[6] A Pakistani investigative commission later reported that the house belonged to Maryam's father. Ibrahim's brother Abrar joined them and got married during this period. Khalid Sheikh Mohammed visited for about two weeks. Bin Laden busied himself recording an audiotape in which he praised mass casualty terrorist attacks in Bali, Moscow, and Jordan and he composed long written statements about the urgency of jihad against Americans and Jews.

Early in March 2003, Pakistani police working with the C.I.A. and the F.B.I. arrested Khalid Sheikh Mohammed in Rawalpindi. Bin Laden and his wife fled Swat three days later. The letters and travel documents seized from K.S.M. provided insights into Bin Laden's support network in Pakistan but no target address. The documents showed that Bin Laden's children and wives had access to passports, visas, and trusted escorts, allowing these family members to move through Karachi and eventually to seek refuge in Iran. Yet the fact that close family members such as Bin Laden's son Saad and two of Osama's older wives went in 2002 to Iran—a Shiite-majority country hostile to Al Qaeda's ideology—suggested that Bin Laden did not have cooperation, or at least not extensive cooperation, from the Pakistani state; otherwise, he would have tried to avoid exposing loved ones to Iran. Later letters make clear that he would have preferred to have all of his family in Pakistan. I.S.I.'s role in the arrests of Al Qaeda leaders such as K.S.M. and Musharraf's willingness to turn detainees over to the Americans would have made clear to Bin Laden that the Pakistani state could not be trusted fully.

The available record contains another gap in Bin Laden's movements over the summer of 2003 but comes back into focus in August of that year, when Bin Laden and Amal moved into a rented two-story home in Naseem Town, a suburb of Haripur, Pakistan. The area was in Pakistan's Pashtun-dominated western province of Khyber Pakhtunkhwa, formerly the Northwest Frontier Province. Ibrahim and Abrar as well as their wives moved in with the Bin Ladens. Osama, who was now forty-five years old, paid each of the Ahmed brothers about 9,000 Pakistani rupees per month, or just over $100, for their services. The house rent was another $150 a month.[7] That year Amal gave birth to a girl, Aaisa, either in a government hospital or in a private clinic. Bin Laden made audiotapes and videotapes throughout this period, including one, released on October 29, 2004, on the eve of the American election, in which he took responsibility for September 11 and threatened more violence against the United States.

During the Haripur sojourn, Ibrahim and Abrar went to work on more sustainable and secure accommodation, in Abbottabad. They acquired land and, no doubt in close consultation with Bin Laden, who came from a family that specialized in construction, designed a multistory compound that could house the emir's growing family with Amal and perhaps other wives and children if they could be brought into Pakistan. The total cost of the project was estimated at several hundred thousand dollars or more.[8] The group moved into the new compound in August 2005. Twelve-foot walls ringed the property; in one place, they rose as high as eighteen feet. Seven-foot walls protected a balcony on the highest floor. The home had no telephone or Internet connections. The occupants burned their own trash. In its design and location, the house stood apart from its neighbors and its walls were unusually high. Yet in a region of drug traffickers, tribal figures living in fear of revenge attacks by rivals, and conservative Pashtun families that sought to keep their wives and daughters in purdah, many people walled off their homes. This layout was only somewhat on the extreme side of the local spectrum of fortress architecture.

The house stood less than a mile from the treed, red-roofed campus of the Pakistan Military Academy, the country's equivalent of West Point, which lay off PMA Road. That proximity presented damning

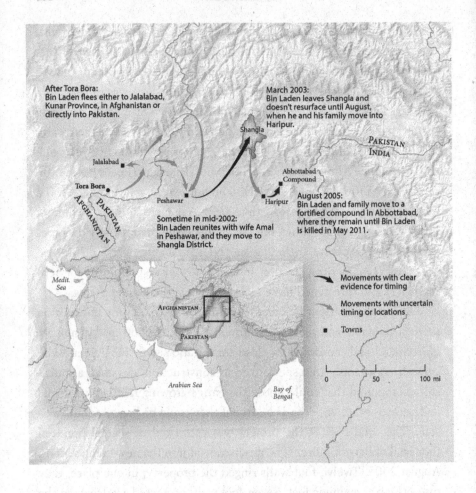

After Tora Bora:
Bin Laden flees either to Jalalabad,
Kunar Province, in Afghanistan or
directly into Pakistan.

March 2003:
Bin Laden leaves Shangla and
doesn't resurface until August,
when he and his family move into
Haripur.

Sometime in mid-2002:
Bin Laden reunites with wife Amal
in Peshawar, and they move to
Shangla District.

August 2005:
Bin Laden and family move to a
fortified compound in Abbottabad,
where they remain until Bin Laden
is killed in May 2011.

Movements with clear
evidence for timing

Movements with uncertain
timing or locations

Towns

circumstantial evidence of connivance with Bin Laden by the Pakistani
state, but the evidence was not conclusive. Was it conceivable that Bin
Laden could live so close to the army's highest seat of officer education
for six years without anyone in uniform or in I.S.I. being aware of his
presence? Kayani later insisted that it was the case. The compound was
not actually visible from the academy. Pakistanis did not routinely get to
know their neighbors in the way that many Americans did, he argued to
American visitors. The army rarely conducted perimeter security sweeps
of neighborhoods around its bases, except in conflict areas; the army was
not under threat in Abbottabad. In October 2009 ten militants disguised

in army uniforms penetrated the walls of General Headquarters in Rawalpindi in a raid that killed fifteen people, including a brigadier and a colonel. It turned out one of the conspirators had rented a house in Rawalpindi and conducted surveillance undetected for two months. In December another Pakistani Taliban suicide bombing cell struck the Parade Lane mosque near G.H.Q., attended almost exclusively by military officers, and killed about forty people, including a two-star general. Obviously if I.S.I. or military intelligence had the wherewithal to detect the cells lurking around supreme headquarters in Rawalpindi it would have done so. *Yes, we are that blind* became the thrust of Kayani's argument about the location of Bin Laden's hideout in Abbottabad.[9]

Of course, Kayani and Pasha made the same argument to American visitors about their supposed lack of knowledge of the hideouts of Taliban leaders in Quetta and Karachi—implausibly so. In Bin Laden's case the Pakistani generals advanced by implication a subtle argument, as the Americans heard it: We lie to you about our access to Taliban leaders, because our relations with the Taliban are a vital national interest of Pakistan, but we are telling you the truth about our lack of access to Bin Laden, because Al Qaeda is our enemy, too.

Bin Laden's lifestyle in hiding was pinched but warmly familial. He arrived on move-in day at Abbottabad with nine items of clothing.[10] He watched satellite television on a tiny black-and-white set—Bin Laden had been a TV news junkie since adolescence. In 2006, Amal gave birth to another daughter, Zainab, and Bin Laden released a handful of audiotapes. In 2007, he released his first video in about three years, to mark the sixth anniversary of September 11. Throughout, he wrote many long, discursive letters to Al Qaeda operatives and international affiliates, letters characteristic of a man with a lot of time on his hands. Some of his writing concerned the proper conduct of revolutionary jihad, such as concentrating on attacking America, avoiding Muslim civilian casualties, and cranking up media campaigns. Sometimes he offered specific instructions about operations or hostage exchanges. He issued what he evidently believed to be binding decisions about Al Qaeda alliances with allies in Iraq, North Africa, and Somalia. He wrote frequently about the welfare of those sons and wives from whom he remained separated.

As the university-educated scion of a modern Arabian business family, Bin Laden had always considered himself an expert on finance, and he distributed detailed if quirky investment advice. In a 2010 letter, he advised that ransom proceeds from the kidnapping of an Afghan should be invested in gold, euros, Kuwaiti dinars, and Chinese renminbi. He was bullish on gold (which usually rose in price whenever the world was engulfed in chaos, which Bin Laden sought to create) and he suggested that his correspondent monitor price fluctuations and buy in at $1,500 an ounce, whenever that was possible.[11]

He was paranoid about American aerial and electronic surveillance capabilities. He urged Al Qaeda allies in North Africa to grow more trees to hide from Predator drones and spy satellites. He asked supporters trying to smuggle his wife and son from Iran to travel only on cloudy days. He repeatedly urged allies to stay out of Waziristan because of the dangers of aerial surveillance and drone strikes. He reminded a colleague considering a media interview that even a trusted journalist "may be under surveillance that neither we nor they can perceive, either on the ground or via satellite." Also, "A chip could be planted in a piece of their equipment." He wrote to two of his sons that Al Qaeda had decided that Waziristan was "well known to the enemy" and that it would be necessary to shift to Peshawar, where C.I.A. drones did not operate. He offered complex instructions about how to slip into Peshawar. He was as paranoid about Iran as he was about the C.I.A. He worried that Iranian doctors might use medical treatment as a pretense to inject his sons with tracking chips. "The syringe size may be normal but the needle is expected to be larger than normal size," Bin Laden wrote. "The chip size may be as long as a seed of grain but very thin and smooth."[12]

In another letter, he noted that "the most important security issues in the cities is controlling children, by not getting out of the house except for extreme necessity like medical care, and teaching them the local language; and that they do not get to the yard of the house without an adult who will control the volume of their voices." He and the Ahmeds rigged a tarp covering the outdoor space in Bin Laden's section of the compound, and he sometimes wore a cowboy hat when he walked in short loops outside.[13]

He did have the ability to call on substantial Al Qaeda funds. He once asked for a draw on his "personal fund" of 30,000 euros, presumably the equivalent of a C.E.O.'s allowance managed by Al Qaeda's finance committee. Bin Laden asked at one point for an accounting of incoming funds by country of origin, indicating that several Gulf States were sources, although his request did not indicate whether the donors were official or private. Bin Laden apparently contemplated arranging for his son Hamzah to migrate to Qatar, and Atiyah Abd al-Rahman queried as to whether he should approach the Qatari embassy in Pakistan to determine whether this was possible or if the "Americans will definitely take him" once he reached the emirate. Al-Rahman thought, on balance, it was better for Hamzah to remain in Iran. "Perhaps the matter is more difficult than you imagine, in terms of the route and searches between us and Peshawar."[14]

On April 26, 2011, Bin Laden wrote what would be his final letter, to al-Rahman. He began by reflecting on the "consecutive revolutions" of the Arab Spring of that year, "a great and glorious event" that would "inevitably change the conditions" for Al Qaeda. The Muslim Brotherhood, then ascending to power in Egypt, was a movement of "half solutions," so it would be incumbent "upon us, the mujaheddin," to "plug that gap." On the Afghan war, he expressed satisfaction that the jihad there was "bleeding down the head of the international apostasy, until it reaches such weakness that the Muslim people have regained some self-confidence and daring."

He added some advice about security: "It is proved that American technology and modern systems cannot arrest a Mujahid if he does not commit a security error that leads them to him. So adherence to security precautions turns their technological advancement into a loss and a disappointment to them."[15]

Bin Laden was about to be discovered even though he had not made a significant security error. Since 2002, the two dozen or so C.I.A. analysts looking for him from the Counterterrorism Center's ground-floor suites in New Headquarters had been trying to identify couriers who might ferry his messages and supply him with money and other support. Abu Ahmed al-Kuwaiti's name surfaced during interrogations of several

Al Qaeda detainees after 2002, but it was not clear whether he was still active. Exactly how the C.I.A. discovered Ibrahim Ahmed's true name, that he was living in Pakistan, and that he might be working with Bin Laden remains unclear. The agency released a version emphasizing help from other intelligence services, cell phone intercepts, and street work by C.I.A. agents in Pakistan who identified Ibrahim's jeep and followed it to Abbottabad.

Operation Neptune Spear, the carefully rehearsed plan to deliver SEALs to Abbottabad by helicopter, launched on May 1 from Jalalabad. The attackers faced disruption early on when one of the two helicopters carrying the assault team crash-landed at the Abbottabad compound. The pilots of the second helicopter then landed in a different place from where they had intended. This led the SEALs to improvise. One team approached the outer building where Ibrahim and his family lived. They pounded on the door with a sledgehammer. Somebody shot at them from inside. They shot back and killed a man who turned out to be Ibrahim. Inside the main house they also killed Abrar, his wife, and then, as they climbed higher up the stairs, Osama's son Khalid. On the top floor, they shot Bin Laden in the head and several times in the chest, as he lay writhing on the floor. The SEALs shot and wounded Amal, but she and Maryam, Ibrahim's widow, survived and were later taken into custody by Pakistani police.[16]

The killing of Osama Bin Laden had many reverberations. It delivered justice for the victims of September 11. It disrupted the founding branch of Al Qaeda and delivered the organization to a turgid successor, Zawahiri. It achieved a significant goal of Barack Obama's surge of troops into Afghanistan, creating political space for Obama to carry out the rapid troop withdrawal from Afghanistan that he increasingly believed was the correct policy. And for anyone who had not yet come to terms with the depths of nuclear-armed Pakistan's disorder or its stew of international terrorists working or at least living side by side with prestigious institutions of the Pakistani state, the raid provided bracing clarity. Among those shocked into recognition were many disgruntled citizens of Pakistan.

On Tuesday, May 4, two days after he announced Bin Laden's killing on national television, President Obama descended to the Situation Room to preside over a Principals Committee meeting called to review American strategy toward Pakistan and Afghanistan now that Bin Laden was eliminated. From Islamabad, Ambassador Munter reported that the atmosphere in Pakistan was one of "cognitive dissonance." He kept taking calls from the Pakistani government, as well as civilian friends and contacts. They all congratulated the United States. But a backlash against the army and I.S.I. was building in the media, egged on by civilian politicians who sensed an opening to recapture authority from Kayani and Pasha. The public discourse in Pakistan during those first days was similar to that in the United States: Either I.S.I. was complicit in sheltering a mass murderer, or it was incompetent. Yet it seemed clear that much or most of the Pakistani public was more offended by the fact that the SEALs had been able to penetrate the country's borders undetected than by the possibility that I.S.I. had sheltered Bin Laden. "Someone will have to answer," Munter said.[17]

Clinton, Panetta, and Gates outdid one another at the table, describing how dysfunctional America's relations with Pakistan had become. It wasn't just that the atmosphere was poisoned by mistrust. It had become almost impossible to get even minor work or accounting completed with the Pakistanis in an orderly way. Everything was frozen, broken after the Raymond Davis affair.

Intercepts of phone conversations by Kayani and Pasha after the Abbottabad raid had them sounding surprised about Bin Laden's whereabouts—or pretending to be surprised—but also captured them expressing envy. "We should have this capability," Kayani said on one call. The Americans marveled: We've been trying to train them up for counterinsurgency operations, including this kind of capability, but they have resisted mightily, as much from pride as anything else. Do they listen to anything we say?

"Look, we know Pakistan is dysfunctional," Obama finally said. "I take that as a given, the baseline. Let's work at what we can do. And let's stop trying to change their minds" about where Pakistan's interests lie.

With that, the president put the final knife into the ambitions of the strategic dialogue and the Kayani memos, 1.0 through 3.0. There were just too many structural obstacles to transforming the relationship, Obama concluded. It was going to be transactional and difficult.[18]

Day by day that May, Kayani's position looked more and more precarious. Among the three-star generals in the corps commanders conference who constituted his privy council, the feelings of anger and humiliation about the raid were described as the worst since the loss of East Pakistan to India in the 1971 war. These emotions were compounded by lingering resentment at the top of the officer corps over Kayani's decision to extend his term as army chief the previous autumn. Intercepts and other reporting showed that senior three-star Pakistani generals at the corps level really wanted Kayani out.

On Friday, May 13, Kayani and Pasha, accompanied by a deputy chief of air force operations, arrived at Parliament House, on Constitution Avenue, in Islamabad's section of broad avenues and grand public buildings. Parliament House was a modern, boxy white building designed by an American architect and opened twenty-five years earlier. The generals sat in an ornate, carpeted chamber before about four hundred senators and members of the National Assembly. Kayani opened with one of his standard PowerPoint briefings, talking over slides that reminded the parliamentarians of how many thousands of Pakistani soldiers and civilians had died in terrorist attacks since 2001 and how many Al Qaeda leaders the army, I.S.I., and police had arrested.[19]

After the PowerPoint, Pasha did most of the talking. He said Pakistan's relationship with the United States had "gone bad" and they would now reassert themselves. "They want to take action on their own on our soil," he said. "We will not allow their boots on our ground." The Americans had "conducted a sting operation on us," with the raid on Abbottabad. Yet the problem was one of military capabilities, and if the United States wanted to conduct such a raid again, they might succeed.

Pasha offered to resign at one point. "I present myself for accountability before any forum, including Parliament," he said. "There was no intentional negligence but an aspect of failure is there." I.S.I. should have known where Bin Laden was, he admitted.[20]

Six days later, Kayani appeared at National Defense University, on the edge of Islamabad, across from a golf club. The main building had an auditorium with a long horseshoe-shaped table. Kayani sat down by himself in full dress uniform with only a file of papers, a glass of water, and an ashtray. He told eighty or so officers and civilian faculty they could ask anything they wished. He lit a cigarette.

"If they don't trust us, how can we trust them?" a colonel asked about the United States.

"In uniform, we tend to see everything in black and white," Kayani answered. "In the real world, there are a lot of gray areas and you have to deal with it."

He described Pakistan as a mortgaged house, with the United States in the role of banker. "We are helpless," he professed. "Can we fight the United States?" The solution was to strengthen the economy, and to raise taxes domestically, so they could end their dependence on Washington and its allies.[21]

By late May American intelligence reports showed that Kayani and Pasha had opened vigorous discussions about how to break off the relationship with America and reorganize around Pakistan's alliance with China. How could they raise money from alternative sources? How could they build their own Chinese-inspired economy with surpluses that could be reinvested in defense? The Obama administration officials who read accounts of these conversations figured that some of the posturing was deliberately constructed for American eavesdroppers, to caution the United States, but that some of it was probably a genuine search for strategic alternatives. There was little room for Kayani to act precipitously. The Pakistani state and its bloated military depended on American, European, Japanese, South Korean, and Australian aid, as well as loans from the International Monetary Fund, to avoid bankruptcy. There might come a day when Chinese-led finance could replace those flows, but it hadn't arrived yet. For the Chinese Communist Party leadership,

Pakistan remained an essential ally, a rare friend, and a long-term check on India. Yet the Chinese government had grown as exhausted by Pakistani dysfunction as the United States had.[22]

After the May 4 meeting in the Situation Room, Obama's national security team decided to try to embrace Pakistan rather than repudiate its army or I.S.I. The C.I.A.'s drone campaign against Al Qaeda and its allies in Waziristan had depended on tacit Pakistani permission, and supply lines to American troops in Afghanistan ran through Pakistani territory. For all its failings, Kayani's army had fought to reduce violence and restore some stability since Pakistan's low point of 2009 and the cabinet did not want to see the Pakistani Taliban revive. Doug Lute, Marc Grossman, and Hillary Clinton, in particular, also hoped that Bin Laden's death might shift the ground favorably in talks with the Taliban. It would certainly make it easier, in a political sense, to carry out the troop withdrawal from Afghanistan that Obama had preannounced at his West Point speech almost eighteen months earlier.

In the documents seized at Abbottabad they soon found evidence that around 2010, Tayeb Agha had traveled from Quetta to deliver a message in person to Bin Laden from the Taliban leadership. Essentially, the message was "If we—when we—return to power in Afghanistan, all things being equal, it would be a good idea if you did not come with us, and if you do come, you will have to maintain a very low profile."[23] This reinforced the hope that the Taliban might be willing to break with Al Qaeda in a comprehensive peace deal.

On his initial visit to Pakistan after the raid, which had been previously scheduled, Marc Grossman met with Brigadier Saad Muhammad, a former I.S.I. station chief in Kabul, who was part of a Pakistani delegation designated to talk regularly to the Americans. "What goes on in the I.S.I. mind?" Saad asked out loud. The I.S.I. had given a concrete proposal to Karzai in April to build a new relationship with Pakistan, which could deliver the Taliban to talks. Now, with Bin Laden dead, "You and others who favor negotiation will be stronger," the brigadier advised.[24]

Biden worked the telephone to Islamabad. Michael Morell at the C.I.A., John Kerry, Mullen, and Clinton flew to Pakistan to try to start to repair the relationship.

Morell met Pasha alone at the I.S.I. director's home. The first fifteen or so minutes were awkward to the point of palpable discomfort; no one knew what to say. Pasha complained about the C.I.A.'s unwillingness to share what it knew about Bin Laden at Abbottabad, and about the Pentagon's unwillingness to inform them about the raid. Morell expressed frustration about I.S.I.'s long-standing work with extremists. He said the Obama administration could not share its secrets about Bin Laden because they believed the information might leak and that Bin Laden would walk away, which was unacceptable. After fifteen minutes, they started talking once more about where to go from here. Pasha called Army House and escorted Morell to a meeting with Kayani after midnight. Both sides felt freer to gripe. The Pakistanis pointed out that the administration was still keeping them in the dark about its talks with the Taliban, a subject of vital interest to them.

"What's the big picture?" Husain Haqqani asked Pasha during this period.

"We're a small country," he answered. "They are the big ones. We have to keep our pride. We have to outmaneuver them. It's all about being smart."[25]

THIRTY-ONE

Fight and Talk

Frank Ruggiero, Jeff Hayes, and Chris Kolenda flew back to Munich in the days following Bin Laden's death. They rehearsed for negotiation with Tayeb Agha, with Kolenda playing the Taliban envoy. They discussed how to use Bin Laden's killing as leverage. The team met Tayeb Agha in the German safe house on May 7, 2011. Ruggiero urged Agha to see Bin Laden's killing as an opening for the Taliban to break with Al Qaeda. "This is a historic opportunity for you to correct your mistakes," Ruggiero said.

Tayeb Agha asked the Americans to define more precisely what a Taliban break with Al Qaeda would entail. (The American side later delivered a nonpaper.) Tayeb Agha said it might take time for him to get firm guidance from the Taliban's underground leadership. "We communicate by courier," he said drily. "Finding good couriers is becoming more difficult" after the events of May 1.

They returned to Tayeb Agha's demand that the United States release senior Taliban prisoners. The Americans informed him that releasing senior leaders from Guantánamo was a nonstarter. Michael Steiner, the German envoy, thought that Agha was willing to compromise and that the Americans were too cautious. The American negotiators worried that Agha might be using the talks solely for prisoner releases, with no real intention to explore a political compromise to end the war or reduce its violence. Agha seemed agitated about the prisoner issue. At one point,

he left the room. One member of the American team heard him throwing up in the bathroom. They thought he might be so upset about the
stalemate over prisoners that it had made him sick, but of course they
could not rule out an aversion to Bavarian food.

The Americans were prepared to continue discussions about a Taliban political office. The politics around prisoner releases in the United
States looked treacherous; an office to pursue peace might be easier. The
Taliban's prospective political office had to be located in Qatar, Tayeb
Agha insisted as the talks went on. This was a position expressing Taliban foreign policy, he explained. The Taliban's political commission had
decided it would not open an office in any country that had military
forces in Afghanistan, in any neighboring country, or in any country
where the presence of such an office might cause a backlash against the
movement. Choosing Saudi Arabia, for example, would provoke a negative reaction from Iran. The governments of the United Arab Emirates
and Turkey were too close to Pakistan. It had to be Qatar. The American
team had decided beforehand to accept this demand, in part because
they were not prepared yet to accommodate prisoner exchanges, Tayeb
Agha's other priority.[1]

A week after the Munich meeting, *Der Spiegel* and *The Washington
Post* carried accounts of the talks and published Tayeb Agha's name for
the first time. Furious, the envoy informed the Americans through his
Qatari intermediaries that he was suspending negotiations. Grossman,
Lute, and others in the Conflict Resolution Cell sought to signal their
regret about the leaks (which were inevitable, given the divisions about
the talks within the Obama administration and the Karzai regime). Hillary Clinton instructed Ruggiero to fly to Qatar to deliver a message that
they wanted to get back on track. The Qataris soon replied that Tayeb
Agha was willing to meet, at least informally.

Ruggiero and Hayes flew to Doha during the first week of July, to the
Sharq resort hotel, a Ritz Carlton property. It featured sharks in its deco-
rating themes. They met Sheikh Faisal bin Qassim Al Thani, the member of the Qatari royal family who had been working as an informal
interlocutor with the Taliban. Later, Tayeb Agha joined them. He handed
the Americans a one-page, unsigned, typed letter in fractured English,

with the boldface word "Message" as its header. It was a letter, the envoy explained, from Mullah Mohammad Omar to President Obama.

It said, in essence, that both leaders had to manage domestic political risks to seek a settlement of their war, but that Omar was willing to be courageous and Obama should be as well. "I made the important decisions for the sake of humanity, and a desire to stop the casualties on both sides, for peace in the country, and for good relations between the two countries after the complete withdrawal of your forces from Afghanistan," the letter began. It rankled, Mullah Omar or his ghostwriter continued, that because the Taliban had extended an olive branch, this was dismissed by the United States as "a sign of our weakness, or subordination, as said by high-ranking officials in your government." He was apparently referring to how Gates, Petraeus, and other officials were quoted in the press. The Taliban had made significant concessions already, the letter continued. These had "negative aspects for us," and yet, "I made them in order to get the above-mentioned objectives," that is, peace and American withdrawal.

Now it was time for President Obama to step up. "I have acknowledged the legitimate hurdles you face regarding Guantanamo prisoners, but still you have to make important and tough decisions in order to get what you have been calling [for] for years." The letter said that Mullah Omar would guarantee that released Taliban prisoners would not return to the war. "I am determined to [sic] what I have said in this regard and I will stick to my words (promises) without hypocrisy.

"We are in the stage of confidence-building and still there is [a] way to get to the stage of negotiations," the letter continued. "We should both listen to each other carefully and act honestly and sincerely so that [we] will have positive impacts on our negotiations in the future." The Obama administration's willingness to allow the Taliban to open a political office in Qatar "is a positive step, and [I] hope you will take steps for the release and transfer of Guantanamo prisoners" and the elimination of sanctions and travel bans on Taliban leaders, "as these are the necessary steps required for confidence building."[2]

It appeared to be the first direct communication from the Taliban's leadership to an American president since N.A.T.O.'s war in Afghanistan began a decade earlier. Of course, everything about Mullah Omar's whereabouts and independence from I.S.I. was a mystery. Nobody could say for sure who had authored the letter.

Tayeb Agha agreed to start talking to the Americans again. They would meet again in Doha the following month. Amid the satisfaction and high public standing the Obama administration enjoyed after knocking off Bin Laden, there was rising hope at the White House—even confidence—that they might be on a path to negotiating an end to the war.

"I'm building on what Holbrooke created, trying to take it to the next level," Marc Grossman told Prince Muqrin, the Saudi intelligence chief, around this time. "President Obama and Secretary Clinton are both serious" about the talks. "To be fair," Grossman added, "a ceasefire is some time away. We have to be sure that they stop suicide bombing, and attacking women's schools."

With a State Department colleague that summer, Grossman was less cautious: "Sometime in 2012," he predicted, "I'm going to get all these guys on an island off the coast of Turkey and hammer out a deal."[3]

I n Islamabad, Ruggiero briefed Kayani about the negotiations but told the general only about half of what he was up to. His reticence had a logic: The Conflict Resolution Cell believed that if a peace negotiation about Afghanistan's future did become serious, the American side would, in effect, be negotiating against I.S.I., which would be aligned with the Taliban, even if it did not control them fully. They could not afford to be too forthcoming in advance about U.S. positions.

Kayani and Pasha remained insistent: If you want peace, you should be talking to the Haqqanis. Ruggiero disclosed that he would be willing to meet Ibrahim Haqqani for exploratory conversations. For most of Obama's war cabinet, the idea of talking to the Haqqanis, as part of a peace process, remained anathema. The network had the blood of Americans on its hands. Without question, the network remorselessly slaughtered Afghan civilians in terrorist attacks in Kabul and elsewhere. It had collaborated with I.S.I. to kill Indian civilians, diplomats, and military officers. It had collaborated with Bin Laden since Al Qaeda's birth. Yet President Obama noted that the Haqqanis were different from Al Qaeda: They lived in the region, it was their home. They were not foreign implants. They could not simply be wiped out. The Haqqanis *were* part of the Taliban—both they and the Taliban leadership said so—and Obama had authorized ambitious confidence-building talks with the Taliban's envoy. Why should the Haqqanis belong to a different category from the Quetta Shura?

On August 10, a few weeks after receiving the letter from Mullah Mohammad Omar, Frank Ruggiero and Jeff Hayes met Ibrahim Haqqani in a room at an Egyptian-themed hotel in Dubai. Clinton and Obama had sanctioned this meeting. Ahmed Pasha, the I.S.I. director, also greeted Ruggiero. As they talked, Pasha translated between English and Urdu.

Haqqani thanked the United States for supporting the mujaheddin during their war of resistance against the Soviet Union. Without that support, they could not have prevailed. He added that the Taliban, including the Haqqanis, were not enemies of the United States, but were only fighting against a foreign occupation. And he undermined I.S.I.'s claim that the Haqqanis were essential to any negotiation: Ibrahim said that the only official channel for peace talks with the Taliban ran through Tayeb Agha. His purpose with the Americans seemed to be to press for the release of a pair of Haqqani network commanders held at Bagram.

Overall, the conversation proved desultory. Ibrahim did not seem very well briefed about what might be possible in negotiations with the United States. He rambled on about how the attempted car bombing at Times Square the previous spring had been an Al Qaeda operation.

After the meeting, Clinton rebuked Kayani for having Pasha in the room, for not clearing that decision in advance. The Pakistanis were puzzled; Pasha believed that he had made clear he would attend, and he did not understand why the Americans would choose to make an issue of it. Wounded and confused, Pasha and Kayani updated their grievances. They had been trying to do the Americans a favor. Yes, Ibrahim Haqqani was not a major commander, but Pasha's plan was to hold two meetings with the family representative and then move to someone higher in the network. Why did there never seem to be room in Washington to give Pakistan the benefit of the doubt?[4]

Obama shuffled his national security cabinet in the summer of 2011. Gates retired from the Pentagon. Obama asked Panetta to move there from the C.I.A. and he decided to appoint Petraeus to replace Panetta. The Obama administration had taken a beating in the 2010 midterm election. There were rumors that Petraeus, a registered Republican, might be induced to run for president in 2012. Petraeus had insisted forcefully to Rahm Emanuel, Obama's influential first chief of staff, that he had no interest: "Look, get it through your head, I'm not going to run for office—mark my words." He repeated this privately to anyone who asked him. Yet politics was an unpredictable business; the C.I.A.'s leadership was a glamorous position, and it offered a way to keep Petraeus inside the administration's fold as the 2012 election arrived.[5]

Four-star military commanders had a mixed record as C.I.A. directors, certainly in the eyes of career agency employees. General Michael Hayden had been mostly successful, despite military airs that sometimes rankled at Langley. Career officers regarded Admiral Stansfield Turner, Jimmy Carter's C.I.A. director, as a stiff-necked prisoner of military culture, an outsider who never connected. By the time a typical general or admiral had his third star pinned on, he had become accustomed to the military's deferential protocols, red carpet travel, and entourages of bag carriers and communication aides. The C.I.A. was a flatter, quirkier organization—the agency was part university campus, part mad science lab, part undercover police force, part paranoid internal affairs department, and part militia. Petraeus had spent his entire adult life in military service, and he had spent the last decade as a highly political general, and as an international celebrity.

Soon after he arrived on the Seventh Floor, Petraeus issued instructions to the kitchen about his highly fastidious runner's diet, heavy on shrimp and quinoa. He went on long bike rides on the weekends with his security detail, expecting his aides to keep him well hydrated. There were plenty of fitness fanatics at the C.I.A., but the cigar-chomping George Tenet or the wine connoisseur Leon Panetta were more of a piece with clandestine service habits of living. And there was not a civilian bureaucracy in Washington that did not relish taking down a leader who had airs. Still, the resentment of Petraeus was rarely more serious than eye rolling. For his part, Petraeus seemed thrilled to be at the C.I.A. He read into Special Access Program files that he previously knew little or nothing about even as a top Central Command general—clandestine operations in Iran, the Arab world, and elsewhere. At dinner with former Pentagon colleagues, he expressed the enthusiasm of a college student: "You wouldn't *believe* all the things we are doing."[6]

What Petraeus lacked in self-awareness he often made up for with political savvy. As a commanding general in Iraq, at Central Command, and in Afghanistan, he had become a master in what spin doctors called strategic engagement. He placed longtime allies from his Pentagon brain trust as fellows in Washington think tanks. He regularly accepted off-the-record lunch and dinner invitations from journalists, public policy scholars, and editorial boards. Petraeus intended to do less of this at the C.I.A., and to stay off the Sunday television talk shows, but one evening in August, the president of the Brookings Institution, Strobe Talbott, hosted a private dinner for Petraeus, to reintroduce the general as the country's top spy. Talbott invited about fifteen newspaper columnists and think-tank types. Petraeus arrived a little late with his biographer, Paula Broadwell, with whom Petraeus happened to be embarking on a secret affair. "She seems to think I'm worth a book," he remarked. At the large table he invited each guest to ask him one question. He was candid about a few personalities but overall said little that he would not have testified to at a congressional hearing. He gave statistics purporting to document that N.A.T.O. was winning the Afghan war. He defended the C.I.A.'s drone program in the Federally Administered Tribal Areas.[7]

Petraeus sought to disarm White House and State Department critics of the Counterterrorism Center's drone operations. He assured Cameron Munter, the U.S. ambassador in Islamabad, that he would never call him out or embarrass him during an interagency meeting, as Panetta had once done. Petraeus also assured Munter that the Counterterrorism Center would bring him into their targeting and decision-making process much earlier, to identify and resolve problems before they escalated into an interagency fight. Even if they did not always follow the ambassador's advice, they would respect his role.

When Munter found himself back in Washington, he was surprised to receive an invitation to have lunch with Petraeus in the C.I.A. director's dining room on the Seventh Floor.

An escort walked Munter past the museum space on the ground floor of Old Headquarters. The C.I.A.'s curators had installed a cheesy diorama of a paramilitary scene in Afghanistan, using wax figures to depict two C.I.A. officers and two Afghan guerrillas in Panjshiri hats. (A little later, the C.I.A. curators installed a display of the AK-47 rifle that had been in Bin Laden's bedroom when he was killed.)

Upstairs, Munter found Mark Kelton, the Islamabad station chief with whom he had clashed repeatedly. Kelton had left Islamabad soon after the killing of Osama Bin Laden, suffering from an acute stomach illness that caused him to lose forty pounds. Some at the C.I.A. suspected, but could not prove, that I.S.I. had poisoned him. Kelton told colleagues that he did not know what to think; it might have been natural causes. He recovered fully.

Now Kelton stood by as Petraeus presented Munter with a service medal in recognition of his contributions to the country. It was vintage Petraeus—ceremony as influence.[8]

Career intelligence analysts at the C.I.A. and across the administration who were working on Afghanistan greeted the Petraeus era at Langley with particular anxiety. The analysts responsible for the annual secret National Intelligence Estimate about the progress of the Afghan war had earlier battled Petraeus, when he was commanding general at I.S.A.F., over what they regarded as his undue optimism. Since 2007, the annual N.I.E. had reached negative judgments about the Afghan war every single year. In late 2010, from Kabul, Petraeus had written an eight-page dissent letter arguing that the analysts were wrong and that he was executing his military campaign plan successfully. It was not unusual for commanding generals to see wars they ran more optimistically than professional intelligence analysts in Washington. While in command of the surge into Iraq, Petraeus had formally dissented from a National Intelligence Estimate in 2007 for being too negative and for not including late-breaking data from the battlefield that he thought showed progress. He had also dissented the following year because he felt the intelligence community was too positive about the gains the forces he commanded had made in Iraq. Now, as the analysts prepared the 2011 N.I.E. on Afghanistan, which was to consider scenarios for the country until 2014, the analysts were again in conflict with Petraeus's successors in the I.S.A.F. military command over how well things were going. The estimate's authors were moving toward six key judgments, none of them encouraging. One was that the next group of political leaders to follow Karzai would be corrupt and unlikely to improve governance. Another was that the goal of establishing capable Afghan National Security Forces at the scale America had planned might not be viable. The C.I.A.'s assessment was "highly skeptical" that the Afghan security forces could be as effective against the Taliban as I.S.A.F. commanders predicted, although they stopped short of predicting an outright collapse of the Afghan National Army.[9]

One resource for the 2011 N.I.E. was the C.I.A.'s District Assessments, the top secret color-coded maps of Afghanistan depicting areas of government control, Taliban control, and "local control." These were still produced twice a year by Tony Schinella's small group of career analysts. As of late 2011, they depicted an eroding stalemate with the Taliban. Petraeus criticized the C.I.A. maps, believing that they understated American military gains. He called the green zone of the Arghandab, where Art Kandarian's brigade task force had paid such a heavy price in lives and limbs the previous year, "transformed." The intelligence community did not give these gains enough credence, he argued.[10]

It was true that the Taliban had been cleared out of many of the grape and marijuana fields where the foot patrols of the 101st Airborne task force had slogged, and that Kandahar City was more secure. It was also true that the "ink spot" premise of the military campaign plan—to concentrate forces to defend major Afghan cities (except in Helmand, where they attacked the drug economy)—had successfully reinforced security in big population centers. Yet other important hypotheses of the military plan had not worked out. "Reintegration," the idea that battered Taliban commanders would defect en masse to the Karzai government, had not materialized. Petraeus told colleagues that he had tried his best to replicate the "Sons of Iraq" success from the surge there, but they just did not have the resources. By 2011, only 5,400 ragged Taliban fighters had come into the reintegration program, by one I.S.A.F. estimate, and some of those seemed to be scammers looking for payoffs.[11]

That summer, Robert Williams, who would become Peter Lavoy's successor as national intelligence officer for South Asia, traveled with U.S. Special Forces for three weeks in Helmand, Kandahar, and Uruzgan, conducting more than fifty interviews with Afghan leaders and civilians. He was leading Petraeus's I.S.A.F. "Red Team" to provide counterintuitive or original analysis on hard problems. He wanted to understand the arc of history in Helmand, from King Zahir Shah in the 1960s to the present. The Afghans he met had very low expectations of any government, including the Taliban's shadow government. New Afghan and foreign occupying regimes entered into their districts and villages from time to time, made extravagant promises, and then became exploitive, one after another, one decade after another. N.A.T.O. and its corrupt Afghan allies, in the form of predatory local police and governors, were only the latest example. In a village in Kandahar Province, Williams met officers of a local police force that had recently apprehended a criminal. They told him they had handed the suspect to the Taliban, to be tried by one of the movement's "shadow" religious courts, because they thought the outcome would be more just than if they sent him to the corruption-riddled district center. The civilians Williams interviewed were not really looking for good government—that seemed beyond imagining. They were fashioning least-bad choices within families, villages, and subtribes, to protect themselves from both the Karzai regime and Taliban-aligned predators. That often involved straddling the U.S.-Taliban war, with some sons enlisted in the Taliban militias and others on the government payroll. Williams heard sympathy for the Taliban's ideology and respect for the movement's swift if ruthless shadow courts. He heard accounts of the Taliban's complaint system and anecdotes about abusive Taliban commanders who were sometimes removed after citizens protested. The Taliban were embedded. They were certainly not defeated.[12]

M arc Grossman met Tayeb Agha in person for the first time late that summer, in Doha. By dispatching Grossman, the Americans signaled that they were ready to elevate the negotiations to a new level, as Mullah Mohammad Omar's "Message" had urged. Grossman now experienced for himself the odd rhythm of talking to Tayeb Agha. Typically, at the negotiating sessions, the Qatari mediators first met separately with the American delegation and served tea. Then Tayeb Agha would arrive, typically wearing a white shalwar kameez, a traditional gown. They assembled in a meeting room to talk across a table for an hour or two. Tayeb Agha usually opened with a prepared statement. Discussion followed. The Qataris by now took copious notes, as did Tayeb Agha, as did American aides supporting Grossman. Later, they would all have a buffet dinner on the compound, mingling and having more informal chats.

Grossman began his first encounter with Tayeb Agha by introducing himself, a little about his career, and then laying out the Obama administration's vision for Afghanistan. He talked about the calendar of major donor conferences and intergovernmental political discussions to support the Karzai government. "We hope the Taliban will be part of it," he said. "Afghanistan will be better. If the Taliban make the right choices, they can be part of it." He explained that he wanted to advance a sequence of confidence-building and negotiating steps that would create a path for the Taliban to join Afghanistan's future.

Tayeb Agha replied, in essence, that he wasn't very interested in all of these plans. The Taliban would not be at the intergovernmental meetings. They were not members of N.A.T.O. He spoke dismissively about Karzai. He turned the discussion quickly to his effort to win the releases of the five senior Taliban prisoners at Guantánamo. That continued to seem to be his principal objective. The Americans continued to prioritize finding a way toward an agreement on a political office for the Taliban. They went into more discussion about what the rules for such an office might be and how they would proceed, step by step.

Over dinner, and in subsequent meetings, Grossman tried to plumb Tayeb Agha's motivations. He had read voluminous intelligence analysis about the envoy but now he tried to ask about his personal history, his family. "We have a job to do," Grossman told him. "It seems to me that if we do our work less people will die. I want to understand if that is your motivation too." Yet he found the answer elusive.

Remarks Tayeb Agha made fed a library of restricted Conflict Resolution Cell cables and memos. It was an eclectic, curious compendium of thoughts and positions. The Taliban envoy said the Afghans were naturally democratic and that the Taliban would win an election if the vote was truly free and fair. He also said, "We recognize the problems from the past, and we have to have qualified people within the government" when the Taliban returned to power. "We have to have good relationships with the outside world. We have to have better relationships with all the Afghan ethnicities," not just Pashtuns.

"Our leadership in Pakistan sends their girls to school and even to university," he remarked one time. "We recognize that this is important for families, and important for society."

He was expansive about the possibilities for a political transition as the American forces withdrew. "We cannot afford to have another power vacuum, like what happened when the Soviets left," he said, which had triggered a civil war. "Whatever agreement comes about, it's going to have to be enforced and monitored," so some kind of international peacekeeping force might be needed. "We need to have positive relations with the United States and with the international community because we tried governing once as an outcast and it didn't work out very well."

Whenever the subject of September 11 came up, Tayeb Agha reverted to a talking point. "We inherited these people," he said, referring to Bin Laden and Al Qaeda. "They had told us they were not going to do these kinds of attacks, and that they had nothing to do with September 11. We told you that we would investigate this and hold them accountable if needed, but that wasn't good enough for you." The Arabs were fellow Muslims; the Taliban couldn't just disown them. About Pakistan, Tayeb Agha was openly disdainful. "Yes, we live there, but we are an independent movement, and we don't respond to what Pakistan wants to do."

At some sessions, Tayeb Agha brought along an aide, Sher Moham-mad Abbas Stanikzai, a former deputy minister during the Islamic Emir-ate. Michael Steiner, the German diplomat, still appeared as well. At one session, the Americans listened with bemusement as Stanikzai uncorked an extemporaneous rant about how perfidious the Americans had been over the years, whereas Germany had always been a great and reliable friend of Afghanistan. To show appreciation, Steiner got up from one side of the table and sat down next to Stanikzai. Just then, the Taliban leader turned to the subject of the Second World War. He pointed out that Afghanistan had been a staunch ally of Adolf Hitler's against Amer-ica and Britain. Steiner froze, betraying as little dismay as possible. The Americans found the scene a little funny—of course, they didn't associ-ate Steiner with Nazism—but Steiner was shocked and embarrassed. These things happened from time to time to German diplomats and it was always hard to take.[13]

Grossman returned from his first direct engagement with Tayeb Agha convinced that the two sides were making progress. He told colleagues that he expected the Taliban to have their political office in Qatar opened within a few months.

As the tenth anniversary of September 11 approached, the Haqqani network organized attack squads to strike directly at American targets in Afghanistan. On September 10, a truck bomb detonated at a N.A.T.O. base south of Kabul, killing five American soldiers and wound-ing more than six dozen; but for luck, the death toll could have been much higher. On September 13, a Haqqani squad infiltrated Kabul and struck the U.S. embassy with mortars and assault rifles. The battle went on for hours. No Americans were killed but five Afghan police died.

I.S.A.F. intelligence sources had warned of the Haqqanis' truck bomb plan about six weeks before it occurred. But they and the C.I.A. could not pinpoint the truck itself as it rolled into Afghanistan. At one point Admiral Mullen called Kayani and asked him to stop the attack. Kayani said he would try, but how could he locate a single truck in all of North Waziristan? Didn't the Americans have a better chance with their technical surveillance? When the attack finally occurred, and lives were lost, the Americans were even more aggravated than usual; they had warned I.S.I. and held the service responsible.[14]

The two deadly Kabul attacks also coincided with secret intelligence reports emanating from I.S.I. It held that Mullah Zaeef, the former Taliban ambassador to Pakistan and Guantánamo prisoner now living in Kabul, had facilitated an American visa for an Al Qaeda operative. The operative, in turn, had joined a plot to carry out car bombings in New York and Washington, to mark ten years since 9/11.

The reporting stretched credulity—how could Zaeef, a known Taliban founder living under Karzai's protection in Kabul, help anyone obtain an American visa? Yet once such specific threat reporting seeped into the American intelligence system it could be self-propagating, unless it could be affirmatively disproved. Based on the report, the Department of Homeland Security issued heightened warnings and extra New York police poured into the streets. American forces raided Zaeef's home in south Kabul; he happened to be away. The threat information passed by I.S.I. turned out to be false.[15]

The Haqqani attacks on Kabul that September infuriated Obama's war cabinet, however. Marine General James Mattis had taken over Central Command, in charge of U.S. military forces in the Middle East, Afghanistan, and Pakistan. His deputy was Admiral Robert Harward, a Navy SEAL who had served multiple tours in Afghanistan. They saw the Haqqanis' strikes as a "game changer." That month, Obama's national security principals embarked on a near-daily series of meetings to coordinate pressure on Kayani, to deter further attacks, and to try to force the general to do something at last about the sanctuary in North Waziristan.[16]

The C.I.A., the I.S.A.F., and the N.S.A. had by now accumulated a rich portfolio of evidence about I.S.I. relations with Sirajuddin Haqqani, his brother Badruddin, and other active network commanders. Cell phone

intercepts of Badruddin Haqqani made clear that his forces had carried
out the truck bomb strike and the embassy assault in September. However, the intercepts did not provide evidence of direct I.S.I. participation. Yet it was clear that the Haqqanis operated with concrete Pakistani
support. The Americans had evidence that the Pakistan Army transported the Haqqanis to Rawalpindi for meetings, and that these discussions concerned military operations in Afghanistan.[17]

Marc Grossman told Kayani that the United States was suspending
direct talks with Ibrahim Haqqani. Yet the envoy also told Kayani that
the American policy still ultimately sought "inclusive" negotiations
among all Afghans. Grossman explained further that the United States
would continue to seek the death or capture of Haqqani leaders unless
they wanted to reconcile with the Karzai government. Kayani was incredulous. "You can't say to the Haqqanis, 'If you don't come here to
talk, we'll blow your brains out.'" But that was in fact the American
position. Grossman and his colleagues thought Kayani was missing the
point. The attack on the American embassy crossed a line—Kayani had
to do everything possible to bring his Directorate S clients under
control.[18]

It got worse. On September 23, a Taliban assassin with a bomb rigged
inside his turban visited the home of Burhanuddin Rabbani, the seventy-
one-year-old leader of the Jamiat-e-Islami party in Afghanistan and the
de facto political leader of the old Northern Alliance. The assassin bent
in greeting, detonated himself, and killed Rabbani. Hamid Karzai had
appointed Rabbani to lead his High Peace Council, a body of diverse
Afghan figures that Karzai hoped might eventually develop a peace deal
with the Taliban, perhaps in concert with European and American negotiations, such as the Obama administration's secret channel with Tayeb
Agha. The attack infuriated him. Karzai was in New York for the United
Nations General Assembly meetings. Michael Steiner met him there.
Karzai signaled that he might have to shut off talks with the Taliban
because the killing of Rabbani might be unforgivable for Karzai's allies in
the old Northern Alliance. The attack also wounded Masoom Stanekzai,
one of Karzai's most important advisers on peace negotiations. It took
Stanekzai months to recover from his wounds in a hospital in India,

which removed a steady voice about the Taliban conundrum from Karzai's inner circle during a critical time.

The Taliban kept escalating their strikes in Kabul and the Americans kept hoping that Kayani would do something about it. That month, Kayani held another round of long, one-on-one conversations with Obama's top advisers. In Abu Dhabi, Kayani met Tom Donilon, the national security adviser. In Seville, at a N.A.T.O. meeting, he talked for hours with Mike Mullen; this was their twenty-seventh face-to-face conversation.

Kayani asked four questions. If there were to be peace talks, who among the Taliban is judged to be reconcilable and who is not? Who does what in the negotiating process? What is the sequencing? And what are the time lines for achieving reductions in violence or a political settlement?

The White House composed a classified paper for Kayani to address these questions. The general said he appreciated the paper, yet his meetings with American officials volleyed back and forth between planning for peace talks and threats about I.S.I.'s role.[19]

"We're at a crossroads," Donilon warned Kayani. If the Haqqani truck bomb had killed seventy American soldiers, the U.S. military would have again attacked inside Pakistan in response, he said. If the Haqqanis continued to hit American targets, "You've really turned your fate over" to the network, he warned.[20]

Mullen was scheduled to testify to the Senate Armed Services Committee on September 22. In the Principals meetings about the Haqqanis that month, Mullen had heard Hillary Clinton denounce the enemy in bloodthirsty language: "We ought to hang every one of them," she had said. Mullen found her remarks bracing and even a little inspiring. Mullen knew that because of his visible relationship with Kayani, he was in a distinctive position to declare publicly that I.S.I. had crossed a line. He decided to speak out. "With I.S.I. support, Haqqani operatives planned and conducted that truck bomb attack, as well as the assault on our embassy," Mullen testified to the Senate committee. "The Haqqani network acts as a veritable arm of Pakistan's Inter-Services Intelligence agency."

The testimony made headlines. To Mullen's dismay, Clinton and Grossman expressed surprise at his statements—surprise that he had seemed surprised by the revelation that I.S.I. backed Haqqani violence.

President Obama also told aides that he thought Mullen was grandstanding. Obama remained firmly committed to the negotiating track with Tayeb Agha; he didn't want it undermined gratuitously.[21]

On October 19, 2011, Hillary Clinton flew in to Kabul on an unannounced visit. With Ryan Crocker, the U.S. ambassador, she met Hamid Karzai at the palace.

"This has been a tough year," Clinton acknowledged. There had been many casualties suffered by the Afghan security forces, and many killings of Afghan civilians, mainly by the Taliban, but also in mistaken actions by N.A.T.O. forces. "We feel for you," she said.

"The Afghan people are united," Karzai told her. "All of them are angry at Pakistan. I'm under immense pressure to do something. Pakistan is the address. How far is the U.S. willing to go?"

"We're willing to take the fight to Pakistan," Clinton assured him. She pointed to the C.I.A. drone war in Waziristan. Yet we also have to talk, Clinton went on. We have to structure peace negotiations. We want transparency and to have Afghans in the room. "Pakistan will also have to be there," she said. "How do we structure the process of talking and fighting?"

Clinton told Karzai about the most recent meeting with Tayeb Agha. There were difficulties, but they were still negotiating for a possible five-to-one exchange of prisoners—the five senior Taliban detainees at Guantánamo in exchange for Sergeant Bowe Bergdahl. If that deal was successful, then Mullah Mansour, Omar's deputy, would lead substantive Taliban negotiations about the war and the future of Afghan politics.

"It has to happen more quickly," Karzai said. "Put a lot more pressure on Pakistan," he advised. "Stir up the Pashtuns. They should realize they're being used as a tool by Pakistan to hurt Afghanistan."[22]

Clinton flew on to Islamabad. She met Kayani. Her message was "We can't get off of talk and fight. This is our policy. We know you think it's contradictory, but *we* don't."[23]

Clinton tried to convince Kayani that the Obama administration was unified on both the fight *and* talk tracks. But Kayani and his advisers, particularly the savvy Washington watcher Maleeha Lodhi, had their own reading. She judged that the White House and the State Department were more invested in a serious exit negotiation with the Taliban than the Pentagon or the C.I.A., which hoped to fight on. With all the high-level American visitors tromping through Islamabad, Kayani and Lodhi had their own exposure to Obama's interagency diversity, one principal at a time.

Kayani told Clinton that America had to determine when fight-and-talk could converge into a single policy. "You have to consider ways that you get some kind of mutual reduction in violence," he insisted. That would be more conducive to a peace process than opening a high-level Taliban office in Qatar, he added.

Clinton tried to clarify the messages Mattis and Donilon had delivered the previous month. "We're not talking about a large military operation" against the Haqqanis, she said. "Can't you just squeeze them?"

"The clarity has to come on the bigger issues," Kayani demurred, meaning how negotiations might end the war and create regional stability. "Then the Haqqanis are part of that."[24]

S oon after Clinton returned to Washington, Tayeb Agha delivered the biggest breakthrough yet: He handed over a proof-of-life video showing that Bowe Bergdahl was still in one piece, in Haqqani custody. The video galvanized the Conflict Resolution Cell at the White House. Here was proof that Tayeb Agha, without ever leaving Qatar, had the ability to communicate even with the Haqqanis. And here was a chance for the Obama administration to bring America's only formal known prisoner of war home.

The video persuaded the White House to move forward with preparations for a prisoner swap, despite the political risks. Jeh Johnson, the Pentagon's top lawyer, negotiated with Qatar's attorney general on a memorandum of understanding that would lay out how the Varsity Five at Guantánamo would be controlled if they were released to Qatar's care.

Leon Panetta, now secretary of defense, faced a legal requirement, imposed by the National Defense Authorization Act of 2011, the main defense spending bill, to certify under his signature that the released prisoners would not pose a threat to American civilians. Overall, analysts outside the Pentagon thought the risk was reasonable to bear. The five Taliban had been out of the war for a decade. They could negotiate and enforce close monitoring by Qatar. But the standard in the law was a high bar and the decision weighed on Panetta.

On a Sunday in mid-November, Denis McDonough, then the deputy national security adviser, called Johnson, counterterrorism adviser John Brennan, and other senior officials to the Situation Room to review the case files of the five senior Taliban prisoners. Harold Koh, the State Department's top lawyer, Avril Haines, the top national security lawyer at the White House, and Michael Morell, the deputy C.I.A. director, attended. Frank Ruggiero was there, too, with Barnett Rubin.

The C.I.A. assessed with "high confidence" that the prisoners, absent some control on their movements, would seek to return to the war, and the agency also had concerns that even if they were banned from travel outside Qatar, they might be used by the Taliban for fund-raising purposes.

Johnson said he had received assurances from the highest levels of Qatar—meaning, from the emir himself—that the five prisoners would not return to violence, nor threaten the United States or its allies. Their families would come to live with them and would provide information. Qatar would watch their associations and place the five into some kind of ideological rehabilitation program, reporting every two weeks.

"None of these individuals has been involved in terrorism," John Brennan reported. "They're just held because they're Taliban." The C.I.A. assessed that Khairkhwa, the former Helmand governor, "could be a threat, but he could also be good for reconciliation."

Over hours, they reviewed the prisoners' files and various intelligence assessments. Daniel Fried, a career diplomat who served as a special envoy in charge of seeking the closure of Guantánamo, argued that the record of Qatar and like Gulf States in preventing international travel by former prisoners was poor. McDonough pushed the group to assess the worst case—what if the five prisoners did go back to the war? Would it really be much of a military setback for N.A.T.O. or the Afghan government? They were looking to bring an American home and to explore a political settlement that could stabilize the region. There were risks in every direction.

"None of these guys are game changers," Brennan said.

The problem, they agreed, wasn't the law; the detainees' case files suggested they were eligible for release. The problem wasn't military risk; these were graying political types, and even if they escaped and tried to fight the United States, they would not alter the war. The problem, as always with Guantánamo, was politics. As Fried put it, "We have to be ready for a hysterical reaction on Capitol Hill." But the main issue for now was finding a way to enforce a travel ban, through Qatar, that would stick.[25]

At Bonn, Germany, in December 2001, Hamid Karzai had been selected as chairman of the post-Taliban interim authority in Afghanistan. Ten years later, with Al Qaeda diminished and Bin Laden dead, but the Taliban on the march, international diplomats reassembled there. The idea was to reaffirm global solidarity with Afghanistan and to support a new phase of Afghan and regional peace negotiations.

Grossman hoped to announce the opening of a Taliban office in Doha within months after the Bonn conference—this would be the biggest advance in diplomacy with the Taliban in a decade. Grossman asked a team of aides to research past negotiations of this character—between Israel and the Palestinians at Madrid, and between factions of the Bosnian war at Dayton, as orchestrated by Holbrooke. Grossman interviewed Henry Kissinger about how the Vietnam talks had been structured. His staff prepared a memo describing a refined approach to decisive negotiations in Turkey, as soon as the summer of 2012, supported by international governments. Most of the classified memoranda of understanding necessary to open the office—providing guarantees about what the office would and would not be used for—had by now been agreed in principle among the Taliban, the United States, and Qatar. Grossman would travel from Bonn to meet Tayeb Agha in Doha,

finalize terms for the Taliban office, and then finalize a Taliban statement denouncing terrorism. The idea was that Hamid Karzai would endorse the Taliban political office as an important step toward peace, as
would many other governments. From that milestone, they would move
quickly toward prisoner exchanges and fuller peace negotiations.

On Sunday, December 4, Grossman and Ryan Crocker met with
Karzai in Bonn.

"As I have told you all along, Mr. President, we're now at a place
where I am going to leave the Bonn Conference in two days and I am going to meet Tayeb Agha and complete the negotiation" on the Taliban's
political office in Qatar, Grossman said.[26]

Karzai blew up. Sometime between meeting Clinton in October and
arriving in Germany, he had concluded once again that the Qatar office
was proof that the United States planned to cut a separate peace with the
Taliban, accommodating Pakistan, at his expense. He now refused to
support the Qatar office on the terms Grossman outlined.

He yelled at them and made wild accusations. "You betrayed me—
you killed Rabbani," he said. He claimed that he had "never heard any of
this" about Grossman's step-by-step plan toward peace talks.

"Excuse me," Grossman replied, "I've seen you once a month" during
the Tayeb Agha saga. He, Ruggiero, and Steiner had kept Karzai fully
informed. On the crazy accusation that they wanted Rabbani dead and
had conspired in his assassination, Grossman said, "You can't talk to us
like that."

He and Crocker were flabbergasted. The next day, Karzai invited
them and Hillary Clinton to join him for lunch at his hotel. He ripped
into Clinton, too, although he refrained from accusing her of murdering
Rabbani. Karzai insisted that only *he* could grant the Taliban the concession of a political office, not the United States.

They were all flummoxed and frustrated, but afterward Clinton said
they had to accept that Karzai was the sovereign leader of Afghanistan.
"Listen, he's our ally," she said. They had many equities in Afghanistan—
troops, N.A.T.O.'s commitments, and counterterrorism programs. "We
have to take his views into account." Grossman agreed. He thought he

could work Karzai's terms forward, that they weren't impossible to manage.

Crocker thought he understood Karzai's decision, and in some respects he agreed with him. These were not Karzai's talks. He could not control them, and the Americans' willingness to talk to the Taliban without Karzai, even preliminarily, signaled his weakness. If the American talks succeeded, Karzai might well lose control of events. If he refused to cooperate, there was less chance that he would become vulnerable.

Grossman canceled his scheduled meeting with Tayeb Agha in Doha and returned to Washington. In January, he flew to Kabul to see if he could bring Karzai back into the negotiation. But in a meeting at the Arg Palace, Karzai presented what some Americans involved came to describe as his three "poison pills," meaning terms that Karzai knew or should have known were too onerous to be accepted. First, the Qataris had to travel to Kabul to explain the Taliban political office to Karzai. Second, there had to be a memorandum of understanding negotiated between Karzai's government and the Taliban. Third, before the office opened, the Taliban had to agree to meet with representatives of the Karzai government. The only positive thing he said about the negotiations to date was that he understood the Americans' humanitarian concern about winning the release of the Taliban prisoner Bowe Bergdahl. He had no objection to a prisoner exchange, including one involving the Varsity Five, if that was the reason. But he was dead set against Grossman's original terms for opening a Taliban political office.

As a diplomat, Grossman was a facilitator, a man of process and professional tradition. All along, he accepted the stated policy of the Obama administration that peace talks were to be Afghan led. He made no effort, as a Holbrooke or Petraeus might have done, to tell Karzai that he was full of crap and that he had to cooperate here and now—that the future of peace in Afghanistan was too important for Karzai to let his ego or his illusions of power stand in the way. Grossman had instructions from Hillary Clinton that there was too much at stake in the alliance with Karzai to blow up the relationship over deal points in this incipient negotiation. If they defied Karzai or bullied him, he might go public and denounce the United States for negotiating secretly with the Taliban without his permission, which would be a devastating accusation in Congress, among other places. The Taliban believed Washington had decisive leverage over Karzai, because he could not survive without their aid; the truth was, Karzai had established decisive leverage over the Obama administration, by taking their pledges of Afghan sovereignty at face value.

In essence, Grossman told Karzai, "Okay, Mr. President, I'll take this forward."[27]

He flew on to Doha to present Karzai's terms to Tayeb Agha. Grossman's assumption was that this might be just another twist in the road that could be negotiated to a compromise. Others on his team thought it was definitely the end of the road. When they were gathered around the table at the Doha compound, Grossman read out Karzai's new requirements. "Our allies, the Afghans, have kind of changed their mind," Grossman conceded, "and we have a responsibility to them."

The Taliban envoy recoiled. He was plainly furious, as were the Qataris. From the Taliban's perspective, Karzai was merely an American puppet, one that depended on American support for money and physical survival. It seemed obvious that Karzai could be forced to do whatever the Americans wanted. Tayeb Agha said he and the Taliban political commission had taken great risks internally to negotiate with the Americans, and now, out of the blue, with some lame reference to Karzai, the Obama administration had upended agreed terms. They had made a deal, down to fine points, for the political office in Qatar. The Americans were tearing up the agreement. They did not seem to hear what Tayeb Agha had been saying on behalf of the Taliban leadership all along: They would not deal with Karzai, a quisling of no legitimacy.

"We reject the role of Kabul Administration in office opening, prisoner transfer [sic] and will only continue talks and negotiations with the United States after office and transfer is concluded," the Taliban reported back in a written message passed by the Qataris. They would not talk to Karzai's representatives "at present stage or negotiation stage" later because it had now been "proved to all that Mr. Karzai is playing in the hands of others and has no power of decision making."[28]

Those at the Pentagon who had been monitoring the talks were appalled. They felt Grossman had been too accommodating of Karzai. They also felt he had envisioned the negotiations too narrowly, and that his plan was just to get Afghans to talk to Afghans after the Taliban had an office address, whereas what was needed was a much more comprehensive, strategic approach worked out with Karzai in advance. In the later search for blame, a number of Grossman's colleagues wondered whether he had done all he should have to keep Karzai and the Pakistanis on his side as the high-risk talks with Tayeb Agha ripened. Grossman seemed to them too careful, too self-protecting. He did not spend the long hours over meals to cultivate Karzai as Zalmay Khalilzad had done. He did not project the forceful energy of Richard Holbrooke. Grossman's defenders admitted that he was no Holbrooke, but argued that he was intelligent, experienced, methodical, and diligent, and that the fault wasn't his, but Karzai's. Another hard truth was that although the president had strongly encouraged the effort, the Obama administration had not brought the full weight of its power or the breadth of its government to the process. Neither the director of the C.I.A. nor the secretary of defense supported Grossman's efforts. They were the ones who, in a pinch, had the clout to try to coerce Karzai. In any event, the failure was a bitter one for the State Department, White House, and Pentagon officials who had been working weekends and endless hours for more than a year to try to negotiate an exit from America's longest war. The two sides traded a few more desultory notes, but in early March 2012, the Taliban announced publicly their withdrawal from negotiations with the United States. In the Taliban's own strategy of fight and talk, they were returning to war.

THIRTY-TWO

The Afghan Hand

Sent: Sunday, April 10, 2011 7:40 AM
To: Loftis Email
Subject: RE: Arrived in Kabul

. . . We finished our classes today. The language classes were very useful, and some of the culture classes were interesting, but there was a lot of PowerPoint as well. Worse yet, it was Afghan PowerPoint. The older I get the harder it is to stay awake during boring presentations.

We have so far had a mullah, some elders, an Afghan general, and a member of parliament come and speak to us. They were all very interesting. . . .

We had a mock shura for the last day of language training. I had to play the part of a village elder, and I had to speak Pashto and sometimes Dari, since the other students are split across both. There's a picture of me in an Afghan hat and shawl looking really tired. . . .

Remember my joke: What kind of Mexican food may or may not happen? (Inshallada.) An Arab American who lives in California liked it and he asked permission to use it. I of course agreed.

John Darin Loftis, a lieutenant colonel in the Air Force, was forty-three when he arrived in Afghanistan on his second tour. He had been drafted into the AFPAK Hands program (for Afghanistan and Pakistan) as a specialist in Afghan languages and culture. He was about five feet eight inches and had a stocky "Celtic build," as his wife Holly put it, referring to his Irish heritage. He had a soft neck, brown hair, and an open face. He was straitlaced, a committed Christian who seemed to go out of his way to identify the best in others. He avoided even mild profanity but could be forthright and direct, even when speaking to superior officers.[1]

Officers who became AFPAK Hands committed to at least two field tours in Afghanistan. Loftis studied foreign languages avidly but he had been reluctant to join because it would require long separations from Holly and their two daughters, Alison, who was twelve, and Camille, who was almost ten. Ultimately, however, senior officers in the Air Force had all but insisted that he become a Hand because of his language ability; he was one of a handful of Pashto speakers in the Air Force. He and Holly felt he had no choice but to serve.

Holly and the girls remained at the family home in Navarre, on the Florida panhandle, near Hurlburt Field, home to the Air Force's First Special Operations Wing. The base had a view of a nearby bay. Airmen enjoyed picnics on the Gulf of Mexico's immaculate beaches. Loftis had been posted at "The Schoolhouse," a facility at the U.S. Air Force Special Operations School. He taught officers and airmen about what they would encounter in Afghanistan. He shared the teaching load with a female Air Force intelligence officer who had immigrated to the United States from Afghanistan at the age of twelve. She spoke native Pashto. Loftis had learned his Pashto at the Defense Language Institute in Monterey, California. The pair became fast friends while devising skits and role-playing games for their curriculum. When new military students arrived, Loftis and his partner would separate the men and women to introduce Afghanistan's gender segregation. They would ask the men to hold hands, as Afghan men do. They dressed female students in burqas so they would know what it was like to wear one. They walked their students through pretend Afghan villages so they could practice talking to wary residents. They recited poems in Pashto and Dari. Among the many roles Loftis played during Schoolhouse skits, he was particularly brilliant as a tea server—even when bantering Air Force generals tried to induce him to speak or break character, Loftis would bow his head and refuse to glance up, to demonstrate his socially prescribed subservience.[2]

He painstakingly taught departing American generals an icebreaker they could memorize in Dari. A man knocks on his neighbor's door and asks to borrow his donkey. The neighbor says he has no donkey. "But I heard it braying." Nope, no donkey, the neighbor insists. Just then arise the sounds of a donkey knocking around inside the house. "Who are you going to believe?" the exasperated man asks. "Me or the donkey?"

The purpose of the AFPAK Hands program was to leverage the expertise of American officers who served multiple tours in Afghanistan, to help win over Afghan hearts and minds. It was a phrase Loftis didn't like "because it can be twisted to just about anything," as he once put it. The Schoolhouse curriculum was one aspect of the counterinsurgency campaign, but it also had a defensive purpose, to prevent misunderstandings between Americans and Afghan partners that might escalate into intimate violence. By 2011, this was a rising problem in the war.

"Everything over there is about relationships," Loftis and his teaching partner emphasized. Yet there was an obvious tension in their curriculum. On the one hand, they taught: Build relationships with Afghans who are your counterparts. At the same time, they warned: Watch your back.[3]

Loftis had grown up in Murray, Kentucky, a town of about fifteen thousand in the southwestern corner of the state. He was the first in his family to attend college, at Vanderbilt University in Nashville. He met Holly Brewer there. They lived in the same foreign-language hall as sophomores; the residents were supposed to speak Spanish as much as possible. She was the daughter of a cardiologist and a schoolteacher. He had little money and made it through Vanderbilt on scholarships and loans. They bonded deeply. They both were children of divorce. They yearned to live abroad. The summer after they graduated, they married and applied to the Peace Corps. They assumed they would go to Latin America because they both spoke Spanish. One day they got a call reporting that they had been assigned to Papua New Guinea, the island nation near the equator in the Pacific, one of the poorest countries in the world.

In 1992, they arrived in the Southern Highlands, a remote forested area populated by the Duna people. They lived for two years in a village that had no electricity and no piped hot water. They both learned Melanesian pidgin, a patois of English, German, and tribal languages. They also acquired a little Duna. The long months of working side by side amid such ingrained poverty "changed our perspective on things—not bleeding heart but more in just learning about development, to see how slowly things can happen and how everything can get caught up in local politics."[4]

In 1994, toward the end of their Peace Corps work, Darin thought about joining the military. He was twenty-six. The Air Force accepted him into Officer Training School in Alabama. Loftis had studied engineering as well as languages at Vanderbilt. Commissioned as a second lieutenant, he became a missile man and worked on classified space and nuclear programs. Holly taught preschool for a while as they moved from base to base. On September 11, 2001, they were living at Wright-Patterson Air Force Base in Ohio. Holly heard the news of the attacks on National Public Radio, then turned on CNN and sat in front of the television most of the day, shocked and transfixed. As George W. Bush's global war on terrorism unfolded, Darin was ordered to Schriever Air Force Base and then Cheyenne Mountain, the Cold War–era nuclear command bunker near Colorado Springs, Colorado. He hoped for a position in the Air Force that would use his gift for languages and enthusiasm for foreign cultures. Eventually, Darin applied to become a regional affairs strategist, an Air Force role that would require him to study a foreign language at Monterey. The application form asked what language he would prefer. Loftis wrote "needs of the Air Force" as his answer. His superiors chose Pashto.[5]

Major Jeffrey T. Bordin arrived in Afghanistan on his latest tour in June 2008. He was a research psychologist who specialized in the causes of failed military and intelligence decision making. He had also spent more than three decades serving in various branches of the military reserves, law enforcement, and the Air National Guard. Among other projects, Bordin had conducted war crimes and human rights investigations in combat zones. After September 11, he deployed to Afghanistan as a civil affairs planner, an adviser on law enforcement issues, and a trainer of the Afghan National Police, working with U.S. Special Forces. He deployed in areas that saw significant combat, such as the Pech Valley, the Korengal Valley, and Nuristan.[6]

Bordin's work contained an emphatic streak of skepticism about commanding generals. His doctoral dissertation at Claremont Graduate School had explored "how elite governmental decision makers come to ignore or refute valid information during their deliberations." The paper began by recounting how, during the late 1930s, naval officers discovered serious quality problems in torpedo manufacturing, yet the officers "acquiesced to both political and organizational pressures to ignore" the defects. Then, in 1942, at the Battle of Midway, nearly a hundred American airmen flew torpedo-armed planes against a vastly superior Japanese force. "Despite the Holocaust they were flying into," Bordin recounted, "every aircrew pressed their attack—many while literally engulfed in flames." Yet their bravery came to naught because "not a single torpedo detonated against a Japanese warship." This failure "enabled the Japanese to launch a devastating counterstrike that culminated in the loss of the USS *Yorktown* and 141 American lives. The title of Bordin's work signaled his perspective on these and similar cases: "Lethal Incompetence: Studies in Political and Military Decision-Making." Early in his career, Bordin worried that he had been too hard on the commanders he chronicled. Later, he decided, "I wasn't hard enough."[7]

By 2010, Bordin had become all too familiar with a disturbing trend: a rising incidence of murder of American and European soldiers by uniformed Afghans who were supposed to be allies. The military called these murders "green on blue" killings. Since the spring of 2007, there had been more than two dozen murder or attempted murder cases in Afghanistan where soldiers or police working alongside American or European forces had turned their guns on their partners, killing at least fifty-eight. By 2010, the pace of fratricidal killings was rising, to the point where an Afghan ally murdered an American or European soldier once a week, on average, according to Bordin's findings. In July, an Afghan soldier killed three British troops in Helmand and then fled to the Taliban. A week later, an Afghan soldier killed two American civilian trainers in northern Afghanistan. The next month, an Afghan employee shot dead two Spanish police officers. Yet no one had ever ordered a study of the problem and its causes.

Bordin had been out on operations with the Afghan National Police in remote areas since 2004. On patrol, he had sometimes felt that he was just as likely to be shot in the back by an Afghan police officer as to be killed by a Taliban insurgent. There were always a handful of Afghan comrades alongside him who had a hard stare that Bordin felt as hostility. He decided that an ethnographic study of the attitudes of Afghan and American soldiers toward one another might be insightful.[8]

The green-on-blue murders rising during 2010—and the shock effect they had on public opinion, particularly in Europe—threatened President Barack Obama's strategy to try to engineer an exit from the Afghan war without leaving violent chaos behind. At the heart of Obama's plan lay the counterinsurgency campaign now led by General Petraeus, which sought to suppress the Taliban long enough to train and equip Afghan security forces so that they could replace American and European troops and allow them to go home, starting in 2011. This expanding training mission required closer and closer interaction between American and European soldiers and Afghan allies. If such collaboration repeatedly gave rise to misunderstandings or resentments that led to cold-blooded murder, the strategy might fail.

It required another tragedy to jolt the Army to take an initial step to investigate as Bordin proposed. On November 29, 2010, in the Pachir Agam district of eastern Nangarhar Province, an Afghan border policeman participating in a joint operation with U.S. soldiers turned his gun on his allies and killed six Americans—the worst mass-murder case involving the United States in the Afghan war to date, and among the worst of its kind in American military history. That attack at last led U.S. Army commanders to authorize a "Red Team" research project about the apparent alienation between Afghan trainees and foreign advisers. Red Team studies at the C.I.A. or in military intelligence seek to step outside prevailing assumptions. Regional Command–East, as the section of the Afghan battlefield to the Pakistani side of Kabul was known, commissioned Bordin to conduct a Red Team study into fratricidal violence in Afghanistan.[9]

He designed his ethnographic research so that it would meet the peer review standards of social science, but in essence the design was simple: The Red Team researchers would ultimately ask more than 600 Afghan soldiers, police, and interpreters, as well as about 120 American soldiers, to talk openly about how they felt about one another. (The team also asked another 136 American soldiers to fill out a questionnaire assessing their Afghan counterparts.) Bordin directly solicited comment on misunderstandings and grievances between the two groups. "Okay, we won't give you the regular 'Smiley Face' answers; we will tell you the truth," an Afghan National Army sergeant told his interviewers.[10]

The research team reached Laghman Province on December 8, 2010. After Christmas, they tramped around Kunar and Nangarhar, through the end of January. They worked on Afghan bases, not American bases. The Afghan soldiers and police they interviewed offered a critique of American conduct that did not sound very different, at times, from the Taliban's critique. The Afghans said that the Americans carried out too many violent night raids; that their home searches looking for insurgents humiliated ordinary Afghans; that they did not respect Afghan women; that they drove local roads arrogantly; that they fired their weapons recklessly if attacked; and that they killed far too many Afghan civilians.

"They get upset due to their casualties, so they take it out on civilians during their searches," one interviewee said.

"They take photos of women even when we tell them not to," said another.

"A U.S. [armored transport vehicle] killed six civilians traveling in a vehicle; it was intentional."

"U.S. soldiers killed two youths. Their mother became a suicide bomber; she was provoked by this atrocity. She went to Paradise as a martyr."

"They cause many civilian casualties; they apologize, but they keep doing it. This isn't acceptable."

Bordin's research team analyzed categories of complaint and built matrices to show which grievances stung most. They identified examples where the Afghan allies attributed violence to Americans that had actually been the Taliban's responsibility.

The American officers and soldiers Bordin interviewed also had a jaundiced view of the Afghans they were training and fighting alongside:

"They are stoned all the time."

"We can't leave anything out; they steal it."

"I wouldn't trust the ANA [Afghan National Army] with anything, never mind my life."

"I was fired on by ANA personnel multiple times during my deployment."

"It would benefit Afghanistan to disband the ANA and start over again."

"We are interfering with Darwinian theory!"[11]

On May 12, 2011, Bordin published a seventy-page paper titled "A Crisis of Trust and Cultural Incompatibility." It provided a raw, highly detailed account of estrangement between American and Afghan allies. The testimony in the report included some from American soldiers who described lethal attacks where they believed Afghan soldiers or police had partnered or been complicit with the Taliban. Bordin found a "rapidly growing systematic threat" and a "crisis of confidence" among the Western trainers preparing the Afghan National Army and police to carry the war against the Taliban on their own.

Bordin was particularly scathing about what he described as a pattern of denial among American commanders. Generals dismissed green-on-blue killings as "isolated" and "extremely rare," Bordin wrote, statements that "seem disingenuous, if not profoundly intellectually dishonest." The willful "cognitive dissonance" of those leading the war "perpetuates an ongoing blindness towards acknowledging this murder problem."[12]

His judgments implicated General David Petraeus, who by now had been named to lead the C.I.A. Petraeus had a doctoral degree in international relations from Princeton. He surrounded himself with Army officers who also were graduate degree holders, many of them social scientists. Yet although he was often described as an intellectual, Petraeus did not have a particularly searching or questioning mind. He projected unshakable confidence and he was masterful at shaping his own reputation. He understood as well that in an era of global media and asymmetric terrorism and insurgency, wars turned as much on what people thought as on the territory they controlled. Bordin's work undermined the public narrative of the Afghan war Petraeus had tried to shape.

Colonel John Angevine had recently arrived at the I.S.A.F. headquarters to run Red Team studies. He read Bordin's report, talked with the author about the possibility of working further together, and, on June 3, 2011, told Bordin that he was going to pass the study up to Petraeus. Three days later, Bordin learned that I.S.A.F. had ordered that his study be classified, to prevent further distribution beyond those with appropriate clearances. The command had also declined to renew his contract and withdrawn an informal offer to further study mistrust between American and Afghan soldiers.

Petraeus said later he had never heard of Bordin, never read the study, and never took any steps to suppress its findings. Angevine had passed the study to Petraeus's command staff but had no way to know whether the general had received it or looked at it. Angevine did conclude that Bordin had broken trust with the command by publishing the study as an open source document in a publicly accessible military knowledge-sharing database before he had authorization from the very top. Bordin thought this was a shoddy excuse for suppressing his findings; he had published through the appropriate channels, in a routine manner. He saw his work as the clarification of inconvenient truths in wartime, in the tradition he had long chronicled, and he believed his work undermined public statements by Petraeus about the war's progress. In any event, I.S.A.F. did not renew Bordin's contract. Someone else in Petraeus's command—it is not clear who—ordered "A Crisis of Trust and Cultural Incompatibility" to be classified. Angevine and other officers in I.S.A.F. discussed Bordin's research and debated his conclusions. The question

was whether cultural incompatibility was really the cause of fratricidal violence or merely one of many contexts in which such intimate
murders occurred, perhaps because of deliberate Taliban infiltration. It
was a sensitive matter because the Bordin thesis of fundamental incompatibility leading to repetitive mass murder offered weary European publics and politicians a clearly lit exit ramp out of an Afghan war
they no longer wanted to fight: We've overstayed, they all hate us, it's
hopeless.[13]

Bordin had no alternative but to go home. He thought the transparent evidence he had assembled spoke amply for itself and that the Petraeus command was in denial. As he departed Afghanistan, he thought
privately, "A lot of people are going to get killed unnecessarily."

Two weeks after Bordin was effectively fired, a *Wall Street Journal*
reporter obtained a copy of the study and wrote about it. A spokes-
woman for Petraeus's command denounced Bordin's work as methodologically flawed and not reliable. The position of Petraeus and his
advisers was that they were aware of the problem of fratricidal violence
and were taking preventive measures, many of them involving classified
security procedures, to stop the killings, to the degree possible. There
was no way to stop all of the insider attacks, but they were alert to the
threat and doing what they could.

As Petraeus departed Kabul for the C.I.A., he and his staff organized
transition briefings for Marine General John Allen, who would take
command of I.S.A.F. on July 18. Petraeus and his lieutenants presented
to Allen at least three formal briefings on the Afghan war. In addition,
the incoming commander dined with Petraeus almost every night. Not
once—not even in staff-level briefings—did Petraeus or his officers mention the trend of fratricidal murder.[14]

Sent: Friday, November 11, 2011 3:10 AM
To: Loftis Email
Subject: Re: Miss you

It has gotten cold here, too. I was on duty last night, and every time I
stepped outside I felt sorry for the guards who were out all night. They

were bundled up, though, and one of them was watching TV in his cell phone.

There's another one who is really friendly and really loud about it. He only speaks Dari, and he's illiterate. When I asked him if he could read, he said, "No, but I can really fight!" and he started maneuvering around with his gun and making sounds. He's a real trip. I've been teaching him one phrase of English a day and he is tickled to death. . . .

I've made really good friends with the janitor who cleans our building at ISAF. Today I introduced him to an AFPAK Hand (Larry, who is still finding his feet in Dari). At the end of our basic conversation Basir said his hope is that our children can be good friends, too.

Another janitor, the one who cleans our part of the MOI building, doesn't have his fingers on his right hand. I finally got close enough to him to ask about it, and after he closed the door he said it had been Taliban cruelty. (I had suspected that.) He then insisted that I translate it for COL Green, who was also in the room. You're the only other ones that I have told. He shakes our hands without any shame or discomfort, though.

He also has nine kids, and I got to meet one of them. COL Green got him a nice Eid present.

I wish it were safe enough to bring you all here so you can see my world. But I like the one at home a lot better. . . .

L, D2

It had been apparent for years that Western military discipline and doctrine might be difficult to teach to Afghan soldiers and police, given that they struggled with high rates of illiteracy and impoverishment. Many American and European training officers had developed a nuanced appreciation of the problem. They did not expect Afghans to celebrate the presence of foreign troops in their country or to perform to the standards of armies in the industrialized world. The training mission was to prepare Afghans well enough to defend their own government and people against a second Taliban revolution, after the Americans and Europeans departed.

"They smoked strong hashish and mild opium. They couldn't map read," recalled Patrick Hennessey, a young British officer who, in 2007, oversaw the training of an Afghan *kandak*, or battalion, in Helmand Province. "They lacked everything that British Army training believed in and taught—and fuck me if most of them hadn't killed more Russians than we'd ever seen. . . . I liked that they had more balls than I ever did to just stand up and say 'Why' or 'No' or 'I don't care if there is a war on and a massive IED threat. I like watermelon so I'm going to steal a car I can't drive and run a Taliban checkpoint in order to go to the market.' I couldn't train them at all."[15]

The potential for misunderstandings between f-bombing Western trainers and pious, prideful Afghan soldiers to erupt into gun violence was a problem "too sensitive to put in the formal briefings," as Hennessey described it, but this gap did not seem to pose a strategic crisis.[16] The murder rate grew only after 2007 as the war's violence spread and as tens of thousands more American, Canadian, and European troops arrived to fight in Afghan towns and villages. It seemed remarkable that Afghans accepted the inevitability of American battlefield errors and the necessity of violent raids on private homes as much as they did. It was hardly surprising that personal bonds on joint bases frayed nonetheless as isolated American units lost discipline, killed civilians in the plain sight of Afghan partners, urinated on household walls in front of Afghan women, shot dogs for sport, or called their Afghan colleagues "motherfuckers," even if the foreigners intended the phrase only in mild censorship.

Increasingly, too, as it became clear that American and European troops would not remain in Afghanistan in large numbers for the long run, trainer and trained harbored distinct assumptions. The Americans and their Canadian and European allies were in a hurry to get the Afghan army and police organized, so they could go home. The Afghan soldiers being trained could not withdraw from the challenge of the Taliban, so they were open to local truces and other improvised, even cooperative strategies with the enemy to avoid direct combat.

During 2011, fratricidal attacks surged in number and lethality. On October 29, an Afghan army trainee at a base in Kandahar Province opened fire on Australian soldiers, killing three of them and wounding seven others before the shooter was felled by return fire. On November 9, an Afghan soldier shot and wounded three Australians in Uruzgan Province. On December 29, an Afghan soldier shot and killed two members of the French Foreign Legion in eastern Afghanistan. Ten days later, during a volleyball game on a base in Zabul Province, an Afghan soldier murdered an unarmed American.

In January 2012, a video of U.S. Marines kicking and urinating on Taliban corpses appeared on YouTube. It went viral and generated news coverage worldwide.

On January 20, on a base in remote Kapisa Province, an Afghan soldier murdered four unarmed French soldiers while they ran for exercise. The killer later told investigators that he was outraged by the abuse video.[17]

One problem was that Afghanistan's Ministry of Defense had no counterintelligence capabilities—no systems or trained personnel to detect Taliban infiltrators or other insiders who posed a threat. The Afghan spy service, the National Directorate of Security, or N.D.S., did have counterintelligence officers. Yet the N.D.S. had roots in Afghanistan's brutal period of Soviet occupation, when the K.G.B. had trained and supported the security service. The Afghan army's leaders had long memories and they did not want K.G.B.-trained officers rooting around in the Afghan National Army's ranks, looking for Taliban spies, inevitably roughing up innocents or torturing suspects into false confessions.

The latest murders revived attention to Bordin's work. General Allen read summaries of the study and looked into its history but he thought that if Petraeus didn't think the work was credible, then it probably wasn't. Allen told colleagues that Bordin seemed too hooked on culture and misunderstanding as a problem between Afghan and American forces. Allen had commanded in Iraq on battlefields where American and Iraqi soldiers fought side by side in circumstances that were at least as challenging as in Afghanistan. Of course, there were frictions, but they were not fatal to the mission and could be overcome with deliberate work. Allen was wary, too, about how politically convenient the "cultural incompatibility" thesis was at a time when public opinion in Europe and America was swinging against the war. Was this reliable social science or just an excuse to go home? Allen's intuition was that the murders more likely constituted an insurgent strategy of infiltration and disruption—a deliberate strike at the core of N.A.T.O. cohesion.[18]

That winter, one of General Allen's lieutenants, Major General Sean MacFarland, put together a self-protection guidebook for N.A.T.O. soldiers, called the "Green on Blue Smartcard." It advised, "The key is for local Commanders to prevent complacency and conduct risk assessments with Green-on-Blue in mind." The Smartcard recommended that N.A.T.O. officers include Afghan partners and promote cultural sensitivity: "Respect Islam," the guidebook suggested, and "avoid arrogance." Commanders should involve Afghan soldiers and officers in patrol briefings and "social/sport activities," the document urged. Yet it also laid out procedures for how to train for gun battles with inside murderers, how to eliminate shooters decisively and quickly, and how to maintain armed vigilance, including the oversight of Afghan allies, "before, during and after military operations."[19]

Wed 2/15/2012 9:44 AM
Holly,

I had another Afghan Hands experience today. General Dawood
invited Nea (another APH in our office) to his house for lunch
today. The main reason was so Nea could talk to his wife about her
health condition so we can try to set up some treatment for her if
necessary. So we donned our civilian clothes and hopped in his
police truck and went to his house. It was an extremely modest setup,
not at all like one might think a general would live in. We had the
standard Afghan meal of rice, bread, beef, chicken, and salad, and
it was tasty. In true Afghan fashion they insisted we eat more
and more. . . .

We believe the reason they live so modestly is that they spend a lot of their money on education. His wife teaches geography and the other two women—I think they were daughters or nieces—teach math, all at the same high school. . . .

Nea also pointed out that the reason he may be waiting so long to pin on his second star is that he is honest, leads an honest-yet-modest lifestyle, and refuses to pay a bribe to get his star pinned on. That's just speculation on our part, but it's plausible. . . .

I just thought you'd like to know of my adventure today. . . .

L, D2

In early 2012, the largest American-run prison in Afghanistan was the detention facility at Parwan, adjacent to Bagram Airfield, about forty miles north of Kabul. Taliban prisoners held there used the facility as a makeshift command center, passing messages to one another and outside. I.S.A.F. had assigned a military police unit and a Theater Intelligence Group counterintelligence team to stop the Taliban prisoners from communicating. In late 2011 and early 2012, the team received "multiple intelligence reports" that the Taliban were using books in the prison library "as a medium of communication within the detainee population."[20]

On February 18, about a dozen American soldiers and civilian linguists searched the prison library. One of the linguists identified books that he thought contained "extremist content." He concluded upon further investigation that perhaps two thirds to three quarters of the library's books and pamphlets "should not be read" by prisoners. On this advice the American counterintelligence team pulled aside about two thousand books and decided to burn them. The team included only a handful of Arabic and Pashto speakers. Only they understood clearly that the books included copies of the Holy Koran.[21]

The team hauled the offending books to a burn pit. Afghan colleagues warned them not to go forward because they feared locals working at the incinerator would recognize religious materials in the load and might react violently. The leader of the American team heard this warning but did not act.

At the burn pit, another Afghan National Army officer and his translator saw Korans in the pile slated for destruction and again warned the Americans to stop. They, too, were ignored. Minutes later, an Afghan civilian employee operating the incinerator noticed that Islamic religious books were on fire. He shouted for help, doused the flames and tried to rescue partially burned Korans. As word spread, more Afghans rushed to the burn pit. The Americans present "became frightened by the growing, angry crowd and rapidly departed the area."[22]

Darin Loftis turned forty-four years old on February 22, 2012. He spoke to Holly that day for ten or fifteen minutes. His colleagues were planning a surprise party for March 28—which Loftis knew about—to celebrate his return home to Florida.

Darin worked for Jean-Marc Lanthier, a Canadian brigadier posted at I.S.A.F. headquarters. He held a shura for I.S.A.F.'s operations group leadership, known as the J-3, most Saturdays. He regarded Loftis as "one of the most brilliant human beings I've seen, in or out of uniform." Loftis could afford to be skeptical about "ambitious generals," as he once called them. He planned to retire from the Army soon and go back to school. In Afghanistan, he would not hesitate to challenge the most senior officers if he felt they had the wrong assumptions. Some of his American and Canadian colleagues "would be dismissive of the Afghan point of view," as Lanthier put it, but Loftis "would always bring us back to the truth." He tried to make them understand why it was important to let the Afghans do it their way, and yet "he hadn't gone native." He would also challenge the Afghans about their assumptions.

Lanthier struggled to assess the rising incidence of fratricidal murder. It was uncomfortable to think the Taliban had the ability to threaten the coalition by placing infiltrators in their midst. But Lanthier and his colleagues felt exceptionally safe at the Ministry of Interior. They assumed the ministry's security guards were reliable because Afghan security had vetted the guards to protect Afghan generals who also worked at the compound.

The Ministry of Interior was a downtown Kabul fortress ringed by iron fences, concrete walls, barbed wire, and armed guards. There were hundreds of Afghan and international troops on the premises or nearby. When Lanthier visited, he walked around without body armor and asked his bodyguard to stand outside his office, to signal to his Afghan colleagues that he trusted them. Afghans were not allowed to carry guns. The compound seemed as secure as any place in Afghanistan.[23]

At Forward Operating Base Lonestar, near Jalalabad, in eastern Afghanistan, American soldiers and military police trained Afghan units. T. J. Conrad Jr., of Roanoke County, Virginia, the married father of a one-year-old son, served as an instructor. He had arrived in Afghanistan only in January. During calls home, he told his father "he felt like on some of the patrols they went on that they were being set up" by the Afghans they were training because they would arrive at target compounds and it seemed that the enemy had been tipped off beforehand.[24]

On February 23, hundreds of shouting Afghans gathered outside the gates of Lonestar to protest the Koran burnings at Parwan.

The Americans shouldered weapons and watched the protesters warily, but held fire. Suddenly an Afghan soldier on the base trained his automatic rifle on his American colleagues.

Conrad sought cover and fired back but the Afghan soon shot him dead. The shooter killed a second American, Joshua Born. Other American soldiers returned fire and wounded the assailant, but he stumbled off the base and into the crowd of protesters.

The base's intelligence unit had launched a surveillance drone that day to watch the protesters. The drone's cameras now followed the shooter as he escaped. Outside Lonestar, four people helped him before a large Pashtun man in civilian dress, who had apparently been waiting for the killer, hoisted the wounded man over his shoulder, carried him half a mile on foot, and then loaded him into a white vehicle. The drone followed as the vehicle sped away but it escaped.[25]

General John Allen called his counterpart, Sher Mohammad Karimi, the Afghan chief of army staff, and proposed that they fly together to Lonestar. In the base's small mess hall, where a large American flag had been hung on the wall, they spoke to survivors.

"There will be moments like this when your emotions are governed by anger and the desire to strike back," Allen said. "These are the moments when you reach down inside and you grip the discipline that makes you a United States soldier. And you gut through the pain. And you gut through the anger. And you remember why we are here. We are here for our friends. We are here for our partners. We are here for the Afghan people. Now is not the time for revenge."

Karimi spoke. "Your sacrifice is not wasted," he said. "This enemy fighting against us is not an enemy of Afghanistan. It is an enemy of the whole humanity. I think we are fighting together for a noble cause."

"We admit our mistake," Allen concluded. "We ask forgiveness. We move on."[26]

O n the afternoon of Saturday, February 25, Darin Loftis went to work in the Interior Ministry office he shared with Major Robert Marchanti, a logistics specialist. Marchanti was forty-eight, a bear-size man with a crew cut. He had served in the Maryland National Guard for twenty-five years. At home in Baltimore, where he had grown up, he had taught physical education in public schools. This was his first Afghan tour. He was trying to learn Dari and Pashto. He ate regularly with Afghans at their dining hall at the Ministry of Interior.

His church back home sent coats and children's gear to him in Kabul that winter. Marchanti distributed the gifts to a local orphanage. For the U.S. Army, his job was to order supplies and manage deliveries around the country.[27]

The room Loftis and Marchanti shared was on the second floor of an auxiliary building on the Interior Ministry compound. Marchanti had mounted a Baltimore Ravens pennant on one wall. A map of Afghanistan hung on another wall. Both men had been caught up that week in conversations about the Koran burnings at Parwan. Loftis had pledged to

Lanthier to draft a paper that explained Islam and Afghan culture to I.S.A.F. soldiers so that, among other subjects, they might better understand the significance of the Koran.

Darin Loftis routinely lingered with Afghans on the Interior Ministry compound. He had only a passing acquaintance with Abdul Saboor, a slight man who kept his head shaved.

Saboor had managed two months earlier to win a transfer from duty as a soldier to a job as an Interior Ministry driver. The new position allowed him greater access to compound buildings.

Early in February, Saboor knocked on the door of the office Loftis shared. He asked to have his picture taken with Loftis, Marchanti, and a third American, Colonel Jim Green. They smiled for the camera.

"I'm checking the Taliban Web site tonight," Loftis joked when Saboor was gone. "Our pictures will probably be there."

Saboor was an ethnic Tajik who spoke Dari and hailed from the Salang area of Parwan Province. This was a profile that seemed to mark him as a reliable American ally, because he belonged to one of the northern Afghan ethnic groups that were in the main ardent enemies of the Taliban. It later emerged, however, that Saboor had left Afghanistan and studied at a Pakistani madrassa before returning to Kabul to take his position at the Interior Ministry.

Shortly after 2:15 p.m. that Saturday, Saboor again entered the office where Loftis and Marchanti worked. They would have had to let him in because a coded lock secured the door; no Afghans were provided with the code, but they routinely were invited in to access the snacks, bottled water, and medicine stored in the room.

Saboor crossed the room, raised a Smith & Wesson 9mm pistol and shot Marchanti in the head.

He shot Darin Loftis in the back; Loftis fell facedown. The killer leaned down and fired again into the back of his victim's head.

Saboor descended the stairs. At the building entrance he told an Afghan colleague that the two American advisers had just shot each other. He walked past security guards and concrete barriers into the streets of downtown Kabul and disappeared.[28]

General John Allen arrived at the compound in a Mine Resistant Ambush Protected transport vehicle, a hulk of plated metal designed to shield occupants from even the heaviest improvised bombs planted on roads by the Taliban. Allen stepped out in full battle gear and climbed to the office where Loftis and Marchanti still lay in pools of blood. He kneeled and prayed over the bodies.[29]

Allen ordered American advisers withdrawn from all Afghan ministries and pledged to develop new protocols that might keep American and European trainers safe. The murders of Darin Loftis and Robert Marchanti on one of the most heavily guarded compounds in Afghanistan, a short walk from the American-led war's command center, stunned I.S.A.F.'s leadership. Despite Bordin's warnings, a few dozen Afghan killers working behind American fences had managed to call the exit strategy of the world's most formidable military alliance into doubt.

It would require another eighteen months of secret intelligence investigations to identify the causes of the green-on-blue murder wave, and to start to stymie its effects.

"What do I tell his family today?" Senator Barbara Mikulski asked Secretary of State Hillary Clinton at a hearing on February 28, 2012, addressing the death of Robert Marchanti.

"Was it worth it? Because they're angry. People in Maryland are angry." Mikulski added of the now decade-old Afghan war, "We went there with the best of intentions."[30]

Holly Loftis flew to Dover Air Force Base, in Delaware, to receive Darin's remains. She met Peggy Marchanti. An honor guard carried their husbands' caskets from the plane.

On March 8, at Hurlburt Field, another dress guard carried Loftis's casket across a tarmac to a funeral service with full honors. The Air Force awarded Darin Loftis a posthumous Bronze Star, his second. The base named a classroom at the Schoolhouse in his memory. Holly's brother, the Reverend Dr. Brian Brewer, led the remembrances. He remembered a photo of Loftis taken during his first Afghan tour, in 2009, when he had served on a Provincial Reconstruction Team in Zabul Province, in the Taliban's heartland. The picture showed Darin offering himself playfully to a group of Afghan children. Referring to the image, Brewer told the mourners, "It is representative of the ideal."[31]

THIRTY-THREE

Homicide Division

A bdul Saboor's murder of Darin Loftis and Robert Marchanti moved the American war command to restudy the threat. That two senior officers could be dispatched with pistol shots to the backs of their heads in a heavily guarded compound in the heart of Kabul suggested that no one or nowhere could be considered safe. The crime recalled nationalistic Afghan uprisings against British occupations of the nineteenth century. In the weeks that followed, the C.I.A. circulated analysis in Washington pointing out that the frequency of insider murders against American and European forces had surged to a rate ten times greater than during the first decade of the war. The murders were on pace to constitute a quarter of all I.S.A.F. fatalities in 2012, an astounding percentage. Nothing like this had happened in Vietnam or during the Soviet occupation of Afghanistan. In fact, as far as the C.I.A.'s analysts could determine, Afghanistan's insider killing spree after 2011 had no precedent in the history of modern counterinsurgency.[1]

Following murders of its soldiers late in 2011, France announced a withdrawal of two thousand combat soldiers from Afghanistan. Australia, Britain, Germany, and Spain all lost soldiers to killings by Afghan soldiers or police they worked alongside. The murder wave pulled at the foundations of every "line of effort" in N.A.T.O.'s campaign—the training of Afghan National Security Forces, the mentoring of Afghan police and technocrats in the ministries, and the resilience of political will in N.A.T.O. capitals to fight on after a decade of effort. The Taliban—or whoever or whatever was the cause of the insider killing—had located "exactly this political-emotional milieu we are in," as a N.A.T.O. diplomat in Kabul put it. "All our capitals are tired. We lost the battle of public opinion three years ago, anyway."[2]

More vexing still, there was no consensus about why these insider killings had surged. Were the killers Taliban infiltrators who had slipped through the N.D.S. vetting system designed to weed out enemy sympathizers from the Afghan National Army and police? Or were they non-Taliban who had become personally aggrieved over slights or insults from N.A.T.O. soldiers and decided to take violent revenge? This was a murder mystery that had become the war's most important strategic puzzle.

Murders of American and European soldiers by Afghan allies spiked slightly in March 2012, and then ground along at an alarming rate of at least several per month into the summer. That year, Ramadan, the Islamic month of fasting and celebration, took place from July 20 to August 19. Ramadan is a time of self-purification, of rituals of affiliation with faith. For individuals susceptible to the call to violent jihad against foreigners, the fasting and celebration in 2012 seemed to have a stimulating effect.

On July 22, in Herat Province, an Afghan policeman shot and killed three N.A.T.O. trainers and wounded a fourth. The next day, in Faryab Province, an Afghan colleague shot and wounded two N.A.T.O. soldiers. Between August 3 and the end of Ramadan, Afghan soldiers or policemen committed at least nine more murders or attempted murders against N.A.T.O. and American troops, killing ten people, including five U.S. Marines, two of those Special Operations officers. During those final two weeks of Ramadan, Afghans attempted to kill Americans or Europeans they worked alongside about once every other day.[3]

Marine General John Allen's chief of intelligence, Mike Flynn's successor, was Robert Ashley, a two-star Army general. He was a silver-haired, sober-faced man whose highly secured offices lay a short walk from Allen's command center at I.S.A.F.'s headquarters in downtown Kabul. Ashley knew well that solving the insider murder problem had become critical. At August's rate of killing, the American plan for a slow, gradual drawdown from Afghanistan looked implausible.

Ashley and Allen established a program of "guardian angels," in which Western commanders appointed armed guards from their own ranks to watch over Afghan allies during joint activities. As the murders picked up during Ramadan, Allen authorized field commanders to appoint even more watchmen if they felt it was needed. But it seemed obvious that the more the Americans tightened their internal security protocols—the more Afghan allies were stripped of their weapons before meetings or endured armed American surveillance on patrol—the more likely it was that these allies would conclude that the Americans were their enemies.

One night that August, Ashley's counterpart in the Afghan National Army, General Abdul Manan Farahi, the head of military intelligence, telephoned. It was unusual to hear from Farahi so late. Ashley stepped outside to take the call.

"My friend, I just want to make sure, with Eid coming up," he said, referring to the celebration of Ramadan's end. "Just minimize the contact with the guys in the field and take care." These were haunted times, Ashley told colleagues, as he relayed Farahi's message.[4]

Ashley decided he needed a fresh mind to analyze the crisis. He turned that autumn to one of the more unusual, naturally gifted characters in the American intelligence community. Marc Sageman, who was then in his late fifties, was a bald, white-bearded forensic psychiatrist and former C.I.A. operations officer. He sometimes favored bow ties and spoke with a still-noticeable French accent. He had been born in Poland but raised as a refugee in France, where his parents had landed after surviving the Holocaust. Sageman matriculated at Harvard University at age sixteen, became a medical doctor, earned another doctoral degree in political sociology, served as a Navy flight surgeon, and then joined the C.I.A. as a case officer. He worked in Pakistan during the 1980s, running frontline C.I.A. contacts with Ahmad Shah Massoud's aides, among other mujaheddin commanders. Later Sageman served as a psychiatrist on the faculty at the University of Pennsylvania, where he studied murder, crime, and terrorism. Sageman was already conducting intelligence investigations for the Army, but not everyone in the command was a Sageman fan. Like some other very smart individuals, he could be dismissive of opinions he found wanting. He was an independent operator, "not a team player," as one general in Washington warned Ashley.

"I have nothing but team players and we don't understand what's going on," Ashley replied.[5]

Sageman agreed to take on the Afghan murder project as a contractor—his title in Ashley's intelligence shop would be "political officer." He flew to Bagram Airfield in mid-October. Sageman had never been in Afghanistan, at least not meaningfully. As a C.I.A. case officer, he had accompanied mujaheddin rebels he armed and financed to the Afghanistan-Pakistan border and symbolically stepped a few yards onto Afghan soil to have his picture taken, but that was it. (The C.I.A. banned case officers from traveling with rebel clients inside Afghanistan, for fear they would be captured and turned into tools for Soviet propaganda.)

As he touched down in Kabul, Sageman was ambivalent. He had a wife and son at home in the Washington suburbs. He had never bought into Obama's counterinsurgency strategy for Afghanistan; it was too ambitious, too disconnected from reality, he believed. But the opportunity to work as a kind of homicide detective was intriguing. And Sageman felt a quiet sense of purpose—to save as many American and European lives as he could by developing insights that might reduce the murder wave, to get as many soldiers and officers as possible safely home from a misbegotten war.[6]

Ashley had won approval for Sageman's assignment in part because the psychiatrist had recently impressed the Army's leadership with his work on another classified, high-priority counterintelligence project. On November 5, 2009, at Fort Hood, Texas, Major Nidal Hasan, an Army psychiatrist, carried out a mass shooting against colleagues on the base, killing thirteen people and wounding more than thirty before he was subdued. It turned out that Hasan had been in contact over the Internet with Anwar Al-Awlaki, an American of Yemeni origin who had become a charismatic Al Qaeda preacher. After Fort Hood, the F.B.I. and American intelligence agencies identified and reviewed American residents who had previously clicked on Awlaki's Web sites or exchanged e-mail with him.

The investigations revealed, among other things, that Awlaki's audience included about one hundred active service members in the U.S. Army. This looked like a classic counterintelligence threat. What if, during the Cold War, the Internet had been around and the Army had discovered that a hundred soldiers and officers were clicking through to the K.G.B.?

The deputy chief of staff of the Army, General Richard Zahner, who oversaw the service's intelligence portfolio, called Sageman. "We have a problem here." Sageman joined the counterintelligence teams looking at the individuals who had clicked on Awlaki's materials. These case-by-case investigations took time, lasting into 2011. In the end, however, the review turned up only one individual, Naser Jason Abdo, the son of a Jordanian father and an American mother, who seemed dangerous. In 2011, Abdo was arrested for conspiring to commit violence against fellow soldiers and was sentenced to life in prison. In the several dozen or so other cases Sageman and Army counterintelligence investigators examined, however, they found no evidence of dangerous jihadi radicalization.

Sageman wrote up a classified analysis and briefed General Martin Dempsey, then the chief of Army staff, in his E-Ring suite at the Pentagon.

"You can't overreact or you will break the Army" by fostering a witch hunt for Muslim traitors, Sageman told the Army leadership. "You have 1.1 million soldiers in the Army. With turnover, we're talking about maybe 10 million soldiers over ten years. And you have two cases: Hasan and Abdo. That's your base rate. Every five years you're going to have some asshole."

Dempsey and other Army commanders grasped the point. For all the anxiety generated publicly by members of Congress and cable TV demagogues, they did not face a strategic counterintelligence threat from Muslim-American soldiers. It was a huge relief.[7]

At Bagram Airfield, Sageman hopped a helicopter to the Kabul airport, then rode in a convoy to I.S.A.F. headquarters. On board the helicopter, he met a young woman, a legal researcher who worked with the judge advocate general's office at Camp Eggers.

"What do you have on the insider attacks?" Sageman asked her.

Not much, she said, so far as she knew. But they exchanged cards and e-mail addresses. It would prove to be a fortuitous encounter.

At I.S.A.F.'s headquarters, the compound of lawns and metal trailers, Sageman met Jeffrey Bordin, the psychologist who had completed the landmark study of mistrust between American and Afghan soldiers early in 2011. They had lunch a few times and visited each other's offices twice. Sageman admired Bordin but found him a little closed and defensive—bruised by experience, at the least. As the problem of insider killings got worse, Bordin had quietly returned to Afghanistan as an Army reservist, to continue his research. The problem for him was that General Allen didn't appreciate his work any more than Petraeus had. Allen's mission was to promote comradeship and cooperation between I.S.A.F. and Afghan soldiers, "shoulder to shoulder," as the slogan went, to allow N.A.T.O. combat forces to leave the battlefield at the end of 2014. Allen believed that the alliance was sound fundamentally, and the Afghans he worked with from day to day did, too; they reinforced Allen's belief that the fratricidal violence was best understood as a Taliban operation. In any event, in 2012, Bordin found that I.S.A.F. had vastly undercounted the true number of fratricidal killings—by as much as 50 percent. The official count of a quarter of all N.A.T.O. fatalities that year was bad enough. If Bordin's estimate was right, I.S.A.F. was effectively at war with the Taliban and Karzai's armed forces simultaneously, an impossible position to sustain. But Allen's staff didn't believe Bordin's numbers. They found the researcher stubborn and headstrong. He was a thorn in their sides. Bordin's position in reply to such criticism was Yes, the truth hurts.[8]

Sageman and Bordin now lived and worked in nearby trailers, by coincidence. They exchanged notes. As a social scientist, Sageman found Bordin's work impressive and methodologically sound. Sageman was inclined to think that there was a direct causal link between the cultural misunderstandings Bordin had documented on the front lines of the "shoulder-to-shoulder" program and the murders Sageman had come to investigate. It seemed apparent to Sageman that international forces had overstayed their welcome. Fratricidal murder might represent only the most extreme outbursts in a chronically frayed atmosphere. The problem was, Sageman had no data. Bordin's interview records did not touch upon the particular killings upending N.A.T.O.; they chronicled day-to-day perceptions among Afghan and American soldiers.

Prior to 2012, N.A.T.O. had not investigated or analyzed insider attacks systematically. Each victimized coalition government handled investigations according to its own procedures. The records were scattered. During 2012, the I.S.A.F. Joint Command, the war's day-to-day headquarters unit, which was located on the north side of Kabul's airport, adopted a new approach. The command created Joint Casualty Assessment Teams—"JCATs," as they were called—to investigate and report on insider attacks immediately after they took place. The teams flew to the site of a murder or attempted killing (more than half of the attacks took place in Kandahar and Helmand), where they would interview witnesses, examine the crime scene, and write up a report within two days. The Joint Command's intelligence unit reviewed these investigations. A brigadier general, Paul Nakasone, oversaw the unit; he ran a department of twenty or so analysts, some from the Defense Intelligence Agency, others civilian. Not too many murder investigations can be resolved in just two days, but the JCATs were intelligence analysts, not detectives working toward an arrest and conviction. The Joint Command's approach effectively prioritized speed over depth, in Sageman's view.[9]

He discovered that Great Britain had dispatched a brigadier of the Royal Dragoon Guards, Tim Hyams, to look at the insider threat across the N.A.T.O. command. His title was chief, insider threat mitigation, and he oversaw a multinational cell of analysts and investigators. In late October, Sageman and Hyams traveled to the Joint Command headquarters to meet with the JCATs' murder investigation squads. But the analysts there told Sageman and Hyams that they had no data. This turned out to be untrue—they had been building a matrix of information about the killings they had investigated. Bureaucratic hoarding of intelligence was commonplace. Hyams did not have high-level clear-ances. The pair went away empty-handed, without even being told that the matrices on the cases existed.

Sageman e-mailed the Army legal researcher he had met on the heli-copter. He asked if she had copies of the "15-6" records of insider murder cases. These were highly detailed files created by the Army's Criminal Investigative Division staff, who looked into violent deaths where some-thing other than straightforward combat might be involved. C.I.D. rec-ords often included extensive interviews with witnesses, reconstructions of crime scenes, and other rich evidence. They were subject to confiden-tiality and privacy rules, however.

The researcher asked her boss, an army lawyer, who wrote Sageman.

"Do you have the names of the victims?" the lawyer asked.

"That I have."

All right, she said, but don't tell anybody about my cooperation.[10]

Ultimately, she sent Sageman records of two dozen insider murder cases that had involved Army personnel. Military C.I.D. investigators had conducted almost all of the reviews. An exception was the case of a female C.I.A. base chief in Kandahar killed by an inside suicide bomber. C.I.A. investigators had looked into that attack. It proved harder to per-suade the Marines to turn over records; they had about ten cases. And there were other cases involving Britain and continental European mili-taries. Of the files Sageman ultimately received, about three fifths in-cluded full 15-6 files, each of which ran to hundreds of pages of interview notes and other documents.

He traveled to Helmand and Regional Command headquarters else-where to talk to some of the investigators as well as other officers who knew the cases. He also interviewed ten confessed murderers being held in Afghan prisons. He began to build his own matrix of forty factors in each shooting—where the Afghan shooter was from, what language he spoke, who the victims were, whether there was evidence of ideological motivation, how the attack had been executed, and so on.

Some of the murders turned out to have little or nothing to do with either personal slights or the Taliban insurgency. In one case, a N.A.T.O.

unit that had been quietly paying off locals with a regular tanker of gasoline rotated out and the incoming unit ceased the practice. The aggrieved
smugglers shot the new soldiers. In three or four cases, Afghan soldiers
who kept young Afghan boys as sex slaves—"chai boys," or tea boys, as the
victims were euphemistically known—fell into apparent crises of conscience over their behavior and decided to purify themselves by joining
the Taliban. To prove they were worthy, they shot up N.A.T.O. soldiers on
their way out. In Helmand, Sageman examined a case where local thugs
involved in protection rackets for truckers decided to join the Taliban, but
were told they had to first kill an American to prove their bona fides. This
morass of corruption, sexual predation, and gang thugs becoming made
men evoked Elmore Leonard's texture of debased human truths, but it
was not obvious how violence of that character might be stopped.

Other cases, however, provided evidence of direct Taliban military
operations. The killing of the C.I.A.'s base chief that autumn was one
such example. A brother of a local police chief in Kandahar defected to
the Taliban and decided to carry out a suicide bombing. Telephone intercepts tracing all the way to Quetta documented the orders the bomber
received. In essence, these orders were "When your brother gets some
V.I.P.s visiting, go and blow yourself up."[11]

As he traveled, Sageman wrestled with the question of whether personal affronts or American arrogance provoked fratricidal murders. In
late November, he investigated a case where there were rumors that the
shooter had been outraged by a story that I.S.A.F. forces had held up a
pregnant Afghan woman's car at a checkpoint, preventing her from getting to the hospital to deliver her baby. The JCAT report of the case
chronicled this motivation. Supposedly, the shooter had learned of the
woman's case and spontaneously attacked. Sageman picked through the
15-6 file, which included dozens of photographs of the attack taken from
soldiers' helmet-mounted cameras. The photos, along with the interviews he conducted, showed that there was no civilian car involved, no
pregnant woman. It was not clear where this story had even come from.
The attacker had approached in a column of combined N.A.T.O. and
Afghan forces, in the back of a pickup with a mounted machine gun. He

had previously decided to join the Taliban and defected on the spot by opening fire at random military targets. Sageman stared at the photos and wondered if other reports about personal or cultural misunderstanding escalating into shootings might also be inaccurate.[12]

As the weeks passed, back at the I.S.A.F. compound, hunched over a restricted computer terminal, Sageman found that communication intercept evidence provided the greatest insights. Because of his previous Army counterintelligence work, Sageman had access to many compartments in the Joint Worldwide Intelligence Communications System, where the Army stored Taliban intercept records, among other sensitive information. Ashley assigned a D.I.A. officer to help. Sageman and the officer extracted names, dates, and details from their 15-6 and other murder investigative files to use in searches to retrieve archived intercepts. Gradually, these transcripts led Sageman to change his thinking about the nature of the problem and to develop a new hypothesis.

The hardest thing to let go of was the "myth," as Sageman began to call it. This was the belief that cultural incompatibility between N.A.T.O. and Afghan soldiers had grown so severe it occasionally turned murderous. Bordin's valid field interviews had created a misleading impression, Sageman concluded. In fact, violence did not follow misunderstanding or resentment very often, Sageman found. In many cases, there was no or very little contact between the victim and the shooter before the murder. In these cases, the shooter behaved more like a mass killer who walked into a mall and fired on shoppers at random.[13]

There were clearly some acts of broad, well-publicized cultural or political provocation—the mistaken Koran burnings at Bagram in February 2012 and, the following month, the mass murder of Afghan civilians carried out by U.S. Staff Sergeant Robert Bales near Kandahar. These incidents had provoked vengeance-seeking insider killings by Afghans. The murders of Loftis and Marchanti were an example. Of course, even their deaths did not arise from intimate misunderstanding between the shooter and his victims. To General Allen, these revenge killings after public events of desecration by Americans belonged to a different category from other insider violence. Altogether, Sageman concluded, there were seven or eight killings caused by cultural provocation, particularly the Koran burning, but these cases were far from a majority.

The Taliban intercept records provided evidence that in many more cases, Afghan soldiers and police changed their minds about which side of the war they wanted to be on. Then, from inside N.A.T.O. bases, these side switchers reached out to Taliban commanders by cell phone to volunteer their services. Or, through social networks, Taliban commanders opened phone conversations with government soldiers or police and recruited them to defect. The Taliban instructed the volunteers to kill N.A.T.O. soldiers and then run away to join the Taliban. As the murders quickened, the visibility of insider killings created stimuli for new defectors. When contacted by volunteers, the Taliban encouraged them to murder N.A.T.O. personnel because the killings made news and sapped Western morale. Encouraging a defector to kill on his way out the gate also resolved the Taliban's own counterintelligence risk, because the shooter wrote his true intentions in blood and erased suspicion that he might be an N.D.S. or C.I.A. infiltrator.

As Kabul nights turned freezing and Christmas neared, Sageman started to write up his findings and analysis. None of it was black and white and plenty of mystery remained. What caused the insider Taliban volunteers to change their minds? This was harder to document because the phone intercepts did not typically reveal motivation and many of the murderers had been killed by return fire or had escaped. In any event, the number of Afghan defectors to the Taliban side was not particularly large or unexpected in such a war dividing families and tribes. It was, rather, the shocking death toll the shooters managed to exact as they switched sides that made them significant.

There remained many cases—perhaps a quarter of the total—where the murderer's motivation was unknown or arose from some extraneous tangle, like corruption rackets. As Sageman was writing, another of these cases turned up on his doorstep.

On Christmas Eve 2012, Joseph Griffin, a forty-nine-year-old

American police trainer from Mansfield, Georgia, was shopping at a stall just outside police headquarters in downtown Kabul. He was looking for a belt buckle for his son, who was back in the States. A thirty-three-year-old female Afghan police sergeant in uniform, who had trained as a sharpshooter, approached Griffin, pulled out a pistol, and shot him dead. The woman then tried to melt away among pedestrians. She was arrested before she could escape.

Sageman hustled over from I.S.A.F. headquarters. He interviewed the shooter at the scene. She seemed to be faking a psychiatric condition, but didn't do it very well. Kabul police raided the woman's house and soon returned with garbage bags of her belongings and dumped them on a table. It turned out that she was an Iranian citizen who had married an Afghan refugee and then moved to Afghanistan with him. She was a Shia—the Islamic sect generally opposed to the Taliban—and she had recently been to the Iranian consulate about returning home. The Kabul police thought the murder was an Iranian operation, but Sageman doubted that. She had no apparent contact with anyone, Iranian or otherwise. He marked her down as another "unknown."[14]

As Sageman completed his analysis, the season of Ramadan jumped out of his numbers. The number of insider attacks had approximately tripled during Ramadan, then returned to its previous rate. This anomaly stood in contrast to the total number of "security incidents" in the Afghan war during the summer. The war's total measured violence had peaked in June and then fallen steadily into the autumn. If Ramadan was not a stimulant of combat, why was it a stimulant of insider murder? Sageman looked back at the less complete data for 2011 and saw a mini-peak of murder during Ramadan that year as well. One of the attackers Sageman interviewed in detention told him that Ramadan "was a time when lots of informal religious discussions took place" among Afghan soldiers and police working with N.A.T.O. The talk "about religion and tradition . . . might have tipped people predisposed to attack I.S.A.F. into actually doing so." Sageman also noticed that several of the murders linked to corruption or the sexual exploitation of children had taken place during Ramadan. The holy month, he wrote, "is a time when people look for redemption, especially people who might have a guilty conscience."[15]

In January, Sageman completed a draft of "The Insider Threat in Afghanistan in 2012." The unclassified version ran to thirty pages with a hundred footnotes. Its main argument sought to debunk the "myth of personal social insensitivity" as a factor in insider murders. His review of all the 2012 cases "failed to detect a single case where direct *personal* social misunderstandings escalated into confrontation ending in a lethal firefight." More general perceived cultural insults did stimulate violence, in about 10 percent of cases, according to Sageman's analysis. But these perceived insults "fell on fertile ground" because a majority of the murderers studied had connected with the Taliban *before* they decided to kill, either because they were recruited while on the inside or because they volunteered. Sageman reported that 56 percent of the inside attackers had "solid" links to the insurgency, another 9 percent had "probable" links, and another 10 percent had "possible" links. These conclusions came substantially from the telephone intercept records he and his D.I.A. colleague had examined. Altogether, 75 percent of the attacks involved shooters who had at least possible prior links to the Taliban. They were not infiltrators, however; they were side switchers.[16]

The killers' motivation was group identification, as Muslims or Afghans, where the terms of membership required violent action against the enemy. In that sense, Sageman's hypothesis was even darker than Bordin's. In theory, cultural misunderstanding might be overcome through training. The broad, fertile belief that American soldiers were occupiers could be addressed only by their departure.

Sageman's findings had one major implication for N.A.T.O. operations. Its forces needed a much more attentive counterintelligence program to monitor the communications of allied Afghan soldiers and police to detect defectors before they acted. If some of the phone conversations Sageman reviewed had been monitored when they took place, killings would have been prevented. "The challenge is to detect people who defect to the insurgency *after* they join" government forces. By Sageman's count, four out of five shooters joined the Taliban after they had been initially vetted for the Afghan army or police; only one out of five was a true sleeper or infiltrator. "Many perpetrators were recruited in place by their peers or superiors, either for ideological or political reasons, especially during Ramadan, or by corrupt commanders trying to reach a compromise with the insurgency."

Sageman's analysis also showed that there was a strong statistical likelihood that when one insider murder took place, another would follow within two days. This copycat pattern in the numbers also had operational implications: After an attack, N.A.T.O. should raise its alert levels for several days. After that, statistically at least, the threat subsided.

The report's bar graphs again created a reassuring sense of clarity, but the case studies Sageman mustered were dismal and evocative of the felony docket in a Mafia stronghold:

> A police checkpoint commander and his deputy had extensive connections to both local insurgents and drug traffickers. The commander also allegedly sexually abused young adolescents who were forced to serve him. He took an interest in a young handsome police recruit of low intelligence. The commander and his deputy encouraged the young recruit to shoot at I.S.A.F. forces accompanying a female USAID civilian inspecting a local school. Prior to the attack, the deputy gave the eventual shooter some opium.
>
> A corrupt army combat outpost commander, who extorted money from local villagers and sexually abused young recruits and had extensive connections to insurgents, encouraged a young soldier to carry out an attack on I.S.A.F., who were transferring the outpost over to the Afghans. The commander claimed that the withdrawing forces would take all the weapons, tanks and vehicles with them. One of his subordinates carried out the attack and the commander organized the escape with the help of insurgents.[17]

All militaries, including the U.S. Army, had to manage criminals in their ranks and the threat of traitors. The practical thing to do was to catch them before they did too much damage. In many of the cases Sageman reviewed, "people within the [Afghan National Security Forces] knew about the plans to carry out an insider attack" in advance. Sometimes, the plot was reported up the Afghan chain of command, "but nothing was done." And nobody told American or European commanders about what was going on. That reflected deeper problems in the Afghan system. "The failure of leadership is often compounded by widespread corruption by A.N.S.F. unit leaders using their position to extort money from local citizens, commercial traffic crossing their area of responsibility, and drug trafficking," Sageman wrote.[18]

Sageman briefed Allen, who embraced the findings, despite the discouraging elements. The analysis affirmed Allen's core belief: American and Afghan government forces were allies who had and would share sacrifice to defeat the Taliban. The problem was not cultural incompatibility. The problem was the insurgency. In truth, Sageman's evidence made clear, it was both; Allen could not do much about Sageman's belief that the presence of international troops in such large and visible numbers was itself dangerously provocative. Sageman had at least identified a counterintelligence task—identifying Taliban defectors after they were vetted at enlistment, but before they struck—that offered a path to improvement as the American withdrawal went on. And he had provided Allen with a framework for talking to Afghan and American troops about the murder wave. The general could use Sageman's evidence to move from "let's hang together" speeches to a rallying cry: "We have a determined enemy."

Sageman's report overturned the analysis earlier circulated by the I.S.A.F. Joint Command intelligence analysts. They had found a much lower percentage of links to the Taliban than Sageman did, and therefore had emphasized the theme of cultural friction. In intelligence bureaucracies, it is common to attack the findings of rival units. Tribalism is a factor, but the disputes can also reflect a healthy marketplace of ideas. The lead Joint Command analyst on the murder wave was a civilian with a bachelor's degree. Her team told Ashley that Sageman was wrong—that he had misclassified his cases, misread the evidence, and ended up with a distorted picture of high Taliban involvement in the killings. According to the Joint Command matrix of cases, only 18 percent of shootings showed links to the insurgency. She and her analysts sent Ashley a long, line-by-line critique of Sageman's report.

Ashley called Sageman in. "We have to resolve this," he said. Sageman explained that his differing conclusions were grounded in intercepts that Joint Command analysts had probably not examined. Ashley appointed what was in effect a three-judge appellate panel—three D.I.A. analysts, including the one who had worked with Sageman. They looked at every case. To support his brief, Sageman pulled documents from six different systems that he had used to accumulate his evidence. In the end, after extensive reviews and debate, the appellate panel downgraded one of Sageman's findings of "definite" links to the Taliban to "probable," but it upgraded another from "probable" to "definite." He felt vindicated.[19]

That winter, Sageman returned to Washington. From there, he helped I.S.A.F. headquarters' "lessons learned" team rewrite standard operating procedures to account for the category of internal defectors he had identified, to monitor their communications and improve vetting. Some of his Pentagon colleagues wanted to send portable lie detectors to Afghanistan. Even though American courts regarded them as unreliable, polygraphs were a routine tool of counterintelligence vetting at the C.I.A. and other American intelligence agencies. Sageman and the other analysts involved didn't think they would work in the environment he had seen in Helmand and Kandahar. The only thing Afghan police and army commanders would use them for would be "to beat the other guy," meaning the detainee, with the machine. Ashley thought the polygraph machines, adapted for use in the Pashto language, were effective, as one part of an array of new measures. These included the deployment of more investigators to support the screening system, Allen's guardian angel programs, and stepped-up efforts to convince Afghan leaders that they had to take greater responsibility.

The new standard operating procedures did not end the insider murder wave. The number of attacks declined in 2013 and 2014, but so did the number and activity of N.A.T.O. troops. During Allen's tour,

his command closed about 500 out of about 835 N.A.T.O. bases and
outposts in Afghanistan. European governments reduced or ended their
military commitments to the Afghan war, but they did not abandon
support for the Karzai government's struggle with the Taliban. Allen
believed the murder rate fell because of the measures taken during and
after Sageman's investigations, not because of the reduction in troop
numbers.

Allen understood Sageman's point about the provocative potential
of the international troop presence. He thought it could be overcome,
but Karzai's public criticism made it harder. Karzai's rhetoric played
into the Taliban's narrative. Once, Allen confronted Karzai in his office
at the Arg.

"Look at the numbers that are in school today," he said. "Look at
the numbers of Taliban we removed that were victimizing your population."

Karzai cited the number of tribal leaders being assassinated in Kandahar and implied that the Americans had a hand in the violence, so as
to sow chaos, so as to have a reason to stay in Afghanistan.

Allen came out of his seat. "We aren't staying. We are going home. If
you're implying that we are committing these assassinations, you need to
tell me."

Karzai backed off. This had become his familiar demeanor. He shared
freely his belief that the United States had a hidden agenda in Afghanistan (otherwise it would do something about Pakistan and the I.S.I.) but
he never went so far as to sever relations with American counterparts
altogether. Later, when Allen's mother died, Karzai called him to offer
personal condolences.

Sageman reflected on what he had learned. He had spent the last
several years studying counterintelligence problems in several settings—
the U.S. Army, the Afghan army and police. The Army also commissioned him to study military traitors during the Cold War period to
determine what insights might be gained. Whether the context was
Soviet-inspired communism or the Taliban or the Islamic State, Sageman concluded, an individual's act of crossing over to the other side was
often about identification, not ideology. It was about feeling a part of

someone else's "imagined community," in the scholar Benedict Anderson's resonant phrase. Such a change of identification might arise from discussions with friends or coworkers. It might arise from provocations like Koran burnings or images of civilian casualties on the battlefield. Sageman now believed that this had implications for American counterterrorism policy. If the United States escalates a conflict violently and visibly, that action would as a side effect contribute to more terrorism. For the Army Sageman served, it would not be a satisfying or popular insight, but it was where the evidence led him.

THIRTY-FOUR

Self-inflicted Wounds

Early in 2012, Doug Lute moved from his cramped office in the West Wing of the White House to a suite on the third floor of the Eisenhower Executive Office Building next door. His walls displayed photos of the smoking rubble in New York after the September 11 attacks, and of President Obama on a tarmac in Afghanistan, talking to American soldiers and to Karzai. Another showed Lute briefing the president. Topographical and demographic maps of Afghanistan and Pakistan were mounted nearby. On the floor was one of those Afghan rugs woven for foreigners depicting an AK-47 and a helicopter gunship. Jeff Eggers, the former Navy SEAL, served as Lute's deputy. The seven other "directors" or professional staff included Jeff Hayes, the D.I.A. analyst who had negotiated with Tayeb Agha. Lute had now been the principal National Security Council specialist on Afghanistan and Pakistan for five years, across two administrations, an unusually long run in such a grinding wartime role. He had started as an operations man, a West Point–credentialed general who could connect White House policy with Pentagon systems. During the first years of the Obama administration, he had evolved into a skeptical but influential coordinator, the guy who seemed to be in every meeting, taking notes, and who could run the back channels at the White House to Tom Donilon or Denis McDonough, who were then Obama's most trusted foreign policy advisers. White paper after white paper, interagency review after interagency review, trip after trip to Afghanistan and Pakistan, Lute mastered the file. He tried to keep his thinking fresh by consulting outsiders. He maintained his somewhat unlikely friendship with Barney Rubin and consulted the State Department adviser regularly.

Lute had become a passionate believer in the necessity of pursuing a peace deal with the Taliban. According to the C.I.A.'s classified District Assessments, despite the American-led combat escalation after 2009, the territory assessed to be under Taliban control had expanded by about 1 percent; the two sides had fought to a draw. If the Taliban could not be defeated militarily, and if the movement was to be prevented from returning to power, the only plausible alternative was some kind of political settlement. After Karzai's demands scuttled the talks with Tayeb Agha, the Qataris initiated a new attempt to get direct talks between the Taliban and the United States back on track. Obama sent word down: He, too, wanted another major effort to get the negotiations restarted.[1]

Kayani had closed American ground supply routes through Pakistan to Afghanistan in retaliation for the deaths of Pakistani soldiers in a violent border incident at Salala late in 2011. The closure of Pakistani routes had forced Central Command and General John Allen to import materials from the north of Afghanistan and by air, at an expense to taxpayers of $100 million more per month compared with the Pakistani option. The impasse had become a politicized, highly public matter of honor, with the Pakistanis demanding an American apology and the Obama administration, still seething over the discovery of Osama Bin Laden at Abbottabad, among other offenses, unwilling to bend. Lute decided to go back to work on the relationship with Kayani.

The first task was to reopen the supply routes. Peter Lavoy, the Pakistan specialist now in charge of Asia-Pacific policy at the Pentagon, negotiated with Sherry Rehman, the new Pakistani ambassador to Washington, and Hina Rabbani Khar, the foreign minister. The Pentagon did have financial leverage—it had suspended the Coalition Support Funds to the Pakistan Army, running into hundreds of millions of dollars annually. There was also $500 million or so in defense equipment that the Pakistanis wanted that had been placed on hold. By late spring Lavoy and his counterparts had sorted out a deal. Hillary Clinton issued a careful statement that acknowledged mistakes on both sides, which the Pakistanis accepted as the apology they had required.

Lute arranged to visit Kayani at Army House in Rawalpindi. He brought Lavoy and, initially, Marc Grossman. (After Grossman left office at the end of 2012, James Dobbins, who had helped to negotiate the original Bonn Agreement, replaced him as the State Department's special envoy.) Lute inaugurated what would become, over the ensuing months, half a dozen long, private, discursive conversations with Kayani at Army House. The purpose was to try to find a way to structure a peace deal that would end the war in Afghanistan or at least greatly reduce its violence. If the Afghan Taliban continued to sow chaos, this would inevitably strengthen the Pakistani Taliban, Kayani's principal domestic insurgent threat. Gradually, in private, they developed a shared commitment to drawing Tayeb Agha and the Taliban political leadership back into talks. They met in the wood-paneled reception room of the bungalow, the room where Kayani's stewards gave prominent display to ancient Chinese vases and other gifts from Beijing. Kayani chain-smoked from his stemmed holder. After each session, the Americans stumbled back to their quarters, typically in the early hours of the morning, their eyes watering and their clothes in need of fumigation. Lute habitually took notes in a government-issued, green cloth-bound notebook, and he would write little tick marks every time Kayani lit up.

After all the recent history—after Kayani 1.0, 2.0, and 3.0, after Raymond Davis and Bin Laden, after the secret negotiations with Tayeb Agha, where the Americans had largely locked Kayani and Pasha out of the channel—Lute's idea now was to come clean. Lute believed that no political agreement with the Taliban, if one could be achieved at all, would be sustainable without Pakistan's participation, even though Tayeb Agha had insisted that the Taliban wanted to negotiate independently with the United States, free from I.S.I. pressure.

For the first time, the Americans told Kayani the whole story about their talks with Tayeb Agha. They narrated the history of the meetings and the confidence-building measures—how Tayeb Agha had delivered a proof-of-life video of Bowe Bergdahl, how he had been able to place certain agreed-upon statements in Taliban media. They told Kayani how far they had gotten in negotiating for prisoner exchanges that would lead to the opening of a Taliban political office in Qatar. And they related the embarrassing story of how Hamid Karzai had blown up that deal.

It was always hard to tell exactly what Kayani knew and didn't know, but he seemed surprised by how far the Americans had gone with Tayeb Agha, how close they were to a meaningful initial agreement, one that would legitimize the Taliban on the international stage. This had been a historical goal of I.S.I. Kayani's take in private on Tayeb Agha's credibility and about the personalities within the Taliban leadership was similar to American analysis. About Karzai, the general was dismissive. The Americans should be able to force Karzai to do what they needed. About the Taliban, the I.S.I.'s client, Kayani sang a different tune. The I.S.I. had "contact but not control" and there was no way Kayani could "deliver" the Taliban to some sort of grand peace bargain.[2]

They also spoke candidly about the military stalemate in Afghanistan. In the first meetings, Kayani had some I-told-you-so to get out of his system. He had, in fact, long expressed doubt about the American faith in military success against the Taliban in such a short time, and also about Washington's hurried, expensive project to enlarge, train, and equip Afghan National Security Forces. For their part, Lute and Lavoy gradually allowed themselves to express "personal views" about the Afghan war, opinions that departed from the Obama administration's public line. Essentially, they told Kayani, Look, Washington understands. The U.S. military does not yet understand, but Washington understands that we aren't going to win in Afghanistan. There is no amount of military effort there that is going to look like victory. And we know the problems and the limits we have with the Afghan government."[3]

The point was, didn't the United States and Pakistan now have a common interest in preventing the Taliban from returning to power via armed revolution? Wouldn't that outcome be even worse for Pakistan than for the United States? A restored Islamic Emirate in Kabul would fire up the Pakistani Taliban and provide them with a deep base for operations against Kayani's military.

Kayani said he agreed. In fact, his army's experiences in the tribal areas since 2008 had led him, by 2012, to an outlook similar to Lute's: *Enough with clear-hold-build-transfer.* He had lost faith in the effectiveness of military clearing operations. And after the annus horribilis of 2011, it was a relief to be freed from the grand ambitions of Plan Pakistan. If this was a transactional relationship, a matter of hardheaded interests, not a deep strategic partnership, then it was possible to let go of some of the emotions of betrayal and disappointment.

Kayani's idea was to approach the problem of reducing violence in Afghanistan subtly, privately, through local managed cease-fires and political experiments in different Afghan provinces. But when Lute and Lavoy pressed Kayani for specifics, they felt he often drifted off into abstraction. The Americans sought to draw the discussions toward a negotiating plan, to revive the suspended talks with Tayeb Agha, to achieve the goals already identified—a prisoner exchange, a Taliban political office in Qatar, and the advancement of comprehensive talks that would include Karzai's government and its democratic opposition.

In April, Ryan Crocker and Marine General John Allen concluded months of negotiations with Karzai over a new strategic partnership agreement between the United States and Afghanistan, one designed to publicly ratify American commitment to Afghanistan's future security. Obama agreed to fly to Kabul to sign the document with Karzai, a symbolic and visible gesture of public diplomacy. Karzai wanted a grand ceremony where elders from across the country would attend. Crocker, too, thought a grand event would send a strong signal. Yet the Secret Service, taking note of the suicide bomber who killed Rabbani with explosives hidden in a turban, insisted that anyone in Obama's presence would have to remove his turban and be fully searched. There was no way Karzai could honorably ask Afghan leaders to subject themselves to such a search. He fulminated and fumed to Crocker and the White House. In the end, Obama stayed six hours in Kabul under cover of darkness, flying by helicopter from Bagram to the Arg for a brief one-on-one with Karzai before they signed at midnight. The president seemed distant and distracted. Karzai offered him tea or coffee, but Obama refused, an insulting breach of local protocol, as the president surely knew by now. In a televised speech from Bagram, Obama acknowledged more directly than ever before his administration's secret talks with the Taliban, and he spoke of "a future in which war ends, and a new chapter begins."

That spring, Kayani announced that Ahmad Shuja Pasha would retire as I.S.I. chief, three and a half years after he took charge. Kayani named General Zahir ul-Islam as Pasha's successor. Islam was a Punjabi whose father had been a brigadier in the Pakistan Army. His most notable physical feature was an impressively bushy mustache. He had most recently served as the powerful corps commander in Karachi. Earlier, he had done a tour as an officer in the I.S.I. section that manipulated domestic politics. Pasha moved to Abu Dhabi to enroll his son in school there.

Barnett Rubin flew to Islamabad to try to understand Pakistan's position after the breakdown with Tayeb Agha. He met twice over the next few months with Major General Sahibzada Pataudi, the I.S.I. director of analysis, as well as his deputy, Brigadier Saleem Qamar Butt, who ran the desk that analyzed the United States. For the first meeting, Rubin rode to I.S.I. headquarters with an embassy note taker. The second time, they agreed to speak more informally. Pataudi served lunch. They agreed that they were talking as individuals, not negotiating for their governments.

"We don't want to be a spoiler, and we don't want the Taliban breathing down our necks for some spite that was never intended," Pataudi said. "We need to see a process out in the open that we can rely on. We can't guarantee anything."

Rubin asked Pataudi what he thought the Taliban's negotiating position would be, if they got that far. The I.S.I. general said he thought the Taliban had matured while in exile. They had started as "young kids just out of the madrassas, eager to kill. When they started to govern, they imposed a tough version of Sharia, and people are afraid that will happen again." Yet over the past ten years of exposure to Pakistan, the international community, traveling to Saudi Arabia and the smaller Gulf States, many Taliban leaders had developed a different worldview. "Look at the new stuff, the idea of women soldiers," Pataudi said. "It all seeps in."

Pakistan's worst fear, he went on, was another civil war in Afghanistan— more drugs pouring into Pakistan, more guns, more warlords. "We'd like to fence the border." The Taliban were on the ascendance, Pataudi believed. The only incentive that might work would be to offer the Taliban a share of political power through a transparent process, after adequate confidence-building measures.[4]

Rubin and Chris Kolenda at the Pentagon coauthored a new classified strategy document. The paper outlined a regional framework, one that could be a basis for negotiations with the Taliban, Pakistan, Karzai, and other Afghan groups, as well as neighboring governments such as China and Iran. Lute and Lavoy agreed that leveraging China's influence over Pakistan could be helpful, even decisive, in developing a durable peace plan, although the idea of involving Iran looked too complicated, given the separate track of nuclear negotiations under way. It was hard for Rubin to inventory how many papers of this ilk he had written or cowritten since arriving at the State Department in 2009. He had never had faith in his government's ability to use its power constructively in Afghanistan, but now his enthusiasm about trying had started to wane. The obstacles seemed so great.

One afternoon that autumn, Rubin arrived at one of the White House visitor gates for a meeting of the Conflict Resolution Cell that had been called to discuss his latest paper. Rubin had a top secret security clearance and was typically cleared into the Eisenhower Executive Office Building without incident. But a guard pulled him aside and said that he would require an escort. The guard called Lute's office but couldn't find anyone. Fed up, Rubin told the officer, "It's okay. If I'm too dangerous to national security to discuss my own paper, I'll leave." He went back to his office at State.

Jeff Eggers, Lute's deputy, soon called him, asked him to return, and apologized. Rubin noted that this had been happening to him throughout his time in government, but only when he visited the White House.

It was a running joke among them: "No Taliban in the White House." Lute asked the Secret Service what was really going on. They told him they couldn't disclose the answer, due to privacy laws.

"Look, if it's because he has contact with some dubious people, and he has phone calls with some dangerous people—he's doing that for us."

No, the reply came. "It's a criminal matter."

When he heard that, Rubin knew right away what it was. At Yale, as an activist with Students for a Democratic Society, he had been arrested several times in connection with protests over the Vietnam War. He had an F.B.I. file. Half a century later, he could hold a top secret clearance but could not walk around the White House without an escort. Eventually, the Secret Service agreed to waive their policy in his case.[5]

The cabinet principals approved the Rubin-Kolenda strategy paper for renewed negotiations with the Taliban on November 30, 2012. Around the same time, through Sheikh Faisal and the Qatari government, the Conflict Resolution Cell revived their confidence-building plan to break the deadlock with Tayeb Agha.

They returned to the idea that opening the Taliban's political office in Qatar would provide a visible, practical springboard to negotiations, a new atmosphere for diplomacy. The two sides could pursue the prisoner exchange plan from there. Earlier, they had tried to resolve all the issues in advance. Now they would concentrate on opening the office and then negotiate about prisoners.

To try that, however, they would have to persuade Hamid Karzai to drop the "poison pill" objections he had made, such as his demand that the Taliban talk to his government first. The Obama administration invited Karzai to Washington for a state visit in January. The visible purpose was to try to coax Karzai into a security agreement that would allow American forces to remain in Afghanistan after 2014. In private, they also worked to move Karzai off his blocking position.

After Karzai and his senior aides settled in at Blair House, National Security Adviser Tom Donilon summoned them to the Situation Room. Lute introduced an intelligence briefing on how the United States saw its future in Afghanistan. The briefing made a factual case that the Taliban were essentially self-sufficient, indigenous, had no meaningful connection to Al Qaeda, and were not owned and operated by I.S.I. The latter finding was a matter of emphasis; even if Directorate S did not run the Taliban's war, was it not culpable for the sanctuary the Taliban leadership enjoyed on Pakistani soil? As Marc Grossman once put it to Kayani during this period, "They're not called the Milwaukee Shura." Still, the briefing challenged Karzai's bedrock belief that his country would not be at war if it weren't for Directorate S and I.S.I. The Afghans erupted into conversation in Dari and Pashto, evidently shocked by the assessment.

Later, Lute explained to Karzai what the intelligence analysis implied about the American mission in Afghanistan after the end of N.A.T.O.-led combat in 2014: The United States would stay on to fight Al Qaeda, not the Taliban. The war against the Taliban—or negotiations to settle the war against the Taliban—would belong to the Afghan government and its security forces, with international subsidies, training, and assistance. It seemed evident to the Americans that this had been the plan all along, but again, Karzai seemed shocked and disoriented. He had never accepted that the Taliban constituted an internal insurgency against his government. In his analysis, they were I.S.I.'s proxy force, mysteriously tolerated by Washington. The Obama administration and Karzai were bound by enormous sacrifices in expenditure and blood, and yet they saw the war in fundamentally different terms.

In their one-on-one, Obama urged Karzai to support a restart of the talks with Tayeb Agha, to drop the "poison pill" terms that had killed the negotiations a year earlier. We need to get past this deadlock, Obama said. He asked Karzai to relent on his condition that the Taliban meet with the Afghan government first. Also, the president went on, they needed to move forward with Qatar. The emirate provided the most credible channel for negotiations. Everybody involved in this—Karzai, the Pakistanis, and American intelligence—assessed that Tayeb Agha was the real deal, Obama said. Let's not mess around with another mediator, he urged.

Karzai said he was open to compromise. His aides worked to develop a joint statement by Karzai and Obama that would carefully describe the

Taliban's prospective office as being for talks—a form of permission for the office granted by Karzai. The statement said Obama and Karzai "would support an office in Doha for the purpose of negotiations" between Karzai's High Peace Council "and the authorized representatives of the Taliban." Qatar then issued its own statement, calling on "the armed opposition to join a political process," so the Taliban could say that it was their concession. Over dinner with Hillary Clinton, who was in her last weeks at the State Department, Karzai agreed that this would be adequate.

The idea was for the Taliban to have a legitimate political address for the first time since 2001 in just a matter of weeks.

O bama had moved Karzai, at least temporarily, but the Afghan president remained thoroughly estranged. "You've failed," Karzai told Zalmay Khalilzad over dinner one night late in 2012, referring to the United States. Karzai could sound despondent and threatening at the same time. "Everything will collapse. The army is rubbish. The government is a puppet. And nobody can hold elections in this country. The Americans did not let me come to an agreement with the Taliban, but I can tell you—I can come to an agreement."[6]

The C.I.A. and other quarters of the intelligence community continued to circulate classified analysis of Karzai's mind-set. The best-informed takes on Karzai accounted for his understandable fears and grievances as well as his misguided fantasies about American designs on South and Central Asia. Prohibited by the Afghan constitution from seeking reelection, Karzai sought to remain relevant and influential as the 2014 vote to choose his successor neared. Being disruptive was one way to do that. It was also plain from Karzai's remarks that, like many political leaders nearing the end of their time in power, he was concerned about his legacy in Afghan history. He was determined to avoid being remembered as an American quisling. Moreover, Karzai believed what he said about the damage done by the American military's home invasions and battlefield mistakes. Yet his theatrical, emotional remarks over the last few years had left Obama and his aides increasingly jaundiced, beyond frustrated. Karzai was not the only one in this relationship who took things personally.

James Dobbins was seventy years old when Secretary of State John Kerry asked him to become the special envoy early in 2013. Dobbins had worked on the Vietnam peace talks as a young diplomat. He supported the Obama administration's outreach to Tayeb Agha but had constrained expectations about how quickly it might produce results. On Karzai, his advice was to wait him out and not become too aggravated. It seemed clear to Dobbins that a majority of the Afghan political class, including all of Karzai's most likely successors, wanted to reach an agreement that would keep some American forces in the country after 2014. If Karzai chose not to sign a deal, his successor would.[7]

Because Karzai believed that the United States could make Pakistan do whatever it wanted, and that the I.S.I. could turn off the Taliban's insurgency effortlessly, their failure to act still seemed to him evidence of malign American intent. He seemed to countenance a theory that the United States was deliberately promoting violent instability in the region in order to control Afghanistan or to make things difficult for Iran and China.

"Mr. President, between Edward Snowden and WikiLeaks, you have several million documents to examine—can you find any mention of such designs?" Dobbins said. "Do you really think I would lie to you about this?"

"Maybe you don't know about the plan," Karzai replied. He referred to there being a "deep state" in America.

"Mr. President, there is no deep state," Dobbins insisted.[8]

Chuck Hagel, who became secretary of defense early in 2013, had a history with Karzai dating to the Bush administration. Hagel flew to Kabul on his first trip abroad as defense secretary. Karzai marked his arrival by issuing public invective, asserting that America was aligned with the Taliban to destabilize Afghanistan. Karzai tried to put off meeting Hagel but eventually agreed to see him one-on-one at the palace.

"Mr. President, this has to stop," Hagel told him. "You may have John McCain and Lindsey Graham and a few senators who will be with you to the end. But that's not where Congress is, that's not where the

American people are. If you keep screwing around with this you're going to find yourself way out alone, because this president will pull the plug on you, and the Congress will too. This country has a belly full of you.

"How do you think this plays out in the American press?" Hagel went on. "We've got kids out here dying, we're spending hundreds of billions of dollars, kids coming back with no legs, and then the blaring headlines are, 'Karzai accuses us of being traitors.'"

Karzai rarely took the bait in these sorts of conversations. The words just seemed to wash over him. "I understand, Mr. Secretary. You and I have known each other a long time. I value what you're telling me."[9]

Because it played into Karzai's paranoia (or, as Karzai might say, confirmed his analysis), the Americans concealed the extent of their collaboration with Kayani after the smoke-filled-room sessions at Army House. Early in 2013, the Qataris worked with the Taliban political leadership to assure the guerrillas that the American desire to revive negotiations with them was legitimate, and that despite the previous failures, the Obama administration would support the opening of a political office in Qatar soon. As for Kayani and I.S.I., the Americans could never quite tell what they were doing with the Taliban leadership. Kayani continued to repeat his "contact but not control" mantra, and the White House did not initially ask him to take action. The fragmentary evidence available reinforced the impression Tayeb Agha gave that he was hostile to I.S.I.; at one point, the Americans learned that I.S.I. had detained members of the Taliban envoy's family in Pakistan and threatened the negotiator if he chose to return to Pakistan.

Although they made no public announcement, the Taliban agreed to return to the talks. There ensued weeks of work on two draft documents. One was called the "Office M.O.U.," or memorandum of understanding. The draft provided that the Taliban could not command or control the insurgency in Afghanistan from the Qatar office. Another provision held that they could not issue propaganda from there. A third was that they could not conduct fund-raising. The Qatari government would finance the office, with no outside contributions, and the money would be monitored by Qatar. Also, the M.O.U. said, the Taliban could not call the office an outpost or embassy of the Islamic Emirate of Afghanistan, as they had named their government while in power during the 1990s. Lute's team came up with a name that the Americans, and later, Karzai, felt was acceptable: the Political Office of the Afghan Taliban. The Taliban representatives stationed there could meet with other diplomats—Europeans, nongovernmental agencies working in Afghanistan, the United Nations. The M.O.U. was to be signed by President Obama and the emir of Qatar. But the Qataris would not go forward unless the Taliban agreed to the final terms. British and Norwegian envoys continued to meet with Tayeb Agha, so they worked as well on bridging the last gaps.

All along, the idea had been that the Taliban would issue a public statement when the office in Qatar opened, repudiating Al Qaeda and terrorism in some fashion. In Washington, Jeff Hayes went back through recent Eid statements issued in the name of Mullah Mohammad Omar. He essentially copied and pasted language previously issued by the Taliban into a single draft statement for the Taliban to release on the big day. ("This sounds like fourth-grade English," as one American participant put it. "This isn't the Marshall Plan.")

British prime minister David Cameron, who was collaborating with Obama on the negotiation, had hosted Karzai and Kayani at Chequers, his country residence, to encourage them to support reconciliation. On April 23, 2013, John Kerry, the secretary of state, also hosted Karzai and Kayani at Truman Hall, the twenty-seven-acre residence of the U.S. ambassador to N.A.T.O. in Brussels. They set up a U-shaped table in the ambassador's living room, looking out on his gardens. Kerry, Karzai, and Kayani took a walk together on the wooded grounds. During the summit, Lute handed Kayani a copy of the draft statement for the Taliban that Hayes had prepared. Kayani had now achieved the position that I.S.I. had always said it sought: negotiating agent for the Taliban.

Kayani insisted that he did not know where Mullah Mohammad Omar was. More than two years later, the Taliban would admit that on the very day Kayani, Karzai, and Kerry met in Brussels, Omar died of tuberculosis in a Karachi hospital. If Kayani knew of the Taliban emir's dire condition, he kept it to himself while working on the statement in Omar's name. None of the Americans involved had a clue. Kayani continued to represent to the Americans that he was carrying messages from Omar. Afghan intelligence did have a sense that Omar might be dead, but it could not prove it to the satisfaction of the Americans. The National Directorate of Security had developed a source with access to a wife of Mullah Omar's. The wife reportedly traveled to Karachi for conjugal visits with her husband every few months. That spring, the source reported that on the wife's regular visit, she had not been able to see him and had gleaned that he had died. But this was a single source, reporting hearsay from an agent that nobody had vetted.

The effort to finalize all the documents for the Qatar grand opening proved to be a grind. They went around and around about the office M.O.U. Karzai remained sensitive about any form of agreement that would appear to elevate the Taliban to a status equivalent to that of his elected government. They finally decided to abandon the memorandum and replace it with a series of letters. The Qatari government would write a diplomatic note, encompassing the previously agreed terms of the M.O.U., addressed to the State Department, assuring the United States that the rules would be followed. And Obama would write a letter to Karzai, essentially offering his own guarantee: no command and control, no fund-raising, and the outpost would be called the Political Office of the Afghan Taliban. Obama also telephoned the emir of Qatar to cement the understanding. It was questionable how firmly these documents bound the Taliban to terms.

The grand opening was scheduled for June. The average daytime high temperature in Qatar during June well exceeds 100 degrees Fahrenheit. Doha sinks into a shimmering torpor. To oversee the preparations, Jeff Hayes, Jarrett Blanc (a deputy to Dobbins), and Barney Rubin flew to Qatar. There were more delays. Rubin and Blanc left before the opening.

At last, it was agreed to debut the office on June 18. A few nights before, a C.I.A.-N.S.A. team of black-bag specialists broke into the Taliban office compound in Doha to plant listening devices. These were offshore specialists who came and went from break-in jobs around the world, focused only on the narrow task assigned them. Once inside, the team members saw firsthand all the preparations the Taliban had made for the grand opening, but they were not briefed on what agreements had been made about the movement's presentation. The team did its work and reported nothing amiss.

Opening day, the Conflict Resolution Cell learned that Al Jazeera was planning live coverage of a debut press conference given by the Taliban at the new office. Lute watched the broadcast in the Eisenhower Executive Office Building. At the State Department, in the special envoy's ground-floor suite, someone had brought champagne. Years of work, long days, endless flights, and hundreds of memos and meetings had finally produced a diplomatic breakthrough that might yet reduce Afghanistan's violence and end some of its suffering.

Al Jazeera's anchor cut to the scene. The screen showed a giant sign behind the speaker's podium that read ISLAMIC EMIRATE OF AFGHANISTAN. Out front of the building, the broadcast showed, was a flagpole. It flew the former black-and-white flag of the Islamic Emirate high above the compound's wall.

"Fuck," Lute announced.

The Taliban had blatantly violated terms Obama had guaranteed to Karzai. The Afghan president reacted furiously and quickly. He announced his withdrawal from the American negotiation effort. Later, in public, he waved around the guarantee letter Obama had sent him, to illustrate that no guarantee of the United States could ever be trusted.

After a round of phone calls, threats, and pleadings, the Taliban removed their Islamic Emirate sign. Rubin was flying back to Qatar. When he landed in Doha his BlackBerry scrolled one panicked message after another. The Americans told the Taliban they had to remove their flag and sign permanently if they wanted to keep the office. The Taliban signaled that they'd rather close it down. Lute sent Rubin over to the Taliban office several days in a row, to document whether the Taliban had pulled down the flag and sign. At first it turned out that they kept raising their prohibited Islamic Emirate flag in the morning, but only to half-mast so that it could not be seen outside the high walls of the compound.

It did not take long for the Conflict Resolution Cell to accept that the fiasco was irreversible and that the negotiations they had met on bi-weekly for three years were dead. They had too many other issues with Karzai—particularly around the continuing security presence in Afghanistan after 2014—to play this losing hand any longer. John Kerry called Karzai and apologized. The United States would not recognize the political office as planned.

The Doha office failure was an episode of remarkable diplomatic incompetence. The decision to replace the office M.O.U. with letters had created too much ambiguity. The Americans mainly blamed Sheikh Faisal. They suspected he had told the Taliban they could call themselves whatever they wanted, without focusing on where that would leave the Obama administration and Karzai. A deputy foreign minister of Qatar stood at the podium in front of the giant prohibited sign at the debut press conference. At the State Department, a senior career foreign officer told colleagues, "The Qataris fucked up every mediation they've been involved with. What made us think this would be any different?"

For others who had given years to the project, the causes of the failure seemed to lie closer to home. How could the most powerful government on Earth, with tens of thousands of troops at war, at a pivotal moment of negotiations aimed at exiting the war, mess up so badly? How could it be that a scholar on contract with the State Department, an aide to a State Department envoy, and a D.I.A. analyst constituted the entire on-the-ground effort to make sure a complicated, vitally important agreement hit the mark at the moment of its announcement? Where was the U.S. embassy? Where was the C.I.A.? "It was so much the amateur hour, Keystone Kops," as a participant in the effort put it. "It was just terrible. Terrible. This is the United States. This is what we do?"

Kayani, too, was stunned at the ineptitude. The message from many of the Pakistanis who had entered the negotiations after the Army House sessions was simple: "How could you guys fuck this up so bad?" For their part, the Taliban had started out believing—insisting, again and again—that the United States was an indispensable party to any negotiation.

After June, they shifted toward thinking that the United States was an "utterly incompetent obstacle to anything they might want to achieve," as the American participant put it.[10]

At the end of 2013, Rob Williams, the national intelligence officer for South Asia, oversaw another National Intelligence Estimate about the Afghan war. It examined several scenarios and found that the level of international support would be the biggest factor determining the future of the Kabul government. If there were no international troops and no international aid available, the regime would likely collapse quickly. One way to interpret the N.I.E. was that the N.A.T.O. troop surge had bought a decent interval before the Afghan government fell under the Taliban's pressure, but unless the United States or its allies were prepared to make a decades-long, South Korea–like commitment to Afghanistan's security, it had bought little more than that. Looking ahead, there was no way that the Kabul regime would be able to pay on its own for the Afghan National Army and police. This meant any forecast of the durability of the Afghan forces had to account for the willingness of Congress, European governments, Japan, and others to write large checks to subsidize Kabul indefinitely. At the C.I.A., officers like Chris Wood, who had been working in the country since the fall of 2001, told colleagues that they were confident the Taliban would be back in power by 2017. The Afghan forces were being asked to take charge of their war very rapidly. At the beginning of 2013, there were about 100,000 international troops in the International Security Assistance Force for Afghanistan. Of those, 68,000 were American, 9,000 were British, 4,400 were German, 3,000 were Italian, and almost 2,000 were Polish. A year later, the total international force had shrunk to about 57,000, with 38,000 troops from the United States. The force was on a fast glide path to fewer than 20,000 international soldiers.[11]

The National Intelligence Estimate pointed out that when the Soviet Union withdrew from its Afghan war in the late 1980s, Moscow was able to hold off the C.I.A.-backed mujaheddin rebels by pouring in subsidies to its client government in Kabul, which was led by former Communists. The numbers were admittedly squishy, but the Soviets poured in between $3 billion and $6 billion annually, in 2011 dollars, the analysis estimated. But Moscow did not have an independently elected Congress to worry about and could print money at will. And the Soviets were willing to provide an enormous amount of equipment by land and air. The estimate raised doubts about the comparable durability of N.A.T.O. and American commitments to Karzai's successor. In the short term, the N.I.E. forecast, the Taliban would gain more territory in the countryside. About the major controversy of the war, the role of I.S.I., it found that to bring the Taliban to heel, it would be necessary to do something about the movement's safe havens in Pakistan, but the analysis also held that the sanctuaries were not the only cause of the Taliban's revival. The movement had its own political objectives—restoration of the Islamic Emirate—that it pursued by guerrilla and terrorist violence, without reference to Pakistan.

C.I.A. analysts had taken a dark view of Afghanistan's prospects for years now. They had been equally confident in 1989 that the Soviet-backed government in Kabul would collapse quickly, and that analysis had proved wrong. President Najibullah's regime fell only after the Soviet Union itself dissolved and its subsidies ended abruptly. James Dobbins was accustomed to reading predictions of doom from his intelligence counterparts. He knew they weren't always right. Afghanistan was not the same country it had been in 1989 or 2001. In the decade since the Taliban's fall, it had undergone rapid urbanization, and there was a new anti-Taliban generation in the cities that enjoyed connectivity to the world and rising literacy rates. He thought it was hard to say how Afghan elites and networks would perform after the withdrawal of the large international military force, although he agreed with the N.I.E.'s forecast that a rapid and complete withdrawal might lead to the collapse of Karzai's government. The willingness of Congress and N.A.T.O. governments to subsidize Kabul adequately was an uncertainty, but it was not a given they would withdraw aid quickly, he argued.[12]

The debacle at Doha left Dobbins and Lute to turn to the forthcoming Afghan presidential election to try to manage the risks of a failed transition at the Arg Palace. Now that he had been proven right about the American talks with the Taliban, Karzai went back to probing for negotiations with the Taliban on his own. In September 2013, Pakistani prime minister Nawaz Sharif released from prison Mullah Baradar, the longtime Taliban number two. The Karzai family had long pointed to Baradar as a potential Taliban peacemaker, but it wasn't clear that this hope had any basis in fact. There were intelligence reports that while in I.S.I. custody, Baradar had suffered a stroke and had become reticent, or that he had stopped taking important medication, or that he had taken too much medication. At least one official who read the reports thought that perhaps Baradar, fearful that he would be forced into talks with Karzai's government, which he still rejected as illegitimate, had somehow figured out a way to become silent. Like Mullah Mohammad Omar's health condition, here was another Taliban mystery inside a mystery, shrouded by I.S.I.

With the Obama administration, Karzai continued to thrash about, refusing to sign an agreement that would allow U.S. forces to remain. The White House leaked word to the press that it might preempt Karzai by adopting a "zero option," a complete pullout of all American forces. At one point during this back-and-forth, early in 2014, Karzai telephoned Zalmay Khalilzad from Kabul to talk about the issue. Karzai was in "broadcast" mode, meaning that he knew his phone was being listened to by diverse intelligence agencies. He spoke with those audiences in mind.

"You should think about the implications if the U.S. decides to go for the zero option," Khalilzad told him, "not only for the current generations of Afghans, and for all that has been accomplished, but for future generations. Once in a while you are confronted with big decisions. And this is perhaps the biggest decision facing Afghanistan since the Soviet departure."

Karzai said that if the United States continued to conduct military operations in which innocent Afghans died, "It is better that they leave than that they stay. They are in bed with Pakistan and they won't restart a peace process, which they could easily do. If they leave, then we will have to deal with Pakistan ourselves, as to what to do."

"Look," Khalilzad said, "if you wanted to show that you are not a lackey of the United States, you have accomplished that. That box has been checked. Now one has to think about the future of thirty million Afghans, as well as future generations. If it all unravels, who knows when it can be brought back together again? You have to think of your responsibility to this, to the people, and to future generations."

"I am very much at peace for the first time," Karzai answered. "I am more at peace than I have ever been because I know this is the right thing to do. Either America stays in a different way or it leaves. If the U.S. leaves, I can explain it to the Afghan people, and they will understand."[13]

THIRTY-FIVE

Coups d'État

R ahmatullah Nabil first took charge of Afghan intelligence in 2010, after Hamid Karzai forced the resignation of Amrullah Saleh, amid Karzai's flirtations with I.S.I. Nabil was not connected to any of the major armed factions from the eras of the Soviet occupation and the subsequent civil war. Before the Taliban's fall, he had worked for a decade in Kabul for the United Nations High Commission for Refugees, as a manager. He remained at the U.N. after Karzai took power, until 2003, when he joined the staff of the new National Security Council at the Arg Palace. Soon, Karzai appointed him to supervise his bodyguards and Palace Protection Service, akin to the United States Secret Service. The job required coordination with the C.I.A., the State Department, European security services, and private contractors. Karzai and his closest advisers wanted a capable manager who was also a reliable Pashtun. Nabil gradually became a trusted member of Karzai's inner circle and watched up close as the president struggled with the pressures of office and became alienated from the United States.

When Karzai removed Amrullah Saleh, he initially appointed another personal confidant, Ibrahim Speenzada, as acting director of N.D.S. But he did not want the job permanently. Karzai summoned Nabil to the palace. "What do you think if I send you to N.D.S.?" he asked.

Nabil had the leadership experience to do the job, he believed, and he said that he would work honestly. "But the biggest problem is, I don't have any political support." N.D.S. officers knew the secrets of powerful politicians and gunmen, they tapped phones, they monitored coup plots and other security threats. The legacy of K.G.B. training and Panjshiri patronage at N.D.S. that had grown up under Engineer Arif and then Amrullah Saleh, both aides to Ahmad Shah Massoud, would be difficult for a Pashtun technocrat to take on, and Nabil had no network of his own to call upon. Yet Karzai insisted.[1]

When Nabil moved into Amrullah Saleh's office that summer, he noticed a framed photograph of Hamid Karzai on the wall and beside it markings that indicated a second picture had been removed. He asked what had been there. It was a photograph of Commander Massoud, one of his new aides explained. Saleh had taken it with him when he departed. Nabil ordered another photo of Massoud mounted in its place. It was going to be difficult to convince his colleagues that he aspired to be a postethnic Afghan patriot, but he had to start somewhere.

Gradually, Nabil educated himself about the secrets he had inherited. He learned about the source networks Saleh had built to watch the Taliban, particularly across the border in Pakistan. One of the most sensitive operations involved the Pakistani Taliban. After C.I.A. drone missiles killed Baitullah Mehsud, the founder of the movement, his brother Hakimullah had succeeded him as emir. During 2009, under Hakimullah's spur, the Pakistani Taliban entered into a full-blown revolutionary war against the Pakistani state, often including I.S.I. The National Directorate of Security was also in a full-blown war against the I.S.I. Under the old adage "The enemy of my enemy is my friend," there seemed scope for Afghan intelligence to cooperate with the Pakistani Taliban. At first, N.D.S. developed sources in the movement only for intelligence collection, Nabil learned. The Pakistani Taliban were present throughout Waziristan, so Mehsud tribal sources could offer helpful information. Hakimullah Mehsud later sent a deputy, Latif Ullah Mehsud, to Kabul, to deepen cooperation. For their part, I.S.I. officers repeatedly told American counterparts that Pakistani Taliban commanders were agents of India and N.D.S. The Americans often discounted these claims;

with reason, they saw the movement as blowback from the Pakistan Army's long succoring of militancy. In any event, while it was not clear what role, if any, India had in Nabil's operation with the Mehsuds, the N.D.S. director and his senior officers had no qualms about signaling to Pakistan that they could always do to Pakistan what I.S.I. did to Afghanistan, even if they had to work with murderous figures like the Mehsud leaders.[2]

In the summer of 2012, Hamid Karzai informed Nabil that he had decided that N.D.S. directors should limit their service to two years. (This would prevent spy chiefs from becoming too powerful.) Nabil accepted the decision. Karzai appointed Asadullah Khalid, the longtime C.I.A. ally, as his successor. Khalid had overseen torture and rough detention for a decade in various posts, going back to his tour as governor of Ghazni Province in 2002, according to various published reports. He had diverse enemies. In December, a suicide bomber met him at a guesthouse in Kabul and detonated his explosives. Khalid was seriously wounded but survived. The N.D.S. eventually concluded that the attack stemmed from a long-term dispute with an Afghan family, dating to Khalid's service as governor in Ghazni. Hamid Karzai was reluctant to remove Khalid from N.D.S. leadership while he recovered from his wounds, but by the summer of 2013, the lack of active leadership at the service had become a problem. Even healthy, Khalid remained a rough "one-man band," as the American embassy had once described him. The Afghan security forces were preparing in late 2013 to take charge of the war from N.A.T.O. Preparations had started for a presidential election in 2014 that would inevitably take place in the midst of violence. N.D.S. needed a devoted, round-the-clock leader. Eventually, Karzai asked Nabil to return as "acting" director.[3]

After the fiasco concerning the Taliban's political office in Qatar, the Obama administration essentially abandoned peace negotiations with the enemy and turned attention to a different field of Afghan politics, the election contest to succeed Hamid Karzai. In October, the Afghan government announced eleven candidates who had qualified to run for president. These included three Pashtuns who had served Karzai at the Arg. Two of them were technocrats who had returned to Afghanistan

from the West after 2001 and had worked as ministers: Zalmai Rassoul
and Ashraf Ghani. The third was Gul Agha Sherzai, the Barakzai strongman. Also in the field was the runner-up from 2009, Abdullah Abdullah, the eye doctor who had been close to Ahmad Shah Massoud.
Abdullah had swallowed his ire about electoral fraud in 2009 in the
hope that his time would come in 2014. Yet the intensification of ethnic
divisions among Afghanistan's elites meant that Abdullah, who was of
mixed family heritage but was identified with the Northern Alliance,
would inevitably face a Pashtun rival. The question was whether this rival would be Rassoul, Ghani, or Sherzai.

Hamid Karzai had been reelected in 2009 while his network of
Pashtun supporters in the war-ravaged south rigged ballot boxes there.
The problems that had given rise to fraud in 2009 had not been solved
since then. Election supervisors were politicized and allied with Karzai.
The systems to prevent fraud schemes from the process of voter registration right through to counting ballots remained vulnerable. And the map
of Afghanistan's violence meant that voters in Pashtun areas, where the
Taliban had the greatest influence, would have more trouble getting to
the polls than citizens in non-Pashtun areas. During 2009, violence and
voter alienation produced turnout rates of 10 percent or less in some
districts of Kandahar and Helmand. The likelihood that this would be
repeated in 2014 provided a motivation for Pashtun leaders to embrace
fraud schemes to counterbalance the problems of Pashtun access to the
polls. It seemed clear that Karzai or his network could mobilize a fraud
campaign similar to the one carried out in 2009 on behalf of any successor Karzai designated. Skillfully, late in 2013 and into 2014, Karzai withheld his endorsement. He stated that he planned to leave politics and
retire in Kabul after his successor's election but Afghan politicians took
it for granted that Karzai would remain active and influential, not least
to protect his family's interests and his own. This logic suggested that
the final choice would come down to Rassoul or Ghani. (Karzai
had pushed Gul Agha Sherzai out of the race in 2009 and he remained a
wild card, an independent power.) Karzai hinted to numerous visitors
that he would back Rassoul, and several candidates who dropped out

early in 2014 endorsed Rassoul, but in the end Karzai appeared to shift his support to Ghani.[4]

On April 5, 2014, millions of Afghans cast their ballots. Election officials reported 6.6 million votes, a turnout better than in 2009 yet well below 50 percent, even before accounting for the likelihood that, as in 2009, a million or more votes were fraudulent. Abdullah won 45 percent, just under the 50-plus-1 percent he required to avoid a second round of voting. Ghani finished second with 31 percent; Rassoul was third with 11 percent. Abdullah had reason to be encouraged. Although he drew his greatest support from Tajik and Hazara areas, the distribution of his votes showed that he had national, cross-ethnic appeal. Yet Pashtun voters had split their support among several candidates. In the second round, if they united around Ghani, the remaining Pashtun candidate, they might overtake Abdullah's advantage.

At N.D.S., after receiving tips about wrongdoing, Nabil's intelligence officers listened to the telephone conversations and monitored the text messages of the election's supervisors and those of powerful Afghan politicians. The intelligence officers could clearly hear these election officials and politicians organizing fraud on a large scale. Nabil brought the evidence to Karzai. The president told him to eavesdrop further, to document what Karzai assumed to be an American conspiracy to interfere with the vote. Karzai didn't know what Washington was trying to accomplish with its intrigues, but after his experience with Holbrooke and other officials in 2009, he readily assumed that the Obama administration was manipulating Afghan politics. Karzai wanted to know "how the U.S. is interfering, whom they are contacting, who is contacting them, and what they are saying."[5]

When N.D.S. officers tapped the phone of Ziaul Haq Amarkhel, the secretary of the Independent Election Commission, which was supposed to organize a clean vote, the officers heard him talking not to American diplomats, but to colleagues in various provinces, apparently instructing them to organize fraud at Abdullah's expense, as Nabil interpreted it. In one conversation, Amarkhel allegedly told provincial officials to "take sheep to the mountains, stuff them, and bring them back," which N.D.S.

interpreted as code for ballot stuffing. Later police found Amarkhel traveling with thousands of blank election ballots.[6]

Nabil worried that if the election collapsed amid fraud allegations, Karzai would blame him and N.D.S. for not warning him. At a National Security Council meeting, Nabil decided to show his hand. "Mr. President," he said in front of Karzai and aides, "I have almost five thousand SIGINT" conversations on file of election officials and allies that show patterns of fraud. Karzai asked for specifics. Nabil retrieved a dozen audio files and transcripts as examples. Karzai seemed to worry about whether Nabil might be part of the American conspiracy that he perceived. In any event, he told the N.D.S. director to take his evidence to Amarkhel's boss, Ahmad Yusuf Nuristani, the chief of the Independent Election Commission. But the matter stalled. Finally, a Tajik N.D.S. officer involved in the eavesdropping, deeply offended by the ethnic slurs he overheard, decided to act on his own. He copied some of the evidence and leaked it to Abdullah.[7]

On June 14, Afghans voted in the second round. Four days later, Abdullah went public with his fraud evidence and demanded that the Independent Election Commission stop counting ballots. He withdrew his observers from the vote-counting process. Amarkhel resigned, without admitting wrongdoing, but that decision was not enough to settle the matter.

"From today onward, we reject all the decisions and activities of the Independent Election Commission," Abdullah announced. "They have no intention to assess the fraudulent votes and separate the dirty votes from the clean votes."[8]

Abdullah's rejection of the constitutional process carried an unsubtle warning that his northern backers might seize power in Kabul by force. The campaign devolved day by day toward the incitement of a new round of ethnic civil war, a rerun of the 1990s. Former allies of Ahmad Shah Massoud aligned with Abdullah stoked the flames. Amrullah Saleh publicly called the Independent Election Commission and the Election Complaints Commission "biased, racist, corrupt." Atta Mohammad Noor, the governor of Balkh Province and perhaps the most powerful officeholder in Abdullah's camp, prepared to declare "our own legitimate government" led by Abdullah. Facebook and other social media platforms became cauldrons of ethnic slander. Germany warned N.A.T.O. allies that Abdullah's supporters intended to violently seize government centers in several provinces and that they might then march on the Arg Palace to occupy it by force.[9]

After thirteen years, the loss of more than a thousand lives, and the expenditure of unfathomable sums of money, the entire American project in Afghanistan looked as if it might terminate in a coup d'état, followed by civil war. President Obama and Secretary of State John Kerry telephoned Abdullah to urge him to stand down and to wait for Kerry to fly to Kabul to try to sort out a peaceful solution. Kerry issued a public statement warning that "any action to take power by extralegal means will cost Afghanistan the financial and security support of the United States and the international community." Ján Kubiš, the United Nations envoy to Afghanistan, negotiated with Ghani and Abdullah on a plan to audit suspicious votes. Kerry landed on July 11. The next night, after whirlwind negotiations at the American embassy, Kerry stood between the two contenders at a press conference as they announced agreement on a new vote-counting plan. They also announced a vague plan to share power in a unity government after the count was completed.[10]

Kerry's Band-Aid diplomacy barely stuck. The two sides squabbled over the vote-counting process. In mid-August, Governor Noor announced that he would not accept any result short of Abdullah's victory and vowed to lead a "civil uprising" if the recount did not ratify Abdullah's election. The C.I.A. quietly arranged, through former officers close to him, for Amrullah Saleh to visit the United States with his family—a cooling-off period during which Saleh could give some private seminars. But the Afghan government continued to crack from within.[11]

Nabil was among those who feared civil war remained imminent. There were posters in Tajik areas of Kabul declaring Abdullah president. Commanders mobilized armed militias openly in the capital. Nabil assured the American embassy that he would try to keep N.D.S. neutral. He wondered how his service might defend the government from violent collapse if Abdullah's supporters attempted a coup or if Ghani tried to preempt Abdullah's supporters violently. Nabil; Rangin Spanta, the national security adviser; Bismillah Khan, the minister of defense; and Umer Daudzai, the minister of interior; discussed the situation. They drafted a statement and discussed holding a press conference where they would declare an interim government, to buy time for the election mess to be sorted out peacefully. Their main concern was to prevent the Afghan army or other security forces from allowing anyone to interfere with the election or push the country toward chaos. Of course, the quartet's intervention would be a kind of coup d'état as well. Yet if they acted together, they might present a powerful, stabilizing, multiethnic group of technocrats who favored a peaceful resolution: the current head of the military, the head of the police, the head of intelligence, and the government's senior national security adviser. They agreed that they would not act yet, but would prepare a statement and proceed only "if the situation is getting out of hand," as Nabil put it, in which case they would "call on people that we should save our country." As a kind of warning shot, some in the group talked about their plan with Matthew Rosenberg, a reporter for *The New York Times*.[12]

"A coterie of powerful Afghan government ministers and officials with strong ties to the security forces are threatening to seize power if an election impasse that has paralyzed the country is not resolved soon," Rosenberg wrote on August 18. Furious, Karzai expelled Rosenberg from the country, informing him that he had been declared a spy with "secret relations." Police escorted the journalist onto a plane. I.S.A.F.'s new commanding general, Joseph Dunford, warned the quartet that if they followed through on their plan, the United States would treat them no differently than the Taliban—as enemies of the state.[13]

Day after day, in four prefabricated warehouses off the highway from Kabul to Jalalabad, the Independent Election Commission oversaw the ballot audit Kerry had negotiated. Ballot boxes stacked six high lined the walls of the Quonset huts. At long plastic tables sat observers from the Abdullah campaign, the Ghani campaign, the international community, and Afghanistan's Independent Election Commission. Each plastic box of ballots had a sticker on it indicating its origins. The ballots themselves were blue, four inches by five inches, with pictures of the candidates and the visual symbols they had chosen to represent them in a still largely illiterate society. (Ghani chose a Koran, Abdullah an image of pen and paper.) Many of the ballot reviews went smoothly, but heated arguments, even fistfights, erupted periodically at the compound. On August 19, protesters swarmed the site, and thugs battled with knives and brass knuckles outside.[14]

The more time passed, the more evident it became that the ballot audit would not resolve the crisis. Ghani's surge of votes in the second round from Pashtun areas racked by violence was inherently suspect. Some analysts guessed that if all the fraud could be identified accurately, Abdullah would have won the election, but not every international analyst agreed. Yet the full audit showed that Ghani had won. It was not released for fear that it would touch off violence, a decision Ghani accepted. In late August, Abdullah again threatened to withdraw from the process. On September 6, Obama again called both candidates to urge them to honor the agreement to finish the count and then form a unity government in which Ghani and Abdullah would share power. The president of the United States was holding Afghanistan together by sheer willpower, one phone call and threat at a time, but the political sand castle his administration had helped to construct in Kabul still appeared to be crumbling.

That same day, September 6, across the border in Pakistan, another mutiny erupted, against the Pakistani military. Thirteen years earlier, on the eve of the American-led attack on Taliban-ruled Afghanistan, Vice President Dick Cheney had warned that a new war in South Asia might lead to such instability that the Pakistan Army could lose control over the country's nuclear weapons. Then Deputy National Security Adviser Stephen Hadley had called this the "nightmare scenario." Now the scenario appeared to be drawing closer to reality.[15]

Zeeshan Rafiq joined the Pakistan Navy as a lieutenant in 2008. He first went to sea two years later, as part of Combined Task Force 150, a twenty-five-nation sea patrol operation that deployed ships from Karachi into the Arabian Sea on counterterrorism and antipiracy missions. The coalition's participants included Pakistan, the United States, and N.A.T.O. navies. Rafiq chose his country's navy after "listening to patriotic songs," and he was motivated to serve. But after a few years, he came to think that the Pakistani military had become "the right hand of these infidel forces" and that his country's generals and admirals "follow American diktats. One signal from America and the entire Pakistan Army prostrates before them," he reflected.[16]

Rafiq once watched an American soldier board a Pakistan Navy ship. Everyone addressed him as "sir" and he was accorded the protocol of an officer even though he was just an enlisted man. In the war between the Muslim faithful and the infidels, Rafiq wondered, "Which side is Pakistan's army on?" The generals who ran his country assisted in the "carpet bombing" of Afghanistan. They turned air bases over to the C.I.A. for drone attacks against Muslims. Rafiq read *Inspire*, Anwar Al-Awlaki's English-language Internet magazine. He studied the biographies of Faisal Shahzad, the would-be Times Square bomber, and Nidal Hasan, the major who went on a shooting rampage at Fort Hood, Texas. He wanted to do something to remind "mujahids around the world" that it was important to "break the grip of infidels over our seas."[17]

Rafiq discovered that another serving Pakistan Navy lieutenant based in Karachi, Owais Jakhrani, who was from Baluchistan, felt similarly. Jakhrani's father was a senior officer in Pakistan's national police. The son nonetheless came to believe that his country had become a slave state of America. Jakhrani's radicalization manifested itself as complaints to navy officers that the service was insufficiently Islamic; an internal investigation of him led to his dismissal.[18]

Sometime during 2014, Jakhrani and Rafiq made contact with Al Qaeda in Waziristan. After Osama Bin Laden's death, his longtime Egyptian deputy, Ayman Al Zawahiri, succeeded him. Zawahiri issued occasional pronouncements but kept a low profile, to avoid Bin Laden's fate. Al Qaeda's local network increasingly consisted of Pakistani militants who had drifted toward the organization and its brand name from other violent groups based in Punjab and Kashmir. One of the leaders of this less Arab, more subcontinent-focused Al Qaeda fought under the name Asim Umar. His real name, according to the investigations of Indian police and intelligence agencies, was Asim Sanaullah Haq, originally an Indian citizen in the state of Uttar Pradesh. He left there in the mid-1990s and ended up in Pakistan, where he joined Harkat-ul-Mujaheddin before moving toward Al Qaeda. During 2014, Rafiq and Jakhrani met him and explained that they could mobilize a sizable group of sympathizers and seize control of an armed Pakistan Navy ship, and then use it to attack the enemies of Islam.

The Pakistan Navy was not merely a conventional surface fleet; it was part of the country's systems of nuclear deterrence. In 2012, Pakistan launched a Naval Strategic Forces Command, meaning a command focused on the deployment of nuclear weapons at sea. The country's military leadership sought to develop a nuclear "triad," akin to that deployed by the United States: that is, systems that would allow the firing of nuclear arms from aircraft, from land bases, or from the sea. The advantage of a triad is that it makes it difficult for an adversary that also has nuclear arms to launch a preemptive strike, because at least some of the targeted country's dispersed nukes and delivery systems would likely survive and could be used in retaliation. While developing their triads, the United States, Russia, Britain, and France placed special emphasis on submarines armed with nuclear missiles because these stealthy undersea vessels would be particularly hard for an enemy to locate and destroy during a first strike. Pakistan had not yet acquired and deployed enough high-quality submarines to place the sea leg of its nuclear triad only with those vessels. Analysts assumed that Pakistan would also consider placing nuclear weapons aboard navy ships that carried cruise missiles with enough range to reach India, which of course was by far the most likely adversary to enter into a nuclear war with Pakistan.[19]

PNS *Zulfiqar*, a Chinese-built seven-story Pakistani frigate, which typically had 250 to 300 sailors and officers aboard, was one such ship. On December 19 and 21, 2012, the frigate reportedly test-fired Chinese-made C-802 Land Attack Cruise Missiles, which have a range of about 180 miles. C-802 missiles can fly as low as 25 meters above the surface of the ocean, making them difficult to detect by radar. The missiles can also be fitted with a small nuclear warhead with a yield of two to four kilotons, or about 15 to 25 percent of the explosive force of the atomic bomb the United States dropped on Hiroshima, Japan, in 1945.[20]

Around the time that it launched its Naval Strategic Forces Command, Pakistan also accelerated its development of small, or "tactical," nuclear weapons like the ones that might fit on C-802 missiles. During the first decade after the invention of the atomic bomb, the United States, too, had built and deployed small nuclear bombs that could be dropped from planes or even fired from special artillery guns. The United States sent the small bombs to Europe and planned to use them on the battlefield against Soviet troops and tanks if a land war erupted across the Iron Curtain. It was only later in the Cold War that the idea of using atomic bombs on a battlefield as if they were just a more potent artillery shell became anathema in most nuclear strategy circles. Nuclear deterrence between the United States and the Soviet Union evolved into an all-or-nothing proposition under the rubric of Mutually Assured Destruction, or M.A.D. At the peak of M.A.D., each side had more than twenty thousand nuclear bombs that were so powerful that any full-on nuclear exchange would have ended human civilization. The effects of nuclear war became so dramatic and unthinkable that it made such a war—or any conventional war that might go nuclear—less likely. That was the theory, at least.

India and Pakistan tested nuclear weapons in 1998. As their version of mutual nuclear deterrence evolved, it displayed some parallels to the position of the United States in Europe during the 1950s. The United States feared a massive conventional blitzkrieg by Soviet forces and saw small nuclear weapons as a way to counter such an invasion. In South Asia, a similar factor was Pakistan's fear of a conventional armored invasion by India. Because India has a much larger military than Pakistan, as well as a larger economy and population, it might be expected to prevail in a long war. Pakistan acquired nuclear bombs to deter India from considering a conventional tank-and-infantry invasion, no matter how provoked India might feel from time to time by Pakistani-sponsored terrorism. For this defense to work, Pakistani generals had to plant doubt in the minds of Indian leaders about whether the generals were really rash enough to be the first to use nuclear weapons in anger since 1945. The development of small or tactical nuclear weapons aided Pakistan in this respect. Small atomic bombs might be dropped on a desert battlefield against Indian troops, away from population centers. Or they might be fired on cruise missiles against an isolated Indian military base. The use of even a small nuclear weapon on a battlefield would likely shock the world and provoke international intervention to end the war, perhaps before India could achieve its war aims. Overall, the existence and deployment of small nukes by Pakistan made it more likely that its generals would actually use them, which in turn deepened doubts in the minds of Indian leaders about how costly a war with Pakistan might become. That is, in Pakistan's twisted and dangerous logic, small nuclear weapons strengthened deterrence. Yet there were obvious downsides. One was that building and spreading out so many small, loose bombs exacerbated the threat that terrorists might try to steal them—or might come across them inadvertently.

Lieutenant Zeeshan Rafiq and former lieutenant Owais Jakhrani knew all about the PNS *Zulfiqar*'s internal security systems. After they made contact with Al Qaeda in 2014, they developed elaborate plans, seemingly derived from Hollywood thrillers, to defeat that security in order to seize control of the ship and its weapons, including its 76mm gun and its C-802 cruise missiles. One part of their plan was to exploit "a particular weakness of the security system," as Rafiq put it, namely, that "the lockers and rooms of officers are not checked."[21]

Rafiq and other officers successfully smuggled weapons aboard the PNS *Zulfiqar* "in batches, in their backpacks," and stowed them in lockers. The next part of their plan was to make duplicate keys to the doors of the missile rooms and the operations rooms "so that these rooms could be accessed without the knowledge" of the ship's commanding officers. Here, too, the insider knowledge of the two lieutenants offered an advantage. They planned to sneak into the magazine room of the 76mm gun to load its shells before they moved to seize control of the ship. They also understood that it was possible to prime and operate both the gun and the C-802 missiles outside of the ship's main operations room, in an alternate area below, on the second deck. The C-802 missiles could be operated manually from the second deck when the missiles' automated system was off—with their duplicate keys, they could accomplish this.

The conspirators also scoped out the armed security guards they

expected to find on the PNS *Zulfiqar*. These were elite commandos from
the Special Services Group. There were typically five Pakistani commandos aboard when the frigate sailed to join N.A.T.O. for operations of
Combined Task Force 150. The commandos were deployed in part to
protect the ship in case Somali or other pirates attacked. Rafiq, Jakhrani,
and their coconspirators devised a plan to kill them or hold them at bay.
First, they would bring two dozen or so coconspirators aboard—some
after the ship was at sea. They would try to avoid any confrontation with
the crew as the PNS *Zulfiqar* sailed toward American and other vessels
operating in the coalition.

Their target was the USS *Supply*, a lightly defended American supply
and refueling vessel. According to Rafiq, the American logistics ship's
defense was assigned to a U.S. Navy frigate that always shadowed it, no
more than a few miles away. When the PNS *Zulfiqar* got close, they
would use their duplicate keys to arm and fire its big artillery gun and its
cruise missiles, to "secretly attack the U.S. ship," as one of the conspirators put it, before the Pakistani crew aboard realized what was happening. They would use the 76mm gun to "destroy" USS *Supply* and then
turn the C-802 cruise missiles on whatever American ship came to its
defense. After they launched their attack on the U.S. Navy, they expected the crew of the PNS *Zulfiqar* to try to stop them, but "since it
doesn't take much time to fire missiles" they would already have done a
lot of damage. At that point, they planned to defend the frigate's armory
so the Pakistani crew could not arm themselves. They also would lock all
the doors and hatches between the second and third decks, to barricade
themselves below. They would take the frigate's commanding officer as
a hostage and force him to order the crew to abandon ship, by donning
life jackets and jumping into the sea. Once in full control of the PNS
Zulfiqar, the conspirators planned to use all of the frigate's weapons—the
76mm gun, "torpedoes, antiaircraft gun, Shalka and C-802 missiles" to
attack "any U.S. Navy ship." They would continue to fight until "the PNS
Zulfiqar was destroyed" or until the mutineers themselves were "killed in
action." They hoped to use the ship's communication systems to reach
"the media and tell the world about this entire operation."[22]

Early in September 2014, Al Qaeda publicly announced a new

branch, Al Qaeda in the Indian subcontinent, under the leadership of Asim Umar, the Indian from Uttar Pradesh. Al Qaeda's leaders explained that they had worked for some time to recruit and unite militants from disparate Pakistani groups. The announcement seemed designed to provide Al Qaeda with new visibility and relevance at a time when the Islamic State had risen to prominence in Syria and Iraq and had started to recruit local allies in Afghanistan and Pakistan. An Al Qaeda member, Hasan Yusuf, explained that the group's main motivation in forming the new branch came "in the wake of the American defeat and withdrawal from Afghanistan. . . . This jihad will not end; America's defeat is only the prelude." A withdrawal that was seen in Washington as an intelligent winding down of an unsustainable war was inevitably understood by jihadists worldwide as a historic victory and a source of new momentum.[23]

On September 6, 2014, in Karachi, at dawn, Rafiq and Jakhrani boarded the PNS *Zulfiqar* in navy uniforms, with their service cards displayed. A number of coconspirators, in marine uniforms, approached through the harbor in a dinghy. An alert Pakistan Navy gunner noticed that the "Marines" were carrying AK-47s, which are not normally issued in the navy. He fired a warning shot. A full-on gun battle erupted. S.S.G. commandos joined the fray to defend the ship. When it was over, by one count, eleven attackers died, including Rafiq and Jakhrani. They never had a chance to access the weapons they had smuggled aboard or to use the duplicate keys they had made to the C-802 missile room.[24]

The Pakistani defense of the PNS *Zulfiqar* was professional and successful. Yet there was a disturbing postscript to Al Qaeda's strike. About six weeks after the attack, India's principal external intelligence service, the Research and Analysis Wing, citing agent reporting from Karachi, informed India's national security adviser that a nuclear warhead had been on board the PNS *Zulfiqar* at the time of the attack. If their plan had succeeded, Rafiq and Jakhrani would have had more on their hands than they expected, by this account. It was possible that India put a false story out to stir up global alarm about terrorism and nuclear security in Pakistan. Yet if the Indian report was accurate, September 6, 2014, would mark the first known armed terrorist attack in history against a facility holding nuclear weapons. Judging by Pakistan's trajectory, it was unlikely to be the last.[25]

On September 14, Ghani and Abdullah completed negotiations on a four-page power-sharing agreement under which the former would become president of Afghanistan, succeeding Karzai, and the latter would appoint a "Chief Executive" of Afghanistan, to run the country day to day. When Abdullah again threatened to back out of the deal a few days later, John Kerry telephoned him and issued a warning on speakerphone to the candidate and about thirty of his aides. "If you don't come to agreement now, today, the possibilities for Afghanistan will become very difficult, if not dangerous," the secretary of state warned yet again. "I really need to emphasize to you that if you do not have an agreement, if you do not move to a unity government, the United States will not be able to support Afghanistan."[26]

Abdullah gave in. At the end of September, a new government limped into being, with Ghani as president. Karzai delivered a bitter farewell speech in which he reiterated his conspiracy theories about American motivations and did not mention the soldiers' lives sacrificed or the billions of dollars expended to develop Afghanistan. "America did not want peace for Afghanistan because it had its own agendas and goals here," Karzai said.[27]

Ghani retained Nabil at N.D.S., the only holdover from Karzai's cabinet. As Kayani and Pasha had done with the waffling Karzai, the new leadership of the Pakistan Army tried to encourage Ghani to cut a deal with Islamabad. Ghani met with Kayani's successor as army chief, Raheel Sharif, and the newest I.S.I. director, General Rizwan Akhtar. As Amrullah Saleh had experienced before him, Nabil found himself cut out of meetings between the president and the Pakistani leadership, uncertain about what sort of accommodation they might be exploring. Nabil later discovered that I.S.I. had installed in the Arg Palace two sets of encrypted hotlines between Ghani and the Pakistan Army and spy service leadership. He eventually resigned. After fitful efforts, Ghani withdrew from negotiations about peace with Pakistan.

From the first days following September 11, America's principal goal in Afghanistan was to destroy Al Qaeda. After more than a decade of effort, Al Qaeda remained active, lethal, and adaptive. Osama Bin Laden and many of his former lieutenants were dead and the ability of the group's original branch in Pakistan and Afghanistan to carry out complex attacks in Europe and America had been greatly reduced. Yet Bin Laden's deputy and successor, Ayman Al Zawahiri, remained in charge, presumably in hiding in Pakistan. New Al Qaeda branches formed in Pakistan to attack India and elsewhere in South Asia carried out well-organized strikes; Al Qaeda in the Indian subcontinent claimed responsibility for the murders of four freethinking Bangladeshi writers, including Avijit Roy, an American citizen. Other Al Qaeda allies based in Pakistan remained active across borders. Some Al Qaeda cells returned to Afghanistan as security there deteriorated. And the broader goal announced by George W. Bush in 2001, to defeat Al Qaeda and its ideological allies worldwide, and to suppress the threat of terror generally, lay in shambles. The Al Qaeda branch seeded in Iraq to challenge the American invasion of that country morphed into the Islamic State, recruited tens of thousands of volunteers to Syria and Iraq, and seized territory there, in Libya and Afghanistan. Its operatives and followers killed hundreds of civilians in France, Belgium, Germany, and elsewhere. In 2014, more than thirty-two thousand people died in terrorist violence worldwide, a record number. This represented a fivefold increase from 2001 and an 80 percent increase from 2013. Almost four out of five deaths from terrorism in 2014 took place in just five countries: Afghanistan, Pakistan, Iraq, Syria, and Nigeria. The first three of those nations remained embroiled in civil violence directly set off by the American-led invasions that followed September 11.

The United States also sought to stabilize and develop Afghanistan, to prevent it from becoming a terrorist sanctuary again. For many Afghans, life did improve as billions of dollars poured in from the United States, European capitals, Japan, the Gulf States, and other donors. The aid was often poorly managed and siphoned off by corrupt Afghan elites and criminal networks, yet it made a difference. Average life expectancy improved from about fifty-five years to just above sixty years. The economy grew almost tenfold, from about $2.5 billion in estimated gross domestic product in 2001 to about $20 billion in 2014. School enrollment quintupled, and after the dark, unplugged years of Taliban rule, nine out of ten Afghans gained access to modern communications, including smart phones. The population grew in size by about half, to thirty million, partly because several million refugees returned home, lured by the growing economy and the promise of peace. Yet Afghanistan nonetheless remained one of the world's poorest countries, with more than a third of its citizens living in poverty, and its government and security forces remained almost entirely dependent on outside subsidies of doubtful longevity.

The war that followed the American-led invasion of 2001 caused about 140,000 deaths directly by the end of N.A.T.O.'s formal combat role in 2014, according to estimates assembled by researchers at Brown University. This compared with the estimated one million to two million Afghan lives lost during the decade after the Soviet invasion. The dead after 2001 included about 26,000 Afghan civilians and about 21,000 Pakistani civilians. The extent of Pakistani losses was one difference from the wars of the 1980s and the 1990s. In those decades, Afghanistan's wars spilled over into Pakistan, in the form of loose weapons, sectarian hatred, and heroin addiction. But there were fewer cases inside Pakistan of terrorism inspired by the ideologies of Al Qaeda and the Taliban. After the American-led intervention, Pakistan gradually fell victim to terrorism carried out in the name of a broader revolutionary Islamic politics. To some extent the country was destabilized by Al Qaeda's opportunistic escape across the border from Afghanistan, under U.S. military pressure, during late 2001 and 2002. But to a much greater extent the violence reflected how Pakistan reaped the price of a state policy that nurtured and accommodated violent jihadi groups.

Hamid Karzai's conspiracy theories notwithstanding, the United States had no coherent geopolitical vision when it counterattacked Afghanistan after September 11, other than perhaps to try to avoid destabilizing Pakistan, a goal it failed to achieve. Gradually, American diplomats, intelligence and military leaders in the second Bush term and then the Obama administration did come to believe that access to at least one or two military bases in Afghanistan would be helpful to counter regional terror groups—even after the withdrawal of the great bulk of American troops, the remaining bases would become a South Asian link in a chain of American counterterrorist outposts from Kurdistan to the Gulf to Djibouti to East Asia. Whether Afghanistan would remain stable enough after 2020 to accommodate such a modest foothold in the region looked questionable.

The rising, embittered skepticism toward Pakistan at the Pentagon, in Congress, and at the C.I.A. engendered by America's experience of the Afghan war after 2001 helped to solidify ties between the United States and India; after 2001, the two countries judged increasingly that they shared a common enemy. Yet India proved to be cautious about working too closely or explicitly with Washington in Afghanistan or the region. The country's noisy democratic politics contained a large strain of skepticism about American power. And India's security establishment remained wary of taking risks in Afghanistan—say, by providing lethal military aid and troops to bolster Afghan forces against the Taliban— that might confirm Pakistan's fears of encirclement and thereby provoke I.S.I. to retaliate by sponsoring more terrorism inside India. The fallout from the Afghan war also persuaded Pakistan's leaders, after 2011, to give up on any strategic partnership with Washington and to deepen ties to Beijing. This effectively opened Pakistani territory to Chinese companies and military planners, to construct transit corridors and bases that might improve China's regional influence and links to the Middle East. Overall, the war left China with considerable latitude in Central Asia, without having made any expenditure of blood, treasure, or reputation.

In the decades after helicopters lifted the last Americans off the roof of the United States embassy in Saigon, a generation of U.S. military leaders and spies lost touch with the challenges of carrying out long expeditionary wars in poor countries in an age of saturated media. As the Soviet Union wobbled and then collapsed, the size and technological advantages of the U.S. military ushered in an era of global battlefield superiority. After September 11, the shockingly rapid triumph of the

C.I.A.-inspired campaign to overthrow the Taliban so exceeded expectations that it blinded some of its architects to their own limitations. No small part of N.A.T.O.'s ultimate failure to stabilize Afghanistan flowed from the disastrous decision by George W. Bush to invade Iraq in 2003. That war inflamed and mobilized deeper resistance to American counterterrorism policy and warfare in the Muslim world. The Taliban's comeback, America's initial inattention to it, and the attraction for some Afghans and Pakistanis of the Taliban's ideology of national resistance under Islamic principles—all these sources of failure cannot be understood in isolation from the Iraq war. The Bush administration committed other unforced strategic errors in conceiving a global war on terror: the prison at Guantánamo and the C.I.A.'s torture of Al Qaeda suspects in secret offshore prisons, for example.

Yet it also seems likely that even without Iraq or Guantánamo the United States would have struggled to achieve many of its goals in Afghanistan. Primarily this was because two administrations led by presidents of different political parties could not resolve essential questions about the conflict. Did they truly believe that Afghanistan's independence and stability was more important than Pakistan's stability? Why did they accept I.S.I.'s support for the Taliban even when it directly undermined American interests and cost American lives? If they were to try to stop I.S.I.'s covert action, what risks were they prepared to take? Inside Afghanistan, which was more important: to work with unsavory but sometimes effective warlords and militias against Al Qaeda and the Taliban, or to promote decent government, even if the attempt to do so created instability? How important was drug enforcement, if the anti-drug campaign risked alienating farmers and laborers in Taliban country? The Taliban might be abhorrent, but did the movement pose a direct threat to the United States? If the Afghan war could be settled only by peace talks that included as much of the Taliban as possible, as many at the highest levels of the Obama administration came to believe after 2010, why was this daunting project left to a secret cell of negotiators and not made a higher, more explicit priority of the United States, as were the comparably risky negotiations with Iran and Cuba undertaken during Obama's second term?

The United States and its allies went barreling into Afghanistan after September 11 because they felt they had no alternative. The complex wars and the political strategies that followed were often reactive, improvised, and informed by illusions. Yet America did not fight alone or for cynical gain. The United States was one of fifty-nine countries, or more than a quarter of the world's nations, to deploy troops or provide other aid to Afghanistan in an attempt to stabilize the country after the Taliban's fall. The motivations of the political leaders, military volunteers, and aid workers who participated in the war varied greatly. For many American and European generals and counterterrorism specialists, the critical mission was security—to deprive Al Qaeda of the territorial sanctuary from which it had been able to organize such a devastating terrorist raid on New York and Washington on September 11. A secondary aim was to prove that the compact of the North Atlantic Treaty Organization—founded on the premise that an attack on one member was an attack on all—had meaning, and that N.A.T.O. could operate if necessary outside its defensive perimeter in the West. Yet many lower-ranking volunteers who came to Afghanistan from around the world after 2001 saw themselves on a humanitarian mission. A more stable and prosperous Afghanistan restored to independence and peaceful sovereignty—restored to its best twentieth-century example of ethnic and linguistic pluralism—might contribute to international security. Yet a strong, rising Afghanistan relieved of some of its recent suffering was, for many of these volunteers, an end in itself.

September 11 made plain how the security of ordinary Afghans was connected to the security of ordinary Americans and Europeans. Yet the problems of restoring stability to Afghanistan proved to be rooted not only in the patterns of terrorism, but also in the country's massive underdevelopment. On September 11, Afghanistan languished at the very bottom of United Nations and World Bank tables measuring poverty and human potential. Even that ranking was a guess, because the country no longer produced reliable statistics. Less than a quarter of all school-age children were enrolled. Girls were even less likely than that to learn to read and write. The wars since 1979 had ripped jagged losses in most Afghan families.

The international community has an unimpressive record of fostering rapid economic development in extremely poor, war-shattered
countries. From the 1980s on, infrastructure investment, trade, and
free-market policies transformed the lives of hundreds of millions of
Asians and Latin Americans, fostering new middle classes and reducing
the risks of war between states. By the 1990s, a number of coastal African nations had embarked on similarly transforming paths of economic
growth, international trade, and middle-class formation. Yet the political
economy of Afghanistan in 2001 had more in common with the world's
most intractable cases: Somalia, Haiti, the Central African Republic, or
the Democratic Republic of Congo.

Both administrations that fought the Afghan war between 2001 and
2014 tolerated and even promoted stovepiped, semi-independent campaigns waged simultaneously by different agencies of American government. The easiest way for the National Security Council and the
president to resolve policy conflicts among the C.I.A., the Pentagon
policy offices, the D.E.A., Central Command, D.I.A., and the State Department was to tell each agency: Do it your way, but follow our broad
guidance. The agencies often interpreted White House policy memos
liberally; the agencies proved to be more inclined to apologize in the
event of a perceived transgression than to implement policy they did not
like. It is hardly surprising that policies riddled with such internal contradictions and unresolved analytical questions failed to achieve the ex-
traordinarily ambitious aim of stabilizing war-shattered Afghanistan.
The war instead became a humbling case study in the limits of American
power. It became a story of mismatched means and ends. Rich, techno-
logically advanced, and often ably staffed, the United States foreign policy, intelligence, and military machine was built for competition with
other states: to win conventional wars against opposing armies, to negotiate treaties with professional diplomats, to patrol sea lanes, or to
steal the secrets of other governments. At those sorts of tasks, the machine remained mostly competent. It was never well equipped to build
good governance in deeply impoverished, violent landscapes or to win
asymmetric conflicts with ideological, media-savvy guerrillas on short
time lines.

The I.S.I. proved to be a formidable adversary, but it was not omnipotent; it suffered from the same corruption and weakness that plagued the entire Pakistani state. America failed to achieve its aims in Afghanistan for many reasons: underinvestment in development and security immediately after the Taliban's fall; the drains on resources and the provocations caused by the U.S.-led invasion of Iraq; corruption fed by N.A.T.O. contracting and C.I.A. deal making with strongmen; and military hubris at the highest levels of the Pentagon. Yet the failure to solve the riddle of I.S.I. and to stop its covert interference in Afghanistan became, ultimately, the greatest strategic failure of the American war.

In the autumn of 2014, the United States military finished the massive project of tearing down or turning over to Afghan forces the sprawling infrastructure built in the country since 2001, to prepare for the official end of N.A.T.O. combat operations at year's end. The United States operated 715 bases around Afghanistan; it would ultimately keep only 12, to carry out the forthcoming mission of advising and assisting the Afghan National Army and police. The Afghan National Army took control of about 225 of the former American bases; the police took another 118. Most of the rest were closed or abandoned. Altogether, the United States handed over to Afghanistan about $900 million of "foreign excess real property"—military hand-me-downs of various kinds—and destroyed another $46 million worth because the items were too sensitive or impractical to transfer. The largest single gift was Camp Leatherneck, the United States Marine base in Helmand, valued at $235 million; the Marines lowered the American flag and flew away in late October.[28]

The war against the Taliban grew deadlier for Afghan civilians and troops during 2014. More than 10,000 Afghan civilians died or suffered injuries during the year, the highest number since the United Nations began counting civilian casualties there in 2009. The U.N. judged the Taliban responsible for almost three quarters of the civilian casualties, through roadside bombings and other indiscriminate attacks, but hard ground battles between Afghan forces and the Taliban also took a heavy toll—more than 3,000 civilian casualties. The Afghan National Army and police suffered 4,634 deaths and many more wounded, a rate of casualties that Lieutenant General Joseph Anderson, a senior American commander in Kabul, termed "not sustainable."[29]

The Taliban consolidated control in rural areas, threatened highways, but captured no major cities. The war remained a bloody stalemate but one in which the government's position—high casualties in the security forces, high rates of desertion and attrition, and paralysis within the new "unity" government of Ghani and Abdullah—looked precarious. By the year's end, the unhappy partners had yet to name a cabinet. On the Taliban's side, there were some signs of fragmentation as opportunists and Pakistani militants repositioned themselves for a post-American war. During the summer and fall, through video messages and fragmentary statements, various Pakistani and Afghan Taliban commanders offered support for the Islamic State. Some of the declarations of allegiance were ecumenical expressions of support for any righteous jihadist movement of the Islamic State's character. Later in the year came more outright defections; the black flags of I.S.I.S. flew in place of Taliban banners in some districts of Nangarhar, Helmand, Farah, and Logar.

On February 15, 1989, the final armored column of the "Limited Contingent of Soviet Forces in Afghanistan," as the Soviet Fortieth Army called itself, crossed over the Friendship Bridge above the Amu Darya River, officially ending Soviet combat operations in the country. (Thousands of Soviet advisers remained behind.) General Boris V. Gromov, the final Soviet commander of the war, sat in the column's last armored personnel carrier. On the bridge, the vehicle stopped and Gromov climbed down. He walked the final yards on foot, never looking back on Afghanistan. On the Soviet side of the border, his teenage son greeted him with a bouquet of flowers.[30]

General John Campbell, the final commander of the International Security Assistance Force for Afghanistan, wanted a less dramatic and final-looking ceremony. The mission was changing but the number of troops in country was not; this was by no means a final withdrawal. He also had to manage security arrangements to be sure the Taliban did not

disrupt his ceremony. On December 28, 2014, a Sunday, Campbell invited Afghan government officials, diplomats, and journalists to a gym-
nasium inside N.A.T.O.'s secure perimeter in Kabul. The ceremony
program noted that attendees should lie flat on the ground in the event
of a rocket attack. A small military brass band played in a corner as
Campbell rolled up the I.S.A.F. flag and unfurled a new green one, em-
blazoned with the words "Resolute Support," as the new advisory mission would be known. Campbell promised a "bedrock partnership" with
Afghanistan. "The road before us remains challenging, but we will triumph," he said. The Taliban issued a statement declaring that "the infidel powers" that had thought they would turn Afghanistan "into their
colony" instead stood on "the brink of defeat." From Washington, President Barack Obama issued a statement of his own. The end of American
combat in Afghanistan was "a milestone for the country," he said. He
thanked the American troops and intelligence officers who had devastated, he said, "the core Al Qaeda leadership, delivering justice to Osama
Bin Laden, disrupting terrorist plots and saving countless American
lives." Finally, Obama went on, after much sacrifice, "The longest war in
American history is coming to a responsible conclusion."[31]

As it happened, the American war in Afghanistan would officially
start again in just over twelve months, this time against the Islamic
State's new Afghan affiliates. The longest war in the country's history
would be longer still.

Epilogue:
Victim Impact Statements

After Abdul Saboor murdered Darin Loftis and Robert Marchanti at the Interior Ministry in February 2012, American and Afghan intelligence and police officers tried to hunt him down. At one point, a signals intelligence operation traced Saboor's cell phone to Iran. Among the Afghan officers who took an interest in the case was General Mohammad Ayub Salangi, a former Kabul police chief who had risen to become deputy interior minister. Salangi worked closely with American and European generals and police trainers; he was an Afghan nationalist who spoke out regularly against the I.S.I., accusing the service of providing military-grade explosives to the Taliban and sending Pakistani commandos in disguise to fight inside Afghanistan. Salangi came from the same area of Parwan Province as Saboor (just to the north of Kabul), so the case had an aspect of personal honor. As months and then years passed, the general made sure that Saboor remained on the wanted list. Early in 2016, after living in Iran for four years, Saboor returned to Parwan. The N.D.S. had instructed local informants to notify the service if he turned up. In the end, it wasn't hard to track him down; that winter, Saboor openly hosted neighbors for discussions about Islam. Police arrested him on March 19 while he was "preaching in favor of the enemies of Afghanistan," as the Interior Ministry put it.[1]

On April 21, in Kabul, the police arranged for Saboor, who was now thirty-two years old, to make a brief appearance before the Afghan

media. He entered a Kabul briefing room in handcuffs, wearing a blind-
fold. A policeman removed the cloth as he stood before microphones.
Saboor introduced himself and recited a verse from the Koran: "God says
it is obligatory upon you to wage jihad against the enemies of your religion, creed, honor and pride." He offered a brief and unrepentant confession. Since the "coalition forces have come to this country, what good
have they done?" he asked. "What is the service they have provided to
this land?" He recalled the burning of the Korans at Bagram Airfield in
early 2012. "I couldn't control myself," he admitted. He was "grateful to
God" and did "not care if I die for this."[2]

In Florida, Holly Loftis learned about Saboor's arrest by text message
from Peggy Marchanti, who had been given some fragmentary information about the case by Army liaisons. Eventually she contacted military
lawyers from the Judge Advocate General's Corps, or J.A.G. Corps.
They explained that Saboor would be tried for murder later in the summer. The families had an opportunity to submit Victim Impact Statements to the court in Parwan. Victim impact evidence—typically,
written statements or videos submitted by family members of crime
victims—is a relatively recent feature of American jurisprudence, at
times controversial, particularly in capital cases, because of the emotional hold such testimony can have on juries. In the redevelopment of
Afghan law and justice after the Taliban's fall, shaped by European and
American finance and advice, Victim Impact Statements became part of
some Afghan proceedings.

The eldest of Holly's two daughters, Alison, was seventeen years old.
For the past few summers, she had participated in Gold Star Teen Ad-
ventures, a program for children of Special Operations soldiers killed in
the line of duty. She had learned scuba diving and had decided to study
marine biology in college. Camille, the younger daughter, was fourteen.
She was enrolled in a preprofessional ballet program and was about to
attend a summer intensive organized by the American Ballet Theatre.
For both girls and Holly, the news of Saboor's arrest and the invitation to
write about the loss of their father and husband turned the spring of
2016 into a season of new emotional trials. Holly tried to seek out

professional counseling for all of them again, although between her work schedule and the constraints of her health insurance network, it wasn't easy.

For her part, Holly had never expected justice for Darin's murder. She thought it was appropriate that Afghans who respected her husband's memory had tracked Saboor down. It wasn't comforting, exactly, but "it came full circle." For four years, she had dreamed from time to time that Darin had come home. The dreams were not of a gauzy, running-through-the-wildflowers reunion, but routine, matter-of-fact. The two of them picked up where they had left off. She talked with Darin about what had happened since he died—who in the military had been difficult with her, who had been kind. Somehow, with Saboor's arrest, it felt to her now as if that fantasy might vanish.[3]

Holly and both of her daughters decided to go ahead and submit Victim Impact Statements. Alison's was "without a doubt the most difficult thing I have ever had to write," as she noted near the start. It ran to several pages. She was thirteen when her father was killed, and "over the last four years I have struggled with heartbreak, grief, anger and devastation." Revisiting her loss after Saboor's arrest had "redoubled all the feelings of bereavement I have had since the Air Force knocked on my door four years ago." She recounted her father's qualities, the richness of their relationship, her memories of him, and her struggle with depression since his death. Over the Memorial Day weekend, she had visited her father's grave at Arlington National Cemetery and played taps on the trumpet. "As I played the tribute for him," she wrote, "I was faced with the truth that my dad will not ever be able to tell me how proud he is of me, or be able to listen to the music that I have composed about his life and death."

She continued, "To the man who murdered my father: You have caused so many people so much deep grief, pain, and agony. You cannot possibly imagine the pain I have endured and continue to endure because of your actions. I would never wish these feelings upon anyone."

Holly's younger daughter, Camille, had turned fifteen since Saboor's arrest. She had been ten when her father was murdered. She composed a five-paragraph statement for the court. "My Dad believed that we all worship the same God," she wrote. "We are all just trying to live our lives in service of God, always trying to be the best person we can be." She continued, "Some people may think it outrageous for me to offer my forgiveness to someone who has changed my life in such an irreparable way, but I can say only this: God forgives us, and he has commanded his people to forgive each other and to live to be more like him. That does not mean I believe there should be no consequences. One may be forgiven, but one must still receive consequences for one's actions. In order to receive forgiveness, one must express remorse. So, my forgiveness will come to you if you are qualified to accept it. . . . I say all this in remembrance of my father."

In her statement, Holly described her long journey with Darin, including their time as Peace Corps volunteers in Papua New Guinea, before her husband joined the Air Force. "In our country, we marry for love," she wrote, "and Darin was the love of my life, my best friend, the person I could trust most in the world, and also the smartest person I know." He held three master's degrees "and wanted to get a Ph.D. as well. He had studied the history and culture of Afghanistan, and he spoke Pashto and Dari. He respected the Afghan people and culture." She quoted a letter Darin had written to his daughters when he deployed to Afghanistan the first time:

> My reasons for going to Afghanistan include an honorable sense of duty to help others. If I had stayed home and not volunteered to go, I would have always wondered what I could have contributed. I don't want to sit around wondering if I could have done something to help their children go to school, their sick people get better, or their poor people have a better life. I don't want to be in the situation where I wonder how I could have helped, and so that's why I'm going to Afghanistan. I know this is the honorable thing to do, and that's why I have to be away from you for a while.

Holly's statement concluded, "I wish to thank General Salangi and the Afghan National Police for continuing to search for the shooter, for never giving up over the last four years, and for bringing this murderer to justice. I also wish to thank the Honorable Chief and Members of the National Security Branch of the Parwan Province Primary Court for hearing my statement and for ensuring that justice be done."[4]

Saboor's trial opened on October 5, 2016. The Afghan prosecutor rose to introduce facts about the defendant. Saboor had a ninth-grade education. He had worked at the Ministry of Education before joining the Ministry of Interior. At one point, he had traveled to Pakistan and studied the Koran at a madrassa in Peshawar. In 2012, after he learned from news reports about the burning of the Korans at Bagram, he carried food to a local mullah and discussed the provocation. He decided that he should act. At the ministry a few days later, he loaded a pistol in the bathroom. He knocked on the door of the office where Loftis and Marchanti worked. He pretended to have a stomach illness and said he needed to get some medicine from a locker. Then he shot the two men to death. As he walked out of the building, he told an Afghan he passed that the sound of gunshots was from the Americans fighting with each other. He dropped his pistol in some trash, traveled to Herat Province, and then on to Iran.

The prosecutor detailed Saboor's confessions after his arrest and presented ballistics evidence about the shootings. Saboor interrupted the proceedings from time to time by reciting verses and parables from the Koran.

Saboor's lawyers denied his guilt and presented several defenses. They said his confessions had been coerced by torture, that members of his family had been wrongfully detained to intimidate him, and that he was not in adequate health to stand trial.

Two American captains read out Victim Impact Statements from the Marchanti and Loftis families.

The prosecutor, in rebuttal of the defense case, played Saboor's confessions on video, where he admitted readily to the shootings.

"What of the video statements you made?" the judge asked the defendant. "You were not being intimidated then, when you made that confession. What do you want this court to do?"

Saboor said that he had done nothing wrong. "God is unblemished," he added.

The court recessed for half an hour. When the judge returned, he found Saboor guilty and sentenced him to twenty years in prison.[5]

Saboor appealed but lost a second hearing; his sentence was upheld. He had one remaining avenue of appeal, to the Supreme Court. Holly realized the case was like a scab that was going to be picked at for a while. She shared the news of the verdict and sentence with her daughters. They did not have much of a reaction. Holly thought that Darin would be satisfied that the sentence was a long prison term instead of the death penalty. It was impossible to speak for him now that he was gone, but he would have said, she thought, that it did not make sense for one more person to die.

During the seven months between March 2016 and the opening of Abdul Saboor's trial, more than 4,500 Afghan soldiers and police died in combat against the Taliban and the Islamic State, and more than 8,500 others were wounded. The casualties were so heavy that within the police forces, at least, they outpaced recruitment of fresh volunteers.[6] Taliban guerrillas threatened the provincial capital of Kunduz in the north and Lashkar Gah, in Helmand, in the south. All of the country's major cities remained in the government's hands but the roads and countryside between them were often controlled or influenced by Taliban guerrillas. The Afghan state Ashraf Ghani and Abdullah Abdullah presided over (when they weren't fighting with each other over prerogatives and power) resembled an archipelago of urban islands supplied by hopping airplanes and helicopters, engulfed by a sea of guerrilla country. The state's geometry resembled the archipelago of Communist-controlled cities the Soviet Union had left behind in 1989, when C.I.A.-backed mujaheddin rebels ruled the countryside, before they finally took Kabul in 1992.

Somewhere between a thousand and three thousand fighters in the armed opposition to Ghani's government now fought under the banner of the Islamic State, mainly in eastern Nangarhar Province. They constituted no more than 10 percent of the country's guerrilla forces; nearly all the

rest remained officially loyal to the Taliban. The Islamic State strengthened in Afghanistan after N.A.T.O.'s withdrawal from combat operations
at the end of 2014 in part because its recruiters exploited confusion over
whether Mullah Mohammad Omar was alive or dead. The Taliban's media operation kept insisting that Omar was alive and well and issued statements in his name. But in July 2015, Uthman Ghazi, the leader of the
Islamic Movement of Uzbekistan, the terrorist organization long affiliated
with Al Qaeda, put out a statement declaring that Mullah Mohammad
Omar was dead and that the I.M.U. would now pledge allegiance to the
Islamic State. When Uzbek and allied fighters attacked Taliban-held villages, they used loudspeakers to lure defectors, shouting, "Mullah Omar
is dead!" Where they managed to take control of villages and districts near
the Pakistan border, they imitated the ruthless methodology of the Islamic State in Iraq and Syria. Fighters beheaded Afghan Hazaras, who
followed the Shia sect of Islam, en masse. They executed other hostages
by bomb and distributed digital videos of their carnage online.[7]

In August, to shore up their position, the Taliban—or I.S.I.—at last
admitted publicly that Mullah Mohammad Omar had died in April
2013, more than two years before. After a brief succession struggle, a
Taliban shura appointed Omar's deputy, Mullah Akhtar Mohammad
Mansour, as the new emir. It had been Mansour who directed Tayeb
Agha's secret negotiations with the Obama administration, and it was he
who had apparently coordinated with Ashfaq Kayani and I.S.I. to produce draft statements under Omar's name at a time when the Taliban's
founding leader lay dying in a Karachi hospital.

In May 2016, less than a year after he officially took charge of the
Taliban, Mullah Mansour was killed by an American drone in Baluchistan, Pakistan, as Mansour returned from Iran in a small convoy of
sport utility vehicles. It wasn't clear why the Taliban's new emir had
been visiting Iran. The Taliban's Deobandi creed of Sunni Islam is anathema to Iran's Shiite theologians; in 1998, the Taliban and Iran grew so
hostile toward one another that they almost fought a war. After 2001,
Iran improved relations with the Taliban, however, to help the movement defeat the United States. Iran's evident motive was to hasten the
withdrawal of American troops and aircraft from bases located so close

to Tehran. More recently, a new wrinkle had entered into Taliban-Iranian relations. Both the Taliban and Tehran feared the rise of the Islamic State. It would make sense if Mansour had visited Iran to receive support or even plan joint operations against this shared enemy, just as they had collaborated against Washington. In any event, after American intelligence officers tracked Mansour and eliminated him, a hard-line cleric from Kandahar, Mawlawi Haibatullah Akhundzada, succeeded to power as the Taliban's third emir.

In late 2016, there were still about 8,400 American troops stationed in Afghanistan. About a quarter of them were counterterrorist forces engaged in direct attacks against any groups officially designated as terrorists by the United States. According to the Pentagon, there were thirteen Foreign Terrorist Organizations, as they were officially labeled under U.S. law, with followers in Afghanistan. There were another seven in Pakistan—altogether, this stew of twenty or so groups amounted to about a fifth of all the Foreign Terrorist Organizations worldwide. Early in 2016, President Obama expanded this aspect of the American war in Afghanistan. He added the local Islamic State affiliate to the counterterrorist mission and authorized direct American strikes against its guerrillas. The rest of the 6,000–plus U.S. forces in Afghanistan provided "advise and assist" support to Afghan forces against the Taliban, or delivered logistics, intelligence, and transport to both military campaigns.[8]

The Pentagon estimated that the Taliban and the Islamic State together controlled about 10 percent of Afghan territory outright. The C.I.A. estimated that it was more like one third. Either way, it was clear that more than half of the Afghan population, mainly in cities, lived under the government's writ, however shaky that writ might be. Kidnapping gangs menaced Kabul and abducted Westerners for ransom or to sell them to the Haqqani network in Waziristan. Hundreds of thousands of urbanized young Afghan men voted with their feet after 2014 and undertook perilous migrations overland to Europe.

It was possible to make a case that this stalemate required—and might eventually reward—continued investments of American support. For one thing, a full withdrawal would all but assure the Taliban's triumph. The arguments made by Pentagon commanders who advocated for remaining in the Afghan war and possibly even expanding American involvement held that a stalemate might be good enough for now. They argued that the Afghan forces' fitful progress and the continued American counterterrorist mission there should be evaluated in a worldwide context. There were many dangerous, ambitious terrorist groups in the Afghan region; the United States required forward bases to check them. The Afghan state was weak, corrupt, and politically paralyzed, it was true, but so were the governments of other emerging nations racked by internal violence. The military stalemate in Afghanistan, these commanders argued, resembled Mexico's struggles with narco-traffickers or Colombia's long war with the F.A.R.C. or Nigeria's internal conflicts with Boko Haram and southern oil smugglers. These had been or remained long, messy, shifting wars, but conflicts where the state, however fragmented and corrupt, remained more or less intact, cooperated with the United States and Europe, received development aid, and repressed terrorists. If the United States remained committed to Afghanistan, these Pentagon commanders would tell President Donald Trump, the government in Kabul might never eliminate armed guerrillas or the Taliban's leadership, but it might achieve an acceptable state of equilibrium and slow progress that would keep the country free from reign by the Taliban or the Islamic State and prevent any rekindling of Al Qaeda or its ilk on Afghan territory. Eventually, the war might yield peace negotiations, as in Colombia. Trump had advocated for withdrawal from Afghanistan, but in August 2017, he accepted the arguments of his generals and announced that his administration would stay committed to the Afghan war.[9]

It was a long way from the modernizing, transforming visions for Afghanistan that had characterized the hubristic heights of the Good War, but even as a template for realism, the Pentagon's vision strained credulity. The rates of casualties and attrition in Afghan forces had already weakened them badly; if this cycle of combat and casualties went on for a few more years, the forces were likely to break down. Also, the Afghan army, the police, and the N.D.S. increasingly were politicized, influenced by Kabul factions and ethnic polarization, and undermined by the paralysis between Ghani and Abdullah. It was hard to imagine how another Afghan presidential election, scheduled for 2019, could improve matters, given the record of the previous two elections. President Ghani's initial plan had been to reduce the war's violence through reconciliation talks with the Taliban and Pakistan, but these efforts had proved to be as treacherous and unproductive for his administration as they had been for the Obama administration's Conflict Resolution Cell.

On the other side of the war, I.S.I.'s support for the Taliban remained steadfast. Ashfaq Kayani finally retired as chief of army staff at the end of November 2013. General Raheel Sharif, his successor, extended the army's influence over Pakistani media and foreign policy. During Sharif's tenure, American commanders in Afghanistan detected no change in Kayani's policies of support and sanctuary for the Taliban. By 2016, Major General Muhammad Waseem Ashraf reportedly ran I.S.I.'s Directorate S. On the Afghan front of external operations, his bureaus seemed to follow a policy of providing as much support for the Taliban as I.S.I. could get away with—just enough to keep the war broiling, while avoiding aid so explicit that it might provoke the international community to impose sanctions on Pakistan or withdraw military sales. The new Pakistan Army regime also continued Kayani's post-Abbottabad policy of probing the possibilities for peace talks with Kabul and increasing reliance on China for economic, military, and nuclear aid.

In August 2016, a helicopter crashed in Logar Province, Afghanistan, in Taliban country to the south of Kabul. The helicopter was painted white, apparently to resemble the helicopters flown by contractors supporting the Kabul government. A Russian pilot and Pakistani military officers were aboard, by some accounts, although there were reports as well that the pilot was a Pakistani-educated British citizen. Taliban commanders facilitated the crew's return to Islamabad within days and burned the helicopter. It was not fully clear whether its supplies were meant for the Taliban or rival Islamic State factions. Pakistan put out an absurd story that the helicopter was on its way to Central Asia for repairs. The area where the aircraft went down has been a supply corridor since the early 1990s from Pakistan for I.S.I. officers aiding guerrillas attacking Kabul. A series of valleys shielded by mountains and gorges provide relatively safe passage for helicopters. Still, I.S.I.'s apparent willingness to defy N.A.T.O. by sanctioning direct covert helicopter supply flights to the Taliban or the Islamic State provided striking evidence of the service's sense of impunity.[10]

For his part, Ashfaq Kayani retired in the Islamabad area, kept a modest profile, and occasionally turned up in civilian dress for conferences about military and foreign policy. Reportedly, some of his family moved to Australia. His former partner at I.S.I., Ahmed Pasha, considered writing a book about his experiences in the military but in the meantime wrote in Urdu about early Pakistani history. Maleeha Lodhi, Kayani's political adviser, became Pakistan's ambassador to the United Nations. Following a conflict with Pasha and I.S.I. that saw him placed under a form of house arrest for a time, Husain Haqqani moved back to the United States and wrote forthrightly in opposition to the Pakistan Army's political influence and I.S.I.'s coddling of extremists.

The American specialists who shaped and debated the country's longest war moved on. Cofer Black joined Blackwater after retiring from government and later joined another C.I.A. contractor as an executive. Rich Blee retired and went into security consulting with Hank Crumpton. Steve Kappes also worked with a private firm involved in intelligence analysis and software. Greg Vogle remained at the C.I.A., was promoted into the Senior Intelligence Service, and ran the C.I.A.'s paramilitary division during the second Obama term. He eventually retired and joined former general Stan McChrystal's consulting firm. In 2015, Chris Wood, also now the equivalent of a three-star general, worked alongside Vogle after succeeding Mike D'Andrea as chief of the C.I.A.'s Counterterrorism Center. He retired about two years later.

Some of the Bush administration's architects of Afghan policy remained involved with the country during the Obama years. Zalmay Khalilzad formed a business with offices on K Street in Washington, D.C., from which he invested in the Middle East and Afghanistan; he also published a memoir. Robert Finn became a lecturer in Turkish history and studies at Princeton University. Following a Taliban attack on the American University of Afghanistan in the late summer of 2016, David Sedney agreed to serve as acting president of the university; he also joined an effort to shore up international commitments to Afghanistan, through a group called the Alliance in Support of the Afghan People. During the Obama years, Steve Hadley worked with John Podesta, the Democratic strategist who would become Hillary Clinton's presidential campaign chairman, on a program by the United States Institute for Peace to support democratic Afghan politics and the 2014 Afghan presidential election. Eliot Cohen returned to Johns Hopkins University; David Kilcullen started a consulting firm and published several books; Brian Glyn Williams also published several books while remaining on the faculty of the University of Massachusetts at Dartmouth.

At the D.I.A., Dave Smith ran Pakistan analysis for several years before retiring. After the secret Taliban negotiations collapsed, President Obama appointed Doug Lute as the United States ambassador to N.A.T.O., where he served until the end of Obama's time in office. Jeff Hayes left Lute's staff to return to D.I.A. Successively, Jeff Eggers and then Peter Lavoy followed Lute at the National Security Council, as Barack Obama's principal specialists on Pakistan and Afghanistan. Lavoy remained in that role until the administration's end, then joined ExxonMobil as an adviser about Asia. Frank Ruggiero ran government relations in Washington for BAE Systems, a British defense company.

At the State Department, Anne Patterson became the U.S. ambassador to Egypt and then assistant secretary of state for the Middle East. Cameron Munter left government and became chief executive of the EastWest Institute. Marc Grossman returned to business consulting; Barnett Rubin returned to his position at the Center on International Cooperation at New York University. Marc Sageman returned to writing about terrorism and served as an expert witness at several terrorism trials.

In addition to consulting and publishing a memoir, Stan McChrystal taught at Yale. David Petraeus pleaded guilty to a misdemeanor for mishandling classified information and joined a large private equity firm in New York. Mike Mullen joined the board of directors of General Motors. Michael Flynn stunned some former colleagues by joining Donald Trump's campaign for the presidency as an outspoken national security

adviser; at the Republican Party convention in Cleveland, he stood onstage and joined the delegates in "Lock her up" chants directed at Hillary
Clinton. Trump then named him national security adviser in his new
administration; he was soon fired after allegations surfaced that he had
misled Vice President Mike Pence about contacts with Russian officials.
General John Allen joined Hillary Clinton's campaign and spoke at the
Democratic convention in Philadelphia.

Hamid Karzai lived for the most part in a Kabul compound behind
high walls, near the presidential palace, received visitors, and was continually rumored to be meddling in Afghan politics. He gave interviews
criticizing the United States for undermining Afghan sovereignty and
insisted, as ever, that there would be no war in Afghanistan if not for
Pakistan and I.S.I. "We are victims," he said.[11]

When the Taliban finally admitted that Mullah Omar was dead,
Tayeb Agha resigned as Omar's supposed negotiator, to avoid "expected
future disputes," as he put it. He continued to spend time in Qatar. An
array of other Taliban leaders joined fitful peace discussions organized
by Pakistan after 2014; they made no progress.[12]

For the Panjshiri commanders and aides who huddled in the garden
of a hospital in Tajikistan in September 2001, debating how to manage
the news of Commander Ahmad Shah Massoud's assassination, the decade and a half following September 11 was transforming and, for many
in the Panjshiri leadership, enriching. Nearly all of Massoud's aides held
cabinet or parliamentary offices during the Karzai years, at one time or
another.

After he left N.D.S., Amrullah Saleh organized a grassroots movement focused on youth and nationalism; he became active on Twitter. In
2017, he returned to government, to oversee reforms of the Afghan security services. President Ghani appointed Engineer Arif as governor of
Panjshir Province. Marshal Fahim died of a heart attack on March 9,
2014, at the age of fifty-seven. His family and followers erected a grand
marble tomb on a barren hillside on the road from Kabul to Panjshir; it
is visible from miles away, resembling the memorial of a Mogul emperor.
The wealth Fahim and his family accumulated after 2001 was visible,

too, in his hometown, Omarz, where he left behind, beside the Panjshir River, a magnificent compound resembling a palace.

The entrance to the Panjshir Valley, near Jabal Saraj, suggests an illustration from a Tolkien novel. The turquoise mountain waters of the Panjshir River, foaming white, roar through a steep and narrow rock gorge toward the Shomali Plains below. The sheer walls and boulders at the valley's mouth create natural gates and barriers that would be difficult for even a heavily armored convoy to breach. Beyond this stone barricade the valley is narrow and protected by high steep walls for several miles. On the eve of September 11, this constituted the front line for Massoud and his holdout Panjshiri forces, one of the last redoubts against full Taliban control of Afghanistan. Almost sixteen years later, Panjshir was again preparing its defenses. As Ghani and Abdullah struggled to govern, as N.A.T.O. governments and voters questioned the cost and trajectory of aid to Afghanistan, it was hard to avoid the possibility that the Afghan war might be cycling back toward where it began before the American intervention following September 11.

The Panjshir looks again to be a defiant redoubt against the Taliban, alongside Hazara areas in the country's central mountains and some other regions of the north. After the Taliban's insurgency revived in 2005, the movement's commanders have occasionally tried to raid the Panjshir Valley, whether for revenge or glory or sport, even though the valley's population is ethnically homogenous and unified in its hostility toward the Taliban and its allies. No Taliban commander or suicide bomber has made it more than a few kilometers up the road from Jabal Saraj before achieving martyrdom.

The Panjshiris' participation in the American-led victory over the Taliban in 2001 has brought the valley many economic rewards, even if corruption and theft by Massoud's lieutenants have diluted the benefits for ordinary farmers and shopkeepers. The main road running north from Jabal Saraj through the valley toward Tajikistan is asphalted and in fine repair. There are new schools and supermarkets groaning with

grapes and melons. The Panjshiris' position as an inner circle of American allies, capable under arms, for the most part reliable under pressure,
created many business opportunities in security contracting, transporta-
tion contracting, and logistics during the surges of American troops into
the country. New stone houses and farms line the river today, ringed by
barbed wire, constructed by the valley families that benefited from war
and reconstruction.

Yet the Panjshir's political and military leadership has fragmented
since 2001. The successor to Massoud elected in the hospital garden,
Marshal Fahim, is gone. None of Massoud's other former lieutenants can
command widespread authority, including Abdullah, who is increasingly
dismissed by Panjshiri colleagues as a self-interested opportunist. The
ideal of Panjshiri solidarity is held together in large measure by a ghostly
symbolic image: Massoud's mournful face, which remains ubiquitous in
Kabul and the valley, in blown-up photographs and posters taped onto
the windshields of Corollas and armored Land Cruisers, plastered on
billboards and in market windows, and at virtually every checkpoint or
bridge. The persistence and mobilizing power of Massoud's memory is
impressive, yet there is a threadbare quality about his hold on Panjshiri
loyalties. Fifteen years after his death, a massive shrine on a mountain
hilltop outside his hometown of Bazarak remains unfinished, a testament to flawed leadership and corruption among his followers. The more
time goes on, the more evident it becomes that the public cult of the
valley's martyred hero remains essential because of the absence of credible living leadership. There are contenders for next-generation political-
military command of the Panjshir, in Massoud's tradition, should the
war require a return to guerrilla fighting. Amrullah Saleh is one credible
possibility. In recent years Saleh has built a whitewashed home by
the rushing water of the Panjshir, just below Massoud's unfinished
shrine. He can look up at his mentor's tomb from his front porch.

Another possibility is Ahmad Shah Massoud's only male heir. Devoted to the anti-Soviet war, Massoud married relatively late, in 1988, to
the daughter of a Panjshiri commander whose family had lived near his
own in the valley for perhaps a century. Massoud's wife delivered a son,

Ahmad, in the year following their union. They had five more children together, all daughters. During the early and mid-1990s, including a few dark years after the Taliban took Kabul, Ahmad lived with his mother in Bazarak, in the heart of the Panjshir Valley. The boy served tea in his father's radio room and slept in a small room with all of his sisters and the occasional caregiver. As the only boy in a famous commander's family, Ahmad received a lot of attention. When the war became rougher, by 1998, when Taliban jets occasionally bombed Panjshir, Massoud shifted his family to Tajikistan and Iran. Ahmad was just twelve years old when Al Qaeda assassinated his father in September 2001.[13]

His mother and uncles groomed him for succession. After high school, he considered attending West Point, but decided instead on Sandhurst, the British military academy, where he could combine military training with university study at King's College in London, which is well known for its war studies department. Ahmad wrote a thesis about whether the Taliban were better understood as a criminal network than an ethnonationalist or ideological movement. (He concluded they were criminals.) He stayed on at City University to earn a master's degree before returning to Afghanistan in 2016.

Ahmad Massoud was now twenty-seven years old. In Kabul, he met a senior C.I.A. officer that summer. The officer told him, "We made two mistakes. We should have listened to your father's warnings about Al Qaeda. And we should never have let you go to Sandhurst," instead of West Point or an American university. Ahmad's plan was to work at the philanthropic Massoud Foundation for a while and travel the country, to build up his public profile before considering an entry into Afghan politics. There are already efforts under way to raise his visibility. On the main road from Kabul to Panjshir, in Charkah, the capital of Parwan Province, supporters have mounted a large billboard depicting Ahmad's photograph alongside his father's. LOOKING AT YOU MAKES US REMEMBER OUR BELOVED ONE, it says.[14]

In September 2016, a few days before the fifteenth anniversary of his father's death, Ahmad Massoud rode in a Land Cruiser to the valley, to visit with supporters and family. On a day bathed in bright sunshine, he met a visitor in Bazarak, on a friend's open porch beside Panjshir River rapids. Ahmad wore a trimmed beard and a pressed, embroidered gown. He is self-possessed, a strong speaker, with a Roman chin and nose; his resemblance to his father is unmistakable. Yet he does not exude great interest in warfare. He learned leadership and military tactics at Sandhurst but also discovered that he hates horses. He has allergies and struggles with an ankle that he once fractured playing soccer. His intention is not to try to live up to his father's reputation as a genius at war, which would be a formidable task, but to convert his father's influence to improve next-generation democratic politics in Afghanistan. "The main thing is that I want to forget about the past," he said. "I want to be part of a generation of peacemakers."

Yet his father's followers seek out Ahmad as their general against the revived Taliban. When the northern city of Kunduz fell briefly to the Taliban, in the late summer of 2015, the incursion set off a panic in the province and in Kabul. Ahmad was still studying in London. His cell phone rang daily as Kunduz residents pleaded for him to come home. "What's your plan?" they asked. "What's your goal? We respected your father. We will follow you."

Ahmad's mother also called him. "Ahmad, what are you doing?" she asked. "I don't care about your studies. I expect you to be on the front lines of Kunduz!"

He paused to reflect on these expectations. "This was *my own mother*," he noted.

He had an out, as it happened—his passport was with British immigration when the Kunduz crisis erupted, and by the time it was returned to him, the government had retaken the city. But this was just a temporary reprieve.

"I don't want a bubble just around myself," Ahmad went on, beside the river. "I want this generation to carry the message and the vision of my father. When my father was there, he was minister of defense," he continued, referring to Ahmad Shah Massoud's position in the mujaheddin government, before the Taliban took Kabul in 1996. "He had an army and a network of commanders. I don't have any of those things. You can't say that to people who are suffering, however."

Afghanistan remained at war. The Taliban remained a vicious enemy, and there were new threats to Panjshir and the country now, such as the Islamic State. He was Commander Massoud's only son, educated at Sandhurst. "Next time," he asked, "what am I going to do when the people knock on my door?"[15]

ACKNOWLEDGMENTS

I am greatly indebted to the many scores of people in the United States, Afghanistan, and Pakistan who agreed to interviews and provided much other assistance during the decade that I conducted research for what became this book. I tried as best as I could to capture with equal empathy the perspectives of decision makers in the three main governments whose antagonisms and confusions drive the book's narrative. Inevitably, I understood the American system best, but I am especially grateful for the long hours offered by Pakistani and Afghan intelligence officers, military officers, cabinet officials, politicians, religious scholars, guerrilla leaders, and many others in those two countries. They did their best to straighten me out but none of my sources or researchers should be judged accountable for errors or misjudgments in the text; I am solely responsible.

In addition to Christina Satkowski and Elizabeth Barber, I owe great thanks to Mustafa Hameed and Derek Kravitz for their interviews, travel, and documentary research.

In Afghanistan, Habib Zahori and Muhib Habibi were intrepid reporting partners. Massoud Khalili was an indispensable friend. Martine van Blijert was a reliable reality check each time I traveled to Afghanistan, and the research she and her team at the Afghanistan Analysts Network produced was rich and independent. I am very grateful as well to Sarah Chayes for her hospitality in Kandahar.

In Pakistan, I owe special thanks to Ahmed Rashid, Najam Sethi, Jugnu Moshin, Waqar Gilani, Zahid Hussain, and Maleeha Lodhi. I first met Ahmed, Najam, and Jugnu when I turned up in Lahore as a wide-eyed rookie newspaper correspondent in 1989. While I was report-ing more recently for this book, it became apparent that we had been holding the same conversations, in the same places, about the same subjects—coup rumors, army succession, I.S.I.'s agenda, American blindness—for almost thirty years. Some things have improved in Paki-stan along the way, but not enough. None of them is responsible for what I have reported and written here.

From India, I was fortunate to have the expertise of Rama Lakshmi and Sajid Shapoo. During the research for this book, I participated in several "track two" meetings among American academic, governmental, and think tank specialists on South Asia and Chinese counterparts, which were invaluable in clarifying Beijing's outlook on Afghanistan and Pakistan.

I started this book while at the New America Foundation, where I was supported by Peter Bergen, Jon Wallace, Victoria Collins, Eric Schmidt, Kati Marton, David Bradley, Rachel White, MaryEllen Mc-Guire, Reid Cramer, and many other friends and colleagues. I finished the project at Columbia University's Graduate School of Journalism. There Sue Radmer and Iris Lee have somehow made the days fit to-gether. I owe thanks as well for support and comradeship from Lee Bol-linger, John Coatsworth, Jane Booth, David Stone, Rick Smith, Paul Neely, Keith Goggin, Simon Lee, Ira Lipman, Janine Jaquet, Paul Schuchert, Ernest Sotomayor, Sheila Coronel, Nick Lemann, Bill Grue-skin, Sam Freedman, Michael Shapiro, LynNell Hancock, Emily Bell, Mark Hansen, June Cross, Betsy West, Kyle Pope, Todd Gitlin, Alisa Solomon, David Hajdu, Jim Stewart, Alexander Stille, Jonathan Weiner, Marguerite Holloway, Richard John, Andie Tucher, Jelani Cobb, Mi-chael Schudson, Mike Pride, and many other wonderful colleagues too many to list without reprinting our directories.

The New Yorker made this book possible by supporting reporting trips to Pakistan and Afghanistan; some of those interviews have turned up in these pages. I am especially grateful to Nick Thompson for his enthusiastic supervision of our quixotic search for Mullah Mohammad Omar. I owe gratitude as well to the editing of Jeff Franks, Nick Traut-wein, Amy Davidson Sorkin, Alan Burdick, and Virginia Cannon. I cannot adequately express my thanks to David Remnick, Dorothy Wickenden, and Pam McCarthy for their backing since I came to the magazine in 2005. And, as ever, the magazine's fact-checkers did some of the best reporting that appeared under my byline. The late Robert Silvers at *The New York Review of Books* was another font of encouragement and insight during these years.

I have been so fortunate to work with Ann Godoff, at what is now Penguin Random House, for more than two decades. On this project again, Ann supported the most ambitious, serious work possible while offering very helpful notes and analysis. Thanks as well, at Penguin, to Karen Mayer, Casey Denis, and Michael J. Burke. Melanie Jackson, my literary agent, has been my steadfast colleague since the early 1980s, and was once again an invaluable reader.

Finally, I am grateful to the friends who went out of their way during the years of this work: David Finkel, Bill Gerrity, Adam Holzman, Glenn Frankel, Bob Kaiser, Phil Bennett, Steve Feirson, Anne Hull, Liz Spayd, Bob Nickelsberg, Ken Zimmerman, Chris Stone, and Michael Greenhouse. As ever I owe the most to the extended Coll clan: Ally, Emma, Max, Rory, John, Susan, Paul, Geoff, Dan, Alex, Aidan, Lilly, Sarah, Katie, Jonny, Kara, Marian, Frank, Phoebe, Hannah, Louisa, Gigi, the Baldwins, the Broadhursts, the Shoemakes, the many dogs I follow on Instagram, and, of course, young Robert, who traveled by road in his mother's tummy to Jalalabad during the making of this book. To the inspiring Eliza, I can only express my deepest love and gratitude.

NOTES

This book is based primarily on more than 550 interviews conducted in the United States, Afghanistan, Pakistan, and Europe between 2007 and 2017 by the author, as well as four researchers, Christina Satkowski, Elizabeth Barber, Mustafa Hameed, and Derek Kravitz. Elizabeth Barber also carried out important additional interviews during 2016 and 2017 while fact-checking the manuscript with its original sources. Many interviewees agreed to multiple sessions or followed up with correspondence. Where possible, we conducted interviews on the record; there are dozens of named individual sources cited below. I also sought contemporary records of events described in the book and was able to rely on such materials in a number of cases. I kept an informal diary of notes from private meetings and conversations I participated in about Afghanistan and Pakistan policy in Washington between 2007 and 2012, when I was both a working journalist at *The New Yorker* and president of the New America Foundation, a policy research institute. The release by WikiLeaks of State Department cables from the embassies in Kabul and Islamabad, through early 2010, also provided an important source of grounding about dates, intelligence reporting, and high-level meetings. The notes below provide a full accounting of the court records, research papers, memoirs, and books by journalists and scholars that I also relied upon throughout.

Chapter One: "Something Has Happened to Khalid"

1. The account of Saleh's meetings in Germany comes primarily from interviews with Saleh, confirmed by two former senior American officials familiar with the program. By Saleh's account, the last shipment he had to move on his own from Frankfurt was handed off by the C.I.A. in early September 2001. The former American officials confirmed that Saleh did have to move nonlethal equipment on his own from Frankfurt that summer, but said there was more than one shipment, and they were less certain of the September timing. For the tangled history of American covert aid and policy toward Massoud between 1997 and 2001, see Coll, *Ghost Wars*, chapters 26–32.
2. Interviews with Saleh. The C.I.A.'s assessment of him is from interviews with four senior intelligence officers who worked with him around this time.
3. All quotations from the interviews with Saleh. London accounts, Massoud controlled just over $60 million: Interview with a former senior intelligence official familiar with the reporting. The World Bank reported Pakistan's G.D.P. as $72.3 billion in 2001.
4. Saleh's biography, ibid. The BBC made a short documentary that touched on Saleh's humanitarian and political work during the early 1990s, *A Town Called Taloqan*. www.youtube.com/watch?v=4n -QrlOeWHo.
5. "We have a common enemy": From an interview with Blee, conducted in 2002. The specific equipment ALEC Station supplied: Berntsen, *Jawbreaker*, p. 57. Berntsen joined a team that visited the Panjshir in March 2000, the last of three C.I.A. visits before worries about Massoud's helicopters caused the supply lines to move back to Dushanbe and Germany. "We were there to capture Zawahiri," Berntsen recalled in an interview, but after C.I.A. headquarters received a report out of Europe that Al Qaeda had identified and targeted the team, they were ordered to leave early. "It was over, a mission that cost millions," according to Berntsen. "We were just in disgust."
6. Quotations from an interview with Blee. This account of ALEC Station's argument to Massoud was confirmed by Saleh as well. On the $150 million covert action program proposed for Massoud, see Coll, *Ghost Wars*, and the "Final Report of the National Commission on Terrorist Attacks Upon the United States," hereafter *The 9/11 Commission Report*, p. 197.
7. Interviews with Saleh.
8. Ibid.
9. Arif's biography, from interviews with Arif. "Scruffy . . . reliable partner": Crumpton, *The Art of Intelligence*, p. 131. Gary Berntsen recalled that Arif's communications and intercept room "resembled a crazy high school experiment . . . a mixture of old French and Russian components wired together." Berntsen, *Jawbreaker*, p. 57.
10. Massoud's intelligence operations and history: Interviews with several former Afghan intelligence officials who worked at the directorate in these years and afterward. Head of Taliban intelligence was a reporting agent: Interview with a senior aide to Massoud who was directly involved.
11. All quotations from interviews with Arif. He also recounts these events in a Dari-language memoir.
12. Interviews with Saleh.
13. The conversation in the Kulyab garden is from interviews with Saleh, Arif, and Abdullah.
14. All quotations are from interviews with Saleh. Blee confirmed Saleh's recollections.

Chapter Two: Judgment Day

1. The description and history of C.T.C.'s office is drawn from interviews with people who worked there in 2001 or visited repeatedly, including Cofer Black and Ed Worthington. Dimly lit and sour smelling, with "Dimly lit and sour smelling": Bennett, *National Security Mom*, p. 15. List of terrorist target branches in C.T.C.: Crumpton, *The Art of Intelligence*, p. 132.
2. Employee survey: "Inspection Report of the DCI Counterterrorist Center Directorate of Operations," C.I.A. Office of Inspector General, August 2001, partially declassified and released, June 10, 2015. Almost six in ten ALEC Station employees: "Office of Inspector General Report on Central Intelligence Agency Accountability Regarding Findings and Conclusions of the Report of the Joint Inquiry into Intelligence Community Activities Before and After the Terrorist Attacks of September 11, 2001," hereafter OIG Accountability Report, June 2005, partially declassified and released, June 10, 2015, p. 73. (The figure was 57 percent.) Cable traffic numbers: Ibid., p. 75. An average of twenty-three reports on Al Qaeda to the F.B.I. per month: Ibid., p. 52. ALEC Station transmitted 1,018 formal reports, called CIRs, between January 1998 and September 10, 2011.
3. Area familiarization operations: Interviews with several people who participated in them for C.T.C. The contractors are "sort of cannon fodder": Author's interview. Billy Waugh, a legendary C.I.A. operative, has described some of the day-to-day overseas surveillance work summarized here in Waugh and Keown, *Hunting the Jackal*.

4. Interviews with Black and Blee.

5. Interview with Black.

6. Interview with Blee, who reviewed his recollection with several of the colleagues working at ALEC Station that morning and reported their combined account to the author in early 2015.

7. "Wherever I go": Interview with Black. "A lot of yelling and screaming": Interview with Allen.

8. 9:40 a.m. videoconference: Tenet, *At the Center of the Storm*, p. 163. Also, *The 9/11 Commission Report*, p. 36.

9. "Let's get out of here": Tenet, ibid., p. 164. "We should stay here": Interview with Allen. He recalled that A. B. "Buzzy" Krongard, the C.I.A.'s executive director or chief administrative officer, also recommended that the group stay put.

10. Tenet, ibid.

11. Schroen, *First In*, p. 14.

12. Alternate campus: Interview with Allen, who worked on continuity of government operations during his long C.I.A. career.

13. "Sir, we're going to . . . absolutely right": Tenet, *At the Center of the Storm*, p. 165. Black confirms the exchange. Other details of the migration to the printing plant and the efforts of the cabinet to communicate are from interviews with Black, Allen, and others present. See also *The 9/11 Commission Report* and Morell, *The Great War of Our Time*, chapter 3.

14. Interview with Worthington. What happened, who did it, what next: Interview with Black.

15. Interviews with several officers who were present.

16. Interviews with Blee and a second C.T.C. officer involved in the debate with Hezbollah branch that morning.

17. All quotations, interview with Blee.

18. Ibid.

19. "Over the last several months": OIG Accountability Report, p. 17. Other headlines: *The 9/11 Commission Report*, pp. 257–59.

20. Tenet, *At the Center of the Storm*, pp. 151–52. Interview with Worthington.

21. "Read one or more": OIG Accountability Report, p. xiv. Four FBI agents opened at least one cable related to Mihdhar's January 2000 visa: Ibid., p. 55. Miller and Rossini have spoken publicly about the blocked cable, i.e., *Newsweek*, January 14, 2015.

22. OIG Accountability Report, p. xiv.

23. Interview with a former C.I.A official.

24. OIG Accountability Report, p. xv.

25. All quotations, interviews with Black.

26. Tenet called Al Qaeda around 3:00 p.m.: Morell, p. 56. "This is a tragedy . . . you cannot imagine": Interview with Saleh, confirmed by Blee.

27. Several C.T.C. employees recounted what they remembered of this speech, before Black confirmed the talk in an interview. The quotations used here are mostly from Black's recollections but a few are from the recollections of officers present.

Chapter Three: Friends Like These

1. The author first met Smith at the U.S. embassy in Islamabad in 1989 while reporting on Pakistan's military for *The Washington Post*. The account of Smith's biography and career comes from multiple interviews with Smith over twenty years, including for this book.

2. As part of the effort to cultivate Mahmud, Smith and the C.I.A. arranged a battlefield tour of Gettysburg. Coll, *Ghost Wars*, pp. 504–11. Mahmud's interests: Correspondence with Mahmud.

3. Stephen Hawking: Grenier, *88 Days to Kandahar*, p. 73.

4. This summary of I.S.I.'s organization is drawn from interviews with serving and former I.S.I. officers, American officials who studied the organization, and published accounts.

5. "Evident personal enthusiasm": Ibid. Mahmud considered: Correspondence from Mahmud.

6. All quotations from author's interviews and contemporary records. Mahmud, in correspondence, confirmed some of the conversation. "That 'Islam is misunderstood' came up during the discussions in nearly all my meetings with the visitors from the West," he wrote. "It was not as a result of my personal belief system but rather because Islam happens to be intrinsic to the regional environment, which the visitors came to discuss in the first place. Misunderstood Islam is still as intrinsic to the regional environment today as it was when 9/11 happened." He wrote without elaboration that the account describing his statements about unity of faith and military command "are misquoted." .

7. Tenet's travel to Pakistan in summer of 2001: Interviews with U.S. officials. Mahmud in Washington: Correspondence from Mahmud. There have been several published accounts of Mahmud's breakfast

with Goss and Graham in the Capitol on the morning of September 11. According to Mazzetti, *The Way of the Knife*, p. 28, Goss planned to provide the I.S.I. chief with a gift, a book about the American Civil War, but in the scramble to evacuate, it was left behind.

8. All quotations, interview with Chamberlin. Musharraf did not respond to requests for comment about Chamberlin's recollections.

9. All quotations from interviews with Smith and contemporary records.

10. "The inconsistency of U.S. attitudes": Correspondence from Mahmud. All other quotations, State Department cable, Washington to Islamabad, September 14, 2001, redacted version obtained by the National Security Archive, George Washington University. See also Woodward, *Bush at War*, pp. 58–59, who published substantially the same talking points.

11. The quotations are primarily from contemporary records. "Come on, General Musharraf" and "Frankly, General Musharraf" are from Chamberlin's recollection, in an interview. The records show that Chamberlin cut Musharraf off a couple of times and challenged him to be more forthcoming, but Chamberlin recalls being less undiplomatic. After Musharraf declared "unstinting" support, Chamberlin went outside and told CNN that Musharraf had agreed. She spoke on camera immediately because she felt she needed "to lock him in so he can't backtrack."

12. "We were on the borderline . . . all the details": Rashid, *Descent into Chaos*, pp. 28–29. "The stakes are high. . .": Bush, *Decision Points*, p. 188. "In almost every conversation": Ibid., p. 213.

13. All quotations from the meeting are from contemporary records.

14. Musharraf, *In the Line of Fire*, p. 216.

15. From author's interviews and contemporary records.

16. Rashid, *Descent into Chaos*, p. 73.

17. Interviews with several retired C.I.A. officers familiar with Wood's work.

18. Interview with McLaughlin.

19. Grenier, *88 Days to Kandahar*, pp. 26–32.

20. Ibid., pp. 79–80.

21. All quotations, ibid., pp. 83–87. Grenier's thinking about making a deal or provoking a Pashtun uprising: Interview with Grenier.

22. All quotations, correspondence from Mahmud.

23. All quotations from author's interviews and contemporary records.

24. Ibid. The quotations in the paragraph beginning "Omar is frightened" are from a declassified State Department cable, Islamabad to Washington, September 24, 2001, obtained by the National Security Archive, George Washington University. Mahmud wrote in correspondence that he never found Omar to be frightened, although he was, at times, angry.

25. Schofield, *Inside the Pakistan Army*, pp. 63–64. Musharraf granted Schofield unusual access to conduct interviews with serving Pakistan Army officers in sensitive positions, including Tarar. Her book contains valuable transcriptions and insights.

26. Grenier, *88 Days to Kandahar*, p. 124.

27. Zaeef, *My Life with the Taliban*, pp. 154–55.

Chapter Four: Risk Management

1. "Rural mind": Interview with a former Taliban officeholder. Battlefield scene, "marvelous party . . . flower-like friend": Zaeef, *My Life with the Taliban*, pp. 42–43.

2. Zaeef, ibid., pp. 63–64.

3. Taliban Sources Project, "The Official Gazette," September 4, 2001.

4. Bashir Noorzai: "Draft Transcript" from Noorzai's interrogation by U.S. defense contractors, filed in *U.S. v. Bashir Noorzai*, United States District Court, Southern District of New York, 81 05 CR. 19. Omar's driver: Linschoten and Kuehn, *An Enemy We Created*, p. 179. Their portrait of the relationship between Bin Laden and Mullah Mohammad Omar, drawn from extensive interviews with Taliban leaders, is the most authoritative available in open sources.

5. "Doubtful": Ibid., p. 214. Crumpton: Author's interview. Taliban edict: Taliban Sources Project, "Mirwais Rahmani His Excellency Amir ul-Mumineen's Order."

6. Strick van Linschoten and Kuehn, *An Enemy We Created*, p. 226. "There was less . . . attack": Zaeef, *My Life with the Taliban*, p. 149. "Where is the evidence . . . supporting the criminal": Author's interview with Zaeef. "Just an excuse": Interview with Rahmani in 2010, in Kabul. He was assassinated in 2012. Taliban editorial of September 23: Taliban Sources Project, "Mirwais Rahmani Editorial: Does America Believe in Negotiations?" "They believed that power . . . defy the world": Author's interview with the former Taliban official.

7. This account of the classified Predator operation that was believed to target Mullah Mohammad Omar on October 7 is drawn primarily from interviews with more than half a dozen participants, including

Scott Swanson, the Predator pilot that night, and David Deptula, an Air Force general who watched the operation in Saudi Arabia and kept contemporaneous notes. In his excellent book *Predator*, the defense journalist Richard Whittle published a groundbreaking account of the operation. The investigative reporter Seymour Hersh broke the first news of the operation soon after it occurred, in *The New Yorker*. This chapter adds several new facts and perspectives, including an account of C.I.A. participation in the decision making, new details about the sequence of events, and details about Central Command decision making in Tampa. For an authoritative account of the September 17 Memorandum of Notification, see Rizzo, *Company Man*, pp. 172–74. Through a spokesman, Franks declined to comment beyond the account provided in his memoir, *American Soldier*.

8. Interviews with participants, ibid.
9. Ibid.
10. Ibid.
11. Franks, *American Soldier*, p. 293.
12. Deptula's notes, shared in an interview.
13. All quotations, author's interview.
14. Ibid.
15. "Will persuade . . .": Deptula's notes. All other quotations, author's interviews. All but one of the participating officers interviewed agreed that the Hellfire killed several presumed guerrillas. The other officer believed there had been no casualties, only that the empty truck was destroyed.
16. Rumsfeld: "Working Paper, October 22, 2001, 1:19 PM," declassified and released by the National Security Archive, George Washington University. Rumsfeld composed the note after Seymour Hersh broke news of the failed operation. Rumsfeld appears to have wanted to make a contemporaneous record of his own actions. Of Franks, he wrote, "I have a feeling he may not have given me the whole story."
17. Gardez, no significant Taliban leadership casualties: From interviews with participants.
18. "Our best human source . . . no response": Grenier, *88 Days to Kandahar*, p. 185. Zaeef, *My Life with the Taliban*, p. 161.
19. "It is very strange . . . Afghan bravery": Franco in Giustozz, *Decoding the Taliban*, p. 272.
20. Author's interviews with former Taliban office holders and Linschoten and Kuehn, *An Enemy We Created*, p. 225.
21. Interviews with C.T.C. officers.
22. Ibid.
23. Ibid.
24. Tenet, *At the Center of the Storm*, p. 263. "Deception indicated": Grenier, *88 Days to Kandahar*, p. 177.
25. "Where are the maps?": Author's interview. "The fact was . . . British maps": Rumsfeld, *Known and Unknown*, pp. 369–70.
26. Woodward, *Bush at War*, pp. 75–78, describes the "Going to War" slide package and its contents. The account here also relies on interviews with participants.
27. September 26: Schroen, *First In*, p. 78. "Given the nature of our world": "Working Paper, October 17, 2001, 11:25 AM," declassified and released, National Security Archive, George Washington University. "Windowless room": Crumpton, *The Art of Intelligence*, p. 175. Assignments: Interviews with former C.T.C. officers.
28. "We were all angry": Interview with Worthington. "When the hearings and the retribution": Interview with Black.
29. Schroen, *First In*, pp. 166–67. Schroen refers to Wood only as "Chris." The airstrip: Author's interviews and Schroen, *First In*, p. 145. All quotations, Schroen, ibid. Dialogue with Global Response Center: Schroen, ibid.
30. Episode with "Lucky": Author's interviews.
31. The description of Prado's work and the scene in the Situation Room is primarily from interviews with several people familiar with his proposal, his team, and the meeting. To my knowledge, the first published account of the presentation in the Situation Room and Cheney's approval was by the intelligence reporter and author Mark Mazzetti, in his book *The Way of the Knife*, p. 10.
32. Bush, *Decision Points*, p. 184. Crumpton, *The Art of Intelligence*, p. 213.

Chapter Five: Catastrophic Success

1. "Clean up": Interview with Dave Smith. "It's in Pakistan's interest": From contemporary records.
2. Ibid.
3. Interview with a European security officer assigned to Kabul during this period. Mahmud Ahmed insisted: Correspondence from Mahmud.

4. All quotations are from contemporary records.

5. Interviews with two Pakistani officials involved in the mission to Washington. See also Rashid, *Descent into Chaos*, p. 79. Blair made no mention of this episode in his memoir, but he was in Washington on November 7 and met Bush. In a press appearance describing what he discussed with Bush, he did not mention any effort at negotiations.

6. "Aggressive philistinism": Grenier, *88 Days to Kandahar*, p. 183.

7. "Felt strongly . . . more difficult": Ibid., p. 207. The essential conflict between Grenier and Schroen was first described in Woodward, *Bush at War*. The account here is informed by the memoirs of several participants as well as interviews with more than six participants.

8. "new, more moderate leadership . . . military one": Schroen, *First In*, p. 163. Schroen is apparently summarizing a contemporaneous cable from Islamabad.

9. "Taliban Bob": Interview with a colleague of Crumpton's. "Taken the side of . . . the southern question": Crumpton, *The Art of Intelligence*, p. 194.

10. "Pakistani drum song": Schroen, *First In*, p. 146. "a blueprint for failure . . . post-Taliban period": ibid., pp. 163–64. Watching on the balcony, "This is all the U.S. Air Force can do?": Interview with Schroen.

11. Kathy Gannon, Khaqzar's account of the Taliban meeting: Gannon, *I Is for Infidel*, pp. 106–7. Schroen, *First In*, pp. 343–44. Gary Berntsen, Schroen's successor leading the C.I.A. team in northern Afghanistan, held the meeting.

12. For a well-informed profile of Karzai's early life and family origins, see Rashid, *Descent into Chaos*. The author has interviewed Karzai twice individually and in groups on other occasions. The *Central Asian Survey* article is in the author's files. Although it is a relatively brief essay, it captures Karzai's preoccupations and his long commitment to Afghanistan's royal and tribal traditions amid various forms of ideological competition.

13. Karzai's arrest: Coll, *Ghost Wars*, p. 286. "Advice . . . nervous": Interview with a former Afghan officeholder involved.

14. Author's interview with the diplomat.

15. "I believed in the Taliban . . . I.S.I.": Rashid, *Descent into Chaos*, p. 14. Karzai wrote in correspondence that he "never met with Mullah Omar."

16. The portrait of Vogle is drawn from interviews with half a dozen colleagues who worked closely with him. References to his career can be found in several books, including those by Crumpton and Grenier, who refer to him only as "Greg." In Berntsen's *Jawbreaker* he appears as "Craig." In the journalist Eric Blehm's account of Hamid Karzai's 2001 guerrilla campaign, *The Only Thing Worth Dying For*, he appears as "Casper."

17. Crumpton, *The Art of Intelligence*, p. 143. Grenier, *88 Days to Kandahar*, p. 139.

18. The quotations here are from interviews with people familiar with Karzai's entry that fall. Grenier, ibid., pp. 145–46, provides a similar account.

19. Ibid., p. 146.

20. "Beyond scandal": Ibid., p. 190. "A lot of reconnaissance": Interview with Crumpton. About Grenier's criticism, Crumpton added, "I couldn't disagree more. . . . Our concern for their welfare was justified. We went as soon as we could. They were under fire when they were landing. . . . The timing was just about right." "Everyone in the U.S. government": Grenier, ibid., p. 194.

21. "Exploiting the absenteeism . . . few heavy weapons": Giustozzi and Ullah, "The Inverted Cycle." Abdul Latif's cook murdered him by poisoning: *The New York Times*, January 6, 2002. Rumors that he was a double agent: Chayes, *The Punishment of Virtue*, p. 67.

22. "That they were making a serious mistake": Grenier, *88 Days to Kandahar*, p. 216. "Posed to the Taliban . . . hazy at best": Ibid., p. 228.

23. Blehm, *The Only Thing Worth Dying For*, p. 129.

24. Interview with Dobbins. "We thought, If he's a Pashtun . . .": Interview with a senior Northern Alliance leader. See also Dobbins, *After the Taliban*.

25. Blehm, *The Only Thing Worth Dying For*, p. 296.

26. Rumsfeld, attendance at Naqibullah's meeting, Rubin, unpublished draft paper. Sherzai and Karzai: Chayes, *The Punishment of Virtue*, p. 60.

27. "Sadly, in terms of our policy . . . ": Interview with Crumpton. "Had been so discredited": Interview with Dobbins.

28. *The Guardian*, October 7, 2001.

29. Franks, *American Soldier*, p. 315.

30. "Drank . . . functional illiterate": Berntsen, *Jawbreaker*, pp. 28–29. Student of Schroen's, Farsi, terrorism operations: Interviews with former colleagues. "Grab-them-by-the-neck": *Jawbreaker*, p. 31. November 26 or 27, "Let's kill this baby": Interview with Berntsen.

31. Cheney: "Tora Bora Revisited: A Report to Members of the Committee on Foreign Relations," United States Senate, November 30, 2009. "Is there any way . . . miss their escape": Crumpton, *The Art of Intelligence*, p. 258.

32. "Almost screamed . . . what we have": Crumpton, ibid., pp. 259–60.

33. Bush, *Decision Points*, p. 202.

34. "I don't give . . . Screw that!": "Tora Bora Revisited."

35. Ibid.

36. DeLong: "Tora Bora Revisited." Edwards: Naylor, *Not a Good Day to Die*, p. 18.

37. "As though someone . . . get Bin Laden": Berntsen, *Jawbreaker*, pp. 297–98. "Done a magnificent . . . strong station chief": Crumpton, *The Art of Intelligence*, p. 261. "Sudden success . . .": Correspondence from Crumpton. "Pretty angry . . . performance": Interview with Berntsen. In correspondence, Crumpton provided a full account of his decision: "Gary was a brilliant and heroic commander, perfect for capturing Kabul and pursuing [Al Qaeda] leadership . . . and would have been a good [chief of station] . . . but I wanted the best so I made a change and selected Rich. If I may use an imperfect World War II analogy, George Marshall did not want Patton doing a job better suited for Eisenhower." The timing of the decision "was driven/dictated by our very success!" The Delta-C.I.A. team forward at Tora Bora killed "hundreds of enemy" and although the operation was "blemished by the failure to capture UBL," that was a function of military and national decision making, Crumpton wrote. He also noted, "Gary was a bluntly honest, profane and passionate battlefield leader but I never once heard a protest about this. . . . I was the commander and he was a rock-solid officer who followed orders. Simple."

38. "A pretty good determination": PBS *Frontline*, www.pbs.org/wgbh/pages/frontline/shows/campaign /interviews/franks.html. Daily memo, "The back door was open": Interview with Allen.

39. Bin Laden's will: Translation from "Tora Bora Revisited," ibid. Interview with Allen.

40. Central Command said it couldn't do it: Interview with Chamberlin. DeLong confirmed this later: "We didn't have the lift," he told Senate investigators. "Tora Bora Revisited."

41. "Tora Bora Revisited."

42. Cheney and Hadley: Bush, *Decision Points*, p. 189. Pentagon warning: Ibid., p. 197. The other risks Bush recalled being forecast before the war began included "mass starvation" in Afghanistan, "an outbreak of civil war" there, and "an uprising by Muslims around the world."

43. Conetta: "Operation Enduring Freedom." Crumpton: *The Art of Intelligence*, p. 260. Crawford: "Civilian Death and Injury in Afghanistan, 2001–2011," http://costsofwar.org/sites/default/files/Crawford AfghanistanCasualties.pdf. Dostum: John Barry, "The Death Convoy of Afghanistan," *Newsweek*, April 25, 2002. Ayoob Erfani, a representative of Dostum, said that "Dostum did not know what happened until a year later. . . . He was with [American] Special Forces in Kunduz. . . . He never ordered it. He never saw it. The commanders in the field, they [made] a decision to transfer" the prisoners.

44. BBC News, December 22, 2001.

Chapter Six: Small Change

1. The description of Kabul Station from that period is from interviews with people who worked there or visited. Naylor, *Not a Good Day to Die*, has a good description, and reports on the bomb dropped in 1997, p. 8.

2. Naylor, ibid., p. 21.

3. Wood was operations chief, thirty to forty case officers: Interviews with former officials familiar with Kabul Station.

4. Interviews with Afghan, American, and European officials familiar with the Omega Team operations.

5. Ibid.

6. Author's interview.

7. "It's a little like *Star Wars*": Interview with a former intelligence official involved. "The big question": Interview with Hurley.

8. "the last battle . . . people I talked to": Naylor, *Not a Good Day to Die*, p. 40. "We had estimates": Interview with Hurley. "Lost a couple . . . how many": Interview with the former intelligence official, ibid.

9. Rehearsals: Interview with Hagenbeck. Also, Naylor, *Not a Good Day to Die*, p. 60.

10. Jalalabad, Peshawar, Kandahar: Bush, *Decision Points*, p. 202. Tajik vendor: Interview with a former intelligence official involved. Imagery analysis of Pakistani regions: Interview with Allen. Members of Bin Laden's close protection party: Maloney, *Enduring the Freedom*, p. 65. The exhumation: *The New York Times*, May 8, 2002.

11. "Just to make sure": Interview with a colleague of Rodriguez.

12. All quotations, interviews with Krongard.

13. Ibid. After authorizing Prince to provide support to Kabul Station, Krongard said he had nothing more to do with Blackwater business while at C.I.A.

14. Gem shows, Concorde: Author's interviews. A former senior American intelligence official quoted Arif as saying he had flown the Concorde more than a dozen times, an estimate cited by a former Afghan intelligence figure as well. In an e-mail, Arif said there was but one instance, out of necessity: "I was supposed to attend a meeting in Paris [at] a specific time and date. . . . Due to the importance of the meeting I was forced to fly by [Concorde] to Paris. That was the only time."

15. From interviews with American and Afghan intelligence officials. Arif's Dari memoir, *9 wa 11 Siptambir*, has a different but overlapping account of his travel to the United States during this period. Suspicions subsided, "Everyone knew . . .": Interview with the colleague.

16. Background of the Afghan intelligence service: Interviews with four Afghan intelligence officials who served in different periods and a European security officer who studied the service.

17. All quotations, $15 million, hundreds of intelligence officers: Author's interviews with Afghan intelligence officials.

18. All quotations, e-mail from Arif.

19. Author's interview.

20. Amy Belasco, "Troop Levels in the Afghan and Iraq Wars." The number rose later in the year, according to military planners.

21. Todd Marzano, "Criticisms Associated with Operation Anaconda." About the lack of unity of command, Hagenbeck said in an interview that General Tommy Franks, his superior at Central Command, "didn't think it would be an issue, but it was." Through a spokesman, Franks declined to comment for this book.

22. Interview with Hagenbeck. Naylor, *Not a Good Day to Die*, p. 375.

23. U.S. Special Forces initially entered the shuttered embassy. The career foreign service officer Ryan Crocker arrived as the first chargé d'affaires. This description of the embassy's condition in late winter is mainly from interviews with Sedney and Finn.

24. Interview with Sedney.

25. "Laughable": Zakheim, *A Vulcan's Tale*, p. 168. "We are not fielding . . . mission clearly": Ibid., p. 129. "You get what you pay for": Interview with Finn.

26. Champagne quotations: Rubin, *Afghanistan from the Cold War Through the War on Terror*, p. 21. Zakheim, *A Vulcan's Tale*, pp. 168–70.

27. "What in retrospect . . . thirty-five thousand dollars": Interview with Sedney. Conditions at the Intercontinental, "There was optimism . . . bring peace" and Kabul University: Fayez, *An Undesirable Element*, p. 65. Bactrian gold objects: *The New York Times*, December 5, 2006.

28. Author's interview with a Western diplomat. "Very respectful": Correspondence from Karzai.

29. "I am calling you . . . very sensitive": Interview with Khalilzad. Karzai kept a car: Interview with Sedney. "The king . . . everybody what to do": Interview with Finn.

30. All quotations, interview with Finn.

31. Interview with Sedney.

32. Rumsfeld-Blee: Interview with a former official present at the meeting. Author's interview. "Do two things," no written campaign plan, no guidance about the A.N.A.'s ultimate size: Interview with McNeill.

33. Bush, *Decision Points*, p. 207.

34. "Don't build Bondsteels": Interview with McNeill. "Anything here . . . not staying long": Interview with McChrystal. "Mafia-owned bar": McChrystal, *My Share of the Task*, p. 77.

35. Karzai and Fahim wanted 250,000: Interview with McNeill.

36. Ibid.

37. "That really got the attention": Former senior military officer who reviewed the attack at the time. False story: *New York Times*, June 13, 2002, quoting Rear Admiral Craig Quigley of Central Command and Colonel Roger King at Bagram saying that investigators had "ruled out" hostile fire as a cause of the incident.

Chapter Seven: Taliban for Karzai

1. Dog fighting: Chayes, *The Punishment of Virtue*, p. 67. Punched people when agitated, knife fight with Mullah Omar, "motherfucker": Peter Maas, "Gul Agha Gets His Province Back, *The New York Times Magazine*, January 6, 2002. The F-word is not explicit, per *Times* style, but strongly implied. Both the Maas profile and the Chayes book are essential journalism about Kandahar after the Taliban.

2. Maloney, *Enduring the Freedom*, p. 189.

3. "A poor listener . . . weak administrator": Kabul to Washington, May 22, 2008, WikiLeaks. Marriages, children, "because she had heard so many good things": Kabul to Washington, January 20, 2009, WikiLeaks. Appeared with boy dressed as a female: Interview with a Western diplomat in Kabul.

4. Spin Boldak revenue, Sherzai's monopolies: Giustozzi and Ullah, "The Inverted Cycle." Cement plant: Chayes, *The Punishment of Virtue*, p. 162. $1.5 million a month: Rashid, *Descent into Chaos*, p. 136. Fifty-two of sixty: Giustozzi and Ullah, "The Inverted Cycle."

5. Affidavit of Bashir Noorzai, *U.S. v. Bashir Noorzai*, United States District Court, Southern District of New York, 81 05 CR. 19, August 8, 2007.

6. Ibid.

7. "Many people take advantage . . . harm their rivals": Transcripts of Noorzai's interviews with American contractors, filed as court documents in *U.S. v. Bashir Noorzai*. In a bizarre sequence of events, two private contractors collecting intelligence for the Pentagon interviewed Noorzai and several of his associates over several days in Dubai in August 2004. They later persuaded Noorzai to travel on to New York the following year. Drug Enforcement Agency agents interviewed him further at a hotel while C.I.A. and F.B.I. personnel listened secretly in an adjoining room. The records of both conversations provide fascinating if fragmentary insights into the Taliban, Gul Agha Sherzai's predatory regime, and American struggles in Kandahar after the Taliban's fall. At the end of the final interviews, the D.E.A. arrested Noorzai on heroin trafficking charges. He was convicted at trial and sentenced to life in prison in 2009.

8. "Beat up . . . made him a hero": Dubai transcripts, ibid.

9. All quotations, Norzai Affidavit and Dubai transcripts, ibid.

10. "Look, the Bonn Conference . . . how to do this": Interview with the American official. "Convinced him": Norzai Affidavit, Dubai transcripts.

11. The account of the C.I.A.'s negotiation with Mutawakil and Archibald's presentation come from interviews with two former U.S. officials familiar with the episode, as do all of the quotations. Archibald declined to comment.

12. All quotations, ibid.

13. All quotations, Noorzai Affidavit.

14. Interview with a senior military officer then deployed in Afghanistan.

15. "CID Report of Investigation," 0064-2004-CID369-69280-5C1N/5Y2E, October 25, 2004, accessed from American Civil Liberties Union database. The Army investigator concluded that he could neither prove nor disprove the specific detainee abuse allegations he had received.

16. Interview with Muñoz.

17. Windsor et al., *Kandahar Tour*, pp. 24–25.

18. Ibid., p. 25.

19. State Department cable, Kabul to Washington, April 18, 2003, WikiLeaks.

20. Rashid, *Descent into Chaos*, p. 250.

21. Interview with Paul Miller, a former C.I.A. analyst and director for Afghanistan at the National Security Council during the Bush administration. In 2008, Miller and a colleague searched their archives to create a chronology of National Security Council principals and deputies meetings held on Afghanistan during the Bush years.

Chapter Eight: The Enigma

1. Kayani in Hawaii: Interview with Shapiro. Fort Leavenworth thesis, National Defense University performance: Interviews with Dave Smith and other U.S. officials who studied Kayani's career.

2. Interviews with U.S. officials who studied Kayani's family connections. Kayani did not respond to requests for comment for this book.

3. All quotations, interview with Smith.

4. Disneyland, "a very smart, intelligent guy": Interview with Smith.

5. Grenier, *88 Days to Kandahar*, p. 290. Grenier's estimate of the number arrested is the most authoritative I have been able to identify. Eventually, Pakistani arrests of Arab and other foreign fighters in 2002 and 2003 may have totaled several hundred.

6. Ibid., p. 318.

7. All quotations, interview with Shapiro.

8. Ibid.

9. All quotations, interview with Crumpton.

10. Interview with McLaughlin.

11. All quotations, interviews with Smith.

12. Ibid.

13. The family biographical details and dates here are from Vahid Brown and Don Rassler's authoritative book about the Haqqanis, *Fountainhead of Jihad*, pp. 28–45. The book draws substantially on translations of Haqqani publications. "His background . . . his personality": Interview with Rocketi.

14. Twelve thousand tons: Yousaf, *The Bear Trap.*

15. Brown and Rassler, op.cit. Case officer operating under nonofficial cover: Interview with a former U.S. official involved in the program.

16. CARE schools: Brown and Rassler, *Fountainhead of Jihad*, p. 108.

17. Ibid., p. 123.

18. All quotations, author's interviews.

19. All quotations, interview with McChrystal.

20. Author's interviews. C.I.A. Document: "C.I.A. Comments on the Senate Select Committee on Intelligence Report on the Rendition, Detention, and Interrogation Program," June 27, 2013, Conclusion 1, p. 3. The document refers to the episode in several partially redacted sentences: "The case of Ibrahim Haqqani is also instructive. The U.S. Military captured him in Afghanistan on 4 May 2003 and brought him to [redacted]. Following review at Headquarters and subsequent direction, [redacted] Station transferred him to [redacted] custody after eight days while working out approvals and logistics for subsequent transfer to U.S. Military custody . . . because Headquarters judged that he did not merit detention by the C.I.A." The redacted words appear to be *Bagram, Kabul,* and *N.D.S.,* respectively.

Chapter Nine: "His Rules Were Different Than Our Rules"

1. The description of operations on the forward bases is from the author's interviews with multiple individuals who served there or visited. All quotations from an interview with an experienced participant. *Mukhalafeen:* Akbar and Burton, *Come Back to Afghanistan*, p. 186. Akbar's account of Abdul Wali's death and the quotations attributed to him in this chapter are mainly drawn from his testimony at the trial of *U.S. v. David A. Passaro,* United States District Court, Eastern District of North Carolina, 5: 04-CR-211-1, which also provides a valuable, on-the-record portrait of the Omega Teams and their environment at the time. Akbar's 2005 memoir with Susan Burton also provides valuable texture.

2. Base description, "Third World cesspool": Trial testimony of Brian Halstead, *U.S. v. David A. Passaro,* ibid.

3. Ibid.

4. Ibid.

5. *Zamanat,* all quotations, trial testimony of Hyder Akbar, *U.S. v. David A. Passaro.*

6. Ibid.

7. Eighty-five percent of C.I.A. interrogators were contractors: "Committee Study of the Central Intelligence Agency's Detention and Interrogation Program," p. 12. Out-of-shape Sylvester Stallone, Jones left after ten or fifteen minutes: Hyder Akbar trial testimony, ibid.

8. "Is there anything . . . tell the truth": Akbar, ibid.

9. "His rules . . . permanent injury": Trial testimony of Matthew Johnson, *U.S. v. David Passaro.*

10. "Got a chair . . . get worse": Ibid.

11. Memorandum of Notification did not mention detention, all cable and memoranda quotations, S.S.C.I., "Committee Study," pp. 11–12.

12. There are numerous published accounts of the C.I.A.'s Rendition, Detention and Interrogation Program before and after 2001. Benjamin and Simon, *The Age of Sacred Terror* and *The Next Attack* provide the perspective of two influential counterterrorism advisers during the Clinton administration.

13. "We couldn't control . . . questions," and about seventy prisoners during the Clinton years: Rodriguez, *Hard Measures,* pp. 51–53.

14. Prado and S.E.R.E.: Interviews with former intelligence officials. Jessen could not be reached for comment and an attorney of record said he was "not able" to pass requests for comment. The S.S.C.I. "Committee Study," p. 21, wrote of Mitchell and Jessen, "Neither psychologist had experience as an interrogator, nor did either have specialized knowledge of Al Qaeda, a background in terrorism or any relevant regional cultural or linguistic experience." In an interview, Mitchell disputed this characterization, saying that he had extensive experience of interrogations at Fort Bragg and received daily intelligence briefings on Al Qaeda after consulting for the C.I.A. in 2001. "My background was in resisting interrogations," Mitchell said. He had also taken "courses in law enforcement." The paper by Jessen and Mitchell is "Recognizing and Developing Countermeasures to Al Qaeda Resistance to Interrogation Techniques: A Resistance Training Perspective." A heavily redacted version was entered as evidence in *Salim v. Mitchell,* CV-15-0286, United States District Court, Eastern District of Washington. In court filings, Jessen and Mitchell denied that they "committed torture, cruel, inhuman and degrading treatment, non-consensual human experimentation and/or war crimes." The lawsuit ended in an

undisclosed settlement in August 2017. Origins of learned helplessness hypothesis: *The New Yorker*, January 14, 2015.

15. Intercepts, task force: Rodriguez, *Hard Measures*, pp. 44–45.

16. PowerPoint presentation, all quotations: S.S.C.I. "Committee Study," p. 22.

17. Tenet briefed Rice and Hadley, who in turn briefed Bush: Interviews with senior officials involved.

18. Proposed conditions for Zubaydah: Ibid., p. 26. "Tremendous influence": Ibid., p. 27. Mitchell later defended: Interview with Mitchell.

19. All quotations, "Committee Study," p. 28.

20. "I did not volunteer . . . all the time": Interview with Black. How some saw his departure: Interviews with former intelligence officials.

21. "To many insiders . . . Middle East hand": Rodriguez, *Hard Measures*, p. 78. "A very biased and unfair": Ibid., p. 28. Funny, sent others to Capitol Hill briefings: Mudd, *Takedown*, pp. 105–6.

22. "Political correctness": Rodriguez, *Hard Measures*, p. 11. "We were under . . . the essence": Ibid., p. 62. Prado: Interviews with participants.

23. "More aggressive" and "thirty days": "Committee Study," p. 62. Mitchell's list, "The thing that is rumored . . . had no idea": Interview with Mitchell.

24. Interviews with former F.B.I. and intelligence officials. "The torture memos": http://nsarchive.gwu .edu/NSAEBB/NSAEBB127/02.08.01.pdf.

25. "A hysteria. . . . the consensus": Author's interview. "We were flying blind . . . what they were doing": Author's interview. Gates: Schmitt and Shanker, *Counterstrike*, p. 230.

26. Interview with Rodriguez. "Were blacked out . . . human waste": "Committee Study," p. 49.

27. "Has issues": Ibid., p. 50. "Sleep deprivation . . . rough treatment," Jessen recommended, Rahman's death: Ibid., p. 54. Jessen has denied any responsibility for Rahman's death.

28. "Many of the same . . . Rahman's death": Ibid., p. 55.

29. According to Mitchell, "We asked for permission to stop using [enhanced interrogation techniques], especially the waterboard. To our surprise, however, headquarters ordered us to continue waterboarding him. . . . At one point Bruce [Jessen] and I pushed back hard and threatened to quit. . . . The officers we were dealing with—mid-level C.T.C. officials—really pissed us off by saying, 'You've lost your spines.' They insisted that if we didn't keep waterboarding . . . and another attack happened in the United States, it would be 'your fault.'" Mitchell, *Enhanced Interrogation*, pp. 72–73. Discovery in a lawsuit filed by the A.C.L.U. against Mitchell and Jessen produced a C.I.A. cable from August 28, 2002, in which C.I.A. personnel at the prison, referring to pressure from ALEC to continue waterboarding, argued, "It is our assessment that if we proceed again to the waterboard, on a general threat question with nothing concrete to focus on, we will risk losing even minimal cooperation afterwards." Rodriguez said in an interview that the reason C.T.C. pressed for more waterboarding was that its analysts possessed "a bunch of videotapes" prerecorded by Abu Zubaydah to "celebrate yet another attack on the U.S." and they felt he was not forthcoming about planning for additional attacks. Eventually, the C.I.A. agreed that Zubaydah was "compliant" and stopped waterboarding him.

30. Tenet, Muller, Rodriguez quotations: Ibid., p. 57.

31. Tenet's December 2002 cable: Trial testimony of Marilyn Dorn, *U.S. v. David A. Passaro*. "Feasible": S.S.C.I. "Committee Study," p. 63.

32. E-mail home: Trial testimony of "Steven Jones," *U.S. v. David A. Passaro*.

33. Trial testimony of Kevin Gatten, *U.S. v. David A. Passaro*.

34. All quotations, ibid.

35. Ibid.

36. Ibid.

37. Ibid.

38. All "Jones" quotations from his trial testimony.

39. All quotations, Passaro's account: Akbar and Burton, *Come Back to Afghanistan*, p. 194.

40. Ibid., pp. 196–98.

Chapter Ten: Mr. Big

1. Interviews with Khalilzad. See also Khalilzad, *The Envoy*, pp. 26–35.

2. Didn't get along with Rumsfeld: Interview with Khalilzad. Rumsfeld: *Known and Unknown*, p. 683.

3. All quotations are from interviews with Khalilzad and nine other former Kabul embassy officials, as well as military officers then in Afghanistan, N.S.C. staff in Washington, and officials at the U.S. embassy in Islamabad. See also Khalilzad, *The Envoy*, pp. 176–89. "Sad and angry": Ibid., p. 175. "Great politician": Ibid., p. 180. "You have your politics": Interview with a former White House official who attended videoconferences between Bush and Karzai.

4. Interview with Harriman.

5. Interview with Barno.

6. Interview with McGowan. McGowan said she recalled being told that security personnel "went back to the scene later." Khalilzad wrote later that after hearing about the incident, he and Barno "decided to put into place new rules to make the protective detail less apt to ride roughshod over civilians." A State Department official said, "As a matter of security, we do not comment on motorcade procedures."

7. *USA Today*, November 27, 2003.

8. "Always ended": Interview with Khalilzad. "*None* of us . . .": Interview with McGowan.

9. DynCorp: Interview with Katherine Brown, an aide to Khalilzad. After "consultation": Correspondence from Karzai. Reading cables: Interviews with U.S. officials familiar with the episodes. In correspondence, Karzai denied that Khalilzad ever attended cabinet meetings.

10. "Are unfair . . . organizational corruption" and $6.5 million, plus support for operations: E-mail from Arif.

11. Salaries frozen: Interview with a senior Afghan intelligence official involved. Schroen: *First In*, p. 357.

12. Interview with Khalilzad.

13. E-mail from Arif. Interview with Saleh.

14. Interview with Saleh.

15. Interview with Barno.

16. Interview with Khalilzad.

17. Ibid., see also Khalilzad, *The Envoy*, pp. 201–3. A Dostum representative said, "Obviously, he does not deny he drinks. But drinking and then calling President Karzai, of course, he denies. He doesn't drink anymore. . . . He has diabetes, high blood pressure. But yes, he loves drinking." As to the account about the B-1, the representative said that Dostum never felt threatened, did not believe the Americans tried to intimidate him, and was pleased that the demands he made about local politics were eventually agreed to by Karzai.

18. All quotations, interview with Khalilzad.

19. All quotations, interview with Barno.

20. Interview with Longhi. E-mail from Khalilzad. Also, *Lawrence Longhi v. Khaled Monawar*, Superior Court of New Jersey, Morris County, L-2619-09. In response to a request for comment, Monawar wrote an e-mail referring to the public court records "as the best place" for an account of the matter and declined further comment.

21. "Discussions took place . . . resources project": Affidavit of Larry Longhi, *Longhi v. Monawar.* "A great idea": Chronology prepared by Longhi, author's files. An attorney for Michael Baker Corp. wrote, "It is my client's policy not to comment on litigation. All that I will say is that Michael Baker has always maintained that Mr. Longhi's claims against it are without merit. That position is supported by the court's entry of a summary judgment order dismissing Mr. Longhi's lawsuit against my client."

22. "Who Is Afgamco?": copy of slide in author's files. "Mr. Big": E-mail records shared by Longhi.

Chapter Eleven: Ambassador vs. Ambassador

1. Taliban circular: Interview with a senior military officer who studied the document at the time. The prevailing view at the embassy: Interview with Sedney.

2. Interview with Barno.

3. All quotations, author's interviews, except "double game," Khalilzad, *The Envoy*, p. 183.

4. Interviews with Powell.

5. Interview with Khalilzad.

6. Interview with Musharraf, with thanks to David Bradley, who arranged the session, which was also attended by other journalists.

7. Interview with the official.

8. All quotations, interview with Khalilzad.

9. Ibid.

10. All quotations, interview with Porch. His books include *The Conquest of Morocco* (1983), *The Conquest of the Sahara* (1984), and *The French Foreign Legion* (1991).

11. All quotations, ibid. Cambridge University Press published *Counterinsurgency* in 2013.

12. Ibid.

13. All quotations, interview with McChrystal, except "We don't know," interview with Porch.

14. Interview with McChrystal.

15. All quotations, interview with Barno.

16. "We're going to get Bin Laden": Interview with Porch.

17. All quotations, interviews with McChrystal and Porch.

18. This account of the transition, and all quotations, come from interviews with several individuals involved, who asked not to be further identified.

19. Hassan Ghul: S.S.C.I. report, p. 371.

20. Interview with Musharraf.

21. Author's interview with the participant.

22. Schofield, *Inside the Pakistan Army*, p. 144.

23. Interviews with the intelligence official, Musharraf, and other American and Pakistani officials involved.

24. Ibid.

25. Mazzetti, Rashid, and other journalists have chronicled Mohammad's killing.

26. "These votes . . . to help": *The New York Times*, November 5, 2004. "Made frequent reference . . . Nashville": State Department cable, Kabul to Washington, November 24, 2005, WikiLeaks.

27. Interviews with Khalilzad, Khalid Farooqi of Hezb-i-Islami, the former Taliban officeholder Arsala Rahmani, and a second former Taliban officeholder involved.

28. Interview with Barno.

29. Interview with Miller.

Chapter Twelve: Digging a Hole in the Ocean

1. Interview with Afghan officials familiar with N.D.S. during this period.

2. Ibid. Kayani did not respond to a request for comment for this book. American officials involved with the efforts to promote cooperation between I.S.I. and N.D.S. confirmed the gist of this tetchy relationship. WikiLeaks cables document several efforts to promote cross-border intelligence sharing during this period and the mutual suspicions that hindered such work.

3. Interview with a senior Afghan official. Rubin, "Saving Afghanistan," summarized and quoted briefly from the study.

4. All quotations, ibid.

5. Rubin, "Saving Afghanistan."

6. Interview with Saleh. Karzai wrote in correspondence that he "can't recall" the findings presented in Saleh's paper.

7. Interview with Kilcullen.

8. Ibid.

9. Interviews with Kilcullen, as well as American and Pakistani military officers. At one point, the United States agreed to supply night-vision goggles to Pakistani forces in the F.A.T.A. but only if they signed the equipment out and returned it immediately after use, like library books. That compromise only deepened Pakistani resentment about how little they were trusted.

10. Interview with Art Keller, a C.I.A. case officer deployed to Pakistan at the time.

11. Ibid.

12. "Stirred up a hornet's nest": State Department cable, Islamabad to Washington, March 10, 2006, WikiLeaks. "Dave, I'm sitting on a powder keg": Interview with Kilcullen. Crocker confirmed the conversation.

13. Interview with a Bush administration official.

14. Interview with Kilcullen.

15. Ibid.

16. "Remarks by President Bush and Prime Minister Manmohan Singh," March 2, 2006, New Delhi, http://2001-2009.state.gov/p/sca/rls/rm/2006/62426.htm.

17. "India Civil Nuclear Cooperation: Responding to Critics," White House release, March 8, 2006, http://georgewbush-whitehouse.archives.gov/news/releases/2006/03/text/20060308-3.html.

18. Decoy convoy: Bush, *Decision Points*, p. 214. See also: State Department cable, Islamabad to Washington, March 29, 2006, WikiLeaks.

19. State Department cable, Islamabad to Washington, April 14, 2006, WikiLeaks.

20. See Clarke, ed., "The Afghan Papers: Committing Britain to War in Helmand, 2005–06," Royal United Services Institute, December 8, 2011. For a thorough Canadian account, see Stein and Lang, *The Unexpected War*.

21. State Department cable, Kabul to Washington, January 11, 2006, WikiLeaks.

22. Interview with Lynch.

23. Akhundzada and opium: *The New York Times*, October 4, 2008. Helmand: Farrell and Giustozzi, "The Taliban at War," pp. 845–71.

24. Ibid.

25. Hennessey, *Kandak*, p. 240.

26. Clarke, "The Afghan Papers," p. 16. "We would be perfectly happy . . .": BBC News, April 24, 2006.

27. Chandrasekaran, *Little America*, p. 48.

28. Clarke, "The Afghan Papers."

29. Ibid.

30. Blatchford, *Fifteen Days*, p. 3.

31. Ibid., pp. 8–12.

32. Horn, *No Lack of Courage*, p. 35.

33. "To defeat . . . traditional areas": Ibid., p. 27. "Charred pieces . . . insurgency here": Smith, *The Dogs Are Eating Them Now*, p. 46.

34. Horn, *No Lack of Courage*, p. 27.

35. Bradley and Maurer, *The Lions of Kandahar*, pp. 101–2.

36. Horn, *No Lack of Courage*, p. 114.

37. State Department cable, Kabul to Washington, April 24, 2006, WikiLeaks.

38. State Department cable, Peshawar to Washington, September 6, 2006, WikiLeaks.

39. All quotations, State Department cable, Kabul to Washington, September 11, 2006.

40. Bush, *Decision Points*, p. 215. Rice, *No Higher Honor*, pp. 444–45.

41. Bush: *Decision Points*, p. 208. First deterioration in 2005, "I had a very good relationship . . . experienced later": BBC Interview, October 3, 2013.

42. All quotations, author's interviews with officials familiar with the events.

43. Ibid.

44. Ibid.

Chapter Thirteen: Radicals

1. British security contacted I.S.I.: "Operation Overt: The Trans-Atlantic Airlines Liquid Bombs Plot," draft chapter by Marc Sageman for his forthcoming book about terrorism cases in Britain. Sageman obtained extensive trial transcripts and other court materials from which his account is drawn. The author is deeply grateful to him for sharing these materials and citations. Rodriguez, *Hard Measures*, confirms aspects of the narrative constructed from trial testimony. Nic Robertson, Paul Cruickshank, and Tim Lister added considerably to the record with their April 30, 2012, report for CNN about a written account by Rashid Rauf about his involvement in both the Underground bombings and the planes bombing conspiracy. The author also conducted interviews with British and American officials involved with the case. A C.I.A. drone reportedly killed Rauf in North Waziristan in November 2008. About 825,000 people of Pakistani origin in England circa 2006: "The Pakistani Muslim Community in England," The Change Institute, Department for Communities and Local Government, March 2009, p. 6. "At least a quarter of a million people": Ibid., p. 53.

2. Sageman, ibid., from trial transcripts.

3. Ibid.

4. Robertson, Cruickshank, and Lister, CNN report, 2012.

5. All quotations, Sageman from Ali's trial testimony. At his trial, Ali admitted his involvement in the preparations but claimed the entire plot was merely to be a harmless demonstration, a kind of theater for political ends, and would not have taken lives. He was convicted and sentenced to at least forty years in prison.

6. All quotations from author's interviews.

7. "Clandestine technical resources . . . too rashly": Rodriguez, *Hard Measures*, pp. 6–7.

8. Ibid., pp. 3–7.

9. Author's interviews.

10. Sageman, from court records.

11. "Compilation of Usama Bin Ladin Statements 1994–January 2004."

12. *The Guardian*: www.theguardian.com/alqaida/page/0,12643,839823,00.html.

13. IntelCenter, "Al Qaeda Messaging Statistics."

14. All translations from the Taliban Sources Project archive.

15. Ibid.

16. Ibid.

17. Ibid.

18. Ibid.

19. Waltz, *Warrior Diplomat*, p. 212.

20. This summary of how ALEC Station analysis evolved is from the author's interviews with half a dozen U.S. intelligence and other officials familiar with its work.

21. "You might kill . . . invading Pakistan": Mazzetti, *The Way of the Knife*, p. 116. Clandestine raid in early 2006: Interview with a senior military officer involved. Mazzetti, pp. 134–35, reported on a clandestine raid in January 2006 against an Al Qaeda compound in Damadola, in the Bajaur agency of the F.A.T.A., that was unannounced at the time. He is probably describing the same raid. The account here is also informed by interviews with former senior U.S. officials involved.

22. "Inroads": Bergen, *Manhunt*, p. 90. Flora and coded messages: Author's interviews. See also Bergen, ibid., p. 83. "When a bird could be heard chirping on one tape, a German ornithologist was called in to analyze the chirps. . . . None of the forensic work . . . ever yielded a useful lead," Bergen writes.

23. Grenier, *88 Days to Kandahar*, p. 377. Interviews with former C.I.A. officials familiar with Goss's experience.

24. "Among the very best . . . handful to manage": Grenier, ibid., p. 379.

25. Ibid., pp. 379–80. Interview with Grenier.

26. Going unilateral as early as 2005: Interviews with senior British intelligence officers who worked with the C.I.A. Task Force Orange, analysts from military reserves, N.S.A. teams: Interview with a senior military officer involved. Predator drones going exclusively to Iraq circa 2005: Grenier, *88 Days to Kandahar*, p. 391. (It was not until Robert Gates became defense secretary in 2007 that drone production increased and the demands of the Iraq war began to ease somewhat.) Uzbek prisoner interrogation, map of Al Qaeda facilities in North Waziristan: Interview with the senior military officer.

27. All quotations, interviews with Hayden and colleagues of Hayden at the C.I.A.

28. "Old Yale . . .": Author's interview.

29. All quotations, ibid.

30. C.T.C.'s budget ran into the billions and was by far the largest organization at C.I.A.: Grenier, *88 Days to Kandahar*, p. 377. "Brilliant operational thinker . . . run at his speed": Author's interview.

31. All Hayden quotations: "A Conversation with Michael Hayden," Council on Foreign Relations, September 7, 2007. Hayden's thinking and approach: Interview with Hayden.

Chapter Fourteen: Suicide Detectives

1. All quotations are from interviews with Williams or unclassified materials from his study.

2. Williams recorded 149 suicide bombings in Afghanistan during 2006. Rashid, *Descent into Chaos*, cites 141, p. 236. *Al Samood:* Taliban Archives, January 6, 2006.

3. Williams, "Mullah Omar's Missiles: A Field Report on Suicide Bombers in Afghanistan," Middle East Policy Council, 2007. The translated quotations from Dadullah are from the Middle East Research Institute, Special Dispatch Series, June 2, 2006, No. 1180, as cited by Williams. In 2006, according to Williams's figures, of the 149 suicide bombings in Afghanistan, 48 took place in Kandahar, where Dadullah Lang helped oversee the Taliban's offensive against Canadian troops, and 24 took place in Khost, the Haqqani stronghold. The Pakistani journalist Syed Shahzad, writing in *Le Monde Diplomatique* in 2006, reported that Dadullah recruited suicide bombers from "Uzbekistan, Tajikistan and Pakistan, as well as Waziristan." British Special Forces and N.A.T.O. aircraft located and killed Dadullah in Helmand in the summer of 2007. According to Stanley McChrystal, Special Forces found him by tracking one of Dadullah's brothers after he was released from prison. See also Giustozzi: "Military Adaptation by the Taliban, 2002–2011," in Farrell, Osinga, and Russel (eds.), *Military Adaptation in Afghanistan*, p. 254. McChrystal, *My Share of the Task*, p. 265.

4. Interviews with Williams.

5. Ibid.

6. "We ought to take a look": Interview with Tony Harriman, then codirector of the Afghan Inter-Agency Operations Group and senior director for Afghanistan at the National Security Council. Paul Miller, who joined the N.S.C. to work on Afghanistan in September 2007, also described the review's essential findings in an interview.

7. Neumann, *The Other War*, p. 168.

8. Interview with Harriman. "We cannot win": Neumann, *The Other War*, p. 145. "Pleased to find . . . do more": Waltz, *Warrior Diplomat*, p. 194.

9. Neumann, *The Other War*, p. 145. "I have wondered in retrospect if we should have asked for more," he wrote later. "Perhaps, after years of unsuccessfully pushing uphill for additional resources, we did not think as expansively as we should have. In any event, it is unlikely that we could have gotten more." Ibid., p. 161. "Got pretty cranky": Interview with Gastright. See also Bush, *Decision Points*, pp. 210–11, and Gates, *Duty*, p. 200. Ultimately, Gates raised the U.S. troop level in Afghanistan to 25,000 by the end of 2007 through the extension of a deployment by the Tenth Mountain Division, but he concluded that he could not do more because of Iraq. In his memoir, Bush describes ordering a troop increase to 31,000 but does not acknowledge that this level was not achieved until April 2008, about eighteen months after the initial decision.

10. Interview with Miller. William Wood, who succeeded Neumann as U.S. ambassador in Kabul during 2007, recalled in an interview a similar scale of total increase in security spending, classified and unclassified, during this period.

11. "President Bush Discusses Progress in Afghanistan, Global War on Terror," http://georgewbush-whitehouse.archives.gov/news/releases/2007/02/20070215-1.html.

12. Gates, *Duty*, p. 197.
13. Interview with Williams.
14. Ibid.
15. Ibid.
16. Bajwa, *Inside Waziristan*, p. 51. His book, published in Pakistan, also contains photos of the facility.
17. Ibid., pp. 48–50.
18. All quotations, interview with Beg.
19. Interview with Zeboulon Taintor, a New York University psychiatrist who worked with suicide bomber recruits in Pakistan.
20. Interview with Williams.
21. All quotations, ibid. Between 2007 and 2010, the number of Taliban attacks using improvised explosives rose from just over 2,200 to more than 14,000. During the same period, the number of suicide bombings remained steady at just over 100 per year.

Chapter Fifteen: *Plan Afghanistan*

1. Rose by about a quarter: "National Drug Control Strategy." It estimates that between 2002 and 2004, opium production increased from 3,400 metric tons to 4,200 tons. Just over 400,000 acres in 2006: "Afghanistan Opium Survey 2006." Just over 90 percent of world supply: "Interagency Assessment of the Counternarcotics Program in Afghanistan." More than three million Afghans: "Afghanistan Opium Survey 2008." $30 versus $500: Jon Lee Anderson, "The Taliban's Opium War," *The New Yorker*, July 9, 2007. Estimated export value, estimated farm gate value: "Afghanistan Opium Survey 2008."
2. Interview with Michael Braun.
3. Ibid.
4. Fearon, "Why Do Some Civil Wars Last So Much Longer Than Others?," pp. 275–301.
5. Interview with Braun.
6. All quotations, interviews with Long and Wankel.
7. This summary of the intelligence debate is from interviews with multiple analysts and policy makers involved. The U.N.'s annual "Afghanistan Opium Survey" provides considerable detail in unclassified documents.
8. Interview with Long.
9. Bush and McNeill, all quotations: Interview with McNeill. Urgent cabinet meeting: Thomas Schweich, "Is Afghanistan a Narco-State?," *The New York Times*, July 27, 2008. More than $1 billion: "Afghanistan Drug Control."
10. Interview with Walters.
11. State Department cable, Kabul to Washington, February 9, 2007, WikiLeaks. The discussion took place on January 28, the day after the "urgent cabinet meeting" on the Afghan opium problem described by Schweich.
12. Rice, *No Higher Honor*, p. 446. After initially granting an interview, Wood did not respond to multiple follow-up requests for comment.
13. Cowper-Coles, *Cables from Kabul*, pp. 18–19. 400,000 acres sprayed aerially in Colombia in 2006: *The New York Times*, May 14, 2015.
14. All quotations, interview with Schweich. Wood said in an interview that while he did advocate for aerial spraying, "I was speculating" and carrying out White House policy.
15. Cowper-Coles, *Cables from Kabul*, and author's interviews with Cowper-Coles.
16. "National Drug Control Strategy." Karzai: *Meet the Press*, September 25, 2006.
17. Task Force 333: Peters, *Seeds of Terror*, p. 120. Also, interview with a senior British national security official involved in the drug policy debates. MI6 frustrations: Interviews with two former British intelligence officers involved.
18. E.P.A. assessment: www2.epa.gov/ingredients-used-pesticide-products/glyphosate. Kakar quotations: Interview with Wankel.
19. "A much more agricultural": Interview with Wankel. Before the cabinet: Neumann, *The Other War*, p. 148. This cabinet meeting took place before Wood arrived in Kabul, but the Afghan cabinet's position never changed. Neumann wrote, "I had never seen the cabinet so eloquent, outspoken, and firm in their views."
20. "This is the most popular chemical": Interview with Wood.
21. "Taliban propaganda would profit": Neumann, *The Other War*. Karzai's attitude: Interviews with Cowper-Coles, Long. Exchange between Karzai and Massoud: Correspondence from Zubair Massoud, a spokesman and son of Ahmad Zia.

22. Interview with Braun.
23. Interview with Schweich, who later held political office in Missouri. In 2015, at the age of fifty-four, he committed suicide.
24. "The question is why": State Department cable, Kabul to Washington, September 8, 2007. "Whether they had any evidence": Kabul to Washington, January 10, 2006.
25. Author's interview.
26. One of the largest ever: United Nations Office of Drugs and Crime, "Afghanistan Opium Survey, 2008." According to the U.N., opium poppy cultivation in Afghanistan set a new record in 2014, at more than 550,000 acres.

Chapter Sixteen: Murder and the Deep State

1. All quotations from interviews with Smith, correspondence with Mahmud.
2. Ibid. Mahmud confirmed the conversation. He wrote, in correspondence, "The views and assessments I shared with my contemporaries in the C.I.A., Pentagon or other American officers were based on dispassionate professional analyses. However, time and events since 9/11 have proven that my advice . . . was not inconsistent with saner voices in the U.S. Indeed, the interest of my own country was always central and paramount. War in our neighborhood was to be avoided if it could. I made all efforts to attain this to the very end. Here is another line from *Ben-Hur:* 'Where there is greatness—great government or power—even great feelings or compassion—error also is great.' So it is with the U.S. But the real test of greatness lies in having the moral courage to recognize the error and having the moral capacity to rectify it."
3. "A machine that operates": Author's interview with Fatima Bhutto in 2007. "A symbol of reform . . .": Rice, *No Higher Honor*, p. 609.
4. Rice, ibid. January 2007: Bhutto, from a manuscript that became the posthumous memoir *Reconciliation*, provided to the author in early 2008 by her longtime adviser Mark Siegel.
5. Author's interview. These and some other passages about Bhutto's murder first appeared in "Time Bomb," *The New Yorker*, January 28, 2008.
6. Ibid.
7. All quotations from the slide deck, which is in the author's files.
8. Taliban warnings: Schofield, *Inside the Pakistan Army*, p. 176. Hyat: State Department Cable, Islamabad to Washington, June 22, 2007, WikiLeaks.
9. Author's interview with Musharraf.
10. Schofield, *Inside the Pakistan Army*, p. 177, captures some of the internal debates in the Army command. Ghazi: Author's interview, in early 2008.
11. Ghazi interview, ibid.
12. Interview with Lavoy in December 2014.
13. "Safe haven": "The Terrorist Threat to the Homeland." "'Hideouts' would be a better description": Musharraf to Senator Dick Durbin, August 7, 2007, as described in State Department cable, Islamabad to Washington, August 11, 2007, WikiLeaks. "How can we navigate . . . ?": From an interview with Lavoy in December 2014.
14. *The New York Times*, October 17, 2007.
15. The author flew to Karachi on Bhutto's plane; the quotations are from the author's interview with her after the initial suicide bombing attack on her procession.
16. "Would go to any length": Ibid. Patterson: State Department cable, Islamabad to Washington, October 23, 2007, WikiLeaks.
17. Ibid.
18. Meeting between Bhutto and Taj: "Report of the United Nations Commission of Inquiry into the Facts and Circumstances of the Assassination of Former Pakistani Prime Minister Mohtarma Benazir Bhutto."
19. Author's interview with Karzai, early 2008.
20. Interview with Rehman; U.N. investigation report.
21. *The Washington Post*, January 4, 2008.
22. The conversation between Patterson and Zardari took place on January 25, 2008, on the eve of the Pakistani election. State Department cable, Islamabad to Washington, January 28, 2008, WikiLeaks.

Chapter Seventeen: Hard Data

1. The account of the District Assessments here comes from interviews with seven Bush administration officials who worked with the maps and debated their findings and implications during 2007 and

2008. Rajiv Chandrasekaran and Graeme Smith are among the journalists who have previously reported on the maps' existence. Schinella took charge of the project in 2009.

2. All quotations from interviews with Cohen and Gordon.

3. Interview with Miller and officials who worked on the maps.

4. Rex Douglass's thesis at Princeton: "Why Not Divide and Conquer? Targeted Bargaining and Violence in Civil War," September 2012, page 184. Also, interviews with Milam and Bruce Kinsey, a foreign service officer who rated hamlets in the field. Eliminating "V" and blending hamlet scores: Correspondence with David Elliott.

5. Elliott, *The Vietnamese War*, p. 857.

6. Author's interviews with officials who used the maps in 2007 and later. It was common in my experience for non-C.I.A. sources to describe the agency's analysts as negative about U.S. prospects in Afghanistan after 2006. Former C.I.A. officials offered little disagreement with that description. They said the agency's pessimistic analysis was factual.

7. The meeting is recounted by Waltz, *Warrior Diplomat*, pp. 204–5, from notes he took. McNeill said quotations attributed to him were not correct, but that the essence of what Waltz reported was accurate, that is, that he defended the war's progress against pessimistic C.I.A. forecasts. In correspondence, Gates endorsed Waltz's account. The account here draws upon Waltz's quotations of Gates and McNeill's memory of his argument.

8. State Department cable, Kabul to Washington, March 28, 2007, WikiLeaks. This Provincial Reconstruction Team survey appears to have been a twice-annual assessment exercise of local political, economic, and security conditions.

9. Ibid.

10. State Department cable, Kabul to Washington, July 10, 2007, WikiLeaks.

11. Ibid.

12. Smith, *The Dogs Are Eating Them Now*, p. 204.

13. All quotations, interview with Cohen.

14. Interviews with multiple American, Afghan, and European officials.

15. Author's interview.

16. Interviews with two participants.

17. Ibid.

18. Karzai and Miliband: Miliband, *The Sunday Telegraph*, February 10, 2008. Karzai, Rice, and Miliband: Rice, *No Higher Honor*, p. 617.

19. *Chicago Tribune*, February 8, 2008.

20. All quotations, author's interview with a participant. Rice and Wood did not respond to requests for comment.

21. All quotations, interview with Hagel, confirmed by Kate Bedingfield, an aide to Biden, and David Wade, an aide to Kerry.

22. All quotations, interview with Hagel, with additions from Bedingfield and Wade, ibid. *The New York Times*, February 8, 2009, first reported the essence of the episode. In correspondence, Karzai remembered a different, similar dinner with Senators John McCain, Lindsey Graham, and Joe Lieberman, at which McCain, not Kerry, assured him that they would get through the emerging sources of tension. McCain, Graham, and Lieberman did visit Afghanistan in December 2008, six weeks before the trio led by Kerry. Both visits probably included tense exchanges, given Karzai's doubts about the United States.

Chapter Eighteen: Tough Love

1. Brown and Rassler, *Fountainhead of Jihad*, pp. 151–52.

2. British conclusion: Interviews with U.S. and British officials involved. Trained by Lashkar: Brown and Rassler, *Fountainhead of Jihad*, p. 152.

3. Interviews with U.S. officials involved.

4. Timing of Kappes visit, Archibald: Interviews with U.S. and Pakistani officials familiar with the trip.

5. All quotations from author's interviews.

6. Akhtar and Taj: State Department cable, Islamabad to Washington, October 8, 2008, WikiLeaks. "He was just a bag man": Author's interview.

7. Principals Committee and National Security Council: Paul Miller notes. C.I.A. proposals: Author's interviews with officials, confirming several previous accounts by journalists, including Woodward, *Obama's Wars*, Mazzetti, *The Way of the Knife*, and Schmitt and Shanker, *Counterstrike*. Expanded target list: Waltz, *Warrior Diplomat*, p. 319.

8. Vogle in Kabul, his views: Author's interviews with N.A.T.O. officials. National Security Council meeting: Schmitt and Shanker, *Counterstrike*, pp. 101–2. "We're going to stop . . . had enough": Woodward, *Obama's Wars*, pp. 4–5.

9. Waltz, *Warrior Diplomat*, p. 318.

10. Interview with Gordon. Summary of the outlooks of Kappes, Lavoy, and Wood from author's interviews with multiple U.S. officials working on Pakistan.

11. Interviews with multiple U.S. and Pakistani officials involved.

12. www.cbsnews.com/news/obama-tours-afghan-war-zone.

13. The author attended Occidental College two years ahead of Obama and maintained a friendship with Chandoo afterward.

14. Notes of conversation between Saleh and U.S. Major General David Rodriguez, March 8, 2008, War Logs, WikiLeaks.

15. All quotations from the lunch meeting from State Department cable, Kabul to Washington, July 24, 2008, WikiLeaks.

16. "Al Qaeda Annual Messaging Volume and Runtime, 2002–29 June 2013." IntelCenter is a counterterrorism analysis company that analyzes open media and other sources.

17. "Timeline of Communications from Mustafa Abu al-Yazid." SITE is a counterterrorism analysis company headquartered outside Washington.

18. All quotations from GEO's translation of the interview, posted by GEO on YouTube, www.youtube .com/watch?v=37GvqPxwFyc.

19. August 28: Paul Miller notes. Civilian victims: Bajwa, *Inside Waziristan*, pp. 111–12.

20. "Good . . . into confidence": State Department cable, Islamabad to Washington, September 3, 2008, WikiLeaks. Kayani statement: Reuters, September 11, 2008. Headlines: Islamabad to Washington, September 12, 2008, WikiLeaks.

21. Cryptologist: "Honor the Fallen," *Military Times*, http://thefallen.militarytimes.com/navy-cryptologic -technician-3rd-class-matthew-j-obryant/3741174.

22. Interviews with U.S. and Pakistani officials involved. Also, Islamabad to Washington, October 8, 2008, WikiLeaks.

23. Islamabad to Washington, January 3, 2009, WikiLeaks.

24. Childhood: *Los Angeles Times*, July 30, 2007. Author's interviews.

25. In addition to interviews, this account draws on "Admiral Mike Mullen," *Harvard Business Review*, June 2012.

26. Interviews with multiple U.S. and Pakistani officials familiar with Mullen's assessment of I.S.I. and his discussions with Kayani that year.

27. Kayani's list, first meeting with Mullen: Interviews with U.S. and Pakistani officials involved. See also Islamabad to Washington, February 11, 2008, and March 24, 2008, WikiLeaks, which document some aspects of Kayani's requests. At a March 4 meeting, Mullen told Kayani that "a U.S. SIGINT team had completed its initial assessment of Pakistan's requirements and that they intended to propose options to assist them in developing a solution."

28. "Fundamentals . . . not a U.S. war": All quotations from author's interviews with Pakistani and U.S. officials involved in the discussions.

29. All quotations, ibid.

30. Ibid.

31. Ibid.

Chapter Nineteen: Terror and the Deep State

1. Pasha's biography is primarily from interviews with senior Pakistani military officers and civilian officials familiar with his career, as well as from interviews with Americans who worked with him. A State Department cable, Islamabad to Washington, October 8, 2008, WikiLeaks, confirms several details.

2. Interview with a Pakistani familiar with the conversation.

3. Schofield, *Inside the Pakistan Army*, p. 79.

4. Interviews with Pakistani military officers and officials familiar with Pasha's thinking, as well as Americans who worked with Pasha.

5. What Pasha believed: Author's interviews, ibid. Extreme nationalist: Interview with an American official who worked closely on Pakistan during this period.

6. "I want my kids . . ." and "Of course we have links . . . what we say": Interview with a U.S. diplomat. Pasha came to understand: Interviews with Pakistani military officers and officials familiar with his thinking.

7. American and N.A.T.O. fatalities by year: icasualties.org. I.E.D. attacks: "IED Metrics for Afghanistan, January 2004–September 2010," Cordesman, et al. Center for Strategic and International Studies, November 2010.

8. Interview with Kilcullen.

9. Interviews with Miller and Wood.
10. From interviews with more than half a dozen former Bush administration officials involved with the Afghanistan policy review.
11. Ibid.
12. Dialogue with Lessard, impressions of trip: Interviews with participants, including Cohen, Gordon, and Long.
13. "Bleed out" time: Interview with Long. "No one in this room": Waltz, *Warrior Diplomat*, p. 215, from his handwritten notes. Hadley to Lute, September 17, sixteen sessions, forty hours, Room 445: Interviews with multiple participants.
14. Interviews with participants.
15. Cable, U.S. Mission N.A.T.O. to Washington, December 4, 2008, WikiLeaks.
16. Interviews with British intelligence and Foreign Office officials involved.
17. All quotations, interview with Cohen.
18. All quotations summarizing the estimate's findings from December 4, 2008, cable from Brussels.
19. Ibid.
20. About forty pages, "The United States is not losing . . .": Interviews with multiple participants in the review, including Cohen.
21. "Detail of Attacks by NATO Forces/Predators in FATA," F.A.T.A. Secretariat, obtained and released by the Bureau of Investigative Journalism. The bureau conducted field interviews and reviews of Pakistani media to supplement the F.A.T.A. records, which appear to be the most authoritative single open source available, but which are also incomplete and based on uncertain reporting methodology.
22. Interview with a pilot at Creech, and other officers closely involved with the program.
23. "Strike policy," briefings, Bashir: State Department cable, Islamabad to Washington, November 20, 2008, WikiLeaks.
24. Reported victims of Bannu strike, headline: Ibid. Zardari: Islamabad to Washington, November 15, 2008, WikiLeaks.
25. All quotations from the final National Security Council meeting, which appears from contemporaneous notes to have taken place on November 20 or November 22, are from Waltz, *Warrior Diplomat*, pp. 220–23, from Waltz's handwritten notes taken at the meeting.
26. Bush, *Decision Points*, p. 218.
27. Translated dialogue: Government Exhibit TR 11/27/2008, *United States of America v. Tahawwur Hussain Rana*, 09 CR 830, United States District Court, Northern District of Illinois. Sajid's background: "Interrogation Report of David Coleman Headley."
28. Two Lashkar camps: Briefing of then Pakistani interior minister Rehman Malik to U.S. embassy Islamabad, State Department cable, Islamabad to Washington, February 6, 2009. "To fight harder" and "pinprick": "Government's Santiago Proffer," *U.S. v. Rana*. The proffer is the prosecution's most authoritative summary of Headley's cooperative testimony about his role in the Mumbai conspiracy. Lakhvi profile: Indian investigation documents, 2010, author's files.
29. Intercepts, all quotations: Author's interviews with individuals familiar with the reports. Also, a State Department cable, Islamabad to Washington, December 5, 2008, makes several references to "UK intelligence" about the attacks that was "passed to I.S.I."
30. Quotations from the author's interviews with participants.
31. Islamabad to Washington, November 30, 2008, WikiLeaks. The cable describes a meeting among Feierstein, Kayani, Pasha, and the "Acting RAO," or Regional Affairs Officer, a common light cover title for the C.I.A. station chief.
32. Puppet of I.S.I. and Dehradun: "Interrogation Report of David Coleman Headley." $30,000, "Spotting and assessing . . .": "Government's Santiago Proffer," op.cit.
33. 100,000 militants, 128 I.S.I. camps: Contemporaneous notes from a briefing in Washington. "Broom" and "strike at my enemies": Islamabad to Washington, December 1, 2008. Hoped it was a shock to the system: Interview with an American official who worked with Pasha.
34. Intelligence study: Author's interviews.
35. Feinstein, "Tribute to John D. Bennett."
36. State Department cable, "Follow-Up on Mumbai Information Sharing," Islamabad to Washington, January 8, 2009, WikiLeaks. I have inferred Bennett's participation. The January 8 cable has dropped earlier references in cable traffic to the "Acting RAO," and describes the "RAO," or Regional Affairs Officer, as having "passed to I.S.I. the three dossiers." Bennett rotated into Islamabad as station chief around this period and served into mid-2009, according to interviews with individuals familiar with his tour. "Fighting the I.S.I.": Interview with Cohen.
37. Bush, *Decision Points*, p. 186.

38. "The Taliban? Legitimate?": Interview with a senior Bush administration official familiar with the meeting. Karzai meeting: Bush, *Decision Points*, pp. 219–20. "You were right": From notes of the contemporaneous account of an aide to Karzai.

Chapter Twenty: The New Big Dogs

1. Biden's furniture, "What do I need to put into Afghanistan now": Contemporaneous notes from a dinner at Biden's residence, February 19, 2009, which the author attended.
2. All quotations, State Department cable, Islamabad to Washington, February 6, 2009, WikiLeaks.
3. "New contract": State Department cable, Kabul to Washington, January 20, 2009, WikiLeaks. "Mr. President . . . the drug problem": From contemporary records describing the conversation. "Mr. Vice President . . . the United States": Author's interview with an Afghan present at the meeting, confirmed in correspondence by Karzai. "The Taliban is your problem": Interview with Kai Eide, then U.N. representative to Afghanistan, who met with Karzai after Biden departed.
4. "Expect more": CNN, January 28, 2009. "Are you with me . . . to the mountains": Contemporary records of a conversation with an Afghan cabinet minister present. In correspondence, Karzai denied that he said, "I will declare jihad and go to the mountains," but accepted the attribution from contemporary records that he had said "The U.S. can leave." "Is not listening to us": Ibid., from a separate conversation with a different aide. Ben Rhodes, a senior communications adviser to President Obama and later deputy national security adviser, said that Sherzai was not explicitly invited to the inauguration. "We didn't have an invite list of foreign leaders. They just come and play it as they wish."
5. Interview with Eide.
6. Notes from the February 19 dinner.
7. Ibid.
8. Panetta, *Worthy Fights*, p. 194.
9. Interview with Obama administration officials involved. Two drone strikes January 23: "Detail of Attacks by NATO Forces/Predators in FATA." South Waziristan strike: Klaidman, *Kill or Capture*, pp. 39–40.
10. Panetta, *Worthy Fights*, p. 203.
11. "Very effective . . . Al Qaeda": Interview with the former intelligence official.
12. Itinerary, briefing about Al-Kini: Interview with a former official familiar with the trip. All quotations from the dinner with Zardari and Pasha are from an interview with a participant.
13. "Open, charming": Author's interview. The conflict between Bennett and Panetta was described by two people familiar with the matter. All quotations from author's interviews. Panetta declined to comment.
14. "An obligation . . . uncomfortable": Panetta, *Worthy Fights*, p. 195.
15. All quotations from Saleh are not from his meeting with Panetta, but reflect what he told another American interlocutor in the same period, according to contemporary records.
16. "As good a partner": Author's interview with the former colleague.
17. "A giant among Pygmies": Interview with Cowper-Coles.
18. The account of the meeting at C.I.A. and all quotations are from interviews with more than one participant as well as contemporary records.
19. Ibid.
20. Terrific subordinate . . . terrible colleague: Author's interview. Diplomacy as jazz improvisation: Author's interview with Holbrooke.
21. Cowper-Coles, *Cables from Kabul*, p. 222.
22. All quotations, interview with a participant.
23. "Desperate": State Department cable, Islamabad to Washington, May 25, 2009, WikiLeaks. Holbrooke flew secretly to Abu Dhabi: Author's interview with an official involved. "Greatest issue . . . Pakistani state": from interviews with participants and contemporary records.
24. www.whitehouse.gov/the-press-office/remarks-president-a-new-strategy-afghanistan-and-pakistan.
25. Meeting scene and all quotations from notes by the author, who was present.
26. Interviews with multiple participants in the Riedel review.
27. See Gates, *Duty*, p. 341. Asked to respond to Gates's criticism, Riedel said, "Gates understood that the previous administration had had no goal, no overarching objective. . . . At the time, in March 2009, Gates was fully on board and backed the review process." Gates was the most influential holdover from the Bush administration, which complicated the situation.
28. "Destroy" to "defeat" and other aspects of the document are from author's interviews with participants, then and later. See also the unclassified paper distilled from the top secret document: www.whitehouse

.gov/assets/documents/Afghanistan-Pakistan_White_Paper.pdf. That Obama felt strongly from the beginning that war aims should not include the Taliban's full defeat: Interview with Ben Rhodes.

29. Ibid. Principals, Biden dissent on political grounds: Gates, *Duty*, p. 342.

30. Ibid., pp. 345–46.

31. "Awkward . . .": McChrystal, *My Share of the Task*, p. 288. Skelton: Ibid., p. 291. Meeting with Kayani: All quotations from an interview with a participant in the meetings, the thrust of which was confirmed by three participants.

32. Interviews with participants, ibid.

Chapter Twenty-one: Losing Karzai

1. Arg Palace: Author's visits. Polished calligraphy, other descriptions: Eide, *Power Struggle over Afghanistan*, p. 16.

2. From author's interviews with diplomats who met frequently with Karzai in this period, as well as correspondence with Karzai.

3. Ibid.

4. "What can we do . . .": Interview with Eide.

5. Interview with Eide.

6. All quotations, interview with the minister.

7. State Department cable, Kabul to Washington, May 2, 2009, WikiLeaks.

8. Interviews with multiple U.S. and N.A.T.O. officials familiar with the intelligence assessments of Karzai.

9. Interview with the official. In correspondence, Karzai denied that he had ever told diplomats that he criticized the Pentagon or American policy in public for political credibility in an election year; the implication of his note was that he was fully sincere in his criticisms, never politically tactical.

10. Karzai's outlook on Afghanistan's geopolitical position: Interviews with multiple diplomats who spoke with him at length during this period, including Khalilzad and Eide.

11. Intercepts, U.S. person issue: Interviews with N.A.T.O. officials familiar with the episode.

12. State Department cable, Kabul to Washington, May 7, 2009, WikiLeaks. Later in May, Khalilzad called Spanta and told him that he would not run. His decision seemed definitive, but it did not end speculation in Kabul that he might seek office in some sort of brokered deal as the election descended into allegations of fraud and manipulation.

13. What Karzai believed: Interview with Eide, who met with Karzai frequently during this period. "The more people who challenge Karzai": Interview with Barnett Rubin.

14. From interviews with four British officials involved in the discussions.

15. Karzai had an account of the meeting, "should be . . . with experience": Interviews with participants, correspondence with Karzai. "Before we took office . . .": Interview with Rubin.

16. Eide, *Power Struggle over Afghanistan*, locations p. 178.

17. "Widely understood . . .": State Department cable, "Is Kandahar Under Siege?," Kabul to Washington, September 28, 2009, WikiLeaks. Holbrooke and Karzai in April: Interviews with two U.S. officials familiar with the meeting.

18. Interviews with participants.

19. Eide, *Power Struggle over Afghanistan*, p. 172.

20. Bijlert, "How to Win an Afghan Election," Afghanistan Analysts Network, February 2009.

21. "The 2009 Presidential and Provincial Council Elections in Afghanistan," National Democratic Institute, www.ndi.org/files/Elections_in_Afghanistan_2009.pdf. The International Election Commission reported turnout at 38 percent. Other credible estimates, accounting for evidence of phantom and fraudulent voting, suggest it may have been as low as 30 to 35 percent.

22. Intercepts, "No unrest . . . goes to the streets": From interviews with participants, contemporary records. Conference call on August 21: Cowper-Coles, *Cables from Kabul*, pp. 234–35. "We had been speaking . . . on an open line," the British envoy writes. "Holbrooke sounded as though he was on his mobile. Afghan listeners reported our every word . . . to Karzai in unusually quick time." The contents of the call are also documented in fragmented form in contemporary records. "We have to respect the process . . . will be disputed": Interviews with participants, contemporary records. Cowper-Coles writes that "Holbrooke was clear" that there "would have to be a second round," a position that would infuriate Karzai. The interviews and records show Holbrooke taking a more ambiguous position. In any event, Holbrooke did soon lobby Karzai insistently to accept a second round, as Cowper-Coles describes.

23. Interviews with participants and contemporary records.

24. "Will say . . . defeat him": Ibid. "One way . . . it's a fact": Author attended the meeting and took notes.

25. Karzai's bodyguard: Interview with Nabil. In correspondence, Karzai wrote that he was never concerned about his Panjshiri guards but confirmed that he had asked Nabil whether he should be concerned, and that Nabil told him that he could rely on their professionalism.

26. "Look, we've all had some tough decisions . . .": *The New York Times*, November 24, 2009. Khalilzad and Kerry: Interviews with officials familiar with the conversations.

27. "Backseat . . . runaway car": Interviews with participants and contemporary records.

Chapter Twenty-two: A War to Give People a Chance

1. This account of I.S.A.F. tactical intelligence in 2009 is drawn from interviews with more than a dozen military and intelligence officers deployed to Afghanistan during this period, including McChrystal. It is also drawn from interviews with American and European military officers and diplomats who worked in or with I.S.A.F., as well as Afghan and N.D.S. officers. The author made several reporting trips to Afghanistan and one to Iraq during this time and conducted many of the interviews in the field, contemporaneously or soon after the events described.

2. Flynn, Pottinger, and Batchelor, "Fixing Intel."

3. Zabul: State Department cable captioned "Outrage Against Coalition Special Ops Increases in Zabul," Kabul to Washington, January 19, 2009, WikiLeaks. I.S.A.F. pedestrian accidents: See, for example, War Logs field entries for November 28, 2008, which describe a British van in Kandahar running over a pedestrian and fleeing the scene, provoking a mob to gather to sack the next foreign vehicle through. These sorts of portraits also drew from D.I.A. and C.I.A. field reporting as yet unpublished but identified in disclosed cables. Examples include D.I.A.'s July 21, 2009, "Kandahar Province Overview" and "C.I.A. Field Memo: Security in Kandahar City . . . May 28, 2009."

4. Interview with participants and contemporary records.

5. State Department cable, Kabul to Washington, August 1, 2009, WikiLeaks.

6. Press reports described aspects of Stone's classified study that summer. Holbrooke described the finding of Taliban command and control within prisons, conducted by cell phone, in contemporaneous discussions with the author.

7. Interviews with participants.

8. Woodward, *Obama's Wars*, Chandrasekaran, *Little America*, and Kaplan, *The Insurgents*, are among the multiple well-sourced accounts of McChrystal's summer review. This summary draws on those and interviews with multiple military officers involved. "District Stability Frameworks" and "It's great to make sure" from a briefing the author attended as a reporter at the Pentagon. "Science project": Interview with the aide.

9. Interviews with participants and contemporary records.

10. All quotations, interviews with participants and contemporary records.

11. McChrystal, *My Share of the Task*, p. 310.

12. When Bob Woodward obtained a copy of the report, the Pentagon prepared an unclassified version that was ultimately published by *The Washington Post* on September 21, 2009. www.washingtonpost .com/wp-dyn/content/article/2009/09/21/AR2009092100110.html.

13. All quotations from interviews with three U.S. officials familiar with the meeting. The dialogue reflects their recollection of the essence of the exchanges, which were reported contemporaneously in diplomatic cables. A version of the meeting was also described in Partlow, *A Kingdom of Their Own*.

14. Interviews with the U.S. officials, ibid.

15. Ibid.

16. All quotations, interviews with participants and contemporary records.

17. State Department cable, Kabul to Washington, October 7, 2009. The cable's author sarcastically called the Pakistani brigadier's remarks about the Quetta Shura "the high point" of the meeting, which took place in Kandahar on September 29. Holbrooke: Author's interview.

18. Interviews with White House officials. See also the Woodward, Chandrasekaran, and Kaplan books cited in note 8 above.

19. Contemporary records, including a reconstructed chronology by a participant.

20. Lavoy's briefings, including the assessment that the Taliban controlled about a third of the population at the time: Interviews with several participants and contemporary records.

21. Ibid. Obama's thinking and frustration: Interview with Ben Rhodes.

22. Ibid.

23. Author's contemporaneous notes of the meeting.

24. All quotations, interviews with participants and contemporary records. $4 billion in the fiscal year beginning October 2009: Chandrasekaran, *Little America*, p. 197.

25. Contemporary records, including a reconstructed chronology by a participant.

26. All quotations, interview with Holbrooke.
27. Kayani: State Department cable, Islamabad to Washington, October 7, 2009, WikiLeaks.
28. At the time there was considerable confusion about how the decision to name a departure date had been reached. The White House did not circulate drafts of the West Point speech containing the announcement for interagency review, corrections, and pleadings, a typical process for policy speeches. Chandrasekaran and especially Kaplan have cleared up the mystery. Obama and his White House advisers kept their own counsel, their accounts report, and then sprang the decision on the war cabinet just after Thanksgiving, presenting it as part of a kind of contract that the president asked his commanders and senior civilian war advisers to support. There was no serious debate outside the White House about the costs and benefits of making the decision public. The summary here draws mainly on Kaplan and Chandrasekaran.
29. All quotations, McChrystal, *My Share of the Task*, p. 357.
30. Kaplan, *The Insurgents*, p. 317, and author's interviews with officials involved.
31. Author's interview with Holbrooke. Obama's comments: Interview with Ben Rhodes. Karzai: State Department cable, Kabul to Washington, November 29, 2009, WikiLeaks. What Karzai recalled later: Correspondence with Karzai. The available contemporary records—WikiLeaks cables and other contemporary records—don't show Karzai advocating for a withdrawal of U.S. forces to bases at this time, but it is certainly a view he developed over time.
32. McChrystal, *My Share of the Task*, p. 358.
33. Text of Obama's speech: www.whitehouse.gov/the-press-office/remarks-president-address-nation-way-forward-afghanistan-and-pakistan. Author's interview with Holbrooke, February 27, 2010.
34. McChrystal: Author's contemporaneous notes of the meeting.

Chapter Twenty-three: The One-man C.I.A.

1. "Alarming . . . U.S. government": Interview with Holbrooke, 2010.
2. All quotations from interviews with participants and contemporary records.
3. Ibid.
4. Ibid.
5. Interview with Rubin.
6. The author attended the meeting and took notes.
7. From interviews with participants and contemporary records.
8. Interview with participants. Remarks by the President: www.whitehouse.gov/the-press-office/remarks-president-address-nation-way-forward-afghanistan-and-pakistan.
9. Interviews with British and American officials involved in the discussions. All quotations, interviews with participants and contemporary records.
10. Ibid.
11. Ibid.
12. Ibid.
13. All quotations are recollections from interviews with six senior international and Afghan officials then in Kabul who either participated in the meetings or received accounts of them soon after from Karzai or his aides. Some of these interviews were conducted by the author in Kabul within days or weeks of the meetings described. Some of the quotations and summarized statements were also recorded in contemporary records reviewed by the author. In correspondence, Karzai wrote that the account of his interactions with Pakistani leaders and Saleh during this period was "not true," without elaborating.
14. Ibid. It was impossible, without access to Afghan or Pakistani records, to resolve the contradictory accounts of N.D.S.-I.S.I. interactions in the aftermath of the attack.
15. Ibid. In correspondence, Karzai confirmed the exchange between Saleh and Kayani and the birth of talks about a new strategic partnership. However, he called the account here of his breakfast with Saleh "not true."
16. All quotations from author's interviews in Kabul in March 2010.
17. Ibid. In correspondence, Karzai denied asking whether there was too much influence in Afghanistan during this period. However, the author recorded these comments contemporaneously, as related by diplomats in Kabul who had just met with the Afghan president.
18. All quotations from the Four Seasons are from author's notes and recorded transcript of the lunch interview. "How Does This Thing End?": from interviews with U.S. officials. White House: Interview with Jones.
19. British intelligence briefing: Interviews with participants and contemporary records. Rubin: Memo in author's files. 106-page paper: Chronology of diplomacy developed by a participant. "Nonhegemonic

South Asia": Contemporaneous interview with a State Department official who read the paper. Holbrooke summary: Interviews with participants.

20. Mid-March videoconference between Obama and Karzai, first in months: Contemporaneous interview with a participant. Obama quotations: CNN, March 28, 2010.

21. All quotations, interview with an Afghan participant in the meeting, the thrust of which was confirmed by a second Afghan participant.

22. All quotations from interviews with participants and contemporary records.

Chapter Twenty-four: The Conflict Resolution Cell

1. Interviews with Holbrooke, his aides, and N.S.C. staff, contemporaneously and later.

2. The author hosted and moderated a presentation by Kayani at the New America Foundation, a public policy institute, on March 25, 2010. He presented the slides at several meetings in Washington that week.

3. In a report for the Atlantic Council, Shuja Nawaz published some of the slides Kayani presented on March 25. "Learning by Doing."

4. Ibid. Later that day, Kayani met National Security Adviser Jim Jones at the White House, according to a chronology prepared by a participant in the visit. Jones presented a written response to the "Kayani 1.0" white paper. At this stage, however, the exchanges broke little new ground.

5. All description from the author's visit to Zaeef's home, April 3, 2010.

6. Interviews with participants in the discussions.

7. All quotations, author's April 3 interview.

8. The I.S.A.F. task forces charged with supervision of Taliban prisoners at Bagram produced these reports annually for several years. *The New York Times* later obtained and published one, based on interviews in 2011, www.nytimes.com/interactive/world/asia/23atwar-taliban-report-docviewer .html?_r=0. Obama's comments: Interviews with participants and contemporary records.

9. Strick van Linschoten, draft monograph for the Afghan Analysts Network, 2016. "Partly due . . . free media": Borhan Osman and Anand Gopal, "Taliban Views on the Future State," forthcoming, as cited by Strick van Linschoten.

10. Interviews with participants.

11. Karachi base swelled to about three dozen, agreement with Zardari and Pasha: Interview with the Pakistani official involved. Baradar's arrest: Mazzetti, *The Way of the Knife*, p. 269, and interviews with U.S. officials knowledgeable about the case. "If you kill him," from an interview with a participant, summarizing the thrust of the American message to I.S.I.

12. Interviews with participants and contemporary records. "The 'truths' Baradar could tell . . .": State Department cable, Islamabad to Washington, February 26, 2010, WikiLeaks.

13. Obaidullah, Ishakzai, "Pakistani prisons are worse . . .": Interviews with participants and contemporary records.

14. Interviews with Obama administration officials who pieced Mansour's profile together after his promotion in 2010. For more on Zakir, see Chandrasekaran, *Little America*, pp. 288–90. For a biography of Mansour, see *The New York Times*, October 4, 2015.

15. Interviews with half a dozen Obama administration officials who worked to clarify the profiles of Taliban leaders and envoys during this period.

16. Ibid.

17. Pasha: Interview with a senior intelligence official who attended.

18. Interviews with several Obama administration officials involved.

19. Conflict Resolution Cell dates: All quotations from interviews with Obama administration officials involved and contemporary records.

Chapter Twenty-five: Kayani 2.0

1. Plea hearing, *United States of America v. Faisal Shahzad*, 10-CR-541, United States District Court, Southern District of New York, June 21, 2010.

2. The chronology and details of the attack are all drawn from documents filed in *U.S. v. Shahzad*, particularly Shahzad's testimony at his plea hearing, the criminal complaint, and the government's sentencing memo of September 29, 2010.

3. This account of Pasha's May 9 meeting with Karzai is drawn from interviews with two people familiar with the meeting and contemporary records of what Karzai told the Obama administration when he arrived in Washington, as well as interviews with participants. Karzai and a senior Pakistani

military officer denied that Pasha proposed a new partnership at the expense of the United States. The Pakistani military officer said the visit "was meant to show support to Afghanistan and President Karzai."

4. Daudzai provided this account to Obama administration officials in June.

5. This account of Karzai's state visit and his discussions with Clinton and others draws on multiple interviews with participants and contemporary records.

6. Ibid.

7. Ibid.

8. Ibid.

9. Ibid.

10. Ibid.

11. "They didn't give me enough . . . legitimacy": Author's interview with the aide. Kayani drops "friendly" at this meeting: Interviews with American and Pakistani officials, as well as contemporary records.

12. All quotations and summary of C.I.A. analysis, ibid.

13. The character of Karzai's doubts about Saleh is from interviews with United Nations and other officials who interacted with him on intelligence and security matters at the time, as well as from Saleh's account of Karzai's accusations against him and Atmar in June.

14. "Brother Taliban-*jan*" is from *The New York Times*, June 2, 2010. The account here draws also on the Afghanistan Analysts Network contemporary blogs of the *jirga* and Reuters reporting of Karzai's remarks.

15. The account of this meeting is from interviews with Saleh and a second senior Afghan official familiar with the meeting. All quotations are from the interviews, which took place between two and four years after the event. Karzai confirmed the general outlines of the exchange, but denied using some of the language attributed to him.

16. Ibid.

17. Sentencing memorandum, *United States of America v. Faisal Shahzad.*

18. Author's interviews with participants and contemporary records.

19. Interviews with Pakistani and American participants in the discussions that summer.

20. Department of State transcript, "Television Roundtable with Pakistani Journalists," July 19, 2010.

21. The author was able to read and take notes from a copy of the letter.

Chapter Twenty-six: Lives and Limbs

1. With gratitude to Tim Hopper for sharing his journal and recollections with researcher Christina Satkowski and Elizabeth Barber. Now-Captain Hopper later earned a graduate degree at Syracuse University and remains in the Army as a health care comptroller in San Antonio. "In one sense, we accomplished a lot," he said in a recent conversation. "In Bakersfield—the Russians never took it. We took back a lot of area. But it didn't last. It doesn't seem like it did. We made transient changes. Nothing that stayed. Was it worth all this? Did we make a difference? I think we did. For certain [Afghan] individuals, who were grateful that we brought their home back. But we were there for only a year. It's hard for them to put their faith in us, because we won't be there. We did what we were told to and we accomplished our mission. But did we change the course of the war? I don't know."

2. No-fly zone south of Highway 1: Interview with Brigadier General William Gayler, then commander of the 101st Combat Aviation Brigade, and with Anthony Carlson, historian at the Command and General Staff College, Fort Leavenworth, who has researched a history of the Strike task force.

3. Memorandum from Tunnell to Secretary of the Army John McHugh, August 20, 2010, www .michaelyon-online.com/images/pdf/secarmy_redacted-redux.pdf. Murder and obstruction charges against soldiers under Tunnell's command: www.cnn.com/2010/US/09/09/afghan.coverup/.

4. Interview with Kandarian. The exchange took place at Fort Campbell in May 2010 when McChrystal and Kandarian accompanied Hamid Karzai to visit American troops headed to Kandahar. Richard Holbrooke had hoped the Fort Campbell trip would rehabilitate Karzai's reputation in the United States by demonstrating his gratitude for the forthcoming American military effort.

5. All quotations, interview with Kandarian.

6. The Strike task force and Kandarian later assembled a "Book of Valor" documenting the specific deaths, wounds, and service awards for meritorious conduct during the brigade's 2010–11 tour of Kandahar. Dates and details of the deaths of Hunter and Park are from the book, interviews with Hunter's family, and interviews with soldiers in the task force.

7. The author traveled with Mullen for *The New Yorker* during part of the admiral's trip; these quotations are from contemporaneous notes.

8. "Sending troops . . . Al Capone": Contemporaneous notes, author's files. "The most powerful . . . needed": State Department cable, Kabul to Washington, February 25, 2010, WikiLeaks. Views within I.S.A.F. about dealing with A.W.K.: Interviews with multiple participants, then and later.

9. Quotations from a contemporaneous interview with a senior U.S. military officer familiar with the exchange.

10. "Sort of unfortunate fact . . .": Author's interview. "Intelligence collectors will have a focus": State Department cable, Kabul to Washington, February 25, 2010, WikiLeaks.

11. "A short, professional": McChrystal, *My Share of the Task*, p. 388. Reggie Love, scene with Petraeus: Interviews with former Obama administration officials involved.

12. C.O.P. design: Interview with Major Kevin Moyer, combat engineer, Second Combat Brigade. "From six kilometers . . .": Interview with Spears.

13. S-2's mapping and analytical work: Interviews with Kandarian and Gayler.

14. Interview with Mandel.

15. All quotations, interview with Strickland.

16. Ibid.

17. Interviews with Strickland and other members of the unit.

18. Interviews with Moyer and Kandarian.

19. Ibid.

20. Unclassified PowerPoint slide decks about the Strike tour.

21. "Secure the People . . .": Ibid. Exercises at Freedom Town: Interviews with multiple soldiers and officers in the Strike task force.

22. Interviews with multiple participants in the compensation and arbitration system, including Kandarian.

23. Interview with Motupalli.

24. Ibid.

25. From a recorded Oval Office conversation on August 3, 1972. http://prde.upress.virginia.edu/conversations/4006748.

26. Author's interviews with White House and N.A.T.O. officials.

27. This account is drawn from the author's interviews with more than half a dozen European and American senior military officers within I.S.A.F., contemporaneous and retrospective, as well as with N.A.T.O. diplomats and senior Afghan security officials who worked with Petraeus during 2010.

28. Ibid. Mock cable: Author's files.

29. All quotations, author's interviews.

30. Rashid, *Pakistan on the Brink*, p. 106.

31. All quotations, interviews with participants and contemporary records.

32. All quotations, interviews with participants and contemporary records.

33. Interview with Strickland.

34. Interview with Kandarian and Strike task force PowerPoint briefing slides from 2010 and 2011.

35. Interview with Hopper.

Chapter Twenty-seven: Kayani 3.0

1. September 13, quotations: Interviews with participants and contemporary records. Gates, *Duty*, p. 501, quotes from the State paper but places a discussion of its categories of corruption in December. He also gives Hillary Clinton personal credit for redrafting the analysis, which he considered "the best I had ever seen on the topic." It is possible that the September paper was revised during the autumn and reviewed again in December, but the author is confident it was first submitted and debated at the September 13 N.S.C. meeting.

2. Ibid. In his memoir, Gates does not report his exchange with Panetta in the Situation Room, but acknowledges, "We ran into a stone wall named Panetta. The C.I.A. had its own reasons not to change our approach." On his comparison of contracting to the Afghan drug trade, Gates was essentially correct. International military and aid spending constituted about 97 percent of Afghanistan's gross domestic product of about $15 billion. American spending was a large portion of that. The farm-gate price of Afghan opium in 2010 was in the range of $600 million to $800 million, according to the United Nations.

3. All quotations from interviews with participants and contemporary records.

4. Interviews with investigators in Kabul, December 2010. Dexter Filkins, "The Afghan Bank Heist," *The New Yorker*, February 14, 2011, which estimated the missing sum at $900 million. Other examples: Interview with Thomas Creal, former forensic accountant, who worked for one of the Kabul-based investigative units. Also, interview with Zac Bookman, former legal adviser to the similar Shafafiyat investigative task force; Andrew Wright, a congressional investigator who studied Host Nation Trucking.

5. Interviews with investigators, ibid.
6. Interviews with participants and contemporary records.
7. Three threads, Cell meetings: Interviews with multiple U.S. and other N.A.T.O. officials involved. Lute and quotations: Interviews with participants and contemporary records.
8. *The New York Times*, September 27, 2010.
9. Interviews with multiple U.S. and other N.A.T.O. officials involved.
10. Mullen and Kayani on his extension: Interviews with senior U.S. and Pakistani military officers. Kayani announced in November 2010 that he would stay on for three more years. "They beat the Russians . . .": Author's interview with Cameron Munter. The author was able to review a copy of the October white paper and take notes. The summary of its contents and the background of Kayani's delivery of it to Obama is also informed by interviews with more than half a dozen U.S. officials who read the paper.
11. All quotations from the author's notes from the document, ibid.
12. "We're sending him a bill . . .": From interviews with participants and contemporary records.
13. Rashid, *Pakistan on the Brink*, chapter 6, provided an early account of the meeting and its context.
14. The quotations from interviews with participants and contemporary records. Nabi and the C.I.A.: Associated Press, May 27, 2015.
15. Interviews with participants and contemporary records.
16. Holbrooke to Clinton: Memo in author's files. December 9: Interview with Abramowitz.
17. Clinton, *Hard Choices*, p. 148.
18. Gates, *Duty*, p. 500.
19. Interviews with multiple participants.
20. All quotations, www.whitehouse.gov/the-press-office/2010/12/16/statement-president-afghanistan-pakistan-annual-review.

Chapter Twenty-eight: Hostages

1. This summary is drawn from interviews with several senior Obama administration officials who worked directly with Pasha during this period.
2. This summary is drawn from interviews with several senior Pakistani officials, intelligence officers, and military officers who worked closely with the Americans during this period.
3. Interviews with two former officials familiar with the document.
4. Interviews with Obama administration officials.
5. Interviews with Akbar. He is a former commercial lawyer trained in Britain who served as an investigator for the National Accountability Bureau, an anticorruption arm of the Musharraf government. Later, however, he moved into human rights work with the independent British-based organization Reprieve. There, Akbar filed strategic litigation in Pakistan on behalf of C.I.A. drone victims, the types of lawsuits common in international human rights promotion strategies worldwide. Akbar said when his work gained press attention, I.S.I. officers visited him to ask what he was doing, but that he convinced them his human rights work was in Pakistan's interests and they left him alone. He said he had no contact with I.S.I. before naming Bank in his lawsuit and that he reached that decision on his own, in collaboration with Reprieve colleagues, after obtaining Bank's name from local journalists. Bank's departure on Morell's plane: Greg Miller, *The Washington Post*, May 5, 2016.
6. Interviews with senior Obama administration officials.
7. Interview with the State Department official.
8. From contemporaneous interviews with two senior Obama administration officials, who had worked for many years in Pakistan and continued to travel the country during the "surge" period.
9. Interviews with Smith and Munter. In 2015, the U.S. embassy in Islamabad said that it was building a compound of about 625,000 square feet. When contacted in 2017, a State spokesperson said the finished compound would occupy 43 acres and include 1,700,000 square feet of "office, support and residential space." According to the Pakistan *Tribune*, the compound could accommodate 5,000 personnel.
10. Interviews with two U.S. intelligence officials familiar with Davis's assignment. The evidence collected from his car by Pakistani police supports their account that in addition to his core work as a security officer for case officer meetings with reporting agents, Davis also did at least some independent surveillance work typical of black-bag contractors used by the C.I.A. in difficult environments.
11. Inventory of Davis's possessions: Police files provided to the author by Pakistani police. The shooting: Davis's written account provided to the Pakistani police after his arrest and interviews with several Pakistani police investigators.

12. Police files and interviews with investigators, ibid.
13. Base chief: Interviews with U.S. officials familiar with the matter.
14. Interview with Mejaz Rehman, a brother of the victim.
15. Interviews with Pakistani police investigators.
16. Ibid. Currency and pistol pouch: Pakistani police files provided to the author. "Seeing the situation": Davis's written statement. "This is not a witch hunt . . .": Interview with Hameed.
17. Interviews with three former senior U.S. officials involved.
18. Police files, interview with Hameed and other police investigators and Pakistani officials involved in the case.
19. Interview with Haqqani.
20. "Is he your boy?": Interview with a Pakistani intelligence officer involved. Mazzetti, *The Way of the Knife*, recounts a closely similar exchange, p. 264.
21. Panetta, *Worthy Fights*, p. 299. Inclined to think I.S.I. knew: From Panetta's interviews following his memoir's publication, particularly with *60 Minutes*.
22. Interviews with Obama administration officials, some contemporaneous with the drafting of the reply memo. Obama and Munter: Interview with Munter.
23. Interviews with several Obama administration officials involved.
24. Ibid.
25. Text of Clinton's remarks: http://kabul.usembassy.gov/sp-021811.html.
26. All quotations from interviews with participants and contemporary records.
27. Panetta, *Worthy Fights*, p. 307.
28. Panetta-Pasha quotations are from the recollection of a senior U.S. official familiar with the conversation. Pakistani officials confirmed the gist of the sequence and content of the discussions.
29. Interview with Conroy and Pakistani police investigators involved.
30. Interview with Irshad.
31. Interviews with several American and Pakistani officials familiar with the final courtroom resolution.

Chapter Twenty-nine: Dragon's Breath

1. *Maliks, Khasadars* present: From witness statements filed in Pakistani court documents seeking redress for the attack. Ledger quotations: From a document maintained by the Federally Administered Tribal Areas secretariat, released by the Bureau of Investigative Journalism (B.I.J.)
2. Author's interview with Jalal and other residents of North Waziristan between 2010 and 2012, when the rate of drone strikes peaked. For a fuller account of their experiences, see Coll, "The Unblinking Stare," *The New Yorker*, November 24, 2014.
3. *The New York Times*, March 17, 2011.
4. All quotations, author's interviews with officials involved. Mazzetti, *The Way of the Knife*, provides a closely similar narrative of these debates.
5. "Drone Wars Pakistan."
6. This summary of Kayani's thinking is drawn from interviews with senior Pakistani military officers as well as American officials who worked with him.
7. All quotations, interviews with officials involved.
8. Suspension of strikes, debate in April: Interviews with senior Obama administration officials involved.
9. Author's interviews, Coll, "The Unblinking Stare."
10. Bajwa, *Inside Waziristan*, pp. 115–16.
11. Analysis from B.I.J. data, see Coll, "The Unblinking Stare."
12. Interviews with American officials familiar with the video feeds and the exchanges with Kayani and Pasha.
13. All quotations from American officials involved in the discussions, recounting the gist of what Karzai and Wood said repeatedly in these private meetings.
14. Interviews with senior military officers involved.
15. All quotations from interviews with participants and contemporary records.
16. Ibid.
17. All details from interviews with participants at State, the White House, the Pentagon, and other agencies involved, as well as from contemporary records.
18. All quotations from interviews with participants and contemporary records.
19. Interviews with Pakistani and American officials familiar with the conversation.
20. "Shouting match": *The New York Times*, May 14, 2011. Pasha reportedly said this while appearing before Pakistan's parliament in camera after the raid on Abbottabad. "There was simply too much risk . . .": Panetta, *Worthy Fights*, pp. 308–9.

21. All quotations from interviews with participants, other officials briefed about the conversation, and contemporary records.

22. Ibid.

Chapter Thirty: Martyrs Day

1. The ceremony can be found on YouTube, www.youtube.com/watch?v=SG150-dsuc8. Or search "Youm-e-Shuhada 2011." The quotations are from *The News*, May 1, 2011, with slight adjustments of the Pakistani paper's translations from Urdu to English.

2. This account is from interviews with senior Pakistani military officers and civilian officials familiar with the chronology, as well as interviews with Pakistani journalists who spoke with Pasha and Kayani during May about the raid.

3. This summary of the twenty-minute call between Kayani and Mullen and Kayani's perspective is drawn primarily from interviews with senior Pakistani and American military officers. The quotations are drawn from the recollections of officers on both sides. "Our people need to understand . . . U.S. operation" is from Bergen, *Manhunt*, p. 237, whose reporting is in accord with the author's independent interviews in Washington and Pakistan.

4. The best available evidence about Bin Laden's exile in Pakistan after 2001 comes from three documentary sources. The first is the 336-page Abbottabad Commission Report, a Pakistani inquiry carried out by a four-member panel during 2011 and 2012 and submitted to the government in early 2013. After Pakistan classified the document, Al Jazeera released it: www.aljazeera.com/news/asia/2013 /07/20137813412615531.html.

   Among hundreds of others, the panel interviewed seven Bin Laden family members or survivors in Ibrahim and Abrar Ahmed's families who described the chronicle of Bin Laden's movements. The second document is a 2012 Pakistani police report obtained by *Dawn* and *The New York Times* that appears to draw more heavily on Amal's testimony than the commission does. Both of the Pakistani reports filter the testimony of witnesses into omnibus findings, so it is hard to know what is left out, but the testimony of the wives appears straightforward. Finally, there are the letters seized from Bin Laden's Abbottabad home and published in several tranches by West Point's Combatting Terrorism Center and the Office of the Director of National Intelligence, such as at www.dni.gov/index.php /resources/bin-laden-bookshelf?start=1. In citing details and quotations in this section, I will use "Abbottabad Commission," "2012 Pakistani Police Report," as summarized in the *Times* on March 29, 2012, and "ODNI letters." "People that he knows": Bin Laden to al-Rahman, October 21, 2010, Combatting Terrorism Center translation.

5. ODNI letters, https://assets.documentcloud.org/documents/2084410/letter-to-shaykh-abu-abdallah -dtd-17-july-2010.txt.

6. "Coach" and Amal's recollection, 2012 Pakistani Police Report. Maryam's version, "beautiful area," and "river behind it": Abbottabad Commission.

7. 9,000 rupees per month: Abbottabad Commission. One hundred fifty dollars per month: Associated Press, April 1, 2012.

8. Bergen, *Manhunt*, p. 124, cites C.I.A. officials making an initial estimate of the low hundred thousand dollars in construction costs. Other estimates ran as high as $1 million or more.

9. This summary of Kayani's argument is drawn from interviews with senior Pakistani military and intelligence officers and civilian officials.

10. Abbottabad Commission.

11. See, for example, ODNI letters, December 3, 2010 (27/12/1431).

12. Surveillance: Ibid. Peshawar, "The syringe size . . .": ODNI letters, January 2017 release, "Letter to sons Uthman and Muhammad."

13. "The most important security issues . . .": Bin Laden to al-Rahman, April 26, 2011, Combatting Terrorism Center translation. Cowboy hat: Abbottabad Commission.

14. 30,000 euros: Bin Laden letter to al-Rahman, September 26, 2010, ODNI translation. "Americans will . . . Peshawar": Al-Rahman to Bin Laden, July 17, 2010, ODNI translation.

15. All quotations, Bin Laden to Al-Rahman, April 26, 2010, Combatting Terrorism Center translation.

16. This account of the shootings is drawn mainly from the memoir of a Navy SEAL on the mission, Mark Bissonnette, who wrote under the pseudonym Mark Owen. Owen, *No Easy Day*.

17. N.S.C. meeting: Author's contemporary interviews in Washington with participants as well as contemporary records.

18. Ibid., quotations from contemporaneous interviews. Obama concluded: Interview with Ben Rhodes.

19. *The New York Times*, May 14, 2011.

20. All quotations, ibid., and from *The Washington Post*, May 14, 2011. The account is also informed by an interview with a senior Pakistani military officer.

21. "If they don't trust us . . . deal with it": BBC Monitoring, GEO "Aapas Ki Baat," June 10, 2011. Mortgaged house, "We are helpless. . . . ": *The New York Times*, June 16, 2011.
22. Contemporaneous interviews with American officials involved in the N.S.C. discussions.
23. Ibid. The quotation is from an interview with an official who read the letter and who summarized its contents.
24. All quotations from contemporaneous notes.
25. Morell, Pasha, and Kayani: Interview with officials familiar with the discussions. Pasha and Haqqani: Interview with Husain Haqqani.

Chapter Thirty-one: Fight and Talk

1. Interviews with six U.S. officials familiar with the negotiations, and contemporary records.
2. The author obtained a copy of the "Message." Its existence was first reported in news accounts in early 2012 and it was referred to in Hillary Clinton's memoir of her State Department years, *Hard Choices*, p. 154.
3. Grossman and Muqrin: Interviews with participants and contemporary records. "Sometime in 2012 . . .": Interview with Munter.
4. Interviews with six American and three Pakistani officials familiar with the meeting.
5. Interviews with participants.
6. Interviews with eight U.S. officials, civilian and military, who worked with Petraeus during this period. "You wouldn't *believe* . . ." from one of those interviews.
7. The author attended the dinner.
8. Interview with Munter. Diorama and Bin Laden's rifle: From interviews with participants and contemporary records.
9. Interviews with ten officers and analysts involved in writing the 2011 N.I.E. who provided assessments for the key judgments. Most of those interviews took place while the estimate was being finished.
10. Ibid.
11. 5,400: From a detailed I.S.A.F. briefing about reintegration at a Royal United Services Institute conference in London in 2012, which the author attended.
12. Author's interviews with multiple participants.
13. Interviews with several officials familiar with the negotiations and contemporary records.
14. Warned about six weeks before: From interviews with both American and Pakistani military officers involved.
15. See "New York on Security Alert amid Warning of 9/11 Terror Threat," *The Guardian*, September 9, 2011, for a flavor of the impact of the threat reporting at the time. The truth was typical of the ambiguous murk from which such threat reporting often arose, according to two U.S. officials familiar with the matter. President Karzai had earlier asked Zaeef to help obtain the release of an Afghan diplomat kidnapped by Al Qaeda. Zaeef had been reluctant; he feared he would be accused of having operational contacts with terrorists. At Karzai's insistence, Zaeef did eventually make inquiries of radical Afghan intermediaries. Later, I.S.I. arrested a man involved in that episode and, while under Pakistani interrogation that was probably not gentle, the detainee fingered Zaeef. Either that, or I.S.I. officers invented the threat story in order to discredit Zaeef, because of his role as a collaborator with Tayeb Agha.
16. Author's interviews with five senior U.S. military officers, in the United States and Pakistan.
17. Ibid. Four of the interviews were contemporaneous with the events described. According to a former Afghan intelligence official with access to N.D.S., the Americans obtained around this time a cell phone video documenting a meeting between Sirajuddin Haqqani and a Pakistani general at which the Pakistanis handed over an arms cache.
18. The quotations are from an interview with a Pakistani participant in the discussions.
19. Interview with the Pakistani participant.
20. David Sanger, *Confront and Conceal: Obama's Secret Wars and Surprising Use of American Power*, New York: Crown, 2012, p. 8.
21. "We ought to hang": Interview with a participant in the meeting. Mullen testimony: *The New York Times*, September 22, 2011.
22. All quotations from interviews with participants and contemporary records.
23. All quotations in this passage are from contemporaneous interviews with Pakistani officials summarizing the discussions.
24. All quotations from interviews with participants and contemporary records.
25. Ibid.
26. Ibid.
27. Ibid.
28. Ibid.

Chapter Thirty-two: The Afghan Hand

1. All e-mail reproduced in this chapter is from Holly Loftis. "Celtic build": Interview with Holly Loftis.
2. Schoolhouse curriculum: Interview with a military officer who participated in the program.
3. "Because it can be twisted": From *Call Me Ehsaan*, a short *New York Times* video documentary by Micah Garen, who filmed Loftis in 2010, when he served on a Provincial Reconstruction Team in Zabul Province. The curriculum: Interview with a former Hurlburt officer, ibid.
4. Loftis bio and all quotations: Interview with Holly Loftis.
5. Ibid.
6. Bordin bio: Interview with Bordin. See also: "Lethal Incompetence: Studies in Political and Military Decision-Making," a 2006 bound issue of a "slightly edited" version of Bordin's 1992 doctoral dissertation, by Nonstop Internet Printing.
7. Bordin, "Lethal Incompetence." "I wasn't hard enough": Interview with Bordin.
8. "A Crisis of Trust and Cultural Incompatibility," declassified Bordin study of May 12, 2011, pp. 13, 55–58. For the full study: http://nsarchive.gwu.edu/NSAEBB/NSAEBB370/docs/Document%2011 .pdf. On patrol in 2004, origins of study: Interview with Bordin.
9. That the study was approved after the November 29 killings: "A Crisis of Trust," p. 6.
10. "Smiley Face": Ibid., p. 7.
11. All quotations, ibid., pp. 12–28.
12. Ibid., p. 5.
13. Interviews with I.S.A.F. military officers involved in the episode.
14. Ibid. Interviews with participants surfaced disagreement about the circumstances of the Bordin paper's publication. In correspondence, Bordin wrote, "Originally, the intelligence officer of the brigade I was working for had classified it as UNCLASSIFIED. It was the policy of that brigade to have their intelligence officer classify all such products. . . . My discordant research findings challenged the veracity of GEN Petraeus' sworn testimony to the U.S. Congress earlier that year. . . . Unfortunately, between the time I had initially reported my findings and recommendations and the time they were finally implemented, over 80 coalition personnel had been murdered." On the other hand, a military officer in the Petraeus command said, "I did my duty. I pursued every aspect of green on blue and it was provided [to Petraeus]. . . . It was very broad and very deep. . . . None of this was swept under the rug."
15. Hennessey, *The Junior Officers' Reading Club*, pp. 16–17.
16. "A Crisis of Trust," p. 5.
17. Marc Sageman, "The Insider Threat in Afghanistan in 2012," unclassified version, p. 9. Sageman conducted an extensive investigation of fratricidal murders in Afghanistan during 2012 for I.S.A.F.'s J-2, or intelligence directorate, in the aftermath of Bordin's work. See chapter 33. Sageman found the Marine urination video was a "major contributing factor" to the murders of the French soldiers in Kapisa. Sageman interviewed the killer in Kabul's Pul-e Charki prison.
18. Interview with Allen.
19. www.documentcloud.org/documents/413327-inside-the-wire-reference-guide.html.
20. "Executive Summary of Findings and Recommendations, Army Regulation (AR) 15-6 Investigation (Allegations That US Service Members Improperly Disposed of Islamic Religious Materials)," March 24, 2012.
21. Ibid.
22. Ibid.
23. All quotations, interview with Lanthier.
24. Interview with Tim Conrad Sr.
25. Interview with a U.S. official who reviewed the video.
26. Allen and Karimi quotations: "General Allen Visits Base Attacked After Koran Burning Protests," www.youtube.com/watch?v=blUTkmysMX0.
27. Interview with Peggy Marchanti.
28. "I'm checking the Taliban Web site": Interview with Green. Office description, profile of Saboor, description of murders and aftermath: From extensive Agent Investigation Reports, including extensive interviews with witnesses, carried out by the Criminal Investigative Division in Kabul, in author's files. Colonel Green retired after the murders. He might have been at the ministry when the attack took place but happened to be away. The killings affected him deeply, he said in a recent interview. He experiences "regrets, nightmares." He was so furious at the Afghan police after the murders that he "wanted to kill them." Even four years later, "I'm very angry and irretrievably biased against the Afghans," he said. He added, "I don't go a day without thinking about this."
29. Interview with Allen.
30. Associated Press, February 28, 2012.

31. Air Force Special Operations Command, www.afsoc.af.mil/News/ArticleDisplay/tabid/136/Article/162715/afghanistan-lost-its-best-friend-loftis-remembered.aspx.

Chapter Thirty-three: Homicide Division

1. C.I.A. analysis summary is from contemporaneous interviews with Obama administration officials familiar with the agency's products on Afghanistan that spring.
2. Author's interview with the N.A.T.O. diplomat.
3. The *Long War Journal* has maintained a database of open source reports of insider killings in Afghanistan, www.longwarjournal.org/archives/2012/08/green-on-blue_attack.php.
4. All quotations from the author's contemporaneous interviews at I.S.A.F. headquarters in Kabul, 2012.
5. Interviews with Sageman.
6. Ibid.
7. Interviews with officials familiar with the work.
8. Ibid., and author's contemporaneous interviews with military officers at I.S.A.F. headquarters, 2012.
9. Ibid.
10. Ibid. Then–Brigadier General Paul Nakasone (later promoted to lieutenant general) said that if Sageman worked solely as a contractor, he would not have been able to access the data he sought from the JCATs, but that he considered it unlikely that no sharing took place. "I know we shared the data with everyone throughout the theater that had a part in this ongoing investigation. . . . This was the most important issue taking place."
11. Ibid. "The Insider Threat in Afghanistan in 2012," unclassified version.
12. Sageman recalled the checkpoint case as the one that first led him to doubt the role of personal affront in murder cases. It was one of several cases where video and photographic evidence from "helmet cams" clarified with hard evidence what had and had not precipitated insider shootings.
13. Interviews with Sageman.
14. Ibid.
15. All quotations, Sageman, "The Insider Threat in Afghanistan in 2012."
16. Ibid.
17. Ibid.
18. Ibid.
19. Interviews with Sageman.

Chapter Thirty-four: Self-inflicted Wounds

1. The account in this chapter of White House–led negotiations with Pakistan, Qatar, and the Taliban during 2012 and 2013 is drawn from extensive interviews with ten Obama administration officials involved, as well as with several senior Pakistani military and intelligence officials and diplomats.
2. Ibid.
3. Ibid.
4. Interviews with Rubin, correspondence from Pataudi. The latter confirmed "the gist" of the conversation and added, "It was believed the Taliban would want a share of the political pie if they were to be encouraged to talk. . . . The Taliban were and as events have shown are on the ascendant even now. What's changed since then is that the government in Kabul has lost a lot of its power and slipped in its ability to govern the country."
5. Quotations from author's interviews.
6. The quotations are from a contemporaneous interview with Abdullah Abdullah, who had just met with Khalilzad. Abdullah related Khalilzad's summary of Karzai's remarks.
7. Interview with Dobbins.
8. All quotations, interview with Dobbins.
9. Interview with Hagel.
10. All quotations from author's interviews with the participants, including Rahmatullah Nabil, then the N.D.S. director.
11. The account of the N.I.E. is from interviews with a senior intelligence official familiar with its findings, as well as other Obama administration officials who read it. I.S.A.F. troop figures: www.nato.int/cps/en/natolive/107995.htm.
12. Dobbins: Author's interview.
13. All quotations, interview with Khalilzad. Karzai confirmed the essence of the exchange.

Chapter Thirty-five: Coups d'État

1. Biography, quotations, interview with Nabil.
2. Ibid. On the N.D.S. relationship with the Mehsuds, see also a *New York Times* report by Matthew Rosenberg on October 28, 2013, and his interview with Nabil, January 16, 2015. According to Nabil, in correspondence relayed through a spokesman, U.S. Special Forces, tipped by N.D.S., arrested Latif Ullah Mehsud in Logar Province in October 2013. N.D.S. asked the Americans to turn him over, but "Secretary of State Kerry stated that Mehsud had blood on his hands and was responsible for the Times Square bomb attempt." Later, however, in December 2014, as part of Afghan president Ashraf Ghani's attempt to forge a new understanding with Pakistan, the United States did release Mehsud to I.S.I. custody, according to Nabil's spokesman.
3. Interview with Nabil, ibid. "One-man band": State Department cable, Kabul to Washington, May 19, 2007, WikiLeaks.
4. Interviews with multiple Afghan cabinet members and palace officials.
5. Interview with Nabil.
6. "Take sheep to the mountains": *The Guardian*, June 22, 2014. Transcripts of the leaked intercepts, as well as an authoritative analysis of the election's patterns of fraud, are at www.afghanistan-analysts.org/elections-2014-36-some-key-documents/.
7. Interview with Nabil and other Afghan officials familiar with the episode.
8. *The New York Times*, June 29, 2014.
9. Saleh: From his Twitter feed. Atta: *The New York Times*, July 8, 2014. German warning: *The New York Times*, July 15, 2014.
10. "Any action to take power": *The New York Times*, July 8, 2014.
11. "Civil uprising": *The Washington Post*, August 14, 2014. Saleh: Interviews with Afghan and American officials involved in the coup prevention effort.
12. Quotations from interviews with Nabil. Other senior Afghan officials involved also described the plan. In correspondence, Spanta denied that the quartet had ever discussed the formation of an interim government. Their focus "was very clear," he wrote, namely, "no interference by Afghanistan's security forces in the electoral or post-election process in 2014." He denied any role or knowledge of how the matter reached *The New York Times*. Spanta also wrote that because he believed the 2014 presidential election "was rigged and massively fraud-infested," he proposed annulling the results, encouraging Karzai to remain in office, and rerunning the poll the following year, simultaneously with parliamentary elections. Karzai and the "international community" rejected this suggestion.
13. *The New York Times*, August 18–20, 2014. "Secret relations": Rosenberg's Twitter feed.
14. Christina Satkowski, who was in Kabul conducting research for this book in August, visited the facility during this period.
15. Cheney and Hadley: Bush, *Decision Points*, p. 189.
16. All quotations are from a translation of a video prepared by Al Qaeda in the Indian subcontinent in the autumn of 2014, which contains interviews with Rafiq, other conspirators, and the A.Q.I.S. emir.
17. Ibid.
18. The Al Qaeda video says Jakhrani retired. *The Wall Street Journal*, September 16, 2014, in one of the few thorough media reports on the attack, quoted unnamed Pakistani officials saying he was dismissed because of his radical views.
19. The Pakistani military announced the Naval Strategic Force Command in a press release, www.ispr.gov.pk/front/main.asp?o=t-press_release&id=2067. The release described the command as "the custodian of the nation's second strike capability" and said that its role would strengthen Pakistan's "policy of Credible Minimum Deterrence."
20. Retired Vice Admiral Kumar Singh, of the Indian Navy, described the PNS *Zulfiqar*'s 2012 tests and the efforts to fit ship-borne cruise missiles with tactical nuclear weapons in a column in the *Deccan Chronicle*, October 8, 2014.
21. Al Qaeda video.
22. All quotations and details of the attack plan, ibid.
23. Alistair Reed, "Al Qaeda in the Indian Subcontinent," The International Centre for Counter-Terrorism—The Hague, Policy Brief, May 2015.
24. *The Wall Street Journal*, September 16, 2014, and several Pakistani media accounts. The press reports leave a number of questions unanswered about how the attack unfolded and how it was thwarted. The Pakistani military seems to have imposed an informal press blackout on the case, although it did announce that naval officers involved who survived the assault were later tried and sentenced to death.
25. Interview with Indian intelligence officials familiar with the reporting.
26. *The New York Times*, September 21, 2014.
27. *The New York Times*, September 23, 2014.

28. Special Inspector General for Afghanistan Reconstruction, www.sigar.mil/pdf/special%20projects /SIGAR-16-23-SP.pdf, as well as related Pentagon reports.

29. United Nations: www.un.org/apps/news/story.asp?NewsID=50111#.V_Pc_GPB9lI. Anderson: Pentagon briefing transcript, www.defense.gov/News/Transcripts/Transcript-View/Article/606959/department-of-defense-briefing-by-lt-gen-anderson-in-the-pentagon-briefing-room. Brown University figures: http://watson.brown.edu/costsofwar/.

30. Ruttig, "Crossing the Bridge."

31. Quotations from Reuters, Al Jazeera, and *Washington Post* coverage of the event on site, December 28, 2014.

Epilogue: Victim Impact Statements

1. Signals operation: Interview with an intelligence official involved. Salangi: Interview with Holly Loftis, who was briefed on the investigation by J.A.G. officers. "Preaching in favor . . .": General Mohammad Zahir, Ministry of Interior, at a press conference, April 21, 2016.

2. All quotations from the April 21 press conference.

3. Interviews with Holly Loftis, with gratitude to Elizabeth Barber.

4. The author is grateful to Camille, Alison, and Holly Loftis for providing copies of their statements.

5. The account of the trial and the quotations are from notes taken in the courtroom by an American military observer and supplied to the Loftis family.

6. Casualty figures, attrition: *The New York Times*, October 12, 2016.

7. Uthman Ghazi statement: www.lawfareblog.com/statement-islamic-movement-uzbekistans-leader -uthman-ghazi-its-been-thirteen-years-we-have-heard-you.

8. Interviews with U.S. military officials at Resolute Support Mission, Kabul, September 2016.

9. Ibid.

10. Helicopter crash details: Interviews with current and former Afghan security officials. The author visited this region of Logar in 2002 and talked with residents about the history of I.S.I. supply to the region through corridors of linked valleys running from the province east toward Waziristan.

11. *Los Angeles Times*, July 10, 2016.

12. "Expected future disputes": BBC News, August 4, 2015.

13. Author's interviews with Ahmad Massoud and other family members, September 2016, in Kabul and Panjshir.

14. Ahmad's biography, ibid. Billboard, from author's travels. Quotations, interviews with Ahmad Massoud.

15. All quotations, author's interview, September 2016.

BIBLIOGRAPHY

Books

Abbas, Hassan. *The Taliban Revival: Violence and Extremism on the Pakistan-Afghanistan Frontier*. New Haven, CT: Yale University Press, 2014.

Adamec, Ludwig W. *Afghanistan: 1900–1923*. Berkeley: University of California Press, 1967.

Ahmed, Mahmud. *Illusion of Victory: A Military History of the Indo-Pak War—1965*. Karachi: Lexicon Publishers, 2002.

Akbar, Said Hyder, and Susan Burton. *Come Back to Afghanistan: A California Teenager's Story*. New York: Bloomsbury, 2005.

Alexander, Chris. *The Long Way Back: Afghanistan's Quest for Peace*. Toronto: HarperCollins, 2011.

Allen, Nick. *Embed: With the World's Armies in Afghanistan*. Stroud, UK: History, 2010.

Bajwa, Abu Bakr Amin. *Inside Waziristan: Journey from War to Peace—Insight into the Taliban Movement and an Account of Protecting People from Terrorists*. Lahore: Vanguard Books, 2013.

Bashir, Shahzad, and Robert D. Crews. *Under the Drones: Modern Lives in the Afghanistan-Pakistan Borderlands*. Cambridge, MA: Harvard University Press, 2012.

Beattie, Doug, and Philip Gomm. *An Ordinary Soldier: Afghanistan: A Ferocious Enemy: A Bloody Conflict: One Man's Impossible Mission*. London: Simon & Schuster, 2008.

———. *Task Force Helmand: A Soldier's Story of Life, Death and Combat on the Afghan Front Line*. London: Simon & Schuster, 2009.

Begg, Moazzam, and Victoria Brittain. *Enemy Combatant: My Imprisonment at Guantánamo, Bagram, and Kandahar*. New York: New Press, 2006.

Benjamin, Daniel, and Steven Simon. *The Age of Sacred Terror*. New York: Random House, 2002.

———. *The Next Attack: The Failure of the War on Terror and a Strategy for Getting It Right*. New York: Times Books, 2005.

Bennett, Gina M. *National Security Mom: Why "Going Soft" Will Make America Strong*. Deadwood, OR: Wyatt-Mackenzie, 2009.

Bergen, Peter L. *Manhunt: The Ten-Year Search for Bin Laden from 9/11 to Abbottabad*. New York: Crown Publishers, 2012.

———. *United States of Jihad: Investigating America's Homegrown Terrorists*. New York: Crown Publishers, 2016.

———, and Daniel Rothenberg. *Drone Wars: Transforming Conflict, Law, and Policy*. New York: Cambridge University Press, 2015.

———, and Katherine Tiedemann. *Talibanistan: Negotiating the Borders Between Terror, Politics and Religion*. Oxford: Oxford University Press, 2013.

Berntsen, Gary, and Ralph Pezzullo. *Jawbreaker: The Attack on Bin Laden and Al Qaeda: A Personal Account by the CIA's Key Field Commander*. New York: Crown Publishers, 2005.

Bhutto, Benazir. *Reconciliation: Islam, Democracy, and the West*. New York: Harper, 2008.

Bishop, Patrick. *3 Para*. London: HarperPress, 2007.

Blair, Tony. *A Journey: My Political Life*. Toronto: Knopf Canada, 2010.

Blatchford, Christie. *Fifteen Days: Stories of Bravery, Friendship, Life and Death from Inside the New Canadian Army*. Toronto: Doubleday Canada, 2007.

Blehm, Eric. *Fearless: The Undaunted Courage and Ultimate Sacrifice of Navy SEAL Team Six Operator Adam Brown.* Colorado Springs, CO: WaterBrook Press, 2012.
———. *The Only Thing Worth Dying For: How Eleven Green Berets Forged a New Afghanistan.* New York: Harper, 2010.
Bordin, Jeffery T. *Lethal Incompetence: Studies in Political and Military Decision-Making.* Nonstop Internet, 2006.
Bowden, Mark. *The Finish: The Killing of Osama Bin Laden.* New York: Atlantic Monthly Press, 2012.
Bradley, Rusty, and Kevin Maurer. *Lions of Kandahar: The Story of a Fight Against All Odds.* New York: Bantam Books, 2011.
Brewster, Murray. *The Savage War: The Untold Battles of Afghanistan.* Mississauga, ON, Canada: J. Wiley & Sons Canada, 2011.
Brown, Vahid, and Don Rassler. *Fountainhead of Jihad: The Haqqani Nexus, 1973–2012.* New York: Columbia University Press, 2013.
Burke, Jason. *The 9/11 Wars.* London: Allen Lane, 2011.
Bush, George W. *Decision Points.* New York: Crown Publishers, 2010.
Call, Steve. *Danger Close: Tactical Air Controllers in Afghanistan and Iraq.* College Station: Texas A & M University Press, 2007.
Chandrasekaran, Rajiv. *Little America: The War Within the War for Afghanistan.* New York: Alfred A. Knopf, 2012.
Chayes, Sarah. *The Punishment of Virtue: Inside Afghanistan After the Taliban.* New York: Penguin Press, 2006.
Clinton, Hillary Rodham. *Hard Choices.* New York: Simon & Schuster, 2014.
Coburn, Noah, and Anna Larson. *Derailing Democracy in Afghanistan: Elections in an Unstable Political Landscape.* New York: Columbia University Press, 2014.
Cohen, Stephen Philip. *The Future of Pakistan.* Washington, D.C.: Brookings Institution Press, 2011.
———. *The Idea of Pakistan.* Washington, D.C.: Brookings Institution Press, 2004.
Coll, Steve. *Ghost Wars: The Secret History of the CIA, Afghanistan, and bin Laden, from the Soviet Invasion to September 10, 2001.* New York: Penguin Press, 2004.
Corera, Gordon. *The Art of Betrayal: The Secret History of MI6.* New York: Pegasus Books, 2012.
Cowper-Coles, Sherard. *Cables from Kabul: The Inside Story of the West's Afghanistan Campaign.* London: HarperPress, 2011.
Crumpton, Henry A. *The Art of Intelligence: Lessons from a Life in the CIA's Clandestine Service.* New York: Penguin Press, 2012.
Dobbins, James. *After the Taliban: Nation-Building in Afghanistan.* Washington, D.C.: Potomac Books, 2008.
Eide, Kai. *Power Struggle over Afghanistan: An Inside Look at What Went Wrong, and What We Can Do to Repair the Damage.* New York: Skyhorse Publishing, 2012.
Elliott, David W. P. *The Vietnamese War: Revolution and Social Change in the Mekong Delta, 1930–1975.* Armonk, NY: M. E. Sharpe, 2003.
Farrell, Theo, Frans P. B. Osinga, and James A. Russell. *Military Adaptation in Afghanistan.* Stanford, CA: Stanford University Press, 2013.
Fayez, Sharif. *An Undesirable Element: An Afghan Memoir.* Edited by Matthew Trevithick. Berlin, Germany: First Draft Publishing.
Fearon, Kate. *City of Soldiers: A Year of Life, Death, and Survival in Afghanistan.* Northampton, MA: Interlink Books, 2012.
Fergusson, James. *A Million Bullets: The Real Story of the British Army in Afghanistan.* London: Bantam, 2008.
———. *Taliban: The True Story of the World's Most Feared Guerrilla Fighters.* London: Bantam, 2010.
Franks, Tommy. *American Soldier.* New York: Regan Books, 2004.
Fury, Dalton. *Kill Bin Laden: A Delta Force Commander's Account of the Hunt for the World's Most Wanted Man.* New York: St. Martin's Press, 2008.
Gannon, Kathy. *I Is for Infidel: From Holy War to Holy Terror: 18 Years Inside Afghanistan.* New York: Public Affairs, 2005.
Gates, Robert Michael. *Duty: Memoirs of a Secretary at War.* New York: Alfred A. Knopf, 2014.
Giustozzi, Antonio. *Decoding the New Taliban: Insights from the Afghan Field.* New York: C. Hurst, 2009.
———. *Koran, Kalashnikov, and Laptop: The Neo-Taliban Insurgency in Afghanistan.* New York: Columbia University Press, 2008.
———, and Mohammad Isaqzadeh. *Policing Afghanistan: The Politics of the Lame Leviathan.* New York: Columbia University Press, 2012.
Grau, Lester W., and Dodge Billingsley. *Operation Anaconda: America's First Major Battle in Afghanistan.* Lawrence: University Press of Kansas, 2011.

Grenier, Robert. *88 Days to Kandahar: A CIA Diary*. New York: Simon & Schuster, 2015.

Ḥaqqani, Husain. *Pakistan: Between Mosque and Military*. Washington, D.C.: Carnegie Endowment for International Peace, 2005.

Hastings, Michael. *The Operators: The Wild and Terrifying Inside Story of America's War in Afghanistan*. New York: Blue Rider Press, 2012.

Hennessey, Patrick. *Kandak: Fighting with Afghans*. London: Allen Lane, 2012.

———. *The Junior Officers' Reading Club*. London: Penguin Press, 2010.

Hirsh, Michael. *None Braver: U.S. Air Force Pararescuemen in the War on Terrorism*. New York: New American Library, 2003.

Horn, Bernd. *No Lack of Courage: Operation Medusa, Afghanistan*. Toronto: Dundurn Press, 2010.

Hussain, Zahid. *Frontline Pakistan: The Struggle with Militant Islam*. New York: Columbia University Press, 2007.

Jennings, Christian. *Midnight in Some Burning Town: British Special Forces Operations from Belgrade to Baghdad*. London: Weidenfeld & Nicolson, 2004.

Jones, Seth G. *Hunting in the Shadows: The Pursuit of Al Qa'ida Since 9/11*. New York: W. W. Norton & Co., 2012.

———. *In the Graveyard of Empires: America's War in Afghanistan*. New York: W. W. Norton & Co., 2009.

Junger, Sebastian. *War*. New York: Twelve, 2010.

Kaplan, Fred M. *The Insurgents: David Petraeus and the Plot to Change the American Way of War*. New York: Simon & Schuster, 2013.

Khalilzad, Zalmay. *The Envoy: From Kabul to the White House, My Journey Through a Turbulent World*. New York: St. Martin's Press, 2016.

Khan, Imran. *Pakistan: A Personal History*. London: Bantam, 2012.

Kilcullen, David. *The Accidental Guerrilla: Fighting Small Wars in the Midst of a Big One*. Oxford: Oxford University Press, 2009.

Klaidman, Daniel. *Kill or Capture: The War on Terror and the Soul of the Obama Presidency*. Boston: Houghton Mifflin Harcourt, 2012.

Laux, Douglas, and Ralph Pezzullo. *Left of Boom: How a Young CIA Case Officer Penetrated the Taliban and Al-Qaeda*. New York: St. Martin's Press, 2016.

Linschoten, Alex Strick van, and Felix Kuehn. *An Enemy We Created: The Myth of the Taliban–al Qaeda Merger in Afghanistan, 1970–2010*. New York: C. Hurst, 2012.

Lippold, Kirk S. *Front Burner: Al Qaeda's Attack on the USS Cole*. New York: PublicAffairs, 2012.

Luttrell, Marcus, and Patrick Robinson. *Lone Survivor: The Eyewitness Account of Operation Redwing and the Lost Heroes of SEAL Team 10*. New York: Little, Brown, 2007.

Mackey, Chris, and Greg Miller. *The Interrogators: Inside the Secret War Against Al Qaeda*. New York: Little, Brown, 2004.

Malkasian, Carter. *War Comes to Garmser: Thirty Years of Conflict on the Afghan Frontier*. New York: Oxford University Press, 2013.

Maloney, Sean M. *Enduring the Freedom: A Rogue Historian in Afghanistan*. Washington, D.C.: Potomac Books, 2005.

Mann, Jim. *Rise of the Vulcans: The History of Bush's War Cabinet*. New York: Viking, 2004.

Mazzetti, Mark. *The Way of the Knife: The CIA, a Secret Army, and a War at the Ends of the Earth*. New York: Penguin Press, 2013.

McChrystal, Stanley A. *My Share of the Task: A Memoir*. New York: Portfolio/Penguin, 2013.

McNab, Andy. *Spoken from the Front*. London: Bantam, 2009.

Meyer, Dakota, and Francis J. West. *Into the Fire: a Firsthand Account of the Most Extraordinary Battle in the Afghan War*. New York: Random House Trade Paperbacks, 2013.

Mitchell, James, with Bill Harlow. *Enhanced Interrogation: Inside the Minds and Motives of the Islamic Terrorists Trying to Destroy America*. New York: Crown Forum, 2016.

Morell, Michael J., and Bill Harlow. *The Great War of Our Time: The CIA's Fight Against Terrorism—From al Qa'ida to ISIS*. New York: Twelve, 2015.

Mudd, Philip. *Takedown: Inside the Hunt for Al Qaeda*. Philadelphia: University of Pennsylvania Press, 2013.

Musharraf, Pervez. *In the Line of Fire: A Memoir*. New York: Free Press, 2006.

Nasr, Vali. *The Dispensable Nation: American Foreign Policy in Retreat*. New York: Doubleday, 2013.

Nawaz, Shuja. *Crossed Swords: Pakistan, Its Army, and the Wars Within*. Oxford: Oxford University Press, 2009.

Naylor, Sean. *Relentless Strike: The Secret History of Joint Special Operations Command*. New York: St. Martin's Press, 2015.

———. *Not a Good Day to Die: The Untold Story of Operation Anaconda*. New York: Berkley Books, 2005.

Neumann, Ronald E. *The Other War: Winning and Losing in Afghanistan*. Washington, D.C.: Potomac Books, 2009.

Nordberg, Jenny. *The Underground Girls of Kabul: In Search of a Hidden Resistance in Afghanistan*. New York: Crown Publishers, 2014.

Owen, Mark, and Kevin Maurer. *No Easy Day: The Firsthand Account of the Mission That Killed Osama Bin Laden*. New York: Dutton, 2012.

Panetta, Leon E., and Jim Newton. *Worthy Fights: A Memoir of Leadership in War and Peace*. New York: Penguin Press, 2014.

Parnell, Sean, and John R. Bruning. *Outlaw Platoon: Heroes, Renegades, Infidels, and the Brotherhood of War in Afghanistan*. New York: William Morrow, 2012.

Partlow, Joshua. *A Kingdom of Their Own: The Family Karzai and the Afghan Disaster*. New York: Alfred A. Knopf, 2016.

Peritz, Aki, and Eric B. Rosenbach. *Find, Fix, Finish: Inside the Counterterrorism Campaigns That Killed Bin Laden and Devastated Al-Qaeda*. New York: PublicAffairs, 2012.

Peters, Gretchen. *Seeds of Terror: How Heroin Is Bankrolling the Taliban and al Qaeda*. New York: Thomas Dunne Books, 2009.

Pfarrer, Chuck. *SEAL Target Geronimo: The Inside Story of the Mission to Kill Osama Bin Laden*. New York: St. Martin's Press, 2011.

Pillar, Paul R. *Intelligence and U.S. Foreign Policy: Iraq, 9/11, and Misguided Reform*. New York: Columbia University Press, 2011.

Porch, Douglas. *The Conquest of Morocco*. New York: Alfred A. Knopf, 1983.

——. *The Conquest of the Sahara*. London: J. Cape, 1984.

——. *Counterinsurgency: Exposing the Myths of the New Way of War*. New York: Cambridge University Press, 2013.

——. *The French Foreign Legion: A Complete History of the Legendary Fighting Force*. New York: Harper-Collins Publishers, 1991.

Rashid, Ahmed. *Descent into Chaos: The United States and the Failure of Nation Building in Pakistan, Afghanistan, and Central Asia*. New York: Viking, 2008.

——. *Taliban: Militant Islam, Oil, and Fundamentalism in Central Asia*. New Haven, CT: Yale University Press, 2000.

——. *Pakistan on the Brink: The Future of America, Pakistan, and Afghanistan*. New York: Viking, 2012.

Rice, Condoleezza. *No Higher Honor: A Memoir of My Years in Washington*. New York: Crown Publishers, 2011.

Risen, James. *Pay Any Price: Greed, Power, and Endless War*. Boston: Houghton Mifflin Harcourt, 2014.

Rizzo, John Anthony. *Company Man: Thirty Years of Controversy and Crisis in the CIA*. New York: Scribner, 2014.

Robinson, Linda. *Tell Me How This Ends: General David Petraeus and the Search for a Way Out of Iraq*. New York: PublicAffairs, 2008.

Rodriguez, Jose A., and Bill Harlow. *Hard Measures: How Aggressive CIA Actions After 9/11 Saved American Lives*. New York: Threshold Editions, 2012.

Rubin, Barnett R. *Afghanistan from the Cold War Through the War on Terror*. Oxford: Oxford University Press, 2013.

Rumsfeld, Donald. *Known and Unknown: A Memoir*. New York: Sentinel, 2011.

Saar, Erik, and Viveca Novak. *Inside the Wire: A Military Intelligence Soldier's Eyewitness Account of Life at Guantanamo*. New York: Penguin Press, 2005.

Sageman, Marc. *Understanding Terror Networks*. Philadelphia: University of Pennsylvania Press, 2004.

Sands, Philippe. *Torture Team: Rumsfeld's Memo and the Betrayal of American Values*. New York: Palgrave Macmillan, 2008.

Scahill, Jeremy. *Dirty Wars: The World Is a Battlefield*. New York: Nation Books, 2013.

Schmidt, John R. *The Unraveling: Pakistan in the Age of Jihad*. New York: Farrar, Straus and Giroux, 2011.

Schmitt, Eric, and Thom Shanker. *Counterstrike: The Untold Story of America's Secret Campaign Against Al Qaeda*. New York: Times Books, 2011.

Schofield, Carey. *Inside the Pakistan Army: A Woman's Experience on the Frontline of the War on Terror*. London: Biteback Publishing, 2011.

Schroen, Gary C. *First In: An Insider's Account of How the CIA Spearheaded the War on Terror in Afghanistan*. New York: Presidio Press/Ballantine Books, 2005.

Scott-Clark, Cathy, and Adrian Levy. *The Siege: Three Days of Terror Inside the Taj*. London: Viking, 2013.

Semrau, Robert. *The Taliban Don't Wave*. Mississauga, ON, Canada: Wiley, 2012.

Shah, Aqil. *The Army and Democracy: Military Politics in Pakistan*. Cambridge, MA: Harvard University Press, 2014.

Shahzad, Syed Saleem. *Inside Al-Qaeda and the Taliban: Beyond Bin Laden and 9/11*. London: Pluto Press, 2011.

Sharma, Sita Ram. *General Pervez Musharraf: Wisest Dictator and Saviour of Pakistan*. New Delhi: Alfa Publications, 2006.

Siddique, Abubakar. *The Pashtun Question: The Unresolved Key to the Future of Pakistan and Afghanistan*. London: Hurst, 2014.

Slahi, Mohamedou Ould, and Larry Siems. *Guantánamo Diary*. New York: Little, Brown, 2015.

Smith, Graeme. *The Dogs Are Eating Them Now: Our War in Afghanistan*. Berkeley, CA: Counterpoint, 2015.

Soufan, Ali H., Daniel Freedman, and Adrian Kitzinger. *The Black Banners: The Inside Story of 9/11 and the War Against Al-Qaeda*. New York: W. W. Norton & Co., 2011.

Southby-Tailyour, Ewen. *3 Commando Brigade: Helmand Assault*. London: Ebury, 2010.

Stein, Janice Gross, and Eugene Lang. *The Unexpected War: Canada in Kandahar*. Toronto: Viking Canada, 2007.

Tankel, Stephen. *Storming the World Stage: The Story of Lashkar-e-Taiba*. New York: Columbia University Press, 2011.

Tapper, Jake. *The Outpost: An Untold Story of American Valor*. New York: Little, Brown, 2012.

Tenet, George, and Bill Harlow. *At the Center of the Storm: My Years at the CIA*. New York: HarperCollins, 2007.

Tootal, Stuart. *Danger Close: Commanding 3 PARA in Afghanistan*. London: John Murray, 2009.

Waltz, Michael G. *Warrior Diplomat: A Green Beret's Battles from Washington to Afghanistan*. Lincoln, NE: Potomac Books, an imprint of the University of Nebraska Press, 2014.

Warrick, Joby. *The Triple Agent: The al-Qaeda Mole Who Infiltrated the CIA*. New York: Doubleday, 2011.

Waugh, Billy, and Tim Keown. *Hunting the Jackal: A CIA Ground Soldier's 50-Year Career Hunting America's Enemies*. New York: William Morrow, 2004.

Weiss, Mitch, and Kevin Maurer. *No Way Out: A Story of Valor in the Mountains of Afghanistan*. New York: Berkley Caliber, 2012.

Whittle, Richard. *Predator: The Secret Origins of the Drone Revolution*. New York: Henry Holt and Company, 2014.

Williams, Gary. *SEAL of Honor: Operation Red Wings and the Life of Lt. Michael P. Murphy, USN*. Annapolis, MD: Naval Institute Press, 2010.

Windsor, Lee, David Anderson Charters, and Brent Wilson. *Kandahar Tour: The Turning Point in Canada's Afghan Mission*. Mississauga, ON, Canada: John Wiley & Sons Canada, Ltd., 2008.

Woods, Chris. *Sudden Justice: America's Secret Drone Wars*. Oxford: Oxford University Press, 2015.

Woodward, Bob. *Obama's Wars*. New York: Simon & Schuster, 2010.

———. *Bush at War*. New York: Simon & Schuster, 2002.

———. *Veil: The Secret Wars of the CIA*. New York: Simon & Schuster, 1987.

Wright, Donald P. *A Different Kind of War: The United States Army in Operation Enduring Freedom (OEF), October 2001–September 2005*. Fort Leavenworth, KS: Combat Studies Institute Press, U.S. Army Combined Arms Center, 2010.

Wright, Lawrence. *The Looming Tower: Al-Qaeda and the Road to 9/11*. New York: Alfred A. Knopf, 2006.

Yousaf, Mohammad, and Mark Adin. *The Bear Trap*. London: Leo Cooper, 1992.

Zaeef, Abdul Salam. *My Life with the Taliban*. Edited by Alex Strick van Linschoten and Felix Kuehn. New York: Columbia University Press, 2010.

Zakheim, Dov S. *A Vulcan's Tale: How the Bush Administration Mismanaged the Reconstruction of Afghanistan*. Washington, D.C.: Brookings Institution Press, 2011.

Journal Articles, Reports, and Manuscripts

"Abbottabad Commission Report." Released by Al Jazeera, July 8, 2013. www.aljazeera.com/news/asia/2013/07/20137813412615531.html.

"Afghanistan Drug Control." General Accounting Office, March 2010.

"Afghanistan Opium Survey 2006," United Nations Office of Drugs and Crime.

"Afghanistan Opium Survey 2008," United Nations Office of Drugs and Crime.

"The Afghan Papers: Committing Britain to War in Helmand, 2005–06." Royal United Services Institute, December 8, 2011.

"Al Qaeda Annual Messaging Volume and Runtime, 2002-29 June 2013." IntelCenter, http://intelcenter.com/reports/charts/AQ-Annual-Messaging-Volume-Runtime/#gs.QfTiclg.

"Al Qaeda Messaging Statistics v3.3." IntelCenter, September 9, 2007. https://intelcenter.com/QMS-PUB-v3-3.pdf.

Belasco, Amy. "Troop Levels in the Afghan and Iraq Wars." Congressional Research Service, July 2, 2009.

Bordin, Jeffrey. "A Crisis of Trust and Cultural Incompatibility: A Red Team Study of Mutual Perceptions of Afghan National Security Force Personnel and U.S. Soldiers in Understanding and Mitigating the Phenomena of ANSF-Committed Fratricide-Murders." N2KL Red Team, May 12, 2011. http://nsarchive.gwu.edu/NSAEBB/NSAEBB370/docs/Document%2011.pdf.

Call Me Ehsaan. Directed by Micah Garen. *The New York Times,* March 23, 2012.

"CID Report of Investigation—Final (C)/SSI—0064-2004-CID369-69280-5C1N/5Y2E." U.S. Army Criminal Investigation Command, 2004.

"Committee Study of the Central Intelligence Agency's Detention and Interrogation Program: Declassified and Redacted Executive Summary." Senate Select Committee on Intelligence, December 3, 2014.

"Compilation of Usama Bin Ladin Statements 1994–January 2004." FBIS Report, 2004.

Conetta, Carl. "Operation Enduring Freedom: Why a Higher Rate of Civilian Bombing Casualties." Project on Defense Alternatives Briefing Report #13, January 18, 2002.

Cordesman, A. H., M. Allison, and J. Lemieux. "IED Metrics for Afghanistan, January 2004–September 2010." Center for Strategic and International Studies, November 2010.

Crawford, Neta C. "Civilian Death and Injury in Afghanistan, 2001–2011." Boston University, September 2011.

———. "Update on the Human Costs of War for Afghanistan and Pakistan, 2001 to mid-2016." Costs of War Project at Brown University's The Watson Institute, August 2016.

"Department of Defense Base Closures and Transfers in Afghanistan: The U.S. Has Disposed of $907 Million in Foreign Excess Real Property." Special Inspector General for Afghanistan Reconstruction, March 2016.

"Detail of Attacks by NATO Forces/Predators in FATA." F.A.T.A. Secretariat, released by the Bureau of Investigative Journalism, January 29, 2014.

"Drone Wars Pakistan: Analysis." New America Foundation, http://securitydata.newamerica.net/drones/pakistan-analysis.html.

"Elections 2014 (36): Some Key Documents." *Afghanistan Analysts Network,* July 8, 2014. www.afghanistan-analysts.org/elections-2014-36-some-key-documents/.

Farrell, Theo, and Antonio Giustozzi. "The Taliban at War: Inside the Helmand Insurgency, 2004–2012." *International Affairs* 89, no. 4 (2014), pp. 845–71.

Fearon, James D. "Why Do Some Civil Wars Last So Much Longer Than Others?" *Journal of Peace Research* 41, no. 3 (May 2004), pp. 275–301.

Feinstein, Dianne. "Tribute to John D. Bennett." Federation of American Scientists. *Congressional Record* 159, no. 26 (February 2013), http://fas.org/irp/congress/2013_cr/bennett.html.

Flynn, Michael T., Matt Pottinger, and Paul D. Batchelor, "Fixing Intel: A Blueprint for Making Intelligence Relevant in Afghanistan." Center for a New American Security, January 2010.

Giustozzi, Antonio, and Noor Ullah. "The Inverted Cycle: Kabul and the Strongmen's Competition for Control over Kandahar, 2001–2006." *Central Asian Survey* 26, no. 2 (September 2007), pp. 167–84.

"Glyphosate." United States Environmental Protection Agency. www2.epa.gov/ingredients-used-pesticide-products/glyphosate.

"Inspection Report of the DCI Counterterrorist Center Directorate of Operations." C.I.A. Office of Inspector General, 2001.

"Interagency Assessment of the Counternarcotics Program in Afghanistan." Inspectors General, U.S. Department of State and U.S. Department of Defense, June 2007.

"Interrogation Report of David Coleman Headley." National Investigation Agency, Government of India, derived from interrogations conducted between June 3 and June 9, 2010.

"Living Under Drones: Death, Injury and Trauma to Civilians from US Drone Practices in Pakistan." Stanford Law School and New York University Law School, September 2012.

Marzano, Todd. "Criticisms Associated with Operation Anaconda." Joint Military Operations Department, Naval War College, October 23, 2006.

"National Drug Control Strategy." Government of Afghanistan, a British-funded report, January 2006.

Nawaz, Shuja. "Learning by Doing: The Pakistan Army's Experience with Counterinsurgency." The Atlantic Council, February 2011.

The 9/11 Commission Report: Final Report of the National Commission on Terrorist Attacks upon the United States, July 2004.

"Office of Inspector General Report on Central Intelligence Agency Accountability Regarding Findings and Conclusions of the Report of the Joint Inquiry into Intelligence Community Activities Before and After the Terrorist Attacks of September 11, 2001." C.I.A. Office of Inspector General, 2005.

Osman, Borhan, and Anand Gopal. "Taliban Views on the Future State." NYU Center on International Cooperation, July 2016. http://cic.nyu.edu/sites/default/files/taliban_future_state_final.pdf.

"The Pakistani Muslim Community in England." The Change Institute, Department for Communities and Local Government, March 2009.

Rassler, Don, Gabriel Koehler-Derrick, Liam Collins, Muhammad al-Obaidi, and Nelly Lahoud. "Letters from Abottobad: Bin Ladin Sidelined?" Combating Terrorism Center at West Point, May, 3 2012. www.ctc.usma.edu/posts/letters-from-abbottabad-bin-ladin-sidelined.

Reed, Alistair. "Al Qaeda in the Indian Subcontinent." The International Centre for Counter-Terrorism—The Hague, Policy Brief, May 2015.

"Report of the United Nations Commission of Inquiry into the Facts and Circumstances of the Assassination of Former Pakistani Prime Minister Mohtarma Benazir Bhutto," April 15, 2010.

Roggio, Bill, and Linda Lundquist. "Green-on-Blue Attacks in Afghanistan: The Data." *The Long War Journal*, updated May 7, 2016. www.longwarjournal.org/archives/2012/08/green-on-blue_attack.php.

Rubin, Barnett. "Saving Afghanistan." *Foreign Affairs*, January–February 2007.

Ruttig, Thomas. "Crossing the Bridge." Afghan Analysts Network, February 15, 2014.

Sageman, Marc. "The Insider Threat in Afghanistan in 2012." Unclassified version in author's files.

———. "Operation Overt: The Trans-Atlantic Airlines Liquid Bombs Plot." Draft chapter, in author's files.

Strick van Linschoten, Alex. Draft monograph for Afghan Analysts Network, 2016, in author's files.

"The Terrorist Threat to the Homeland." National Intelligence Estimate, unclassified excerpts released July 17, 2007.

"Timeline of Communications from Mustafa Abu al-Yazid." SITE Intelligence Group, 2010. http://news.siteintelgroup.com/blog/index.php/about-us/21-jihad/123-timeline-of-communications-from-mustafa-abu-al-yazid.

"Tora Bora Revisited: A Report to Members of the Committee on Foreign Relations." United States Senate, November 30, 2009.

"The 2009 Presidential and Provincial Council Elections in Afghanistan." National Democratic Institute. www.ndi.org/files/Elections_in_Afghanistan_2009.pdf.

Waldman, Matt. "The Sun in the Sky: The Relationship Between Pakistan's I.S.I. and Afghan Insurgents." Crisis States Discussion Papers, Destin Development Studies Institute, London School of Economics, June 2010.

Watson, Bryan G. "Executive Summary of Findings and Recommendations, Army Regulation (AR) 15-6 Investigation (Allegations That US Service Members Improperly Disposed of Islamic Religious Materials)." United States Army, 2012.

Documents

"C.I.A. Comments on the Senate Select Committee on Intelligence Report on the Rendition, Detention, and Interrogation Program." The Director, Central Intelligence Agency, released December 8, 2014. www.cia.gov/library/reports/CIAs_June2013_Response_to_the_SSCI_Study_on_the_Former_Detention_and_Interrogation_Program.pdf.

"COMISAF Initial Assessment (Unclassified)," released August 30, 2009. www.washingtonpost.com/wp-dyn/content/article/2009/09/21/AR2009092100110.html.

Defense Procurement and Acquisition Policy Archives, 2010. www.acq.osd.mil/dpap/ops/archive/2010/ops_news_10.html.

George W. Bush White House Archives. "Rebuilding Afghanistan" and other collections. 2001–2009. https://georgewbush-whitehouse.archives.gov.

"Inside the Wire Threats—Afghanistan (Green-on-Blue) Smartcard," February 2, 2012. www.documentcloud.org/documents/413327-inside-the-wire-reference-guide.html.

Inter Services Public Relations (ISPR). "Naval Chief Inaugurates Naval Strategic Force Headquarters," May 19, 2012. www.ispr.gov.pk/front/main.asp?o=t-press_release&id=2067.

Lawfare. "Statement from the Islamic Movement of Uzbekistan's Leader Uthman Ghazi: 'It's Been Thirteen Years Since We Have Heard from You Mullah Muhammad Omar,'" July, 1, 2015. www.lawfareblog.com/statement-islamic-movement-uzbekistans-leader-uthman-ghazi-its-been-thirteen-years-we-have-heard-you.

Massoud, Ahmad Shah. "Massoud's Letter to the People of America," 1998. www.afghan-web.com/documents/let-masood.html.

Michael Yon Online Magazine. "Memorandum from Tunnell to Secretary of the Army John McHugh," August 20, 2010. www.michaelyon-online.com/images/pdf/secarmy_redacted-redux.pdf.

National Security Archive. "Memorandum for Alberto R. Gonzales, Counsel of the President: Re: Standards of Conduct for Interrogation Under 18 U.S.C. §§ 2340-2340A," August 1, 2002. http://nsarchive.gwu.edu/NSAEBB/NSAEBB127/02.08.01.pdf.

National Security Archive, Electronic Briefing Book No. 122. "Prisoner Abuse: Patterns from the Past,"
    May 12, 2004. http://nsarchive.gwu.edu/NSAEBB/NSAEBB122/.
NATO, Archive ISAF Placemats, 2007–2016. www.nato.int/cps/en/natolive/107995.htm.
Office of the Director of National Intelligence. "Bin Laden's Bookshelf." Declassified materials released
    between 2015 and 2017. www.dni.gov/index.php/resources/bin-laden-bookshelf?start=1.
Presidential Recordings Program at the University of Virginia's The Miller Center. "Richard Nixon and
    Henry A. Kissinger on 3 August 1972," 2014. http://prde.upress.virginia.edu/conversations/4006748.
Strick van Linschoten, Alex, Felix Kuehn, and Anand Gopal, eds. "Taliban Sources Project." A Thesigers
    Project, Michael Innes, ed. talibansourcesproject.com.
United Nations News Centre. "In Afghanistan's Deadliest year, Civilian Casualties Top 10,000 in 2014—
    UN," February 18, 2015. www.un.org/apps/news/story.asp?NewsID=50111#.V_Pc_GPB9lI.
U.S. Department of Defense, News Transcripts. "Department of Defense Briefing by Lt. Gen. Anderson
    in the Pentagon Briefing Room via Satellite from Afghanistan." www.defense.gov/News/Transcripts/
    Transcript-View/Article/606959/department-of-defense-briefing-by-lt-gen-anderson-
    in-the-pentagon-briefing-room.
U.S. Department of State. "Department of State transcript: 'Television Roundtable with Pakistani Jour-
    nalists,'" July 19, 2010. www.state.gov/secretary/20092013clinton/rm/2010/07/145009.htm.
U.S. Department of State Archive 2001–2009. "Afghanistan" and other collections. https://2001-2009
    .state.gov.
U.S. Embassy Kabul, U.S. Official Speeches and Statements. "Remarks by Secretary of State Hillary Clin-
    ton, Launch of the Asia Society's Series of Richard C. Holbrooke Memorial Addresses," February 18,
    2011. http://kabul.usembassy.gov/sp-021811.html.
White House. "White Paper of the Interagency Policy Group's Report on U.S. Policy Toward Afghanistan
    and Pakistan," March 2009. www.whitehouse.gov/assets/documents/Afghanistan-Pakistan_White
    _Paper.pdf.
White House Briefing Room. Presidential remarks and statements 2009–2017. www.whitehouse.gov
    /briefing-room.
WikiLeaks. "Cablegate," "The Guantanamo Files," and other collections. https://wikileaks.org.

Court Documents

Lawrence Longhi v. Khaled Monawar, Superior Court of New Jersey, Morris County, L-2619-09.
Suleiman Abdullah Salim et al. v. James E. Mitchell and John Jessen, United States District Court, Eastern
    District, Washington, CV-15- 0286-JLQ.
United States of America v. Bashir Noorzai, United States District Court, Southern District of New York,
    81 05 CR-19.
United States of America v. David A. Passaro, United States District Court, Eastern District of North Caro-
    lina, 5: 04-CR-211-1.
United States of America v. Faisal Shahzad, 10-CR-541, United States District Court, Southern District of
    New York.
United States of America v. Tahawwur Hussain Rana, 09 CR-830, United States District Court, Northern
    District of Illinois.

INDEX

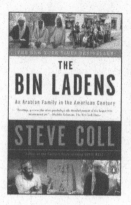 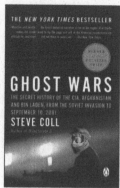 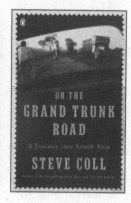